CLIFTON M. MILLER LIBRARY
Washington College
Chestertown, MD 21620-1197

PRESENTED IN MEMORY OF

Dr. Robert Gray

BY

Betty Gray

Useful Reference Series No. 30

INDEX TO ONE-ACT PLAYS

AN INDEX TO
ONE-ACT PLAYS

COMPILED BY

HANNAH LOGASA, Ph.B.
LIBRARIAN, UNIVERSITY HIGH SCHOOL, THE UNIVERSITY OF CHICAGO

AND

WINIFRED VER NOOY, B.L.S.
REFERENCE LIBRARIAN THE UNIVERSITY OF CHICAGO LIBRARIES

BOSTON
F. W. FAXON COMPANY
1924

Copyright, 1924
By F. W. FAXON CO.
BOSTON

VAIL-BALLOU PRESS, INC.
BINGHAMTON AND NEW YORK

TABLE OF CONTENTS

	PAGE
Preface	3
How to use this index	3
Abbreviations and symbols used in this index	5
Key	11
Titles	36
Authors	203
Subjects	263
Collections	277

PREFACE

This index contains over 5000 titles of one-act plays written in English or translated into English from a foreign language, published since 1900. Although the index is not complete, it is comprehensive and serviceable.

HOW TO USE THIS INDEX

The key is the bibliographical identification of a play. Key letters refer to book in which play may be found. Magazine references are given the identification used by the Reader's Guide to Periodical Literature.

The title index contains full information about the individual play, e. g., author, number and kind of characters, setting or background, suitability for elementary or high school pupils, and letters which refer to the Key showing in what book or magazine the play may be found. Refer to the title index from author, subject and collection indexes.

ABBREVIATIONS

*	suitable for children.
†	suitable for high school.
‡	suitable for junior high.
anon.	anonymous.
Apr.	April.
Aug.	August.
b.	boy.
c.	children.
Dec.	December.
Feb.	February.
g.	girl.
il.	illustrated.
Jan.	January.
July	July.
June	June.
m.	men.
Mar.	March.
May	May.
n. d.	no date.
Nov.	November.
Oct.	October.
s.	servant.
Sc.	scene.
Sept.	September.
tr.	translated or translator.
w.	women.

AN INDEX TO ONE-ACT PLAYS

KEY TO BOOKS INDEXED

A B	Arkwright, Ruth. Brownikins and other fancies. Lond. Darton, n. d.
A B B	Abbott, Keene. Hair Trigger Smith. Omaha, Nebr. Keene Abbott, 1909.
A B F	Abercrombie, Lascelles. Four short plays. Lond. Martin Secker, 1922.
A E	Anderson, Mrs. Isabel. Everyboy and other plays for children. N. Y. Shakespeare Press, 1914.
A L Q	Alquist, Joan. The wooing of Mary of Magdela. Denver, Colo. Joan Alquist, 1921.
A N D	Andreev, Leonid. Love of one's neighbor. N. Y. Albert and Charles Boni, 1914.
A N P	Antigo Publishing Co. Plays. Antigo, Wis. Antigo Pub. Co., n.d.
A O	Alabama Centennial Com'n. Series of children's plays in commemoration of the close of a century of statehood. Montgomery, Ala. Paragon Press, 1919.
A P	Aldis, Mary. Plays for small stages. N. Y. Duffield, 1915.
A P P	Ames. Theatrical plays. Lebanon, Ohio. March Bros., n. d.
A S	American School Peace League. Bost. n. d.
A U	Augier, Émile. Four plays. tr. from the French by Barrett H. Clark. N. Y. Knopf, 1915.
B	Baker, Walter H. & Co. Plays. Bost. Walter H. Baker, n. d.
B A	Baring, Maurice. Diminutive dramas. Lond. Martin Secker, n. d.
B A B	Baker, Walter H. & Co. Plays in pinafores. Bost. Walter H. Baker, 1916.
B A C	Baker, Walter H. & Co. Merry Christmas plays and entertainments by various authors. Bost. Walter H. Baker, 1916.
B A D	Bangs, John K. The real thing and three other farces. N. Y. Harper, 1909.
B A L	Baldwin, Sidney. Five plays and five pantomimes. Phila. Penn, 1923.
B A N	Baldwin, Charles C. (Charles Gordon, pseud.) Airy nothings; or, What you will. N. Y. Sturgis & Walton, 1917.
B A O	Bantock, Leedham & Greenbank, Percy. Man the life boats. Washington, D. C. J. D. Milans, 1908.
B A P	Bax, Clifford. Polite satires. Lond. Medici Society, 1922.
B A Q	Barrington, Pauline B. When the young birds go. Los Angeles, Calif. C. C. Parker, 1915.
B A R	Barton, George E. The pipe of desire and other plays. Bost. Old Corner Book Store, 1905.

B A S	Barne, Kitty. (Mrs. Eric Streatfield) Susie pays a visit. Lond. J. Curwen & Sons, n. d.
B A T	Baker, George M. & others. Ten plays for boys. Bost. Walter H. Baker, 1918.
B A X	Baxley, Isaac R. Poems and plays. Vol. I. San Francisco, Calif. A. M. Robertson, 1921.
B B	Bynner, Witter. A book of plays. N. Y. Knopf, 1922.
B B C	Burrows, Edith M. & others. Cheery comedies for Christmas. Bost. Walter H. Baker, 1915.
B B S	Burrows, Edith; Bridgham, Gladys R. & others. Short plays for small players. Bost. Walter H. Baker, 1915.
B D	Browne, Horace B. Short plays from Dickens. Lond. Chapman & Hall, 1908.
B E	Barrie, James M. Echoes of the war. N. Y. Scribner, 1918.
B E C	Beith, John H. (Ian Hay, pseud.) The crimson cocoanut and other plays. Bost. Walter H. Baker, 1913.
B E J	Bell, Lady. Nursery comedies. N. Y. Longmans, Green, 1918.
B E L	Bellini, Gabriel. The triumph of remorse. N. Y. J. W. Fawcett, 1916.
B E P	Benton, William B. Poems. Vol. III. (Chrysanthemum ed.) N. Y. William B. Benton, 1915.
B E S	Betts, Frank. Saga plays. N. Y. Longmans, Green, 1917.
B E T	Barrie, James M. "Der tag"; or, The tragic man. N. Y. Scribner, 1914.
B E Y	Brown-Evarts, Edith. Young folks' dialogues and dramas. Chic. M. H. Donohue, 1902.
B F	Beach, Lewis. Four one-act plays. N. Y. Brentano's, 1921.
B F R	Bechhofer, C. E. Five Russian plays with one from the Ukrainian. N. Y. Dutton, 1916.
B H	Barrie, James M. Half hours. N. Y. Scribner, 1914.
B H P	Bullivant, Cecil H., ed. Home plays: a collection of new, simple and effective plays for boys and girls. N. Y. Dodge Pub. Co., n. d.
B J P	Benavente, Jacinto. Plays. tr. by Underhill. N. Y. Scribner, 1917.
B J P 2	Benavente, Jacinto. Plays. Second series. tr. by Underhill. N. Y. Scribner, 1918.
B J P 3	Benavente, Jacinto. Plays. Third series. tr. by Underhill. N. Y. Scribner, 1918.
B K G	Botomley, Gordon. Gruach and Britain's daughter. Bost. Small, Maynard, 1921.
B K L	Bottomley, Gordon. King Lear's wife, and other one-act plays. Bost. Small, Maynard, n. d.
B L	Bloxam, E. E. Little pageant plays for children. Lond. Wells, Gardner, Darton, n. d.
B L C	Barbee, Lindsey. Cinderella and five other fairy plays. Chic. T. S. Denison, 1922.
B L K	Block, Etta, tr. One-act plays from the Yiddish. Cincinnati. Stewart Kidd, 1923.
B L O	Block Publishing Co. Plays. N. Y. Block Pub. Co., n. d.
B L P	Barbee, Lindsey. Let's pretend. Chic. T. S. Denison, 1917.
B M	Belmont, Mrs. O. H. P. & Maxwell, Elsa. Melinda and her sisters. N. Y. Robert J. Shores, 1916.

B O	Brown, Alice. One-act plays. N. Y. Macmillan, 1921.
B O T	Bottomley, Gordon. The riding to Lithend. Portland, Maine. Thos. B. Mosher, 1910.
B P	Bennett, E. Arnold. Polite farces. N. Y. Doran, n. d.
B R	Bell, Lady and Richmond, Mrs. Herbert. The cat and the fiddle book. N. Y. Longmans, Green, 1922.
B R A	Branch, Anna H. The shoes that danced and other poems. Bost. Houghton, Mifflin, 1905.
B R B	Brunner, Emma B. Bits of background in one-act plays. N. Y. Knopf, 1919.
B R C	Branch, Anna H. The heart of the road, and other poems. Bost. Houghton, Mifflin, 1901.
B R D	Branch, Anna H. Rose of the wind, and other poems. Bost. Houghton, Mifflin, 1910.
B R E	Breed, James E. Every credit man. Portland, Oregon, J. E. Breed, 1916.
B R I	Brand, Alfred. The infernal masculine and other comedies. Bost. Cornhill Co., 1918.
B R O	Broido, Louis. The enemies of Israel. Cincinnati, Ohio. Cincinnati Dept. of Synagogue and School Extension. Union of American Hebrew Congregations, 1917.
B R P	Brighouse, Harold. Plays for the meadow and plays for the lawn. N. Y. French, 1921.
B R Q	Brown, Alice. Joint owners in Spain. Chic. Little Theatre, 1914.
B R W	Bell, May. What of the night? and other sketches. Lond. Arthur H. Stockwell, 1918.
B S	Barnum, Madalene D. School plays for all occasions. Newark, N. J. Barse & Hopkins, 1922.
B S B	Benton, Rita. Bible plays. N. Y. The Abingdon press, 1922.
B S C	Benton, Rita. The star-child and other plays. N. Y. Writers Pub. Co., 1921.
B S D	Benton, Rita. Shorter Bible plays. N. Y. Abingdon press, 1922.
B S M	Benavente, Jacinto. The smile of Mona Lisa. Bost. Richard G. Badger, 1912.
B T	Barker, Granville. Three short plays. Bost. Little, Brown, 1917.
B U	Burbank, Barbara & others. Comedies for young folks. Bost. Walter H. Baker, 1902.
B U E	Buckton, A. M. Eager heart. Lond. Methuen, 1904.
B U J	Bugbee, Willis N. Jolly Christmas book. Syracuse, N. Y. Willis N. Bugbee, n. d.
B U P	Bugbee, Willis N. Plays. Syracuse, N. Y. W. N. Bugbee, n. d.
B U R	Burkham, Lucie T. When the land was young. Cincinnati, Ohio. D. A. R. Chapter, 1909.
B Y L	Bynner, Witter. The little king. N. Y. Kennerley, 1914.
B Y R	Byrne, Lee. Quarry slaves. Bost. Poet-lore, 1914.
B Y T	Bynner, Witter. Tiger. Lond. D. J. Rider, 1914.
C 1	Cohen, Helen L., ed. One-act plays by modern authors. N. Y. Harcourt, Brace, 1921.
C 2	Cohen, Helen L. The junior play book. N. Y. Harcourt, Brace, 1923.

C A	Calderon, George. Eight one-act plays. Lond. Grant Richards, 1922.
C A C	Cameron, Margaret. Comedies in miniature. N. Y. McClure, Philips, 1903.
C A I	Caine, Hall. The iron hand. N. Y. McConnell Printing Co., 1916.
C A M	Camp Outfitting Co. Plays. N. Y. Camp Outfitting Co., n. d.
C A N	Campbell, Evangeline. The husking bee. Haverhill, Mass. Franklin P. Stiles, 1910.
C A P	Cannan, Gilbert. Four plays. Lond. Sidgwick & Jackson, 1913.
C A R	Carr, Albert. The cowboy and the lady. Hill City, So. Dakota. Albert Carr, 1912.
C B	Chambers, C. I. The Boy Scouts' book of plays. Lond. Well, Gardner, Darton, 1914.
C B I	Clark, Barrett H. Representative one-act plays by British and Irish authors. Bost. Little, Brown, 1921.
C C	Cauldwell, Samuel M. Chocolate cake and black sand. N. Y. Putnam, 1917.
C C C	Carter, Elsie H. Christmas candles. N. Y. Holt, 1915.
C D	Craig, Anne A. T. The dramatic festival. N. Y. Putnam, 1912.
C D L	Colum, Padraic. Dramatic legends and other poems. N. Y. Macmillan, 1922.
C E	Cannan, Gilbert. Everybody's husband. N. Y. Huebsch, 1917.
C F	Clark, Barrett H. Four plays of the Free Theatre. Cincinnati. Stewart Kidd, 1914.
C F A	Chapman, John J. Four plays for children. N. Y. Moffat, Yard, 1908.
C F P	Carolina folk-plays. N. Y. Holt, 1922.
C F S	Conger, Margaret L. Folk story plays for children. N. Y. James A. McCann, 1920.
C H	Cleather, Dorothy. A handy book of plays for girls. Chic. Saalfield Pub. Co., n. d.
C H A	Chapin, Harry L. Poems and plays. N. Y. The Shakespeare Press, 1915.
C H B	Chamberlain, Basil H. Japanese poetry. Lond. John Murray, 1911.
C H C	Chaplin, Alice W. A play a month for female characters. Bost. Walter H. Baker, 1917.
C H D	Chékhov, Anton. Plays. Second series. N. Y. Scribner, 1912.
C H E	Chékhov, Anton. Plays. tr. from Russian by Marian Fell. Vol. I. N. Y. Scribner, 1916.
C H F	Corbin, John. Husbands, and The forbidden guests. Bost. Houghton, Mifflin, 1910.
C H U	Churchill, E. P. The special rehearsal. Peoria, Ill. Frank Brown, 1907.
C J	Cabell, James B. The jewel merchants. N. Y. McBride, 1921.
C K	Crocker, Bosworth. Humble folk. Cincinnati. Stewart Kidd, 1923.
C L	Crocker, Bosworth. The last straw. N. Y. Frank Shay, 1917.
C L A	Clark, Milton F. The scoop. San Francisco, Calif. M. E. Clark, 1907.

CLD	Clements, Colin C. Plays for a folding theatre. Cincinnati. Stewart Kidd, 1923.
CLE	Clemenceau, Georges. The veil of happiness. N. Y. T. M. Cleland, 1920.
CLF	Cleugh, Dennis. The violet under the snow. Lond. Simpkin, Marshall, 1915.
CO	Cooke, Marjorie B. Dramatic episodes. Chic. Dramatic Pub. Co., 1904.
COC	Cockrell, Maud. Golliwog in Fairyland. Bost. Le Roy Phillips, 1921.
COI	Coit, Henry A. War's end. Los Angeles, Calif. Clyde Brown, 1917.
CON	Converse, Florence. The blessed birthday. N. Y. Dutton, 1917.
COV	Cowan, Sada. The state forbids. N. Y. Kennerley, 1915.
COW	Code, Grant H. When the fates decree. Pittsburgh, Pa. Peabody High School, 1914.
COX	Cox, Ethel L. Poems lyric and dramatic. Bost. Richard G. Badger, 1904.
CT	Chapin, Harold. Three one act plays. N. Y. French, 1921.
CU	California University, Little Theatre Workshop. Plays of the University of California Little Theatre Workshop. University of California. Little Theatre Press, 1922.
DA	Dix, Beulah M. Allison's lad and other martial interludes. N. Y. Holt, 1910.
DAA	Davis, Malcolm W. Plays. N. Y. Malcolm W. Davis, 1915.
DAB	Davis, M. E. M. A bunch of roses and other parlor plays. Bost. Small, Maynard, 1903.
DAD	Daly, Arnold. The dominant male, essays and plays. N. Y. Moffat, Yard, 1921.
DAF	Davis, Richard H. Farces. N. Y. Scribner, 1906.
DAG	Denton, Clara J. The program book. N. Y. J. Fischer & Bros., 1910.
DAH	Denton, Clara J. All the holidays. Chic. A. Flanagan, 1905.
DAI	Denton, Clara J. When the curtain rises. Program book. Vol. II. N. Y. J. Fischer & Bros., 1909.
DAK	Dakota playmakers. Plays. University of North Dakota, 1920.
DAL	Dakota Playmaker plays. First series. Four one-act plays on Colonial themes. Bost. Walter H. Baker, 1923.
DAN	Daniel, C. W. Plays. Lond. C. W. Daniel, n. d.
DAO	Dane, Essex. One act plays. Bost. Walter H. Baker, 1923.
DEM	Demarest, William T. Plays. Marmoreneck, N. Y. W. T. Demarest, n. d.
DEP	Denison, T. S. Plays. Chic. T. S. Denison, n. d.
DF	Dunsany, Lord. Five plays. Bost. Little, Brown, 1914.
DFN	Dunsany, Lord. A night at an inn. N. Y. Sunwise Turn, 1916.
DFO	Dunsany, Lord. Plays of near and far. N. Y. Putnam, 1922.
DFP	Dunsany, Lord. Plays of gods and men. Bost. John Luce, 1917.
DIC	Dickinson, Thomas H., ed. Chief contemporary dramatists. Bost. Houghton, Mifflin, 1915.

16   AN INDEX TO ONE-ACT PLAYS

DK	Dell, Floyd. King Arthur's socks and other village plays. N. Y. Knopf, 1922.
DL	Denison, Emily. H. The little mother of the slums and other plays. Bost. Gorham Press, 1915.
DLP	Dalkeith, Lena. Little plays. Lond. T. C. & E. C. Jack, n. d.
DM	Down, Oliphant. The maker of dreams. Lond. Gowans & Gray, 1914.
DO	Dopp, Katharine E. Homer and David. (From an essay by Edward E. Hale) Westwood, Mass. Ariel Press, 1903.
DOF	Domestic and Foreign Missionary Society. Voices from everywhere. N. Y. The Domestic and Foreign Missionary Society, 1914.
ROR	Dorsen, Helen. Power of loyalty. N. Y. Moffat, Yard, 1918.
DOT	Doty, Harry M. Plays. Chatham, N. Y. Harry M. Doty, n. d.
DOW	Downing, Henry F. & Downing, Mrs. H. F. Placing Paul's play. Lond. Francis Griffiths, 1913.
DP	Dreiser, Theodore. Plays of the natural and the supernatural. Bost. John Lane, 1916.
DPA	Drinkwater, John. Pawns: three poetic plays. Lond. Sidgwick & Jackson, 1917.
DPF	Dargan, Olive T. & Peterson, Frederick. The flutter of gold-leaf and other plays. N. Y. Scribner, 1922.
DPN	Dowson, Ernest. The poems of Ernest Dowson. N. Y. John Lane, 1917.
DPO	Dowson, Ernest. The Pierrot of the minute. Portland, Maine. Mosher, 1913.
DPP	Dramatic Publishing Co. Plays. Chic. Dramatic Pub. Co., n. d.
DR	Drinkwater, John. The storm. Birmingham, Eng. John Drinkwater, 1915.
DSE	Davis, R. H. & Sheehan, P. P. Efficiency. N. Y. Doran, 1917.
DU	Duran, Leo, tr. Plays of old Japan. N. Y. Thomas Seltzer, 1921.
DUN	Dunn, Fannie W. What shall we play? (A dramatic reader) N. Y. Macmillan, 1916.
ED	Educational Publishing Co. The first flag and other patriotic plays and exercises. Bost. Educational Pub. Co., 1917.
EDG	Edgar, Mary S. The wayside piper. N. Y. National Board of Y. W. C. A., 1915.
EG	Egbert, Frank H. Capitulation of Mr. Hyleigh. Hamilton, Ohio. Brown & Whitaker, 1906.
EL	Ellis, Mrs. Havelock. Love in danger. Bost. Houghton, Mifflin, 1915.
ELA	Ellis, Mrs. Havelock. The subjection of Kezia. Stratford-on-Avon. Shakespeare Head Press, 1908.
ELT1	Eliot, Samuel A., Jr., ed. Little Theatre classics. Vol I. Bost. Little, Brown, 1917.
ELT2	Eliot, Samuel A., Jr., ed. Little Theatre classics. Vol. II. Bost. Little, Brown, 1917.
ELT3	Eliot, Samuel A., Jr., ed. Little Theatre classics. Vol. III. Bost. Little, Brown, 1921.
ELT4	Eliot, Samuel A., Jr., ed. Little Theatre classics. Vol. IV. Bost. Little, Brown, 1922.

E P	Eldridge. Plays. Franklin, Ohio. Eldridge Entertainment House, n. d.
E R	Ervine, St. John G. Four Irish plays. Dublin. Maunsel, 1914.
E R A	Ervine, St. John G. The magnanimous lover. Dublin. Maunsel, 1912.
E T	Elkins, Fenton B. Three tremendous trifles. N. Y. Duffield, 1919.
E T E	Elwes, Mary. Temporary engagements and other plays. Lond. Francis Griffiths. 1920.
E V	Evans, Della J. Two plays and a preface. Bost. Richard G. Badger, 1921.
E V M	Evans, Florence W. The ride home, poems, with "The marriage of Guineth." Bost. Houghton, Mifflin, 1913.
E W	Ehrmann, Max. The wife of Marobius. N. Y. Kennerley, 1911.
F E	Foucher, Laure C. Effie's Christmas dream. Bost. Little, Brown, 1912.
F E N	Fenollosa, Ernest & Pound, Ezra. 'Noh'; or, Accomplishment. N. Y. Knopf, 1917.
F E R	Ferrer, Linna M. Bobby's dream. Bost. Quincy Prevocational Center. Boston Public School, 1921.
F E T	Fay, Frederic L. & Emerson, M. A. Three plays for boys. (International Com'n of Young Men's Christian Ass'n.) N. Y. Association Press, 1919.
F F	Fitzmaurice, George. Five plays. Bost. Little, Brown, 1914.
F G	Fotheringham, E. M. & Gemmell, John. Tiny plays for tiny people. N. Y. French, 1921.
F I	Fischer, J. & Bros. Plays. N. Y. J. Fischer & Bros., n. d.
F I L	Fillmore Music House. Plays. Cincinnati, Ohio. Fillmore Music House, n. d.
F L	Flanagan, A., Co. Plays. Chic. A. Flanagan, n. d.
F L E	Fleming, Charles L. The telephone. Phila. R. S. Joyce, 1903.
F L S	Flying stag plays. N. Y. Egmont Arens, n. d.
F O	Foley, James W. Sing a song of Sleepy Head. N. Y. Dutton, 1922.
F O S	Four Seas Co. Plays. Bost. Four Seas, n. d.
F P	Fitzgerald. Plays. N. Y. Fitzgerald Pub. Corporation, n. d.
F R	France, Anatole. The man who married a dumb wife. N. Y. Lane, 1915.
F S 1	47 workshop. Plays. First series. N. Y. Brentano's, 1918.
F S 2	47 workshop. Plays. Second series. N. Y. Brentano's, 1920.
F S 3	47 workshop. Plays. Third series. N. Y. Brentano's, 1922.
F S D	French, Samuel. French's Standard Drama. N. Y. French, n. d.
F S J	Frank, Florence K. Jael. Chic. Little Theatre, 1914.
F S P	Frank, Maude M. Short plays about famous authors. N. Y. Holt, 1915.
F U	Fuller, Alice C. Dramatized stories, myths, and legends. Franklin, Ohio, Eldridge Entertainment House, 1913.
G 1	Grange plays—Number one. One-act plays. Compiled by J. W. Darrow. N. Y. Chatham, 1914.

G 2	Grange plays—Number two. One-act plays. Compiled by J. W. Darrow. N. Y. Chatham, 1915.
G 3	Grange plays—Number three. Pub. by J. W. Darrow. N. Y. Chatham, 1915.
G A L	Gascoin, Catherine B. The lumber room and other plays. N. Y. Vaughan & Gomme, 1914.
G A T	Garnett, Louise A. Three to make ready. N. Y. Doran, 1923.
G B A	Goodman, Kenneth S. Barbara. (Stage Guild plays) N. Y. Vaughan & Gomme, 1914.
G D	Greene, Clay M. The dispensation and other plays. N. Y. Doran, 1914.
G D L	Greene, Kathleen C. The little boy out of the wood and other dream plays. N. Y. Lane, 1917.
G F	Goodlander, Mabel R. Fairy plays for children. Chic. Rand McNally, n. d.
G G	Gordon, Leon. The gentleman Ranker and other plays. Bost. Four Seas, 1919.
G I	Gregory, Lady Isabelle A. The image and other plays. N. Y. Putnam, 1922.
G I A	Gibson, Wilfrid W. Battle and other poems. N. Y. Macmillan, 1917.
G I B	Gibson, Wilfrid W. Borderlands and Thoroughfares. N. Y. Macmillan. 1914.
G I D	Gibson, Wilfrid W. Daily bread. N. Y. Macmillan, 1916.
G I E	Gibbins, J. R. Becoming an American. Eden, Idaho. J. R. Gibbins, 1920.
G I I	Gregory, Lady Isabelle A. Irish folk-history plays. Second series. N. Y. Putnam, 1912.
G I P	Gibson, Wilfred W. Poems, 1904-1917. N. Y. Macmillan, 1912-1917.
G I S	Gibson, Wilfrid W. Stonefolds. Lond. Elkin Mathews, 1916.
G J	Goddard, Harold. The sisters. Swarthmore, Penn. H. Goddard, 1914.
G O	Gould, Felix. The marsh maiden. Bost. Four Seas, 1918.
G O R	Gordon, Henry. Thirst. N. Y. New Rochelle, 1912.
G P	Glaspell, Susan. Plays. Bost. Small, Maynard, 1920.
G P C	Glaspell, Susan. The people, and Close the book. N. Y. Shay, 1918.
G Q	Goodman, Kenneth S. Quick curtains. Chic. Stage Guild, 1915.
G Q A	Goodman, Kenneth S. More quick curtains. Chic. Stage Guild, 1923.
G R	Griffith, Benjamin L. C. Plays and monologues. Phila. Penn Pub. Co., 1901.
G R A	Griffith, William. Candles in the sun. Chic. The Bookfellows, 1921.
G R E	Greve, Clifford. The militant God and some sonnets, verses and rhymes. Kansas City, Burton Pub. Co., 1918.
G R F	Grendon, Felix. Will he come back? N. Y. New Review Pub. Ass'n., 1916.
G R L	Graham, Manta S. Light weights. Bost. Cornhill Pub. Co., 1921.

GRN	Greenwald, M. Our uncle from the West. N. Y. Leo Feist, 1912.
GRS	Grossman, Samuel S. The Purim players. Phila. J. H. Greenstone, 1911.
GRY	Gregory, Lady Isabelle A. The full moon. Dublin, Ireland. Lady Gregory, 1911.
GRZ	Gregory, Lady Isabelle A. New comedies. N. Y. Putnam, 1913.
GS	Gregory, Lady Isabelle A. Seven short plays. N. Y. Putnam, 1903.
GSS	Galsworthy, John, Six short plays. N. Y. Scribner, 1915–1921.
GT	Gerstenberg, Alice. Ten one-act plays. N. Y. Brentano's, 1921.
GU	Gunnison, Binney. New dialogues and plays for young people, ages fifteen to twenty-five. Adapted from the popular works of well-known authors. N. Y. Hinds, Hayden, & Eldredge, 1905.
GUB	Guptil, Elizabeth F. & Hunting, Ema S. & others. Bright ideas for Christmas. Lebanon, Ohio. March Bros., 1920.
GUC	Guptill, Elizabeth F. The complete Hallowe'en book. Lebanon. Ohio. March Bros., 1915.
GUD	Guptill, Elizabeth F. Guptill's new Christmas book. Lebanon, Ohio. March Bros., 1915.
GUI	Guild, Thacher H. The power of a God and other one-act plays. Urbana, Ill., University of Illinois Press, 1919.
GUT	Guptill, Elizabeth F. Twelve plays for children, humorous, wise and otherwise. Chic. Beckley-Cardy, 1916.
GW	Gibson, Wilfrid W. Womenkind. N. Y. Macmillan, 1912.
HA	Housman, Laurence. Angels and ministers. Lond. Cape, 1921.
HA4	Housman, Laurence. Angels and ministers: four plays of Victorian shade and character. N. Y. Harcourt, Brace, 1922.
HAB	Housman, Laurence. False premises: five one-act plays. Oxford, England. Basil Blackwell, 1922.
HAD	Henderson, Mrs. Alice C. Adam's dream and two other miracle plays for children. N. Y. Scribner, 1909.
HAE	Haslett, Harriet H. Dolores of the Sierra and other one-act plays. San Francisco, Calif., Paul Elder, 1917.
HAG	Hagedorn, Hermann. The horse thieves. Bost. H. Hagedorn, 1909.
HAH	Hazard, Rowland G. How Robin Hood once was a Wait: a miracle play or Christmas masque. S. P. C. Providence R. I., 1912.
HAL	Hale, Harris G. & Hall, Newton M. The story of Jacob. Bost. Pilgrim Press, 1906.
HAN2	Hankin, St. John. Dramatic works. Vol. II. N. Y. Kennerley, 1912.
HAN3	Hankin, St. John. Dramatic works. Vol. III. N. Y. Kennerley, 1912.
HAP	Housman, Laurence. Possession. Lond. Cape, 1922.
HAR	Housman, Laurence. The wheel: three poetic plays on Greek subjects. N. Y. French, 1920.
HAS	Halman, Doris F. Set the stage for eight. Bost. Little, Brown, 1923.

HAT	Harnwell, Anna J. The sin of Ahab. N. Y. Doran, 1922.
HB	Harper's book of little plays. Selected by Madalene D. Barnum. N. Y. Harper, 1910.
HD1	Harvard Dramatic Club. Plays. N. Y. Brentano's, 1918.
HD2	Harvard Dramatic Club. Plays. Second series. N. Y. Brentano's, 1919.
HE	Heath, Lilian M. Enjoyable entertainments. Bost. United Society of Christian Endeavor, 1913.
HEA	Hewlett, Maurice. The Agonists: a trilogy of God and man. N. Y. Scribner, 1911.
HER	Herbach, Joseph. The rehearsal. Phila., J. H. Greenstone, 1911.
HES	Hervilly, Ernest. Sayonara. ed. by Kenneth S. Guthrie. Brooklyn, N. Y. Comparative Literature Press, 1912.
HF	Houghton, Stanley. Five one-act plays. N. Y. French, 1913.
HH	Hill, Frederick T. High School farces. N. Y. Stokes, 1920.
HHA	Hill, Edward G. The House of Aegeus and other verse. Louisville, Ky., The Standard Printing Co., 1920.
HM	Hofmannsthal, Hugo H., elder von. Madonna Dianora. (Contemporary Dramatists series) Bost. Richard G. Badger, 1916.
HO	Hope, Winifred A. Friends in bookland. N. Y. Macmillan, 1921.
HOL	Holloway, Pearl; Freeman, Carolyn, and others. The Paramount Christmas book. Chic. Meyer & Bros., 1922.
HOM	Houghton, Mifflin Co. Plays. Bost. Houghton, Mifflin, n. d.
HOR	Holley, Horace. Read-aloud plays. N. Y. Kennerley, 1916.
HOT	Howard, Katharine. Two plays and a rhapsody. First edition. San Diego, Calif., Katharine Howard, 1916.
HP	Hagedorn, Hermann. Poems and ballads. N. Y. Macmillan, 1913.
HPS	Hagedorn, Hermann. The silver blade. Berlin. Alfred Unger, 1907.
HPT	Hagedorn, Hermann. A troop of the guard and other poems. Bost. Houghton, Mifflin, 1909.
HS	Hunter, Rex. Stuff o' Dreams and other plays. Chic. T. S. Denison, 1919.
HT	Holt, Florence T. They the crucified and Comrades: two war plays. Bost. Houghton, Mifflin, 1918.
HU	Huxley, Aldous L. Mortal coils. N. Y. Doran, 1922.
HUB	Hubbard, Louis H. Telling the truth. Belton, Texas. Lone Star Play Co., 1907.
HUC	Hubbard, Eleanore. Citizenship plays: a dramatic reader for upper grades. Chic. Benj. H. Sanborn, 1922.
HUD	Hubbard, Eleanore. Little American history plays for little Americans. Chic. Benj. H. Sanborn, 1919.
HUG	Hughes, Richard. The sisters' tragedy. Oxford, England. Basil Blackwell, 1922.
HVS	Heidenstam, Verner von. The soothsayer. Bost. Four Seas, 1919.
HW	Hare, Walter B. The white Christmas and other Merry Christmas plays. Chic. T. S. Denison, 1917.
I	Irish, Marie; Denton, Clara J.; Smith, Laura R., & others.

AN INDEX TO ONE-ACT PLAYS 21

        Thirty new Christmas dialogues and plays. Chic. A. Flanagan, 1909.

I C   Irish, Marie. Choice Christmas dialogues and plays. Dayton, Ohio. Paine Pub. Co., n. d.

I D   Irwin, Grace L. Drawing room plays. San Francisco, Calif. Paul Elder, 1903.

I L   Irish, Marie. Little people's plays. Chic. T. S. Denison, 1913.

I P   Irish, Marie. Practical dialogues, drills, and marches. Chic. A. Flanagan, 1900.

I P P   Irish, Marie. Plays and comedies for little folks. Chic. A. Flanagan, 1912.

I P R   Irish, Marie. The primary Christmas book. Dayton, Ohio. Paine Pub. Co., 1922.

I P T   Izumo, Takeda. The pine-tree. N. Y. Duffield, 1916.

I W   Iwaski, Yozant and Hughes, Glenn. Three modern Japanese plays. Cincinnati. Stewart Kidd, 1923.

J B   Johnston, Emma L. & Barnum, Madalene D. A book of plays for little actors. Chic. Am. Book Co., 1907.

J E   Jenkins, Hester D. Five playlets, written for the Department of Social Betterment. Brooklyn, N. Y. Bureau of Charities, 1915.

J E P   Jex, John. Passion playlets. Bost. Cornhill, 1918.

J F   Jennings, Gertrude. Four one-act plays. N. Y. French, 1914.

J O   Jones, Henry A. The theatre of ideas, a burlesque allegory, and three one-act plays. N. Y. Doran, 1915.

J O A   Johnson, Gertrude E. Dialects for oral interpretation. N. Y. Century, 1922.

J O N   Jones, Horatio S. "The Cracker." Kansas City, Mo. H. S. Jones, 1922.

K E   Keating, Miss E. H. Dramas for boys. N. Y. French, n. d.

K E N   Kennedy, Charles R. The necessary evil. N. Y. Harper, 1913.

K I   Kinnick, Claude. As advertised. Alliance, Ohio. Claude Kinnick, 1921.

K L   Kleber, Frank T. Three plays. N. Y. Frank T. Kleber, 1922.

K L E   Kleber, Frank T. Triangle No. V333. N. Y. Frank T. Kleber, 1917.

K M A   Kreymborg, Alfred. Plays for Merry Andrews. N. Y. Sunwise Turn, 1920.

K M P   Kreymborg, Alfred. Plays for poem-mimes. N. Y. The Other Press, 1918.

K M R   Kreymborg, Alfred. Puppet plays. N. Y. Harcourt, Brace, n. d.

K P   Knickerbocker, Edwin Van B., ed. Plays for classroom interpretation. N. Y. Holt, 1921.

K P P   Kraft, Irma. The power of Purim and other plays. Designed for Jewish religious schools. Phila. Jewish Publication Society of America, 1915.

K T   Kennedy, Charles R. The terrible meek. N. Y. Harper, 1912.

L A   Langner, Lawrence. Another way out. N. Y. Frank Shay, 1916. (Washington Square players)

L A F   Langner, Lawrence. Five one-act comedies. Cincinnati, Ohio. Stewart Kidd, 1922.

L A N   Lang, Edith. A Christmas story. Bost. Beacon Press, 1917.

	L B	Lisle, Clifton. Boy scout entertainments. Phila. Penn Pub. Co., 1918.
	L C	Lewis, B. Roland, ed. Contemporary one-act plays. N. Y. Scribner, 1922.
	L E	Leonard, Sterling A., ed. The Atlantic book of modern plays. N. Y. Atlantic Monthly Press, 1921.
	L E E	Lee, Agnes. The sharing. Bost. Sherman, French, 1914.
	L E L	Leland, Robert D. The barbarians. Bost. Poetry-Drama, 1915.
	L E N	Leonard, Martha. The dream of wings. Mt. Kisco, N. Y. North Westchester Pub. Co., 1918.
	L E O	Leonard, William E. Glory of the morning. Madison, Wis. William E. Leonard, 1912.
	L E T	Leslie, Noel. Three plays. Bost. Four Seas, 1920.
	L L P	Lord, Katharine. The little playbook. N. Y. Duffield, 1920.
	L L R	Lord, Katharine. Little playbook plays. N. Y. Katharine Lord, 1915.
	L L S	Lord, Katharine. Plays for school and camp. Bost. Little, Brown, 1922.
	L O	Loving, Pierre, ed. Ten minute plays. N. Y. Brentano's, 1923.
	L S	Luques, E. Antoinette. The snow image and other plays for children. Bost. Walter H. Baker, 1914.
	L U	Lütkenhaus, Anna M. Plays for school children. N. Y. Century, 1915.
	L Y	Lyttelton, Edith. A Christmas morality play. Lond. Elkin Mathews, 1908.
	L Y A	Lyttelton, Edith. The thumbscrew. N. Y. Longmans, Green, 1911.
PS 634 M3	M A	Mayorga, Margaret G., ed. Representative one-act plays by American authors. Bost. Little, Brown, 1919.
	M A C	McGeoch, Daisy. Concert cameos. N. Y. French, 1922.
	M A E	Maeterlinck, Maurice. A miracle of Saint Anthony, and five other plays. N. Y. Boni and Liveright, 1917.
PQ 2625 A5 P.42	M A F	Maeterlinck, Maurice. Pelleas and Melisande; Alladine and Palomides; Home. tr. by Richard Hovey. N. Y. Dodd, Mead, 1918.
	M A G	Maeterlinck, Maurice. Plays. Second series. tr. from French by Richard Hovey. N. Y. Duffield, 1906.
	M A H	Maeterlinck, Maurice. Plays of Maurice Maeterlinck. Vol. I. tr. by Richard Hovey. Chic. Herbert S. Stone, 1894.
PQ 2625 A41	M A I	Maeterlinck, Maurice. The intruder. tr. from French by Richard Hovey. N. Y. Dodd, Mead, 1911.
	M A J	McLaren, Ian. The Duchess entertains. Toronto, Canada. W. S. Johnston, 1917.
	M A K	McLaren, Ian. The estaminet. Toronto, Canada. W. S. Johnston, 1917.
	M A M	MacMillan, Mary Louise. The shadowed star. Cincinnati, Ohio. Consumers League of the City of Cincinnati, 1908.
	M A P	March Bros. Plays. Lebanon, Ohio. March Bros., n. d.
	M A R	Marmer, Archie. Makers of America. Bost. Richard G. Badger, 1919.
	M A S	Marsh, Charles A. & Rowland, H. O. The challenge of the Cross. Sioux City, Ia., C. A. Marsh, 1915.
	M A T	Martin Studios, ed. Pathfinders. Conn. Willimantic, 1916.

AN INDEX TO ONE-ACT PLAYS

M B	Mackay, Constance D. The Beau of Bath and other one-act plays of eighteenth century life. N. Y. Holt, 1915.
M B F	Mackay, Constance D. The Forest Princess and other masques. N. Y. Holt, 1916.
M B M	Mackay, Constance D. Memorial day pageant. N. Y. Harper, 1910.
M B P	March Bros. Petite plays. Lebanon, Ohio. March Bros., 1912.
M C	Middleton, George. Criminals. N. Y. Huebsch, 1915.
M D	Mayne, Rutherford. The drone and other plays. Dublin. Maunsel, 1912.
M D T	Mayne, Rutherford. The troth. Dublin. Maunsel, 1909.
M E	Middleton, George. Embers and other one-act plays. N. Y. Holt, 1911.
M F	Moeller, Philip. Five somewhat historical plays. N. Y. Knopf, 1916.
M F H	Merington, Marguerite. Holiday plays. N. Y. Duffield, 1910.
M F P	Merington, Marguerite. Festival plays. N. Y. Duffield, 1913.
M H	Manners, J. Hartley. Happiness and other plays. N. Y. Dodd, Mead, 1914.
M H H	Mackay, Constance D. The house of the heart and other plays for children. N. Y. Holt, 1909.
MI F	Millward, Florence M. Four short plays. Lond. Joseph_William, 1922.
MI M	Middleton, George. Masks. N. Y. Holt, 1920.
MI P	Middleton, George. Possessions. N. Y. Holt, 1915.
MI S	Missionary Education movement of U. S. and Canada. Plays. N. Y.
MI T	Middleton, George. Tradition. N. Y. Holt, 1913.
M L	McGurrin, C. H. A light from another world. (American Dramatic series) Bost. Gorham Press, 1915.
M L G	Masefield, John. Good Friday. Garden City, N. Y. Letchworth, 1916.
M L S	Masefield, John. The locked chest and The sweeps of Ninety-eight. N. Y. Macmillan, 1916.
M M	MacMillan, Mary. More short plays. Cincinnati. Stewart Kidd, 1917.
M O	Moorman, Frederic W. Plays of the ridings. Lond. Elkin Mathews, 1919.
M O A	Moran, Mabel M. The Shakespeare Garden Club. Larchmont, N. Y. Larchmont Garden Club, 1916.
M O L	Morley, Malcolm. Told by the gate and other one-act plays. Bost. Gorham Press, 1916.
M O O	Moylan, Thomas K. "Oh Lawsy Me!" and "Movies." Dublin James Duffy, 1917.
M O P	Monroe, Harriet. The passing show: five modern plays in verse. Bost. Houghton, Mifflin, 1903.
M O Q	Morgan, Edward. A son of the greater fatherland. San Francisco, Calif., Edward Morgan, 1916.
M O R	Moorman, Frederic W. Plays of the Ridings. Lond. Elkin Mathews, 1919.
M O S	Mosher, John C. Sauce for the Emperor. N. Y. Frank Shay, 1916.

M O T	Moore, Thomas S. Tragic mothers. Lond. Grant Richards, 1922.
M O Y	Moylan, Thomas K. Uncle Pat. Dublin. James Duffy, 1913.
M P	Morningside plays. Frank Shay, ed. N. Y. Frank Shay, 1917.
M P P	Mackay, Constance D. Plays of the pioneers: a book of historical pageant-plays. N. Y. Harper, 1915.
M P Y	Mackay, Constance D. Patriotic plays and pageants for young people. N. Y. Holt, n. d.
M P Z	Merington, Marguerite. Picture plays. N. Y. Duffield, 1911.
M R	Moses, Montrose J., ed. Representative one-act plays by Continental authors. Bost. Little, Brown, 1922.
M S	Macmillan, Mary. Short plays. Cincinnati. Stewart Kidd, 1913.
M S L	Milne, A. A. First plays. Lond. Chatto & Windus, 1919.
M S M	Milne, A. A. Second plays. Lond. Chatto & Windus, 1921.
M S T	Mackay, Constance D. The silver thread and other folk plays for young people. N. Y. Holt, 1910.
M T	Marks, Jeannette. Three Welsh plays. Bost. Little, Brown, 1912.
M T A	Masefield, John. Poems and plays. Vol. II. N. Y. Macmillan, 1918.
M T C	Moses, Montrose J., ed. A treasury of plays for children. Bost. Little, Brown, 1921.
M T P	Manners, J. Hartley. Three plays. N. Y. Doran, 1920.
M T T	MacMillan, Mary. Third book of short plays. Cincinnati. Stewart Kidd, 1922.
M U B	Musset, Alfred de. Barberine and other comedies. Chic. Dramatic Pub. Co., 1911.
M W	Monkhouse, Allan. War plays. Lond. Constable, 1916.
M Y	Mackaye, Percy. Yankee fantasies. N. Y. Duffield, 1912.
M Y S	Mackaye, Percy. Sanctuary. N. Y. Frederick A. Stokes, 1913.
N A	Norton, Ida G. Club stunts. La Junta, Colo. Ida G. Norton, 1922.
N C	Noyes, Alfred. Collected poems. Vol. III. Lond. W. Blackwood & Sons, 1921.
N C B	Noyes, Alfred. A Belgian Christmas Eve. N. Y. Stokes, 1915.
N E	Newton, Alma. The blue string and other sketches. N. Y. Duffield, 1918.
N I	Nirdlinger, Charles F. Four short plays. N. Y. Kennerley, 1916.
N O	Noel, Joseph. Three plays and a curtain raiser. N. Y. Claridge Press, 1916.
N O B	Noble, Kate W. A Colonial tea. Waterbury, Conn. Melicent Porter Chapter, D. A. R., 1915.
N O R	Norton, Louise. Little wax candle. N. Y. Claire Marie, 1914.
N R	Noyes, Alfred. Rada. N. Y. Stokes, 1918.
N T	Neihardt, John G. Two mothers. N. Y. Macmillan, 1921.
O	Oxford pamphlets, 1914–15. Lond. Oxford University Press, 1915.

AN INDEX TO ONE-ACT PLAYS 25

O D   O'Brien, Seumas. Duty and other Irish comedies. Bost. Little, Brown, 1916.

O MC   O'Neill, Eugene G. The moon of the Caribbees and six other plays of the sea. N. Y. Boni & Liveright, 1919.

O P   Olcott, Virginia. Plays for home, school, and settlement. N. Y. Moffat, Yard, 1916.

O P A   Olcott, Virginia. Patriotic plays for young people. N. Y. Dodd, Mead, 1918.

O P P   Oppenheim, James. The pioneers. N. Y. Huebsch, 1910.

O R   O'Dea, Mark. Red Bud women: four dramatic episodes. Cincinnati. Stewart Kidd, 1922.

O S   Oliver, Margaret S. Six one-act plays. Bost. Richard G. Badger, 1916. (American Dramatists series)

O S T   Ostrovsky, Alexander. Plays. tr. and ed. by George R. Noyes. N. Y. Scribner, 1917.

O T   O'Neill, Eugene G. Thirst and other one-act plays. Bost. Gorham Press. 1914.

P 1   Provincetown plays. First series. N. Y. Frank Shay, 1916.

P 2   Provincetown plays. Second series. N. Y. Frank Shay, 1916.

P 3   Provincetown plays. Third series. N. Y. Frank Shay, 1916.

P A   Poole, Evan. An age of steel. Lond. Heath, Cranton & Ouseley, 1913.

P A B   Palmer, Mrs. Martha R. The best seller. Salt Lake City, Utah. Mrs. Martha Royle Palmer, 1913.

P A D   Painton, Edith F. A. U. Dialogues and plays for entertainment days. Chic. Beckley-Cardy, 1917.

P A P   Paine Publishing Co. Plays. Dayton, Ohio. Paine Pub. Co., n. d.

P A R   Parker, Oliver P. The Wren. Memphis, Tenn. National Drama Co., 1923.

P A S   Painton, Edith F. A. U. Specialty entertainments for little folks. Chic. Beckley-Cardy, 1917.

P B   Pape, Lee. The bravest thing in the world. Phila. Penn Pub. Co., 1917.

P C   Pemberton, May. Christmas plays. N. Y. Crowell, 1915.

P C P   Practical Publishing Co. Christmas plays for children. Series I. Westfield, N. J. Practical Pub. Co., 1916.

P E T   Peixotto, Eustace M. Ten boys' farces. Bost. Walter H. Baker, 1916.

P F   Peabody, Josephine P. Fortune and men's eyes. Bost. Houghton, Mifflin, 1900.

P H   Phelps, Pauline & Short, Marion, eds. Sixteen two-character plays. N. Y. Edgar S. Werner & Co., 1906.

P HI   Phillips, Stephen. Lyrics and dramas. N. Y. John Lane, 1913.

P I   Pillot, Eugene. My lady dreams. Bost. Rockwell & Churchill Press, 1922.

P L   Play-bits: fragments for concert folk. N. Y. French, 1922.

P L A   Plays for amateur actors. New edition. Lond. C. Arthur Pearson, 1921.

P L N   Pleasant, Lillian. Their godfathers from Paris. N. Y. E. A. Fink, 1915.

P M	Parker, Mary M. Monologues, stories, jingles and plays. Chic. Frederick J. Drake, 1917.
P O	Poole, Madeline. The elf that stayed behind and other plays for children. Bost. Walter H. Baker, 1918.
P O T	Potter, Dorothy. Under the eagle: three plays with a Prologue and Epilogue. Bost. Gorham Press, 1916.
P P	Payne, F. Ursula. Plays for Anychild. N. Y. Harper, 1918.
P P C	Payne, F. Ursula. Plays and pageants of citizenship. N. Y. Harper, 1920.
P P D	Payne, F. Ursula. Two war plays for schools. Brooklyn, N. Y. Training School for teachers. Bulletin No. 11, 1918.
P P P	Penn Publishing Co. Plays. Phila. Penn Pub. Co., n. d.
P R	Parsons, Margaret G. Red letter day plays. N. Y. Womans Press, 1921.
P R I	Pritchard, George A. Prohibition Mother Goose. N. Y. Christian Nation Pub. Co., 1921.
P R Z	Pearse, Padraic. Collected works. Dublin. Maunsel, 1917.
P S	Pearse, Padraic. The singer and other plays. Dublin. Maunsel, 1918.
P T	Pinski, David. Ten plays. tr. from the Yiddish by Isaac Goldberg. N. Y. Huebsch, 1920.
P T K	Pinski, David. King David and his wives. tr. fr. Yiddish by Isaac Goldberg. N. Y. Huebsch, 1923.
P T S	Pinski, David and others. Six plays of the Yiddish Theatre. tr. and ed. by Isaac Goldberg. Bost. John W. Luce, 1916.
P T T	Pinsky, David & others. Six plays of the Yiddish Theatre. Second series. tr. & ed. by Isaac Goldberg. Bost. John W. Luce, 1918.
P U	Purcell, Lewis. The pagan. Dublin. Maunsel, 1907.
P WP	Plays with a punch. Bost. Walter H. Baker, 1916.
Q	Quinton, Pauline B. The locust flower and The celibate. Bost. Sherman, French, 1916.
R A	Rand, Kenneth. The Dreamer and other poems. Bost. Sherman, French, 1915.
R A A	Rawson, Graham S. The stroke of Marbot and two other plays of Napoleonic times. Lond. T. Fisher Unwin, 1917.
R C	Robinson, Lennox. Two plays; Harvest; The Clancy name. Dublin. Maunsel, 1911.
R D	Raeder, Henry. A dream of liberty. Chic. Peterson, 1903.
R E	Rein, A. E. Plays. Milwaukee, Wis., A. E. Rein, n. d.
R E E	Reely, Mary K. Daily bread; A window to the south; The lean years; one act plays. N. Y. H. W. Wilson, 1919.
R E F	Reely, Mary K. Early Ohios and Rhode Island Reds. Minn. Perine Book Co., 1921.
R E M	Remington Co., Norman. Plays. Norman Remington. Baltimore, Md., n. d.
R E P	Repertory plays. Lond. Gowans & Gray, Bost. Le Roy Phillips, n. d.
R F	Roberts, Morley. Four plays. Lond. Nash, 1911.
R I	Rice, Cale Y. The immortal lure. Garden City, N. Y. Doubleday, Page, 1911.
R I S	Rice, Wallace. Suggestions for giving six little plays for Il-

	linois children. State of Illinois. Illinois Centennial Commission, 1918.
R I T	Riley, Alice C. Ten minutes by the clock and three other plays for out-door or in-door production. (Drama League Junior play series) N. Y. Doran, 1923.
R O	Rogers, Thomas B. Five plays. Lond. Philip Allan & Co., 1920.
R O A	Roberts, Charles V. H. Octavia and New poems. N. Y. The Torch Press, 1918.
R O B	Robinson, Reed. His charity patient. San Diego, Calif. Keeler & Gillrup, 1914.
R P	Richards, Laura E. The pig brother play-book. Bost. Little, Brown, 1915.
R S	Richardson, Grace. Summer snow and other fairy plays. Chic. Saalfield Pub. Co., 1916.
R T	Robinson, Lennox. Two plays: Harvest; The Clancy name. Dublin. Maunsel, 1911.
R U	Russell, Mary M. Dramatized Bible stories for young people. N. Y. Doran, 1921.
R U E	Ruschke, Egmont W. "The echo" and "A bit o' verse." Bost. Stratford, 1918.
S A	Schnitzler, Arthur. Anatol. (Paraphrased by Granville Barker) Bost. Little, Brown, 1917.
S A A	Schnitzler Arthur. Anatol; Living hours; The Green Cockatoo. tr. by Grace I. Colbron. (Modern Library of World's Best Books) N. Y. Boni and Liveright, 1917.
S A B	St. Nicholas book of plays and operettas. Second series. N. Y. Century, 1916.
S A D	Sanders, Helen F. Petalesharoo, and The Star Brave. Butte, Montana. McKee Printing Co., 1910.
S A I	St. Clair, Winifred. The snubbing of Fanny. Lond. F. Griffiths, 1914.
S A M	Saunders, Louise. Magic lanterns: a book of plays. N. Y. Scribner, 1923.
S A N	Santayana, George. A Hermit of Carmel and other poems. N. Y. Scribner, 1901.
S A Q	Sargent, Fred L. Omar and the Rabbi. Cambridge, Mass. Harvard Cooperative Society, 1909.
S A R	Sargent, Herbert C. Pierrot playlets. N. Y. French, 1920.
S A S	Sackville, Lady Margaret. Selected poems. Lond. Constable, 1919.
S A X	Saxon, Edward. The spirit of Kiwanis. Lexington, Ky. Kiwanis Club, 1921.
S B	Schafer, Barbara L. A book of one-act plays. Indianapolis. Bobbs-Merrill, 1922.
S C I	Stevenson, Augusta. Children's classics in dramatic form. Book 1. Bost. Houghton, Mifflin, 1911.
S C 2	Stevenson, Augusta. Children's classics in dramatic form. Book II. Bost. Houghton, Mifflin, 1909.
S C 3	Stevenson, Augusta. Children's classics in dramatic form. Book III. Bost. Houghton, Mifflin, 1908.
S C 4	Stevenson, Augusta. Children's classics in dramatic form. Book IV. Bost. Houghton, Mifflin, 1910.

S C H	Stapp, Emilie B. & Cameron, Eleanor. Happyland's fairy grotto plays. Bost. Houghton, Mifflin, 1922.
S C O	Shay, Frank, ed. Contemporary one-act plays of 1921. (American) Cincinnati. Stewart Kidd, 1922.
S C P	Schindler, A. J. Plays. (single) Bloomfield, N. J., A. J. Schindler, n. d.
S C T	Smith College. Theatre Workshop plays: an anthology, 1918–1921. Northampton, Mass. The Theatre Workshop, Smith College, 1921.
S C W	Schnitzler, Arthur. Comedies of words. Cincinnati. Stewart Kidd, 1917.
S E	Seymour, Mrs. Arthur T. The protest of the trees, and Flossie's Alphabet lesson. (Two blue bird plays) Bost. Walter H. Baker, 1918.
S E A	Searle, Katharine. Three war sketches. Cambridge, Mass. Powell Printing Co., 1916.
S F	Sutro, Alfred. Five little plays. N. Y. Brentano's, 1914.
S F A	Sutro, Alfred. Women in love: eight studies in sentiment. Lond. George Allen, 1902.
S F H	Smith, Laura R. Helps and hints for Hallowe'en. Lebanon, Ohio. March Bros., 1920.
S F R	Smith, Evelyn. Form-room plays—Junior book. N. Y. Dutton, 1920.
S G	Schnitzler, Arthur. The green Cockatoo and other plays. Lond. Gay & Hancock, n. d.
S G A	Schnitzler, Arthur. Gallant Cassian. tr. from German by Adam L. Gowans. Lond. Gowans & Gray, 1914.
S H	Shaw, George B. Heart break House; Great Catherine, and Playlets of the War. N. Y. Brentano's 1919.
S H A	Shaw, George B. Misalliance; The Dark Lady of the Sonnets; and Fannie's first play. N. Y. Brentano's, 1914.
S H B	Shaw, George B. Androcles and the lion; Overruled; Pygmalion. N. Y. Brentano's, 1914.
S H C	Shaw, George B. John Bull's other island and Major Barbara. N. Y. Brentano's, 1907.
S H S	Shaw, George B. The Doctor's dilemma; Getting married; and the Shewing up of Blanco Posnet. N. Y. Brentano's, 1915.
S H V	Sharp, William. Vistas; The gypsy Christ, and other prose imaginings. N. Y. Duffield, 1912.
S I	Sindelar, Joseph C. Bright entertainments for Christmas. Chic. Beckley-Cardy, 1922.
S I A	Sindelar, Joseph C. The new Christmas book. Chic. A. Flanagan, 1910.
S I J	Sidgwick & Jackson, Publishers. Plays. Lond. Sidgwick & Jackson, n. d.
S I P	Sinclair, Upton. Plays of protest. N. Y. Kennerley, 1912.
S I S	Sisters of Mercy. Plays. Chic. Sisters of Mercy, St. Patrick's Academy, n. d.
S L	Shay, Frank & Loving, Pierre, ed. Fifty contemporary one-act plays. Cincinnati. Stewart Kidd, 1920.
S M	Strindberg, August. Mother love. Phila. Brown Bros., 1910.
S MS	Strindberg, August. Swanwhite. Phila. Brown Bros., 1909.
S O	Someple, (pseud.) Mother Goose dramatized. Lebanon, Ohio. March Bros., 1923.

S O B	Soble, Mae S. (Mrs. John J. Soble) Bible plays for children. N. Y. Jas. T. White, 1919.
S P	Smith, Nora A. Plays, pantomimes and tableaux for children. N. Y. Moffat, Yard, 1917.
S P C	Shaw, Bernard. Press cuttings. N. Y. Brentano's, 1901.
S R	Smith, Howard F. Blackberryin'. Bost. Rockwell & Churchill Press, 1922.
S S	Smith, Alice M., ed. Short plays by representative authors. N. Y. Macmillan, 1920.
S S C	Skinner, Eleanor L. & Skinner, Ada M. Children's plays. N. Y. Appleton, 1918.
S S E	Syrett, Netta. Robin Goodfellow and other fairy plays for children. Lond. Lane, 1918.
S S F	Syrett, Netta. Six fairy plays for children. Lond. Lane, 1903.
S S G	Syrett, Netta. The fairy doll and other plays for children. N. Y. Dodd, Mead, 1922.
S T	Sobel, Bernard. Three plays. Bost. Gorham Press, 1913.
S T A	Stigler, W. A. Three plays: "Where east meets west"; "Be sociable"; "Little owl." Memphis, Tenn. The National Drama Co., 1923.
S T B	Stanton, Frank J. Norwich, N. Y., F. J. Stanton, n. d.
S T D	Stevens, Henry B. All alone in the country. Durham, N. H. New Hampshire College Extension office, 1921.
S T E	Stevens, Henry B. A cry out of the dark. Bost. Four Seas, 1919.
S T F	Stevenson, Augusta. The puppet Princess. Bost. Houghton, Mifflin, 1915.
S T G	Stage Guild plays. Chic. Stage Guild. N. Y. Frank Shay. N. Y. Donald C. Vaughn. N. Y. Vaughan & Gomme, n. d.
S T I	St. John, Christopher & Thursby, Charles. The Coronation. International Suffrage shop, 1911.
S T K	Stewart Kidd, Publisher. Plays. Cincinnati. Stewart Kidd, n. d.
S T N	Stoll, Lillian. Trying them out. Atchinson, Kansas. J. Hellener, 1921.
S T O	Strindberg, August. Plays. Second series. tr. by Edwin Bjorkman. N. Y. Scribner, 1913.
S T P	Strindberg, August. Plays. Third series. tr. by Edwin Bjorkman. N. Y. Scribner, 1914.
S T Q	Strindberg, August. Plays. Vol. I. tr. by Edwin Bjorkman. N. Y. Scribner, 1912.
S T R	Sturgis, Granville F. Little plays for all occasions. Bost. Cornhill Pub. Co., 1923.
S T U	Stuart, Muriel. Poems. Lond. William Hememann, 1922.
S T V	Shay, Frank, ed. A treasury of plays for men. Bost. Little, Brown, 1923.
S T W	Shay, Frank. A treasury of plays for women. Bost. Little, Brown, 1922.
S T Z	Sudermann, Hermann. Morituri: three one-act plays. tr. from the German by Archibald Alexander. N. Y. Scribner, 1910.
S U	Sudermann, Hermann. Roses: four one-act plays. tr. by Grace Frank. N. Y. Scribner, 1916.

S UO	Sutherland, Evelyn G. In office hours. Bost. Walter H. Baker, 1900.
S UR	Sutherland, Evelyn G. Po' white trash and other one-act dramas. Chic. Herbert S. Stone, 1900.
S Y	Symons, Arthur. Tragedies. N. Y. John Lane, 1916.
S YS	Synge, J. M. Riders to the sea. Bost. John W. Luce, 1911.
S YT	Synge, John M. The Tinker's wedding; Riders to the sea; and The Shadow of the glen. Dublin. Maunsel, 1911.
S YU	Synge, J. M. The shadow of the glen, and Riders to the sea. Lond. Elkin Mathews, 1911.
T A	Taft, Grace E. Chimalman and other poems. N. Y. The Cameo Press, 1916.
T BJ	Tarkington, Booth. Beauty and the Jacobin. N. Y. Harper, 1912.
T C	Tagore, Rabindranath. Chitra. N. Y. Macmillan, 1914.
T CS	Tagore, Rabindranath. Sacrifice and other plays. N. Y. Macmillan, 1917.
T E	Telford, Mary E. The children's Christmas dream. Chic. L. L. Henry, 1916.
T H	Thomason, Caroline W. Plays for children in French and English. il. by Mary Rose Donovan. Phila. Penn Pub. Co., 1922.
T HO	Thomas, Edith M. The White messenger and other war poems. Bost. Richard G. Badger, 1915.
T HR	Thorp, Josephine. The treasure chest. Chic. Old Tower Press, 1922.
T KP	Thorp, Josephine & Kimball, Rosamond. Patriotic pageants of today. N. Y. Holt, 1918.
T MP	Tullar-Meredith. Plays. N. Y. Tullar-Meredith, n. d.
T N	Theis, Grover. Numbers and other one-act plays. N. Y. Nicholas L. Brown, 1919.
T O	Tobin, Bertha Irene. Recitations, drills and plays for children. Bost. Walter H. Baker, 1921.
T OW	Townley, Morris M. Two plays. (American dramatist series) Bost. Gorham Press, 1916.
T PF	Torrence, Ridgely. Plays for a Negro Theatre. N. Y. Macmillan, 1917.
T RH	Tucker, Louise E. & Ryan, Estelle L. Historical plays of Colonial days. N. Y. Longmans, Green, 1912.
T RU	True, Mary E. In moonbeams. Madison, Wis. Extension Division of the University of Wisconsin, n. d.
T T	Thorne-Thomsen, Mrs. Gudrun. A tramp and a nights lodging. Chic. Chicago School of Civics and Philanthrophy, 1917.
T U	Tupper, Wilbur S. Six short plays. Bost. Four Seas, 1922.
T UR	Turrell, Charles A., tr. Contemporary Spanish dramatists. Bost. Richard G. Badger, 1919.
U S	U. S. Commission on training camp activities. (War Dept.) Plays. 1918–19.
U W	University of Washington. Plays. Seattle, Wash. University of Washington Press, 1921.
V 1	Vagabond plays. First series. Baltimore. Norman, Remington, 1921.

AN INDEX TO ONE-ACT PLAYS

V A	Varney, Alice S. Story plays old and new. Book three. Chic. American Book Co., 1915.
V C	Van Derveer, Lettie C. Christmas doings: a group of little Christmas plays, entertainments and recitations. Bost. Walter H. Baker, 1920.
V E	Verga, Giovanni & others. Plays of the Italian Theatre. tr. by Isaac Goldberg. Bost. John W. Luce, 1921.
V G	Viereck, George S. A game at love and other plays. N. Y. Brentano's, 1906.
V I	Viets, Edward. The masque of morning and other poems. Bost. Four Seas, 1921.
V O	Vosburgh, Maude B. The health champions. Bost. Tuberculosis League, 1921.
W A	Walker, Stuart. Portmanteau adaptations. Cincinnati. Stewart Kidd, 1921.
W A A	Waley, Arthur. The Nō plays of Japan. N. Y. Knopf, 1922.
W A K	Walker, Francis. The Prince's pigeon. San Diego, Calif., F. Walker, 1916.
W A L	Walker, Dugald S. Dream boats. Garden City, N. Y. Doubleday, Page, 1918.
W C	Wilde, Percival. Confessional and other American plays. N. Y. Holt, 1915.
W C B	Wickes, Frances G. A child's book of holiday plays. N. Y. Macmillan, 1916.
W C P	Wagstaff, Blanche S. Colonial plays for the school-room. Designed for class-room work in sixth and seventh grades. Bost. Educational Pub. Co., 1912.
W E	Wilde, Percival. Eight comedies for Little Theatres. Bost. Little, Brown, 1922.
W E D	Wilde, Percival. Dawn with The Noble lord; The traitor; A house of cards; Playing with fire; The finger of God. N. Y. Holt, 1915.
W E N	Wentworth, Marion C. War brides. N. Y. Century, 1915.
W E P	Werner & Co., Edgar S. Plays. N. Y. Edgar S. Werner, n. d.
W E S	Westermayr, A. J. Yoshivara. N. Y. Appeal Printing Co., 1916.
W F	Whitworth, Goeffrey. Father Noah and other fancies. N. Y. Robert M. McBride, 1919.
W H	Waugh, Constance E. Holiday plays for girls. Lond. Wells, Gardner, Darton, n. d.
W H P	Whitmark & Sons, M. Plays. N. Y., M. Whitmark & Sons, n. d.
W I	Williams, E. Harcourt. Four fairy plays. N. Y. French, 1920.
W I A	Williams, Joseph. Plays. Lond. Joseph Williams, n. d.
W I F	Wilson, Lillian P. The fruit of toil and other one-act plays. Indianapolis. Bobbs-Merrill, 1916.
W I P	Wisconsin plays. Thomas H. Dickinson, ed. N. Y. Huebsch, 1914.
W I P 2	Wisconsin plays. Second series. N. Y. Huebsch, 1918.
W I T	Williams, Frayne. Three Oriental plays. Los Angeles, Calif., J. A. Alles, 1921.

W J	Wells, Carolyn. Jolly plays for holidays. Bost. Walter H. Baker, 1903–1914.
W M	Walker, Stuart. More Portmanteau plays. Cincinnati. Stewart Kidd, 1919.
W N	Wright, Harriet S. New plays from old tales. N. Y. Macmillan, 1921.
W O	Woodman, Rhea. The Bobby Bennett plays for children. Chic. Dramatic Pub. Co., 1922.
W O H	Wolfrom, Anna. Human wisps: six one-act plays. Bost. Sherman, French, 1917.
W O O	Woolf, Henry. The dream book. Cincinnati. Ark Pub. Co., 1915.
W P	Walker, Stuart. Portmanteau plays. Cincinnati. Stewart Kidd, 1917.
W R	Wendell, Barrett. Raleigh in Guiana; Rosamond, and a Christmas masque. N. Y. Scribner, 1902.
W R P	Wetzel, Rosener. Plays. N. Y. Wetzel, Rosener, n. d.
W S	Walker, Stuart. Six who pass while the lentils boil. Cincinnati. Stewart Kidd, 1921.
W S P	Washington Square Plays. Garden City, N. Y. Doubleday, Page, 1916.
W T	Watts, Mary S. Three short plays. N. Y. Macmillan, 1917.
W T C	Wilcox, Constance. Told in a Chinese garden and four other fantastic plays for out-doors or in-doors. N. Y. Holt, 1920.
W U	Wilde, Percival. The unseen host and other war plays. Bost. Little, Brown, 1917.
W W	Wentworth, Marion G. War brides. N. Y. Century, 1915.
W W S	Webber, James P. & Webster, Hanson H. One-act plays for secondary schools. Bost. Houghton, Mifflin, 1923.
W Y	Willard, Ellen M. Yuletide entertainments. Chic. T. S. Denison, 1910.
Y A	Young, Stark. Addio; Madretta, and other plays. Chic. Dramatic Pub. Co., 1912.
Y A T	Young, Stark. Three one-act plays. Cincinnati. Stewart Kidd, 1921.
Y C 2	Yeats, William B. Collected works in verse and prose. Vol. II. Lond. Chapman & Hall, 1908.
Y F	Yeats, William B. Four plays for dancers. N. Y. Macmillan, 1921.
Y H	Yeats, William B. The hour-glass, and other plays. N. Y. Macmillan, 1904.
Y I	Yeats, William B. Poems. Lond. T. F. Unwin, 1904.
Y J	Yeats, William B. The green helmet and other poems. N. Y. Macmillan, 1912.
Y K	Yeats, William B. The King's Threshold and On Baile's Strand. (Vol. III of Plays for an Irish Theatre) Lond. A. H. Bullen, 1904.
Y O	Young, Stark. The twilight saint. Amherst, Mass., S. Young, 1921.
Y P 2	Yeats, William B. The poetical works, vol. II. Dramatic poems. N. Y. Macmillan, 1907.
Y P P	Yeats, William B. Plays in prose and verse written for an Irish Theatre. N. Y. Macmillan, 1922.

YR	Yeats, William B. Responsibilities: poems and a play. Churchtown, Ireland. The Cuala Press, 1914.
YS	Yeats, William B. The shadowy waters. Acting ed. Lond. A. H. Bullen, 1907.
YU	Yeats, William B. & Gregory, Lady Isabelle A. The Unicorn from the stars. N. Y. Macmillan, 1908.

PERIODICALS WHICH CONTAIN PLAYS

American Magazine. N. Y. Phillips Publishing Co.
American Poetry Magazine, published for the American Literary Association. Milwaukee, Wis.
Asia; journal of the American Asiatic Association. N. Y.
Atlantic Monthly. Boston, Houghton, Mifflin
Bibleot. Portland, Me. Thomas B. Mosher
Canadian Magazine. Toronto, Ontario Pub. Co.
Century. N. Y. Scribner
Chapbook. London, Poetry Bookshop
Charaka Club. Proceedings. N. Y.
Colliers, the national weekly. N. Y. P. F. Collier
Cosmopolitan. N. Y. International Magazine Co.
Delineator. N. Y. Butterick Publishing Co.
Dial. N. Y. Dial Publishing Co.
Double-dealer. New Orleans, Double Dealer Publishing Co.
Drama. Chicago, Dramatic Publishing Co.
Dramatist. Easton, Pennsylvania.
English Review. London, Duckworth.
Everyland. West Medford, Mass. Everyland Publishing Co.
Forerunner, ed. by Charlotte Perkins Gilman. Charlton Co. N. Y.
Forum. N. Y. Forum Publishing Co.
Gael, The. N. Y. Gael Publishing Co.
Good Housekeeping. N. Y. International Magazine Co.
Granite Monthly. Concord, H. H. Metcalf.
Harper's Bazaar. N. Y. Harper and Bro.
Harper's Monthly Magazine. N. Y. Harper and Bro.
Harvard Monthly. Cambridge, Mass.
Hearst's Magazine. N. Y. International Magazine Company
International: a review of two worlds. N. Y. Moods Publishing Co.
Journal of Home Economics. Geneva, N. Y. American Home Economics Association
Journal of the Outdoor Life. N. Y. Journal of the Outdoor Life Publishing Co.
Ladies' Home Journal. Philadelphia, Curtis Publishing Co.
Liberator. N. Y. Liberator Publishing Co.
Little Review. N. Y. Margaret C. Anderson.
Little Theatre Magazine. San Francisco
McClure's Magazine. N. Y. S. S. McClure
Metropolitan. N. Y. E. Butterick
Midland, a magazine of the middle west. Iowa City, Ia.
Moods, the magazine of personality. N. Y. Moods Publishing Co.
New England Magazine. Boston, New England Magazine Co.
Nineteenth Century. N. Y. Leonard Scott Pub. Co.
Open Court. Chicago, Open Court Pub. Co.
Pacific Review. Seattle, University of Washington Press
Play-book, The. Madison, Wis.
Poet-lore. Bost. R. G. Badger
Poetry. Chicago.
Poetry and Drama. London, The Poetry Bookshop
Poetry Review. Lond. Erskine Macdonald
Putnam's Monthly and the Critic. N. Y. G. P. Putnam

Quarterly Journal of Speech Education. Ann Arbor, National Association
    of Teachers of Speech
St. Nicholas. N. Y. Century Co.
Samhain, ed. for the Irish literary theatre by W. B. Yeats. Dublin, Sealy,
    Bryers and Walker
Seven Arts. N. Y. Seven Arts Publishing Co.
Smart Set. N. Y. Ess Ess Publishing Co.
Stagelore. N. Y. Wetzel, Rosener and James
Stratford Journal. Boston. The Stratford Co.
Studies,' an Irish quarterly review of letters, philology and science. Dublin,
    Educational Company of Ireland
Texas Review. Austin, Texas, Univ. of Texas
Theatre Arts Magazine. N. Y. Theatre Arts
Twentieth Century Magazine. Bost. Twentieth Century Co.
Woman's Home Companion. Springfield, Ohio. Crowell Pub. Co.
Yale Sheffield Monthly. New Haven, Conn.

TITLE LIST

A

* **A. B. C. capers.** Soemple. For primary grades or kindergarten 14b., 14g. Sc. Interior. EP
A. D. 2000. E. Preston. Farce. 10m., 4w. Sc. A boxing ring. PL
* **Abe Lincoln and little A. D.** Marguerite Merington. Lincoln's birthday play. 4b. Sc. Library. MFH
Abigail. David Pinski. A Biblical drama. 2w., 7m., chorus. Sc. David's camp. PTK PTS
Abishag. David Pinski, trans. from the Yiddish by Isaac Goldberg. 4m., 1w., 2 chorus groups. Sc. Sleeping chamber in palace in ancient Palestine. PTK
* **About angels.** Laura E. Richards. 1b., 4g. Sc. A road. RP
Abraham and Isaac, adapted from the Pageant of the Barbers and Wax-Chandlers in the Chester cycle of miracles. 4m., 1w., chorus. Sc. Space immediately before the altar of a chapel. ELT2
* **Abraham Lincoln and the little bird.** Emma L. Johnston and Madalene D. Barnum. 4b. Sc. A road. JB
* **Abraham Lincoln: rail-splitter.** Constance D'Arcy Mackay. 6b., 4g. Sc. Lincoln's kitchen and living-room. MPY
Absent minded. Clarence I. Freed. 3m., 1w. Sc. Living room. FP
† **Absolution of Bruce, The.** Graham Price. Historical play about Robert Bruce. 10m. Sc. Room in the Bishop's palace. REP
Acacia cottage. B. Orange. Comedy. 1m., 4w. Sc. Drawing-room at Acacia cottage. FSD
Academy picture, An. Ethel Chillingworth. 3m., 2w. Sc. Combined studio and living room. WIA
Accomplice, The. Abigail Marshall. 6m. Sc. Well furnished bedroom in a large hotel. STV
According to Darwin. Percival Wilde. 3m., 2w. Sc. A cheap tenement in the slums of New York. WC, Forum 54: 488–504, Oct. 1915.
Acid drops. Gertrude Jennings. 1m., 6w. Sc. Workhouse ward for women. JF
Action! Holland Hudson. Melodramatic farce. 12m. Sc. Packing room. STV
Actress, The. Franz Molnar and Joseph Teleki. 2w. Sc. Drawing room of apartment. Smart Set 33: 119–122, Mar. 1911.
Adam Goodwon. Frank J. Stanton. Farce. 2m., 1w. Sc. Up-to-date office. STB
Adam's apple. Harold Simpson. Sentimental comedy. 2m., 2w. Sc. Sitting room. FSD
* **Adam's dream.** Mrs. Alice Corbin Henderson. Miracle play. 3b., 1g., Chorus. Garden of Eden. HAD
Adder, The. Lascelles Abercrombie. Verse. 3m., 1w. Sc. Before the charcoal-burner's hut. ABF, Poetry and Drama 1: 100–119, March 1913.
Addio. Stark Young. 3m., 1w. Sc. In a bakery. YA, YAT

Admiral Peters. W. W. Jacobs and Horace Mills. Comedy. 2m., 1w. Sc. Interior. FSD

Adopting an orphan. Ida G. Norton. 1m., 5w. Sc. Orphan's home. NA

‡ **Adoption of Bob, The.** Marie Irish. 4b., 6g. Sc. Living room BUP

Advertising for a husband. Charles S. Bird. 3m., 2w. Sc. Interior. FSD

Ægean, The. Isaac Rieman Baxley. Play of famous Sculpture. 4m., 2w. Sc. Studio overlooking the Aegean Sea. BAX

Affected young ladies, The. Jean-Baptiste Poquelin Moliere, translated from the French by Barrett H. Clark. 5m., 4w., chorus. Sc. Elaborate room in a house in Paris in the seventeenth century. FSD

Affinities. Vernon Woodhouse. Tragical farce. 3m., 1w. Sc. Room in a bachelor's flat. FSD

After all. Harriet Monroe. Verse. 1m., 1w., chorus. Sc. Pathway in hell. MOP, Poet-Lore 12: 321–326, July–Sept. 1900.

After Euripides' "Electra." Maurice Baring. Farce. 6m., 5w. Sc. A room in the house of Congras at Athens. BA

After the bargain sale. Willis N. Bugbee. Comedy. 2m., 2w. Sc. Sitting room. MBP

After the circus. Lawrence Chenoweth. Farce. 4m., 3w. Sc. Railway depot. APP

† **After the honeymoon.** Wolfgang Gyalui, translated from the German by Barrett H. Clark. 1m., 1w. Sc. Well furnished sitting room. FSD

After the honeymoon. Wallace Nisbet. Farce. 2m., 3w. Sc. Reception room. FP

After the play. Harry W. Osborne. 1m., 3w. Sc. Interior. DEP

After-dinner speaker, The. Lewis Allen. At least 16m. Sc. Banquet hall. Smart Set 42: 99–101, Ap. 1914

Aftermath, a one-act play of negro life. Mary Burrill. 3m., 3w. Interior negro cabin. Liberator 2: 10–14, Ap. 1919

Afternoon walk, The. Henri Lavedan. 1m., 4b. Sc. On a quay. MR, Poet Lore 28: 403–406, Vacation 1917.

Afterwards. Marion Roberton. 2w., 1g. Sc. Young girl's bedroom. WIA

Agatha Steel. Wilfrid Wilson Gibson. Verse. 2w. Sc. Room in tenements. GID, GIP

Agression won. Harry Lorenzo Chapin. 1m., 1w. Sc. Living room CHL

Ain't women wonderful? H. P. Powell. 5w. Sc. Interior. PPP

Alarm, The. Marion Roger Fawcett. Vaudeville sketch. 4m. Sc. Interior of a small grocery store. PWP

Alarm of fire, An. Helen Sherman Griffith. Comedy. 3m., 5w. Sc. Interior. B

Alchemist, The. Bernice Lesbia Kenyon. 6m. Sc. A dark and dingy room in Milan in the 15th century. STV

† **Alice's blighted profession.** Helen C. Clifford. 8g. Sc. Modern business office. FP

Aliens, The. Charles Hanson Towne. 4m., 3w. Private art gallery in New York City. McClure's 47: 12–13, 76, May 1916.

All alone in the country. Henry Bailey Stevens. 1m., 2w. Sc. Living room of farm house. STD, Granite Monthly 52: 239–248, June 1921

* **All America eleven, The.** M. N. Beebe. 12b. Sc. Unimportant. B

All clear. J. Hartley Manners. Play of the World War. 3m., 1w., 1b., 1g. Sc. Little room in a tenement house. MTP

All for the cause. Lindsey Barbee. Red Cross play, war background. Comedy. 10w. Sc. Interior. DEP

All gummed up. Harry Wagstaff Gribble. Satirical comedy. 3m., 2w. Sc. Consulting rooms of a doctor's office. SCO

* **All his fault.** Clara J. Denton. Christmas play. 2b., 3g., chorus. Sc. Interior. I

All in the family. William Wallace Whitelock. 2m., 1w. Sc. Living room of country cottage. Smart Set 34: 49–50, May 1911

All on a summer's day. Lindsey Barbee. Comedy. 1m., 6w. Sc. Summer hotel. DEP

All on account of an actor. Louis L. Wilson. Farce. 6w. Sc. Parlor of summer hotel. PPP

All Soul's eve. Katherine Officer. 3m., 4w. Sc. Large room with massive furniture. International 7: 14–15, Jan. 1913

All Souls' night's dream, An. Frederic W. Moorman. Yorkshire dialect. 2m., 2w. Sc. Corner in the church yard of a Yorkshire market town. MO, MOR

All stars; or, a manager's trials. O. E. Young. Farce. 4m., 1w. Sc. Interior. DPP

All the world loves a lover. Hobart Sommers. Comedy. 1m., 9w. Sc. Room in a finishing school. PPP

* **All the year 'round.** Ellen M. Willard. 2b. Sc. Interior. WY

Allied occupations. Manta S. Graham. 3m., 3w. Sc. Hair dressing and manicure parlor. GRL

† **Allison's lad.** Beulah Marie Dix. 6m. Sc. Upper chamber of a village inn in England. DA, KP, MA

Allotments. G. E. Jennings. 2w. Sc. Interior. FSD

Almost everyman. Helen H. Austin. 7m., 4w., others. Sc. Courtroom. Quarterly Journal of Speech Education 5: 45–53, Jan. 1919.

Along the quays. Henry Lavedan. 2m., 1w., 1b. Sc. Along the quay MR, Poet Lore 28: 385–390, Vacation 1917.

Alternative, The. Florence M. Millward. 1m., 3w. Sc. Living room in a workman's flat. MIF

Altruism. Karl Ettlinger. Translated from the German by Benjamin F. Glazer. 13m., 6w., chorus. Sc. Parisian café by the Seine. SL

Amateur rehearsel of Hamlet. Herbert C. Sargent. Farce. 8m., 2w. Sc. Interior. SAR

Amateurs, The. Raymond M. Robinson. Burlesque. 4m., 1w. Sc. Library. PPP

Ambassador's daughter, The. Caroline Duer. 3m., 2w. Sc. Small drawing room. Smart Set 5: 49–57, Nov. 1901.

* **Ambition in Whitechapel.** Irma Kraft. Shabnot. 1b., 5g. Sc. A very shabby living-dining room in back of a shop. KPP

* **America, the beautiful, democracy's goal;** a pageant. Margaret Knox and Anna M. Lütkenhaus. Any number of children. Sc. Unimportant. St. Nicholas 47: 738–744, June 1920.

America passes by. Kenneth Andrews. 2m., 2w. Sc. Living room of a small flat in Chicago. B, HD1

* **America pays her debt to France.** Eleanore Hubbard. Great War background. 2b., 3 chorus groups. Sc. Lafayette's tomb in Paris. HUD

American bar, The. Herbert C. Sargent. Farce. 4m., 2w. Sc. Saloon. SAR

American idea, The. Lily Carthew. Play of Jewish life at the present time. 3m., 2w. Sc. Parlor. B

Amethyst remembrance, An. McVay Sumner. 2m., 1w. Sc. Morning room of a metropolitan hotel. Smart Set 3: 57–60, Feb. 1901

Among the lions. George Middleton. 2m., 6w. Chorus. Sc. Elaborate drawing-room. MIM, Smart Set 51: 327–336, Feb. 1917

Among the nightingales. Aldous Huxley. 5m., 3w. Sc. Terrace outside hotel. Smart Set 63: 71–88, Nov. 1920

Anachronism at Chinon, An. Ezra Pound. 2m. Sc. Clear space in front of an inn. Little Review 4: #2 p. 14–21, June 1917

Anatol's wedding morning. Arthur Schnitzler, translated from the German. 3m., 1w. Sc. Room in bachelor apartment. SAA

And forbid them not. Louise Morey Bowman. 1m., several ghosts. Sc. Not indicated. Poetry 13: 306–307, Mar. 1919

Andromeda unfettered. Muriel Stuart. Verse. 1m., 1w., 2 choruses. Sc. Not indicated. STU, English review 32: 483–492, June 1921

Angel intrudes, The. Floyd Dell. Comedy. 3m., 1w. Sc. Washington Square by moonlight. DK, FLS

* **Anita's secret; or, Christmas in the steerage.** Walter Ben Hare. 1m., 9b., 7g. Sc. Steerage of a large ocean going vessel. HW

Annajanska, the Bolshevik empress. George Bernard Shaw. 4m., 1w. Sc. General's office in a military station on the east front in Boeotia. SH

Anniversary, The. Anton Tchekoff. 2m., 2w., many chorus characters. Sc. Private office in a bank. CHD

Anonymous letter, An. Kenyon Nicholson. 2m., 1w. Sc. Sitting room of a bungalow. Smart Set 65: 73–83, May 1921

Another man's place. Marion Wilder. 2m., 2w. Sc. Sitting-room in Dutch house in colonial New York. DAL

Another way out. Lawrence Langner. 2m., 3w. Sc. Studio. LA, LAF, SL

* **Answer, The.** Josephine Thorpe. Pageant. 125 children. Sc. A great hall or garden. TKP

Answering the phone. Elizabeth Guptill. Farce. 3w. Sc. Living room. TMP

Antick: a wayside sketch, The. Percy Mackaye. 2m., 3w., chorus. Sc. Dusty country road. MY

Anybody family on Sunday morning, The. Hester A. Hopkins. 2m., 2w., 1b., 1g. Sc. Interior. TMP

Aoi no Uye (Princess Hollyhock); revised by Zenchiku Ujinobu. Nō play of Japan. 3m., 2w. Chorus. Sc. Stage. WAA

Apocryphal episode, An. Mary MacMillan Historical farce. 2m., 2w. Sc. In the center of a grassy open space. MTT

Apollo in Hades. Laurence Housman. Verse. Greek mythology. 7m., 3w. chorus. Sc. Hall of black pillars in which Hades is enthroned. HAR

* **April's lady,** a little play for Arbor Day. Carolyn Wells. 15w. Background of trees. Ladies Home Journal 33: 38, April 1916

* **Arbor Day.—"Anychild helps the baby tree"** F. Ursula Payne. 3c. Chorus. Sc. Room in any house. PP

Arduin. Cale Young Rice. Verse. 3m., 1w. Sc. Ancient science laboratory in Egypt. RI

Aren't they wonders? Charles Frederic Nirdlinger. Holiday tragedy. 2m., 2w. Sc. Office of architect. NI

Aria da capo. Edna St. Vincent Millay. 4m., 1w. Sc. Stage set for a Harlequinade. SL, Chapbook #14. Aug. 1920.

Ariadne in Naxos. Maurice Baring. Farce. 1m., 1w., 1 servant. Sc. Room in Ariadne's house. BA

Ariadne in Naxos. Maurice Hewlett. Verse. Ancient Greece. 3m., 2w., chorus of women. Sc. Sandy shore of the island of Naxos. HEA

Arrival of a rival, The. Percy Fendall and Fred Emmey. Farce. 2m. Sc. Interior. FSD

Arrival of Reuben, The. W. M. Bugbee. College play. Comedy. 5m., 5w. Sc. Study room at college. BUP

Art clubs are trumps. Mary Moncure Parker. 6w. Sc. Interior. B

Art for art's sake. Grace Luce Irwin. Farce. 2m., 3w. Sc. Living room of women's apartment. ID

Art for breakfast. W. C. Parker. Farce. 2m., 2w. Sc. An artist's studio. PPP

Artful automaton. Arthur Law. 2m., 2w., Sc. Drawing room WIA

Artist, a drama without words, **The.** H. L. Mencken. 9 or more m. 8 or more w., Sc. Auditorium, seats and stage. Smart Set 49: 79–84, August 1916.

Artist and the materialist, The. Alma Newton. 2m. Sc. Studio. NE

Artist-mother and child (from the picture "Mme Lebrun and her daughter" by Lebrun) Marguerite Merington. 1w., 1c., Sc. Picture frame. MPZ

As a pal. Leon Gordon. 2m., 2w. Sc. Cheap suburban lodging house. GG

As advertised. Claude Kinnick. 5m., 4w. Sc. Interior. KI

As good as gold. Laurence Housman. Morality play of St. Francis of Assisi. 7m. Sc. Side of a hill. FSD

As it will be. Elizabeth F. Guptill. 2m., 1w. Sc. A disordered kitchen. MBP

As Molly told it. Marion Paul, pseud. of Pauline Phelps and Marion Short. 2w. Sc. Sitting room in a country house. WEP

‡ **As ye sew.** Dorothy Critchton. Doll's missionary play. 2b., 10g. Sc. Living room. EP

Asaph. William O. Bates. 3m., 2w. Sc. Corner of front yard of house in New Jersey village. Drama 10: 227–235, Mar.–Ap. 1920.

Ashes. Eleanor Custis Whiting. 2m., 1w. Sc. Dingy room in cheap rooming house. Poet Lore 33: 423–438, Autumn 1922.

Ashes of roses. Constance D'Arcy Mackay. 3w., 1m., 1s. Sc. Bare white-washed walls of a dressing room in the theatre. MB

Ask no questions and you'll hear no stories. Arthur Schnitzler. 2m. Sc. Charming flat used by bachelor. SA

Assisted order, An. Alex. Ricketts. 1m., 1 man's voice and 1 woman's voice over telephone. Smart Set 1: 150, June 1900.

Assumption of Hannele, a dream poem. Gerhart Hauptmann, tr. by G. S. Bryan. 7m., 4w. Sc. Room in almshouse. Poet Lore 20: 161–191, May–June 1909.

* **At anchor.** Louise E. Tucker and Estelle L. Ryan. Mayflower story. 4b., 1g., chorus. Sc. Deck of the Mayflower. TRH

At "Jenny Wren's." Horace B. Browne. From Dickens' Our Mutual Friend. 3m., 2w. Sc. Parlor. BD

At night all cats are gray. Robert Garland. 3m., 1w. Sc. Smoking room of a home. Smart Set 48: 247–259, Mar. 1916.

‡ **At old Mobile.** Marie Bankhead Owen. Historical. 14b., 6g., chorus. Sc. Esplanade before the fort. AO

At retreat; a dramatic fancy of the Civil War. Arthur A. Blunt. 3m., 2w. Sc. Interior. B

At the barricade. Evelyn G. Sutherland. Franco-Prussian war, background for the play. 5m., 6w. Sc. Barricade. SUP

At the chasm. Jaroslav Vrchlicky, pseud. of Emil Bohnslav Frida, trans. from the Bohemian by Charles Recht. 2m., 1w. Sc. Plainly furnished library of a home. Poet Lore 24: 289–308, Autumn 1913.

At the church door. Mary MacMillan. 2m., 2w. Sc. Vestibule of an old and very aristocratic church in New York City. MM

At the club. Jacque Morgan. 22m. Sc. Club's barber shop. Smart Set 47: 251–254, Sept. 1915.

At the depot; a character play. Anne M. Palmer. 10m., 7w., 6c. Sc. Interior of depot. TMP

* **At the door of the igloo,** by an Alaskan Missionary. 2b., or g. Sc. Outside an Eskimo hut. DOF

At the edge of the wood. Kenneth Sawyer Goodman. 6m., 2w. Sc. Open space at the edge of an old wood. GQA

At the end of the rope. Edith M. Levy. 4m., 2w. Sc. Outer office of theatrical manager. SCT

At the flowing of the tide. Edward J. O'Brien. 1m., 1w. Sc. Poor cottage. Forum 52: 375–386, Sept. 1914.

At the goal. Harriet Monroe. Verse. 1m., 1w. Sc. Exquisitely furnished bedroom. MOP

At the Golden Goose. M. Lefuse. English Historical play. 2m., 2w. Sc. Interior. FSD

At the Grand Central. Frances Aymar Mathews. 2w. Sc. Ladies' waiting room in station. WEP

At the Hawk's well. William Butler Yeats. 6m. Sc. Bare space before a wall. YF

At the junction. Charles S. Bird. Farce. 3m., 2w. Sc. Interior. B

* **At the library.** Clara J. Denton. Valentine's Day play. 4g. Sc. A parlor. DAH

At the milliner's. Mabel H. Crane. Comedy. 8w. Sc. Milliner shop from inside. FSD

At the movies. Harold B. Allen and Joseph Upper. Farcical novelty. 2m., 2w. Sc. Interior. FSD

At the play. Edward E. Piaggio. Curtain raiser. 3m., 3w. Sc. Theatre in England. FSD

At the ribbon counter. Gertrude E. Jennings. 3w. Sc. Dry goods store. FSD

At the setting of the sun. Pierre Louys, trans. from the French by E. H. Pfeiffer. 1m., 1w. Sc. Unimportant. LO

At the shrine. Stark Young. 1m., 1w. Sc. A room in an old fashioned house. YAT, Theatre Arts Mag. 3: 196–203, July 1919.

At the sign of the cleft heart. Theodosia Garrison. Verse. 1m., 1w. Love's shop, Arcadian way. Smart Set 4: 91–96, July 1901.

At the sign of the silver spoon. Lucine Finch. 1m., 3w. Sc. Tea room in New York. Smart Set 38: 73–77, Oct. 1912.

At the sign of the thumb and nose. Alfred Kreymborg. Satire. 6m., 1w. Sc. A small inn. KMA

At the turn of the year. Mark Forrest. 2m., 3w., Sc. Living room in manor house in Virginia. American Poetry Mag. 1: 15–28, May 1919.

At the window. Lillian F. Chandler. 2m., 5w. Sc. Living room. FSD

At Whitsuntide. L. D. G. Bentley. 3m., 1w. Sc. Living room at rectory. New Eng. Mag. n. s. 42: 331–9, May 1910.

Atoms. Robert Gruntal Nathan. 2m., 1w. Sc. Study. Harvard Monthly 57: 31–38, Nov. 1913.

Atsumori. Seanii. Nō play of Japan. 3m., chorus. Sc. Stage. WAA

Attuned. Alice Gerstenberg. 1w. Sc. Boudoir. GT

Aubrey closes the door. Cosmo Hamilton. 3m., 1w. Sc. Interior FSD

Auction at Meadowville, An. Alice C. Thompson. 1m., 7w. Sc. Interior. B

Augustus does his bit. George Bernard Shaw. 2m., 1w. Sc. Mayor's parlor in the town hall of Little Pifflington. SH

Augustus in search of a father. Harold Chapin. 3m. Sc. A square in the West End of London. REP

Aulis difficulty, The. Maurice Baring. Historical farce. 3m., 2w., 1s. Sc. Agamemnon's tent at Aulis. BA

Aunt Abigail and the boys. Lillie Fuller Merriam. Farce. College play. 8m., 2w. Sc. College boy's room at Harvard. B

Aunt Bessie. Wilfred T. Coleby. 2m., 2w. Sc. Parlor. FSD

Aunt Columbia's dinner party, a patriotic play. Mary R. Gamble. 4m., 3w., Fairies, children. Sc. Unimportant. Ladies Home Journal 34: 28, June 1917.

Aunt Deborah's first luncheon. Laura M. Adams. 7w. Sc. Handsomely furnished living room. EP

* **Aunt Grundy.** Olive Allen. Moral play. 2b., 4g. Sc. Parlour. BHP

Aunt Harriet's night out. Ragna B. Eskil. Comedy. 1m., 2w. Sc. Interior. DEP

* **Aunt Jane visits school.** Jeanette Joyce. 2w. any number of children. Sc. Modern school room. MAP

Aunt Jerusha's quilting party. Laura M. Parsons. 4m., 12w. Sc. Rustic. B

Aunt Matilda's birthday party. Alice C. Thompson. Comedy. 11w. Sc. Interior. DEP

Aunt Mehetible's scientific experiment. Emma E. Brewster. Farce. 6w. Sc. Interior B

* **Aunt Penelope.** Constance E. Waugh. 6g. Sc. Drawing-room. WH

* **Aunt Sabriny's Christmas.** Elizabeth F. Guptill. 7g. Sc. Interior. EP

Aunt Sally Saunders' health crusade. Ida G. Norton. 2w. Sc. Interior. NA

Aunty. John M. Francis. Farce. 2 m., 2w. Sc. Interior. DED

Author's evening at home, The. Alice Dunbar. (Mrs. Paul Laurence Dunbar) 1m., 1w. Sc. Library. Smart Set 2: 105–106, Sept. 1900.

* **Authorship.** John Gemmell. 1b. Sc. Room. FG

Autocrat of the coffee-stall. Harold Chapin. 6m. Sc. A large well-equipped coffee stall. CT, Theatre Arts Mag. 5: 125–141, Ap. 1921.

Autumn. Pierre Loving. 2m., 2w. Sc. Spacious living room. Drama 13: 61–63, Nov. 1922.

Autumn fires. Gustav Wild, trans. from the Danish by Benjamin F. Glazer. 8m. Sc. Room in old men's home. SL

Aux Etuves de Weisbaden, A. D. 1451. 2m. Sc. Pool in the woods. Little Review 4: 12–16, July 1917.

Avenger, The. Clarendon Ross. Fantasy. 2m. Sc. Upper room of a castle. Drama 8: 329–339, Aug. 1918.

Avenue, The. Fenimore Merrill. 4m., 8w. Sc. Outside Fifth Ave. shop window. Drama 10: 53–57, Nov. 1919.

Avenues. Dorothy Butts. 1m., 1w. Sc. Cabin. SCT

Awakening of Barbizon, The. Clay M. Greene. Comedy. 4m., 1w. Sc. Courtyard of an old castle. GD

Awoi no Uye. Ernest Fenollosa and Ezra Pound. Nō play of Japan. 1m., 1w., chorus. Sc. Japanese background. FEN

Axin' her father, a negro farce. O. E. Young. 2m., 3w., Sc. Interior. DEP

Aya No Tsuzumi. (The damask drum) Seami. Nō play of Japan. B 2m., 1w., Sc. stage. WAA

B

* **Babushka, The.** Elsie Hobart Carter. 24c. Sc. Interior of a Russian hut. CCC

Baby carriage, The. Bosworth Crocker. 2m., 2w. Sc. Ordinary tailor shop in England. CK, SL

* **Baby New Year.** Ruth Arkwright. 3b. Sc. A snowy country. AB
* **Baby show, The.** Elizabeth F. Guptill. 4b., 3g. Sc. Not important. GUT
* **Baby show, The.** Marie Irish. 1b., 12g. Sc. Stage. IPP

Babylonian captivity, The. Lésya Ukáinka. Historical. 1m., 3 chorus groups. Sc. A wide plain. BFR

* **Baby's ill!** John Gemmell. 1b., 1g. Sc. Room. FG

Bachelor club's baby, The. Louise Rand Bascom. Christmas play. 9m., 1w., 1c. Sc. Bachelor's club. EP

Bachelor's baby. Katherine Kavanaugh. 2m., 2w. Sc. Studio. FP

Bachelor's club, The. Effie W. Merriman. 13m. Sc. Interior. DPP

Bachelor's reverie, A. Grace B. Faxon. 1m., 9w. Sc. Interior. B

Back from the Philippines; or, Major Kelly's cork leg, an Irish farce. O. E. Young. 5m., 3w. Sc. Parlor in a hotel. FP

Back of the ballot. George Middleton. Woman suffrage farce. 4m., 1w. Sc. Interior. FSD

Back of the yards. Kenneth Goodman Sawyer. 2m., 1w., 1b., 1g. Sc. Kitchen of a small flat in the district back of the Chicago Stock Yards. GB, GQ

Backtown spirits; or, two under the table. Farce. O. E. Young. 3m., 1w. Sc. Interior. APP

Backward child, A. H. L. Pemberton. Farce comedy. 1w., 1g. Sc. Private school-room. PH

Bad beginning, A. Ernest Grant White. Comedy. 4m., 2w. Sc. Sitting room of hotel suite. FP

* **Bad case of microbes, A.** Rea Woodman. 1b., 2g., Sc. Living room. WO

Bad debts. Margaret Searle. 3m., 2w. Sc. Living room. FSD

* **Bad temper bureau, The.** E. M. Fotheringham. Verse. 5b., 5g. Sc. Ticket office at back of stage. FSD

Bag o' dreams, The. Margretta Scott. 3m., 6w., 2b., 1g. Sc. Park with trees. Drama 11: 131–132, Jan. 1921.

† **Bairnies' Saturday night.** Edith F. A. U. Painton. Scotch dialect. 1b., 2g. Sc. Interior. PAD

† **Bank account, The.** Howard Folsom Brock. 1m., 2w. Sc. Living room of a shabby flat. HD1, Harvard Mo. 58: 33–50, Apr. 1914.

† **Bank robbery; a take-off, The.** Max Ehrmann. 5m. Sc. Front of a money safe. SB

* **Banker's strategy, The.** Eleanore Hubbard. Financial play. 4b., chorus. Sc. Bank in New York in 1816. HUC

Barbara. Kenneth Sawyer Goodman. 2m., 2w. Sc. Living room of bachelor apartment. FSD, GBA, GQ

Barbara. Jerome K. Jerome. 2m., 2w. Sc. Simple interior. B

Barbara Roscorla's child. Arthur Symons. 2m., 2w. Sc. Dining hall of manor in Cornwall. Little Review 4: 25–36, Oct. 1917.

‡ **Barbara the Great.** Julia Martin. 5b. Sc. Country store. EP

Barbara's wedding. J. M. Barrie. 4m., 2w. Sc. A sitting-room of a country cottage. BE

Barbarians, The. Robert DeCamp Leland. Great War play. 6m. Sc. A barber shop in Provencia. LEL

Bardwell vs. Pickwick. Charles Dickens, adapted by J. Hollingshead. 6m., 2w. Sc. Court room. B

Bargain, The. Wilbur S. Tupper. 1m., 3w. Sc. Simply furnished living room in California. TU

Bargain day. Mary H. Flanner. Comedy. 2m., 1w., 1 baby. Sc. Interior of apartment. FSD

‡ **Barnaby Lee.** Anna M. Lütkenhaus. Dramatization of Barnaby Lee by John Bennett. Historical play of early New York. 7b., 1g., chorus groups. Sc. Coast of New Amsterdam. LU

Barrington's "At Home," The. John Kendricks Bangs. Farce. 2m., 3w. Sc. Drawing room of a parsonage. BAD

Batch of proverbs, A. B. M. Morris. 1m., 1w. Sc. Interior. APP

Bathroom door, The. Gertrude Jennings. Comedy. 3m., 3w. Sc. Hall leading to bathroom. FSD

Bathsheba. David Pinski, tr. by Isaac Goldberg from the Yiddish. 4m., 1w., 1 chorus group. Sc. Roof of the King's Palace in ancient Palestine. PTK

‡ **Battle of Manbilla, The.** Marie Bankhead Owen. Historical. Spanish invasion of Florida. 19b., 3g., Chorus. Sc. Fort in distance. AO

* **Battle of the days.** Grace Richardson. 11c. Sc. Nursery. RS

Baucis and Philemon. Frances Gillespy Wickes. 8c. Chorus. Sc. A hut on the hillside. WCB

AN INDEX TO ONE-ACT PLAYS

Be sociable. W. A. Stigler. Comedy. 6m., 4w. Sc. Office. STA

Beanstalk, The. John Chapin Mosher. 1m., 1w. Sc. Leaf on a beanstalk. Smart Set 60: 83–87, Dec. 1919.

† **Beau of Bath.** Constance D'Arcy Mackay. Fanciful play with historical characters. 2m., 1w. Sc. Room of faded splendor. MB, WWS

Beautiful despot, the last act of a drama, The. Nicholas Evréinov. 5m., 3w. Sc. Luxuriously furnished room. BFR

Beautiful nun, The. David Pinski. 2m., 4w. Sc. Small chapel of a nunnery. PT

* **Beautiful song, The.** Augusta Stevenson. 12c. Many choruses. Sc. A meadow. SC1

Beautiful story, The. Percival Wilde. 1m., 1w., 1c. Sc. Dignified room with cheerful fire. WC

Beautiful thing, The. Murray Leinster and George B. Jenkins, Jr. 2m., 2w. Sc. Mezzanine floor of a good hotel. Smart Set 59: 89–95, Aug. 1919.

† **Beauty and the Jacobin.** Booth Tarkington. 3m., 2w., chorus. Sc. Lodging house in Boulogne-sur-Mer during the French Revolution. C1, TBJ

Beauty versus the beast. Malcolm Morley. 1m., 1w. Sc. Comfortably furnished bachelor's quarters. MOL

* **Because he loved David so.** Irma Kraft. The closing of school. 3g. Sc. Narrow alley outside of clothing shop in a small town in Pennsylvania. KPP

† **Because it rained.** Alice W. Chapin. 4g. Sc. Room in a cottage. CHC

Becket saves Rosamund. Binney Gunnison. Adapted from "Becket" by Tennyson. English historical play. 3m., 2w. Sc. Secret bower in a forest in England. GU

† **Becoming an American.** J. R. Gibbins. Americanization school play. 8m., chorus. Sc. Courtroom. GIE

Bedroom suite. Christopher Morley. 2m., 1w. Sc. A show window in a department store. Outlook 133: 79–82, Jan. 10, 1923.

* **Bee hive, a play for Labor Day, The.** Madalene D. Barnum. 17c. Sc. Interior of a beehive. BS

Before breakfast. Eugene G. O'Neill. 1m., 1w. Sc. A small room serving as kitchen and dining room. P3, STW

Before breakfast. Githa Sowerby. Comedy. 2m., 2w. Sc. Interior. FSD

Before the dawn, a melodrama. Wilson Hicks. 2m., 1w. Sc. Waiting room of village railway station. Smart Set 61: 71–75, Feb. 1920.

Before the fairies came to America, masque. William Griffith. Verse. 8 char. elves, fairies etc. International 10: 316–318, Oct. 1916.

Before the Pixies came to America. William Griffith. Fairy play for grown-ups. 4m., 6w., Chorus. Sc. Forest of Arden. GRA

Before the play begins. Georgia Earle. 2m., 1w. Sc. Room for rehearsal of play. DEP

Before the rummage sale. G. S. Shephard. 14w. Sc. Interior. FSD

Beggar and the king. Winthrop Parkhurst. 3m. Sc. Chamber in a palace overlooking the courtyard. LE, STV Drama 9: 62–74, Feb. 1919.

* **Beginning of negro slavery, The.** Louise E. Tucker and Estelle L. Ryan. 4b., chorus. Sc. River front of old Jamestown. TRH

Behind a Watteau picture. Robert Emmons Rogers. Fantasy in verse. 6m., 2w., chorus. Sc. Great gilt frame as if the play were a painting. B

Behind the black cloth. Kenneth Sawyer Goodman. Melodrama. 3m., 1w. Sc. Room in a sanatorium. GQA

* **Behind the khaki of the scouts,** a girl scout pageant. Fannie Moulton McLane. 12w. and girl scouts. Sc. Large auditorium. St. Nicholas 50: 386–389, Feb. 1923.

Behind the lines. Helen Bagg. Great War comedy. 10w. Sc. Room in a hotel used for a Red Cross workroom. PPP

Behind the Purdah. Eden Gardener. 3m., 3w. Sc. Courtyard of palace in India. Asia 20: 273–276, April 1920.

* **Behind the rain curtains.** Edith Burrows. 17c., chorus. Sc. Interior. PPP

† **Behind the screen.** Alice W. Chaplin. 5g. Sc. Library in a home. CHC

* **Being a hero.** Clara J. Denton. 2b. Sc. Interior. MBP

Being the fly. Lillian P. Wilson. 3m., 2w. Sc. office. WIF

Belgian baby, The. Fenton B. Elkins. Farce. 2m., 2w. Sc. Sitting room in a flat. ET

Belgian Christmas eve, A. Alfred Noyes. Great War play. 2m., 1w., 1g., chorus. Sc. Room in a Doctor's house in Belgium. NC, NCB

† **Belles of Canterbury, The.** Anna Bird Stewart. 11w. Sc. Room in a dormitory. FSD

Ben-Hur and Iras. Binney Gunnison. Adapted from "Ben-Hur" by Lew Wallace. 1m., 1w. Sc. A home in Antioch. GU

Benjamin, Benny and Ben. Anthony E. Wills. Farce. 8m., 4w. Sc. Interior. FP

* **Benjamin Franklin: journeyman.** Constance D'Arcy Mackay. 3b., 2g. Sc. Room in a tavern. MPY

Benkei on the bridge. (Hashi-benkei) Hiyoshi Sa-ami Yasukiyo. Nō play of Japan. 3m., chorus. Sc. Stage. WAA

† **Beresford benevolent society.** (Author not given) 1b., 7g. Comedy. Sc. Unimportant. BU

* **Bernard Palissy, enameller to his Majesty.** Augusta Stevenson. 10b., 7g., chorus. Sc. Cottage living room. SC4

* **Best children in the world, The.** Lady Bell. Comedy. 1b., 2g. Sc. Unimportant. BEJ

Best man, The. Eleanor Maude Crane. Comedy. 2m., 2w., Sc. Vestry room of a church. FSD

† **Best seller, The.** Martha Royle Palmer. 30 or more women or girls. Sc. City library. PAB

* **Best wish, The.** F. E. Bloxam. 2b., 7g., many choruses. Sc. Woodland. BL

Bet; or, an old story retold, The. Darcy Leverson. 5m., 2w. Sc. Country inn. WIA

Betrayal, The. Padriac Colum. Melodrama. 3m., 1w. Sc. Inn in Ireland in 18th century. Drama 11: 3–7, Oct. 1920.

Betrothed, The. Wilfrid Wilson Gibson. Verse. 2w. Sc. Fishing village. GID, GIP

Betsey's boarders. O. E. Young. Farce. 2m., 2w., Sc. Third floor corridor in a boarding house. BUP

Betsy Trotwood at home. Horace B. Browne. From Dickens' David Copperfield. 2m., 2w., 1b. Sc. Front garden. BD

Betsy Baker; or, Too attentive by half. John Maddison Morton. Farce. 2m., 2w. Sc. Parlor. PPP

Better son, a domestic drama. Isaac Goldberg. 2m., 1w. Sc. Dining room of an apartment of family of moderate means. Stratford Journal 3: 169–180, Oct. 1918.

* **Betty Jane's Christmas dream.** Glenn H. Isenberger and Susie E. Isenberger. Christmas play. 43b., 9g. Sc. Girl's bedroom in a well-to-do-home. MAP

Betty's ancestors. Emma M. Hunting. 2m., 12w. Sc. A quaint old room. PPP

Betty's butler. Frances H. Schreiner. Comedy. 1m., 3w. Sc. Library of a home. B

Between fires. Grover Theis. 2m., 1w. Sc. Living room of a fisherman's hut. TN

Between the soup and the savory. G. E. Jennings. 3w. Sc. Interior. FSD, JF

Beyond. Alice Gerstenberg. 1w. Sc. Limitless space. GT, MA

Bibi, or the Japanese foundling. Ruth Arkwright. 3g. Sc. Japanese room. AB

Big Kate. Charles Frederic Nirdlinger. Play of Catherine the Great of Russia. 3m., 2w. Sc. Room in the Winter Palace at St. Petersburg in 1780. NI

Big scene, The. Arthur Schnitzler. 4m., 1w., 1b. Sc. An apartment in a fashionable hotel. SCW

Bill Perkins' proposin' day. Helena A. Ffeil. Rustic comedy. 2m., 2w. Sc. Country living room. DPP

Billie's first love. Grace Griswold. Comedy. 2m., 2w. Sc. Studio. FSD

Bills. John M. Francis. Farce. 2m., 1w., Sc. Apartment in New York. FSD

Billy's chorus girl. Clara B. Batchelder. Comedy. 2m., 3w. Sc. Interior. DEP

Billy's mishap. Viola E. Brown. 2m., 3w. Sc. Interior. DEP

Bird child, The. Lucy White. 2m., 2w., 1c. Sc. Law office in small town. International 8: 337–339, Nov. 1914.

Bird in the hand. Sigmund B. Alexander. 4m., 3w. Sc. Corridor off the ball room in a summer hotel. WHP

Bird in the hand. Laurence Housman. 3m., 1w. Sc. Study of a scientist. FSD

Bird's nest, a fantasy. Tracy D. Mygatt. 3m., 1w. Sc. Garden outside a cottage. B

* **Birds' story of the trees, The.** Anna M. Lütkenhaus. Arbor Day play. 5c. Sc. Out of doors. LU

* **Birth of a nation's flag, The.** Ellen Jess. Excellent school play. 6b., 13g. Sc. Interior. EP

Birth of a soul, The. William Sharp. Symbolic. 3m., 4w. Sc. Austerely furnished bedroom in old city of Flanders. SHV

Birth of God, The. Verner von Heidenstam. Translated from the Swedish. Religious speculation. 8m. Sc. Street of the Sphinxes in Karnak. FOS

† **Birthday ball, The.** Marjory Woods. Revolutionary War background. 5w., 1s. Sc. Colonial living room in Washington in 1792. FSD

* **Birthday candles.** Margaret C. Getchell. 1b., 2w., fairies and elves.

Sc. Old fashioned parlor. Woman's Home Companion 44; 23, Aug. 1917.

Birthday of the Infanta. Stuart Walker. 5m., 2w. Sc. Royal balcony overlooking a garden. WA

* **Birthday of the Infanta, The.** Harriet Sabra Wright. From the story by Oscar Wilde. 3b., 2g., chorus. Sc. A room in a palace. WN

Birthday party, The. Hjalmar Bergström. Translated from the Danish. 1m., 8w. Sc. Room with a fireplace. MR

Biscuits and bills. O. B. DeBois. Comedy. 3m., 1w. Sc. Dining room. FP

† **Bishop's candlesticks, The.** Normal McKennell. From Victor Hugo's Les Miserables. 3m., 2w. Sc. A plainly furnished kitchen. FSD

Bit o' stuff, A. Wilfred T. Coleby. 2m., 2w., Sc. Room in a lodging house. FSD

Bit of instruction, A. Evelyn G. Sutherland. Comedy. 2m. Sc. Bachelor sitting room. SUP

Bit of nonsense, A. Kate Thomas. Farce. 8w. Sc. Plainly furnished sitting-room in a boarding school. FSD

Bit of old Chelsea, A. Mrs. Oscar Beringer. 4m., 1w. Sc. Studio. FSD

Bit of the world, A. Edgar Allan Woolf. 2m. Sc. Squalid room in the tenements. Smart Set 32: 121–126, Dec. 1910.

Biteless dog, The. Israel Solon. 1m., 1w. Sc. University campus in June. Smart Set 42: 97–102, Jan. 1914.

Black death or Ta-ün (plague), The. A Persian tragedy. M. E. Lee. 2m., 2w., servants. Sc. Persian harem. Poet Lore 28: 691–702, Winter 1917.

Black Madonna. William Sharp. Fanciful. Verse. 1m., 1w., 4 choruses. Sc. A forest. SHV

Black sheep, The. Leon Kobrin. Tr. from the Yiddish by Isaac Goldberg. 3m., 2w. Sc. A study. PTT

† **Black tie, The.** George Middleton. 1m., 2w., 1s., 1c. Sc. Upstairs sitting room. MIP

Black trouble, A. Dorothy Cleather. 3w., 1s. Sc. Dining room. CH

Blackberryin'; a comedy. Howard Forman Smith. 5w. Sc. Berry house on a farm. SR, STW

Blank cartridge. Georges Courteline. 1m., 1w. Sc. Plainly furnished bedroom. International 8: 211–215, July 1914.

Blessed Baby, see **That blessed baby.**

† **Blessed birthday, The.** Florence Converse. Christmas miracle play, 9b., 9g., chorus. Sc. A well in Nazareth during the life of Christ. CON

Blind, The. Maurice Maeterlinck. Translated from the French. 7m., 6w., 1c., 1 dog. Sc. An ancient forest. MAH. MAI, MR

† **Blind.** Senmas O'Brien. Irish comedy. 3m. Sc. Street in a country town in Ireland. FS

* **Blind men and the elephant, The.** Augusta Stevenson. 7b., Sc. Roadside. SC2

Blockade. Olivia Howard Dunbar. 3m., 2w., 1g. Sc. Rear of a house in a New Hampshire village. Theatre Arts Magazine 7: 127–142, April 1923.

Blood money. Curtis Dunham. 4m., 1w. Sc. Consulting room of a doctor's office. US

Blood o' Kings. June Dransfield. 9m. Sc. Bedroom in the brickyard region of the Hudson Valley. STV

Blood Royal. Evan Poole. French historical play. 9m., chorus of men. Sc. King's chamber in the 16th century. PA

Blood will tell. Sallie Kemper. Comedy. 4w. Sc. Drawing room in house in Richmond, Virginia. B

Bloodybush edge. Wilfrid Wilson Gibson. Verse. 3m. Sc. Remote spot on border of England. GIB, GIP

Blue and green. Alfred Kreymborg. Puppet play. Shadow play. 1m., 1w. Sc. Among trees. KMR

Blue Harlequin, The. Maurice Baring. Fantastic farce. 3m., 1w. Sc. A London street. BA

Blue morning glory, A. Moritz Jagendorf. 2m., 1w. Sc. Grecian chamber. International 8: 95–97, 104, Mar. 1914.

Blue pincushion, The. M. Q. Dixon. 1m., 2w. Sc. Boudoir. Smart Set 4: 137–139, May 1901.

* **Blue pump, The.** Clara J. Denton. 2b. Sc. Interior. MBP

Blue sphere, The. Theodore Dreiser. 6m., 2w., chorus. Sc. Kitchen of a poor family. DP, Smart Set 44: 245–252, Dec. 1914.

Blue vase, The. Frayne Williams. Chinese play in free verse. 1m., 1w. Sc. House in ancient China. WIT

Bluebeard. Lindsey Barbee. 1b., 2g., Sc. Turkish house. BLC

Bluebeard. May Bell. 2m., 3w. Sc. Upper chamber in an Arabian palace. BRW

* **Bluebeard.** Caroline W. Thomason. 6b., 5g., Sc. Bluebeard's drawing-room. PPP, TH

Blunted age, The. Agnes Lee. 1m., 2w. Sc. Living room. Poetry 19: 71–73, Nov. 1921.

* **Bo-Peep's Christmas party.** Elizabeth F. Guptill. Mother Goose play. 6b., 8g. Sc. Interior. EP

* **Boastful giant, The.** Marie Irish. Christmas play. 3b., 2g. Sc. Interior. IC

* **Boastful weathervane.** Clara J. Denton. Verse. Christmas play. 10b. Sc. Out door scene. I

‡ **Boasts and a bruise.** A. L. Westlake. 4g. Sc. Girls' class room. FSD

Boatswain's mate. W. W. Jacobs and Herbert N. Sargent. Farce. 2m., 1w. Sc. Interior. FSD

Bobbie settles down. Gertrude E. Jennings. Comedy. 1m., 3w. Sc. Interior. FSD

* **Bobby's dream.** Linna M. Ferrer. 5b., 1g. Sc. A school room. FER

* **Bob's and Tom's Thanksgiving.** Clara J. Denton. Thanksgiving day play. 2b. Sc. Interior. DAH

Boccaccio's untold tale. Harry Kemp. 2m., 2w., 1s., 2 voices, chorus. Sc. A simply furnished room. SL

Bogie men, The. Lady Isabella Augusta Gregory. Irish comedy. 2m. Sc. A shed near a road. GRZ, Forum 49: 28–40, Jan. 1913.

Bohemians, a farce of poverty. Abraham Raisin, trans. from the Yiddish by Isaac Goldberg. 8m., 1w. Sc. Room of a lodging house. Stratford Journal 6: 111–120, Ap.–June, 1920.

* **Bolo and Babette.** Henry Bailey Stevens. 9b., 3g. Sc. Slope of a pasture. STE

"Bombast and platitudes." Dorothy Potter. 3m. Sc. Comfortable library of a bachelor's apartment. POT

Bombastes in the shades. Lawrence Binyon. Historical characters. 4m., 1w., 1c. Sc. Cool green glade. O

Bonds of marriage, The. Aleister Crowley. Play to increase the sale of Liberty Bonds. 2m., 1w., Sc. Living room of apartment. International 12: 88–91, March 1918.

‡ Bone of contention, The. Genevieve K. McConnell. Fairy melodrama. 4b., 8g. Sc. Child's bedroom. B

Bonnie Dundee. Frank Richardson. Historical background of the English commonwealth. 4m., 2w. Sc. An oak chamber in England of the 17th century. FSD

* Bonnie's Christmas Eve. Jay Clay Powers and Irene M. Childs. 3b., 1g. Sc. Cabin in Canadian Northwest. BAC

Boob, The. J. C. McMullen. Comedy of business life. 4m., 1w. Sc. Private office. B

Book agent, The. Louis A. La Shere. Farce. 2m., 2w. Sc. Any interior. APP

Booklegger, The. Curtiss LaQ Day. 5m., 1w. Sc. College study. Smart Set 66: 75–80, Dec. 1922.

Bookmaker's shoes, The. Earle Mitchell. 2m., 1w. Sc. Living room in plainly furnished flat. Smart Set 30: 131–136, March 1910.

Boor, The. Anton Tchekoff. Trans. from Russian by Hilmar Baukhage 1m., 1w., 1s. Chorus. Sc. Well furnished reception room in Russian house. CHD, FSD, LC, SL

Borrowed luncheon, A. Helen Sherman Griffith. 5w. Sc. Interior. DEP

Borrowers' day. Jessie E. Henderson. Rural comedy. 5m., 6w. Sc. Unimportant. PPP

* Boston Tea Party, The. Constance D'Arcy Mackay. 9b. Sc. Tavern. MPY

Bottled in bond, a tragic farce of our times. Glenn Hughes. 2m., 2w. Sc. Ordinary living room. Drama 13: 170–173, Feb. 1923.

† Bound east for Cardiff. Eugene O'Neill. 11m. Sc. Seamen's forecastle of a British tramp steamer. OMC, P1

* Bouquet of rose spirits.—— 8b., 18g. Sc. An open glade. BBS

Box of powders, A. Pauline Phelps and Marion Short. Farcical romance. 1m., 1w. Sc. Handsomely furnished drawing room. PH

Boy and a girl, A. Alfred Sutro. 1m., 1w. Sc. Park of a London house. Colliers 34: 16–17, Jan. 7, 1905.

† Boy comes home, The. A. A. Milne. Great War background. 2m., 3w. Sc. Interior of dignified home. MSL, WWS

* Boy who found Christmas, The. Louise Rand Bascom. Christmas play. 4b., 2g., chorus. Sc. Street. GUB

Boy will, The. Robert Emmons Rogers. Drama of boyhood of William Shakespeare. 3m., 2w. Main room of an inn. C1, Harvard Monthly 43: 238–249, Jan. 1907.

* Boy's Christmas, A. Ellen M. Willard. 3b. Sc. Interior. WY

Boy's proposal. Arthur Eckersley. Comedy. 2m., 1w., 1b. Sc. Drawing room. FSD

Boys will be girls, a girlsterious extravaganza. Sherman F. Johnson. 2m., 24w. Sc. Interior. B

Bracelet, The. Alfred Sutro. 4m., 3w., 1s. Sc. Dining-room. FSD, SF

Branded Mavericks. H. O. Stechhan and Maverick Terrell. 5m. Sc. Combination saloon and ranch house in Texas. Smart Set 42: 133, March 1914.

Brass door-knob, The. Matthew Boulton. 1m., 1w. Sc. Interior. FSD

* **Brave foresters.** Marie Irish. Forest conservation play. 6b. Sc. Unimportant. IPP

* **Brave little tomboy, A;** play of the Revolution. Elizabeth F. Guptill. 7b., 6g. Sc. Unimportant. EP

* **Bravest thing in the world,** a comedy of childhood. Lee Pape. 2b., 5g. Sc. Nursery. PB, PPP

Bread, butter and romance. Mary Moncure Parker. Comedy. 1m., 3w. Sc. Any room. DEP

Breakfast at eight. Ronald Gow. 4m. Sc. Library in a country house. FSD

Breakfast breeze. W. Macfarlane. Farce. 1m., 2w., 1s. Sc. Around the breakfast table. PL

Breaking the engagement. W. C. Parker. Farce. 2m., 1w. Sc. Hotel parlor. B

Breaking the ice; or, A piece of holly. Charles Thomas. Romantic comedy. 1m., 1w. Sc. Room in a country inn. PH

* **Brethren,** a play for Peace Day. Madalene D. Barnum. 12m., 2w., chorus. Sc. Green plateau. BS

* **Brewing of brains, A;** Constance D'Arcy Mackay. A Lincolnshire folk play. 1b., 2g. Sc. A kitchen. MST

Bridal, The. Wilfrid Wilson Gibson. Verse. 1m., 2w. Sc. A lonely shepherd's cottage. GIA, GIP, GIS

Bridal trip, A. Harry Hurst. Comedy. 2m., 2w. Sc. Drawing room. FSD

Bride and the burglar. Florence Lewis Speare. Comedy. 2m., 1w. Sc. Living room of a new unoccupied bungalow. FSD

Bride from home, A. Willis Steell. A vaudeville sketch. 1m., 2w., 1c. Sc. Room in a tenement. PWP

Bridegroom, The. Lajos Biro, trans. from the German by Charles Recht. 5m., 6w. Sc. Room with bridal gifts. Drama 8: 154–175, May 1918.

Bride's Christmas tree, a Christmas play. Beatrice Herford. 4m., 4w. Sc. New York apartment. Ladies Home Journal 28: 14, 64, Dec. 1911.

Bride's crown, The. Zakarias Topelius, trans. by Elizabeth J. Macintire. 2m., 1w. Sc. Great hall of a castle. Poet Lore 28: 595–599, Autumn 1917.

Bridges. Clare Kummer. 2m., 1w. Sc. Inner office of a business firm. FSD

Bright idea. Arthur Law. 2m., 2w. Sc. Drawing room. WIA

Bright morning, A. Serafin and Joaquin Alvarez Quintero, trans. from the Spanish by Carlos C. Castillo and E. L. Overman. 2m., 2w. Sc. Lonely place on a public promenade in Madrid. Poet Lore 27: 668–679, Winter 1916

Brink of silence, The. Esther E. Galbraith. 4m. Sc. Interior of a log house on a rocky island. MA

Brogues of Kilavain Glen. Fairy play for grown-ups. 2w., 6c., chorus. Sc. Glen in Ireland. FL

Broken bars, The. Anna Wynne. Modern morality play. 10m., 10w. Sc. Ballroom. FSD

Broken engagement, A. Alice C. Thompson. Comedy. 4w. Sc. Parlor. FSD

* **Broken picture, The.** Marie Irish. Christmas play. 2b., 2g. Sc. Living room. IC

Brother Dave. Willis Steell. 1m., 2w. Sc. Farmhouse kitchen. PWP

† **Brother Sun.** Laurence Housman. About St. Francis of Assisi. Sc. Camp of the Saracens before Damietta. C2

Brotherhood of veterans.——Any number of characters. Ladies Home Journal 23: 41, Feb. 1906.

Brothers. Lewis Beach. 3m. Sc. Small room in shanty. BF, SL

Brothers. Richard Burton. Humanitarian play. 2m., 1w. Sc. Interior. FSD

* **Brothers and sisters.** E. E. Bloxam. 17c. Sc. Unimportant. BL

* **"Brownie night,"** a Hallowe'en entertainment for rural schools. Nan L. Mildren. Any number of children. Sc. Unimportant. Ladies Home Journal 30: 106, Oct. 1913.

* **Brownies' vacation.** Elizabeth F. Guptill. 9b. Sc. Santa Claus' kitchen. FIL

* **Brummy Crock.** E. M. Fotheringham. Fantasy. 8b. Sc. School room. FSD

Bubble's troubles. James Madison. Farce. 4m., 2w. Sc. Parlor. US

Bud's baby. Edwin Holt. 3m. Sc. Interior of miner's cabin. US

Buffer, The. Alice Gerstenberg. 2m., 3w., 1c. Sc. Living room. GT

Builders, The; B. Russell Herts. A dramatic dialogue in verse. 1m., 1w. Sc. Woods. Moods 2: 24–31, Aug.–Sept. 1909.

Bull-terrier and the baby, The. Helen M. Givens. 2m., 2w. Sc. Private sitting room in a country hotel. Ladies Home Journal 23: 15, Oct. 1906.

Bumps. Lillie Davis. Phrenology farce. 3w. Sc. Interior. B

Bunch of roses, A. M. E. M. Davis. 4m., 4w. Sc. Sitting room. DAB

Bunk. Henry Clapp Smith. Burlesque melodrama. 6m., 1w. Sc. Behind the stage. FSD

Bunkered. Bertha Moore. 2w. Sc. Lounge of a hotel. FSD

Burden, The. Elma Ehrlich Levinger. Play of Jewish life. 3m., 1w. Sc. Living room of a Jewish family on the East side. B

Burglar, The. Margaret Cameron. Comedy. 5w. Sc. Sitting room. CAC, FSD

Burglar alarm, The. R. MacDonald Alden. Comedy. 3m., 3w., chorus. Sc. Well furnished parlor. G1

Burglar and the girl. Matthew Boulton. 1m., 1w. Sc. Drawing room of a country house. FSD

Burglar who failed, The. St. John Emile Clavering Hankin. 1m., 2w. Sc. Bedroom. HAN3

Burglar's welcome. Harry L. Newton. 1m., 1w. Sc. Interior. DPP

* **Buried treasure.** Katharine Lord. 5b., 3g. Sc. Back yard of a house. LLS

Burlesque pantomine. Herbert C. Sargent. Burlesque farce. 5m., 3w. Sc. A forest dell. SAR

Bushido from "Terakoya" or "Matsu." Takeda Idzumo. Japanese play. 18m., 3w., 9b. Sc. Stage with two levels. ELT3

Business is business. Harry L. Newton. 2m., 1w. Sc. Office. DEP

Business meeting, A. Arlo Bates. Comedy. 10w. Sc. Interior. B, Ladies Home Journal 20: 15, March 1903.

‡ **Buster.** Violet M. Methley. 6b. Sc. Dining room. FSD

Busy day in Bangville, A. Ethelyn Sexton. Comedy. 9m., 11w., 1b., 2g. Sc. Country store and post office. EP

Butcher's daughter, The. Granville Forbes Sturgis. 3m., 1w. Sc. 1. Street or country road. Sc. 2. Living room back of butcher shop. STR

Butterfly, The; a morality. George S. Viereck. 4m., 2w., chorus. Sc. A sleeping chamber. VG, International 11: 156–159, May 1917.

"Butting in" in French. Adele Luehrmann. 1m., 1w. Sc. Drawing room in New York City home. Smart Set 31: 125–127, Aug. 1910.

* **Buying a day.** Rea Woodman. 1b., 3g. Sc. Sitting room. WO

Buying a house. Herbert C. Sargent. Farce. 1m., 1w. Sc. Interior. SAR

Buying a suit for Jimmy. Anne M. Palmer. Comedy. 3m., 6w. Sc. Clothing-store. PPP

By Miho's pine-clad shore, a Noh play, trans. from the Japanese text by Yone Noguchi. 1m. and fishermen, 1 fairy, chorus. Pacific Review 2: 235–240, Sept. 1921.

By mutual agreement. R. A. Brandon and George Bull. 2m., 1w. Comedy. Sc. Interior of lawyer's office. FSD

By ourselves. Ludwig Fulda. 3m., 2w. Sc. Dining room of home. SS Poet Lore 23: 1–24, Jan.–Feb. 1912.

By-product, A. Manta S. Graham. Great War background. 5m. Sc. Improvised officers' headquarters in a deserted farmhouse. GRL

By the Sumida River. Colin Campbell Clements. 2m., 1w., spirit of her boy child, chorus. Sc. Banks of the Sumida River. Poet Lore 31: 166–175, Summer 1920.

By their words ye shall know them. Serafin and Joaquin Alvarez Quintero, trans. from the Spanish. 2m., 1w. Sc. Corner of the courtyard of apartment house in Seville. MR, Drama 7: 26–39, Feb. 1917.

By woman's wit. A. Louis Elliston. 2m., 1w. Sc. Room in a handsome apartment. B

* **Bye, Baby Bunting.** Someple (pseud.) Christmas play. 11c. Sc. Interior with grate fire. SO

Bygones. Miriam Nichelson. 2m., 1w. Sc. Private room in smart restaurant. Smart Set 51: 81–92, March 1917.

C

Cabman and the lady, The. William D. Emerson. 2m., 1w. Sc. Exterior. DEP

Cain. R. E. Rogers. 1m., 1w. Sc. Barren plain of Cush. Harvard Monthly 41: 259–260, Feb. 1906.

* **Cake, The.** Laura E. Richards. 14c. 1 dog. Sc. A road. RP

Calamity Jane, R.N. Major William Price Drury. Comedy. 5m., 2w. Sc. Pensioners' ward. FSD

Calegula's picnic. Maurice Baring. 9m., many choruses. Sc. Large banqueting table. BA

Call, The. Wilfrid Wilson Gibson. Verse. 2m., 1w. Sc. Engine house of a fire station. GID, GIP

‡ **Call of God, The.** Mae Stein Soble. Bible play of Moses. 7b. Sc. Mountain. SOB

* **Call of Samuel, The.** Rita Benton. Bible play. 8b., 1g. Sc. Before the door of the tabernacle. BSD

* **Call to the youth of America.** Rosamund Kimball. 23c., choruses. Sc. Hall. TKP

Calpurnia's dinner party. Maurice Baring. Historical farce. 1m., 1w., 1s. Sc. Room in Julius Caesar's house. BA

Calvary. William Butler Yeats. 9m. Sc. Bare space. YF

‡ **Camp fire Cinderella, A.** Mrs. Arthur T. Seymour. Camp fire play. 6g. Sc. Sitting room. B

‡ **Camp-fire girl, The.** Edith F. A. U. Painton. 1b., 3g. Sc. A camp fire PAD

Campbell of Kilmhor. J. A. Ferguson. Historical play of Mary Stuart. 4m., 2w. Sc. Interior of a lonely cottage. LE, REP

Camping. Daisy McGeoch Comedy. 3m., 3w. Sc. Out doors with tent in foreground. MAC

Capitulation of Mr. Hyleigh. Frank Howard Egbert. 3m., 2w. Sc. Office. EG

Caprice, A. Alfred de Musset. Comedy. 1m., 2w. Girl's room in Paris. MUB, Poet Lore 33: 395–419, Autumn 1922.

† **Captain of the gate.** Beulah Marie Dix. 6m. Sc. Upper room of a gate house of Bridge of Cashala. DA, LE

Captain Walrus: or, The game of three. Alexander H. Laidlaw, Jr. 1m., 2w. Sc. Interior. FSD

Capture of Ozah, The. Helen P. Kane. Indian play. 2m., 2w. Sc Indian lodge of the 18th century. FSD

* **Captured year, The.** Frances Gillespy Wickes. 22c. Sc. Halls of Father Time. WCB

Carlos among the candles. Wallace Stevens. 1m. Sc. Semicircular room with two long tables. Poetry 11: 115–123, Dec. 1917.

Carnival, The, a divine comedy in one act. Paul Eldridge. 15m., 8w., others. Sc. An ordinary garden. Double Dealer 5: 4–29, Jan. 1923.

Carrots. Jules Renard, trans. from the French of Alfred Sutro. 1m., 3w. Sc. Courtyard of an old prison like building. FSD

Carrying out a theory. Willard Spenser. Comedy. 4m., 1w. Sc. Hotel dining room. PPP

Case of duplicity. Helen Sherman Griffith. 1m., 2w. Sc. Interior. PPP

* **Case of Mrs. Kantsey Know.** Myra Williams Jarrell. 2b., 7w., 1g. Sc. Disorderly sitting room. Drama 12: 210–212, March 1922.

* **Case of Sophronia.** Marjorie Benton Cooke. 5g. Sc. Dormitory of a girl's school. DPP

Case of spoons; or, The Baroness Sorato's garden party. Japanese farce. Eunice T. Gray. 3m., 5w. Sc. Indoors or out doors, in Japanese garden. FSD

Casey's daughter, Mary Ann, an Irish farce. J. R. Farrell. 2m. Sc. Interior. APP

AN INDEX TO ONE-ACT PLAYS 55

† **Cash concern, A.** E. M. Fotheringham. Farce. 7b. Sc. Shop for ladies' hats. FSD

Casino gardens, The. Kenyon Nicholson. 5m. Sc. Orchestral platform of Casino gardens. Smart Set 64: 77–83, March 1921.

Cast rehearses, The. A. L. Tildesley. 5w. Sc. Sitting room. B

* **Casting of lots.** Abraham Burstein. Purim play. 4b., 4g., choruses. Sc. Living room. BLO

Castle Botherem. Arthur Law. 3m., 3w. Sc. Kitchen. WIA

* **Cat and dog.** Lady Bell. Comedy. 1b., 1g. Sc. Unimportant. BEJ

Cat and the cherub, The. Chester B. Fernald. 7m., 2w. Sc. A street in the Chinese quarter in San Francisco. FSD

* **Cat and the fiddle, The.** Lady Bell. 5c. Sc. Room in a boarding house. BR

* **Cat and the mouse, The.** Augusta Stevenson. 1b., 2g. Sc. A garret. SC3

Cat-boat, The. Percy Mackaye. Fantasy. 2m., 2w. Sc. A small work shop. MY

* **Cat that waited, The.** Augusta Stevenson. 3g. Sc. A garden. SC1

Catesby. Percival Wilde. Comedy. 1m., 1w. Sc. Veranda of a summer hotel. WE

Catherine Parr. Maurice Baring. Historical farce. 1m., 1w., 1s. Sc. Breakfast chamber in the Palace of King Henry VIII. BA

Cathleen Ni Hoolihan. William Butler Yeats. Irish Play. 3m., 3w., chorus. Sc. Inside of an Irish cottage. YH, YU, YPP. Samhain. 1902 pp. 24–31.

Caught. Morris M. Townley. Burglar play. 2m. Sc. Room in darkness. TOW

Caught at last. Dwight Spencer Anderson. 1m., 2w. Sc. Masquerade ball. APP

* **Cave of precious things.** Alice Wangenheim, adapted by K. W. Hinks. 1w., 5b., 2g., band of thieves. Sc. Nursery. Journal of Home Economics 11: 215–220, May 1919.

Cease Fire! Katharine Parry and John R. Collins. 11m. Sc. Interior. FSD

* **Census man, The.** Elizabeth F. Guptill. 2b., 1g. Sc. Sitting room. GUT

Césaire. Jean Schlumberger. 3m. Sc. Interior of fisherman's hut. Living Age 312: 106–15, Jan. 14, 1922.

Challenge of the cross. Charles A. Marsh and H. O. Rowland. Sacred drama. 8m., choir. Sc. Interior. MAS

Champagne. Isaac Loeb Perez, tr. from the Yiddish. 5w. Sc. A poor cellar dwelling. BLK

Chance at midnight. Charles Stewart Walsh. 2m., 1w., 1c. Sc. Library of home. FP

Change-house. John Brandane. 3m., 2w. Sc. Interior of change house in 1752. REP

Changeling, The. W. W. Jacobs and H. C. Sargent. 2m., 1w. Sc. Kitchen. FSD

* **Chanukah sketch.** Ruth E. Levi. Jewish holiday play. 12c., chorus. Sc. Large room. BLO

Charlie Barringer, the second of five sketches from a county poor farm. John Joseph Martin. 3m. Sc. Bedroom at the county farm. Theatre Arts Magazine 5: 242–248, July 1921.

* **Charlie's pop-corn.** Clara J. Denton. Thanksgiving Day play. 2b., 1g. Sc. Plain living room. DAH

Charming Leandre. Theodore de Banville, trans. from the French by Barrett H. Clark. Comedy. 2m., 1w. Sc. Deserted square in the neighborhood of the Luxembourg gardens in Paris in 18th century. FSD

* **Charter oak, The.** Eleanore Hubbard. Self government play. 6b., chorus of boys. Sc. General court in colonial Hartford, Conn. HUC

Chaste adventures of Joseph. Floyd Dell. Comedy. 3m., 2w. Sc. A room in Potiphar's house. DK

Cheat of pity, The. George Middleton. 1m., 1w., 1s. Sc. A dark room, a drawing room fashionably furnished. MIT

Cheezo. Lord Dunsany. 4m., 2w. Sc. Interior of a big house. DFO

* **Cherry-Blossom princess, The.** Gladys Evelyn Warren. 1b., 3g., chorus. Sc. The palace garden. BHP

Cherry Blossom River, The. Colin Campbell Clements. 3m., 1w., chorus. Sc. A street in Tsukuski. Poet Lore 31: 159–165, Summer 1920.

* **Cherry pie.** Louise E. Tucker and Estella L. Ryan. Maryland in raiding time. 4b., 3g. Sc. Living room. TRH

Chi-Fu, a play with masks. William Justema, Jr. 2m., 1w. Sc. Tumbledown hut of a fisherman in China. Drama 13: 356–370, Aug.–Sept. 1923.

Child, The. Wilfrid Wilson Gibson. Verse. 1m., 1w. Sc. A garret in the slums. GID, GIP

Child in the house, The. Marjorie Benton Cooke. Satirical sketch. 4w., 1c. Sc. Drawing room. CO

Child in the house, The. Homer Hildreth Howard. Temperance play. 2m., 2w., 1 baby. Sc. Basement room in a tenement house. FSD, Poet Lore 24: 433–444, Winter 1913.

Child of God, The. Louise Driscoll. 2m., 3w. Sc. Dining room of small house. Seven Arts 1: 34–46, Nov. 1916.

Children and the Evangelists, The. Margaret Otey Tomes. A Nativity play. 17m., 6w., choir. Sc. Dark background. Drama 11: 58–60, Nov. 1920.

* **Children in the Great War.** Wallace Rice. 4b., 4g. Sc. A clearing in the woods. RIS

* **Children of France.** Wallace Rice. 4b., 4g. Sc. A clearing in a wood. RIS

Children of Granada. Margaret Scott Oliver. A Spanish play. 7m., 2w., chorus. Sc. Courtyard of Alhambra in Granada. OS

* **Children of the Christmas spirit.** Anita B. Ferris. 8b., 9g., choir. Sc. Room in a home. Everyland 6: 33–37, Dec. 1914.

* **Children of the Civil War.** Wallace Rice. 4b., 4g. Sc. A clearing in a wood. RIS

* **Children of the Illini.** Wallace Rice. 4b., 4g. Sc. A clearing in a wood. RIS

Children of the sunrise. Julia P. Dabney. 10m., 6w., shepherds and attendants. Sc. Forest glade. Poet Lore 26: 653–693, Nov.–Dec. 1915.

* **Children's Christmas dream, The.** Mary E. Telford. 24c. Sc. Living room. TE

* **Children's hour, The.** Gladys Ruth Bridgham. 7b., 12g. Sc. A study. BBS

* **Child's play.** Laura E. Richards. 2b. Sc. A roadside. RP

Chimalman. Grace E. Taft. Verse. Ancient Aztec. 3m., 3w. Sc. A forest glade. TA

China pig, The. Evelyn Emig. 3w. Sc. Living room of moderate priced apartment. STW, Poet Lore 33: 439–450, Autumn 1922.

Chinese lily. Paula Jakobi. 1m., 7w. Sc. Laundry of a woman's prison. Forum 54: 551–566, Nov. 1915.

Chinese love. Clare Kummer. Chinese life. 4m., 2w. Sc. Interior. FSD

‡ **Chips off the old block.** E. M. Peixotto. Farce. 4b. Sc. A street PET

Chitra. Rabindranath Tagore. 3m., 1w., chorus. Sc. Not given. TC

* **Chocolate cake and black sand.** Samuel Milbank Cauldwell. A dream play. 1b., 3g. Sc. Little girl's bedroom. CC

Choice, The. Allan Monkhouse. Play of the Great War. 1m., 3w. Sc. Sitting room of a country cottage. MW

Choice of a tutor, The. Denis von Vizin. 5m., 3w., s., chorus characters. Sc. Room in a Russian house of the well-to-do. BFR

Choir rehearsal, The. Clare Kummer. 2m., 2w. Sc. Interior. FSD

Choosing a career. Gaston A. de Caillavet, trans. from the French by Barrett H. Clark. 3m., 1w. Sc. A simple room in a hotel in France. FSD

Chorio. Ernest Fenollosa and Ernest Pound. Noh play of Japan. 4m., chorus. Sc. Laid in China. FEN

* **Christening of Rosalys.** Netta Syrett. A pastoral. 4b., 3g. Chorus. Sc. Part of the Palace garden. SSG

Christening robe, The. Anne L. Estabrook. Comedy. 1m., 3w. Sc. A pleasant tenement kitchen. B

* **Christmas.** Alice Summer Varney. 7b., 7g. Sc. A large room with a decorated tree in the center. VA

* **Christmas "Anychild preparing for Christmas"** F. Ursula Payne. 7c., chorus boys and girls. Sc. A room in any house. PP

* **Christmas at Holly Farm.** Clara J. Denton. 4b., 5g., chorus. sc. Handsome interior. I

* **Christmas at Punkin Holler,** a Christmas play. Elizabeth F. Guptill. 2w., 7b., 8g. Sc. A schoolroom. PAP

* **Christmas at Skeeter Corner.** Elizabeth F. Guptill. 5b., 5g. Sc. An old fashioned school. MAP

† **Christmas at the cross roads.** Elizabeth F. Guptill. 9b., 12g. Sc. Old fashioned country schoolhouse. MAP

* **Christmas babes in the woods.** Corinne Rockwell Swain. 3b., 4g., 2 chorus groups. Sc. Woods in winter. SAB

* **Christmas bargain, A.** Ellen M. Willard. 2g., Sc. Modern room. WY

* **Christmas benefit, A.** Marjorie Benton Cooke. 3b., 1g. Sc. Dressing room in a theatre. DPP

* **Christmas beyond the trenches.** Seymour S. Tibbals. Play about the orphans of the Great War. Any number of Characters. Sc. In the trenches. EP

* **Christmas box, The.** Madeline Poole. 3b., 3g. Sc. A cottage across the water. PO

Christmas boxes. M. E. M. Davis. 4m., 4w. Sc. Sitting room. DAB

* **Christmas brownie, The.** Elsie Hobart Carter. 24c. Sc. Nursery. CCC

Christmas burglar, The. Mary H. Flanner. 3m., 1w. Sc. A professor's study. FSD

* **Christmas carol or the miser's Yuletide dream.** (Adapted from Dickens' Christmas Carol.) Walter Ben Hare. 10m., 5w., 4b., 4g. Sc. A dark dreary office. HW

Christmas chime. Margaret Cameron. Comedy. 2m., 2w. Sc. Living room in a country house. CAC, FSD

* **Christmas conspiracy, The.** Elizabeth Woodbridge. 14c. Sc. Dimly lighted sitting room. SAB

* **Christmas cookies, The.** Marie Irish. Christmas play. 3b., 3g. Sc. Kitchen. IPR

* **Christmas dinner, The.** Marie Irish. Christmas play. 2b., 3g. Sc. Kitchen. IC

* **Christmas dream, A.** Elizabeth F. Guptill. Dream play with Mother Goose characters. 5b., 5g. Sc. Interior. MAP

* **Christmas eve.** Sidney Baldwin. Christmas play. 50c. Sc. Stage. BAL

Christmas eve at the Mulligans. Marie Irish. 2m., 3w., 2b., 2g. Sc. Living room. PAP

Christmas eve with Charles Dickens, A. Maude Morrison Frank. 8m., 6w., many chorus characters. Sc. Poorly furnished but neat room. FSP

* **Christmas for all nations,** a play in rhyme. Elizabeth F. Guptill. 5b., 6g. Sc. Interior. MAP

* **Christmas for Santa Claus, A.** W. H. Gardner. 2b., 9c. School children. Ladies Home Journal 20: 26, Dec. 1902.

* **Christmas gifts of all nations.** Carolyn Wells. 2b., 2g., 3 chorus groups. Sc. Palace of Father Christmas at the North Pole. WJ, Ladies Home Journal 29: 86, 91, Dec. 1912.

Christmas guest. Sara Kingsbury. 1m., 3w., 1c. Sc. Cheerful kitchen of a home. Drama 8: 455–461, Nov. 1918.

* **Christmas guest:** a miracle play after the manner of the 16th century, The. Constance D'Arcy Mackay. 8c. Sc. Hall of a 16th century house. MHH

* **Christmas harvest,** an exercise for the presentation of gifts by Sunday Schools. Edna Randolph Worrell. 1w., any number of children. Ladies Home Journal 33: 42, Dec. 1916.

* **Christmas idea, The.** Alice Cook Fuller. 5g. Sc. Living room. EP

* **Christmas in Leipsic.** John Jay Chapman. Verse. 2b., 3g., chorus. Sc. Sitting room. CFA

* **Christmas in Mother-Gooseville.** Eleanor Allen Schroll. Verse. 15c. Sc. Interior. FIL

* **Christmas in Rhyme-land.** May Pemberton. Musical play. 9c. Sc. Interior of a small cottage. PC

* **Christmas in the air.** Marie Irish. 6b., 5g. Sc. Inside of street car. I

* **Christmas in the forest.** Netta Syrett. 1b., 1g., 4 chorus groups. Sc. A cottage room. SSG

* **Christmas influence.** Marie Irish. 4b., 5g., Sc. Poorly furnished room. I

* **Christmas joke.** Elizabeth F. Guptill. 12b., 12g. Sc. Interior. MAP

* **Christmas journey, A.** Marie Irish. 3b., 2g. Sc. A street. I

* **Christmas message, The.** Margaret G. Parsons. 12c. Sc. Interior. PR
  Christmas miracle play: the pageant of the Shearman and Tailors in the Coventry Cycle of Miracles. Samuel A. Eliot. ed. 13m., 1w. Sc. An inner and an outer stage. ELT1
† **Christmas mix-up or Mrs. Santa Claus Militant.** Belle Elliot Palmer. 6b., 3g. Sc. Interior. EP
* **Christmas morality play, A.** Edith Lyttelton. 11c. Sc. Poorly furnished room. LY
* **Christmas mystery, A.** Elizabeth Guptill. 13b. Sc. Any interior. EP
  Christmas mystery, A. Jane Judge and Linwood Taft. To be used as a part of a community Christmas sing. 4m., 1w. Sc. Outside of the stable in Bethlehem. Drama 11: 60–62, Nov. 1920.
* **Christmas of the little pines, The.** Emma Larson. 3m., 15 or more children. Sc. Forest. Woman's Home Companion 44: 29, Dec. 1917.
* **Christmas party, A.** Marguerite Merington. 2m., 1w., 7b., 3g. Sc. Nursery. MFP
‡ **Christmas picture, The.** Lettie C. VanDerveer. 5g. Sc. Living room. VC
* **Christmas pitcher, The.** Augusta Stevenson. 6b., 5g., Many chorus characters. Sc. A palace. SC1
  Christmas present, A. Arthur Schnitzler. 1m., 1w. Sc. Side street. SA, International 4: 6–7, June 1911.
* **Christmas rainbow, A.** Adeline Hohf Beery. 4b., 4g. Sc. Interior. FIL
  Christmas shopping. Arthur Schnitzler, trans. from the German. Anatol play. 1m., 1w. Sc. Street in Vienna. SAA
* **Christmas shopping.** Beulah Smith. Comedy. 4b., 8g. Sc. Toy shop. WEP
* **Christmas speakin' at Skagg's Skule.** Marie Irish. 6b., 8g. Sc. School room of olden times. PAP
* **Christmas spirit, The.** Sidney Baldwin. Christmas play. 13c. 2 chorus groups. Sc. Field bordered by trees. BAL
‡ **Christmas stars.** Anne E. Williamson. 5b., 5g. Sc. Cozy living room. PCP
* **Christmas stockings.** Arthur Guiterman. 1m., 1b., 1g. Nursery. Ladies Home Journal 22: 28, Dec. 1904.
‡ **Christmas story, The.** Rita Benton. 16c., chorus. Sc. Stable at Bethlehem. BSB
* **Christmas story, A.** Edith Lang. With music. 14b., 10g. Sc. In a forest. LAN
* **Christmas strike, A.** Edith M. Burrows. 4b., 3g. Sc. Out-of-doors before the Cave of the North Wind. BBC
* **Christmas surprise for Mother Goose, A.** Marie Irish. 4b., 8g. Sc. Living room. I
* **Christmas sympathy.** Marie Irish. 4b. Sc. Street. I
  Christmas tale, A. Maurice Bouchor, trans. from the French by Barrett H. Clark. 2m., 2w., 1g. Sc. Room serving as living room and studio. FSD
  Christmas tree, The. Laurence Housman. 1m., 1w., 1c. Sc. A cottage interior. HAB. Drama 11: 75–76. Dec. 1920.
* **Christmas tree in New England, A.** Louise E. Tucker and Estelle L.

Ryan. How the Puritans kept Christmas. 3b., 2g. Sc. Living room. TRH

* **Christmas tree joke, A.** Lindsey Barbee. 7b., 7g. Sc. Living room. BLP

* **Christmas visitors from other lands.** Marie Irish. 4b., 6g. Sc. Living room. I

* **Christmas wishes.** Marie Irish. 2b., 3g. Sc. Living room. I

* **Christmas with the Mulligan's.** Walter Ben Hare. 2w., 5b., 5g. Sc. The Mulligan's front room. HW

Chrysanthemums, Japanese comedy. A. C. Wallace. 2m., 2w. Sc. Room in a Japanese house. FSD

Chuck: an orchard fantasy. Percy Mackaye. 3m., 1w. Sc. In the shadow of an appletree. MY

Ci-devant, The. Michael Arlen. 1w., 1 voice. Sc. Bedroom in a London house. Dial 69: 125–131, Aug. 1920.

* **Cinderella.** Alice Cook Fuller. 6b., 4g. Sc. Home of Cinderella. FU

Cinders. Lily Tinsley. 1m., 1w. Sc. Interior. FSD

Cin'n'buns. F. H. Schreiner. 2m., 2w. Sc. Interior. B

Circles. George Middleton. 1m., 1w. Sc. Sitting room. MIP

* **Circus, The.** Alice Summer Varney. 6h., 6g. Sc. A street leading to a school house. VA

Cissy's engagement. Ellen Lancaster Wallis. 2w. Sc. Interior. FSD

City pastorals. William Griffith. Verse. 3m. Sc. Living room.
  Spring. International 9: 178–180, June 1915.
  Summer. International 9: 219–222, July 1915.
  Autumn. International 9: 250–252, Aug. 1915.
  Winter. International 9: 278–279, Sept. 1915.

Civilization. Mary S. Watts. 5m., 5w. Sc. Patio of a ranch house. WT

Claims, The. Louise Rand Bascom. 7m., 1w., 1c. Sc. General's office. MBP

Clancy name, The. Lennox Robinson. 5m., 3w., chorus. Sc. Living room of an Irish farmhouse. RC, RT

Class of '56, The. Thacher Howland Guild. 5m. Sc. Library of a pleasant old country house. GUI

* **Class ship.** Edith F. A. U. Painton, Dramatization of Longfellow's "The Building of the Ship" 3b., 8g. Sc. Any large room. DEP

Clearly and concisely. Robert Higginbotham. Comedy. 1m., 1w. Sc. Interior. FSD

Clemency, written for the American School Peace League. Beulah Marie Dix. 3m., 1w. Sc. Old fashioned house in a foreign country. AS

Cleopatra. Isaac Rieman Baxley. Roman and Egyptian historical play. Verse. 3m., 3w. Sc. Cleopatra's tower. BAX

Cleopatra in Judea. Arthur Symons. Historical. Blank verse. 7m., 3w. Sc. Hall in the palace of King Herod in Jerusalem. SY, Forum 55: 643–660, June 1916.

Clerical error, A. Henry Arthur Jones. Comedy. 3m., 1w. Sc. Interior. FSD

* **Clever cock, The.** Augusta Stevenson. 2b. Sc. In the woods. SC1

* **Clever kid!** Violet M. Methley. Boy Scout play. 3b. Sc. Corner of a field. FSD

* **Clever kid, The.** Augusta Stevenson. 2b., 1g. Sc. A pasture. SC2

Cliff of tears, a lyrical drama. Kenneth Rand. Verse. Play of ancient Greece. 2m., 1w. Sc. Altar on an island coast. RA

Clinging vine, The. Rachel B. Gale. Comedy. 16w. Sc. Room of a woman's club. B

Clod, The. Lewis Beach. Civil War play. 4m., 1w. Sc. Kitchen of a farmhouse. BF, WSP

Close call, A. Grace Luce Irwin. Farce. 1m., 5w. Sc. Interior. B

† **Close the book.** Susan Glaspell. Comedy. 3m., 5w. Sc. Library of a home. GP, GPC

Closed door. Edmund Elliot Shepherd. 2m., 2w. Sc. Library. Smart Set 31: 131–137, June 1910.

Closet, The. Doris F. Halman. 4w. Sc. Narrow, dim corridor. HAS

* **Closing day at Beanville school.** Willis N. Bugbee. 7b., 7g. Sc. School room. BUP

Cloud descends, The. Maxwell Bodenheim. 4w. Fantastic. Sc. Small waterpool. Poetry 14: 295–300, Sept. 1919.

Cloudy day, A. Benjamin L. C. Griffith. Farce. 1m., 1w. Sc. Living room. GR

* **Clytie.** Alice Fuller Cook. 4b., 9g. Sc. Forest by the sea side. FU

Coats. Lady Isabelle Augusta Gregory. Irish comedy. 3m. Sc. Dining room of a hotel. GRZ, Metropolitan 36: 40–42, May 1912.

Coats and petticoats. Rachel Baker Gale. Comedy. 1m., 7w. 2 chorus groups. Sc. Interior. B

† **Cobbler's bargain.** Mrs. C. F. Fernald and Olivia L. Wilson. Musical comedy. 1b., 1g. Sc. Shoe maker's shop. BAB

* **Cock and the fox.** Evelyn Smith. Adapted from Chaucer. 10c. Sc. Farmyard. SFR

* **Cock Robin.** Someple. (pseud.) 8b., 7g. Sc. Open place in the woods. SO

Cockcrow. L. M. Taylor. Based on old Scottish ballad "Clerk Saunders." 1m., 1w. voice. Sc. Massive hall of the 14th century. Poet Lore 33: 118–127, Spring 1922.

Coda, The. Charles Stratton. 1m., 2w. Sc. Small library of a home. Drama 8: 215–232, May 1918.

Codicil, The. Paul Ferrier. Trans. by Elizabeth Lester Mullin. 3m., 1w. Sc. Chateau de Chantenay. Poet Lore 19: 193–206, Summer 1908.

* **Colette of the Red Cross.** Margaret Getchell. 8g. Sc. Living room. FSD

College chums, The. Harry L. Newton. Comedy. 2m. Sc. Street. WHP

College days. John K. Stafford. Farce. 11m., 1w. Sc. Hotel lobby. FSD

College joke, A. Granville Forbes Sturgis. Comedy. College play. 3m. Sc. Typical college room. STR

Colloquy in Hades, A. Edward Goodman. 2m. Sc. Misty gray setting. Moods 1: 151–153, March 1909.

† **Colombine.** Reginald Arkell. Fantasy. 5m., 1w. Sc. A Roman camp in England. WWS

Colonel and the lady, The. Dawson Milward and Homan Clark. Comedy. 3m., 2w. Sc. Quarters in English barracks. FSD

* **Colonial school.** Eleanore Hubbard. Educational play. 10b., chorus. Sc. School room in colonial Boston. HUC

† **Colonial tea, A.** Kate Woodward Noble. 5w. Sc. Parlor. NOB
* **Colonial Virginia.** Blanche Shoemaker Wagstaff. American history play. 1b., 3g. Sc. A colonial parlor. WCP
* **Color fairies, The.** Elizabeth F. Guptill. 10g. Sc. No special scenery. GUT

Colour-sergeant, The. Brandon Thomas. 4m., 1w. Sc. Interior. FSD

Columbine. Colin Campbell Clements. 2w. Sc. Bedroom. CLD. STW, Poet Lore 21: 588–595, Winter 1920.
* **Columbus Day.** "Columbus helps Any Child." Ursula F. Payne. 10c. Sc. Room in any home. PP

Comala. Reginald R. Buckley. 4m., 1w., warriors. Sc. Island off a northern coast. Poetry Review 6: 233–250, May–June 1915.

Combat with the dragon. Ethel Louise Cox. Verse. Old Norse background. 3m., 2w., chorus. Sc. A wild rocky pass in a mountain. COX

Come Michaelmas. John Keble Bell. (Keble Howard, pseud.) Comedy 2m., 2w. Sc. Parlour of a farm. FSD

Comedie Royall, A. Evelyn G. Sutherland. Historical background. 4m., 2w. Sc. Audience chamber of Queen Elizabeth in 1580. SUP

Comedy of the exile, A. Isabella Howe Fiske. 3m., 2w., 1 dog. Sc. Living room in House of Tobit in Ninevah. Poet Lore 17: 51–58, Spring 1906.

Comforter, The. Laurence Housman. English political farce. 3m., 1w., 1s. Sc. Sitting room in house on Downing street. HA, HA4
* **Coming home to Grandma's.** Edith F. A. U. Painton. Thanksgiving play. 5g. Sc. Sitting room. PAS

Coming of Annabel, The. Alice C. Thompson. 6w. Sc. Sitting room. B

Coming of Columbine, The. Eric Lyall. 2m., 1w. Sc. Garrett with sloping roof. Poetry Review 11: 178–181, July–Aug. 1920.
† **Coming of Fair Annie, The.** Graham Price. Based on the old ballad "Love Gregor." 2m., 2w. Sc. Hall of a Scottish castle. WWS

Coming of Hippolytus, The. Margaret Sackville. 2w. Sc. High tower overlooking the sea. Poetry 3: 40–45, Nov. 1913.

Coming of the Prince, The. William Sharp. Imaginative. Verse. 4m., 1w. Sc. A great forest. SHV

Commission, A. Weedon Grosmith. 3m., 2w. Sc. Studio. FSD

Committee on matrimony, A. Margaret Cameron. Comedy. 1m., 1w. Sc. Drawing room. CAC

Common ground. Eleanor Whiting. 1m., 2w. Sc. Small, barely furnished room in New England farmhouse. Poet Lore 32: 140–148, Spring 1921.

Compromise of the King of the Golden Isles, The. Lord Dunsany. 13m. Sc. Audience room. DFO

Compromising Martha. Keble Howard. Comedy. 1m., 1w. Sc. Living room. FSD

Confederates, The. Pauline Phelps and Marion Short. Romantic comedy. 1m., 1w. Sc. Garden lighted by Chinese lanterns. PH

Confession, The. Pearce Bailey. 2m., others. Sc. Prison cell. Charaka Club Proceedings 5: 56–71, 1919.
† **Confessional, The.** Marjorie Benton Cooke. 1m., 1w., 1s. Sc. Drawing room. CO

Confessional. Percival Wilde. 3m., 2w., 1s. Sc. Parlor window of a trim cottage. WC

Confidence, A. Elizabeth Jordan. 2w. Sc. Living room of home. Harper's Bazaar 43: 447–50, May 1909.

Conflict, The. Clarice Vallette McCauley. 1m., 3w. Sc. Kitchen of old fashioned farmhouse. REM, SCO, STW, VI

Conquest of Helen, The. Ralph W. Tag. Comedy. 3m., 2w. Sc. Handsomely furnished room. FP

Consarning Sairey "Uggins." Sailor play. Wilfrid Blair. 3m., 1w. Sc. Low ceilinged room. WIA

Conscript Fathers, a forecast, **The.** J. D. Simpson. 7m. Sc. Barrack room. English Review 27: 208–212, Sept. 1918.

Considerable courtship. Bessie Blair Smith. Farce. 2m., 2w. Sc. Interior. PPP

Conspirators, a Christmas play, **The.** Ralph Henry Barbour. 2m., 2w. Sc. Richly furnished dining room. New England Magazine 37: 425–32, Dec. 1907.

Constant lover, The. St. John Hankin. Comedy. 1m., 1w. Sc. Glade in a wood. FSD, HAN2, SL, Smart Set 38: 133–142, Oct. 1912. Theatre Arts Magazine 3: 67–77, April 1919.

Conversation, The. Edgar Lee Masters. 2m. Sc. Unimportant. Poetry 7: 55–59, Nov. 1915.

‡ **Conversion of Mrs. Slacker, The.** F. Ursula Payne. Great War play. 2b., 7g. Sc. Any room. PPD

Conversion of Nat Sturge. Malcolm Watson. Comedy. 3m., 1w. Sc. Interior. FSD

Convert, A. Clematis White. 1m., 2w. have speaking parts, 20 dinner guests. Sc. Dinner table set for 20. Smart Set 35: 103–106, Nov. 1911.

Converted suffragist. Katharine Kavanaugh. 3w., 1 baby. Sc. Interior. FP

Converting Bruce. Edith J. Broomhall. Farce. 2m., 2w. Sc Living room. B

Converts. Harold Brighouse. Comedy. 3m., 1w. Sc. Inside a Salvation Army Barrack in London. REP

Convict on the hearth, The. Frederick Fenn. 6m., 5w. Sc. Combined living room and dining room. FSD

Cooks and cardinals. Norman C. Lindau. 4m., 2w. Sc. A kitchen. FS2

* **Cooky, The.** Laura E. Richards. 3g. Sc. Nursery. RP

Corner in hearts, A. Edna Randolph Worrell. Christmas play. 5m., Sc. Reading room of a country club. MAP

Corner in strait-jackets. Amelia Sanford. Farce. 2m., 6w., 3c. Sc. An office. B

Coronation, The. Christopher St. John and Charles Thursby. Suffrage play. 7m., 1w., chorus. Sc. Hall adjacent to a church. STI

Correct thing, The. Alfred Sutro. A study in sentiment. 1m., 1w., 1s. Sc. Drawing room of a pleasant little house. SFA

Cosher, The. Malcolm Morley. 2m., 2w. Sc. Interior of a poor tenement in London. MOL

Cost of a hat, The. Bosworth Crocker. 2m., 2w. Sc. Kitchen in a flat in a tenement house. CK

† **Cottage on the moor, The.** E. E. Smith and D. L. Ireland. Historical

English play of cavaliers and roundheads. 4m., 1b. Sc. Cottage on a lonely moor. WWS

Counsel retained. Constance D'Arcy Mackay. 2m., 1w., chorus elements. Sc. Poverty stricken room. MB

Count Festenberg. Felix Salten. Trans. by Alfred B. Kuttner. 5m., 1w. Sc. Ostentatious hotel drawing room. International 3: 23–28, Jan. 1911.

Countess Cathleen. William Butler Yeats. 3m., 3w., many chorus characters. Sc. 1. Room with lighted fire, Sc. 2. A wood. YP2

Countess Mizzie. Arthur Schnitzler. Trans. from the German. Comedy. 7m., 2w. Sc. Garden. MR

‡ **Country cousin, A.** Edith F. A. U. Painton. 1b., 2g. Sc. Any stage or platform. PAD

Couple of heroes, A. Katharine Kavanaugh. Comedy. 3m., 1w. Sc. Interior. DEP

* **Courage.** Kate Harvey. 4b., 2g. Sc. A Dutch kitchen. BHP

* **Course of true love.** Anne A. Craig. Harlequin farce. 9b., 2g. Sc. A street in front of an inn. CD

Court comedy, A. Marjorie Benton Cooke. 1m., 2w. Sc. Ante room of palace. CO

Court of fame, The. Mary V. Duval. Play of great women. Has pageant qualities. 20w. Sc. Classical stage setting. HI

Court singer, The. Frank Wedekind. Trans. from the German. 6m., 2w. Sc. Pretentiously furnished room in a hotel. MR

Courting the widow. Paul Marion. Irish characters. 1m., 1w. Sc. Interior of a country kitchen. WEP

⨏ **Courtship of Miles Standish, The.** Eugene Presbery. 2m., 2w. Sc. Room in a Colonial house. FSD

Cousin Tom. Robert C. V. Meyers. Comedy. 2m., 1w. Sc. Interior. PPP

Coward, The. Robert G. Nathan. 1m., 2w. Sc. Bare attic studio. Harvard Monthly 58: 20,–March 1914.

Cowboy and the baby, The. Dr. Albert Carr. Farce. 6m., 2w., 1c. Sc. Inside a depot. CAR

Cowboy-Jim. Fred H. James. Romance of the far west. 1m., 1w. Sc. Girl's bedroom. Stagelore p. 89, Feb. 1912.

Cow-herd and the weaving maid, The. Shen Hung. Based on Chinese folk-lore. 2m., 2w. Sc. Laurel woods. Drama 11: 404–408, Aug.–Sept. 1921.

Crack in the bell, The. Grover Theis. 2m., 1 chorus. Sc. Independence Square. TN

"**Cracker, The.**" Horatio S. Jones. U. S. Civil War melodrama. 5m., 3w. Sc. Kitchen in the home of a physician in Missouri. JON

Cranberry corners. Alice Marie Donley. Comedy. 2m. Sc. Grocery and postoffice combined. G3

Creditor, The. August Strindberg. Trans. from the Swedish. 2m., 1w., 1s., chorus characters. Sc. A drawing room in a watering place. SL, STO Poet Lore 22: 81–116, Spring 1911.

Crepuscule. Pierre Louys, a romance trans. by Blanche S. Wagstaff. 1m., 1w. International 6: 102, Oct. 1912.

Cressmans, The. M. F. Hutchinson. 5m., 7w. Sc. Drawing room. WIA

Crier by night, The. Gordon Bottomley. Verse. 2m., 2w. Sc. Interior of a cottage. BKL, Bibelot 15: 298–331, Sept. 1909.

Criminals, an unpleasant play in tableaux. Gustaf of Geijerstam, trans. from the Swedish by Roy W. Swanson. 2m., 3w. Sc. Peasant's cottage. Poet Lore 34: 186–209, Summer 1923.

Criminals, a play about marriage. George Middleton. 2m., 2w. Sc. Cozy sitting room. MC

Crimson cocoanut, The. John Hay Beith (Ian Hay, pseud.) Farce. 4m., 2w. Sc. London restaurant. BEC, US

Crimson lake, The. Alice Brown. 8m. Sc. Dining room of an ostentatiously Bohemian restaurant. BO

Cripples, The. David Pinski. 5m. Sc. A city square. PT

Crispin, rival of his master. Alain-René Le Sage. Trans. from the French by Barrett H. Clark. Comedy. 4m., 4w. Sc. Street scene in Paris in 18th century. FSD

Criss cross. Rachel Crothers. 2m., 1w. Sc. Tastefully furnished sitting room. FP

Critics' catastrophe, a probable possibility, **The.** Herman Schuchert. 6m., 1w. Sc. Dining room of an exclusive club. Little Review 2: 20–27, April 1915.

Critics; or, a New play at the Abbey: being a little morality for the Press, **The.** St. John G. Ervine. 5m. Sc. Lobby of the Abbey Theatre, Dublin. ER

Crooked man and his crooked wife. Kenneth L. Andrews. 2m., 1w. Sc. A musty looking room in a Chinese house. PWP

Crooks. Nathan Kussy. 5m. Sc. Library in a home on Riverside Drive. US

* **Crow and the fox, The.** Augusta Stevenson. 1b., 2g. Sc. A high tree in a grove. SC3

‡ **Crowning of Columbia;** a patriotic fantasy. Kathrine F. Carlyou. 25b., 24g. Sc. Large room or platform. B

* **Crowning of peace, The.** Nora Archibald Smith. Patriotic. 3b., 2g. Sc. Goddess of Liberty at back of stage. SP

* **Crowning of the Dryads.** Martha B. Bayles. May Day dream. Arbor day celebration. 32c. Sc. In the heart of an ancient wood. LU

Crows. Betti Primrose Sandiford. 2m., 1w. Sc. Parlor of middle class Canadian home. Canadian Magazine 58: 397–405, March 1922.

Crowsnest, The. William F. Manley. 3m. Sc. On board of old coasting ship. FS3

Cruet of marigolds, The. John McClure. 1m., 1w. Sc. Oasis in Ethiopian sands. Smart Set 66: 73–75, Nov. 1922.

Crystal gazer, The. Leopold Montague. Comic sketch. 2w. Sc. Drawing room. FSD, PH

* **Cuckoo!** E. E. Bloxam. 12c. Sc. A wood. BL

Cuckoo's nest, The. F. Roney Weis. Comedy. 3m., 3w. Sc. Living room. B

Cul-de-sac. Essex Dane. 1m., 2w. Sc. Doctor's office. DAO

Culprit, The. May Bell. Comedy. 2m., 2w. Sc. Study in a comfortable home in Johannesburg. BRW

Culprit, The. Percival L. Weil. 3m., 1w. Sc. Well furnished room in house. Smart Set 39: 129–142, Feb. 1913.

Cult of content, The. Noel Leslie. Fantastic morality. 11m. and w. Sc. Interior of the Court of Interpretation in the Palace of Dreams. FOS

Cupboard love. Herbert Swears. 18th century costume comedy. 2w. Sc. Boudoir. FSD

Cupid in the kitchen. Ada Leonora Harris. 1m., 2w. Sc. Kitchen in London lodging house. PLA

Cupid mixes things. Sara Henderson. Valentine comedy. 5m., 6w., 2g., 3b. Sc. A wooded park. MAP

Cupid's column. Dorothy D. Calhoun. Farce. 2m., 3w. Sc. Combination dining and living room. FP

Cupid's trick. Preston Gibson. Valentine playlet. 4m., 1w. Sc. Interior. FSD

Cure for husbands. George M. Rosener. Comedy. 2m., 2w. Sc. Interior. Stagelore p. 186, Feb. 1912.

Cure for hypnotism, A. Asa Steele. Farce. 2m., 1w. Sc. Sitting room. PPP

Cure for indifference. Geoffrey Wilkinson. 4w. Sc. Interior. FSD

Cure for jealousy, A. George V. Hobart. Comedy. 3m., 2w. Sc. Sample room in a hotel. US

Cure that failed, The. Gertie de S Wentworth-James. 1m., 3w. Sc. Drawing room in a small house. PLA

Curiosity of Kitty Cochraine. Miriam Michelson. 3m., 4w. Sc. Bare chamber in New York debtor's prison in 1790. Smart Set 37: 133–142, May 1912.

* **Curly locks.** Someple. (pseud.) 5b., 4g. Sc. Kitchen. SO

Curtain, The. Hallie F. Flanagan. 4m., 2w. Sc. Small room in New York apartment. Drama 13: 167–169, Feb. 1923.

Curtains, The. Cloyd Head and Mary Gavin. 7m., 3w. Sc. Darkened stage, steps in background. Poetry 16: 1–11, April 1920.

Cycle, a play of war. Witter Bynner. 2m., 2w. Sc. Library in the home of a Prussian officer. BB

D

"D. H. S." Lucie Conway. Farce. 1m., 2w. Sc. Quiet spot outside a ball room. FSD

Daggers and diamonds. Katharine Prescott Moseley. Satire on radicalism. 2m., 2w. Sc. Interior. B

Daily bread. Mary Katharine Reely. Slum play. 1m., 4w. Sc. Kitchen-living room in a tenement. REE

Daimyo, The. Translated from the Japanese by Leo Duran. 5m., 2w. Sc. Wooded mountains in Japan in 18th century. DU

* **Daisy, The.** Alice Sumner Varney. 9c. Sc. Edge of a ditch beside a garden. VA

Dakota widow, A. Grace Livingston Furniss. Comedy. 1m., 2w. Sc. Drawing room. FSD

Dame Greel o' Portland town. Constance D'Arcy Mackay. 14m., 4w. Sc. Tavern at Portland, Maine. MPP

Dance of death, an interlude. E. Hamilton Moore. 4m., 2w. Sc. Southern garden. Poetry Review 2: 61–71, Feb. 1913.

Dance of the seven deadly sins. Arthur Symons. 2m., 1w. Sc. Large empty room. English Review 30: 481–485, June, 1920.

Dancing dolls. Kenneth Sawyer Goodman. 4m., 7w. Sc. Inside of a tent, used as dressing room. GQ, GQA, STG

Dandy dolls, The. George Fitzmaurice. 4m., 2w., 3c. Sc. Kitchen. FF

Dane's dress suit case. Robert C. V. Meyers. Farce. 2m., 1w. Sc. Interior. B

Dangers of peace, The. Graham S. Rawson. French historical play of Napoleonic times. 6m., 3w. Sc. Room in Paris. RA

* **Daniel Boone: Patriot.** Constance D'Arcy Mackay. 9b., chorus. Sc. An open woodland. MPY

* **Daniel Boone's snuff box.** Eleanore Hubbard. Historical play of the settlement of the U. S. 3b., chorus group. Sc. Indian village in the Kentucky woods. HUD

Dunny. Anna Wolfrom. 2m., 3w. Sc. Sitting room. WOH

Dante in Santa Croce of the Raven, trans. from the Italian of Arturo Graf by Rudolph Altrocchi. 3m., choir. Sc. Cloister of a monastery. Harvard Monthly 46: 94–102, May 1908.

Dardanelles puff-box, The. J. R. Milne. 2m., 2w. Sc. Library of a country house. Smart Set 62: 77–83, May 1920.

Dark lady of the sonnets, The. G. B. Shaw. Elizabethan background. 3m., 3w. Sc. Terrace of a Palace overlooking the Thames. SHA, English Review 7: 258–269, Jan. 1911.

Dark man at the feast, The. Francis M. Livingston. 20m. and w. Sc. Banquet. Smart Set 3: 115–118, April 1901.

† **Dark of the dawn, The.** Beulah Marie Dix. 4m. Sc. Living room. DA

Darktown social betterment s'ciety, The. W. T. Newton. Negro farce. 7m., 8w. Sc. Interior. BUP

Daughter of Japan, A. F. D. Bone. 3m., 1w. Sc. Interior of Japanese house. FSD

* **Daughter of Jephthah, The.** Rita Benton. Bible play. 1b., 2g., 2 chorus groups. Sc. Before the door of a tent. BSB

Daughter of men, The. Katharine Kavanaugh. Political play. 3m., 2w. Sc. Library. DPP

David Garrick's masterpiece. Fred H. James. 18th century English life. 4m., 2w. Sc. A handsome parlor. WRP

Dawn, The. Alma Newton. 1w., 1c. Sc. Interior. NE

Dawn. Rita Wellman. 2m., 1w. Sc. Small room in a Russian military hospital. Drama 9: 89–102, Feb. 1919.

Dawn. Percival Wilde. 2m., 1w., 1c. Sc. Inside a rough shack. WED, Smart Set 44: 115–123, Nov. 1914.

Dawn of the sunset. Robert Hillyer. 5m. Sc. Country road. Harvard Monthly 60: 125–126, June 1915.

* **Day after the circus.** Clara J. Denton. 2b. Sc. Interior. MBP

* **Day before Christmas, The.** Carolyn Wells. 7b., 6g., chorus. Sc. A schoolroom. WJ, Ladies Home Journal, 21: 16, Dec. 1903.

Day in court; burlesque on a justice of the peace's court, **A.** Jay Clay Powers. 5m., 2w. Sc. Court room. B

Day of dupes, The. J. Hartley Manners. Allegory. 4m., 1w., 1s. Sc. Boudoir. MH

Day of the Duchess. Alice C. Thompson. Farce, comedy. 12w. Sc. School parlor. B

Day that Lincoln died, The. Prescott Warren and Will Hutchins. 5m., 2w. Sc. Exterior. B

* **Days of long ago, The.** Marie Irish. Verse. 3g. Sc. Afternoon tea IPP
* **De Soto and the Indians.** Marie Bankhead Owen. Alabama Centennial play. 8b., 8g. Sc. School playground. AO
Deacon Brodie. Binney Gunnison. Adapted from a play by Henley and Stevenson. 5m., 1w. Sc. Platform. GU
† **Deacon's hat, The.** Jeannette Marks. 3m., 3w. Sc. A little shop. LC, MT, SB
Deacon's sweetheart, The. Frank Kennedy and A. S. Hoffman. 2m. Sc. Interior. DPP
Dead are singing, The. Carl Hauptmann, trans. by Mary L. Stephenson. 7m., 1w. Sc. Lonely battlefield. Texas Review 1: 250–256, Ap. 1916.
Dead eyes, The. Hanns Deinz Ewers. 3m., 7w. Sc. Hillside outside Jerusalem. International 11: 176–183, June 1917.
Dead poet, The. Stark Young. Verse. 1m., 2w., 1c. Sc. Deep in a forest glade. YA
Dead saint, The. Bertha Hedges. 3m., 1w. Sc. Stone wall with arched gateway. Sc. 2. Room with bare walls. Drama 12: 305–309 June–Aug. 1922.
† **Dear departed, The.** Stanley Houghton. Comedy. 3m., 3w. Sc. Interior. FSD, HF
Dearest thing in boots, The. Edna I. MacKenzie. 2m., 4w. Sc. Store. PAP
Death: a discussion. Robert W. Woodruff. 6m. Sc. Back parlor. Smart Set 44: 213–216, Dec. 1914.
Death and the dicers, adapted from "The Pardoner's Tale" by Chaucer. Frederick Schenck. 7m., 1w. Sc. Roadside tavern. Harvard Monthly 48: 195–206, July 1909.
Death and the fool. Hugo von Hofmannsthal. Trans. from the German by Elizabeth Walter. 5m., 2w. Sc. Studio. BAG, MR, Poet Lore 24: 253–267, Vacation 1913.
Death and the young man. Lee Simonson. 3m., 2w. Sc. Grove of yew and cypress. Harvard Monthly 45: 80–84, Nov. 1907.
Death in fever heat, A. George W. Cronyn. 3m., 1w., 2 sup. Sc. Dining room of forlorn western hotel. SL
Death of Agrippina, The. Arthur Symons. Historical. Blank verse. 4m., 3w. Sc. Nero's villa. SY
Death of Alcestis. Laurence Housman. Ancient Greek play. Verse. 4m., 2w., chorus. Sc. Underground garden of Proserpine. HAR
Death of Alexander, The. Maurice Baring. 2m., 2w., 2s., chorus characters. Sc. A bedroom in Alexander's palace. BA
* **Death of Balder.** Evelyn Smith. From a Norse legend. 11c., chorus. Sc. Out of doors. SFR
Death of Hippolytus, The. Maurice Hewlett. Tragic play of ancient Greece. Verse. 3m., 2w., chorus. Sc. A rocky coast. HEA
Death of Titian, The. Hugo von Hofmannsthal. Trans. from the German by John Heard, Jr. 8m., 3w. Sc. Curtain or tapestry background. FOS
Death speaks. Egmont W. Ruschke. Fantasy. 2m. Sc. A country churchyard. RUE
Death-stone, The. Basil Hall Chamberlain. Japanese lyric drama. 1m., 1w., chorus. Sc. Moor in Japan. CHB

AN INDEX TO ONE-ACT PLAYS 69

Debit and credit. August Strindberg. Trans. by Emil Schering 5m., 4w. Sc. Beautifully furnished room in a hotel. Poet Lore 17: 28–44, Autumn 1906.

Debutante, The. F. Scott Fitzgerald. 5m., 4w. Sc. Bedroom. Smart Set 60: 85–96, Nov. 1919.

"Deceivers." William C. De Mille. 2m., 1w. Sc. Living room of home in suburbs. FSD

* **Declaration of Independence.** Eleanore Hubbard. 13b., chorus of boys. Sc. Independence Hall, Philadelphia. HUC

* **Decoration Day "Anychild meets Memory."** F. Ursula Payne. 12c., chorus. Sc. A room in any house. PP

Decree Nisi, The. Joshua Bates. 2m., 2w. Sc. Private sitting room at a London hotel. Smart Set 28: 117–124, July 1909.

Defeat. John Galsworthy. Great War play. 1m., 1w. Sc. A room. GSS

Deirdre. William Butler Yeats. Verse. Irish folklore background. 6m., 1w. Sc. A guest house in a wood. YC2, YP2, YPP

Delayed birthday, A; a Hanukah play. Emily Goldsmith Gerson. Jewish holiday play. 2m., 3w. Sc. A pretty room. BLO

Deliverer, The. Lady Gregory. Tragic comedy. 8m., 3w. Sc. Steps of a Palace at the Inver of the Nile. GII

Delta wife, The. Walter McClellan. 1m., 1w. Sc. Interior of southern cabin. Double Dealer 4: 271–278, Dec. 1922.

Demigod, The. Helen Cheyney Bailey. 3m., 3w. Sc. Living room of a working man's house. Drama 8: 505–514, Nov. 1918.

Democracy's king. Arnold Daly. Leading diplomats in the World War. 9m., a number of children. Sc. Orchard in autumn. DAD

Demon's shell, The. Trans. from the Japanese by Yone Noguchi. 2m. Sc. Not given. Poet Lore 17: 44–49, Autumn 1906.

Dent's office boy. Charles M. Stuart. 3m. Sc. Office. DPP

* **Departure, The.** Louise E. Tucker and Estella L. Ryan. Early days of Harvard College. 2b., 2g. Sc. Living room. TRH

Depot lunch counter, The. Frank Dumont. 13m., 2w. Sc. Depot lunch room. PPP

Derby. Helen Gentry. Tragedy. 2m., 2w., 1b. Sc. Interior. CU

Derelict, The. Clarendon Ross. 2m., 1w. Sc. Shabby genteel room in a lodging house in 1871. Poet Lore 30: 601–607, Winter 1919.

Derelicts. George Calderon. 3m., 3w., chorus. Sc. A hotel garden. CA

Derelicts. Preston Gibson. 1m., 1w. Sc. Poorly furnished garret. FSD

Dervorgilla, a tragedy. Lady Gregory. 6m., 3w. Sc. Green lawn outside garden wall. Samhain pp. 13–27, 1908.

Desert, The. Colin Campbell Clements. 3m., 6w. Sc. A lonely place in the desert outside Jerusalem. CLD

Deserter, The. Lascelles Abercrombie. Verse. 5m., 4w. Sc. In front of a cottage in the country. ABF, Theatre Arts Magazine 6: 237–254.

Detective Keen. Percival Knight. 4m., 1w. Sc. Well furnished hall drawing room. US

Devil's gold, The. Sara Jefferis Curry. Dramatization of Chaucer's Pardoner's Tale. 9m. Sc. Before and behind a curtain. STV

Devil's star. F. J. Newboult. 3m., 1w. Sc. Interior. FSD

* **Dew necklace, The.** Charles McEvoy. 4c., chorus. Sc. A wood with a hollowed-out oak tree. FSD

Diabolical circle, The. Beulah Bornstead. 3m., 1w. Sc. Living room. DAL, LC

Diadem of snow, A. Elmer L. Reizenstein. 3m., 2w. Sc. Room in Russia furnished in execrable taste. Liberator 1: 26–33, April 1918.

Dianthe's desertion. Helen P. Kane. Revolutionary war play. 4w. Sc. Colonial interior. PPP

Dick's sister. Norman McKinnel. 1m., 1w. Sc. Sitting room. FSD

Did it really happen? Zoe Akins. 3m., 1w. Sc. Small study. Smart Set 52: 343–352, May 1917.

Did it really happen? Alfred Brand. Comedy. 2m., 3w. Sc. Old fashioned comfortable room. BRI

* **Diego's dream,** a play for Columbus birthday. Madalene D. Barnum. 13c., chorus characters. Sc. A school room in Spain. BS

Dies Irae. Frederick W. Wendt. 1m., 1w. Sc. Poorly furnished attic. Smart Set 34: 117–121, July 1911.

Difference in clocks, A. Ethel Livingston. 1m., 1w. Sc. Interior. B

Difficult border, The. Doris F. Halman. Fantasy. 2m., 3w. Sc. Edge of a strange wood. HAS

‡ **Ding-a-Ling.** E. M. Peixotto. Farce. 6b. Sc. Employment agency. PET

Dinner at seven sharp. Annabel Jenks and Tudor Jenks. 5m., 3w. Sc. Interior of a modest house. B

Dinner at the club. Eulora M. Jennings. Comedy. 6w., 2c., 1s. Sc. Reading room of a woman's club. FSD

Dinner for two. R. C. Carton, pseud. of R. C. Critchett. 3m. Sc. Interior. FSD

Dinner table, The. Edwin L. Sabin. 2m., 2w., 1b. Sc. Dinner table. Century 90: 159–160, May 1915.

Dinner with complications, A. Marjorie Benton Cooke. 3m., 3w. Sc. Drawing room. CO

* **"Dinner's served!"** Frederick Trevor Hill. Farce. 4b., 1g. Sc. Inside of negro cabin. HH

Diplomacy. David Pinski. 6m., 1w., many chorus characters. Sc. Spacious ante-room of the Chancellor's office. PT

† **Disastrous announcement.** Burney Gunnison. Adapted from David Copperfield by Dickens. Comedy. 1m., 3w., 1 dog. Sc. Parlor. GU

Disciples of art. Adele Luehrmann. 4m., 8w., chorus. Sc. Gallery in the Louvre. Smart Set 33: 57–59, Feb. 1911.

* **Discouraged worker, A.** Elizabeth F. Guptill. Christmas play. 3b., 3g. Sc. Santa's kitchen. GUD

Discussion with interruptions, A. Kate McLaurin. 2m., 1w. Sc. Elegantly furnished dining room. Smart Set 26: 125–127, Dec. 1908.

Dispatches from Washington. Charles Chambers Mather. Revolutionary War play. 3m., 5w. Sc. Front yard of Colonial house. B

Dispensation, The. Clay M. Greene. 4m. Sc. Private audience chamber in the Vatican. GD

AN INDEX TO ONE-ACT PLAYS 71

Dissolution. Arthur Schnitzler. Trans. from the German. Anatol play. 2m., 1w. Sc. Interior. SAA

District visitor, The. Richard Middleton. 2m., 1w. Sc. Living room. English Review 15: 497–505, Nov. 1913.

Divided attentions. Evelyn Simms. Comedy. 1m., 4w. Sc. Parlor in a summer hotel. DEP

Division between friends, A. Horace B. Browne. From Dickens' Martin Chuzzlewit. 1m., 2w. Sc. Apartment. BD

Dizzy's dilemmas. Charles Ingersoll Brown. 4m. Sc. Interior. Farce. BAT

Do men gossip? Orrin Breiby. Comedy. 5m., 1w. Sc. Men's club on ladies' day. FSD

Doctor Auntie. Alice Brown. 2m., 2w. Sc. A pleasantly furnished sitting room. BO

Doctor Faustus. Christopher Marlowe. Edited by Samuel A. Eliot. 19m., 1w., chorus characters. Sc. Some arrangement whereby there may be room for three sided action. ELT1

"Dod gast ye both!" a comedy of mountain moonshine. Hubert Heffner. 6m., 1w. Sc. A dense thicket in the mountains. CFP

Dog, The. Bosworth Crocker. 4m., 2w. Sc. A magistrate's court. CK

Dog, The. Doris F. Halman. 2m., 1b., several voices. Sc. Interior of shack in Maine woods. HAS

Dog days. Herbert Swears. 5w. Sc. Interior. FSD

* **Doing away with Christmas.** Marie Irish. 5b., 5g. Sc. Ordinary stage. IC

* **Doll shop, The.** Helen Langhanke and Lois Cool Morstrom. 43c. Sc. Interior of a shop. EP

* **Doll show, The.** Edith F. A. U. Painton. 3b., 7g. Sc. Interior. PAS

Dollar, A. David Pinski. 5m., 3w. Sc. Cross-roads at the edge of a forest. LC, PT, Stratford Journal 1: 27–41, June 1917.

Dolls, a Christmas nonsense play. Louise Van Voorhis Armstrong. 11w. Sc. A pleasant room. Drama 11: 52–57, Nov. 1920.

* **Dolls on dress parade, The.** Effa E. Preston. For primary grades. 18 or more c. Sc. Interior of a doll shop. PAP

* **Doll's playhouse, The.** Ruth Selman. 1b., 4g. Sc. Playhouse. BAB

* **Doll's symposium, The.** Elizabeth F. Guptill. 17c. Sc. Toy shop. MAP

* **Dolly dialogue.** Carolyn Wells. 8c. Sc. A nursery. St. Nicholas 34: 156–7, Dec. 1906.

Dolly Madison's afternoon tea. Emily Herey Denison. 5w., 1s. Sc. Drawing room of the President's mansion. DL

Dolly's week-end; or, The tale of the speaking tube. Florence Warden. 4m., 4w. Sc. Sitting room of a cottage. WIA

Dolores of the Sierra. Harriet Holmes Haslett. Mexican episode. 1m., 1w. Sc. Rocky gulch. HAE

Domestic dilemma, A. Grace Luce Irwin. Farce. A golf play. 2m., 2w., 2s. Sc. Front room of a suburban residence. ID

Dominant male, The. Arnold Daly. A comment on suffrage. 2m., 1w. Sc. 1. Lonely hut. Sc. 2. Exterior of French watering resort. PAD

Don Juan duped. Algernon Boyeson. 2m. Sc. Terrace of a Swiss hotel. Smart Set 33: 131–140, April 1911.

Don Juan's failure. Maurice Baring. 1m., 1w. Farce. c. Drawing room. BA

Don't bother Anton. E. J. Freund. 8m., 2w., 3c. Sc. Sitting room. ANP

* **Don't count your chickens until they are hatched.** Alice Sumner Varney. 3b., 3g. Sc. Outside a barn. VA

Don't do that. Jeanette Nordenshield. 1m., 2w. Sc. Interior. FSD

Doom of Admetus, The. Laurence Housman. Verse. Ancient Greek play. 4m., 5w., 1b., chorus. Sc. Chamber in an ancient Greek house. HAR

Doom of Metrodorus, The. John McClure. 3m. Sc. Cafe in Cairo. Smart Set 66: 71–73, Nov. 1922.

Door, The. Charles W. Stokes. Canadian drama. 3m., 1w. Sc. Simple setting. Canadian Magazine 58: 498–502, Apr. 1922.

Door must be open or shut, A; a proverb, Alfred de Musset. 2m. Sc. Interior. MUB

Doorway, The. Harold Brighouse. 2m., 1w. Sc. Narrow street in business section of London. WIA

* **Dora: her flag.** Virginia Olcott. Play of patriotism. 1b., 1g. Sc. Kitchen of a city home. OPA

Dormer windows. Alice Raphael. 3m. Sc. Yard of a small house. Drama 11: 418–420, Aug.–Sept. 1921.

Dormitory girls, The. Edward A. Paulton. 2m., 8w. Sc. Dormitory in a young ladies' boarding school. US

* **Dose of his own medicine, A.** Elizabeth F. Guptill. 2b., 1g. Sc. Unimportant. GUT

Dot entertains. Elizabeth F. Guptill. 1m., 1g. Sc. Parlor. MAP

* **Double Christmas gift, A.** Marie Irish. Christmas play. 3b., 5g. Sc. Reception room of orphan asylum. IC

Double cross. Roi Cooper Megrue. 3m. Sc. Interior of small country railroad station. Smart Set 34: 123–128, Aug. 1911.

Double cross, The. Frank Stayton. 2m., 1w. Sc. Sitting room. FSD

Double-crossed. Charles C. Mather. 3m., 3w. Sc. Well furnished apartment. B

Double deception, A. Arthur Lewis Tubbs. 2m., 3w. Sc. Interior. B

Double dummy. Erna S. Hunting. 1m., 1w. Sc. Studio. B

Double miracle. Robert Garland. 4m., 1w. Sc. Before a mountain shrine. VI, Forum 53: 511–527, April 1915.

Double negative, a problem playlet. Francis M. Livingston. 1m., 1w. Sc. Boudoir. Smart Set 7: 158–160, May 1902.

Doubtful victory, or, Love's stratagem. Frank Dumont. Farce. 2m., 2w. Sc. Handsome interior. FSD

Dove uncaged, The. E. Hamilton Moore. Fantasy. Convent play. 5w., chorus. Sc. An Italian convent. FSD

Down in Paradise alley. Henry L. Newton. 1m., 1w. Sc. Interior of shanty in slums of New York. WHP

Dowry and romance. Rose C. Meblin. Comedy. 1m., 2w. Sc. Best room in American colonial house. DAL

Dragon's claws, The. Grant Carpenter. 3m., 1w. Sc. Living room in Chinese home in Chinatown. Smart Set 42: 135–141, April 1914.

Dralda bloom, The. Leon Cunningham. 9m., 4w. Sc. Porch of king's palace. Poet Lore 30: 553–566, Winter 1919.

Drama class of Tankaha, Nevada, The. Mary Aldis with Harriet Calhoun Moss. 2m., 7w., 2s. Sc. Sitting room. AP

Drama of the future, The. Joseph P. Healy. 7m., 2w. Sc. Office of manager of Electric Theatre, N. Y. Smart Set 7: 147–148, Aug. 1902.

Dramatists at home, The. Howard Keble (pseud. of John Keble Bell. 1m., 1w. Sc. Interior. FSD

Drawback, The. Maurice Baring. Farce. 1m., 1w. Sc. Corner in Kensington Garden. BA

Dream, The. Theodore Dreiser. 11m. Sc. 115th and Broadway, N. Y. Seven Arts 2: 319–333, July 1917.

Dream assassins, The. Rollo Peters. 2m. Sc. Dim place between high old houses. Forum 54: 117–118, July 1915.

‡ **Dream boats.** Dugald Stewart Walker. Fantasy. 5b., chorus. Sc. Picture within a picture frame. WAL

‡ **Dream book, The;** story of Chanukkah. Henry Woolf. 5b., 2g. Sc. A modern home. WOO

A dream come true, a play and pageant based on the history of the Red Cross. Edna Randolph Worrell. 1m., 2w., many others. Sc. Interior Italian villa at Solferino, Italy. Ladies Home Journal 35: 112, 118, Nov. 1918.

* **Dream-lady, The.** Netta Syrett. 3b., 6g., chorus characters. Sc. A garden. SSF

* **Dream lesson,** fairy play. Josepha Marie Murray. Lesson in contentment. 16g. Sc. Interior. EP

Dream maker, The. Blanche Jenning Thompson. Fantasy. 2m., 9w. Sc. Outside Pierrot's house. Drama 12: 197–199, March 1922.

Dream of a spring morning, The. Gabriele D'Annunzio. Trans. by Anna Schenck. 3m., 4w. Sc. Covered portico in ancient Tuscan villa. Poet Lore 14: 6–36, Oct. 1902.

Dream of an autumn sunset, The. Gabriele D'Annunzio, trans. by Anna Schenck. 2m., 4w. Sc. Outside a villa of a Venetian patrician. Poet Lore 15: 6–29, Spring 1904.

* **Dream of Christmas eve, A.** Ina Home. Dream play. 1b., 2g. Sc. Unimportant. FSD

Dream of liberty, A. Henry Raeder. 2m., 1w. Sc. Simply furnished room of the 15th century. RD

Dream of wings, The. Martha Leonard. Pageant play of aviation. 9m. Sc. Unimportant. LEN

* **Dream on Christmas eve.** Ina Home. 13c. Sc. Room occupied as a bed room. FSD

Dream stone. Oswald H. Davis. 2m., 1w. Sc. Highroad outside town. Poetry Review 6: 218–232, May–June 1915.

* **Dream-toy shop, The.** Jessie M. Baker. Christmas play. 4b., 6g. Sc. Child's bedroom. SAB

Dreaming of the bones. William Butler Yeats. 5m., 1w. Sc. Bare room. YF, Little Review 6: 1–14, Jan. 1919.

Dreamy kid, The. Eugene O'Neill. 1m., 3w. Sc. Bedroom in a New York tenement. SCO, Theatre Arts Mag. 4: 41–56, Jan. 1920.

Dregs. Frances Pemberton Spencer. Melodrama. 3m., 2w. Sordid looking room. MA

Dress rehearsal, A. Mrs. S. F. Carroll. 2m., 3w. Sc. Interior. PPP

Dress rehearsal of Hamlet. Mary MacMillan. 10w. Sc. Bare dressing room of modest little theatre. MM

Dressing gown, The. Robert C. V. Meyers. Farce. 3m., 3w. Sc. Parlor. PPP

Drifting cloud, The. Tudor Jenks. Comedy. 1m., 1w. Sc. Dining room in a flat. G1

Drums of Oude, The. Austin Strong. Play of India. 6m., 1w. Sc. Store room in an ancient palace. US

Dryad, The. Mary MacMillan. 2m., 1w. Sc. An open square in a city. MM

Dryad, The. George Sterling. 1m., 2w. Sc. Glade in a forest. Smart Set 58: 81–86, Feb. 1919.

† **Dryad and the deacon, The.** William O. Bates. Fairy play. 1m., 1w. Sc. Huge oak tree in center of a wooded glade. SB, Drama 10: 217–219, Mar.–Apr. 1920.

Duchess entertains. Ian McLaren. Comedy. Great War background. 8m., 3w. Sc. Empty stage. MAJ

Duchess of Doherty Court. Alfred Holles. Comedy. 1m., 1w. Sc. A kitchen. FSD

Duchess of Pavy. Adapted from John Ford's Love's Sacrifice. 5m., 4w., 2s. Sc. A stage. ELT3

Duke and the actress, The. Arthur Schnitzler. Trans. by Hans Weysz. 16m., 2w., noblemen, actors etc. Sc. Prospere's Inn in 1789. Poet Lore 21: 257–284, July–Aug. 1910.

* **Dulce et Decorum club, The.** Marguerite Merington. 2b., chorus b. and g. Sc. Room. MFH

Dumb and the blind. Harold Chapin. 2m., 2w. Sc. Top room in a tenement. REP

† **Dumb-cake, The.** Arthur Morrison and Richard Pryce. 1m., 2w. Sc. Kitchen of an almshouse. FSD

Dumb waiter, The. Helen Sherman Griffith. Farce. 5w. Sc. Room. B

Duped. Emily Herey Denison. 2m., 2w., 1s. Sc. Library. DL

† **Dust of the road.** Kenneth Sawyer Goodman. 3m., 1w. Sc. Living room of a comfortable and fairly prosperous farmer of the Middle West. GQ, STG

Dusty path, The. Wilfred T. Coleby. 1m., 2w. Sc. Nursery. FSD

Duty. Seumas O'Brien. Comedy. 5m., 1w. Sc. Back kitchen of a country public house. OD

Dying pangs. Arthur Schnitzler. 2m. Sc. Bachelor's apartment. SA

Dyspeptic ogre. Percival Wilde. Comedy. Modernized fairy play. 3m., 9w. Chorus. Sc. Dining room and Kitchen. WE

E

* **Each in his own place.** Augusta Stevenson. 5c. Sc. A tiny house. SC3

* **Eager heart.** A. M. Buckton. Verse. Christmas mystery play. 7b., 3g., chorus characters. Sc. Stage with adequate lighting devices. BUE

Early Ohios and Rhode Island reds. Mary Katharine Reely. Comedy. 2m., 3w. Sc. Simply furnished living room. REF

Early snow, a Noh play. Komparu Zembo Motoyazu. Trans. from the Japanese by Arthur Waley. 4w., chorus. Sc. Temple of Izumo. Poetry 15: 317–320, March 1920.

* **Easter miracle.** Della Shaw Harvey. 10g. Sc. Flower bed. BAB

* **Easter morning.** Mrs. Alice Corbin Henderson. A play of the Resurrection. 7b., 3g. Sc. Before the tomb of Jesus. HAD

* **Easter rabbit.** Louise E. Tucker and Estelle L. Ryan. Early days of New York. 4b., 4g., chorus characters. Sc. An open field. TRH

Eastland waters. Agnes Lee. 1m., 2w. Sc. Not given. Poetry 7: 234–235, Feb. 1916.

Easy mark, An. Innis Gardner Osborn. Farce. 5m., 2w. Sc. Interior. B

Easy terms. Katharine Kavanaugh. Domestic comedy of installment house troubles. 2m., 1w. Sc. Interior. DEP

Easy victim, An. Herbert Grissom. 1m., 1w. Sc. Breakfast room. Smart Set 8: 109–110, Nov. 1902.

Eboshi-ori. Miyamasu. Noh play of Japan in the 16th century. 9m., 1w., chorus. Sc. Japanese inn. WAA

* **Echo, The.** Emma L. Johnston and Madalene D. Barnum. 2b. Sc. Beside a mountain. JB

Echo, The. Egmont W. Ruschke. Comedy. 5m., 5w. Sc. Home. Sc. Home of a well-to-do family in a small town. RUE

Echo. Joseph T. Shipley. 1m., 1w. Sc. 1. Darkness, Sc. 2. Restaurant. LO

"Edge o' dark" Gwen John. 5m., 1w. Sc. Parlor-kitchen of a two room cottage. English Review 12: 592–603, Nov. 1912.

Edge of the wood. Katharine Metcalf Roof. 4m., 1w., 1b., dryads, fairies etc. Sc. A wood. Drama 10: 196–199, Feb. 1920.

Editor in chief, comedy of a newspaper office. Charles Ulrich. 10m. Sc. Editorial room. DEP

Eether or eyther. Robert C. V. Meyers. Farce. 4m., 4w. Sc. Interior. B

Efficiency. Bertram R. Brooker. 5m., 1w. Sc. Office International 8: 180–183, June 1914.

Efficiency. R. H. Davis and P. P. Sheehan. 3m. Sc. Private audience chamber of an Emperor. DSE

* **Effie's Christmas dream.** Laure Claire Foucher. Adapted from Alcott's A Christmas dream and how it came true. 4b., 7g., 4 chorus groups. Sc. Sitting room. FE

Eight hundred rubles. John G. Neihardt. Verse. 1m., 2w. Sc. Combined living room and kitchen of a peasant house. NT, Forum 53: 393–402, Mar. 1915.

Eight-thirty sharp. Jasmine Stone Van Dresser. 1m., 2w., 2b., 1 dog. Sc. Upstairs sitting room of a modern home. Delineator 99: 20–21, Jan. 1922.

Elaine, a poetic drama. Mildred Weinberger. 6m., 5w. Sc. Glade in the forest. Poet Lore 34: 72–110, Spring 1923.

Elder Eel. Lord Boleskine. 9m., 2w., others. Sc. Market place. International 12: 83–85, March 1918.

Elder Jenkins' reception. Willis N. Bugbee. Negro farce. 7m., 8w. Sc. Living room. BUP

Election of the roulette, The; a play of Russian life, 1850. William

Byron Mowery. 7m., 1w., 3c. Sc. Hut of a prisoner. Poet Lore 33: 525–536, Winter 1922.

Electra, a shavio-sophoclean tragedy. R. M. Arkush. 2m., 3w., chorus, 1 dog. Sc. Living room of middle class New York apartment. Harvard Monthly 41: 198–206, Jan. 1906.

Electric man. Charles Hannan. 3m., 2w. Sc. Sitting room. FSD

Elegant Edward. Gertrude E. Jennings and E. Boulton. Comedy. Crook play. 4m., 1w. Sc. Interior. FSD

* **Elf child, The.** Constance D'Arcy Mackay. 10c. Sc. A forest. MHH

* **Elf that stayed behind, The.** Madeline Poole. 1b., 5g. Sc. Lawn. PO

Elizabeth's young man. Louise Seymour Hasbrouck. Farce. 1m., 3w. Sc. Interior. B

Ella's apology. Alfred Sutro. A study in sentiment. 1m., 1w. Sc. Interior. FSD, SFA

Ellen. Horace Holley. 2w. Sc. Living room of small cottage. Stratford Journal 1: 54–57, March 1917.

Elopement, The. Harold P. Preston. Farce. 2m., 1w. Sc. Interior. DEP

Elopements while you wait. Caroline D. Stevens. 2m., 2w. Sc. Garden. Drama 13: 184–187, Feb. 1923.

Elopers, The. Paul Merion. 1m., 2w. Sc. Interior. FSD

* **Elsie in Dreamland.** J. Clay Powers. Fantastical play for children. Sc. Sc. Interior. EP

Elusive Alonzo, The. Mrs. Edmond La Beaume. Play of artist life. 3m., 2w. Sc. Studio. BUX

* **Elves and the shoe-maker, The.** Mabel Goodlander. 9c., chorus group. Sc. Shoemaker's shop. GF

Emancipated, The. James Platt White. 4m., 3w. Sc. Reception room of an apartment. Harvard Monthly 31: 184–204, Feb. 1901.

Emancipated ones, The. Elise West Quaife. Satirical comedy. 1m., 6w. Sc. Interior. FSD

Embalming Ebenezer, Ethiopian farce. Herbert P. Powell. 3m. Sc. Interior. PPP

Embarrassed butler, The. John Keble Bell. 3m., 1w. Sc. Dining room. FSD

Embers. George Middleton. 2m., 1w., 1s. Sc. Sitting room. ME

Embryo. Percival Wilde. Comedy. 3m., 2w. Sc. Stage on which "Black Art" can be carried out. WE

Emerson club, The. Effie W. Merriman. Comedy. 7w. Sc. Interior. DPP

Emigration. Herbert C. Sargent. Farce. 2m. Sc. Interior. SAR

Employment office. Jessie A. Kelley. Farce. 18w. Sc. Employment office. FSD

Empty city, The. Trans. directly from the Chinese by Ding U Doo. 6m., armies. Sc. Not given. Stratford Journal 6: 49–56, Jan.–Mar. 1920.

Empty lamp. Forrest Halsey. 1m., 1w., 1b. Sc. Large old fashioned room in a comfortable boarding house. Smart Set 34: 123–130, May 1911.

Empty shrine, The. Lillian P. Wilson. 1m., 2w. Sc. The front of a cottage. WIF

* **Enchanted garden, The.** Constance D'Arcy Mackay. 10c., chorus characters. Sc. A garden. MHH

* **Enchanted garden, The.** Netta Syrett. 11c. Sc. An old fashioned garden. SSG

* **Enchanted gate, The.** Sidney Baldwin. An elf play. 8b., 1g. Sc. A lane. BAL

Encounter in the forest, An. Louise E. Tucker and Estelle L. Ryan. Early days in Massachusetts. 5b. Sc. Forest clearing. TRH

End of the game. Otto S. Mayer. 3m., 1w. Sc. Parson's study. Moods 1: 272–281, June–July, 1909.

End of the rainbow. James Plaisted Webber. Rhymic verse. Pierrot play. 2m., 3w. Sc. Wood. B

End of the way, The. Evelyn G. Sutherland. Robin Hood play. 1m., 1w. Sc. Hall of an ancient castle. SUP

* **Endless tale, The.** Augusta Stevenson. 3b., 1g., many chorus characters. Sc. The king's palace. SC2

Enemies. Neith Boyce and Hutchins Hapgood. 1m., 1w. Sc. A living room. P2

‡ **Enemies of Israel, The.** Louis Broido. Hanukkak fantasy. 36c. Sc. Parlor. BRO

Enemy, The. Beulah Marie Dix. Written for the American School Peace League. 5m. Sc. Room of a mountain cabin. AS

Engaging Janet. Esther W. Bates. Farce. 7w. Sc. Study. PPP

Enigma. Floyd Dell. 1m., 1w. Sc. Room with a table. DK, Liberator 5: 14–16, April 1922.

Enter Dora—exit Dad. Freeman Tilden. 4m., 1w. Sc. Office in rear of country store. Ladies Home Journal 39: 15, 53–55, May 1922.

Enter the hero. Theresa Helburn. Comedy. 1m., 3w. Sc. Sitting room. FLS, SL

Entr' acte. Mary MacMillan. 1m., 2w. Sc. Handsomely furnished room. MS

Ephraim and the winged bear. Kenneth Sawyer Goodman. 3m., 2w., 1s. Sc. Library. GQ, STG

Episode, An. Arthur Schnitzler. 2m. Sc. Bachelor's rooms. SA SAA International 4: 23–24, July 1911

Episode, An. Lillian P. Wilson. 3w. Sc. Boudoir. WIF

Escape. E. P. Parr. 2m., 2w. Sc. Interior of cottage near a prison. FSD

Estaminet, The. Ian McLaren. Great War background. 8m., 2w. Sc. Estaminet of army camp. MAK

‡ **Esther.** Rita Benton. Bible play. 20c., chorus. Sc. Either indoors or out-of-doors. BSB

Eternal masculine, The. Hermann Sudermann. 5m., 4w., 1c., chorus. Sc. State apartment in a royal palace. STZ

Eternal mystery, The. George Jean Nathan. 2m., 1w., 1b. Sc. Room in a modern house. Smart Set 39: 137–142, April 1913.

Eternal presence, The. André Dumas. Trans. by Carrée Horton Blackman. 1m., 1w. Sc. Young man's bedroom. Poet Lore 29: 459–468, Autumn 1918.

Eternal song, The. Marc Arnstein, tr. from the Yiddish. Labor play. 2m., 2w. Sc. A small garret room in a large city. BLK

Etiquette of the occasion. Louise Rand Bascom. Comedy. 2w. Sc. Kitchen. MBP

Eugencial wedding, A. Owen Hatteras. 4m., 5w., guests. Sc. Surgical amphitheatre. Smart Set 41: 63–67, Oct. 1913.

Eugenically speaking. Edward Goodman. 3m., 1w. Sc. A room richly but tastefully furnished. WSP

Evening at Helen's, An. Kate Thomas. 7w. Sc. Interior. FSD

Evening musicale, An. May Isabel Fisk. 3w., 3m., several guests. Sc. Conventional drawing room. Smart Set 10: 111–114, July 1903.

Evening of truth. Charles Battell Loomis. 4m., 4w., other guests. Sc. Drawing room of handsome apartment. Smart Set 14: 93–96, Nov. 1904.

* **Evening rice.** William H. Jefferys. Missionary play about China. 7b. Sc. A hospital ward. DOF

* **Ever-Ever land, The.** Lindsey Barbee. 16b., 17g. Sc. Woodland. BLP

† **Ever young.** Alice Gerstenberg. 4w. Sc. Corner of the lobby of a hotel at Palm Beach. SB, STW, Drama 12: 167–173, Feb. 1922.

Everybody's husband. Gilbert Cannan. 1m., 5w. Sc. Girl's bed chamber. CE

* **Everyboy.** Isabel Anderson. Morality play. 14b. Sc. Stage. AE

* **Every boy.** Anna M. Lütkenhaus. Morality play. 1b., chorus of boys. LU

‡ **Everychild.** Content S. Nichols. A school morality play. 9c. Sc. No stage setting. SAB St. Nicholas 42: 358–9, Feb. 1915.

Everycreditman; morality play of business. James E. Breed. 14m. Sc. Office. BRE

* **"Everygirl"** Rachel Lyman Field. Morality play. 9g., 1 chorus group. Sc. Garden. SAB

† **Every senior.** Pearl Hogrefe. Morality play. 8g. Sc. College girl's room. FP

Everystudent, his encounters in pursuit of knowledge. Edith Everett. Morality play. 14b., 13g. Sc. A student's room. FL

‡ **Evil that men do lives after them, The.** E. M. Peixotto. 3b. Sc. Dilapidated hotel. PET

Excellent receipt, An. Charles H. E. Brookfield. 1m., 2w. Sc. Drawing room. FSD

† **Exchange, The.** Althea Thurston. 4m., 1w. Sc. An office. LC, SB

Exemption. Alice Norris-Lewis. Great War background. 2m., 8w. Sc. Living room. MAP

Exile, The. Amy Josephine Klauber. Play about Dante. 8m. Sc. Large room in an Italian palace. Poet Lore 33: 246–254, Summer 1922.

Extra! The newspaper minstrels are out! Helen J. Ferris. 5w., chorus. Ladies Home Journal 37: 142, Sept. 1920.

† **Extracting a secret.** Binney Gunnison. From a book by F. M. Crawford. 1m., 1w. Sc. Sitting room. GU

Extreme unction. Mary Aldis. 1m., 4w. Sc. Screened space about a bed in a hospital ward. AP, Little Review 2: 31–37, Apr. 1915.

Eyes of faith. Marie Doran. Americanization play. 9w. Sc. Interior. FSD

† **Eyes to the blind.** Thomas B. Rogers. 1m., 2w. Sc. Kitchen. RO

F

Facing reality. Floy Pascal. 2m., 2w. Sc. Living room moderately well furnished. Poet Lore 33: 451–457, Autumn 1922.

† **Fads and fancies.** Eleanor Maud Crane. 17g. Sc. Fashionable millinery establishment. FP

Failures. Belford Forrest. 3w. Sc. Boudoir in house in Paris. Smart Set 49: 223–232, July 1916.

Failures, The. George Middleton. 1m., 1w. Sc. Parlor in small apartment in Rome. ME

* **Fair play.** Clifton Lisle. Boy Scout, football play. 8b., chorus. Sc. Training room in school gymnasium. LB

† **Fairest spirit, The.** Carolyn Wells. Girls' Commencement play. 18w. or g. Sc. Temple on Mt. Olympus. Ladies Home Journal 32: 15, 72, June 1915.

* **Fairies' child, The.** Gertrude Knevels. 12c. Sc. A glade in the fairies' forest. PPP

* **Fairies' Christmas, The.** Mary A. Benson. 12 fairies. Ladies Home Journal 20: 32, Nov. 1903.

Fairies' plea. Maude Morrison Frank. An interlude for Shakespeare Day. 3m., 4w., chorus characters. Sc. A woodland. FSP

Fairy, The. Octave Feuillet. Trans. from the French by Barrett H. Clark. Verse. Romantic comedy. 3m., 2w. Sc. Small parlor in country cottage in France. FSD

* **Fairy and the cat, The.** Augusta Stevenson. 1b., 5g. Sc. A palace. SC1

* **Fairy and the witch, The.** A. D. Nelson. Allegorical sketch for Hallowe'en. 7c., chorus. Sc. Clearing in a forest. EP

* **Fairy doll, The.** Netta Syrett. 2g., 7 dolls. Sc. Nursery. SSG

* **Fairy frolic, A.** Edith M. Burrows. 32c. Sc. Fairyland. FI

* **Fairy Good-will.** Geo. B. Masslich. Christmas play. 3b., 2g., chorus. Sc. Any school. BEQ

* **Fairy minstrel of Glenmalure.** Anna M. Lütkenhaus. Dramatized from work of Edmund Leamy. 4b., 4g., chorus. Sc. A forest. LU

* **Fairy ring, The.** Marjory Benton Cooke. 2b., 3g., chorus of b. and g. Sc. In a wood. DPP

Faith. Margaret Evans. 1m., 2w. Sc. Small kitchen of a colored family's home on Armistice day. Poet Lore 33: 132–137, Spring 1922.

Faithful James. B. C. Stephenson. Farce. 5m., 2w. Sc. Interior. FSD

† **Falcon, The.** Alfred Lord Tennyson. Verse. 2m., 2w. Sc. Italian cottage. WWS

Fallen God, The. William Sharp. 1m., 3 chorus groups. Sc. A vast hollow among barren hills. SHV

Fallen idol. Helen Sherman Griffith. Farce. 4w. Sc. Parlor. PPP

† **Fame and the poet.** Lord Dunsany. 3m. Sc. Poet's room in London. DFO, LE, Atlantic 124: 175–184, Aug. 1919.

* **Familiar quotations.** Patty Pemberton Bermann. 17c., chorus. Sc. A parlor. HB

Family exit, The. Lawrence Langner. Comedy. 4m., 3w. Sc. A room in the Immigration office at Ellis Island. LAF

"**Family's pride, The.**" Wilfrid Wilson Gibson. Verse. 4w. Sc. Cottage at dawn. GID, GIP

Famine and the ghost. Doris F. Halman. Fantasy. 1m., 1w., 1b. Sc. A room in a little old house falling to decay. HAS

† **Fan and two candlesticks, A.** Mary MacMillan. 2m., 1w. Sc. A room at the end of a great hallway in a fine Georgian mansion. MS, STK

Fancy dress. Gerald Dunn. Comedy. 3m. Sc. Rooms in a flat. FSD

Fancy free. Stanley Houghton. 2m., 2w. Sc. Writing room of an apartment hotel. CBI, FSD, HF

Fantasie impromptu. Rosalind Ivan. 1m., 1w. Sc. Hall of a New York apartment house. Drama 11: 233–236, April 1921.

† **Far-away Princess, The.** Hermann Sudermann. 2m., 7w. Sc. An inn situated above a watering place in Germany. LC, SU

Farce of the worthy master, Pierre Patelin, the lawyer as transcribed from the Mediaeval French by Maurice Relonde. 4m., 1w. Sc. Street scene in little town in France about 1400. Poet Lore 28: 343–364, Summer 1917.

Farewell supper, Arthur Schnitzler. 2m. Sc. Private room in a restaurant. SA, SAA

Farewell to the theatre. Granville Barker. 1m., 1w. Sc. Musty law office. BT, English Review 25: 390–410, Nov. 1917.

Faro-Jane. Fred H. James. 1m., 2w. Sc. Interior of elegantly furnished apartment. WRP

Faro Nell. Willis Steell. 6m., 1w. Sc. Picturesque interior. B PWP

Farrell case, The. George M. Cohan. 6m., 2w., policeman. Sc. Office. Smart Set 63: 63–68, Oct. 1920

Fascinating Mrs. Osborne. Julie Helene Bigelow. 1m., 1w. Sc. Woman's sitting room in N. Y. Smart Set 35: 129–134, Dec. 1911.

* **Fashionable calls.** Rea Woodman. 3g. Sc. Living room. WO

Fast Friends. Re Henry. Comedy. 2w. Sc. Sitting room. PH

Fata Deorum. Carl W. Guske. Historical. Verse. 6m. Sc. A room in Roman house about 15 A. D. SCO

† **Fatal pill, The.** Granville Forbes Sturgis. Farce. 2m., 2w. Sc. Sitting room. STR

Fatal rubber, The. Maurice Baring. Historical farce. 2m., 2w. Sc. Room in the Palace of the Louvre. BA

Father, The. Colin Campbell Clements. 5m., 2s., chorus. Sc. 1 Place outside Japan. Sc. 2 Room in Palace. Poet Lore 31: 187–196, Summer 1920.

Father changes his mind. J. Willard Lincoln. Farce. 4m., 5w. Sc. Kitchen of farmhouse. PPP

Father Noah. Geoffrey Whitworth. Verse. Biblical play. 4m., 1w., 1c. Sc. The hold of the Ark. WF

* **Father Time and his children.** Marguerite Merington. New Year's Day play. 1b., 12g. Sc. A sun dial or a clump of rocks. MFP, St. Nicholas 36: 236–40, Jan. 1909.

* **Father Time's Christmas treat.** Frank I. Hanson. 42c. Sc. Court room EP

* **Feast in the wilderness.** George Archibald March. Children's play for Christmas. 3b., 1g. Sc. A very bare room. MAP

Feast of the Holy Innocents, The. S. Marshall Ilsley. 5w. Sc. A little old-fashioned parlor. WIP2

Fee Fo Fum. John Chapin Mosher. 1m., 1w. Sc. Room in a Palace. Seven Arts 1: 602–615, April 1917.

Feed the brute. George Paston. 1m., 2w. Sc. Living room in a workman's model dwelling. FSD

Female of the species, The. Benjamin Russel Herts. 1m., 4w. Sc. Library. International 9: 152–154, May 1915.

Fennel. Jerome K. Jerome. Trans. from the French of Francois Coppée. 3m., 1w. Sc. Italian interior. FSD

Ferry, The. Wilfrid Wilson Gibson. Poetic. 2m., 1w. Sc. Living room of the ferry house. GIA, GIP, GIS

Festival of Bacchus, The. Arthur Schnitzler. Trans. from the German by Pierre Loving. 4m., 2w., chorus. Sc. Railroad waiting room SCW, International 10: 303–10, Oct. 1916.

Festival of Pomona. Constance D'Arcy Mackay. 1m., 2w., choruses. Sc. Level sward with trees on three sides. Drama 5: 161–171, Feb. 1915.

Fever ward, The. Franz Rickaby. Comedy. 4m., 2w. Sc. Room in a sanitorium. B

Fiat Lux (Let there be light). Faith Van Valkenburgh Vilas. Modern Christmas mystery play. 3m., 1w. Sc. Simple interior. FSD

Fickle Juliet. Catherine Bellairs Gaskoin. 2m., 2w. Sc. Drawing room. GAL

† **Fidelitas.** H. Hoyle Wharte. A Roman tragedy. 5b. Sc. Dungeon in the castle. FSD

Field of enchantment, The. Zakarius Topelius. Trans. by Elizabeth J. Macintire. 2m., 3w. Sc. Raspberry field when the berries are ripe. Poet Lore 28: 584–589, Autumn 1917.

1588 (Fifteen hundred and eighty-eight.) Walter Pearce. Historical comedy. 4m., 1w. Sc. Room in an old inn. FSD

Fifth commandment, The. Edward Hale Bierstadt. 2m., 1w., 1b. Sc. Living room of warden's quarters in Riverside Prison. Drama 10: 317–321, June 1920.

† **Fifth commandment, The.** Stanley Houghton. 2m., 2w. Sc. Sitting room of Mrs. Mountain's house. HF

Fifth commandment, The. Willis Steell. 3m., 1w. Sc. Handsomely furnished drawing room. B

Figs and thistles. Wilbur S. Tupper. A morality play. 5m., 6w. Sc. Study. TU

"Figuratively speaking." Fenton B. Elkins. Farce. 3m., 2w. Sc. Boudoir. ET

Figureheads. Louise Saunders. 2m., 2w., 1s. Sc. Darkened stage. SAM

Finders-keepers. George Kelly. 1m., 2w. Sc. Living room. SCO

* **Finding of the first arbutus, The.** Agnes Miller. A play for the "Mayflower" anniversary. 1m., 1w., 4c., 3 voices. Sc. A wood near Plymouth. St. Nicholas 47: 550–553, April 1920.

* **Finding the Mayflowers.** Blanche P. Fisher. A puritan play for children. 1b., 8g. Sc. Study. B

* **Finer shades of honor, The.** Marjorie Benton Cooke. 8b., 9g. Sc. Interior DPP

Finger of God, The. Percival Wilde. 2m., 1w. Sc. Living room. SL, WED

Finis. William Sharp. Fanciful verse. 2m., 2w. Sc. An obscure wood. SHV

Finish of Pete, The. Edwin Baker. Burlesque. 4m. Sc. Doctor's office. DPP

Finished coquette, A. Frances Aymar Mathews. 5m., 5w. Sc. Morning room in a country house. WEP

Finnigan's finish. Howard Amesbury. Farce. 1m., 1w. Sc. Interior. APP

* **Firefly night.** J. M. Dorff. Fairy children's play. 17c., chorus group. Sc. Deep dark woods. LO

* **Fire-spirits.** Margaret G. Parsons. Hallowe'en play. 4b., 3g. Sc. Room of a Puritan farm house. PR

First aid. Helen Bagg. Great War comedy. 3m., 3w. Sc. A field hospital. PPP

"First aid." Joan Edridge and Richard Edridge. Unconventional comedy. 1m., 2w. Sc. Green space in a wood. FSD

First aid to the wounded. Harold Montague. 1m., 1w. Sc. Sitting room. FSD

* **First American flag, The.** Geoffrey E. Morgan. Historical play of the U. S. Revolution. 3b., 1g. Sc. Colonial room. ED

* **First American library.** Eleanore Hubbard. Educational play. 10b., 1g. Sc. Franklin's stationery shop in Philadelphia. HUC

First born, The. Wilfrid Wilson Gibson. Verse. 1m., 1w. Sc. Cottage. GID, GIP

* **First Christmas, The.** Ellen M. Willard. 2g. Sc. Simple interior. WY

First Christmas eve, The. Kathleen C. Greene. Miracle play. 3m., 1w., 1c. Sc. A hut in the hills of Britain. GDL

* **First crop of apples, The.** Louise E. Tucker and Estelle L. Ryan. Providence in Colonial Days. 3b., 3g. Sc. Meadow. TRH

* **First flag, The.** Marguerite Merington. Fourth of July play. 4b., 3g. Sc. A small shop in Colonial days. MFH

* **"First in war, The."** Eleanore Hubbard. U. S. Revolutionary War play. 4b., 5g., chorus of b. HUD

First locust, The. Hugh Mytton. 2m., 1w. Sc. Drawing room. FSD

First love—and second. Gwendolen Overton. 1m., 2w. Sc. Library in a country house. Smart Set 3: 141–146, Jan. 1901.

* **First May baskets, The.** Frances Gillespy Wickes. 10c., chorus. Sc. The forest. WCB

‡ **First temptation, The.** Mae Stein Soble. Play of Adam and Eve. 3b., 1g. Sc. Garden of Eden. SOB

* **First Thanksgiving, The.** Blanche Shoemaker Wagstaff. American Colonial play. 4b., 2g. Sc. A colonial kitchen. WCP

* **First Thanksgiving Day, The.** Agnes Miller. 9b., 3g. Sc. A room in a Colonial house. SAB

* **First Thanksgiving dinner, The.** Marjorie Benton Cooke. Historical play. 7b., 5g. Sc. Colonial kitchen. DPP

First time, The. Bosworth Crocker. 3m., 2w. Sc. Matron's room in a police station. CK

* **First winter, The.** Louise E. Tucker and Estelle L. Ryan. Hardships of the Puritans. 4b., 1g. Sc. Interior of Puritan home. TRH

* **Fishing on dry land.** Augusta Stevenson. 4b., 3g., chorus characters. Sc. Before the king's palace. SC2

Five birds in a cage. G. E. Jennings. 3m., 2w. Sc. Underground in a street railway. FSD

Five in the morning. Hermann Hagedorn. Dramatic poem. 4m. Sc. Room on the top floor of a cheap boarding house in N. Y. HPT

* **Flag day. "Anychild and her flag."** F. Ursula Payne. 30c. Sc. A room in any house. PP

* **Flag makers, The.** Edna Randolph Worrell. Play for Children's Day and Flag Day. 14c. and others. Ladies Home Journal 32: 40, May 1915.

* **Flag of courage, The.** Emma Gray Wallace. Allegorical temperance play. Any number of children. Sc. Unimportant. EP

Fleeing flyer, The. F. J. Vreeland. Farce. 4m., 3w. Sc. Sitting room. FP

† **Fleurette and Co.** Essex Dane. 2w. Sc. Sitting room in Hotel. B, DAO

Flight of Helen, The: A fragment. George Santayana. Verse. 2m., 2w. Sc. Not given. Harvard Monthly 36: 53–56, Apr. 1903.

Flight of the herons, The. Marietta C. Kennard. 3m., 2w. Sc. Prison cell in Russia. Drama 14: 97–98, 107, Dec. 1923.

Flitch of bacon, A. Eleanor Holmes Hinkley. An eighteenth century comedy. 6m., 1w. Sc. A room with a fireplace. FS2

Flittermouse. Mary Katherine Reely. Farce comedy. 1m., 3w. Sc. Living room of a summer cottage. Drama 14: 104–107, Dec. 1923.

† **Florist shop, The.** Winifred Hawkridge. 3m., 2w. Sc. A florist shop. HD1

* **Flossie's alphabet lesson.** Mrs. Arthur T. Seymour. Blue bird play. 3g. Sc. Room. SE

Flower of Yeddo, A. Victor Mapes. A Japanese comedy in verse. 1m., 3w. Sc. Room in little Japanese country house. FSD

Flutter of the goldleaf, The. Olive T. Dargan and Frederick Peterson. 4m., 2w. Sc. Laboratory in attic of cottage. DPF, Charaka Club. Proceedings 3: 29–42, 1910.

* **Fly-away land.** Ella Feist. Fantasy. 2b., 8g. Sc. Garden. FSD

* **Foam maiden, The: a Celtic folk play.** Constance D'Arcy Mackay. 1b., 2g. Sc. A room in a fisherman's house. MST

Fog. Eugene G. O'Neill. 3m., 1w., 1c., chorus. Sc. Life-boat of a passenger steamer. OT

† **Followers.** Harold Brighouse. A "Cranford" sketch. 5w. Sc. Parlor of Cranford house. C2, WWS

Fond delusion. Eugene Verconsin. Farce. Trans. from the French by C. F. and F. M. Brooks. 3w. Sc. Neatly furnished boudoir. PPP

Fond of Peter. John Kendall. Comedy. 1m., 2w. Sc. Interior. FSD

Food: tragedy of the future. William C. DeMille. Satire. 2m., 1w. Sc. Kitchen. FSD

Fool, The. Isaac Rieman Baxley. Play of medieval life. 5m., 4w. Sc. Portico and terrace of a palace. BAX

Fool and his money, A. Laurence Housman. 3m. Sc. A country road. HAB

Fooling father. Raymond M. Robinson. 3m. Sc. Living room in a country home. B

* **Foolish Jack.** Lady Bell. Comedy. 1b., 1g. Sc. Unimportant. BEJ

Football game. Sara King Wiley. Comedy. College play. 4m., 1w. Sc. Parlor in a college hall. FSD

Foothills of fame. May Rose Nathan. Farce. 1m., 6w. Sc. Living room. WEP

For all time. Rita Wellman. 1m., 3w. Sc. Sitting room. SL

For distinguished service. Florence Clay Knox. 3w. Sc. An exquisitely furnished boudoir. STW

For ever and ever. Henri Lavedan. Trans. from the French. 1m., 1w. Sc. In a wood outside Paris. MR, Poet Lore 28: 391–396, Vacation 1917.

For freedom. Irene Jean Crandall. 1m., 3w. Sc. Office in a skyscraper in the loop. FSD

For her sake. Benjamin L. C. Griffith. 3m., 1w. Sc. Poorly furnished living room. GR

For king and country. Noel Leslie. 3m., 2w. Sc. Living room of shop in village in England. LET

For lack of evidence. M. Lefuse. English 18th century life. 3w. Sc. Sitting room. FSD

For love and honor. Florence Gerould. Revolutionary War play. 2m., 1w. Sc. Colonial room. DEP

For she's a jolly good fellow. Rupert Hughes. 5m., 1w. Sc. A country road. US

For the defendant—with costs. F. E. Baily. Comedy. 1m., 2w. Sc. Drawing room. PLA

For the sake of Peggy; a child welfare play. R. B. Eskil. 11w., 10c. Sc. Interior. DEP

* **For you and me.** Laura E. Richards. 2g. Sc. Out of doors. RP

Forbidden fruit. Jay George Smith. Comedy. 2m., 1w., 2s. Sc. A large living room in a chateau. SCO

Forbidden guests, The. John Corbin. Tragedy. 3m., 3w. Sc. Library and sitting room of a city house. CHF

Forced friendship, A. Robert C. V. Meyers. Farce. 2m., 2w. Sc. Interior. PPP

* **Forest of Every Day, The.** Lindsey Barbee. 5b., 7g. Sc. A forest. BLP

* **Forest spring: an Italian folk play, The.** Constance D'Arcy Mackay. 2b., 2g. Sc. A deep wood. MST

* **Forewarned is forearmed.** Eleanore Hubbard. Weather Bureau play. 8b. Sc. Observation station of a Weather Bureau. HUC

† **Forfeit, The.** Thomas B. Rogers. 2m., 2w., 1b. Sc. Manager's office. C2, RO

Forget-me-nots. Benjamin L. C. Griffith. A curtain raiser. 2m. Sc. Interior. GR

Forgotten souls. David Pinski. 1m., 2w. Sc. Workroom in a tailoring establishment in a Russian provincial town. PTS, SL

Fortescues' dinner party, The. Catherine Bellairs Gaskoin. 1m., 1w. Sc. Sitting room. GAL

Fortissimo music society. Grace Hilton Chamberlin. Farce. 16w. Sc. Lodge room. EP

† **Fortune and men's eyes.** Josephine Preston Peabody. (Mrs. Lionel S. Marks) 7m., 2w., 1c., chorus characters. Sc. Interior of "The Bear and the Angel," South London. C1, PF

Fortune favors fools, a musical comedy at the Court of the Czar. Ivan Narodny. Trans. by Maria Ossipovna Miller. 4m., 3w. Sc. Green room of the Imperial Vaudeville. Poet Lore 23: 305–319, Autumn 1912.

AN INDEX TO ONE-ACT PLAYS

Fortune tellers, The. H. R. Abbott. 3m., 2w. Sc. Tent. FSD
† **Fortunes of war.** Louise Latham Wilson. Farce. Play of girls' college life. 1m., 5w. Sc. Room in a sorority house. PPP
Found in a closet. Carlton Van Volkenburg. 1m., 3w. Sc. Room in a lodging house. FP
Fountain of youth, The. Constance D'Arcy Mackay. Fantasy. 3m., 2w., chorus characters. Sc. A clearing in a forest. MPP
Four adventurers, The. Katharine Kavanaugh. 4w. Sc. Living room in a flat. FP
Four-flushers, The. Cleves Kinkhead. 2m., 2w., 1s. Sc. Receiving room of a hotel suite. HD2
* **Four little fir trees.** Minnie E. Burgess. Christmas play. 4c. Sc. Unimportant. PCP
Four of a kind. Constance Wilcox. A play for a boat. 5m. Sc. Deck of a small sailing craft. WTC
Four who were blind. Colin Campbell Clements. A satirical fantasy. Great War background. 5m. Sc. Interior of a coffee house in Jerusalem during General Allenby's occupation of Palestine. STV
Fourteen. Alice Gerstenberg. 2w., 1s. Sc. Dining room. GT, Drama 10: 180–184, Feb. 1920.
Fourth act, The. Basil Macdonald Hastings. 2m., 1w. Sc. Interior. FSD
Fourth man, The. Austin Philips and Edward Cecil. Adapted from Austin Philip's short story of the same name. 5m. Sc. Hotel. FSD
* **Fourth of July, The.** Emma L. Johnston and Madalene D. Barnum. 4b. Sc. State house of Philadelphia. JB
* **Fox and the crow, The.** Emma L. Johnston and Madalene D. Barnum. 2b. Sc. A tree. JB
Fox's grave (Kitsune zuka). Ancient Japanese farce; trans. by Michio Itow and Louis V. Ledoux. 3m. Outlook 133: 306–308, Feb. 14, 1923.
Françoise' luck. George de Porto-Riche. 3m., 2w. Sc. Studio. CF, MR, SL
Fraternity. Pauline H. Lazaron. Jewish College play. 10m. Sc. College room. BLO
† **Freckles.** Violet M. Methley. School play. 4g. Sc. School room. FSD
Freddy goes to college. Dwight Everett Watkins. Farce. 3m., 2w. Sc. Interior. B
Freddy's great aunt. Ella Crane Wilkinson. 7w. Sc. Ladies waiting room of railway station. FSD
Free speech. William L. Prosser. 7m. Sc. Courtyard of a Russian prison. FS1
Freedom. John Read. 6m. Sc. The trusty's cell in a penitentiary. P2, STV
† **Freedom of the Press, The.** George M. Baker. Farce. 8b. Sc. Editorial sanctum. BAT
French as he is spoke. Tristan Bernard. Adapted by Gaston Mayer. 6m., 2w. Sc. Hotel in London. FSD
French maid and the phonograph, The. Madalene Barnum. 8w. Sc. Sitting room. FSD
French without a master. Tristan Bernard; trans. from the French by Barrett H. Clark. Farce. 5m., 2w. Sc. A small office in a hotel. FSD

Fresh air fiend, The. Louise Rand Bascom. Comedy. 2m., 2w. Sc. Stage shows two rooms to the audience. MBP

Friend husband. Irving Dale. Comedy. 2w. Sc. Interior. DEP

* **Friend in need; or, How "The Vicar of Wakefield" found a publisher.** Maude Morrison Frank. 2b., 3g. Sc. London lodgings of Oliver Goldsmith. SAB, St. Nicholas 42: 47–51, March 1915.

Friendly tip. Katharine Kavanaugh. 1m., 3w. Sc. Handsome room in an apartment. FP

Friendly waiter, The. Horace B. Browne. From Dickens' David Copperfield. 1m., 1b. Sc. Coffee-room of an inn. BD

‡ **Friends in bookland.** Winifred Ayres Hope. Play for Children's Book-Week. 10b., 19g. Sc. Home-like living room. HO

Fritzchen. Hermann Sudermann. 5m., 2w. Sc. Drawing room. STZ

* **Frolic of the bees and the butterflies.** Sister Clementia. Any number of boys and girls. Sc. In the woods. SIS

From death's own eyes. George S. Viereck. 1m., 2w. Sc. Tastefully furnished room. VG, International 10: 80–83, Mar. 1917.

From kitchen maid to actress. Katharine Kavanaugh. 1m., 1w. Sc. Interior. DPP

Fruit of toil, The. Lillian P. Wilson. 2m., 1b. Sc. Ordinary living room of the poor. WIF

Fudge and a burglar. Alice C. Thompson. Boarding school play. 5w. 3 others who do not speak. Sc. Girls' school dormitory. DEP

Full moon, The. Lady Gregory. Comedy. 5m., 3w. Sc. A shed close to Coon Station, Ireland. GRY, GRZ

Full of the moon, The. Gertrude Herrick. An Irish play. 2m., 2w. Sc. A cottage kitchen in poor section of town. Poet Lore 31: 379–392, Autumn 1920.

‡ **Fun at Five Point School.** Elizabeth Guptill. Burlesque. 7b., 10g. Sc. An old fashioned school room. EP

Fun in a photograph gallery. James F. Parsons. Farce. 6m., 10w. Sc. Waiting room of a photograph gallery. DEP

Funeral march of a marionette, The. Arthur H. Nethercot. Fantasia. 5m., 5w. Sc. Simple room in the castle. Poet Lore 31: 232–242, Summer 1920.

Funiculi Funicula. Rita Wellman. Play of ideas. 2m., 1w. Sc. Small Washington Square apartment. MA

Furnace, The. Wilfrid Wilson Gibson. Verse. 1m., 2w., 2c. Sc. A room in the tenements. GID, GIP

Futurists, The. Mary MacMillan. 8w. Sc. Parlor in 1882 in which an early Woman's Club meeting is taking place. MS

G

G for George, Berta Ruck, 3w, Sc. Spare bedroom in a country house. PLA

Gabe's home run. William Giles and Josephine Giles. Negro comedy. 1m., 1w. Sc. Country road. RE

Gainsborough lady, A. From the picture, "The Dutchess of Devonshire" by Gainsborough. Marguerite Merington. 1m., 1w. Sc. A frame. MPZ

Galahad Green. Clifford Bax. 2w. Sc. Living room of an apartment. New Age 30: 260–263, March 16, 1922.

Galatea of the Toy-shop. Evelyn G. Sutherland. Fantasy. 1m., 1w. Sc. Interior of the work room of a German toy-shop. SUP

Gallant Cassian. Arthur Schnitzler. Trans. from the German. A puppet-play. 3m., 1w. Sc. A garret-room in a small German town of the 17th century. SGA, Poet Lore 33:507–520, Winter 1922.

Gambetta's love story. Thomas Barclay. 2m., 1w. Sc. Comfortable study. Fortnightly 120:1–7, July 1923.

Game, The. Louise Bryant. A morality play. 2m., 2w. Sc. An out-of-door setting. Pl

Game at love, A. George S. Viereck. 1m., 2w. Sc. An elegant boudoir. VG, International 11:48–51, Feb. 1917.

Game of chess, The. Kenneth Sawyer Goodman. 4m. Sc. A wainscoted room in the house of Alexis. GQ, STG

Game of chess. Alfred Sutro. A study in sentiment. 1m., 1w. Sc. Drawing room of ocean liner. FSD, SFA

Game of comedy, A. Sherwin Lawrence Cook. 2m., 1w. Sc. An apartment in Lyons, France. B, PWP

Gaol gate, The. Lady Gregory. 1m., 1w. Sc. Outside the gate of Galway Gaol. GS

Garafelia's husband. Esther Willard Bates. 4m., 1w. Sc. A large New England kitchen. HD2

Garden, The. Florence Kiper Frank. Verse. 3m., 3w. Sc. Beautiful garden. Drama 8:471–493, Nov. 1918.

Garden, The. Ludwig Lewisohn. Verse. A modern morality play. 4m., 3w., chorus. Sc. Garden with high walls. International 10:44–47, Feb. 1916.

Garden of the west, The. Louise Driscoll. 1m., 1w. Sc. The desert. Poetry 13:138–145, Dec. 1918.

Gargoyle, The. George Middleton. 2m. Sc. Room in a house in the suburbs. ME, Smart Set 27:97–103. April 1909.

Garret, The. Wilfred Wilson Gibson. Verse. 1m., 1w. Sc. A garret in the slums. GID, GIP

Gaspers, an episode. Sewell Collins. 2m., 1w. Sc. Bench in a shelter at the foot of a cliff at a seaside resort. FSD

† **Gassed.** Bessie W. Springer. Comedy. 5b. Sc. Interior. FSD

Gastone the animal tamer. Ercole Luigi Morselli. Trans. from the Italian and ed. by Isaac Goldberg. 1m., 3w. Sc. Room in a huge circus wagon. VE

Gate of dreams, The. Dion Clayton Calthrop. Historical play of the U. S. Civil War. 4m., 2w., chorus. Sc. Garden in the south. FSD

Gate of wishes, The. Mary MacMillan. 1m., 1w., chorus. Sc. Top of a hill. MS, Poet Lore 22:467–476, Winter 1911.

Gazine globe, The. Eugene Pillot. 1m., 2w. Sc. Unfurnished room in house in South Sea Islands. LC, Stratford Journal 3:225–234, Nov. 1918.

* **Gee Whiz, The.** Mrs. Isabel Anderson. 3b., 2g., choruses. Sc. Cabin of a ship. AE

Geminae. George Calderon Farce. 3m., 2w. Sc. Private sitting room in an Edinburgh Hotel. CA

Genius, The. Horace Holley. 1m., 1b. Sc. Front porch of a small farmhouse in New England. HOR

Genjo. Ernest Fenollosa and Ernest Pound. Noh play of Japan. 5m., 1w., chorus. Sc. On the road to China. FEN

Gentle assassin, The. J. Kenyon Nicholson. 1m., 2w. Sc. Kitchen of attractive home. Smart Set 62: 83–89, June 1920.

Gentle furniture shop, The. Maxwell Bodenheim. 4m., 1w., 1g. Sc. Furniture shop. Drama 10: 132–133, Jan. 1920.

Gentle janitor, The. Clara J. Denton. Farce. 2m., 6w. Sc. Hall of an apartment house. DAI

Gentle jury. Arlo Bates. Farce suitable for women's clubs. 1m., 12w. Sc. Plain room. B

Gentleman next door, The. Horace B. Browne. Adapted from Dickens' Nicholas Nickelby. 1m., 2w. Sc. Garden. BD

Gentlemen all. R. A. Allen. 3m. Sc. Waiting room of a station. Smart Set 63: 73–79, Dec. 1920.

* **Gentlemen of Virginia.** Louise E. Tucker and Estelle L. Ryan. 4b. Sc. Wilderness. First English settlement in America. TRH

Gentlemen, the King. Binney Gunnison, adapted from "Gentlemen, the King" by Robert Barr. 11m. Sc. A rough hunting lodge in the wilderness. GU

* **Geographical squabble, A.** Anna M. Lütkenhaus. 17c. Sc. Court room. LU

Geometrically speaking. Harlan Thompson. 4m., 1w. Sc. Living room. Smart Set 56: 75–83, Nov. 1918.

George. H. K. Gornall. 4m., 2w. Sc. Kitchen. FSD

* **George Washington and the cherry tree.** Emma L. Johnston and Madalene D. Barnum. 3b. Sc. Garden. JB

* **George Washington's fortune.** Constance D'Arcy Mackay. 5b., 1g. Sc. An open woodland glade. MPY

* **Georgia debtors, The.** Blanche Shoemaker Wagstaff. Play of Colonial American history. 3b. Sc. Out of doors in Georgia in Colonial days. WCP

Germ hunters, The. E. J. Freund. 3m., 5w. Sc. Sitting room. ANP

Germelshausen. Marion Ellet. 3m., 2w., chorus. Sc. Inn. SCT

Gettin' acquainted. Georgia Earle. Comedy of a small town. 1m., 2w. Sc. New England sitting room. DEP

Getting rid of Father. A. E. Whitman. Comedy. 3m., 1w. Sc. Simple room. DEP

Getting the range. Helen S. Griffith. Great War play. 2m., 7w. Courtyard of an inn in provincial France. B

Getting unmarried. Winthrop Parkhurst. 1m., 1w. Sc. Dining room of apartment. Smart Set 54: 91–99, April 1918.

† **Gettysburg: a woodshed commentary.** Percy MacKaye. 1w., 1w. Sc. Woodshed of a farm house. C1, LE, MY

Ghost of Jerry Bundler. W. W. Jacobs and Charles Rock. 7m. Sc. Commercial room in an old-fashioned hotel. FSD

† **Ghost story, The.** Booth Tarkington. 5m., 4w., 1s. Sc. Pleasant living room. STK, Ladies Home Journal 39: 6–7, 126, 128, 129, 131, March 1922.

Gift, The. Marie H. Foley. Bible background. 2m., 1w., 1b., 1g. Sc. Interior of home in Judea—A. D. 23 FSD

Gift of Asia, The. Claude Bragdon. 2m. Sc. A rustic shelter overlooking a lake in the Adirondacks. Forum 49: 349–355, Mar. 1913.

* **Gift of time, The.** Constance D'Arcy Mackay. A Christmas masque. 32c. Sc. The palace of time. MBF
* **Gifted givers, The.** Alice Cook Fuller. Christmas play. 5b., 4g. Sc. Living room. MAP
Gimlet, The. Maurice Donnay. Trans. from the French by Barrett H. Clark. 1m., 1w. Sc. Study of bachelor's apartment. Stratford Journal 3 : 267–278, Dec. 1918.
Giorgione. Cale Young Rice. 4m., 2w. Verse. Sc. A painter's workshop. RI
Girl and the outlaw, The. Katharine Kavanaugh. 2m., 1w. Sc. Interior of a hut. DPP
Girl and the undergraduate, The. Grace Cook Strong. Comedy. College play. 5m., 2w. Sc. Living room. PPP
Girl in the coffin, The. Theodore Dreiser. 4m., 3w. Parlor of house of well-to-do workingman. DP, Smart Set 41 : 127–140, Oct. 1913.
Girl to order, A. Bessie Wreford Springer. Comedy. College play. 5m., 1w. Sc. Interior. FSD
Girl who paid the bills. Nina Rhoades. Comedy. 2m., 4w. Sc. Attractive interior. B
Girls, The. Mabel H. Crane. Comedy. 9w. Sc. Comfortable sitting room. FSD
Girls over there, The. Marie Doran. Patriotic play. 8w. Sc. Living room comfortably furnished. FSD
Giuseppina. Thomas Littlefield Marble. 3m., 2w. Sc. Private dining room in Italian restaurant. DPP
Glenforsa. John Brandane and A. W. Yuill. Scotland in the 18th century. 2m., 2w. Sc. Large room serving as library and dining room. REP
Glimpse into the theatres. R. B. J. 2m., 1w. Sc. Office of theatrical manager. International 8 : 193–4, June 1914.
Glittering gate, The. Lord Dunsany. 2m. Sc. A lonely place. DF
Gloom; or, **The old grey barn.** E. Preston. 4m., 3w. Sc. A room in a Russian house. PL
Glorious game, The. Beulah Marie Dix. American school peace league play. 6w. Sc. Living room in a simple house in a foreign country. AS
Glory of the morning. William Ellery Leonard. Indian play. 2m., 1w., 1b., 1g. Sc. Before an Indian wigwam. LEO, WIP
Gloves, a fragment of the eternal duet. Gilbert Cannan. 1m., 1w. Sc. End of a hotel corridor. Theatre Arts 4 : 160–165, Apr. 1920.
* **"Go and come."** Laura E. Richards. 1b., 2g. Sc. Overlooking a garden. RP
Go-between, The. Harry L. Newton. Dramatic comedy. 1m., 2w. Sc. Living room. B
Goal, The. Henry Arthur Jones. 4m., 2w. Sc. Dressing room in a very richly furnished apartment. CBI, JO, American Magazine 63 : 451–461, March 1907.
Goat, The. Dorothy Massingham. Comedy. 1m., 3w. Sc. Interior. FSD
Goat alley. Ernest Howard Culbertson. 3m., 3w., 3c. Sc. Sitting room of a negro's squalid dwelling. SCO
* **Goblin guests.** Grace Richardson. Valentine play. 4b., 1g. Sc. Nursery. RS

* **Goblins, The.** Madeline Poole. 6b., 2g. Sc. Cottage on the edge of a forest. PO

God of my faith. J. Hartley Manners. Great War play. 2m. Sc. Room in a London house. MTP

† **God of quiet, The.** John Drinkwater. Verse. 8m. Sc. A road at summit of a hill outside a beleaguered city. DPA

God of the newly rich wool merchant, The. David Pinski. 6m., 2w., chorus. Sc. A vast temple-like hall in a private home. PT

God of the wood, The. Claude M. Girardeau. A garden play. 8m., 2w., parrot, image. Sc. A ruined shrine in the centre of a wood. Drama 10: 305–307, June 1920.

Gods, The. Iao Sabao. From the Coptic. 3m. Sc. Fanciful, top of the earth. International 12: 86–87, March 1918.

God's outcast. J. Hartley Manners. Great War play. 1m., 1w. Sc. Isolated railway station. MTP

‡ **Going shopping.** Clara J. Denton. 1g., 1b. Sc. Interior. MBP

Going to school in China. Janet Ogden. 2b., 2g. Sc. Street in a Chinese town. Everyland 5: 112–113, March 1914.

* **Going to school in Mother Goose Land.** Elizabeth Guptill. 5b., 9g. Sc. Interior. B

Gold brick, The. Willard Bassett. Farce. 6m. Sc. Interior. DPP

Gold bricks. No author given. 3m., 2w. Sc. Interior. ANP

Gold circle, The. Thomas Wood Stevens. Fantastic ancient oriental play. 6m., 4 chorus groups. Sc. Pool. STV

* **Gold in California.** Eleanore Hubbard. The settlement of the U. S. 4b. Sc. Hut on the banks of a stream in California. HUD

† **Golden arrow.** James Plaisted Webber. 2m., 1w. Sc. A monastery garden. B

* **Golden bucket, The.** Augusta Stevenson. 2b., 1g. Sc. The woods. SCL

‡ **Golden calf, The.** Mae Stein Soble. Old Testament play. 4b., chorus. Sc. A mountain side. SOB

† **Golden doom, The.** Lord Dunsany. 9m., 1g., 1b., chorus of m. Sc. Outside the King's great door in ancient Babylon. CBI, DF, KP, Poetry and Drama 1: 431–442, Dec. 1913.

* **Golden gifts.** Julia K. Nusbaum. Jewish. Biblical. Fairy. 5b., 5g. Sc. Before the curtain. BLO

* **Golden touch, The.** Alice Cook Fuller. 7b., 1g. Sc. Forest. FU

Golden wedding, The. Dora H. Stockton. Thanksgiving Day play. 5m., 3w., chorus. Sc. Plainly furnished sitting room. G1

* **Golliwog in Fairyland; or, How Edward the Teddy Bear became a knight,** a fairy play. Maude Cockrell. 18c., chours, Sc. A dell in the wood. COC

Gone abroad. Evelyn Gray Whiting. Comedy. 4w. Sc. Interior. B

Goo-goo. Phil R. Wilmarth. 3m., 2w. Sc. Absolutely plain room. DEP

Good bargain, A. Lord Dunsany. 5m. Sc. A crypt of a monastery. DFO, Smart Set 63: 73–78, Sept. 1920.

Good-bye, a parlor comedy. Arlo Bates. 2w. Sc. Not given. Ladies' Home Journal 20: 8, Jan. 1903.

Good-bye! Jules Renard; trans. from the French by Barrett H. Clark. 1m., 1w. Sc. Small drawing room in apartment in Paris. Smart Set 49: 81–93, June 1916.

* **Good-bye all!** Edith F. A. U. Painton. Closing day of school. Any number of children. Sc. School room. PAS

Good dinner, A. Mary Stewart Cutting. 4m., 4w. Sc. Drawing room prettily furnished. Ladies' Home Journal 22:5, 48, Feb. 1905.

Good Friday. John Masefield. Verse. 7m., 1w. Sc. Paved court outside the Roman citadel in Jerusalem. MLG, MTA

* **Good housewife and her labors, The.** Margaret Lynch Conger. Irish folk story. 1b., 1g., chorus. Sc. Roadside cottage in Ireland. CFS

* **Good intentions.** E. M. Fotheringham. 1b., 1g. Sc. Any room. FG

* **Good little girl, A.** Marie Irish. 3b., 3g. Sc. Sitting room. IL

"Good men do, The." Hubert Osborne. Historical play. 3m., 4w., 1s. Sc. Living room in England 1616 FS1

Good old days, The. Alice Thompson. Dream play of Colonial times. 11w. Sc. Colonial room. DEP, PPP

* **Good Samaritan, The.** Rita Benton. Bible play. 12b. Sc. Road. This play may be given out of doors. BSD

Good woman, A. Arnold Bennett. Farce. 2m., 1w. Sc. Drawing room of plainly furnished apartment. BP, SL

Good woman, A. George Middleton. 1m., 1w. Sc. Flat in large city, modest but comfortable. MA, MIP

* **Goodys Grumble's cottage.** Virginia Olcott. Play of the Red Cross. 4g. Sc. Gloomy room. OPA

Goose, The. Manta S. Graham. 1m., 2w. Sc. Boudoir. GRL

Goose feather bed, The. Willis N. Bugbee. Farce. 4m., 1w. Sc. Interior. MAP

* **Gooseherd and the goblin.** Constance D'Arcy Mackay. 8c. Sc. A bit of woodland. MHH

* **Governor's proclamation, The.** Clara J. Denton. Thanksgiving Day play. 2b., 5g. Sc. Kitchen in Colonial days. DAH

Goya in the cupola. Thomas Walsh. Verse. 2m. Sc. Scaffold in San Antonio. Century 89:701–704, Mar. 1915.

Grace Mary. Henry Arthur Jones. A tragedy in the Cornish dialect. 6m., 2w., chorus. Sc. Exterior of Inn on the North Cornish coast. JO

Gracie. Bessie Springer Breeme. Comedy. 6b., or m. Sc. Cottage sitting room. FSD

* **Graduate's choice.** F. A. U. Painton. Graduation morality. 12g. Sc. May be given indoors or out of doors. DEP

* **Graduation at Gayville.** Willis N. Bugbee. 12c. Sc. A platform. BUP

* **Graduation Day; "The graduation of Anychild."** F. Ursula Payne. 19c. Sc. Any school. PP

Graft. Harry L. Newton. Political play. 4m., 1w. Sc. Interior. DEP

Grammar. Eugene M. Labiche. Trans. from the French by Barrett H. Clark. 4m., 1w. Sc. Room in a house in the suburbs of Paris. FSD

* **Grammar play, A.** Anna M. Lütkenhaus. 40 or more c. Sc. Unimportant. LU

* **Grandfather's bright Christmas plan.** Marie Irish. Christmas play. 2b., 5g. Sc. Living room. IC

Grandmother, The. Lajos Biro. Trans. from the German by Charles

Recht. 3m., 7w. Sc. Broad sunny terrace in Hungary furnished with garden furniture. SL, Drama 8: 176–196, May 1918.

Grandmother Rocker, a costume play. Tracy D. Mygatt. 12m. and w. Sc. An old room in an old house. B

* **Grandmother's cat.** Elizabeth F. Guptill. 3g. Sc. Not important. GUT

Grandpa. S. Decatur Smith, Jr. Farce Comedy. 2m., 2w. Sc. Interior. PPP

Granny Boling. Paul Green. 4m., 3w., neighbors. Sc. Living room of better class negro home. Drama 11: 389–394, Aug.–Sept. 1921.

Granny Maumee. Ridgely Torrence. 3w. Sc. Living room in an old cabin. TPF

Granny's Juliet. Herbert Swears. 3w. Sc. Small drawing room. FSD

Grapejuice. E. J. Freund. 7m. Sc. Office. ANP

* **Grasshoppers and the ants, The.** Anne A. T. Craig. An Aesop's fable play. 9c., 2 chorus groups. Sc. A field beside an ant hill. CD

Gray overcoat, The. William R. Randall. 3m. Sc. Interior. Detective play. FSD

Gray parrot, The. W. W. Jacobs and C. Rock. 4m., 2w. Sc. Interior. FSD

Great doughnut corporation, The. T. S. Denison. Farce. 3m., 5w. Sc. Office. DEP

* **Great feast, The.** Laura E. Richards. 5g. Sc. Nursery. RP

Great hope, The. Elma Ehrlich Levinger. 2m., 1w. Sc. Interior of a hovel. Stratford Journal 5: 231–235, Oct.–Dec. 1919.

Great medical dispensary, The. Larry Vane. Farce. 6m. Sc. Doctor's office. DEP

Great noontide, The Patrick Kearney. Satire. 4m., 2w., others. Sc. Meeting hall of the Nietzschean Community of the Creating Ones. Drama 11: 109–113, Jan. 1921.

Great Protestant association, The. Horace B. Browne. From Dickens' Barnaby Rudge. 4m. Sc. Room. BD

* **Great sale, The.** Clara J. Denton. Christmas play. 5b., 3g., chorus. I

Great Winglebury duel, The. George M. Rosener. From Charles Dickens. Farce. 6m., 3w. Sc. Interior of an Inn. Stagelore p. 89, Feb. 1912.

Greater than war. Asa Steele. Great War play. 3m., 1w. Sc. Lonely house near the battlefields of France. PPP

Greater voice, The. Blanche Shoemaker Wagstaff. 1m., 1w. Sc. Edge of a wood. International 8: 365–366, Dec. 1914.

* **Greatest day in the year, The.** Carolyn Wells. 4b., 20g. Sc. Palace of time. WJ

* **Greatest gift, The.** Anne A. T. Craig. Spring festival play. 8c., 3 chorus groups. Sc. Center of an open space. CD

‡ **Greatest gift, The.** Katharine Lord. Christmas play. 28c., chorus. Sc. A busy street of shops. LLR

* **Greatest gift, The.** Carolyn Wells. Christmas play. 10b., 11g. Sc. Court room of the Palace of gifts. WJ, Ladies Home Journal 30: 32, 58, 59, Dec. 1913.

Grecian urn, The. Arthur H. Nethercot. Verse. 5m., 1w., villagers. Sc. Wooded spot. Poet Lore 33: 142–147, Spring 1922.

Greek vase, The. Maurice Baring. Farce. 2m. Sc. A garret on the top floor of a squalid house in Rome. BA

Green coat, The. Alfred de Musset and Emile Augier. Comedy. 3m., 1w. Sc. Room in the Latin Quarter. FSD

Green cockatoo, The. Arthur Schnitzler. Trans. from the German. 19m., 3w., chorus. Sc. Wine-room of the "Green Cockatoo." SAA, SG

Green-eyed monster, The. Adolph Klauber. 3m., 1w. Sc. Studio in an old-fashioned house in Greenwich Village. Smart Set 42: 133–141, Jan. 1914.

Green helmet, The. William B. Yeats. Heroic farce. 6m., 2w., chorus. Sc. Log house. YT, YPP, Forum 46: 301–321, Sept. 1911.

Green scarf, The. Kenneth Sawyer Goodman. 1m., 1w. Sc. City park. GQA, STG

Gretna Green. Constance D'Arcy Mackay. 1m., 2w. Sc. A room that is a trifle shabby, furnished in 18th century manner. MB

Gringoire, the ballad monger. Theodore De Banville. Trans. from the French by Arthur B. Myrick. 4m., 2w., pages, servants, etc. Sc. Room in Tours in 1469. DPP, Poet Lore 27: 129–163, Spring 1916.

Groove, The. George Middleton. 2w. Sc. Bedroom of cottage in small village. MIP

Grotesques. Cloyd Head. 3m., 3w. Sc. Black background, conventionalized design. Poetry 9: 1–30, Oct. 1916.

Group of poems. A. C. Inman.
    Dialogue 1m., 1 spirit. Sc. Anywhere. Stratford Journal 1: 32–34, Winter 1917.
    Fate. 1m., 1w. Sc. Large bare prison cell. Stratford Journal 1: 25–31, Winter 1917.

Growing old together. Colin Campbell Clements. 2m., 1w., chorus. Sc. Forest of pine trees. Poet Lore 31: 176–180, Summer 1920.

* **Growing up.** E. E. Bloxam. 3m., 8w. Sc. A meadow. BL

Gruach. Gordon Bottomley. 5m., 6w., 1b., 1g. Verse. Historical. Sc. Hall of a small black stone castle in early Scotland. BKG

Guest for dinner, A. Lewis Beach. 4m. Sc. A large, cold formal room. BF

Gutter of time, The. Alfred Sutro. 1m., 1w. Sc. Interior. FSD, SFA

H

Hachi No Hi. Seami. Noh play of Japan. 3m., 1w., chorus. Sc. Stage. WAA

Hagoromo. Ernest Fenollosa and Ezra Pound. Noh play of Japan. 2m., 1w., chorus. Sc. Japanese exterior. FEN

Hagoromo. Seami. Noh play of Japan. 2m., 1w., chorus. Sc. Stage. WAA

Hair trigger Smith. Keene Abbott. Based upon the Shot by Pushkin. Russian play. 3m., 1w. Sc. Parlor of an old fashioned Colonial House in Virginia. ABB

Haku Rakuten. Seami. Noh play of Japan. 3m., chorus. Sc. The coast of Bizen, Japan. WAA

Hal, the highwayman. H. M. Paull. 4m., 2w. Sc. Interior. FSD

Half-back's interference, A. M. N. Beebe. 10m. Sc. A farmhouse. B

Hall of laughter, The. Thomas B. Rogers. 2m., 4w., chorus. Sc. Lobby of a side show of a Fair. RO

Hall-marked. John Galsworthy. Satire. 4m., 4w., 2 dogs. Sc. Sitting room and veranda of a bungalow. GSS, Atlantic 113: 845–851, June 1914.

* **Hallowe'en carnival and wax-work show, A.** Laura Rountree Smith. 14c. Sc. Stage. SFH

* **Hallowe'en puppet play.** Laura Rountree Smith. 8c. Sc. High on the hill. SFH

Ham and eggs. Abercrombie Lascelles. Verse. 2m., 1w., 1c. Chapbook #34, Feb. 1923.

Hamlet's brides. Sara Hawks Sterling. Burlesque on Shakespeare. 1m., 5w. Sc. Ordinary parlor. B

Hand of Siva, The. Kenneth Sawyer Goodman and Ben Hecht. Melodrama. Great War background. 5m. Sc. Room in a small French hotel. STV

Hand of the Prophet, The. Margaret Scott Oliver. An Arabian episode. 2m., 2w., chorus. Sc. A room in an Arabian house in festive preparation for a wedding. OS

Hands and the man. Rex Hunter. 2w. Sc. Breakfast room. HS

Hands in the box, The. Leo Duran, translator. From the Japanese. 2m., 11w., 2c., chorus. Sc. Reception room of Japanese palace in 17th century. DU

Handy Solomon. Ralph W. Tag. Farce. 2m., 2w. Sc. Interior. FP

"Hang it!" Herbert C. Sargent. Farce. 2m., 2w., 1b. Sc. Dining room. PL

Hanging out the wash. Katharine E. Smedley and Anne Buzby Palmer. Negro play. 3w. Sc. Back yard. PPP

* **Hanging up the stockings.** Clara J. Denton. Christmas play. 2b., 1g. Sc. Sitting room. DAH

Hannah gives notice. Alice C. Thompson. Comedy. 4w. Sc. Interior. FSD

Hanrahan's oath. Lady Gregory. 3m., 3w. Sc. A wild and rocky place. GI, Little Review 4: 6–16, 33–38, Nov. 1917.

* **Hans and Grethel.** Alice Cook Fuller. 1b., 3g. Sc. Interior. FU

Happiness. J. Hartley Manners. 2m., 2w. Sc. Comfortable furnished room of a modern apartment house. MH

Happy day, The. Octavia Roberts. Farce. 7w. Sc. Living room. B

Happy ending. Bertha Moore. Romantic pathos. 2w. Sc. Cozy sitting room. PH

Happy families. Aldous Huxley. 3m., 2w., 1g. Sc. Conservatory. Little Review 7: 18–30, Sept. 1919.

* **Happy man, The.** Rita Benton. From the "Enchanted shirt" by John Hay. 13b. Sc. Room in the King's palace. BSC

Happy Prince, The. Oscar Wilde. Dramatized by Lou Wall Moore and Margaret F. Allen. 2m. Sc. Public Square with a golden bronze statue of the Happy Prince. Poet Lore 27: 406–410, Vacation 1916.

Happy returns. Essex Dane. 10w. Sc. Drawing room. DAO

Happy thought, The. Jeanette Marks. 4m., 5w., others. Sc. Village square. International 6: 36–38, July 1912.

* **Happyville school picnic, The.** Willis N. Bugbee. 8b., 9g. Sc. An open space. BUP

† **Harbor of lost ships, The.** Louise Whitefield Bray. 3m., 1w. Sc.

Interior of cottage on an island off the coast of Labrador. HD2

Hard heart, The. M. A. Kister, Jr. 6m., 2w., 1c., chorus characters. Sc. Dining room. FS3

Hardy perennials. Arthur Meeker, Jr. 2m., 3w. Sc. Sitting room of summer cottage in Massachusetts. Drama 13: 292–296, May—June 1923.

* **Hare and the hedgehog, The.** Augusta Stevenson. 2b., 1g. Sc. A cabbage field. SC2

* **Hare and the tortoise, The.** Augusta Stevenson. 2b., 2g. Sc. A meadow. SC1

Harlequin. Colin Campbell Clements. 2m., 1w. Sc. Garden of a small village inn. Poet Lore 31: 579–587, Winter 1920.

Harrison. V. Fetherstonhaugh. 4m., 4w. Sc. 1. A steamship. Sc. 2. A hotel. Smart Set 43: 129–141, July 1914.

Hartleys, The. Arthur Eckersley. 2m., 3w. Sc. Interior. FSD

Harvest, The. T. W. Hanshew. 2m., 2w., 1b. Sc. Boudoir at Riverside cottage on the Thames. Smart Set 26: 118–133, Nov. 1908.

Haste makes waste. Harriette Wilbur. Farce. 2m., 1b. Sc. Drug store. MAP

Hat at the theatre. Anne Palmer. Farce. 6m., 2w. Sc. Interior of the theatre. TMP

Hatching a conspiracy. Horace B. Browne. From Dickens' Barnaby Rudge. 1m., 1w. Sc. A kitchen. BD

Hatching the lucky egg. E. J. Freund. Comedy. 2m., 2w. Sc. Room in a farmhouse. ANP

"Hatred." Katharine Searle. Great War background. 2m., 3w. Sc. House in a coast town in England during the Great War. SEA

Hatsuyuki. (Early snow.) Koparu Zembo Motoyasu. Noh play of Japan. 4w., chorus. Sc. Great temple at Izumo. WAA

Hattie. Elva DePue. 2m., 3w. Sc. Room in a New York tenement. MA, MP

Haunted chamber, The. Grace Griswold. Romantic comedy. 2m., 2w. Sc. Haunted room in a castle. FSD

* **Haunted gate, The.** Edyth M. Wormwood. Hallowe'en play. 3b., 7g. Sc. Interior. EP

Haunted hat-shop, The. Max Michelson. 1m., 2w., voice. Sc. Millinery shop. Poetry 17: 233–237, Feb. 1921.

He is coming. Alvilde Prydz. Trans. from the Norwegian by Hester Coddington. 1m., 5w. Sc. Old fashioned sitting room in small country house. Poet Lore 25: 230–244, Summer 1914.

He said and she said. Alice Gerstenberg. 1m., 3w. Sc. Living room. GT

He, she and it. William Muskerry. Matrimonial comedy. 1m., 1w. Sc. Boudoir. PH

Head of Romulus, The. Sydney Grundy. From the French of Eugene Scribe. 3m., 3w. Sc. Drawing room. FSD

* **Health champions, The.** Maude Batchelder Vosburgh. Modern health crusade. 21c. Sc. No special scenery required. VO

Heart of a clown, The. Constance Powell-Anderson. Harlequin play. Fantasy. 2m., 2w. Sc. Outskirts of a village fair. REP

Heart of a tenor, The. Frank Wedekind. 5m., 3w. Sc. Large hotel room in city in Austria. Smart Set 40: 129–141, June 1913.

* **Heart of Pierrot, The.** Margretta Scott. 4b., 5g., c. Sc. Quaint little street. SB Drama 10: 200–202, Feb. 1920.

Hearts. Alice Gerstenberg. 4w. Sc. A fashionable drawing room. GT

Hearts to mend. H. A. Overstreet. Pierrot play. Fantasy. 2m., 1w. Sc. Living room, dining room and kitchen combined. STK

* **Heathen Chinee, The.** Frederick Trevor Hill. Farce. 5b., 1g. Combination bedroom, dining-room and kitchen. HH

Heirloom, The. Thomas B. Rogers. 1m., 1w. Sc. Library of an old mansion. RO

Heirs-at-law. Anthony E. Wells. Comedy. 3m., 5w. Sc. Interior. FSD

Helen. Edward Storer. 3m., 1w. Sc. Palace of King Menelaus. International 9: 17–20, Jan. 1915. Poetry and Drama 2: 153–165, June 1914.

† **Helen and Modus.** Adapted from "The Hunchback" by Sheridan Knowles. Comedy. 1m., 1w. Sc. Corridor before a parlor. GU

Helena's husband. Philip Moeller. Historical comedy. 3m., 1w., 1s. Sc. A Greek interior. MF, SL, WSP

Helios, a fragment. Gerhart Hauptmann. Trans. from the German by Carlos S. Wupperman. 7m. Sc. Kitchen of an old castle. Moods 1: 101–107, Jan. 1909.

Helping Charlie. V. D. Hyde. Comedy. 2m., 2w. Sc. Parlor of a flat. FOS

Helpless couple, A. M. J. Williams (M. Hayman). 3w. Sc. A green between two cottages. FSD

Henkers Mahlzeit. Alicia Ramsey. 5m., 1w. Sc. Small room in the Bastile. Smart Set 30: 123–131, Feb. 1910.

Henry wakes up. Florence M. Millward. Comedy. 1m., 2w. Sc. Sitting room in a clean lodging house. MIF

Henry, where are you? Beulah King. 1m., 6w. Sc. Veranda of a country house. B

Her busy day or an experience in housekeeping. James C. Richards. (J. R. Condrin, pseud.) Farce. 7m., 5w. Sc. Interior. B

Her Christmas hat. Walter Ben Hare. Farce. 4m., 5w. Sc. Living room in apartment. HW

Her deaf ear. Arlo Bates. Farce. 2m., 3w. Sc. Interior. B

Her dearest friend. Rosmary Rees. 1m., 2w. Sc. Poorly furnished sitting room. FSD

Her final answer. Edward Brewster Sheldon. 3m., 2w. Sc. Boudoir. Harvard Monthly 44: 103–117, Apr. 1907.

Her first assignment. Gladys Ruth Bridgham. Comedy. 10w. Sc. Drawing room. B

Her first scoop. Lindsey Barbee. Comedy. 1m., 3w. Sc. Interior. DEP

Her happiness. Horace Holley. 1m., 1w. Sc. Interior. HOR

Her neighbor's creed. Margaret Cameron. 1m., 1w. Sc. Library in a home. CAC

Her nephew-in-law elect. Helen P. Kane. Farce. 3w. Sc. Interior. PPP

Her old sweethearts, a 30 minute parlor play. Eleanor H. Porter. 10m., 1w. Sc. Comfortable living room. Ladies' Home Journal 27: 17, 90, 92, April 1910.

Her picture Rachel E. Baker. Comedy. 2m., 2w. Sc. Studio. PWP

Her scarlet slippers. Alice C. Thompson. Comedy. 4w. Sc. Interior. PPP

Her second time on earth. Harry L. Newton. Comedy. 1m., 1w. Sc. Interior. B

Her service flag. Helen Sherman Griffith. Great War play. 4w. Sc. Interior. PPP

Her story. Katharine Searle. Great War background. 4w. Sc. Sun parlor of convalescents Home. SEA

Her tongue. Henry Arthur Jones. Comedy. 3m., 2w. Sc. Private hotel. JO

Her uncle's boots. Mrs. Myrtle B. Carpenter. Farce. 7g. Sc. Living room. B

Her victory. Eleanor Maud Crane. Comedy. 17w. Sc. Studio. FP

Her vote. H. V. Esmond. Comedy. 1m., 2w. Sc. Interior. FSD

Her weekly allowance. Jessie A. Kelley. Farce. 9m., 7w. Sc. Interior. B

* **Herbert's discovery.** Marie Irish. Christmas play. 2b. Sc. Living room. IC

Hermit of Carmel. George Santayana. Verse. Early Christianity. 2m. Sc. A ravine amid the slopes of Mount Carmel. SAN

Hero, The. Alice Brown. 3m., 1w., chorus. Sc. Interior of fisherman's cottage. BO

Hero in pink, The. Orrick Johns. A Greek tragedy. 3m., 42w. Sc. Any drawing room. Smart Set 48 : 201–202, Mar. 1916.

Hero and heroine. Herbert Swears. Melodramic absurdity. 1m., 1w. Sc. Cottage. FSD

Hero of Santa Maria, The. Kenneth S. Goodman and Ben Hecht. 6m., 1w. Sc. Living room. SCO, STG

Heroes. Grace Luce Irwin. 2m., 5w. Sc. Sitting room in an old mansion. ID

* **Hiawatha.** Marie Irish. From Longfellow's "Hiawatha." Verse. 8b., 2g. Sc. Wood scene with wigwam. IPP

Hicksville bungler, The. Chester A. Griffin. Small town newspaper farce. 7m., 3w. Sc. Newspaper office. DEP

Hidden harmonies. Evelyn Simms. Comedy. 2m., 3w. Sc. Interior. DEP

Hidden love. Floyd P. Cowan and Robert T. Hardy. 1m., 1w. Sc. Dining-room. FSD

* **High Jinks along the milky way.** Vincent Van Marter Beede. A romance of the Zodiac. 6b., 2g. Sc. Airy apartment in palace. HE

† **High school clothes line, The.** Iowa State College, Ames, Iowa. Home Economics Division. 5 or more g. Sc. Living room. Journal of Home Economics 13 : 169–174, Apr. 1921.

Higher good, The. Thacher Howland Guild. 10m. Sc. Game room of a mission in N. Y. GUI

‡ **Highway robbers, The.** Eleanor Allen Schroll. 12b. Sc. A street. FIL

Hilarion. Josephine Howell-Carter. 5m., 1w. Sc. Sunny glade in an old wood. Poet Lore 26 : 374–392, Summer 1915.

Hildetua. George B. Seitz. 3m., 1w. Sc. Interior rude vikings' hut in 8th century. Smart Set 32 : 143–150, Sept. 1910.

* **Hilltop.** Louise Ayres Garnett. 6b., 2g., chorus. Sc. A clearing before a thatched cottage. GAT, Drama 11 : 277–283, May 1921.

Hippodrome horror, a nightmare drama. Leila Waddell. 1m., 1w Sc. Not given. International 12 : 94–95, March 1915.

Hiram and the peddlers. Willis N. Bugbee. 5m., 2w. Sc. Plain living room. BUP

Hiram Jones' bet. May E. Countryman. Farce. 1m., 2w. Sc. Sitting room. B

‡ **Hired girl's dream, The.** Charles Noel Douglas. Fantastic dream play. 23c. Sc. Kitchen. WHP

Hired man's courtship, The. A. K. Cripps. 4m., 3w. Sc. Dining room. EP

His best day. Matthew Boulton. 1m., 1w. Sc. Interior. FSD

His chance. Herbert A. Mann. Comedy. 4m. Sc. Stage of a New York theatre. PWP

His charity patient. Reed Robinson. 2m., 1w. Sc. Waiting room in a doctor's office. ROB

His city girl . . . Ward Macauley. Comedy. 4m., 3w. Sc. Interior. PPP

His dinner for two. Franklin Johnston. Comedy. 1m., 1w. Sc. Sitting room in N. Y. apartment. FP

His exceptional mother-in-law. Mrs. Frederick W. Pender. 1m., 2w. Sc. Drawing room. WEP

His father's son. Helen Morrison Howie. Farce comedy. 2m., 2w. Sc. Sitting room, dining room combination in cosy flat. PPP

His favorite flower. Laurence Housman. English political farce. 2m., 1w. Sc. Room in fine old English mansion. HA, HA4

His first case. George Albert Drovin. Farce. 1m., 1w. Sc. Law office. PPP

His good genius. Arthur M. Heathcote. Comedy. 1m., 2w. Sc. Study. FSD

His helpmeet. Arthur Schnitzler. Trans. from the German by Pierre Loving. 4m., 1w., 1s. Sc. Elegantly furnished room in a summer resort. SCW, International 9 : 207–211, July 1915.

His honor. O. M. Dennis. 3m., 1w. Sc. Library in the home of a Mayor in a large city. Smart Set 35 : 129–134, Nov. 1911.

His imitation sweetheart. Elliott Flower. Comedy. 1m., 2w. Sc. Parlor of a home. Ladies' Home Journal 25 : 12, 55, Feb. 1908.

His Japanese wife. Grace Griswold. Comedy contrasting the East with the West. 3m., 3w. Sc. Attractive room. FSD

His lordship. M. E. M. Davis. 5m., 3w. Sc. Lawn. DAB, G1

His lordship, the burglar. Edith M. Willett. Comedy. 2m., 1w. Sc. Pretty drawing room in an American summer resort. PPP

His luck. Horace Holley. 2w. Sc. Living room in a small flat. HOR

His lucky day. Thayer Susan Bowker. Farce. 2m., 1w. Sc. Golf Club house. B

His Methodist foot. Vance C. Criss. Farce. 3m., 6w. Sc. Interior. B

His model wife. Helen F. Bagg. Comedy. 3m., 7w. Sc. Studio. PPP

His mother's face. Marguerite Merington. From the picture "Une Fete Champetre" by Watteau. 1m., 1w., 1c. Sc. Room divided by screen into two parts. MPZ

His old sweethearts. Mrs. George T. Palmer. 1m., 11w. Sc. Not given. Ladies' Home Journal 26 : 13, 82, Nov. 1909.

His return. Percival Wilde. Comedy. 1m., 3w. Sc. Boudoir. WE

His second girl. Mary MacMillan. 3m., 3w. Sc. Large Beautiful old fashioned sitting room. MM

His sisters. Beulah King. Farce. 1m., 8w. Sc. Living room. FP

"His soul." Eleanor M. Crane. Farce. 2m., 2w. Sc. Studio. FSD

His widow's husband. Jacinto Benevente. Trans. from the Spanish by John Garrett Underhill. 4m., 3w. Sc. Reception room. BJP, SL

His wife's place. Adapted from the story by C. B. Kelland. 2m., 2w. Sc. Living room. DAK

* **Historical Hallowe'en, An.** Laura Rountree Smith. 16c. Sc. Unimportant. SFH

History repeats itself. Dawson Milward. 1m., 1w. Sc. Drawing room in a house in London. FSD

Hoka priests, The. Zenchiku Ujenobu. Noh play of Japan. 4m. Sc. Stage. WAA

Holbein in Blackfriars. K. S. Goodman and T. W. Stevens. Historical comedy. 6m., 2w. Sc. Holbein's studio. STG

Holed out in one. Claude Radcliffe. Farce. 2m., 3w. Sc. Smoking room. FSD

Holiday. Wilfrid Wilson Gibson. Verse. 1m., 3w. Sc. Room in a tenement. GID, GIP

Holiday, The. Emile Mazaud. Trans. by Ralph Roeder. 4m., 1w. Sc. Garden of a modest villa near Paris. Theatre Arts Magazine 6: 33–61, Jan. 1922.

† **Holly Tree Inn.** Mrs. Oscar Beringer. Adapted from the story by Charles Dickens. 3m., 4w. Sc. Old fashioned parlor decorated for Christmas. FSD

* **Holly wreath, The.** Emilie Blackmore Stapp and Eleanor Cameron. A December play. 8b., 8g., 5 chorus groups. Sc. A forest. SCH

* **Holy scenes of Christmas, The.** Alice Crary. A cantata. 3b., 1w., chorus. Sc. Any church. Ladies' Home Journal 20:32, Nov. 1903.

Home. Maurice Maeterlinck. Trans. from the French. 3m., 2w., chorus. Sc. An old garden planted with willows. MAF, MAG

† **Home and Mother.** Alice W. Chapin. 6g. Sc. Living room. CHC

Home coming, The. Ralph Cheever Dunning, 1m., 1w. Sc. Room in house half-demolished by shell-fire. Poetry 7: 179–181, Jan. 1916.

Home from college. Marion Short and Pauline Phelps. College play. 4m. Sc. Sitting room. FSD

Home guard, The. Jennie S. Smith. Comedy. 8w. Sc. Interior. PPP

Home of the free, The. Elmer L. Reizenstein. 2m., 2w. Sc. Living room in the home of the Burkes. MP

† **Home run, A.** Anthony J. Schindler. 10b. Sc. Open landscape. SCP

† **Homer and David.** Katharine E. Dopp. Adapted from an essay by Edward E. Hale. Historical play. DO

* **Homesteaders' Christmas, The.** Eleanore Hubbard. Homestead distribution. 4b., 1g. Sc. Pioneer's homestead in Wisconsin. HUC

* **Honest Abe, an interlude for Lincoln's birthday.** Madalene D. Barnum. 5m., 1w., 1c. Sc. Cross-roads store. BS

* **Honest critic, An.** Augusta Stevenson. 7b., many choruses. Sc. Palace. SC4

‡ **Honest Peggy.** Alice C. Thompson. Farce. 8g. Sc. Interior. DEP

* **Honest woodcutter, The.** Mabel R. Goodlander. 2c., 2 chorus groups b. and g. Sc. In the woods with a stream at one side. GF

* **Honest woodman, The.** Augusta Stevenson. 2b., 1g. Sc. A river bank. SC1

† **Honesty's the best policy.** Edith Brown-Evarts. 3b., 2g. Sc. Interior. BEY

Honeymoon, A. Author not given. 1m., 1w. Sc. Not given. Smart Set 14: 146, Oct. 1904.

† **Honeymoon, The.** Mrs. C. F. Fernald and Olivia L. Wilson. 3b., 5g. Sc. Cosily furnished room. BAB

Honi Soit, a satire on circumstantial evidence. Maverick Terrell, 1m., 1w. Sc. Parts of three rooms. Smart Set 54: 71–75, Jan. 1918.

Honor—and the girl, a parlor love play. Grace S. Richmond. Dramatized from the story by G. S. Richmond "Their Christmas eve." 1m., 1w. Sc. Cozy bachelor's sitting room. Ladies' Home Journal 20: 12, Feb. 1903.

Honor cross, The. M. E. Lee. 3m., 2w., and people of the village. Sc. Interior of neatly furnished cottage. Poet Lore 27: 702–706, Winter 1916.

Honor of Danzo. Trans. from the Japanese by Leo Durin. 3m., 1w., chorus. Reception room of Golden Turtle Inn in Japan 17th century. DU

† **Honor of the class, The.** Eleanor Maud Crane. 9g. Sc. Study in a select boarding school for young ladies. FSD

* **Honorable Miss, The.** Katharine Lord. 3b., 8g. Sc. Interior of a Japanese house. LLS

Honorable Togo. Harl McInroy. 3m., 1w. Sc. Sitting room in well furnished flat in N. Y. Drama 11: 410–413, Aug.—Sept. 1921.

Honors easy. Albert E. Drinkwater. English life in 18th century. 1m., 2w. Sc. A mansion at a distance from the highway. FSD

Honors even. Belford Forrest. 3m., 1w. Sc. Refectory which was formerly a monastery. Smart Set 53: 71–79, Dec. 1917.

Hoops. Wilfrid Wilson Gibson. Verse. 2m., 6c. Sc. Big tent-stable of a traveling circus. GIB, GIP

Hoosier school. William Giles and Josephine Giles. Farce. 4m., 6w. Sc. Country school. FP

Hooverizing Internationalle. Rebecca P. Abrahamson. Great War food play. 10w. Sc. Apartment. FSD

Horse thieves, The. Hermann Hagedorn. 4m., 2w. Sc. Kitchen of a ranch house. HAG

Hotel Comfort. W. Hanson Boyce. Farce. 1m., 1w. Sc. Interior. APP

Hour glass, The. William Butler Yeats. A morality play. 5m., 1w., 2c. Sc. A large room. DIC, Y3, YH, YU, YPP (In prose), The Mask 5: 327–346. 1913. (New version)

Hour of earth, An. Theodosia Garrison. 1m., 3w. Sc. Library. Smart Set 9: 153–157, March 1903.

Hour of greatness, The. Morley Roberts. Mystery. 4m., 1w. Sc. Room in an old house in medieval Pisa. RF

Hour of Prospero. C. E. Lawrence. Play about Shakespeare. 3m., 3w. Sc. Shakespeare's garden at New Place. Nineteenth Century 92: 685–696, Oct. 1922.

Hour of recognition, The. Arthur Schnitzler. Trans. from the German by Pierre Loving. 2m., 1w., 2s. m. and w. Sc. Dining room in a home in Vienna. SCW, International 10: 167–174, June 1916.

House, A. Ford Madox Hueffer. Verse. 4m., 2w., 12 characters. Chapbook 21: 2-4, March 1921. Poetry 17: 291-310, March 1921.

House, The. George Middleton. 1m., 1w. Sc. Room in an apartment hotel suite. MIM

House across the way. Katharine Kavanaugh. 1m., 1w., Sc. Interior. DPP

House fairy, The. Laurence Housman. 2w., 1c. Sc. A cottage interior. HAB

House of Aegues, The. Edward G. Hill. Verse. Greek play. 4m., 3w., chorus. Sc. A forest glen in Peloponnesia about 600 B. C. HHA

* **House of brick, The.** Augusta Stevenson. 4b. Sc. A turnip field. SC1

House of candles, The. Wilfred Wilson Gibson. Verse. 3w. Sc. Cottage. GID, GIP

House of cards, A. Percival Wilde. 1m., 1w. Sc. Exquisitely furnished room in a fashionable New York apartment house. WED

House of life, The. Katherine Howard. Fantastic. Fanciful. 1m., 1w. Sc. Earth. HOT

House of rest, The. Louis Noel. 1m., 1w. Sc. Interior of the Paris morgue. NO

* **House of the heart, The.** Constance D'Arcy Mackay. Morality. 12c. Sc. A heart shaped room. MHH

* **House that Jack built, The.** Someple, pseud of Gladys Lloyd. 11c. Sc. In front of a little house. MAP

* **How a prince was saved.** Augusta Stevenson. 6b., chorus characters. Sc. Out doors in Arabia. SC1

How a woman keeps a secret. Frank Dumont. Comedy. 10w. Sc. Interior. PPP

* **How Bienville saved Mobile.** Marie Bankhead Owen. Alabama Centennial play—historical. 11b., 5g. Sc. Living room of a French soldier's widow. AO

How Billy helped things along. Dramatic Art Class of the Steele High School, Dayton, Ohio. 2m., 3w., 1c. Sc. Room in a cheap apartment house. Quarterly Journal of Speech Education 4: 437-447, Oct. 1918.

* **How Christmas was saved.** Catharine Markham. 16c. Sc. Interior. SAB

How he lied to her husband. George B. Shaw. 1m., 1w. Sc. Drawing room of an apartment. SHC

How Nellie made good. Marie Doran. 9w. Sc. Interior. FSD

* **How Robin Hood once was a wait.** Rowland Gibson Hazard. A miracle play or Christmas masque. 7b., 1g., chorus. Sc. Winter in a forest. HAH

* **How sleep the brave.** Madalene D. Barnum. Interlude for Memorial Day. 8c. Sc. Entrance to a cemetery. BS

* **How the Christmas song was found.** Lilian Pearson. 14 or more c. Sc. Woodland. EP

* **How the Indians planted powder.** Louise E. Tucker and Estelle L. Ryan. Colonial days in Massachusetts. 4b., 1g. Sc. Field at an end of an Indian village. TRH

How the ladies earned their dollar; or, Mrs. Toploft's scheme. Orissa W. Gleason. Burlesque of Ladies Benevolent Society. 13w. Sc. Interior. B

How the shrew was tamed. M. A. Rask. Farce. 4m., 3w. Sc. Interior. FSD

How the story grew. O. W. Gleason. Suitable for women's clubs. 8w. Sc. Interior. B

How the vote was won. Cicely Hamilton and Christopher St. John. Comedy. Suffragette play. 2m., 8w. Sc. Interior. DPP

How they kept her. Vernon Woodhouse. Play of the servant problem. 2m., 4w. Sc. Drawing room. FSD

How to reduce. Ida G. Norton. Comedy. Any number of women. Sc. Interior. NA

Hulks, The. James Farrington. 4m., 1w. Sc. Poverty stricken living room in Paris in 1800. Smart Set 33 : 123–132, Jan. 1911.

Human nature. Floyd Dell. Morality play. 3m., 1w. Sc. Boundless blue space. DK

* **Humane citizens.** F. Ursula Payne. Kindness to animals play. 2b., 4g., chorus. Sc. A balcony. PPC

Humble pie. W. D. Emerson. Comedy. 3m., 1w. Sc. Interior of hut in the backwoods. DPP

Humpty Dumpty. Bertram Bloch. Fantasy. 7m. and any no. of Mother Goose folk. Sc. Artist's studio. Poet Lore 32 : 76–97, Spring 1921.

* **Humpty Dumpty.** Mrs. Herbert Richmond. 4b., 2g., chorus. Sc. One side of a village street. BR

* **Hundred, The.** Elsie Hobart Carter. 6g. Sc. Dressing room. CCC

† **Hundredth trick, The.** Beulah Marie Dix. 4m. Sc. Dim, wainscoted parlor in a great manor house. DA

Hunger. Eugene Pillot. Fantasy. 4m., 1w. Sc. A great gray tower. MA, Stratford Journal 2 : 19–28, June 1918.

Hunter, The. John T. Frederick. 2m., 1w., attendants. Sc. Great room in an old palace. Stratford Journal 1 : 38–41, Sept. 1917.

Hunting for Hapgood. Frank H. Shepard. Farce. 4m., 2w. Sc. Hallway of a hotel. B

Husband in clover, A. H. C. Merivale. Matrimonial comedy. 1m., 1w. Sc. Breakfast room. PH

Husband's advice. Tom Masson. 2m., 1w. Sc. Not given. Smart Set 6 : 160, Feb. 1902.

Husking bee, The. Evangeline Campbell. 4m., 3w., 1g. Sc. A country barn. CAN

† **Hyacinth Halvey.** Lady Gregory. 4m., 2w. Sc. Outside of a post office in a little town. GS, LC, Samhain 1906, pp. 15–35.

Hyacinths. Tacie May Hanna. 3w. Sc. Living room in home of moderate comforts. Drama 12 : 338–341, Sept. 1922.

Hymen à la mode. Mary L. Pendered. 1m., 1w. Sc. Not given. Smart Set 32 : 127–130, Sept. 1910.

† **Hypnotism.** Newell Bent. 3m., 8w. Sc. Interior. Farce. B, BAT

I

* **I have a little nut tree.** Someple, pseud. About 60b. and g. Sc. Garret. SO

Ibsen revisited. Floyd Dell. 1m., 1w. Sc. Middle-class interior. DK

Iceman, The. Laurence Ditto Young. Farce. 2m., 2w. Sc. Interior. PPP

Ici on parle français. Thomas J. Williams. Farce. 3m., 4w. Interior. FSD

* **Idowanna.** Dorothy Waldo. Play for children. 2w., 5c. Sc. Nursery. B

Idyll. Hugo von Hofmannsthal. Trans. from the German by Charles Wharton Stork. 2m., 1w. Verse. Sc. Open village smithy. Drama 7: 169–175, May 1917.

* **"If don't believe is changed into believe."** Lindsey Barbee. 21b., 15g. Sc. A woodland. BLP

‡ **If I were Bob.** M. A. Emerson. Scout play. 5b. Sc. Camp fire. FET

If morning glory wins. Helen Bagg. Comedy. Racing play. 2m., 2w. Sc. Interior. PPP

† **If Shakespeare lived today.** Lord Dunsany. 5m. Sc. Room in the Olympus Club. DFO, Atlantic Monthly 126: 496–508, Oct. 1920.

Ikeniye. (The pool sacrifice) Seami. Noh play of Japan. 4m., 2w. Sc. Japanese Inn. WAA

Ikuta. Zembo Motoyasu. Noh play of ancient Japan. 2m., 1w., 1 child chorus. Sc. Stage. WAA

Ile. Eugene O'Neill. 5m., 1w. Sc. Cabin on board the steam whaling ship. LE, OMC, SL, Smart Set 55: 89–100, May 1918.

* **I'll try, a grammar play.** Elinor Murphy. 1m., 5w., 12 characters. Sc. Library of a home. St. Nicholas 48: 256–260, Jan. 1921.

Illuminatti in drama libre, The. Alice Gerstenberg. 1m., 1w. Sc. Before the curtain of a stage. GT

I'm going! Tristan Bernard. Trans. from the French by Barrett H. Clark. Comedy. 1m., 1w. Sc. Room in an apartment. FSD

Imaginary aunt, An. William Muskerry. Comedy. 4w. Sc. Sitting room. FSD

* **Imaginary Tommy.** Elizabeth F. Guptill. 1b., 1g. Sc. Sitting room. GUT

Immortal, The. Carl Glick and Bernard Sobel. 1m., 3w. Sc. Interior of a castle. Poet Lore 32: 441–453, Autumn 1921.

Immortal Gulick, The. Otto S. Mayer. 2m., 1b., 1w. Sc. Golf links. Moods 2: 66–78, Oct.–Nov. 1909.

I'm sorry—it's out! Gertrude E. Jennings. Comedy. Humor in a library. 7w. Sc. Interior. FSD

Immortal lure, The. Cale Young Rice. Verse. 2m., 2w. Sc. Before a hermitage in Ancient India. RI

† **Impertinence of the creature, The.** Cosmo Gordon-Lennox. 1m., 1w. Sc. A boudoir leading from a London ball-room. CBI, FSD

Importance of being a roughneck, The. Robert Garland. Burlesque. 3m., 1w. Sc. Studio. REM, V1

Importance of being early. Winthrop Parkhurst. 2m., 2w. Sc. Living room. Smart Set 50: 229–240, Nov. 1916.

Imposition. Max Miller. 3m., 1w., 1c. Sc. Room with faded wall paper. UW

Impromptu. Dana Burnet. 4m., 2w., others. Sc. Before the King's palace. Bookman 57: 267–73, May 1923.

Improving a husband. Helen M. Givens. 1m., 1w. Sc. Comfortable living room. Ladies' Home Journal 24: 10, 67, March 1907.

In a doctor's office. Jeanette Joyce. 3m., 7w. Sc. Waiting room of a famous specialist. MAP

In a park. Arthur William Murdock. 4m., 2w., 3g., 1b., others. Sc. Small park beside a river. Harvard Monthly 45:39–45, Oct. 1907.

In a tenement. Hester Donaldson Jenkins. Tenement play. 3m., 4w. Sc. Kitchen. JE

* **In a toy shop.** Effa E. Preston. Christmas play for primary grades. 18 or more c. Sc. In a toy shop. PAP

* **In a Valentine box.** Margaret G. Parsons. 1b., 3g., chorus. Sc. Stage to represent the inside of a Valentine box. PR

* **In Arcady.** Netta Syrett. 2b., 2g., chorus. Sc. A drawing room. SSF

In Aunt Chloe's cabin. Evelyn Greenleaf Sutherland. Negro comedy. 13w., 4c. Sc. Interior of a negro cabin. SUO

* **In bad company.** Augusta Stevenson. 5b., 2g., chorus. Sc. A corn field. SC1

* **"In bells and motley," or The May Queen.** Rita Strauss. 4b., 3g., chorus. Sc. Village Green. BHP

* **In Betsy Ross's time.** Sara E. Kirk. U. S. Revolutionary war play. 8c. Sc. Colonial room. ED

In Dixie land. Seymour S. Tibbals. Burlesque. 11m., chorus. Sc. Lawn on a plantation. EP

In far Bohemia. Evelyn G. Sutherland. 1m., 2w. Sc. Bare room in a city lodging house. SUP

In front of Potter's. Frank G. Tompkins. 3m. Dual personality. Sc. Before the dimly lighted window of Potter's restaurant. STV

In garrison. C. E. Freybe. 5m. Sc. Workroom in the fortress. Poet Lore 26:499–511, Vacation 1915.

In heaven. Mary MacMillan. Great War play. Farce. 4m. Sc. In Heaven. MTT

In his house. George Middleton. 1m., 2w. Sc. Room in an apartment hotel. ME, Smart Set 29:124–132, Sept. 1909.

In honor bound. Sidney Grundy. 2m., 2w. Sc. Simple interior. B

In hospital. Thomas H. Dickinson. 3m., 2w. Sc. A large room next to the operating room of a hospital. WIP

* **In moonbeams.** Mary E. True. 1b., 4g., chorus. Sc. Room in a Foundling's home. TRU

In my day. Ruth O'Hanlon. 3m., 3w. Sc. Library in a home in a small city. SCT

In 1999. William C. DeMille. Play of the future. Satire on woman suffrage. 2m., 1w. Sc. Handsomely furnished apartment. FSD

In office hours. Evelyn Greenleaf Sutherland. Comedy. 6m., 3w. Sc. Doctor's office. SUO

In other people's shoes. Harold Sander. Comedy of boarding school life. 8w. Sc. Sitting room of a boarding school. FP

In the Ballingers' box. Harold Susman. 2m,. 2w. Sc. Box at the opera. Smart Set 30:65–66, April 1910.

In the dark. Lillian Bennet-Thompson and George Hubbard. 2m., 1w., 1c. Sc. Interior. FSD

In the dark. Theodore Dreiser. 14m., 1w., many chorus characters. Kerry Patch adjoining the car yards. DP, Smart Set 45:419–425, Jan. 1915.

In the dark. Perez Hirschbein. 3m., 2w. Sc. Rooms in a deep cellar. PTS

AN INDEX TO ONE-ACT PLAYS 105

 In the darkness. Dan Totheroh. 2m., 2w. Sc. Lean-to of a cabin. LO

 In the dusk of day. Maurice Relonde. 2m., 2w. Sc. Farmhouse kitchen. International 12: 136–138, May 1918.

* **In the east.** Clara J. Denton. Christmas play. 6b., 2g. Sc. Interior. SI

† **In the good greenwood.** Margery Benton Cooke. A Robin Hood play. 16m. Sc. Forest. DPP

 In the harem. David Pinski, tr. from the Yiddish by Isaac Goldberg. 3m., 9w., 2 chorus groups. Sc. Great hall of the harem in a palace in ancient Palestine. PTK

 In the house of the poet. Isaac Rieman Baxley. Play of the time of Nero. Historical characters. 4m., 2w. Sc. House in ancient Pompeii. BAX

 In the library. W. W. Jacobs and H. C. Sargent. 5m. Sc. Interior. FSD

† **In the light of the manger.** William O. Bates. Prophetic fantasy. 1m., 2w., 1c. Sc. Interior of a humble Bethlehem home in the days of King Herod. SB, Drama 11: 102–103, Dec. 1920.

* **In the market place.** Rea Woodman. 1b., 2g. Sc. Living room. WO

 In the marshes. Felix Gould. Dramatic suspense and mood. 1w. Sc. Interior of a cottage with the storm of the marshes outside. GO

 In the morgue. Sada Cowan. 3m., 1 voice. Sc. In a morgue. SL, Forum 55: 399–407, Apr. 1916.

 In the net. Percival Wilde. Comedy. 4m. Sc. Large simple room in a building occupied by a large manufacturing concern. WE

 In the ravine. Percival Wilde. Great War play. 2m. Sc. A snowy ravine in the Italian Alps. WU

 In the shadow of the glen. J. M. Synge. 3m., 1w. Sc. Cottage kitchen. Bibelot 19: 269–295, August 1913. Samhain 1904. pp. 34–44.

 In "The Spirit of '76." Jules Ferrar. Great War play. 3m. Sc. Library of a home in New York. FSD

 "In the spring a young man's fancy." Comedy. No author given. 1m., 7w. Sc. Sitting room in a Paris hotel. DPP

 In the trenches "Over there." Ragna B. Eskil. Great War play. 10m., 5w. Sc. A dugout. DPP

 In the zone. Eugene O'Neill. Dramatic episode. 8m. Sc. Seaman's forecastle of a British tramp steamer. MA, OMC

 In time of war. Mary Elwes. 3w., 1g. Sc. Drawing room. ETE

 In Toscana tavern. Wilbur S. Tupper. Tragedy. 3m., 1w. Sc. Room used as office and dining room in the foreign quarter of New York. TU

* **In union there is strength.** Alice Sumner Varney. 9b. Sc. Near a pleasant tree. VA

* **In witchcraft days.** Constance D'Arcy Mackay. 17c. Sc. An open glade. MPY

 In wrong. Katharine Kavanaugh. Comedy. 2m., 1w. Sc. Fire escape. DEP

 Inasmuch, a Christmas entertainment. Janet Prentiss. Any number of children. Sc. Large room hung with national colors. Everyland 5: 29–35, Dec. 1913.

 Inasmuch as ye have done it unto the least. Margaret Jeffery Hobart. Missionary play. 2m., 2w. Sc. Buddhist temple. DOF

Inca of Perusalem, The. George Bernard Shaw. 3m., 2w., 1s. Sc. Hotel sitting room. SH

Incident, An. Leonid Andreyev. Trans. from the Russian. 3m. Sc. An unfurnished factory. MR, Poet Lore 27: 171–179, Spring 1916.

Incog. Miss E. H. Keating. Farce. Proverb play "Fine feathers make fine birds." 7m. Sc. Large room in a village in France during the reign of Louis XV KE

Incompatibles, The. Horace Holley. 1m., 1w. Sc. Corner table in a Broadway restaurant. HOR

* **Independence Day.** Eleanore Hubbard. U. S. Revolutionary War play. 7b., 3g., chorus. Sc. Outside the old State house in Philadelphia. HUD

† **Independent Flynn.** Alice W. Chapin. 5g. Sc. An employment office. CHC

* **Indian gifts.** Louise E. Tucker and Estelle L. Ryan. 2b., 2g. Sc. Interior of John Alden's house. TRH

* **Indian story, An.** Blanche Shoemaker Wagstaff. U. S. Colonial play. 6b., 2g. Sc. Pioneer kitchen. WCP

Indian summer. Pierre Loving. 2m., 1w. Sc. Private supper room in a hotel. LO

Indian summer. Henri Meilhac and Ludovic Halvey. Adapted from the French by Barrett H. Clark. 2m., 2w. Sc. A small parlor. FSD

Indifference of Jerry, The. Beulah King. 2m., 4w. Sc. Living room. EP

Infernal masculine, The. Alfred Brand. Comedy. 1m., 3w. Sc. Dressing room in a charming apartment. BRI

Ingenuous grandmother. Mary Vaux Whitford. 2m., 3w. Sc. A well furnished room looking out upon a terrace and garden. SCT

Ingiald Evilheart. Frank Betts. Old Norse play. 7m., 1w. Sc. Hall of a Norse castle. BES

Ingrate, The. No author given. 4m., 2w. Sc. Room in one of the older buildings in Harvard Yard. Harvard Monthly 36: 17–40, March 1903.

Innocence rewarded. No author given. 8m., 3w. Adapted from the Vicar of Wakefield by Goldsmith. Sc. Room in prison. GU

Innocent and Annabel. Harold Chapin. 1m., 3w. Sc. Living room. CT

Innocent villain, An. Grace Luce Irwin. Farce. 1m., 5w. Sc. Dining room of an old family residence. ID

Inspiration of the play, some confessions of a woman playwright. By the Interviewer and Clare Kummer. 2m., 2w., a dog. Sc. Room in apartment in N. Y. overlooking Central Park. Forum 61: 307–316, March 1919.

Intangible, The. Egmont W. Ruschke. 2m., 2w. Sc. Comfortably furnished room. RUE

Interior. Maurice Maeterlinck. Trans. from the French by William Archer. Verse. Gloomy atmosphere. 4m., 5w., 1c., chorus. Sc. An old garden. MAE

Interloper. No author given. 2m., 2w. Sc. Handsomely furnished library. Harvard Monthly 30: 82–86, April 1900.

Interlude. Federica More. Trans. from the Spanish by Audrey Alden. 1m., 1w. Sc. A salon. SL

Interlude in the life of St. Francis, An. Alice Raphael. 2m., 1w. Sc. Courtyard of an Inn in Assissi. Drama 11: 37–40, Nov. 1920.

Interrupted proposal, An. Arlo Bates. 3m., 4w. Sc. Interior. B, Ladies' Home Journal 23 : 10, Feb. 1906.

Interviewed. Roi Cooper Megrue. 2m., 1w. Sc. Library of a New York house. Smart Set 32 : 121–130, Nov. 1910.

Intimate acquaintance, An. Grace Luce Irwin. Farce. 5w. Sc. Hotel sitting room. ID

Intruder, The. Maurice Maeterlinck. 3m., 3w., 1s. Sc. Dimly lighted room in an old country house. C1, MAE, MAH, MAI, SL

Intruder, The. Ethelyn Reed. 2m., 2w. Sc. Bedroom of a country home. Smart Set 36 : 133–138, March 1912.

* **Invention of the rat trap, The.** Samuel Milbank Cauldwell. A romantic historical play. 5b., 1g. Sc. Room in the palace of the Chinese emperor. CC

Inventor, The. Harriet Holmes Haslett. 1m., 2w. Sc. A cheap lodging house bedroom. HAE

Inventor and the king's daughter, The. David Pinski. 11m., 2w., 1s., chorus characters. Sc. A large hall of a palace. PT

Invitation to the ball, An. Harry L. Newton. Comedy. 1m., 1w. Sc. Handsome parlor. WHP

* **Iosagan.** Padriac H. Pearse. Verse. Irish religious play. 6b. Sc. Sea strand beside a village. PRZ

Iphigenia in Tauris, an English version from Euripides. Witter Bynner. 5m., 3w. Sc. On the seashore before a great temple. BB

Irene obliges. Florence M. Millward. Farcical comedy. 1m., 2w. Sc. Sitting room in a London flat. MIF

Irish invasion, An. Alice C. Thompson. Comedy. 8w. Sc. Parlor. B

Irish stew, An. Jeff Branen. Farce. 6m., 4w. Sc. Interior. DEP

† **Irish washerwoman, The.** Mrs. C. F. Fernald and Olivia L. Wilson. 1b., 1g. Sc. Kitchen. BAB

Iron Ann, The. Arthur Grahame and Adelaide St. Claire. Farce. 2m., 2w. Sc. Sitting room of a flat. FSD

Iron hand, The. Hall Caine. Great War play. 9m. Sc. French chateau. CAI

* **Is Santa Claus a fraud?** Carolyn Wells. 17b., 9g. chorus group. Sc. Court. WJ, Ladies' Home Journal 27 : 9–10, 71, Dec. 1909.

Is the editor in? T. S. Denison. Farce. 5m., 2w. Sc. Office of country newspaper. DEP

Is your name Smith? Edith K. Dunton. Comedy. 5m., 3w. Sc. Apartment sitting room. PPP

"Isabel." Clara J. Denton. Farce. 2m., 2w. Sc. Handsome interior. DAI

† **Island sea-dreams, The.** Eustace Hargrave. 6b. Sc. Boy's bedroom. FSD

Isle of Chestnuts, miracle play. Wallace Irwin. 4m., 2w., several m. and w. Sc. Densely wooded desert isle. Collier's 42 : 23–4, Mar. 20, 1909.

Isosceles. Walter Ben Hare. Burlesque on play plots. 2m., 1w. Sc. Elaborate living room. B

Isotta's trump. Martha Tritch. Comedy. 1m., 5w. Sc. Private sitting room of an Italian pension. SCT

It, the usual play with the usual ending. Richard Florance. 2m., 1w. Sc. A study. Smart Set 47 : 85–90, Dec. 1915.

It ain't my fault. Katharine Kavanaugh. Boarding school comedy. 3m., 3w. Sc. A school for young ladies. FP

It behooves us. Doris F. Halman. Comedy of conservation. Great War play. 2m., 2w. Sc. Dining room. FSD

† **It isn't done.** Carl Glick. Comedy. 3m. Sc. Any outdoor scene. STV

It might happen again. Joseph Bernard Rethy. 5m., 4w. Sc. Inside of vault in cemetery near N. Y. International 10: 203–207, July 1916.

It never happens, a comedy of the somewhat improbable. Winthrop Parkhurst. 2m., 1w. Sc. Front parlor. Smart Set 56: 77–87, Dec. 1918.

It passes by. Harriet Monroe. Verse. 3m., 5w. Sc. Drawing room. MOP

It was the Dutch. William Giles and Josephine Giles. 3m., 2w. Sc. Hotel office. RE

It's great to be crazy. J. J. Stein. Farce. 2m., 1w. Sc. Parlor of inn. PPP

It's spring. Claudia Lucas Harris. Fantasy. 1m., 2w., 17 characters. Sc. Little town in distance. Drama 11: 245–250, Apr. 1921.

It's the poor that 'elps the poor. Harold Chapin. 7m., 6w. Sc. A living sleeping room. CT

Ivory tower, The. Elizabeth Macintire and Colin Clements. 3m., 1w. Sc. Desert spot with slender white tower in center. Poet Lore 30: 127–137, Spring 1919.

J

Jack and his queen, A. Harry L. Newton. Comedy. 2m., 1w. Sc. Bachelor den. WHP

Jack and Jill and a friend. Cicely Hamilton. Comedy. 2m., 1w. Sc. Interior. FSD

* **Jack and Jill:** founded on portions of the story by Louisa M. Alcott. S. Decatur Smith Jr. 7m., 8w. Sc. Boy's den. Ladies' Home Journal 24: 14–73, Dec. 1906.

Jack and John. William Birdsley Benton. Verse. Comedy. 2m., 2w. Sc. A beautiful farm. BEP

Jack for every Jill, A. Will D. Felter. Comedy. 4m., 4w. Sc. Parlor. FP

* **Jack Frost's surprise.** Laura Rountree Smith. Hallowe'en play. 14b., 1g. Sc. Unimportant. SFH

* **Jack-I-the-Green.** Margaret G. Parsons. May day play. 5b., 4g., chorus groups. Sc. Green in the outskirts of a city. PR

† **Jackdaw, The.** Lady Gregory. 4m., 2w. Sc. Interior of a small general shop at Cloon. GS

Jack's brother's sister. Pauline Phelps and Marion Short. 1m., 1w. Sc. Sitting room in college. B

Jack's house. Alfred Kreymborg. A cubic play. 1m., 1w. Sc. Small room. KMP, KMR

Jack's predicament. Giselle d'Unger. Comedy. 1m., 3w. Sc. Bachelor's den. DPP

* **Jack's visitors; or, the schoolboy's dream.** Lillian Stair Schreiner. Patriotic and historical. 8b., 7g. Sc. Any interior. APP

Jael. Florence Kiper Frank. Poetic. 1m., 2w. Sc. Interior of tent. FSJ

Jake and his pa. William Giles and Josephine Giles. Comedy. 5m., 4w. Sc. Interior of farm-house. APP

James and John. Gilbert Cannan. 3m., 1w. Sc. Parlor of a little house. CAP, CBI

* **January styles.** Rea Woodman. 4g. Sc. Sitting-room. WO

Japanese romance, A. Fred H. James. Russo-Japanese war. 1m., 1w. Sc. Japanese garden. Stagelore Feb. 1912. p. 141.

Jason and Medea. Maurice Baring. Farce. 1m., 2w. Sc. Room in the house of Jason. BA

Jasper's troubles. Theodore A. Doucet. Farce. 3m., 1w. Sc. Interior. APP

Jean. Donald Colquhoun. Repertory plays no. 7. 2m. Sc. Interior of Scotch cottage. REP

Jean-Marie. Andre Theuriet. Translated from the French by Barrett H. Clark. 2m., 1w. Sc. Interior of a Breton farm-house. The World's best plays by celebrated European authors. FSD

Jeanette. Frederick C. Patterson. 2m., 1w. Sc. Interior of cabin of French trapper. Smart Set 31: 129–134, Aug. 1910.

Jeanne D'Arc at Vaucouleurs: A romantic drama for the stage. Will Hutchins. 5m., 3w. Sc. Interior of cottage in France 1429. Poet Lore 21: 97–148, March–April 1910.

Jennie knows. Bernard Sobel. 3m., 6w. Sc. Simple, attractive drawing room. ST

Jephthah's daughter: A biblical drama. Elma Ehrlich Levinger. Prize play of Drama League of America. 5m., 6w. Sc. Interior. C2, FSD

Jerry and a sunbeam. Cosmo Hamilton. 1m., 1w. Sc. Interior. FSD

‡ **Jerry's job.** Raymond M. Robinson. Boy Scout play. 5b. Sc. Business office. LB, PPP

Jest, The. Paul Eldridge. 4m., 2w. Sc. Living room in summer home. Stratford Journal 3: 22–35, July 1918.

Jester, The, what might have happened between the second and third acts of "The Jesters." Robert Rogers. 4m., 1w. Sc. Ruined garden of old chateau. Harvard Monthly 46: 171–188, July 1908.

Jet. Esther Shepherd. 1m., 6w. Sc. Fashionable apartment. UW

Jewel merchants, The. James Branch Cabell. Comedy. 2m., 1w. Sc. Walled garden in Florence, Italy in 15th century. CJ, Smart Set 65: 67–81, July 1921.

Jewels of Cornelia, The; a health play, James A. Tobey. 9w., 3m., 1g., 1b. Sc. Modern boudoir. Journal of the Outdoor Life 19: 42–45, Feb. 1922.

Jezebel. Dorothy Stockbridge. Historical. 2m., 2w., 2s. Sc. Room in the royal palace in Jezreel overhanging the wall of the city. SCO

Jezebel. Robert Gilbert Welsh. 6m., 3w., others. Sc. Courtyard of Jezebel's palace. Forum 53: 647–660, May 1915.

Jimmy. A. Patrick Jr. 2m. Sc. Interior. FSD

* **Jimmy's ghosts.** Cecil J. Richmond. Hallowe'en play. 7 or more c., chorus. Sc. Bedroom of a little boy. EP

Jim's beast. George Middleton. 5m., 4w. Sc. A corner in the Hall of Paleontology of a Public Museum. MIM

John Arbery's dream. Catherine Bellairs Gaskoin. Dream play. 5m., 6w. Sc. Orchard. GAL

John Bargrave, Gentleman. John E. Grinnell. 4m., 2w. Sc. Interior of richly furnished house in Colonial Virginia. DAL

John Clayton, actor. Rida Johnson Young. 2m., 1w. Sc. Typical bachelor's den. WHP

Johnson's busy day. George Elberon. Comedy. 5m. Sc. Interior. DPP

Joint owners in Spain. Alice Brown. 4w. Sc. A large comfortable bedroom in an Old Ladies Home. BO, BRQ

* **Joke, The.** Elizabeth F. Guptill. 4b. Sc. Schoolyard. MBP

* **Jolliest Christmas ever, The.** Elizabeth F. Guptill. 1b., 1g., chorus groups. Sc. Interior. GUB

† **Jones family, The.** Edith Brown-Evarts. 3b., 1g. Sc. Plain room. BEY

Jones versus Jones. Florence Lewis Spare. 1m., 3w. Sc. Library in home. FSD

Jonesville board of Assessors, The. H. M. Doty. Rural Comedy. 6m., 2w. Sc. Assessor's room in town hall. DOT

Journey, The. Olive Tilford Dargan. 3m., 2w. Sc. Room in a Chinese farm house. DPF

Journeys end in lovers' meeting, a fifteen minute parlor play. Paula Mendel and Arthur Guiterman. 1m., 2w. Sc. Parlor of Old Post Inn at Tarrytown on the Hudson. Ladies' Home Journal 19: 9, Feb. 1902.

* **Joy of giving, The.** Marie Irish. Christmas play. 3b., 1g. Sc. Living room. IC

Jubilee, The. Anton Chekov. Trans. from the Russian by Olive Frances Murphy. 4m., 2w. Sc. Office of President of a bank. BFR, Poet Lore 31: 616–628, Winter. 1920.

Jubilee (Feest). Herman Heijermans. 7m., 2w. Sc. Prison Director's office. Drama 13: 325–331, July 1923.

Judge Offerheimer's first case. James F. Parsons. Farce. 11m., 2w. Sc. Court room. APP

Judge's secret. Adolph E. Reim. Melodrama. 1m., 2w. Sc. Interior. RE

Judgment of Indra, The. Dhan Gopal Mukerji. Indian play. 4m. Sc. Outer court of a monastery. SL, STV

* **Judgment of Solomon.** Rita Benton. Bible play. 6b., 2g., 1 baby, chorus. Sc. Hall of justice. BSD

* **Judith and Ariel.** Hester Donaldson Jenkins. Fresh air play. 15c. Sc. Disorderly looking room. JE

Julie. August Strindberg. Trans. by Arthur Swan. Tragedy. 3w. Sc. Large kitchen in manor house in Sweden. Poet Lore 22: 161–194, Summer 1911.

* **June magic.** Katharine Lord. 2b., 5g., chorus of g. Sc. A garden. LLP

* **Juniper baby, The.** Clara J. Denton. 3g. Sc. Sitting room. MBP

Junk: or, One of those Sunday mornings. Henry Clapp Smith. Comedy. about a group of amateur actors. 5m., 3w. Sc. Interior. FSD

Juno's bird. Alice Cook Fuller. 3b., 2g. Sc. Throne room. FU

* **Jurisprudence.** Seurnas O'Brien. Comedy. 9m., 1w. Sc. Room in court house at Ballybraggan. OD

Just a little mistake: Comedy. Elizabeth Gale. 1m., 5w. Sc. Interior. B
Just advertise. Mrs. George Cobb. Comedy in short episodes. 1m., 2w. Sc. Living room of small apartment. B
Just as well. J. Hartley Manners. 1m., 2w., 1s. Sc. Morning room of town-house in Mayfair. MH
Just before dawn. Granville Forbes Sturgis. Revolutionary war play. 4m., 2w. Sc. Living room of the inn. STR
Just like a story. Dorothy Cleather. 5w., chorus characters. Sc. A cottage room. CH
Just like a woman. William Giles and Josephine Giles. Farce. 1m., 1w. Sc. Interior. APP
Just like a woman. Lewis Carabel Munger. Comedy. 3m., 3w. Sc. Sitting room in a farm house. DEP
Just neighborly. Alexander Dean. 2m., 2w. Sc. Kitchen sitting room of a small home in New England. Drama 12: 10–12, 56–62. Oct.–Nov. 1921.
* **Just plain Dot.** Edith Paintor. Commencement play. 5b., 9g. Sc. Living room. EP
Just plain Jones. Harry M. Doty. Rural comedy. 4m., 4w. Sc. Sitting room. DOT
Just two men. Eugene Pillot. 2m. Sc. Bow of a coastwise freighter. STV
Just women. Colin C. Clements. 7w. Sc. Living room. FSD
* **Justice Whiskers' trial.** Mrs. Isabel Anderson. 3b., 3g., chorus groups. Sc. Vegetable garden in autumn. AE

K

Kagekiyo. Seami. Noh play of Japan. 2m., 2w. Sc. Stage. WAA
Kagekiyo. Ernest Fenollosa and Ezra Pound. Noh play of Japan. 2m., 2w., chorus. Sc. Japanese exterior. FEN
Kakitsubata. Ernest Fenollosa and Ezra Pound. Noh play of Japan. 1m., 1w., chorus. Sc. Japanese exterior. FEN
Kakitsuhata. Motokiyo. From the notes of Ernest Fenollosa and finished by Ezra Pound. 1m., 1w., chorus. Sc. Out of doors in Japan. Drama 6: 428–435, Aug. 1916.
Kanawa; a crown of iron spikes. Motokiyo. Trans. from the Japanese by T. Ochiai. Japanese classical drama. 3m., 1w. Sc. Not given. Poet Lore 23: 222–224, Summer 1912.
Kantan. No author given. Noh play of Japan. 7m., 1w., chorus. Sc. Japanese inn. WAA
Kara. George A. Crain. 3m., 3w. Sc. Room in apartment in N. Y. DAK
Katie's new hat. Alice C. Thompson. Farce. 6w. Sc. Sitting room. DEP
* **Katjen's garden.** Katharine Lord. 12c. Sc. Garden in front of a cottage in a Dutch town. LLP
Katy did. Rachel Crothers. 3m., 1w. Sc. Private law office. Smart Set 27: 129–136, Jan. 1909.
* **Katy in Gooseland.** Charles Barnard. 25 or more c. Sc. Yard in front of a house. HI

Kayoi Komachi. Ernest Fenollosa and Ezra Pound. Noh play of Japan. 2m., 1w., chorus. Sc. Japanese village. FEN

Keep your eye on the ball. Harry L. Newton. Comedy. 1m., 1w. Sc. Parlor. WHP

Keeping Christmas. Harriette Wilbur. Several c. Sc. Not given. Ladies' Home Journal 31: 34, Dec. 1914.

Keeping up appearances. W. W. Jacobs. Farce. 2m., 1w. Sc. Miserably furnished room. FSD

Keepsakes. Arthur Schnitzler. 1m., 1w. Sc. Prettily furnished sitting room. SA

Ketcham pardon, The. William and Kenneth Ellis. 4m. Sc. A library. American Poetry Magazine 1: 16–28, Aug. 1919.

Kettle sings, or the domestic conscience. Caroline S. Wild. Comedy. 1m., 10w. Sc. Interior. DPP

* **Key, The.** Edith Burrows. 16b., 17g. Sc. Comfortable modern living room. BBS

Kid curlers. Dorothy Waldo. Farce. 2m., 2w. Sc. Interior. B

‡ **Kidnapping, The.** Helen Clifford Wilbur. 6g. Sc. Music room. WEP

Killing time. Mary Moncure Parker. Fantasy. 2m., 1w. Sc. Springtime in a lovely wood. PM

King, The. Padraic H. Pearse. Irish morality play. 9m., 5b. Sc. A green before a monastery. PRZ, PS

King, The. Robert Emmons Rogers. 6m., 1w., dancing girls. Sc. Palace terrace of Herod. Harvard Monthly 47: 134–144, Jan. 1909.

King and commoner. Louise Saunders. 4m., 3w., chorus. Sc. Clearing in the forest. To be played out of doors. SAM

* **King Alfred and the cakes.** Lena Dalkeith. Early English historical play. 3b., 1g. Sc. Hut. DLP

* **King Alfred and the cakes.** Augusta Stevenson. 3b., 1g., many chorus characters. Sc. A forest in England. SC2

King Alfred and the neat-herd. Maurice Baring. Historical farce. 2m., 1w. Sc. Interior of a Neat-Herd's hut. BA

King Arthur's socks. Floyd Dell. Comedy. 1m., 3w. Sc. Living room of a summer cottage in Maine. DK, P1

* **King Christmas.** L. A. Sharp. 5b., chorus. Sc. Room with a raised platform. PCP

* **King Foxy of Muir Glacier.** Mrs. Isabel Anderson. 4b., 1g., chorus. Sc. Palace. AE

King laughs, The. Haakon M. Chevalier. Tragic fantasy. 3m., 2w., chorus. Sc. Audience hall of palace. CU

King Lear's wife. Gordon Bottomley. Verse. 2m., 7w. Sc. Bedchamber in a bungalow. BKL

King of the Jews, The. A passion play, Maurice Browne. 8m., 6w. guards and attendants. Sc. Foot of Calvary. Drama 6: 496–529, Nov. 1916.

King of the Jews, The. Frank Harris. 1m., 1w. Sc. Jerusalem. English Review 8: 8–12, Apr. 1911.

* **King of the year, The.** Ellen M. Willard. 17c. Sc. Throne room in a palace. WY

King Rene's daughter. Henrik Hertz. Trans. from the Dainsh by T. Martin. 6m., 2w. Sc. Garden. B, FSD

* **King Robert of Sicily.** Rita Benton. From poem by Longfellow of same title. 14b., 1g., 4 chorus groups. Sc. Throne-room. BSC

AN INDEX TO ONE-ACT PLAYS 113

King who had nothing to learn, The. Leon M. Lion. Fantastic comedy. 1m., 1w., 1b., 1g. Sc. Interior. FSD

King without peer. William Watson. 2m., minstrel behind the scenes. Sc. Palace of Alfred the Great. Fortnightly Review 93: 791–797, May 1910.

* **Kingdom of love, The.** Frances E. Christian. Christmas play. 34c. Sc. Room with Christmas decorations. EP

‡ **King's choice, The.** Ruth Levi. A Purim sketch. Jewish holiday play. 2b., 15g. Sc. Throne room. BLO

* **King's good friend, The.** Augusta Stevenson. 3b. Sc. The woods. SC1

King's letters, The. Evan Poole. Historical. 5m., 2w. Sc. Nobleman's house in 16th century. PA

King's threshold, The. William Butler Yeats. Verse. Irish background. 11m., 3w., chorus of w. Sc. Steps before the palace of the King. YC2, YK, YP2, YPP

Kinuta. Ernest Fenollosa and Ezra Pound. Noh play of Japan. 1m., 3w. Sc. Japanese background. FEN

Kiri no Meijiyama, a Noh drama in Japanese syllabics. S. Foster Damon. 3m., 2w., chorus. Sc. Not given. Dial 68: 205–213, Feb. 1920.

Kisses. S. Jay Kaufman. 2m., 4w. Sc. Drawing room. Smart Set 47: 259–266, Nov. 1915.

Kleptomaniac, The. Margaret Cameron. Comedy. 7w. Sc. Boudoir. CAC, FSD

Knave of hearts, The. Louise Saunders. 6m,. 4w., 6c. Sc. Stage. LE

Knave's move, The. William Brown Meloney. 4m., 1w. Sc. Back room of a saloon. US

Knight's return, The. George Santayana. Sequel to "A hermit of Carmel" Verse. Medieval Christian life. 1m., 2w. chorus. Sc. Wooded lawn before the gate of a castle. SAN

Knitting club, The. Helen S. Griffith. Comedy. Great War Background. 9w. Sc. Drawing room. B

Knitting girls count one, The. Elsie West Quaife. Patriotic play. 6w. Sc. Interior. FSD

Knot of white ribbon, A. Alice C. Thompson. 3w. Sc. Old fashioned parlor. PPP

* **Knotty problem, A.** Frederick Trevor Hill. Boy Scout farce. 6b., 2g. Sc. Parlor. HH

Knut at Roeskilde. Philip Merivale. Verse. Tragedy. 4m., 2w. chorus groups. Sc. Hall in an Iceland house of long ago. FOS

Kumasaka. Zenchiku Ujinobu. Noh play of ancient Japan. 2m., chorus. Sc. Stage. WAA

Kyogen (The bird catcher in hell) Esashi Juo. Farce. 2m., chorus. Sc. Hell. WAA

L

Ladies at twelve. George O'Neil. 2m, 1w. Sc. Living room. Smart Set 55: 73–80, July 1918.

Ladies of Athens. Mrs. M. A. Lipscomb. Comedy. 8w. Sc. Room in house in ancient Greece. WEP

Ladies strike, The. Helen Sherman Griffith. Farce on the servant problem. 8w. Sc. Employment office. PPP

Lady Anne. Doris F. Halman. Fantasy. 2m., 3w. Sc. Hall of a very old English country house. HAS

Lady Betty's burglar. Marjorie Benton Cooke. Colonial. 2m., 1w. Sc. Boudoir. CO

Lady cook, The. E. Lawrence Jenkins. 2m., 4w. Sc. Parlor. HI

Lady Flora's namesake. E. C. Herring. 1m., 1w. Sc. Modern room. FSD

Lady loses her hoop, The, a sad tale in sadder verse. Leisa Graeme Wilson. 2m., 1w., 5c. Sc. London park. Drama 12: 279–280, May 1922.

Lady of the hairpins, The. Mary Fenollosa. 1m., 5w. Sc. Upper story room in a Tokio Tea House. Smart Set 25: 140–149 Aug. 1908.

Lady of the opera house, The. Fanny Cannon. 2m., 2w. Sc. Interior. DEP

Lady Servant, A, or, Mistress for an hour. Will C. Sites. 1m. 1w. Sc. Interior. APP

Lady to call, A. Based on a story by Madeline Poole. Carl W. Pierce. 3w. Sc. Old fashioned sitting room. B

Lady with a dagger, The. Arthur Schnitzler. Translated from the German by Helen Tracy Porter. 2m., 1w. Sc. Small room in a picture gallery. SAA, Poet Lore 15: 1–18, Summer 1904.

Lady with the mirror, The. An Allegory. Rita Wellman. 2m., 2w. Sc. The Lady's temple. Drama 8: 299—316, Aug. 1918.

* **Ladybird.** Emma L. Johnston, Madalene D. Barnum. 4g. Sc. Yard JB

Lady compassionate, The. Katherine Kirker. 1m., 1w., 2b., 1 baby. Sc. Large room in Dante's home, Florence. Poet Lore 33: 239–245, Summer 1922.

* **Lafayette's toast.** Augusta Stevenson. 11b., chorus of boys. Sc. Banquet hall. SC4

Lais. Isaac Rieman Baxley. Grecian episode. 6m., 1w. Sc. Out-of-door banquet at Corinth. BAX

Lamma's Eve. Edith Randolph. Fantasy. 2m., 1w. Sc. Interior Susan's cottage. Poet Lore 32: 288–306, Summer 1921.

Lamp, The. George Calderon. 2m., 1w., 1b. Sc. Outside a rough open hut in the forest. CA

Lamp, The. Edward Heyman Pfeiffer. 1m., 2w. Sc. Large room in a villa. International 7: 108, 110—111. April 1913.

Lamp of God, The. Morley Roberts. 2m., 4w. Sc. An old high garret with sloping walls and a dormer window. RF

Lamp of Heaven, The; a Chinese play. Jessica Belle Welborn-Smith. Boxer Rebellion in China. 3m., 2w. Sc. Palace in Pekin. FOS

Land of heart's desire, The. William Butler Yeats. Verse. 3m., 2w., 1c. Sc. Irish kitchen interior showing hearth. CBI, FSD, LE, YI, YP2, Bibelot 9: 179–213, June 1903.

* **Land of vacation, The.** Bertha Iren Tobin. 16c. Sc. Fairyland. TO

Land of the Aionwas, The. A masque. Edwin Ford Piper. Historical play about Marquette and Joliet. 8m. speaking, 50 other Sc. Woods on Iowa shore of Mississippi. Midland 8: 59–77, Feb. 1922.

Land of unborn children, The. Maurice Maeterlinck. Chapter from his Bluebird. 2w., 3b., children. Sc. Woodcutter's cottage. Ladies' Home Journal 27 : 13–14, Jan. 1910.

Laodice and Danae. Gordon Bottomley. Verse. 1m., 8w., Chorus Sc. A lofty chamber. BKL, FOS

Large order, A. H. S. Griffith. 1m., 2w. Sc. Interior. B

‡ **Lark, The.** Katharine Lord. 7m., 5w. Sc. Before an Indian lodge. LLR

Larry. Harold Sander. Farce. 4m., 4w. Sc. Public room of hotel. FP

‡ **Last day of school, The.** Edith Brown-Evarts. 13b., 5g., chorus Sc. Schoolroom. BEY

‡ **Last day of the term, The;** a play for eight girls in one act. H. M. Paull. 8g. Sc. Classroom. FSD

Last drop, The. Lancelot Bellinger and Guy Moyston. 3m. Sc. Interior. FSD

Last faring, The. Hermann Hagedorn. Verse. 2m. Sc. Unimportant. HP

Last man in, The. William B. Maxwell. 6m., 1w. Sc. Parlour of a humble tavern. REP

Last masks. Arthur Schnitzler. Translated from the German. 5M., 1w. Sc. In the public hospital, Vienna. SAA

Last of the Cragills, The. Rita Johnson Young. 1m., 1w. Sc. Dining room of an old southern mansion. WHP

Last of the Lowries, The. Paul Greene. 1m. 3w. Sc. Kitchen of a rude dwelling place. CFP

Last race, The. H. Hoeffer McMechan. 1m., 2w. Sc. Jockey's room in trainers' quarters. WEP

Last rehearsal, The. Irene Jean Crandall. 2m., 3w. Sc. Room. DEP

‡ **Last rehearsal, The.** E. M. Peixotto. Farce. 6b. Sc. Disorderly stage. PET

Last sitting, The. Marguerite Merington. From the picture "Mona Lisa." 1m., 1w. Sc. Artist's studio in Florence in the 16th Century. MP2

Last straw, The. Bosworth Crocker. 2m. 1w., 2b. Sc. Kitchen in a basement flat. CK, CL, LC, MA

Last visit, The. Hermann Sudermann. Translated from German 5m., 3w. Sc. Richly furnished room in garrison quarters. SU

Last woman, The. George Soule. 6m., 1w. Sc. Council room. Little Review 1 : 20–25, Feb. 1915.

Late delivery, A. John Hay Beith. 3m., 2w. Sc. Dining room. BEC

Laugh and grow wise. Frederick J. Pohl. 8m., 2w. Sc. Fanciful interior. FSD

Laughing gas. Theodore Dreiser. 7m. chorus. Sc. Operating room in a hospital. DP, Smart Set 45 : 85–94, Feb. 1915.

Laughter and song. Archibald Humboldt. Farce, 3m., 5w. Sc. Interior. MAP

Laughter in court. Captain John Kendall. 4m. Sc. Den in a comfortable residence. FSD

Law. Lester Luther. 3m., 3w. Chorus of children. Sc. Stage entirely black. Forum 53 : 776–779, June 1915.

Law-suit, The. Roderick Benedix. Translated by B. H. Clark. 5m. Sc. Interior. FSD

Lawyer's mistake, A. James Burghlie. 3m., 1w. Sc. Large, well-furnished sitting room near Paris. Smart Set 31: 125–136, May 1910.

Lay figure, The. Morley Roberts. 1m. 1w. Sc. Painter's studio. RF

Lazarus. Anna Hempstead Branch. Dramatic verse. 3m., 4w., 1b., 1g., chorus. Sc. Exterior. BRC

Laziest man in the world, The. Carl Webster Pierce. Comedy. 4m. Sc. Room in an apartment. FSD

Leading lady, The. Anita Fallon. Farce-Comedy. Sc. An elegantly furnished boudoir. B

Lean years, The. Mary Katharine Reely. 2m., 2w. Sc. Front porch of a prosperous southern farm house. REE

‡ **Learning lessons.** Mrs. C. F. Fernald and Olivia L. Wilson. 2b. 2g., Chorus. Sc. School room or sitting room. BAB

† **Leave the woman out.** Leon Gordon and Charles King. 3m. Sc. Room which is study, workroom, and library combined. GG

† **Left.** Mrs. C. F. Fernald and Olivia L. Wilson. 1b., 1g. Sc. Waiting room of depot. BAB

Legacy, The. Pierre C de C. Translated from French by Barret H. Clark. 3m., 3w. Sc. Outside a French house in the 18th century. FSD

Legend. Floyd Dell. 1m., 1w., Sc. A small room. DK

Legend of Saint Nicholas, A. Beulah Marie Dix. 9m., 2w., 2s. Sc. Bare stage. Poet Lore 25: 473–495, Autumn 1914.

‡ **Lend a hand.** Frederic Leighton Fay. Scout play. 8b. Sc. Camp. FET

L'eroica. Cesare Lodovici. Translated from the Italian by Petronelle Sombart. 5m., 5w. Sc. Garden with handsome villa at one side. Poet Lore 34: 159–176, Summer 1923.

Lesson in harmony, A. Alfred Austin. 2m., 1w. Sc. Exterior. FSD

Letter, The. Mary Aldis. 3m. Sc. Writing room of a club. AP

Letter from home. Seymour S. Tibbals. Thanksgiving play. 4m. Sc. Reading room of club. EP

Letter of introduction, A. Ward Macauley. 3m. 2w. Sc. Sitting room. PPP

Liberty thrift girls, The. Marie Doran. Great War. 8w., 1b. Sc. Living room. FSD

Licensed. Lawrence Langner. 1m., 2w. Sc. Parlor. LAF

Lie, The. Ludwig Lewisohn. 2m., 2w. Sc. Library of attractive apartment. Smart Set 41: 137–142, Dec. 1913.

Lie that Jack built, The. Georgia Earle. Comedy. 2m., 2w. Sc. Interior. DEP

Life. J. M. Machado de Assis. Translated from Portuguese by Isaac Goldberg. 4m. Sc. A rock, horizon in distance. Stratford Journal 5: 117–129, Sept. 1919.

* **Life beyond, The.** Rita Benton. From the story by Mrs. Gatty. 10b. Sc. Stage with upper and under platforms. BSC

* **Life in New York.** Blanche Shoemaker Wagstaff. Colonial. 1b., 1g. Sc. Kitchen in old New York. WCP

Life insurance. Herbert C. Sargent. Farce. 1m., 1w. Sc. Interior. SAR

Life is a dream. Basil Hall Chamberlain. ed. Japanese lyric drama. 3m., chorus. Sc. Chinese village inn, 8th century. CHB

Life is a dream. Colin Campbell Clements. 3m., chorus. Sc. Yard of a village inn, Kantumu. Poet Lore 31: 204–209, Summer 1920.

Life is always the same. Louise Gebhard Cann. 1m., 1w. Sc. Large room in a rancher's house. Drama 9: 1–20, May 1919.

Light, The. Frances Gillespy Wickes. 15c. Sc. The hearth-room of America. WCB

Light-bearer, The. Tapanmohan Chatterji. Translated from the Bengali by the author. Symbolic. 6m., others. Sc. Very dark room. Drama 8: 383–389, Aug. 1918.

Light from another world, A. C. H. McGurrin. 2m., 1w. Sc. Drawing room in a Fifth avenue mansion. ML

Light gray or dark. Margaret Macnamara. 1m., 2w. Sc. London tenement attic. DAN

Light in the window, The. Theodore Dreiser. 10m., 7w. Sc. Living room and street scene at the same time. DP, International 10: 6–8, 32, Jan. 1916.

Light of other days, The. Laura Spencer Portor. From her story The Christmas dance at Red Oaks. 2m., 3w. Sc. Library of old southern home. Ladies' Home Journal 23: 20, Dec. 1905.

Light of the star of peace, The. Elizabeth Montgomery. Any number of players. Sc. a grotto. Ladies' Home Journal 35: 87. Dec. 1918.

Lighting of the Christmas tree, The. Josephine L. Palmer and Annie L. Thorp. From The Christmas Guest of Selma Lagerlöf. 3m. 2w., 2b. Sc. Living room. FSD

Lighting of the torch, The. Fannie R. Buchanan. Masque. 8m., 2w., Indians, pilgrims, spectres, etc. Sc. Woods with rustic altar at the back. Drama 10: 350–354, July–Sept. 1920.

Lights of happy land, The. Marion Short. 1m., 3w. Sc. Sitting room in typical New Orleans home. FSD

Like a book. Grover Theis. 4m., 3w. Sc. Studio-apartment and section of hallway leading to it. TN

Like father like son, a bit of domesticity. Leila Weekes Wilson. 2m., 1w. Sc. Motor car on country road. Drama 13: 188–191 Feb. 1923.

Likely story, A, a roadside comedy. Laurence Housman. 4m., 1w Sc. Road on the outskirts of a town. FSD

Likes o' me, The. Wilfred T. Coleby. 3m., 2w. Sc. Squalid little shop. FSD

Lima beans. Alfred Kreymborg. Farce. 2m. 1w. Sc. Dining room. KMP, KMR, MA, P3

Lincoln's birthday, Anychild learns from Lincoln. F. Ursula Payne. 15c. Sc. Room in any house. PP

Line of life, The. Leo Sarkadi. 4m., 3w., 1 parrot. Sc. Magnificent hall in London town house. International 10: 341–346, Nov. 1916.

Line of no resistance, The. Percival Wilde. 1m., 2w. Sc. Living room. FSD

Link, The. August Strindberg. Translated from Swedish. 22m., 3w., chorus. Sc. Court room. STQ

Lion and lady, The. Marjorie Benton Cooke. 1m., 1w. Sc. A study. CO

* **Lion and the mouse, The.** Emma L. Johnston, and Madalene Barnum. 2b. Sc. A wood. JB

Listening. John Redhead Froome, Jr. 3w. Sc. Interior of a simple house. Poet Lore 28: 422–431, Vacation 1917.

Literati, The. Theodosia Garrison. 8m., 4w. Sc. Drawing room. Smart Set 13: 149–150, May 1904.

Literature. Arthur Schnitzler. Translated from German by Pierre Loving. 2m. 1w. Sc. Sitting room. SAA, SCW, SL, International 9: 331–336, Nov. 1915.

Lithuania. Rupert Brooke. 5m., 2w. Sc. Inside a hut in Lithuania. STK

* **Little birds, The.** Emma L. Johnston and Madalene D. Barnum. 4g. Sc. A nest in a tree. JB

Little black devil, The. Gordon V. May. The effect of a hindu image. 2m., 1w. Sc. Interior. DEP

Little blue guinea-hen, The. Martel de Janville, Comtesse de, Sibylle Gabrielle Marie Antoinette de Riquetti de Mirabeau. Translated by R. T. House. 5m., 4w. Sc. Large room with Empire furnishings. Poet Lore 30 : 60–80, Spring 1919.

Little boy out of the wood, The. Kathleen Conyngham Greene. 1w., 1b. Sc. Skirts of a small wood near Epping forest. GDL

* **Little Bridget.** Netta Syrett. 1b., 4g., chorus. Sc. Kitchen in an 18th century farmhouse. SSF

Little Co-ed. Harry Osborne. 1m., 1w. Sc. Interior. B

Little Columbine. Granville Forbes Sturgis. Columbine play. 3m., 2w. Sc. Little home of Pierrot and Pierrette. STR

* **Little Doubt.** Mrs. Isabel Anderson. 4b., 2g., chorus. Sc. Forest with falling snow. AE

Little Face. Roland Oliver. 5m., 5w. Sc. Cave dwellings in forest clearing. Smart Set 44 : 131–141, Sept. 1914.

* **Little fish, The.** Augusta Stevenson. 2b. Sc. River shore. SC1

Little fowl play, A. Harold Owen. Farce. 2m., 2w., 1b. Sc. Interior. FSD

Little game with fate, A. Louise Lathans Wilson. Comedy. 4m., 3w. Sc. Sitting room. DPP

* **Little gray lady, The.** Emile Blackmore Stapp and Eleanor Cameron. A November play. 5b., 5g., 1 group of g. Sc. Attractively furnished child's bedroom. SCH

* **Little helpers.** Louise Fallenstein Gauss. Christmas play. 16b., 2g., chorus group. Sc. Simple living room. PCP

* **Little heroes.** David Pinski. 6c. Sc. A large living room in a peasant's house, which has been damaged by canonading. PT, PTT, Stratford Journal 1 : 17–24, June 1917.

* **Little homemakers.** Virginia Olcott. Play of conservation. 4g. Sc. Kitchen in an American home. OPA

* **Little housekeepers.** Marie Irish. 4g. Sc. Kitchen. IPP

* **Little Jack's Christmas.** Elizabeth F. Guptill. Any number of children. Sc. Interior. EP

* **Little John joins the band of Robin Hood.** Alice Cook Fuller. Robin Hood play. 2b., chorus. Sc. Forest. FU

Little Johnny. John Drinkwater. 10m., 4w., others. Sc. Assize Court. English Review 33 : 292–309, Oct. 1921.

† **Little king, The.** Witter Bynner. Historical play of the French Revolution. 2m., 1w., 2c. Sc. In the temple at Paris, a room in which was imprisoned Louis XVII the Boy-King of France. BB, BYL, Forum 51 : 605–632, April 1914.

* **Little Miss America and the happy children.** Mary Moncure Parker. Jingle history of the U. S. 24c. Sc. Platform or schoolroom. B

Little Miss Enemy. Harry L. Newton. 1m., 1w. Sc. Interior of Palm Beach hotel. DEP

* **Little Miss Muffet.** Mrs. Herbert Richmond. 2g. Sc. Nursery. BR
* **Little mortal child, The.** Gladys LaDue Evans. 1b., 1g., 4 wood folk. Sc. Sheltered nook in the woods. Poet Lore 32: 409–415, Autumn 1921.

Little mother, The. A. J. Schindler. Comedy. 5m., 3w. Sc. Poorly furnished room. SCP

Little mother of the slums, The. Emily Hervey Denison. 6m., 5w. Sc. Palatial office of a large business concern. DL

‡ **Little owl.** W. A. Stigler. Indian play. 7c. Sc. Open space in the woods. STA

* **Little people of Autumn.** Virginia Olcott. Sc. Sc. A potato field. OP
* **Little Petsy.** Lady Bell. Comedy. 3g. Sc. Unimportant. BEJ
* **Little pilgrims.** Louise E. Tucker and Estelle L. Ryan. 5b., 1g., chorus characters. Sc. Deck of the Mayflower. TRH
* **Little pilgrim's progress, A.** Constance D'Arcy Mackay. Morality play. 12c. Sc. An inn. MHH, St. Nicholas 37: 60–3, Nov. 1909.
* **Little pink lady, The.** Lindsey Barbee. 6g. Sc. Room with open window. BLP

Little red mare, The. O. E. Young. Farce. 3m. Sc. Kitchen of a farmhouse. FP

* **Little red riding hood.** Alice Cook Fuller. 2b., 2g. Sc. Interior. FU

Little shepherdess, The. Andre Rivoire. Trans. from the French by Barrett H. Clark. 1m., 2w. Sc. In the woods. FSD

Little silver ring, The. Edward Knoblauch. 2w. Sc. Interior. FSD

* **Little sparrow, A.** Emma L. Johnston and Madalene D. Barnum. 2b. Sc. A wood. JB

Little stone house, The. George Calderon. 5m., 2w. Sc. Sitting room in a Russian house in a provincial town. CA, REP, SIJ, SL

Little supper, The. Philip Moeller. A comedy of the Grande Maitresse. 2m., 1w., 1s. Sc. A little pavilion in the park of the chateau of Lucienne. MF

Little tiff, A. Newell Bent. Farce. 6m. Sc. Interior. B

* **Little Tuk's dream.** E. Harcourt Williams. Adapted from Hans Andersen. 5b., 3g. Sc. Bedroom. WI

Little wax candle. Louise Norton. Farce. 2m., 2w., 1g. Sc. A grey bedroom. NOR

Living. Lillian P. Wilson. 3w., 1c. Sc. Stage with effect of mystery. WIF

Living dead, The. F. Carmichael Brunton. A fantasy. 6m., 2w. Sc. Cemetery. International 11: 31–32, Jan. 1917.

Living hours. Arthur Schnitzler. Trans. from the German. 3m. Sc. Carefully tended garden in a suburb of Vienna. LO, SAA, Translated by Colin Clements and Alice Ernest. Stratford journal 4: 155–166, Mar. 1919; Trans. by Helen Tracy Portor. Poet Lore 17: 36-45, Spring 1906.

Local and long distance. H. Manley Dana. Farce. 1m., 6w. Sc. Interior. B

Locked chest, The. John Masefield. 3m., 1w., chorus. Sc. A room MLS, MTA, SS

Locked door. Malcolm W. Davis. Play of organized charity. 2m., 2w. Sc. Small bare attic room. DAA

Locust flower, The. Pauline Brooks Quinton. Fantasy. 1m., 1w., 7 shades. Sc. Garden. Q

Logical extreme, The. George Soule. 1m., 1w. Sc. Private dining room in a General's house in Berlin. Little Review 1 : 3–6, Jan. 1915.

* **Lonely little evergreen tree, The.** Lettie C. Van Derveer. 2b., 2 chorus groups. Sc. Stage represents snowy out door scene. VC

† **Lonesome like.** Harold Brighouse. 2m., 2w. Sc. Interior of a cottage in a village. CBI, LE, REP

Long live the empress! Louis Gilmore. 4m., 2w. Sc. Apartment of Empress Catherine in the Winter Palace. Double Dealer 3 : 26–36, Jan. 1922.

Long time ago, A. Floyd Dell. Fantasy. 3m., 2w. Sc. Courtyard of a palace. DK, Forum 51 : 261–277, Feb. 1914.

Long voyage home. Eugene O'Neill. 8m., 3w. Sc. Bar of a low dive on London water front. OMC, Smart Set 53 : 83–94, Oct. 1917.

Longing. George Calderon. Fantastic subjective drama. 5m., 5w., 3c., chorus. Sc. A bedroom. CA

Look after Louise. Charles Frederick Nirdlinger. 3m., 1w. Sc. Living room. NI

* **"Look of things, The."** Clara J. Denton. 3g., 2 chorus groups b. and g. Sc. Not given. I

Look out for Hezikiah. Louise Rand Bascom. Farce. 3m., 1w. Sc. Office of the college dean. MAP

Looking for more; or, Turn about is fair play. C. M. Lindsey. Farce. 4m., 2w. Sc. Drawing room. B

Looking for trouble. J. Barnes and Abel Beaman. 6m. Sc. Interior. B

* **Looking-glass, The.** Major P. Trevor. 3b., 4g. Sc. Interior. FSD

* **Lord Malapert of Moonshine Castle.** E. S. Brooks. 5b., 5g., 2 chorus groups. Sc. A garden. SAB, SAC

Lord of the Harvest, The. Laurence Housman. Morality. 6m., 1w., 2c. Sc. Ground floor of a mill. FSD

† **Lord's prayer, The.** François Coppée. Trans. from the French. Play of the French Revolution. 3m., 3w., chorus. Sc. Room on ground floor with windows overlooking a garden. WWS

Lord's will, The. Paul Greene. 1m., 2w. Sc. Kitchen dining room of tenant house in eastern North Carolina. Poet Lore 33 : 366–384, Autumn 1922.

Loser, The. Paul Eldridge, 2m., 1w. Sc. Comfortable living room. Drama 11 : 166–170, Feb. 1921.

Losing game, A. Lady Augusta Gregory. 6m., 2w., others. Sc. Kitchen in farmer's cottge. The Gael 21 : 384–388, Dec. 1902.

‡ **Lost but found.** E. M. Piexotto. Farce. 8b. Sc. Office of The Home for Lost Boys. PET

† **Lost colors, The.** Edith F. A. U. Painton. 1b., 2g. Sc. Stage with desk and chairs. PAD

* **Lost firewood, The.** Emilie Blackmore Stapp and Eleanor Cameron. An October play. 5b., 5g. 5 groups g. Sc. A forest. SCH

* **Lost pocketbook, The.** Marie Irish. 3b., 2g. Sc. Out of doors. IPP

Lost saint, The. Douglas Hyde. Trans. by Lady Gregory. 2m., 6c. Sc. Large dining room. Samhain Oct. 1902. p. 19–23.

Lost sheep. Belford Forrest. 2m., 4w. Sc. Garden of London villa. Smart Set 50: 71–75, Oct. 1916.

† **Lost silk hat, The.** Lord Dunsany. 5m. Sc. Fashionable London street. DF

* **Lost toys.** May Pemberton. 9c. Sc. In a wood. PC

† **Lost village;** eighteenth century and twentieth century contrast. Margaret F. Hill. U. S. Colonial history. 6m., 5w., chorus. Sc. Commons of a Massachusetts village. MAP

Lottie sees it through. Ragna B. Eskil. Great War play. 3m., 4w. Sc. Scantily furnished living room. DEP

Louis Quinze Salon, The; or, A friend of Mrs. Robinson. Richard Butler Glaenzer. 2m., 1w. Sc. Art gallery. Smart Set 24: 102–104, Feb. 1908.

Louise. J. H. Speenhoff. Trans. from the Dutch by A. V. C. Huizinga and Pierre Loving. 2m., 1w., 1s. Sc. Large fashionably appointed room. SL

Love among the lions. Lewis Beach. Farce. 2m., 2w. Sc. A gaudily furnished room in a New York apartment house. BF

Love behind the scenes. Mary Moncure Parker. Stage play. 2m., 1w. Sc. Back of the stage. PM

Love child, The. Frederick Fenn and Richard Pryce. 1m., 1b., 5w. Sc. Living room poorly furnished. English Review 4: 409–420, Feb. 1910.

Love conquers revenge. Binney Gunnison. Adapted from "The Cipher Dispatch" by Robert Byr. 2m., 2w. Sc. Bare room. GU

Love-fibs. Margaret Macnamara. Rustic comedy. 2m., 1w. Sc. Kitchen in English cottage. DAN

* **Love flower, The.** Bell Eliott Palmer. 1b., 16g. Sc. Indoors or out. Lawn or garden scene. EP

Love in a French kitchen, a mediaeval farce. Trans. from the old French by Colin C. Clements and John M. Saunders. 1m., 2w. Sc. French kitchen in the middle ages. Poet Lore 28: 722–729, Winter 1917.

Love-in-idleness. E. M. Lent. 1m., 3w. Sc. Interior. FSD

Love magic. Gregorio Martinez Sierra. Trans. from Spanish by John Garrett Underhill. 3m., 2w., 1g. Sc. Pierrot's garden. Drama 7: 40–61, Feb. 1917.

Love me, love my dog. Lady Speyer. 3m., 1w. Sc. Drawing room. Smart Set 58: 73–82, Jan. 1919.

Love of one's neighbors. Leonid Andreyev. Trans. from the Russian by Thomas Seltzer. Satire. 15m., 7w., 1c., man chorus characters. Sc. A wild place in the mountains. AND, SL

Love of women, The. Frederic Arnold Kummer. 5m., 1w. Sc. Living room of a miser in Russia. Smart Set 28: 123–130 Aug. 1909.

Love passage, A. W. W. Jacobs and Philip E. Hubbard. 3m., 1w. Sc. Steamer cabin. FSD

Love pirate, The. Grace Ford. 2m., 3w. Sc. Living room. FSD

Love potion, The. Ernest S. Jaros. Farce. 3m., 3w. Sc. Interior. DEP

Love suit. A. W. Gordon Smythies. Romantic comedy. 1m., 1w. Sc. Morning room. WEP

Love test, The. Harry Lorenzo Chapin. 3m., 2w. Sc. A hacienda in California. CHA

Love test, The. Anonymous. 1m., 3w. 7 scenes. Drawing rooms and dining rooms. Smart Set 2: 145–156, Dec. 1900.

Lovebird's matrimonial agency. Harold Sander. 3m., 4w. Sc. Parlor. FP

Lovliest thing, The. Roland Pertwee. 3m., 3w., 1g., voices. Sc. Comfortable and rather pretentious living room. Ladies' Home Journal 39 : 10–11, 150, 152–154, 157, 158, Dec. 1922.

Lover, The. Gregorio Martinez Sierra. Trans. from the Spanish by John Garrett Underhill. 1m., 2w. Sc. Salon in a Royal Palace. MR, Stratford Journal 5 : 33–44, July 1919.

Love's diplomacy. Maurice Hageman and F. A. Small. Comedy. 2m., 2w. Sc. Interior. DPP

Love's heavy burden. Yone Noguchi. Noh play of Japan. 4m., 1w., chorus. Sc. Not given. Poetry Review 10 : 18–22, Jan. 1919.

† **Love's stratagem,** (Author not given) Verse. Comedy. 2b., 2g. BU

Love's young dream. Agnes M. Miall. 2w. Sc. Sitting room. FSD

Love's young dream. Robert Garland. 1m., 1w. Sc. Poorly furnished bedroom. Smart Set 40 : 83–87, Aug. 1913.

Loving cup, The. Alice Brown. 4m., 9w. Sc. Interior. B, BO, Woman's Home Companion 40 : 11–12, 55, 56 May 1913.

Lucinda's whim. H. S. Mackaye. Farce. 3m., 2w. Sc. Interior FSD

* **Luck of Santa Claus, The.** B. C. Porter. 33c. Sc. Santa's workshop. FP

Luck of war, The. Gwen John. 3m., 3w. Sc. A kitchen living room in England. REP

* **Luckiest girl, The.** Alice C. Thompson. Comedy. 4g. Sc. Interior. DEP

Luckiest man, The. Thomas Grant Springer and Edward Gage. 2m., 1w., Sc. Living room of city apartment. Smart Set 37 : 135–141, July 1912.

* **Lucky Hallowe'en, A.** Eleanore Hubbard. Play of the settlement of the U. S. 2b., 3g., chorus. Sc. Log cabin in the woods of what is now Ohio. HUD

Lucky Peter. Robert Higginbotham. 4m., Sc. Waiting room of physician. FSD

Lucullus's dinner party. Maurice Baring. Historical farce. 2m., 3w., 1s. Sc. Room in Lucullus' house. BA

* **Lucky Locket.** Lady Bell. 3g. Sc. Drawing room. BR

Lumber room, The. Catherine Bellaiis Gaskoin. 1m., 1w. Sc. Almost empty lumber room. GAL

Lunch in the suburbs, A. Helen G. Ludington. Farce. 10w. Sc. Parlor. FSD

M

"M - R - S". Della J. Evans. 3m., 4w. Sc. Living room. EV

* **Maccabean case, A.** Irma Kraft. Hanukkah play. 10b., 3g. Sc. Living room. KPP

McDonough's wife. Lady Isabelle Gregory. Irish comedy. 1m., 2w., Sc. A very poor room GRZ

† **Mad! Mad!** Alice W. Chaplin. 5g. Sc. Reception room in a private school for girls. CHC

Madame. Granville Forbes Sturgis. Psychology of a woman. 3m., 1w. Sc. Boudoir. STR

Madame de Portment's school. E. C. Wilkinson. 6w. Sc. Room in a boarding school. FSD

Made in Heaven. J. J. Bell. 1m., 1w. Sc. A ball room. Smart Set 19: 82–83, July 1906.

Made in Heaven. Mathilde Shapiro. Comedy. 2m., 3w. Sc. Living room in New York apartment. SCT

Mademoiselle Plato, an unplatonic object lesson. Curtis Dunham. 2m., 2w. Sc. Studio in New York. Smart Set 40: 133–140, Aug. 1913.

Mademoiselle Prudence. Thomas Littlefield Marble. 1m., 1w. Sc. Interior. PPP

‡ **Mademoiselle's mistake.** Clara J. Denton. 2g. Sc. Rooms of a dancing teacher. EP

Madhouse, The. Henry Bailey Stevens. 6m., 1w. Sc. 1 Garden in front of madhouse walls. Sc. 2. Madhouse library. STE

Madman on the roof, The. Kau Kikuchi, tr. from the Japanese. Modern Japan. 5m., 2w. Sc. Backyard of a Japanese house. IW

Madonna. George Middleton. 2m., 1w., 1s. Sc. Living room and library combined. ME

Madonna Dianora. Hugo von Hofmannsthal. Trans. from the German by Harriet Betty Boas. 1m., 1w., 1s. Sc. Garden of a palace in France. HM, SL

Madretta. Stark Young. 2m., 1w. Sc. Levee in Mississippi. YA, YAT

Maeterlinckian moving day, A. Corinne Rockwell Swain. 3m., 3w., 1b. Sc. Neglected garden at back of house. Smart Set 37: 117–120, June 1912.

* **Maggie Ann.** E. M. Fotheringham. 3g. Sc. Sitting room. FG

* **Magic chest.** Jean Ross. Hallowe'en play. 12c. Sc. Room in a medieval castle. MAP

Magic glasses, The. George Fitzmaurice. 3m., 3w. Sc. Kitchen interior. FF

Magic sea shell, a play for the sea shore, The. John Farrar. 5b., 2g., several others. Sc. Dock at edge of pool. Bookman 57: 511–520, July 1923.

Magic tabloid, The. Dorothy Cleather. 2w. Sc. Drawing room. CH

Magic theatre, The. Trans. from "El Retablo de las maravillas" of Cervantes by Edith Fahnstock and Florence Donnell White. 8m., 3w., townspeople. Sc. None given. Poet Lore 32: 234–243, Summer 1921.

Magical city, The. Zoe Akins. 10m. 4w. Sc. Luxurious private sitting room in N. Y. hotel. Forum 55: 507–550, May 1916.

Magnanimity. Seumas O'Brien. Comedy. 8m., chorus. Sc. Back parlor of a country public house. OD

Magnanimous lover, The. St. John G. Ervine. Irish play. 3m., 2w. Sc. Kitchen and living room of a cottage in a North Irish village. CBI, ER, ERA

Maid, The. Beulah King. Comedy. 1m., 7w. Sc. Study of a fashionable summer home. FSD

† **Maid of France.** Harold Brighouse. 3m., 2w. Sc. Square in a French town before the statue of Jeanne d'arc C1, REP

Maid of honour, A. Edward G. Hemmerde. Play of England at the time of the Puritan Revolution. 6m., 1w. Sc. Interior. FSD

Maid to order. Helen Sherman Griffith. Farce of boarding school life. 6w. Sc. Interior. B

Maid's prologue, The. Arthur Ketchum. 2m., 3w. Sc. Hillside Poet Lore 25 : 206–209, Summer 1914.

Maiden over the wall. Bertram Bloch. Fantasy. 2m., 1w. Sc. Garden. Drama 8 : 436–453, Aug. 1918.

Major explains, The. W. R. Walkes. 1m., 1w. Sc. Drawing room FSD

"Make-believe." E. C. Rackstraw and W. Muskerry. Comedy. 2m., 2w. Sc. Living room. FSD

† **Maker of dreams, The.** Oliphant Down. Fantasy. Pierrot play. 2m., 1w. Sc. Room in an old cottage. Cl, CBI, DM, FSD, REP

Maker of men, A. Alfred Sutro. A study in sentiment. 1m., 1w. Sc. A little sitting room. FSD, SFA

Makeshifts. Gertrude Robins. 2m., 2w. Sc. Sitting-room. CBI

* **Making a flag.** Bertha E. Bush. United States Revolutionary War play. 1b., 3g., chorus. Sc. Room in a colonial house in Philadelphia. ED

Making a man. Emma Beatrice Brunner. 2m., 2w. Sc. Interior BRB

* **Making the best of things.** Clara J. Denton. May day play. 5b., 5g. Sc. Sitting room. DAH

Malinda and the Duke. Mary Bonham. Farce. 2m., 6w. Sc. Sitting room. BUP

Man about the place, The. Harold Brighouse. 3m., 6w. Sc. Lawn BRP

Man about town, A. Stanislaus Stange. 4m. Sc. An elegant interior. WHP

Man and a maid, A. Helen M. Palmer. 2m., 2w. Sc. Interior. PPP

Man and his wife, A. Colin C. Clements. Farce from the Japanese. 2m., 1w. Sc. Japanese interior. FSD, Poet Lore 31 : 197–203, Summer 1920.

Man can only do his best, A. Kenneth Sawyer Goodman. 6m., 2w. Sc. An attic room. GQ

† **Man from Brandon, The.** J. M. Taylor. Football theme. Farce. 3m., 4w. Sc. Interior. B

Man hunt, The. Harlan Thompson. 2m., 1w. Sc. Pleasant bedroom. Smart Set 59 : 87–98, June 1919.

Man in the bowler hat, The. A. A. Milne. 3m., 1w. Sc. Ordinary sitting room. Ladies' Home Journal 40 : 5, 106, 108, 111–112, Apr. 1923.

Man in the stalls, The. Alfred Sutro. 2m., 1w. Sc. Sitting room of a little flat. CBI, FSD, SF

Man in the street, The. Louis N. Parker. 2m., 1w. Sc. Interior FSD

Man masterful, The. George Middleton. 2w. Sc. Room in a flat. ME, Forum 42 : 369–382, Oct. 1909.

Man next door, The. Edwin Bateman Morris. Farcical comedy. 2m., 2w. Sc. Hall in a modern apartment building. PPP

Man of the world, A. Marie von Ebner-Eschenbach. Trans. by R. T. House. 3m. Sc. Bachelor apartment comfortably furnished. Poet Lore 22 : 128–133, Spring 1911.

† **Man on the kerb, The.** Alfred Sutro. 1m., 1w. Sc. An underground room, bare except for a little broken furniture. FSD, SF, SS

Man outside, The. Helen Bagg. Farce. 3m., 1w. Sc. Library of a home. PPP

Man proposes. Sidney Grundy. 1m., 2w. Sc. Simple interior. FSD

Man the life boat. Leedham Bantock and Percy Greenbank. 4m., 1w. Sc. Interior of sea Captain's cottage. BAO

Man to order, A. Kate Masterson. 2m., 1w. Sc. Hallway of country club. Smart Set 4: 155–157, May 1901.

Man upstairs, The. Augustus Thomas. 2m., 2w., 1s. Sc. Dining room. US

Man who came back. Katharine Kavanaugh. 1m., 2w. Sc. Interior. DEP

† **Man who couldn't say "No," The.** Claudia Lucas Harris. 2m., 2w., 1c. Sc. Sitting room. SB

* **Man who didn't believe in Christmas, The.** Mary Austin. 1m., 2w., 10b., 4g. Sc. Living room of modern house. St. Nicholas 45: 156–162, Dec. 1917.

Man who never worried, The. H. R. Luck. Comedy. 5m., 2w. Sc. Interior of cafe in France. CU

Man who stole the castle. Tom Gallon and L. M. Lion. 4m., 2w. Sc. Interior. FSD

Man with the bundle, The. Frayne Williams. Persian play of paradox. 7m. Sc. An underground eating house in Persia. WIT

Mandarin coat, The. Alice C. D. Riley. 2m., 3w. Sc. Handsome drawing room in California. Drama 13: 132–135, 141–143, Jan. 1923.

* **Manger service.** Rita Benton. Christmas Bible play. 14c., chorus. Sc. Chancel of the church or platform. BSD

† **Manikin and minikin.** Alfred Kreymborg. 1b., 1g. Sc. Conventional parlor seen through oval frame. A bisque play of fancy. KMP, KMR, LC, STW, WWS

Manners and modes. Marjorie Benton Cooke. A satire. 9w. Sc. Millinery shop. CO

* **Manners make the man.** E. E. Bloxam. 20c. Sc. Nursery. BL

Man's honor, A. S. Decatur Smith, Jr. 2m., 1w. Sc. Interior. PPP

Mansions. Hildegarde Flanner. 1m., 2w. Sc. Living room. SL

Mantle of the Virgin, The. Vida Ravenscroft Sutton. A miracle play. 3m., 14w. Sc. Shrine and altar of the Virgin in a chapel. Drama 12: 71–79, 99–100, Dec. 1921.

Marah. May Bell. 3w., 5c. Sc. Small bare chamber of rugged stone, gloomy and neglected. BRW

March of truth, The. Katharine Searle. Great War background. 2m., 1w. Sc. Wine cellar in the war zone in France. SEA

March wind, A. Alice Brown. 2m., 1w., 1c. Sc. A farmhouse kitchen. BO

Margot. Hermann Sudermann. Trans. from the German. 3m., 2w. 1s. Sc. Lawyer's office. SU

Marie recites. Elizabeth F. Guptill. 1b., 4g. Sc. Boarding house parlor. GUT

Marionettes, a modern fantasy. Gilbert Vivian Seldes. 1m., 1w. (No scene given.) Harvard Monthly 57: 124–129, Jan. 1914.

* **Marjorie's garden.** Sidney Baldwin. Fairy play. 10 or more c. Sc. A garden. BAL

Markheim. Zellah Macdonald. 3m., 1w. Sc. Old curiosity, jewelry and clock shop in London. MP

Marquise and woman, an incident during the reign of terror. Claude Askew. 1m., 1w. Sc. Small room leading out of the Salle des Morts in the Conciergerie. Smart Set 7: 83–86, July 1902.

Marriage, The. Douglas Hyde. 2m., 1w., neighbor. Sc. A cottage kitchen. Poet Lore 20: 135–145, Mar.–Apr. 1909.

Marriage certificate, The. Anna Wolfrom. 2m., 1w., 2b., 1g. Sc. Interior of a wooden shack. WOH

Marriage has been arranged, A. Alfred Sutro. Comedy. 1m., 1w. Sc. Conservatory. FSD, SF, Collier's Weekly 29: 11, 14, June 14, 1902.

Marriage made easy. D. T. Praigg. 2m., 2w. Sc. Interior. MAP

Marriage of Dotty, The. Clare Thornton. 2w. Sc. Drawing room. PLA

Marriage of Guineth, The. Florence Wilkinson Evans. Verse. 7m., 3w., 1b, chorus. Sc. A hall in a French château in mediaeval times. EVM

Marriage of little Eva. Kenyon Nicholson. 3m., 3w. Sc. Star's dressing room in opera house. Smart Set 65: 75–85, Aug. 1921.

† **Marriage proposal.** Anton Pavlovich Chekhov. English version by Hilmar Baukhage and Barret H. Clark. 2m., 1w. Sc. Sitting room in a Russian house. FSD

Marriage will not take place, The. Alfred Sutro. 2m., 2w. Sc. Interior. FSD

† **Marriages are made in heaven—and elsewhere.** Graham Price. 2m., 2w. Sc. Interior of a rectory. REP

Married lovers, The, Harold Sanders. 2m., 4w. Sc. Interior. FP

Married to a suffragette. Willis N. Bugbee. 4m., 3w. Sc. Sitting room. MAP

Marrying Belinda. Grace Cooke Strong. Farce. 4m., 4w. Sc. Interior. B

Marrying money. Alice L. Tildesley. 4w. Sc. Room in a bachelor girls' apartment. B

Marse Covington. George Ade. 5m. Sc. At a steel door of a gambling house. US

Marsh maiden, The. Felix Gould. Fantasy. 1m., 1w., 10 voices. Sc. Living room of the Peat-gatherer's home. GO

Martha Dixon's parlor. Burns Kattenberg. 1m., 10w. Sc. Interior. FSD

Martha plays the fairy. Keble Howard. Comedy. 2m., 3w. Sc. Cottage. FSD

Martha the soothsayer. John K. Bell. (K. Howard, pseud.) Comedy. 2m., 3w. Sc. Interior. FSD

Martha's mourning. Phoebe Hoffman. Comedy. 3w. Sc. A Kitchen. MA, Drama 8: 111–121, Feb. 1918.

Martyrdom of Ali, The. Adapted from the Persian miracle play of Hasan and Husain. Trans. under the direction of Sir Lewis Pelly. Historical. 10m., 2b., 5w. chorus groups. Sc. Stage in two levels. ELT4

Martyrs, a life-study, The. William C. DeMille. 1m., 1w. Sc. Dining room. Smart Set 18: 159–160, Feb. 1906.

Mary Ann. Helen P. Hoornbeek. New England dialect. 5w. Sc. FP

Mary! Mary! Charles Crittenton Baldwin. (George Gordon, pseud.)

Shakespeare play. 12m., 1w. Sc. Taproom of the Mermaid Tavern in 1599. BAN

Mary's wedding. Gilbert Cannan. 2m., 2w., 2s., chorus. Sc. Living room in a cottage. CAP, REP, SL

Mask, a tragedy, The. Laura Sherry. 1m., 2w. Sc. Italian interior. The Play-book 2 : 3–26, Feb. 1915.

Masks. Perry Boyer Corneau. 1m., 1w. Sc. Small pleasantly furnished living room. Drama 12 : 234–236, April 1922.

Masks. George Middleton. 2m., 2w. Sc. Doorway from public stairs opening immediately upon the living room. MIM

Masks and men. Sarah Humason. Romantic make-believe play. 8m., 1w. Sc. An English inn in the 17th century. FSD

* **Masque of conservation, A.** Constance D'Arcy Mackay. 21c., chorus. Sc. An American woodland. MBF

Masque of evening, Edward Viets. Verse. Fanciful. 3m., 1w. Sc. Meadow. VI

Masque of morning, The. Edward Viets. Verse. Fanciful. 2m., 6c. Sc. A small grassy knoll. VI

* **Masque of Pomona, The.** Constance D'Arcy Mackay. 1b., 2g., 4 chorus groups. Sc. A glade. MBF

* **Masque of the Pied Piper, The.** Katharine Lord. 11b., 1g., Many chorus characters. Sc. Out of doors. LLS

Masque of the two strangers, The. Lady Alice Egerton. 3m., 11w. Sc. Out of doors—greenwood. C1

Masque of women poets, A. Amelia Josephine Burr. 25w. Sc. Simple stage. Stratford Journal 1 : 13–33, March 1917.

Masqueraders; or, A game of dominoes, The. Louise Emile Dubry. Trans. by L. A. Bradbury. 6m., 4w., chorus. Sc. Ante-room adjoining a ball room. WEP

‡ **Massasoit's illness.** Louise E. Tucker and Estelle L. Ryan. 4b., chorus characters. Sc. A wigwam. TRH

Master, The. Padriac H. Pearse. Verse. Irish play. 10m. Sc. A little cloister in a woodland. PRZ, PS

Master of the house, The. Stanley Houghton. 4m., 2w. Sc. Parlor. HF

‡ **Master skylark.** Anna M. Lütkenhaus. Adapted from the book by John Bennett. Shakespeare play. 6b., 3g., chorus. Sc. Out of doors in Stratford in time of Shakespeare. LU, MTC

Master wayfarer. J. E. Harold Terry. A happening of long ago. 3m., 1w. Sc. Parlor of an inn in England in 18th century. FSD

Masterpiece, The. Malcolm Morley. 2m., 2w. Sc. Apartment in Montmarte Paris. MOL

Matchmaker, The. Everett H. Rupert. Comedy. 2m., 1w. Sc. Living room of bachelor apartment in N. Y. FSD

Matchmakers. Seumas O'Brien. Comedy. 3m., 3w. Sc. Parlor. OD

Mate, The. Arthur Schnitzler. 4m., 1w., 1s. Sc. An artistic room. SG

Mates. Wilfred Wilson Gibson. Verse. 1m., 2w. Sc. Cottage. GID, GIP

Matinata. Lawrence Langner. Comedy. Pierrot play. 2m., 1w. Sc. Small room in a large city. LAF, SCO

Matrimonial fog. Florence Clay Knox. Comedy. 3m., 1w. Sc. A secluded corner on the veranda of a country club. B

Matrimonial tiff. Harold Sanders. 2m., 1w. Sc. Neatly furnished room. FP

Matrimonial venture, A. Charles S. Bird. Farce. 2m., 3w. Sc. Reception room. FSD

† **Matter of duty, A.** Binney Gunnison. Adapted from "The Dolly Dialogues" by Anthony Hope. Comedy. 1m., 1w. Sc. Afternoon tea. GU

Matter of husbands, A. Ferenc Molnar. English text by Benjamin Glazer. 2w. Sc. Drawing room. LO

Maw Moseley's courtin' lamp. Emily Hewitt Leland. 1m., 2w. Sc. Cabin in the Kentucky mountains. G2

† **May.** Alice W. Chaplin. 5g. Sc. Living room. CHC

May baskets new, a springtime playlet. 2m., 2w., 4c., choruses. Sc. Out of doors. Woman's Home Companion 45 : 39, 81, May 1918.

May-day. Constance D'Arcy Mackay. 1m., 2w. Many chorus characters. Sc. Interior of a Puritan home. MPP

* **Mayflower compact, The.** Eleanore Hubbard. Love and order. 9b., chorus. Sc. Cabin of the Mayflower. HUC

Maypole morning. Harold Brighouse. Historical background. 5m., 4w., chorus. Sc. Green near Tunbridge Wells in 1665. BRP

Me and Betty. Ragna B. Eskil. Comedy of rural life. 2m., 5w. Sc. Room in a house in a village. DEP

"Me and my diary." Gertrude E. Jennings. 1m., 5w. Sc. Interior. FSD

* **Meaning of Thanksgiving Day.** Carolyn Wells. 4m., 8w. Sc. Harvest Hall. PPP, Ladies' Home Journal 38 : 30, 79–80, Nov. 1921.

Mechanical Jane. M. E. Barber. 3w. Sc. Sitting room. FSD

Meddler, The. Henry Bailey Stevens. The voice of love. 6m., 1b. Sc. A room just off the street in an old-fashioned house. STE

Medea. Thomas Sturge Moore. Verse. Greek drama. Suitable for chamber presentation. 3m., 4w. Sc. Curtain. MOT

† **Medicine show, The.** Stuart Walker. 3m. Sc. On bank of a river within sight of a town. SL, WP

Meet my wife. Harry L. Newton. Comedy. Dramatic incident. 2m., 1w. Sc. Parlor. WHP

Meeting, The. R. E. Rogers. 4w., 3m. Sc. Tapestry chamber in Polenta's house at Ravenna. Harvard Monthly 42 : 148–153, May 1906.

* **Meeting of the ghosts, The.** Marie Irish. 3b., 3g. Sc. Sitting room. IP

Melinda and her sisters. Mrs. O. H. P. Belmont and Elsie Maxwell. Suffrage play. 6m., 13w., chorus. Sc. Pretentious garden. BM, BMM

Melodrama. J. R. Milne. 2m., 2w. Sc. Living room. Smart Set 60 : 95–99, Sept. 1919.

Melon thief, The. Trans. from the Japanese by Yone Noguchi. 2m. Sc. A melon patch. Poet Lore 15 : 40–42, Spring 1904.

Melon thief, The. From a mediaeval Japanese farce by Shigeyoshi Obata. 2m. Sc. A melon patch. Drama 10 : 104–107, Dec. 1919.

Member for literature, The. Maurice Baring. Political farce. 5m., many chorus characters. Sc. A platform in a hall in Battersea. BA

* **Memorial Day.** Eleanore Hubbard. 5b., 4g., chorus. Sc. Cemetery. HUD

* **Memorial day pageant.** Constance D'Arcy Mackay. 43c., chorus. Sc. Out of doors or a large stage. MBM

Men not wanted. Bell Elliott Palmer. 8w. Sc. Interior. DEP

Men who loved Mamie, The. C. W. Hogg. 2m. Sc. Interior. FSD

Meow! Fannie Cannon and Alice E. Ives. Comedy. 2w. Sc. Sitting room. DEP

Mere man, A. Edith Palmer Painton. 1m., 5w. Sc. Parlor. EP

Merediths entertain, The. Whitney Darrow. 2m., 4w. Sc. Living room. PPP

† **Merry Christmas.** Alice W. Chaplin. 4g. Sc. Room in a hotel in a South Dakota town. CHC

* **Merry Christmas Jake.** Marie Irish. Christmas play. 3b., 2g. Sc. Interior. IC

Merry death, A. Nicholas Evreinov. A Harlequinade. Trans. from the Russian. 4m., 1w. Sc. A room in which there is a bed. BFR, MR

* **Merry Jerry.** Mrs. Isabel Anderson. 3b., 1g., chorus. Sc. Courtyard of the palace of Neptune. AE

Merry merry cuckoo, The. Jeanette Marks. Verse. 3m., 2w. Sc. A garden. MA, MT, SS, The Dramatist 4: 291–300, Oct. 1912. Metropolitan 36: 45–47, July 1912.

Merry widow hat. Helen Sherman Griffith. Farce. 5w. Sc. Interior. B

* **Merrymount.** Constance D'Arcy Mackay. 11b., 8g. Sc. An open glade. MPY

Message of Lazarus, The. C. E. Laurence. 1m., 2w. Sc. Doorway of house in Bethany. Nineteenth Century 91: 170–6. Jan. 1922.

* **Messenger birds, The.** Edna Randolph Worrell. Christmas play. Any number of children. Sc. Interior. GUB

Metal checks, The. Louise Driscoll. Verse. 2m. Sc. Bare room scantily furnished. Poetry 5: 49–54, Nov. 1914.

Michael. David Pinski. Authorized translation from the Yiddish by Isaac Goldberg. 3m., 1w., 1s. Sc. Garden of King Saul. PTK, Stratford Journal 2: 27–35. April 1918.

* **Middle of the night, The.** E. M. Fotheringham. 2b., 2g. Sc. Nursery. FG

Midnight marauders, The. Frank Dumont. Farce. 5m., 2w. Sc. In front of a house. WHP

Midnight trespasser. No author given. 1m., 1w. Sc. Handsome room. DPP

Midsummer eve. Gordon Bottomley. Verse. 2m., 5w. Sc. Interior of an old barn. BKL

† **Miggs' revenge.** No author given. Adapted from Dickens' Barnaby Rudge. 1b., 1g. Sc. Street. BAB

Milestones. Arthur Schnitzler. Trans. from the German. Anatol play. 1m., 1w. Sc. Interior. SAA

Militant God. Clifford Greve. Tragedy. 2m., 1w. Sc. Interior of cabin near volcano in Mexico. GRE

† **Military and medicine.** Edith Brown-Evarts. From the comedy of Colman "The Poor Gentleman." 2b. Sc. Interior. BEY

* **Mill that ground hot porridge, The.** Augusta Stevenson. 11b., 3g. Sc. Out of doors. SC1

* **Miller, his son and their donkey, The.** Augusta Stevenson. 6b., 6g. Sc. A bridge, near a town, not far from a fair. SC3

Millet group, A. Marguerite Merington. From the picture "The Angelus" by Millet. 3m., 4w., 1c. Sc. A large frame. MPZ

Millions in it, Edwin Bateman Morris. Comedy. 5m., 1w. Sc. Interior. PPP

Milly dear. Alice Brown. 2m., 2w. Sc. A charmingly furnished sitting room. BO

Miniature, The. Walter Frith. 2m., 2w. Sc. Interior of a flat. FSD

Mining agent, The. Fred H. James. Comedy. 1m., 1w. Sc. Business office. Stagelore p. 205, Feb. 1912.

Minister pro tem, A. Katharine Kavanaugh. Comedy. 4m., 2w. Sc. Interior. DEP

† **Minister's daughter, The.** Clara J. Denton. Christmas play. 1b., 4g. Sc. Plain interior. SI

‡ **Minister's dream, The.** Katharine Lord. Thanksgiving fantasy of Puritan life. 6b., 7g., chorus of b. Sc. Living room. LLP, LLR

Minister's first at home, The. John Kendrick Bangs. 2m., 3w. Sc. Drawing room of parsonage. Ladies' Home Journal 26: 16, 90–91, Mar. 1909.

‡ **Minister's messenger, The.** Evangeline L. Bretherton. 14g. Sc. Large unadorned room with simple furniture. FSD

Ministers of grace. J. Hartley Manners. 3m., 2w. Sc. Library in fine house in London. Smart Set 38: 129–142, Sept. 1912.

Minister's wife, The. Helen Sherman Griffith. Farce. 6w. Sc. Interior. PPP

Minos, King of Crete. Maurice Hewlett. Verse. Ancient Greek theme. Tragic. 9m., 1w. Sc. Sea wall at Cnossus. HEA

* **Minty-Malviny's Santa Claus.** Elsie Hobart Carter. 3b., 4g. Sc. Interior of handsome lodging house in New Orleans. CCC

Minuet, A. Louis N. Parker. French Revolution play. 2m., 1w. Sc. Living room of gaoler's quarters. FSD, Century 89: 370–376, Jan. 1915.

Miracle of the corn, The. Padraic Colum. Irish legend. 3m., 4w., 1c. Sc. Interior of farmhouse in Ireland in olden times. CDL, Theatre Arts Magazine 5: 323–332, Oct. 1921.

Mirage. George M. P. Baird. 2m., 4w. Sc. Roof of an adobe house in a Hopi Pueblo. SCO, STK

Mirror of time, The. Cyril Wentworth Hogg. 1m., 1w. Sc. Cosy room adjoining a dining room. FSD

‡ **Mirth-provoking school room, The.** Emily David. Farce. 6b., 8g. Sc. Rural school room. FL

Mis' Mercy. Louise Whitefield Bray. 3m., 2w. Sc. Old fashioned kitchen. FS3

† **Miss Burnett puts one over.** Ethelyn Sexton. College play. 6g. Sc. College dormitory. EP

Miss Burney at court. Maude Morrison Frank. 2m., 3w., 1s. Sc. Fanny Burney's drawing room. FSP

† **Miss Civilization.** Richard Harding Davis. 4m., 1w., chorus. Sc. Dining room of a country house. DAF, FSD, Collier's Weekly 34: 16–17, 20–21, Dec. 3, 1904.

Miss Deborah's pocket book. Alice C. Thompson. 6w. Sc. Parlor. PPP

* **Miss Dobson.** Lady Bell. Comedy. 4g. Sc. Unimportant. BEJ

Miss Doulton's orchids. Margaret Cameron. Comedy. 3m., 3w. Sc. Living room of suburban home. CAC

Miss Jones, journalist. J. Butler Haviland. 1m., 1w. Sc. Interior. B

† **Miss Judith Macan.** Binney Gunnison. Adapted from Charles Lever's Charles O'Malley. Comedy. 4m., 1w., chorus characters. Sc. Drawing room. GU

Miss Julia. August Strindberg. Trans. from the Swedish. Naturalistic. 1m., 2w. Sc. A large kitchen. STO

† **Miss Maria.** Maude B. Vosburgh. Dramatization of a story by Margaret Deland. 3m., 3w. Sc. Old fashioned sitting room. FSD

Miss Myrtle says "Yes." Mark O'Dea. 1m. 3w. Sc. Village millinery store. OR

Miss Oliver's dollars. Emillie Callaway. Farce. 8w. Sc. Interior. B

Miss Parkington. May E. Countryman. Farce. 1m., 3w. Sc. Interior. B

* **Miss Poinsettia: Christmas play.** Lillian Schreiner. 5b., 19g. Sc. Any interior. EP

Miss Squeers' tea-party. Horace B. Browne. Adapted from Charles Dickens' Nicholas Nickleby. 2m., 2w. Sc. Parlor. BD

Miss Susan's fortune. Alice C. Thompson. Comedy. 6w. Sc. Interior. PPP

Miss Tassey. Elizabeth Baker. 5w. Sc. Dormitory for the use of the women of a commercial establishment. CBI, SIJ

Miss Todd's vampire. Sally Shute. Comedy. 1m., 4w. Sc. Sitting room. B

Missing card, The. John Hay Beith. (Ian Hay, pseud.) 2m., 2w. Sc. Drawing room. BEC

Missing guest, The. Roland K. Young. 3m., 3w. Sc. Dining room of apartment on Riverside Drive. Smart Set 50: 79–82, Dec. 1916.

Missing liner. C. Gordon Kurtz. 1m., 1w. Sc. Handsomely furnished room. STB

Mistake at the manor, A. Maude Morrison Frank. 2m., 1w., 3s. Sc. Dining hall. FSP

Mistake in identity, A. Benj. L. C. Griffith. 2w. Sc. Ladies' sitting room in a hotel. GR

Mistletoe. Anne M. Mitchell. Adapted from the story by Alice Brown. 2m., 3w. Sc. Kitchen. DAK

* **Mistletoe and holly.** May Pemberton. 5c. Sc. A bare scantily furnished kitchen. PC

Mistletoe and Holly-berry, an old English Christmas play. Marie J. Warren. Any number of characters. Sc. Kitchen of a farm. B

* **Mistress Mary gives a garden party.** Mabel R. Goodlander. 13c. Sc. Stage. CF

Mistress Runaway. M. Lefuse. Romantic comedy. 4w. Sc. Parlor of small inn in England in early 19th century. FSD

Mobswoman; or, The cry of Ishmael, The. Leon M. Lion and W. Strange Hall. 2m., 2w. Sc. Brightly furnished room. FSD

Model growl. Agness Electra Platt. Store window wax figure comedy. 1m., 8w. Sc. Store window. WEP

Modern autocrat, The. Louise Collins. A comedy of cross purposes. 1m., 1w. Sc. Breakfast room. Smart Set 8: 157–158, Dec. 1902.

Modern child. Julien Gordon. (Mrs. Van Rensselaer Cruger) 1w. 1g. Sc. Piazza and a hammock. Smart Set 1: 79–85, May 1900.

Modern daughter, A. Julien Gordon (Mrs. Van Rensselaer Cruger) 2w. Sc. Drawing room in N. Y. Smart Set 1: 77–82, April 1900.

Modern dialogue. Oliver Herford. 1m., 1w. Sc. On Manhattan Island. Smart Set 7: 53–54, Aug. 1902.

Modern Harlequinade, A. Colin Campbell Clements. Poet Lore 31: 579–603. Winter 1920.

Modern masque, A. Mary MacMillan. 3m., 4w. Literary background. Sc. An open green. MS

Modern menage, A. Harriet Holmes Haslett. Tragic farce. 3m., 1w., 1c. Sc. Living room of a bungalow. HAE

Modern minuet, A. Harriet Monroe. Verse. 1m., 1w. Sc. Small room opening into a dance hall. MOP

Modern Mother, A. Julien Gordon. (Mrs. Van Rensselaer Cruger) 1m., 2w. Sc. 1. A drawing room. Sc. 2 The garden. Smart Set 1: 79–86, Mar. 1900.

Modern prodigal, A. Horace Holley. 2m. Sc. Well furnished library of a home. HOR

† **Modesty.** Paul Hervieu. Trans. by Barrett H. Clark. Comedy. 2m., 1w. Sc. Parlor. FSD, LC

Mollie and the milliner. Marianne Stayton. Farce. 1m., 3w. Sc. Hat shop. FSD

Mollusk or suffragette? Elizabeth Overstreet Cuppy. 3m., 3w. Sc. Cozy living room. Putnam's 7: 172–181, Nov. 1909.

* **Molly's Christmas tree.** Willis N. Bugbee. 4b., 6g. Sc. Living room. BUJ

* **Molly's New Year's party.** Emilie Blackmore Stapp and Eleanor Cameron. A January play. 8b., 6g., 17 chorus groups. Sc. Sitting room. SCH

Monday, a lame minuet. Alfred Kreymborg. 6w. Sc. Box like landing of New York tenement. KMA, Drama 10: 264–271, May 1920.

Monkey's paw, The. William Wymark Jacobs and Louis N. Parker. Superstition. 4m., 1w. Sc. Interior. FSD

Monsieur Galespard and Mademoiselle Jeanne. John V. Craven, Jr. 2m., 1w. Sc. A Parisian restaurant. Smart Set 70: 69–73, March 1923.

Monsieur Lamblin. George Ancey. Trans. from the French by Barrett H. Clark. 1m., 3w., 1s. Sc. Stylish drawing room. SL, Stratford Journal 1: 34–45, March 1917.

* **Monster in the garden, The.** Lady Bell. Comedy. 1b., 3g. Sc. Unimportant. BEJ

Mood of a moment, The. George S. Viereck. 2m., 1w., chorus. Sc. Small room off of main drawing room. VG, International 11: 13–16, Jan. 1917.

Moon of the Caribbees, The. Eugene O'Neill. 17m., 4w., chorus m. Sc. Forward section of main deck of British tramp steamer. OMC, Smart Set 55: 73–86, Aug. 1918.

* **Moon's silver cloak, The.** Augusta Stevenson. 10c Sc. The sky. SC1

Moon tide. Colin Campbell Clements. 2m. Sc. Shack at end of an old deserted wharf. CLD

Moonshine. Arthur Hopkins. 2m. Sc. Hut of a moonshiner in the mountains of N. C. FSD, LC, Theatre Arts Magazine 3: 51–62, Jan. 1919.

Moonshine. Laurence Housman. Pierrot play. 4m. Sc. Night in a quiet street. HAB

Morals and circumstance. Bertram Bloch. 2m., 3w. Sc. Sunparlor of country home. Smart Set 58: 87-95, April 1919.

More time out. Carolyn F. Rice. Farce. 7w. Sc. Interior of employment agency. MAP

Morituri: Teias. Hermann Sudermann. Trans. from the German. 8m., 2w., chorus. Sc. Before the king's tent. MR, Poet Lore 9: 330-352, July-Sept. 1897.

Mormonizing. Daisy McGeoch. Comedy. 2m., 8w. Sc. Sitting room. MAC

Morning after the night before, The. Harry L. Newton. Domestic comedy. 3m., 1w. Sc. Drawing room. WHP

Morning after the play, The. W. Steell. Comedy. 2m., 3w. Sc. Attractive interior. B

Morning call, A. Charles Dance. Romantic comedy. 1m., 1w. Sc. Drawing room. PH, WEP

Morraca. Winthrop Parkhurst. 5m., 3w. Others. Sc. Great reception hall in court of the king of the Chaldeans. Drama 8: 536-574, Nov. 1918.

Mortal coils. Aldous Huxley. 4m., 3w. Sc. Terrace outside an Italian hotel. HU

* **Moses in the bulrushes.** Rita Benton. Bible play. 5g., 1c. chorus. Sc. A marshy place by a river. BSD

Moth balls. Sallie Kemper. 3w. Sc. Sitting room in cottage. B

Mother, The. Wilfrid Wilson Gibson. Verse. 2w., 1c. Sc. Lonely moorland cottage. GID, GIP

Mother and son, tr. from the Yiddish. J. Halpern. 3m. 2w. Sc. Room in the house of the old Rabbi in a small Polish village. BLK

* **Mother Autumn and North Wind.** Eleanor L. Skinner and Ada M. S. Skinner. 9c. Sc. An open place. SSC

* **Mother Goose and her flock.** Marie Irish. 10b., 10g. Sc. Unimportant. IPP

* **Mother Goose Christmas, A.** S. Decatur Smith, Jr. 21 characters. Sc. Nursery. Ladies' Home Journal 25: 19, 75, Dec. 1907.

* **Mother Goose garden.** Constance Wilcox. 6b., 6g. Sc. A garden. WTC

* **Mother Goose up-to-date.** Hester Donaldson Jenkins. A health play. 5b., 6g. Sc. Empty platform. JE

* **Mother Goose's Christmas party.** Winnie Saunders. Christmas play. 1b., 11g. Sc. Unimportant. FIL

* **Mother Goose's gosling.** Elizabeth F. Guptill. Play containing songs with music. 7b., 9g. Sc. No scenery. DEP

Mother-love. Gertrude Buck. 1m., 3w. Sc. Maggie's sewing room—shabbily furnished. Drama 9: 1-30, Feb. 1919.

Motherlove. August Strindberg. 4w. Sc. Interior of a fisherman's cottage. SM

‡ **Mother love finds a way.** Mae Stein Soble. Bible play—Moses 8g. Sc. Scantily furnished room in a rude hut in ancient Egypt. SOB

* **Mother Nature's trumpeter.** Sidney Baldwin. Admits of dancing in the play. 12 or more c. Sc. Under the forests in early spring. BAL

Motherly love. August Strindberg. 4w. Sc. Room with window. STW

Mother-of-pearl. Gertrude Jennings. Comedy of slums of London. 1m., 2w. Sc. Button stall. FSD

Mothers, The. Mrs. Havelock Ellis. 1m., 2w. Sc. Cornish farm kitchen. EL

† **Mothers.** George Middleton. 1m., 2w. Sc. Living room in a large apartment hotel. MIT

Mothers of men. Percival Wilde. Great War background. 2w. Sc. Sumptuously furnished drawing room. WU

Mothers on strike; or, Local number one. Carl Webster Pierce. Comedy. 3m., 3w. Sc. Interior. B

Motor mishap, A. Malcolm Morley. Comedy. 2m., 1w. Sc. The Bath High Road. MOL

Mountain She-Devil, The. Yone Noguchi. 2w., 1s., chorus. Sc. None given. Poet Lore 29: 447–451, Autumn 1918

* **Mouths, The.** Christina G. Rossetti. A pageant. 6b., 6g., many chorus groups. Sc. A cottage with its grounds. MTC

"**Movies.**" Thomas King Moylan. Irish farce. 5m., 2w. Sc. An Irish country roadside. MOO

Mr. and Mrs. P. Roe. Martyn Johnson. 1m., 3w. Sc. Attic chamber in slum tenement. Drama 13: 92–95, Dec. 1922.

Mr. Brent's wife. James Regnart. 4m., 2w. Sc. Narrow garden at back of a house on the "North Shore." Harvard Monthly 32: 96–110 May 1901.

Mr. Editor. Ward Macauley. Comedy. 7m., 2w. Sc. Newspaper office. PPP

Mr. Enright entertains, a possibility. Avery Abbott. 5m., 3w., 1g. Sc. Tasteful dining room. Poet Lore 34: 127–144, Spring 1923.

* **Mr. February Thaw.** Emilie Blackmore Stapp and Eleanor Cameron. A February play. 7b., 1g., 2 chorus groups g. Sc. Poorly furnished attic. SCH

Mr. Fraser's friends. Wilbur S. Tupper. A satire. 5m., 1w. Sc. Simple interior. TU

Mr. George's shooting gallery. Horace B. Browne. From Charles Dickens' Bleak House. 5m., 1w. Sc. Living room at a "shooting gallery" BD

Mr. Guppy's proposal. Horace B. Browne. From Dickens' Bleak House. 1m., 1w. Sc. A room. BD

Mr. Icky, the quintessence of quaintness. F. Scott Fitzgerald. 3m., 1w., several c. Sc. Exterior cottage in West Suffolkshire. Smart Set 61: 93–98, March 1920.

Mr. Lorelei, a folk comedy. Paul Armstrong. 1m., 2w. Sc. Living room in a new house. Smart Set 48: 233–242, Jan. 1916.

Mr. McArdle's guest. D. S. Maddox. Farce. 3m., 1w. Sc. Plainly furnished dining room. B

Mr. Micawber's prospects. Horace B. Browne. From Dickens' David Copperfield. 3m., 1w. Sc. Room in London. BD

Mr. Pecksniff's pleasant family party. Horace B. Browne. From Dickens' Martin Chuzzlewit. 4m., 5w. Sc. Room. BD

Mr. Richey changes his mind. Lee Owen Snook. Christmas play. 4m., 4w., chorus. Sc. Office of department store. EP

Mr. Shakespeare at school, a short play for women. Caroline Duer. 10w. Sc. School room. Smart Set 7: 65–73, June 1902.

Mr. Sprigg's little trip to Europe. Comedy. Dream play. 1m., 10w. Sc. Interior. PPP

Mr. Steinmann's corner. Alfred Sutro. A study in sentiment. 2m., 2w. Sc. Sumptuously furnished drawing room. FSD, SFA

Mr. Venus's shop. Horace Browne. From Dickens' Our Mutual Friend. 2m., 1b. Sc. A shop. BD

Mr. Willoughby calls. John Jex. 3m., 1w. Sc. Music room. JEP

Mrs. Bompton's dinner party. Bernard Sobel. 6m., 10w. Sc. Dining room of handsome residence. ST

Mrs. Busby's pink tea. Mary Moncure Parker. Comedy. 1m., 7w. Sc. Interior. DPP

Mrs. Carver's fancy ball. Maisie B. Whiting. Comedy. 4m., 3w. Sc. Interior. DEP

Mrs. Coulson's daughter. Elizabeth Gale. 11w. Sc. Sitting room. FSD

Mrs. Elwell's paper. J. L. Harbour. Comedy. 1m., 4w. Sc. Interior. G2

Mrs. Flynn's lodgers. H A. Kniffin. 4m., 1w. Sc. Combined bedroom and studio. FSD

Mrs. Forrester's crusade. C. Leona Dalrymple. Farce against slang. 1m., 2w. Sc. Interior. FPD

† **Mrs. Hardcastle's journey.** Binney Gunnison. Adapted from Goldsmith's "She stoops to conquer." Comedy. 3m., 1w. Sc. The back of a garden. GU

Mrs. Harrison. John Masefield. 3m., 1w. Sc. Room. MTA

Mrs. Harwood's secret. Binney Gunnison. Adapted from Mrs. Oliphant's "The story of a Governess." 5m., 4w. Sc. An unoccupied wing of a house. GU

Mrs. Hazenby's health. Curtis Brown. 1m., 3w. Sc. Drawing room. WIA

Mrs. Hoops-Hooper and the Hindu. Mary Moncure Parker. Comedy 12w. Sc. Living room. DEP

Mrs. Jenkins' brilliant idea. Jessie Kelley. Comedy. 8w. Sc. Room. DEP

Mrs. McGreevy's boarders. Ward Macauley. 6m., 5w. Sc. Back parlor of a boarding house. PPP

Mrs. Mack's example. Flora Bigelow Dodge. 1m., 2w. Sc. 1. Drawing room, Sc. 2. Bedroom. Sc. 3. Sitting room. Smart Set 5: 51–66, Sept. 1901.

* **Mrs. Marconi.** E. M. Fotheringham. 2b., 1g. Sc. Sitting room. FG

Mrs. Molly. Rachel Crothers. 1m., 2w. Sc. Boudoir in a summer cottage. Smart Set 27: 104–113, Mar. 1909.

† **Mrs. Pat and the law.** Mary Aldis. 2m., 2w., 1c. Sc. A small poor room in tenement flat. AP, MA

Mrs. Pipp's waterloo. Ellis O. Jones. 2m., 2w. Sc. Reception room of a home. Woman's Home Companion 41: 23–24, Apr. 1914.

* **Mrs. Pollywigs and her wonderful wax works.** Anna M. Lütkenhaus. 25c. Sc. Platform of a concert hall. LU

Mrs. Potiphar pays a call. Samuel D. McCoy. 1m., 2w. Sc. Billiard room of residence of Prince in Egypt. Smart Set 37: 123–125, May 1912.

Mrs. Potter buys a present. Harold Susman. 1m., 1w., Sc. Jeweler's shop. Smart Set 32: 107–108, Nov. 1910

* **Mrs. Randy's Christmas.** Ellen M. Willard. 6g., 2b. Sc. Bare room. WY

* **Mrs. Santa Claus, militant.** Bell Elliott Palmer. Christmas comedy. 5b., 4g. Sc. Living room. EP
Mrs. Snagby's guests. Horace B. Browne. From Dickens' Bleak House. 2m., 3w. Sc. Drawing room. BD
Mrs. Stubbin's book agent. Henry Cutler Stearns. Farce. 3m., 2w. Sc. Sitting room. DEP
Mrs. Sullivan's social tea. Laura Frances Kelley. Comedy of the newly rich. 1m., 12w. Sc. Gaudily furnished room. DEP
Mrs. Tibbs boarding house. Horace B. Browne. A play from Dickens. 5m., 5w. Sc. Parlor of a boarding house in London. BD
* **Mrs. Tubb's telegram.** Katharine M. Rice. Comedy. 4w., 3b., 2g., other c. Sc. Kitchen. St. Nicholas 32: 344–355, Feb. 1905.
Much too sudden. Alice C. Thompson. Comedy. 7w. Sc. Parlor. B
Mud. Isabel McKinney. 3m., 1w. Sc. Interior of commodious and snugly built log cabin. Poet Lore 30: 417–427, Autumn 1919.
Muddle-Annie. Harold Chapin. 2m., 5w. Sc. Parlor. REP
* **Muffin man, The.** John Gemmell. 1b. Sc. Unimportant. FG
Mulan. Torao Taketomo. 2m., 2w., villagers. Sc. Room in village house in Northern China. Asia 19: 1258–1261, Dec. 1919.
Mummers' play, The. J. Kinchin Smith. Verse. 9m. Sc. Not given. Theatre Arts Magazine 7: 63–68, Jan. 1923.
Murderer, The. Clarendon Ross. 2m. Sc. Depths of a forest. Poet Lore 30: 596–600. Winter 1919.
‡ **Murdering the language.** Edith F. A. U. Painton. 6b., 6g. Sc. A bare room. PAD
Murdering Selina. Margaret Scott Oliver. 4m., 2w., 1b. Sc. Interior of a frame restaurant in the park. OS
* **Mushroom meadow, The.** Catharine A. Morin. 14c. Sc. A damp green meadow. BHP
Music hath charms. Grace Luce Irwin. Farce. 1m., 1w. Sc. Poor room in a players' boarding house. ID
Music hath charms. Gerald Pioneer. College comedy. Baseball. 16m. Sc. Interior. FSD
Mustard plasters, The. George H. Willard. Comedy. 1m., 1w. Sc. Drawing room. DPP
My friend's in town. Emily Herey Denison. 1m., 1w. Sc. Library in a fashionable apartment. DL
My lady dreams. Eugene Pillot. 4w., 2c. Sc. Lady's boudoir. PI, STW
† **My lady's lace.** Edward Knoblock. 2m., 2w. Sc. Garden of a small Dutch house of about 1660. WWS
My Mexican rose. Katharine Kavanaugh. Comedy. 2m., 2w. Sc. Garden. DPP
My milliner's bill. William Clark Stewart. Farce. 1m., 1w. Sc. Interior. FSD
My son Arthur. Mary F. Kingston. Comedy. 2m., 8w. Sc. Office of summer hotel. FP
My tailor. Alfred Capus. Trans. by Barrett H. Clark. 1m., 2w. Sc. Drawing room of Paris apartment. Smart Set 54: 75–84, Feb. 1918.
My wife's husband. Hilton Coon. Farce. 3m., 4w. Sc. Interior. APP
Mysterious will, The. Harold Selman. Comedy. 2m., 1w. Sc. Interior. FSD

Mystery, a one-act comedietta containing a moral for young gentlemen. Hulbert Footner. 2m., 3w. Sc. Sitting room. Woman's Home Companion 39: 8–9, 69, Jan. 1912.

Mystery of Beacon Hill. Emily Herey Denison. 2m., 1w., 1g., 1s. w. Sc. Living room of a log-house. DL

‡ **Mystic seven; or, The law of the fire.** Mrs Arthur T. Seymour. Camp fire play. 8g., chorus. Sc. Sitting room. B

N

Nakamitsu. Basil Hall Chamberlain. Japanese lyric drama. 4m., 1b., chorus. CHB

† **Nance Oldfield.** Charles Reade. 3m., 2w. Sc. Interior of an English home in the eighteenth century. B

* **Nanny Etticoat.** Someple. (pseud.) 32c. Sc. Interior. SO

Napoleon and the sentry. P. B. Corneau. 3m., 1w. Sc. Sentry's post. DPP

Napoleon's barber. Arthur Caesar. 3m., 1w. Sc. An 18th century barber shop in a small French village. SCO

Nari-Kin. Yozan T. Iwasaki, tr. from the Japanese. Farce of modern Japan. 5m., 2w. Sc. Dwelling in the poor quarter of Asaka.

* **Narrow escape, A.** Louise E. Tucker and Estelle L. Ryan. John Smith and Pocohontas play. 6b., 1g. Sc. Small glade in a forest. TRH

Narrow squeak, A. Lillian Bennet Thompson and George Hubbard. Comedy. 3m., 1w. Sc. Office. FSD

* **Nature play in a city school, A.** Anna M. Lütkenhaus. 30c. Sc. Schoolroom. LU

* **Naughty comet, The.** Laura E. Richards. 7b., chorus b. Sc. Courtyard of large building. RP

Nazareth. Laurence Housman. Morality. Childhood of Christ. Verse. 10m., 2w., 1c. Sc. The Carpenter's shop. FSD

† **Neath the scepter of Susan.** Margaret G. Parsons. 2b., 10g. Sc. Boarding school about 1840. PR

Necessary evil, The. Charles Rann Kennedy. 2m., 2w. Sc. Sitting room. KEN

† **Neighbors, The.** Zona Gale. Picture of village life. Suitable for women's clubs. 2m., 6w. Sc. Plain room. B, WIP

Nellijumbo. Stuart Walker. 4m., 2w., chorus characters. Sc. Room. WA

† **Nelson touch, The.** F. Fenn. 3m., 2w. Sc. English inn at time of Napoleon. FSD

Nero's Mother. Stephen Phillips. Ancient Rome. 2m., 3w. Sc. Chamber in a villa on the shore of Lucrine Lake. PHI

Nest, The. John Jex. 2m., 3w. Sc. Interior of a bungalow. JEP

Nettle, The. Ernest Warren. Romantic comedy. 1m., 1w. Sc. Poorly furnished room. PH

Neuters, The. David Carb. 1m., 2w. Sc. Living room of a bungalow. Harvard Monthly 47: 167–172, Jan. 1909.

Never stretch your legs in a taxi. S. N. Behrman. 3m., 1w. Sc. Inside of veteran taxi. Smart Set 62: 71–76, Aug. 1920.

‡ **Nevertheless.** Stuart Walker. 1m., 1b., 1g. Sc. A room just upstairs. SB, WP, WWS

New age, The. David Carb. 5m., 9w. Sc. Room in rural house in Virginia. Harvard Monthly 50: 7–20, May 1910.

New day, The. William T. Demarest. An Arabian play. 5m., 3w. Sc. A Bedouin camp. DEM

New England fable, A. Ludwig Lewisohn. Verse. 4m., 3w. Sc. Woodland. International 10: 116–119, April 1917.

New man in town, A. Clara J. Denton. Farce. 8w. Sc. Handsome interior. DAI

‡ **New names for old.** Alice V. Carey. A safety first play. 12c. Sc. Interior of American dining room. FSD

New professor, The. Frances Aymar Mathews. Comedy. 12w. Sc. Interior. DPP

New Pygmalion and Galatea, The. Sylvan Drey. 3m., 2w. Sc. Modern office building. FSD

New race. Anna Wolfrom. 3m., 2w., chorus. Sc. Facade of an ancient and dilapidated cathedral in N. Y. WOH

* **New Red Riding-hood, The.** E. S. Brooks. 2b., 1g. Sc. Neatly furnished parlor. SAB, SAC

New reporter, The. Franklin Johnston. Farce. 6m., 2w. Sc. Editorial office. FP

New school-ma'am, The. C. H. McArthur. 2m., 1w. Sc. sitting-room. B

New word, The. J. M. Barrie. 2m., 2w. Sc. A dining room. BE

* **New-Year's Day.** "The resolutions of Anychild." F. Ursula Payne. 7c. Sc. Anyhouse. PP

News from home. William Giles and Josephine Giles. Comedy. 1m., 1w. Sc. Interior. APP

† **Newsy wins.** Eunice G. Hussey. Book play. 15g. Sc. Corner of the Public Library. PPP

* **Next day, The.** Clara J. Denton. Christmas play. 3g. Sc. Sitting room. I

* **Nick Bluster's trick.** Eleanor L. Skinner and Ada M. Skinner. 2b., 6g. Sc. A cave beside a brook. SSC

Night. Sholom Ash. Yiddish play. 5m., 3w. Sc. Night in a market place. SL

Night. James Oppenheim. Poetic drama. 4m., 1w. Sc. Hilltop. FLS

Night after; or, Rameses of Mummy row, The. Arthur Blanchard. 11m. 1w. Sc. Interior. B

† **Night at an inn, A.** Lord Dunsany. 8m. Sc. A room of an inn. C1, DFN, DFP

† **Night-before-Christmas dream, The.** Carolyn Wells. 11m. or b., 3w. or g., many others. Sc. 1. Child's bedroom. Sc. 2. School room. Ladies' Home Journal 33: 36, 111, Nov. 1916.

Night brings a counselor. Lillian Saunders. 1m., 1w. Sc. Office. Drama 13: 251–253, April 1923.

Night in Alexandria, A. Ludwig Lewisohn. 2m., 2w. Sc. Lofty chamber. Moods 2: 143–153, Dec. 1909–Jan. 1910.

Night in Tappan, A. O. B. Dubois. Farce comedy. 2m., 3w. Sc. Dining room. FP

Night of light, The. Louis Kaplan. A Jewish holiday play. 4m., 4w. Sc. Sitting room in a Jewish home. BLO

Night of the wedding, The. Richard Duffy. 1m., 2w. Sc. Room in an old fashioned tenement in N. Y. Smart Set 25: 80–90, May 1908.

Night-shift, The. Wilfrid Wilson Gibson. Verse. 4w. Sc. Cottage in the early morning. GID, GIP

Night watch. Kathleen C. Greene. 4m., 1w. Sc. Interior of fisherman's cottage. GDL

Night watches. Allan Monkhouse. Great War play. Comedy. 3m., 1w. Sc. Ante-room to the wards in a small Red Cross hospital. MW

Night wind, a play of Greenwich village, **A.** Witter Bynner. 2m., 2w. Sc. A dingy coffee-room in Greenwich Village. BB

* **Nimble-Wit and Fingerkin.** Constance D'Arcy Mackay. 9c. Sc. A somewhat dark room. NHH

* **Ninepin Club, The; or, Flora the Queen of Summer.** Caroline A. Creevey and Margaret E. Sangster. 32c. Sc. Room in a private boarding house. HB

Ninth night, The. Victor Dyk. Trans. from the Bohemian by Cyril Jeffrey Hrbek. 2m., 2w. Sc. Living room. Poet Lore 29: 90–101, Jan.–Feb. 1918.

Ninth waltz, The. R. C. Carton (pseud. of R. C. Critchett.) Comedy. 1m., 1w. Sc. Interior. FSD

Niobe. Thomas Sturge Moore. Verse. 3 voices. Sc. Screen or curtain. MOT

Nishikigi. Motokiyo. Trans. by Ernest Fenollosa. 2m., 1w., chorus. Sc. Not given. Poetry 4: 35–48, May 1914.

No admittance. Evelyn Gray Whiting. Farce. Amateur housekeeping. 7w. Sc. Interior. B

* **No Christmas in the house.** Marie Irish. 2b., 3g. Sc. Living room. I

* **No crown.** Clara J. Denton. 2b., chorus. Sc. Soldier's camp with tents. DAI

* **No girls admitted.** Edyth M. Wormwood. 4b., 4g. Sc. Interior. EP

* **No man is above the law.** Eleanore Hubbard. Obedience. 4b., chorus. Sc. Interior of a house in New York City in 1880. HUC

No peddlers admitted. Jeanette Joyce. 2m., 1w. Sc. Business office. MAP

* **"No presents."** Clara J. Denton. Christmas play. 5b. Sc. A street. I

No servants. Gertrude E. Jennings. 1m., 5w. Sc. Interior. FSD

No smoking. Jacinto Benavente. Trans. from the Spanish by John Garrett Underhill. 2m., 2w., chorus. Sc. A compartment in a first class railway carriage. BJP2, Drama 7: 78–88, Feb. 1917.

† **Noble lord, The.** Percival Wilde. Comedy. 2m., 1w. Sc. A secluded spot in the Maine woods. WED

"Noblesse oblige." William C. DeMille and John Erskine. 3m., 1w. Sc. Hunting lodge in 1358. Smart Set 21: 72–81, Jan. 1907.

Nocturne. R. L. Roeder. 2 char. Sc. Small room in castle. Moods 1: 4–9. Nov. 1908.

Nocturne. Anthony Wharton. Comedy. 2m., 3w. Sc. Lodgings in a London suburb. FSD

Noon. Edward Viets. Verse. Fanciful interlude. 2m. Sc. A pleasant meadow. VI

Norah makes a cake. Louise Rand Bascom. Comedy. 2w. Sc. Bare room. MBP

* **North-pole expedition, A.** Marie Irish. 7b. Sc. Deck of a ship. IPP

Northern light, A. William Sharp. Psychic poetic. 2m., 1w. Sc. A desolate district of North Scotland. SHV

Not a bit jealous. Frank Dumont. Comedy. 2m., 1w. Sc. Parlor. PPP

Not at home. Benjamin L. C. Griffith. 2m. Sc. Interior. GR

Not at home. Henry Lavedan. Trans. from the French. 2m., 2w., 1s. Sc. Comfortable sitting room. MR, Poet Lore 28: 407–413, Vacation 1917.

Not in the lessons. Mark O'Dea. Comedy. 2m., 2w. Sc. Boarding house in a village. OR

Not in the regular army. William Sidney Hillyer. Darky farce. 10m. Sc. Office. DPP

Not on the bills. Arthur Lewis Tubbs. Farce. 2m., 2w. Sc. Manager's office in a theatre. PPP

Not on the programme. Gladys Ruth Bridgham. Comedy. 3m., 3w. Sc. Interior. B

‡ **Not so bad after all.** Edith Brown-Evarts. Farce. 6b., 6g. Sc. Sitting room. BEY

† **Not wanted—a wife.** Edward B. Fenn. Farce. 3b. Sc. A college room. BAT

Nowadays call, A. Madeline Bridges. 2w. Sc. Not given. Smart Set 23: 119–120, Oct. 1907.

Numbers. Grover Theis. 2m., 2w. Sc. Officer's quarters at a considerable distance from the front. TN

Nursery maid of heaven, The. Thomas Wood Stevens. Miracle play. 3m., 6w. Sc. 1. Chapter room of convent. Sc. 2. Cell in convent SL

Nyanysa, a Zulu play. Edith S. Lyttelton. 5m., 3w., w. and c. Sc. Interior of a round Kaffir hut. Nineteenth Century 70: 321–338, Aug. 1911.

O

O Joy San. Katharine Kavanaugh. Japanese comedy. American marriage. 2m., 4w. Sc. Japanese interior. DEP

O-Ume's gods. Cale Young Rice. Verse. 2m., 2w. Sc. A room in a house near the sea in ancient Japan. RI

Oak settle, The. Harold Brighouse. 3m., 2w. Sc. Interior of a farmhouse. FSD

Object lesson, An. Frederick Sargent. Dramatic episode. 2m., 1w. Sc. Drawing room. FSD

Obsequies, The. J. L. Morgan. 9m., 2w., many others. Sc. Veranda of a fashionable residence. Smart Set 55: 81–86, June 1918.

Obstacle, The. Stephanie Damianakes. Satire. 2m., 1w. Sc. Studio. CU

Octavia. Charles V. H. Roberts. Play of the Roman Empire. 3m., 3w., chorus. Sc. A chamber in a villa. ROA

Odd streak, The. Roland Pertwee. 4w. Sc. Drawing room. FSD

Off Nags Head; or, The Bell buoy, a tragedy of the North Carolina coast. Dougald MacMillan. 2m.. 3w. Sc. Fisherman's hut. CFP

O'Flaherty, V. C. George B. Shaw. 2m., 2w. Sc. At the door of an Irish country house. SH, Hearst's 32: 87–91, 158–160, 1917.

* **Oh Dear!** Laura E. Richards. 4b., 2g. Sc. Room. RP

Oh! Helpless man! Edgar Morette. Housing problem play. 2m., 2w. Sc. Simple interior. B

Oh Lawsy me! Thomas King Moylan. Irish farce. 4m., 2w. Sc. Two back gardens in the suburbs of Dublin. MOO

‡ **Ola, or a Christmas present for Mother.** John H. Macdonald. Christmas play. 2b., 3g. Sc. Sitting room. TMP

Old class reunion, The. Willis N. Bugbee. 7m., 7w. Sc. School hall or assembly room. BUP

* **Old friends together.** Myrtle C. Cherryman. Christmas play. 7b., 5g. Sc. Parlor. DAH

Old King, The. Remy de Gourmont. Trans. by Richard Aldington. 3m., 3w., pages, servants. Sc. In castle. Drama 6:206–231, May 1916.

† **Old lady shows her medals, The.** J. M. Barrie. 3m., 4w. Sc. A poorly furnished room in a basement flat. BE

Old maid's venture, A. Elma M. Logie. Comedy. 3w. Sc. Old fashioned parlor. B

* **Old man and his grandson, The.** Augusta Stevenson. 3b., 1g. Sc. Interior of a house. SC3

* **Old Mother Goose.** Somepla (pseud.) 30c. Sc. Before the door of Mother Goose. SO

Old order, The. Evelyn Emig. 1m., 2w. Sc. Old fashioned sitting room in the U. S. Poet Lore 32:586–595, Winter 1921.

Old order, The. Sara Neumann. 3m., 3w. Sc. Kitchen of typical West Side Chicago flat. Drama 11:147–150, Feb. 1921.

Old Ragpicker. Theodore Dreiser. An episode. 4m., 1w., chorus characters. Sc. Street corner in lower West Side in N. Y. DP

Old ship, The. Clara J. Denton. FI

Old shoes. Anna Wolfrom. 4m., 2w. Sc. Old-time restaurant. WOH

Old stuff. Trelawney Dangerfield. 1m., 2w. Sc. Living room. Smart Set 52:77–82, June 1917.

* **Old tight-wad and the victory dwarf.** F. Ursula Payne. 2b. Dining room. PPC

* **Old toys, The.** Netta Syrett. 12c. Sc. Nursery. SSE

* **Old uncle Pat gives his consent.** Marie Irish. 2b., 1g. Sc. Sitting room. IPP

Old wife's tale. George Peele. Adapted from the old English play. 14m., 6w., 3b., 4 chorus groups. Sc. Room in a cottage in early England. ELT3

Old woman, The. Marjorie Allen Seiffert. Morality play. 3m., 2w. Sc. None. Poetry 13:204–208, Jan. 1919.

* **Old woman and her pig, The.** Somepla. (pseud.) 14c. Sc. Kitchen which opens out upon a road. SO

Old year and the new, The. Percival Chubb. Dramatization for New Year's Eve of Hawthorne's "The Sister Years." 3m., 2w. Sc. Outside the city hall. Drama 10:110–111, Dec. 1919.

Omar and the Rabbi. Fred LeRoy Sargent. Fitzgerald's trans. of the Rubaiyat of Omar Khayyam and Browning's Rabbi Ben Ezra arranged in dramatic form. 5m., 3w. Sc. A garden. SAQ

† **On bail.** George Middleton. 2m., 1w. Sc. Living room of a small flat. MIT, Smart Set 39:135–141, March 1913.

On Baile's strand. William Butler Yeats. Verse. 5m. chorus. Sc. Great hall in ancient house in Ireland. YC2, YK, YP2, YPP

On black ice. M. Churchill. 1m., 1w. Sc. Cozy dining room. Harvard Monthly 30 : 106–109, May 1900.

* **On Christmas eve.** Constance D'Arcy Mackay. 11c. Sc. Bare living room. MHH

* **On the dyke.** Clara J. Denton. 2b., 2g., chorus. Sc. On one of the dykes in Holland. DAG

On the high road. Anton Tchekoff. 7m., 3w., 1s., chorus. Sc. Interior of tavern in South Russia. CHD

On the highway. Anton Chekhov. Trans. from the Russian by David A. Modell. 8m., 3w. Others. Sc. Interior of tavern in South Russia. Drama 6 : 294–322, May 1916.

* **On the old plantation.** Harriet Sabra Wright. 6b. Sc. A cotton gin-house. WN

* **On the path of the child.** Anna Wynne. Morality play. 10c. Sc. Unimportant. DPP

On the pier. Laura Sherry. 1m., 1w. Sc. A pier in the river. WIP2

On the road. Wilfred Wilson Gibson. Verse. 2m., 1w. Sc. Hedge by the highway. GID, GIP

On the sight-seeing car. Ernest M. Gould. 7m., 2w. Sc. Any square in any city. PPP

On the staircase. Frances Aymar Mathews. Comedy. 1m., 1w. Sc. On the staircase in a house. WEP

On the stairway of life in seven ages. Mrs. Harry Alston Williams. 6m., 12w. Sc. A series of tableaux. FSD

On the threshold. Wilfred Wilson Gibson. Verse. 1m., 2w. Sc. Lonely cottage, GIA, GIP, GIS

On the threshold. Perez Hirchbein. Trans. from the Yiddish by Isaac Goldberg. The old and the new generation. 4m., 2w. Sc. An old fashioned room. PTT

On the tower. Sara Teasdale. 2m., 1w. Sc. Top of battlemented tower of a castle. International 4 : 41–42, Aug. 1911.

On the Veldt. Frederick C. Patterson. 2m., 1w. Sc. Room on farm in South Africa. Smart Set 29 : 113–117, Dec. 1909.

On vengeance height. Allan Davis and Cornelia C. Vercill. 2m., 2w. Sc. Cabin in the Tennessee mountains. FSD, REM, V1

On with the new. Felicia Goddard. 1m., 1w. Sc. Opera box. Smart Set 9 : 83–85, Feb. 1903.

* **Once upon a Christmastime.** Carolyn Wells. 15b., 9g. Sc. Clearing in a forest in winter. Ladies' Home Journal 31 : 75, Nov. 1914.

One a day. Caroline Briggs. Fantasy. 5m. Sc. A trench somewhere in France. MP

One by one, a mortality play. Harlan Thompson. 2m., 2w. Sc. Hall of top floor of apartment building. Smart Set 59 : 93–107, May 1919.

One cannot think of everything. Alfred de Musset. Comedy. 3m., 2w. Sc. Interior MUB

One day awake, a morality without moral. Harold Monro. 6m., 2w., 13 or more other char. Sc. Black curtains and a grey screen. Chapbook 32 : 1–32, Dec. 1922.

One day more. Joseph Conrad. 4m., 1w. Sc. Exterior of cottages near the sea wall. English Review 15 : 16–25, Aug. 1913. Smart Set 42 : 126–141, Feb. 1914.

‡ **100 per cent American.** Dorothy D. Calhoun. Comedy. Great War background. 14g. Sc. Reception room. FP

$100,000 club paper, The. Barbara T. Ring. 4m., 5w. Sc. Interior. B

One may spin a thread too finely. Ivan Tourguenieff. Trans. by Margaret Gough. 5m., 4w. Sc. Sitting room, richly furnished. Fortnightly 91 : 786–804, April 1909.

One of the old guard. Constance Campbell. 1m., 3w. Sc. Study. FSD

One war babe. Rebecca Forbes Sturgis. Tragedy. Great War play. 3m., 2w. Sc. Room in the cottage of a very poor German peasant. STR

* **One way to capture a fort.** Eleanore Hubbard. Historical-English-French rivalry in America. 2b. Sc. Inside a fort on the Mississippi river. HUD

* **Oneida's dream.** Virginia Olcott. A play of the camp fire. 8g. Sc. Open forest woodland. OPA

Onesimus. Wilbur S. Tuper. Biblical play. 4m., 1w. Sc. Portico of house in Colossae in 63 A. D. TU

* **"Only a girl!"** Eleanore Hubbard. Settlement of the U. S. 4b., 1g., 3 chorus groups. Sc. Block house. HUD

Only jealousy of Emer, The. William Butler Yeats. 7m., 1w. Bare space against the wall of any room. YF, Poetry 13 : 175–193, Jan. 1919.

† **Op-o'-me-thumb.** Frederick Fenn and Richard Pryce. 1m., 5w. Sc. Work room of a laundry. CBI, FSD

Open door, The. May Harris. 3m., 1w. Sc. Veranda of cottage at twilight. Smart Set 20 : 60–67, Oct. 1906.

Open door, The. Alfred Sutro. 1m., 1w. Sc. Drawing room. FSD, SF

† **Open or shut?** Binney Gunnison. Adapted from "Proverb" by Alfred de Musset. Comedy. 1m., 1w. Sc. Drawing room. GU

Operation, The. Wilfred Wilson Gibson. Verse. 1m., 2w. Sc. Room in tenements late at night. GID, GIP

Orangeman, The. St. John G. Ervine. Irish play. 3m., 1w. Sc. Kitchen of workmen's home in Belfast. ER

* **Oranges and lemons.** Lady Bell. 5b., 2g., chorus. Sc. Street. BR

Orator of Zapata City, The. Richard Harding Davis. 8m., 1w. Sc. Western court room. DP, DPP

† **Organizing a society.** Edith F. A. U. Painton. 3b., 5g. Sc. School room. PAD

Orpheus among the shades. Lady Margaret Sackville. Verse. 2m., 5w. Sc. Hades. SAS

Orthodoxy. Nina Wilcox Putnam. 18m., 11w., chorus. Sc. Interior of a church. Forum 51 : 801–820, June 1914.

Other fellow, The. Maverick Terrell. 2m. 1w. Sc. Living room. Smart Set 43 : 91–92, Aug. 1914.

Other one, The. Arthur Ketchum. 3m. Sc. A clear space under a railroad bridge. FS3

Other one, The. Charles Townsend. Comedy. Farce. 1m., 2w. Sc. Sitting room. FP

Other room, The. H. M. Paull. 3m., 2w. Sc. Professor's study. Nineteenth Century 90 : 807–818, Nov. 1921.

Other side, The. David Carb. 3w. Sc. Untidy living room. Harvard Monthly 52 : 44–49, April 1911.

Other voice, The. S. vK. Fairbanks. A novelty. 3 voices. Sc. River

flowing in open country with lights of a great city on its banks. B
Other woman, The. Louise Closser Hale. 2w. Sc. Drawing room of apartment. Smart Set 34: 107–113, June 1911.
Other woman, The. Ellis Kingsley. 2w. Sc. Interior. B
Our aunt from California. Madalene Demarest Barnum. 6w. Sc. Interior. FSD
Our Aunt Robertina. Mary Kyle Dallas. 4m., 3w. Sc. Plain interior. B
"Our Career." Edna Riese. Comedy. 5m., 4w. chorus. Sc. Reception room. FSD
* **Our choice.** Margaret Knox. Graduation play. 7g. Sc. Interior. LU
Our first performance; or, Not accustomed to the stage. W. C. Parker. 6m., Sc. Interior. DPP
* **Our friends the food.** Hester Donaldson Jenkins. Food play. 19c. Sc. Anywhere. JE
Our kind. Louise Saunders. 2m., 1w. Sc. Summer cottage. SAM, Smart Set 64: 73–84, Feb. 1921.
Our lady of the moon, a phantasy. G. Murray Atkin. 1m., 1w. Sc. Garden in full bloom. Canadian Magazine 55: 466–470, Oct. 1920.
Our Mary. Granville Forbes Sturgis. Comedy. Servant girl play. 1m., 1w. Sc. Breakfast room. STR
Our minister's bride. Evelyn Watson. 8w. Sc. Parlor. FSD
‡ **Our mother's aid society.** Edith Brown-Evarts. 6g. Sc. sitting room. BEY
* **Our uncle from the west.** M. Greenwald. Christmas play. 5b., 7g. Sc. Parlor. GRN
Outcast, The. August Strindberg. Trans. from the German of Emil Schering by Mary Harned. 2m. Sc. Simple room in the country. Poet Lore 17: 8–21, Autumn 1906.
Outcasts. Gilbert V. Seldes. 2m., 1w. Sc. Cheerful living room. Harvard Monthly 53: 122–125, Jan. 1912.
Outclassed. Carl Glick. Melodramatic comedy. 4m. Sc. Barn. STV, Smart Set 56: 83–93, Sept. 1918.
† **Outcome of a secret, The.** Mary M. Russell. 2b., chorus. Sc. Village street. RU
Outside, The. Susan Glaspell. 3m., 2w. Sc. Room in a house which was once a life saving station. GP
† **Outsider, a college play, An.** Wilhemen Wilkes. Basket ball play 7g. Sc. College girl's den. B
Outwitted, a society sketch. Bob O' Link (pseud.) 3w. Sc. Interior. FP
Outwitted. Harry L. Newton. Comedy. Dramatic novelty. 1m., 1w. Sc. Reception room in hotel in Europe. B
Over age. Emma Beatrice Brunner. 1m., 4w. Sc. Living room. BRB
Over the hills. John Palmer. 2m., 2w. Sc. Dining room of attractive home. Smart Set 46: 227–235, June 1915.
* **Over the hills and far away.** Someple (pseud.) 18c. Sc. An open space before a wall. SO
Overruled. George Bernard Shaw. Marriage theme. 1m., 1w. Sc. Retired corner of the lounge of seaside hotel. SHB, English Review 14: 179–197, May 1913. Hearst's Magazine 23: 681–96, May 1913.
Overtones. Alice Gerstenberg. 4w. Fashionable living-room GT, WSP

Owin' to Maggie. John Jason Trent. Comedy. 3m., 4w. Sc. Interior of lodging house. B

Oysters. Alice C. Thompson. Farce. 9w. Sc. Interior B

P

P. G's, The. Catherine Bellairs Gascoin. Farce. 3m., 4w. Sc. 1. Sitting room, Sc. 2. Dining-room. GAL

P's and Q's. Anna Nathan Meyer. Farce comedy. 2m., 2w. Sc. Interior. FSD

Packet for Popsy, A. Evelyn Simms. 1m., 3w. Sc. Interior. PPP

Packing. Daisy McGeoch. Comedy. 1m., 2w. Sc. Any interior. MAC

Paddly pools. Miles Malleson. Fairy play. 6b., 3g., 2 chorus groups. Sc. Stage strewn with toys. C2

Pagan, The. Lewis Purcell. 7m., 1w. Sc. Enclosure about a house of roughly squared logs in Ulster, Ireland in the 6th century. PU

‡ **Page from the past, A.** Marjorie Benton Cooke. Play of ancient Egypt. 4g. Sc. Interior DPP

* **Pageant of hours.** Constance D'Arcy Mackay. 14c. Sc. A greensward. MHH

Pagoda slave, A. Charles Keeler. A play of Burma. 5m., 3w., others. Sc. Interior of Buddhist monastery. Drama 12: 163–166, Feb. 1922.

Pair of burglars. Byron P. Glenn. Farce. 2m., 2w. Sc. Interior. B

Pair of knickerbockers, A. Eden Phillpotts. 1m., 1w. Sc. Interior. FSD

Pair of lunatics, A. W. R. Walkes. Romantic farce. 1m., 1w. Sc. Interior of lunatic asylum. FSD, PH

Pamperers, The. Mina Loy. 3m., 4w. Sc. Living room. Dial 69: 65–78, July 1920.

Pan in ambush. Marjory Patterson. 2m., 5w. Sc. Old-fashioned garden somewhere in England. REM, VI

† **Pan of fudge, A.** Maude Burbank. Boarding school comedy. 6w. Sc. Interior. B

Pan passes northward. John Hanlon. 1m., 2w. Sc. Woodland. Smart Set 61: 67–72, April 1920.

Pan pipes, a fairy tale. Constance Wilcox. 2m., 2w. Sc. A wooded hillside. WCT

Pandora's box. J. Gordon Amend. A play for a dancer. 2w. Sc. Massive room, richly furnished with tapestries and antique furniture. LO

* **Pandora's box.** Seymour S. Tibbals. Fairy play with Greek setting. 3b., 4g. Sc. Quaint old-fashioned room with woodland background. EP

Pantaloon. J. M. Barrie. 3m., 1w. Sc. A parlor. BH

Pants and the man. Harlan Thompson. 5m., 2w. Sc. Pressing Shop. Smart Set 53: 91–99, Nov. 1917.

Panurge's sheep. Henri Meilhac and Ludociv Halevy. Trans. from the French by Barrett H. Clark. Comedy. 2m., 2w. Sc. A richly furnished drawing room. FSD

* **Papa and mama.** Eduardo Barrios. Trans. by Willis Knapp Jones. Sc. 1b., 1g., 1c. Sc. Street of humble homes. Poet Lore 33: 286–290, Summer 1922.

Paper match, A. E. W. Burt. 2m., 2w. Sc. Interior. B

Paper money. William H. Jefferys. Missionary play of China. 1w., 1c. Sc. In front of a Buddhist temple in China. DOF

Paper wedding. Charles Nevers Holmes. Comedy of the first anniversary. 1m., 5w. Sc. Interior. DEP

Paracelsus. Arthur Schnitzler. Verse-poetic. 4m., 2w. Sc. Well furnished home. SG

* **Paradise of children, The.** Gladys S. Warren. Pandora play. 4b., 2g., chorus. Sc. Room with window looking out on the garden. BHP

Parents' progress, The. George Paston. 3m., 3w. Sc. Drawing room. FSD

Pariah. August Strinderg. Trans. from the Swedish. 2m. Sc. Simply furnished room in a farm house. STO

Paris and Aenone. John Hall Wheelock. 1m., 1w., chorus. Sc. Mount Ida. Harvard Monthly 44: 142–150, May 1907.

Paris doctor, The. Harold Brighouse. 3m., 1w. Sc. An old garden of a small fishing village in Brittany. BRP

Parkin Bros. George Calderon. Comedy. 3m. Sc. Back parlor. CA

* **Parlement of foules, The.** Evelyn Smith. Adapted from Chaucer. 17c. Sc. Garden. SFR

Parliament of servants, A. Louise Latham Wilson. Comedy. 5w. Sc. A parlor. DPP

† **Parlor patriots, The.** Dorothy Donnell Calhoun. Society satire with Great War background. 12g. Sc. Reception room. FP

Parrot cage, The. Mary Shaw. 7m., Sc. Cage. DPP

Parted by Patience. Bessie Blair Smith. Farce. 2m., 3w. Sc. Interior. PPP

Parted sisters, The. F. Ursula Payne. Patriotic allegory in verse. 2m., 8w. Sc. None required. FSD

Parthenon, The. Isaac Rieman Baxley. Play of famous architecture. 4m., 1w. Sc. Studio. BAX

Parting, The. Kenneth Sawyer Goodman. Melodrama. 3m., 1w. Sc. Attic. GQA

* **Party in Mother Goose land, A.** Effa E. Preston. 33c of primary grades. Sc. Interior. PAP

Pa's new housekeeper. C. S. Bird. Farce. 3m., 2w. Sc. Living room. B

Passè. McElbert Moore. 4m., 2w. Sc. Interior. FSD

Passing of Hiawatha, The. Constance D'Arcy Mackay. 9m., 6w., 2c., many chorus characters. Sc. An Indian encampment. MPP

Passing of Lilith, The. William Sharp. Symbolic poetic, visionary. 3m., 1w., 2 chorus groups. Sc. Primal Eden. SHV

Passing of the magi, The. Eduardo Zamacois. Trans. from the Spanish. Comedy. Children's festival play of Spain. 7m., 4w., 1g. Sc. In a private house in the suburbs of a Castilian city. TUR

Passing shadow, The. Leo Sarkadi. 2m. Sc. Scantily furnished bedroom. International 10: 237–239, Aug. 1916.

Passion of Père Hilarion, The. William Sharp. Dramatic poetic. 2m., 1w. Sc. A small dark room, opening from the sacristy of the Church of Notre Dame. SHV

Paste cut paste. Louise Closser Hale. 3w. Sc. Drawing room of home. Smart Set 36: 125–132, Jan. 1912.

Pastor of Jena, The. Graham S. Rawson. French historical background—Napoleonic times. 9m., 1w., chorus. Sc. Simple living room. RA

Pat the apothecary. O. E. Young. Farce. 6m., 2w. Sc. Office of beauty specialist. DEP

† **Patelin.** Guillaume Alecis. Adapted from the farce "Maitre Pierre Patelin." 4m., 1w., 1b., 1g., chorus. Sc. Double scene on same stage. ELT2

Pater Noster. François Coppee. Trans. from the French by Will Hutchins. Verse. 6m., 2w. Sc. Room in a simple house in France. FSD

‡ **Pathfinder.** Martin Studios, Editor. 4b., 2g., chorus. Sc. Primitive forest in Canada. Indian camp in background. MAT

Patriots. Sara King Wiley. Historical background—American Revolution. 3m., 2w. Sc. Large and pleasant kitchen in farmhouse. FSD

* **Patriot's parade, The.** Marjorie H. Davis. Patriotic play. 2b., 1g., 4 chorus groups. Sc. Unimportant. FL

Patron of art, A. Dora Adele Shoemaker. Farce. 7w. Sc. Reception room. PPP

* **Pat's excuse.** No author given. 1b., 1g. Sc. Kitchen. BBS

Pat's matrimonial venture. Ward Macauley. Comedy. 1m., 2w. Sc. Interior. DEP

Patty packs a bag. David Garrow. Comedy. 1m., 2w. Sc. Sitting room of a small house in a seaside town. FSD

Pauline Pavlovna; arr. for play presentation, poem by Thomas Bailey Aldrich, stage business by Marion Short. 1m., 1w. Sc. Ante-camber to grand ball-room in Winter Palace in St. Petersburg, Russia. WEP

Pavement artist, The. Herbert C. Sargent. 2m., 1w. Sc. Unimportant. SAR

Pawns. Percival Wilde. Great War play. 6m. Sc. A swampy forest. WU

Paying the Piper. Frances Aymar Mathews. 1m., 6w. Sc. Elaborately furnished drawing room. WEP

Peace. George Calderon. Farce. 3m. Sc. Interior. CA

Peace at home. George Courtelaine. Trans. by F. C. Fay. 1m., 1w. Sc. Library. International 7: 365–366, 380–382, Dec. 1913.

Peace at home. Georges (Courteline) Moinaux. Trans. from the French by Leroy James Cook. 1m., 1w. Sc. Workshop of a literary man. Poet Lore 29: 331–334, May–June 1918.

Peace manoeuvers. Richard Harding Davis. 3m., 1w. Sc. Interior. FSD

Peace on earth. Van Vechten Hostetter. 4m., 1w., several others. Sc. Bedroom of a fine New York hotel. Smart Set 62: 93–95, July 1920.

Peace that passeth understanding, The. John Reed. A fantasy. 12m. Sc. Salon in Paris which was meeting place of the Peace Conference. Liberator 2: 25–31, Mar. 1919.

Peacemaker, The. E. M. Bryant (pseud. of E. M. B. Boak). 2m., 3w. Sc. Interior. FSD

Peacemaker, The. Derby Brown. 3m., 3w. Sc. Interior. B

Peck of trouble, A. Alice C. Thompson. Comedy. 5w. Sc. Sitting room. B

Peggy, a tragedy of tenant farmer. Harold Williamson. 4m., 2w., 1c. Sc. Bare room in a tenant shack. CFP

† **Peggy's predicament.** Eleanor Maud Crane. Farce comedy. 5g. Sc. Kitchen in a modern New York apartment. FP

Peg's little sister. Anne M. Mitchell. 3m., 2w. Sc. Living room. DAK

* **Pen and the inkstand, The.** Augusta Stevenson. 8b. Sc. A poet's room. SC4

Penelope's affinity. Mary C. Russell. Suitable for women's clubs. 8w., chorus. Sc. Living room. B

* **Pennsylvania incident, A.** Blanche Shoemaker Wagstaff. Play of American colonial history. 1b., 3g. Sc. A colonial room. WCP

Penny bunch, A. A. Neil Lyons and Vera Beringer. Comedy. 1m., 2w. Sc. Street. FSD

Penultimate test, The. Leslie T. Peacocke. 2m., 2w. Sc. Richly furnished smoking room in London home. Smart Set 37: 135–142, June 1912.

People, The. Susan Glaspell. 10m., 2w. Sc. Office of a radical newspaper. GP, GPC

People who die. Alfred Kreymborg. Dream play. 1m., 1w. Sc. In front of a curtain. KMP, KMR

Peregrinations of Polly, The. Helen P. Kane. Comedy. 3w. Sc. Prettily furnished room. FP

Perfect church, The. Grace S. Richmond. 3m. Sc. Village square. Ladies' Home Journal 38: 115, June 1921.

‡ **Perfect holiday, The.** Evelyn Smith. From Louisa M. Alcott. "Little women." 1b., 7g. Sc. Shabby sitting room. SFR

Perfect jewel maiden, The. Trans. from the Japanese by Yone Noguchi. 3m., 1w. Sc. None. Poet Lore 28: 334–337, Summer 1917.

Perfect machine, The. Arthur Scott Craven and J. D. Beresford. 1m., 1w. Sc. A study. English Review 26: 393–408, May 1918.

Perhaps. Grace Livingston Furniss. Comedy. 2m., 1w. Sc. Apartment in a hotel in N. Y. FSD

Person in the chair, The; a revelation, Francis Shaw. 3m., 7w. Sc. Living room in city house. Drama 11: 171–174, Feb. 1921.

Petalesharoo. Helen Fitzgerald Sanders. Verse. Indian history play. Based on James' expedition to the Rocky Mountains, 1819–1820. 4m., 3w., chorus. Sc. A clearing in a dense wood. SAD

Peter. Harry Osborne. Farce. 1m., 2w. Sc. Interior. B

Peter Donelly. Mary Macmillan. 1m., 3w. Sc. Comfortable well-to-do library. MTT

* **Peter Grief.** Olive Allen. Moral play. 3b., 6g. Sc. A parlor. BHP

‡ **Ph.D., The.** Clara J. Denton. 3g. Sc. Sitting room. MBP

Pharaoh's knob. Edith J. Craine. 2m., 11w. Sc. Lobby in a summer hotel. FP

* **Pheasant's eggs.** C. I. Chambers. Scout play. 11b., 1g. Sc. A path near a wood. CB

Philanthropy. Frank G. Tompkins. 2m., 2w. Sc. The maid's room off the kitchen. LO

Philip the king. John Masefield. Historical play of Spain. 7m., 1w., chorus. Sc. Little dark cell in palace. MTA

† **Philosopher of Butterbiggens, The.** Harold Chapin. Comedy of Scotch life. 2m., 1w., 1b. Sc. Room in tenement. FSD, JOA, LE, REP

Philosophers. Morris Colman. Satire. 2m., 1w. Sc. Backyard of apartment house. Smart Set 60: 87–94, Oct. 1919.

Philosophers, The. Rollo Peters. 5m. Sc. Not given. Forum 54: 240–241, Aug. 1915.

* **Philosophy and fairies.** E. E. Bloxam. 20c. and chorus. Sc. A nursery. BL

Phipps. Stanley Houghton. 2m., 1w. Sc. Sir Gerald's library. HF

† **Phoebe Louise.** Bernard Sobel. 1m., 2w., 1c. Sc. Luxurious living room. SB

Phoenix, The. Laurence Irving. 2m., 2w. Sc. Interior. FSD

Phonograph, The. David Pinski. 14m., 11w., chorus characters. Sc. Room in a home in a remote Russo-Yiddish town. PT

Photographer's troubles, A. Jessie A Kelley. Farce. 4m., 8w. Sc. Photograph gallery. FSD

Physical torture club, The. Willis N. Bugbee. 2m., 2w. Sc. Bare Interior. MAP

Pianissimo, an intermezzo. Alfred Kreymborg. 2m. Sc. Park bench. KMR Poetry 20:175, July 1922.

Piazza parleys. Charles Battell Loomis. 1m., 1w. Sc. Hotel piazza in White Mts. Smart Set 12:95–97, Dec. 1903.

* **Pickett's Christmas party.** Marie Irish. Christmas play. 4b., 3g. Sc. Living room. IC

Pickled polliwog. O. E. Young. Farce. 3m., 2w. Sc. Kitchen. APP

† **Pickles, bonbons and temper.** Alice W. Chaplin. 4g. Sc. Sitting room. CHC

Pictures. Horace Holley. 2m., 1w. Sc. A studio in Paris. HOR

Picturing. Daisy McGeoch. Comedy. 5m., 3w. Sc. In a cinema. MAC

Pie. Lawrence Langner. Comedy. 2m., 2w. Sc. A comfortable room in an apartment. LAF

Pie-dish, The. George Fitzmaurice. 4m., 2w. Sc. Interior of farmhouse kitchen. FF

Pie in the oven, The. John Joy Bell. 2m., 2w. Comedy. Sc. Kitchen of a cottage in the country. REP

* **Piece of cheese, A.** Augusta Stevenson. 3b. Sc. A kitchen. SCI

Piece of ivory, A. Florence Lincoln. 2m., 2w. Sc. Comfortable library. Harvard Monthly 52:56–57, April 1911.

Pierrot by the light of the moon. Virginia Church. A fantasy. 2m., 3w. Sc. Moonlit garden. Drama 9:139–148, Feb. 1919.

Pierrot in Paris. Colin Campbell Clements. 2m., 3w. Sc. Under an awning of a café in the Latin quarter. CLD

† **Pierrot of the minute, The.** Ernest Dowson. Dramatic fantasy. 1m., 1w. Sc. Glade in the Parc du Petit Trianon. B, C1, DPN, DPO, FSD, SL

Pilgrims' holiday, The. Vida R. Sutton. American colonial history. 7m., 2w., chorus. Sc. 1. Prologue before curtain. Sc. 2. Pilgrim's house interior. FSD

* **Pilgrims in Holland, The.** Louise E. Tucker and Estelle L. Ryan. 2b., 2g. Sc. Garden. TRH

* **Pine tree, The.** Mabel Goodlander. 5c. Sc. In the forest. GF

Pine tree, The. Takeda Izumo. 3m., 3w., 9c., 1s., chorus. Sc. Class room in a Japanese school. IPT

* **Pink scarf, The.** Duckie Smith. Christmas play. 8g. Sc. Interior. MAP

* **Pioneer boys and girls.** Wallace Rice. 4b., 4g. Sc. A clearing in a wood. RIS

Pioneers, The. Constance D'Arcy Mackay. 3m., 5w., many chorus characters. Sc. Natural clearing in the Primeval forest. MPP

Pioneers, The. James Oppenheim. Verse. 5m., 2w. Sc. Stage. OPP

Pious Aeneas. Maurice Baring. Historical farce. 1m., 1w., 2s. Sc. Room in Dido's palace at Carthage. BA

Pipe of desire, The. George Edward Burton. 2m., 1w., chorus. Sc. A level spot covered with grass. BAR

Pipe of peace, A. Margaret Cameron. Comedy. 1m., 2w. Sc. Dining room. CAC, FSD

Piper's pay, The. Margaret Cameron. Comedy. 7w. Sc. Boudoir. FSD

Pirates. Colin Campbell Clements. Mid-Victorian comedy. 7w. Sc. Living room. FSD

Pitiless policeman, The. George (Courteline) Moinaux. Trans. from the French by H. Isabelle Williams. 3m. Sc. Office of the Clerk of the District Court. Poet Lore 28: 217–230, Spring 1917.

Pixy, The. Mrs. Havelock Ellis. 3m. Sc. A Cornish farmhouse kitchen. EL

Pizarro and Rolla. Binney Gunnison. Adapted from Sheridan's Pizarro. Historical play of Spain. 2m., 1w. Sc. Tent on the battlefield. GU

Placing a play. Harry P. Mawson. 6m., others. Sc. Grill room, Thespians' club. Smart Set 22: 121–124, May 1907.

Placing Paul's play, miniature comedy. Mr. and Mrs. Henry F. Downing. Comedy of playwright's. 2m., 1w. Sc. Study. DOW

* **Plaie for Merrie May tyme; wherein ye scholars go a-masking.** Johnston Grosvenor. With dances and music. 15c. Sc. Ye village green. MAP

Playgoers. Arthur Pinero. 2m., 6w. Sc. Morning-room in a fine house in London. FSD

Play lovers, The. Labor Day musical play with a moral. Carolyn Wells. Several c. Sc. Pleasant green field. Ladies' Home Journal 39: 13, 127, Aug. 1922.

Playing gooseberry; a society comedy. Evelyn Simms. 2m., 2w. Sc. Sitting room. FP

* **Playing rabbit.** Elizabeth F. Guptill. 8c. Sc. Unimportant. GUT

Playing the game. Leon M. Lion and Austin Philips. Comedy. 3m., 2w. Sc. Manager's office in bank. FSD

Playing with fire. Percival Wilde. Comedy. 1m., 2w. Sc. Kitchen. WED

* **Playroom, The.** Doris F. Halman. Fantasy. 2b., 4g. Sc. Interior of a stable belonging to a city house. FS2, HAS

"Play's the thing, The." Ferdinand Reyher. A dramatic nightmare. 20 or more m. and w. Sc. Living room. Smart Set 46: 99–110, May 1915.

‡ **Pleasant surprise, A.** Edith Brown-Evarts. Farce. 3b., 3g. Sc. Library. BEY

Please pass the cream. Charles Nevers Holmes. Comedy. 1m., 1w. Sc. Dining room. DEP

Plot of Potzentausend, The. Miss E. H. Keating. Comedy. 10m. Sc. Large room in frontier village in Germany in 18th century. KE

Plumber, The. Louise Rand Bascom. Comedy. 1m., 1w. Sc. Bare room. MBP

Plume of feathers, A. Gulielma Penn and R. Fitzjohn. Comedy. 3w. Sc. Poorly furnished room in lodging house in London. FSD

Po' white trash. Evelyn G Sutherland. 4m., 4w. Sc. Dilapidated cabin exterior in Georgia. SUP

* **Pocohontas in London.** Louise E. Tucker and Estelle L. Ryan. 3b., 4g. Sc. Ante chamber in fashionable house in London. TRH

Poet at the court of Pan, A. Lady Margaret Sackville. Verse. 2m., 5w. Sc. A green field. SAS

Poetry and prose. Z. Levin. Trans. from the Yiddish by Isaac Goldberg. 1m., 1w. Sc. Room in East Side tenement. PTT

Poet's club, The. M. N. Beebe. Farce. 11m. Sc. Interior. B

Poet's heart. Maxwell Bodenheim. 3m., 2w. Sc. Purple wall framing a window. Little Review 4: 21–24, July 1917.

‡ **Poet's well, The.** Mrs. Alice C. Riley. 5b., 2g., chorus groups. Sc. Garden. RIT

Poet's wife. May Harris. 2w. Sc. Large comfortable living room. Smart Set 44: 55–59, Oct. 1914.

Pokey or the beautiful legend of the amorous Indian. Philip Moeller. A cartoon comedy. 6m., 3w. Sc. On top of a tall cliff. MF

Poland—1919. David Pinski. 12m., 4w., 5c., chorus. Sc. A spacious dark cellar. PT

Police matron, The. Carl Glick and Mary Hight. Melodrama. 3m., 2w. Sc. Office of police matron in Chicago police station. B

Political editor, The. Comedy of newspaper and political life. Charles Ulrich. 3m., 1w. Committee room of state capitol. DEP

‡ **Political promises.** E. M. Peixotto. Farce. 7b. Sc. Office. PET

Political pull. J. J. Jackson. Comedy. 3m., 3w. Sc. Drawing room. B

Pollen picks a wife. Ward Macauley. 5m., 4w. Sc. Library of a home. PPP

* **Polly puts the kettle on.** Lady Bell. 6g. Sc. Cottage. BR

Polyxena, from the "Hecuba" of Euripides. Samuel A. Eliot. ed. 3m., 3w., 2s., chorus. Sc. An open space between the sea and the Achaian camp. ELT1

Pompadour's protegé, The. Kate Jordan Vermilye. 2m., 2w., 1b. Sc. Gardens of Versailles in 1757. Smart Set 12: 75–87, Sept. 1903.

Pool, The. R. L. Roeder. Symbolic comedy. 4w. Sc. Enchanted forest. Moods 1: 196–207, Ap.–May, 1909.

* **Pool of answers, The.** Anne A. T. Craig. Idyllic play. 5b., 6g., 2 chorus groups. Sc. An opening among forest trees. CD

Poor Harold. Floyd Dell. 1m., 3w. Sc. Room in Washington Square South. DK

Poor house, The. Louise Driscoll. 2m., 2w. Sc. Kitchen in cottage on Hudson. Drama 7: 448–460, Aug. 1917.

Poor John. Gregorio Martinez Sierra. Trans. by John Garrett Underhill. 5m., 5w. Sc. Formal garden. Drama 10: 172–180, Feb. 1920.

* **Poor little boy.** Virginia Olcott. Play of garden production. 6c. Sc. An open space. OPA

"Poor old Jim." William C. DeMille. 2m., 1w. Sc. Sitting room. FSD

Poor relations. Mrs. E. H. Keating. Proverb play. "Love me, Love my dog." 7m. Sc. Interior. KE

Poorhouse, The. Douglas Hyde. Trans. by Lady Gregory. 3m., 2w. Sc. Poorhouse ward. Samhain Sept. 1903 pp. 19–24.

Popopelka. Lawrence Vail. 1m., 2w. Sc. Beach of desert island. Smart Set 64: 89–97, Jan. 1921.

Popping by proxy. O. E. Young. Farce. 2m., 4w. Sc. Neatly furnished room. B

Poppy seller, The. Kathleen C. Greene. 3m., 1w., 1b. Sc. Room in a besieged castle. GDL

† **Popular Dick, The.** Edith F. A. U. Painton. Comedy. 5b., 4g. Sc. Room with large dictionary on stand in corner. PAD

Porcelain and pink. F. Scott Fitzgerald. 1m., 2w. Sc. Downstairs in a summer cottage. Smart Set 61: 77–85, Jan. 1920.

Portrait, The. Thacher Howlad Guild. Fantasy. 7m., 2w. Sc. A castle hall, long ago. GUI

Portrait, The. Florine R. Wormser. 2m., 2w. Sc. Sitting room of a luxuriously furnished house. Smart Set 28: 76–83, June 1909.

Portrait of Tiero, The. Zoe Akins. 6m., 2w. and others. Sc. Room in Italian villa in 16th century. Theatre Arts Magazine 4: 316–337, Oct. 1920.

Portrait on the wall. Edward Goodman. 3m., 1w. Sc. Library. Moods 2: 11–19, Aug.–Sept. 1909.

Possession. Laurence Housman. A peep-show in Paradise. 2m., 5w. Sc. The everlasting habitations. HA4 HAP

Possession. George Middleton. 1m., 2w., 2s. Sc. Broad entrance hallway of a luxuriously appointed residence. MIP

Post of honor, The. Evan Poole. Historical play of France. 3m., 3w., chorus. Sc. Boudoir in King's chateau in the 16th century. PA

Postal orders. Rowland Pertwee. Farce. 1m., 4w. Sc. Post office. FSD

† **Postman's knock, The.** Barbara Burbank. ed. 2b., 2g., Sc. Kitchen. BU

Post-script, The. Emile Augier. Trans. from the French by Barrett H. Clark. 1m., 1w., 1s. Sc. Elegantly furnished room. AU

Pot boiler, The. Alice Gerstenberg. A satire. 5m., 2w. Sc. A stage only half set for rehearsal. GT, SL

Pot-luck. Gertrude Robins. Farce. 3m., 1w. Sc. Room in a cottage. FSD

Pot of broth, A. William Butler Yeats. 2m., 1w. Sc. Cottage kitchen. YH, YPP   The Gael 22: 310–313, Sept. 1903.

* **Pot of gold, The.** Augusta Stevenson. 4b. Sc. Vineyard. SC2

* **Potentate of Weatherdom, The.** Margaret G. Parsons. May day play. 14c. Sc. An open green. PR

Potter Thompson. Frederic W. Moorman. Play of King Arthur of the Round Table legend in Yorkshire dialect. 9m., 3w. chorus. Sc. 1. Potter's workshop in 15th century. Sc. 2. Out of doors. MOR

Power of a God, The. Thacher Howland Guild. 3m., 1w. Sc. Doctor's office. GUI

Power of flattery, The. Violet Clarke. 3w. Sc. Hat-shop, Paris. Smart Set 8: 143–145, Oct. 1902.

* **Power of loyalty;** a war time play. Helen Dorsen. Great War background. 20c. Sc. 1. Living room. Sc. 2. Bed room. DOR

* **Power of Purim.** Irma Kraft. 4b., 7g. Sc. Outskirts of a small village. KPP

† **Prairie princesses.** Binney Gunnison. Comedy. 2m., 4w., 1s. Sc. Richly furnished drawing room in an English castle. GU

Preferences. Fairfax S. Rogers. 3m., 1w. Sc. Small sitting room in hotel in Boston. Harvard Monthly 39: 180–192, Jan. 1905.

Prelude. (To "Creation" a drama.) 1m., 1w., several voices and choruses. Sc. Misty scene. Seven Arts 1: 240–259 Jan. 1917.

Press cuttings. Bernard Shaw. 3m., 3w. Sc. Office. SPC

Pressing matter, A. Brandon Hurst. 1m., 1w., 1b. Sc. Studio. WHP

Pretty bequest. Malcolm Watson. 3m., 2w. Sc. Interior. WIA

Previous engagement, The. Percival Wilde. Comedy. 1m. Sc. Living room of a modestly furnished bachelor's apartment. WE

Price of coal, The. Harold Brighouse. 1m., 3w. Sc. Colliery village. REP

Price of fame, The. Walter R. Matthews. 1m., 1w. Sc. Dining room. FSD

* **Price of liberty, The.** Eleanore Hubbard. Financial play. 5b. Sc. Federal Hall in Colonial N. Y. HUC

Price of orchids, The. Winifred Hawkridge. 4m., 2w. Sc. Inside a florist shop. Smart Set 47: 103–119, Oct. 1915.

Price of popularity, The. Mrs. Edmond LaBeaume. 1m., 1w. Sc. Dressing room. BUX

† **Pride against pride.** Binney Gunnison. Adapted from Westlund Marston's Donna Diana. 4m., 2w., chorus. Sc. Hall in a palace. GU

Pride and charity; or, A game of pinochle. Fred H. James and George J. Wetzel. 3m., 1w. Sc. Elegant drawing room.

Pride of the family, The. Agnes L. Crimmins. 3m., 1w. Sc. Kitchen of New England farm. B

Pride of regiment. F. D. Bone. 2m., 1w. Sc. Interior. FSD

Prim Miss Perkins, The. Harry LaMarr. 1m., 1w. Sc. Sitting room of farm house. B

* **Primrose lane, a May-day play for out of doors.** Cornelia Meigs. 3m., 3w., c. Sc. The edge of a wood. St. Nicholas 46: 641–647, May 1919.

Prince of court painters, The. Constance D'Arcy Mackay. 1m., 1w. Sc. Living room in cottage in 18th century. MB

Prince of Semberia, The. Branislav Nooshich. Trans. by Luka Djurichich and Bertha W. Clark. 10m., 1w., others. Sc. Enclosure before prince's house. Poet Lore 33: 85–96, Spring 1922.

Prince Patiomkin. Louise Gilmore. 4m., 1w. Sc. Salon communicating with Empress Catherine's private apartments in 1776. Double Dealer 3: 144–154, March 1922.

Prince who was a piper, The. Harold Brighouse. 5m., 8w., chorus. Sc. Palace garden. BRP

Prince's pigeon, The. Francis Walker. Japanese play. 1m., 2w., 2b. Sc. Room in the tower of a Japanese castle. WAK

* **Princess and a churn, A.** Virginia Olcott. A play of human fitness. 2g. Sc. Cottage. OPA

Princess and the countess, The. Binney Gunnison. Adapted from R. L. Stevenson's Prince Otto. 2w. Sc. Room in palace. GU

* **Princess and the crystal pipe, The.** Beulah Folmsbee. 6b., 5g. Sc. Old fashioned garden. St. Nicholas 48: 61–65, Nov. 1920.

* **Princess and the pixies, The.** Constance D'Arcy Mackay. 8c., chorus characters. Sc. A bare room. MHH

* **Princess and the swineherd, The.** Lena Dalkeith. From Hans Andersen. 2b., 3g., chorus. Sc. Hall in a palace. DLP

Princess' choice, The. Margaret Rabe. 13m., 5w., others. Sc. Grove in a garden. Quarterly Journal of Speech Education 5: 279–286, May 1919.

* **Princess Fragoletta.** Netta Syrett. 14c., chorus groups. Sc. Palace garden. SSE

* **Princess in the fairy tale, The.** Constance Wilcox. Fantastic. 6b., 9g. Sc. A garden. WTC

Princess innocence, The. Mary Moncure Parker. 8w. Sc. Out of doors in a wood. PM

* **Princess Moss-Rose.** Marguerite Merington. For Everychild's birthday. 8m., 4w., 3 animals, many chorus characters. Sc. Hall of a castle. MFP

Princess on the road, The. Kathleen C. Greene. 1m., 1w., chorus. Sc. Street of a country village. GDL

‡ **Princess Parsimonia.** E. M. Fotheringham. 4b., 3g. Sc. Outside the Palace. FSD

* **Princess Pocahontas.** Constance D'Arcy Mackay. 10b., 13g., chorus characters. Sc. An open glade. MPY

* **Princess Rosy cheeks.** Effie Sammond Balph. 2c. 8 chorus groups. Sc. Child's bedroom. EP

‡ **Prindle's proposal.** Marie Irish. 7b., 5g. Sc. In the wildwood. IL

Prinzessin von Barnhof. Eulora M. Jennings. Farce. 1m., 6w., 1s. Sc. Room in a German castle. FSD

* **Priscilla, Myles and John.** Marguerite Merington. Thanksgiving play. 2b., 2g. Sc. Living room in a log cabin in Plymouth Colony. MFH

Priscilla's room. Louise Latham Wilson. Farce. College play. 4m., 2w. Sc. Room in a student's apartment house. BUP

Prisoner, The. Clarendon Ross. 2m., 1w. Sc. Attic bedroom. Poet Lore 29: 590–595, Winter 1918.

Privy council, A. Major W. P. Drury and Richard Pryce. English literary characters—Pepys. 3m., 4w. Sc. English interior. FSD

Prize, The. John Bargate. Satire on women's bridge clubs. 4m., 3w. Sc. Interior. FSD

† **Prize of learning, The.** Edith Brown-Evarts. Adapted from Mrs. Crowley's "Who's the dupe?" 5b., 2g. Sc. Drawing room. BEY

Prize picture, The. Herbert C. Sargent. Farce. 1m., 1w. Sc. Studio. SAR

Problem of the hour. Mrs. E. LaBeaume. 5w. Sc. Apartment in a hotel. BUX

Prodigal son. Harry Kemp. Comedy. 3m., 2w. Sc. A hill town in Galilee sometime before the beginning of the Christian era. FLS Smart Set 52: 83–93, July 1917.

Professional visit. Rudolph Raphael. Comedy. 2m., 1w. Sc. Doctor's office. B

* **Professor Frog's lecture.** Eleanor L. Skinner and Ada M. Skinner 3b., 1g., chorus. Sc. Hill near a pond. SSC

Professor of love, The. Katharine Kavanaugh. Comedy. 3m., 3w. Sc. Library in a home. DPP

Professor's truant gloves, The. Elliott Palmer Bell. 1m., 1w. Sc. Interior. FP

AN INDEX TO ONE-ACT PLAYS

Progress. St. John Ervine. 1m., 2w. Sc. Professor's study. Saturday Evening Post 194: 10–11, 40, 42, 45–46, Feb. 11, 1922.

* **Prohibition Mother Goose.** Anna Pritchard George. 24c. Sc. Living room. PRI

Prologue. Carl Glick. 3m. Sc. A bridge, a street or a corner of a park under an arc light. Poet Lore 33: 553–562, Winter 1922.

Prologue for a marionette theatre. Hugo von Hoffmannsthal. Englished by Pierre Loving. 1m., 1w. Sc. Clearing in a wood. LO International 10: 103–104, April 1916.

Prometheus Pyrphoros. Joseph Trumbull Stickney. 3m., 2w., voices. Sc. The plain of Haimonia. Harvard Monthly 31: 45–64, Nov. 1900.

Promise, The. Evan Poole. Historical. 5m., 1w., chorus. Sc. King's palace in France in 16th century. PA

‡ **Promised land, The.** Mae Stein Sobel. 5b., 5 chorus groups. Sc. Tabernacle of the people of Israel. SOB

Proof of the pudding, The. Percy O. Martin. Farce. 2m., 1w. Sc. Pleasant room in a villa in the suburbs. PLA

Proposal, The. Frances Aymer Mathews. Romantic comedy. 1m., 2w. Sc. Tastefully furnished drawing room. WEP

Proposal, The. Anton Chekhov. 2m., 1w. Sc. Drawing room. CHD International 8: 150–155, May 1914.

Proposal in grandma's day, A. Jeannette Joyce. 2m., 2w. Sc. Kitchen. MAP

Proposing. Daisy McGeoch. Comedy. 2m., 2w. Sc. Unimportant. MAC

Proposing by proxy. Arthur Helliar and Harold Montague. 1m., 1w. Sc. Interior. FSD

Pros and cons, The. Gertrude Jennings. 1m., 3w. Sc. Drawing room of middle-class people. JF

Protegée of the mistress, A. Alexander Ostrovsky. Trans. from the Russian by George R. Noys. Scenes from Russian village life. 4m., 4w., chorus characters. Sc. Part of a densely grown garden on a Russian estate. OST

* **Protest of the trees, The.** Mrs. Arthur T. Seymour. Blue bird play. Sc. Sc. Forest. SE

* **Proud finger-ring, The.** Augusta Stevenson. 2b., 3g. Sc. Bedroom. SC2

* **Provident society, The.** Edith F. A. U. Painton. Thrift play. Any number of children. Sc. Platform. PAS

Public worrier, The. George M. Vickers. 5m., 2w. Sc. Office. PPP

* **Pumpkin Pie Peter.** Marie Irish. Thanksgiving Day play. 6b., 5g. Sc. Interior. PAP

Punch and Go. John Galsworthy. Comedy. 8m., 2w. Sc. Stage of a theatre set for a dress rehearsal. GSS

* **Punch and Judy.** No author given. 9b., 1g., 3 animals. Sc. Punch and Judy arrangement. MTC

Punk; or, The amateur rehearsal. Henry Clay Smith. 3m., 4w. Sc. Interior. FSD

* **Puppet Princess, The; or, The heart that squeaked,** Augusta Stevenson. Christmas play. 6b., 7g., chorus. Sc. Palace. HOM STF

* **Purim players.** Samuel S. Grossman. Jewish holiday play. 8b., 5g. Sc. Room in a house. GRS

* **Puritan Christmas, A.** Virginia Olcott. 2b., 2g. Sc. A cottage kitchen in early Salem. OP

* **Puritan prank, A.** Madeline Poole. Thanksgiving Day play. 4b., 4g. Sc. School in Puritan New England. PO

Purple youth. Robert DeCamp Leland. 2m., 1w. Sc. Studio. FOS

Pursuing a mother-in-law. Ad. H. Gibson. 2m., 1w. Sc. Office of chief of police. APP

* **Puss in boots.** Alice Cook Fuller. 8b., 1g. Sc. House of the miller's son. FU

† **"Put to the test"** Edith Brown-Evarts. 1b., 1g. Sc. Nicely furnished room. BEY

Putting it across. George C. Hollander. 5m. Sc. Sitting room in bachelor's quarters. FSD

Putting it over on father. J. W. Lincoln. 2m., 1w. Sc. Office. PPP

Putting up a prosperous front. Flot Pascal Cowan. 2m., 4w. Sc. Interior. EP

Q

"Q." Stephen Leacock and Basil MacDonald Hastings. 3m., 1w. Sc. Interior. FSD

* **Quaker way, The.** Madeline Poole. Revolutionary War. 3b., 4g. Sc. Living room of a Quaker home inside the British lines. PO

* **Quakers in New England, The.** Louise E. Tucker and Estelle L. Ryan. Salem witchcraft. 2b., 5g. Sc. House in old Salem. TRH

Quarry slaves. Lee Byrne. Ancient Sicily. 4m., chorus. Sc. Sicilian underground quarry. BYR

Quay of magic things, The. John Chapin Mosher. 5m., 7w. Sc. Scene along the Seine embankment. Drama 10: 188–191, Feb. 1920.

Queen and Emperor. Marguerite Merington. From the picture "Queen Louisa" by Richter. 8m., 3w., 1c., 2s. Sc. A hall of a house in Tilsit in 1807. MPZ

Queen Anne cottages. M. E. M. Davis. 4m., 4w., chorus. Sc. Cottage by a lake. DAB

Queen Catherine. Binney Gunnison. From Shakespeare's Henry VIII. 2m., 1w., chorus. Sc. Room in palace. GU

* **Queen Christmas.** Carolyn Wells. 10b., 4g. Sc. Interior. PPP Ladies' Home Journal 37: 32, 52, Dec. 1920.

* **Queen Flora's court.** Netta Syrett. A masque of flowers. 34c. Sc. A wood. SSE

Queen: God bless her! The. Laurence Housman. Scene from home-life in the Highlands. Queen Victoria. 3m., 1w. Sc. Garden tent on the lawn of Royal residence. HA, HA4

* **Queen loving heart.** Jean Ross. May Day play. 11c., chorus. Sc. Unimportant. EP

Queen of diamonds, The. Katharine Kavanaugh. Detective play. 3m., 2w. Sc. Interior. DEP

Queen of hearts, The. Gladys Ruth Bridgham. 3m., 3w. Sc. Interior. B

Queen of hearts, The. Ian Hay (pseud. of Ian Hay Beith). 2m., 2w. Sc. Interior. PPP

Queen of Sheba, The. Stark Young. Verse. 2m., 2w. Sc. A Gothic chamber. YA Theatre Arts Magazine 6: 152–164, April 1922.

Queen's crags, The. Wilfrid Wilson Gibson. Verse. 2m., 1w. Sc. A fantastic group of rocks. GIB, GIP English Review 13: 169–182, Jan. 1913.

Queen's enemies, The. Lord Dunsany. 9m., 2w., chorus char. Sc. An underground temple in Egypt. DFP

Queen's hour, The. Clarice Vallette McCauley. Springtime morality play. 1m., 2w. 7 char. without speaking parts. Sc. Garden with hedge at back. Drama 10: 295–300, June 1920.

Queen's messenger, A. J. Hartley Manners. 1m., 1w., Sc. Interior. FSD

* **Queen's offer, The.** Clara J. Denton. 18b., 1g., chorus. Sc. Office of Queen. DAI

Quest of an ancestor, The. Roy Melbourne Chalmers. 2m., 1w. Sc. Public library. Smart Set 7: 160, June 1902.

* **Quest of Christmas, The.** Julia Martin. 12c. Sc. Room with Christmas tree. EP

Question of division, A. Marianne Stayton. Comedy. 2w. Sc. Girl's special sitting room in country home. FSD

Question of fidelity, A. George S. Viereck. 1m., 1w. Sc. A library furnished with massive elegance. VG International 10: 121–123, Apr. 1917.

Question of morality, A. Percival Wilde. Comedy. 3m., 1w. Sc. Drawing room. MA, WC Century 90: 609–617, Aug. 1915.

Question of sex, A. Arnold Bennett. Farce. 2m., 2w. Sc. Drawing room. BP

Questioning fate. Arthur Schnitzler. Trans. from the German. Anatol play. 2m., 1w. Sc. Interior. SAA

Quick and the dead, The. Fenton B. Elkins. Satire. 4m., 1w., 1s. Sc. Private hall in a house. ET

* **Quick news.** Clara J. Denton. 5b. Sc. Unimportant. MBP

Quiet evening at home, A. Mary Moncure Parker. Comedy. 3m., 2w., 2c. Sc. Young bachelor's room. PM

Quiet game, A. Henri Becque. Trans. by Sheba Harris. 4m. Sc. Corner of cafe. Playbook 1: 7–19, Dec. 1913.

Quiet hotel, The. Frank Dumont. Farce. 1m., 2w. Sc. Country hotel lobby. PPP

Quiet little dinner, A. Thomas Cobb. 3m., 4w. Sc. Drawing room. PLA

Quilting party in the thirties, A. Evelyn G. Sutherland. 6m., 4w. Sc. An old fashioned kitchen. SUO

* **Quite by ourselves.** Lady Bell. Comedy. 1b., 2g. Sc. Unimportant. BEJ

Quod wrangle, The. Oliphant Down. Farce. 5m., 1w. Sc. Interior. FSD

R

Rabbit-hutch, The. George Sterling. 1m., 3 char. (rabbits) Sc. Rabbit hutch. Smart Set 60: 123–124, Sept. 1919.

Rada. Alfred Noyes. Great War play. 3m., 2w. Sc. Living-room of a prosperous village doctor in the Balkans. NR

† **Radio Christmas or Christmas in Room 326, A.** J. MacCulp Wick 9g., chorus. Sc. Room in a Y. W. C. A. EP

Rag doll, A. Evangeline M. Lent. 1m., 3w. Sc. Luxuriously furnished reception room in N. Y. Smart Set 28: 100–110. May 1909.

Raggles' corner. Bertha M. Wilson. Farce. 2m., 5w. Sc. Street in Bowery of N. Y. PPP

Raimond released. Binney Gunnison. Adapted from The Vespers of Palermo by Mrs. Hemans. Verse. Historical Sicily. 2m., 1w. Sc. Before the gates of Palermo. GU

Rain. Dana Burnett. 6m., 1w. Sc. Kitchen of home in a small town in Maine. Drama 14: 20–23, Oct. 1923.

Rain. Horace Holley. 1m., 1w., 2b., 1g. Sc. Parlor of hotel in the White Mountains. HOR

Raising the wind. W. H. Neall. Tribulations of a playwright. 3m., 3w. Sc. Poorly furnished room. PPP

Ramlet o'Puce, A. A. McClure Warnock. Irish play. 2w. Sc. Roadside in Donegal. JOA

* **Rather a prig.** Lady Bell. Comedy. 1b., 1g. Sc. Unimportant. BEJ

Rather rough on Robert. J. W. Lincoln and James Montgomery. Farce. 3m., 2w. Sc. Interior. PPP

* **Raven man, The.** Katharine Lord. 3b., 6g. Sc. On the shores of a lake. LLS

Razor, The. Kichizo Makamura, tr. from the Japanese. Modern Japanese play. 5m., 1w. Sc. Interior of a village barber-shop near Tokyo. IW

Reader, The. Ada Tully Ammerman. Comedy. 6w., 1g. Sc. Reception room in N. Y. boarding house. FSD

Reading. Daisy McGeoch. Comedy. 3m., 4w. Sc. A living room. MAC

Real doctor, The. Frank Dumont. 1m., 1w. Sc. Interior. FSD

Real people, The. Charles Frederic Nirdlinger. Circus play. 3m., 1w. Sc. Dressing room of a circus tent. NI

Real price or Stranger than fiction, The. William H. Jefferys. Missionary play. China. 2m., 3w. Sc. On a Chinese street. DOF

Real "Q," The. Maverick Terrell and H. O. Stechhan. 3m. Sc. Main room of doctor's suite. Smart Set 35: 129–136, Sept. 1911.

Real thing, The. John Kendrick Bangs. Farce. 2m., 5w. Sc. Office. BAD Harper's Bazaar 43: 134–143, Feb. 1909.

Realist, The. Rosa Rosenthal. 1m., 2w. Sc. Attractive living room. SCT

Reason, The. George Middleton. 2m., 2w. Sc. Sitting room. MIM Smart Set 53: 89–97, Sept. 1917.

Rebound, The. Louis Benoit Picard. Trans. from the French by Barrett H. Clark. Comedy. 4m., 2w. Sc. Room in a house in Paris in the 18th century. FSD

* **Reception for Santa Claus, A.** Willis N. Bugbee. 7b., 5g. Sc. Plainly furnished room. BUJ

Recklessness. Eugene G. O'Neill. 2m., 3w. Sc. Library of a summer home in the Catskills. OT

Reckoning, A. Percival Wilde. 2m. Sc. Barber shop. B

Recoiling vengeance, A. A. Louis Elliston. 3m., 2w. Sc. Handsome apartment. B

Recollections. Malcolm Mosley. Matrimonial duologue. 1m., 1w. Sc. Sitting room. MOL

AN INDEX TO ONE-ACT PLAYS

Rector, The. Rachel Crothers. 1m., 6w. Sc. Study in a country parsonage. FSD

Red feathers, The. A. A. Milne. Fantastic operetta. 3m., 2w. Sc. Living room of a country house. MSL

Red flag, The. Kenneth Sawyer Goodman. Comedy. 4m., 2w. Sc. Living room of summer home. GQA

Red or white? William Maynadier Browne. 2m., 2w. Sc. Library in private home. PWP

Red parasol, The. Alice C. Thompson. Comedy. 8w. Sc. Interior. DEP

Red pearls, heard in a revery. Agnes Lee. Verse. 2 voices. Sc. Not given. International 10: 310, Oct. 1916.

Red roses. Granville Forbes Sturgis. Tragedy. 2m., 1w. Sc. Private box in a Paris café. STR

Red turf. Rutherford Mayne. 4m., 1w. Sc. A peasant kitchen in Ireland. MD

* **Redeeming their characters.** C. I. Chambers. Scout play. 9b. Sc. Scout's camp. CB

Reflected glory. Helen Sherman Griffith. Farce. 6w. Sc. Women's room in railroad station. PPP

Reform. Marjorie Benton Cooke. 2w. Sc. Bachelor-maid's apartment. CO

Reforming Bertie. Charles Saxby. 1m., 2w. Sc. Breakfast room. FSD

Registry office, The. Herbert C. Sargent. Farce. 4m., 3w. Sc. Interior. SAR

† **Rehearsal, The.** Maurice Baring. Farce. 13m. Sc. Globe Theatre, 1595. BA

Rehearsal, The. Joseph Herbach. 5m., 2w. Sc. Sitting room. HER

Rehearsal. Christopher Morley. 6w. Sc. Bare stage. STW

Rehearsal, The. Mary Moncure Parker. Comedy. 4m., 4w. Sc. Out of doors. PM

† **Rehearsing the program.** Edith F. A. U. Painton. 1b., 3g. Sc. Schoolroom. PAD

Relations. George M. Rosener. 3m., 1w. Sc. Interior. FP

Release. Edward H. Smith. Tragedy. 5m. Sc. County jail in up state New York. REM, STV, VI

Renaissance. Holger Drachmann. Trans. from the Danish by Lee M. Hollander. 4m., 2w., chorus. Sc. Room in house in Venice. Poet Lore 19: 369–419, Winter 1908.

Rescue, The. Rita Creighton Smith. 3w. Sc. Old fashioned living room. HDI

Resemblance, The. Alice Leal Pollock and Aura Woodin Brantzell. 3w. Sc. Apartment in fashionable hotel. Smart Set 33: 12 127–134, Feb. 1911.

Respective virtues of Heloise and Maggie, The. Randolph Bartlett. 1m., 3w. Sc. Luxurious apartment in N. Y. hotel. Smart Set 48: 73–80, Feb. 1916.

Rest cure, The. Marie Muggeridge. 1m., 1w. Sc. Sitting room. FSD

Rest cure, The. Gertrude Jennings. 1m., 2w., 1s. Sc. A small bedroom in a nursing home. JF

Restaurant episode, A. Alfred Lester. Farce. 1m., 1w. Sc. Restaurant. FSD

Restville auction sale, The. S. Decatur Smith, Jr. 5m., 5w. Sc. Auction room. PPP

Retribution. Seumas O'Brien. Comedy. 3m., 1w. Sc. Bedroom in a country lodging house. OD

Return, The. Edward J. Morgan. 2m., 1w. Sc. Peasant's one-room hut in North Russia. Drama 11 : 119–121, Jan. 1921.

Return of Alcestis, The. Laurence Housman. 5m., 3w., chorus m. and w. Sc. A chamber in the house of Admetus, King of Pherae. FSD

Return of Christmas, The. John Kendrick Bangs. Farce. 3m., 2w., 1b., 1g. Sc. Drawing room. BAD

Return of Harlequin, The. Colin Campbell Clements. 1m., 1w. Sc. Small living room with fireplace. CLD Poet Lore 31 : 596–603, Winter 1920.

Return of Letty. Alice C. Thompson. 6w. Sc. Room in a country home. PPP

Return trip, The. Ford Douglas. 7m. Sc. Cemetery. Smart Set 70 : 71–74, April 1923.

Returning the calculus. Louise Latham Wilson. College comedy. 4m., 5w. Sc. A college girl's room. PPP

Rev. Peter Brice, Bachelor, The. Beulah King. 7w. Sc. Sitting room. B

† **Revolt, The.** Ellis Parker Butler. School play. 1m., 8w., chorus. Sc. Class room of girl's academy. FSD

* **Revolt of Santa Claus, The.** Ednah Proctor Clarke. 10b., 7g. Sc. Interior of Santa Claus's house. Ladies' Home Journal 19 : 19, Dec. 1901.

* **Revolt of the Holidays, The.** Edward Irenaeus Stevenson. 24c., ballet. Sc. A large drawing room. HB

* **Revolutionary days.** Blanche Shoemaker Wagstaff. Colonial history of U. S. 2b., 5g. Sc. Colonial room. WCP

* **Rhoecus.** Alice Cook Fuller. A dramatization of the legend. 6 or more c. Sc. Unimportant. FU

Rialto and the drama, The. Joseph Bernard Rethy. 4 char. Sc. Dark street in N. Y. International 12 : 95, Mar. 1918.

Ricardo and Viola. S. A. Eliot, ed. From "The Coxcomb" of Beaumont and Fletcher. 11m., 4w. Chorus characters. Sc. Elizabethan tavern room. Fore-stage with grey-brown curtains. ELT1

* **Rich citizens.** F. Ursula Payne. 1b., 10g., chorus. Sc. Path in a city park. PPC

† **Rider of dreams, The.** Ridgely Torrence. 2m., 1w., 1c. Sc. Night in a room used for kitchen, dining room and laundry by a colored family. SS, JOA, TPF

† **Riders to the sea.** John Millington Synge. 1m., 3w., chorus characters. Sc. A cottage kitchen. CBI, C1, DIC, LE, SYS, SYT, SYU Bibelot 19 : 247–268, July 1913. Poet Lore 16 : 1–11, Spring 1905. Samhain p. 25–33, 1903.

Riding to Lithend, The. Gordon Bottomley. Poetic. 9m., 9w. chorus characters. Sc. Hall in a house in South Iceland. BKL, BOT, LE Bibelot 16 : 3–62, Jan.–Feb. 1910.

Rights of the soul, The. Giuseppe Giacosa. Trans. from the Italian by Theodora Marcone. 2m., 1w., 1s. Sc. Living room in a villa. SL Stratford Journal 2 : 26–43, Feb. 1918. (Trans. by Isaac Goldberg.)

"Riley." Herman D. Levinson. Play of Jewish life. 2m., 2w. Sc. A plain reception room. BLO

Rim of the world, The. Floyd Dell. Fantasy. 2m., 2w. Sc. Room in a palace. DK

Ring, The. Mary MacMillan. Historical background. 4m., 4w. 2s. Sc. House of Peter Dodsley. MS

Ring-around-a-Rosie. Gladys Ruth Bridgham. Comedy. 2m., 2w. Sc. Sitting room. B

Ripening wheat. Anna Wolfrom. 2m., 2w. Sc. Low narrow room in a house in Western Canada. WOH

Rise up, Jennie Smith. Rachel L. Field. Great War patriotic play. 1m., 3w. Sc. Dressmaking shop. FSD

† **Rising of the moon, The.** Lady Gregory. 4m. Sc. Side of a quay in a seaport town. DIC, GS, WWS The Gael 22: 376–378, Nov. 1903. Samhain pp. 45–52, 1904.

Rival speakers; or, The judge and the major. Frank Dumont. 3m. Sc. Room in a hotel. WHP

River of light, The. Neilson Morris. 6m., 2w. Sc. Interior. FSD

Road agent, The. Charles Ulrich. Melodramatic western drama. 3m., 1w. Sc. Western cabin. DEP

Roadhouse in Arden. Philip Moeller. A whimsicality. 4m., 2w. Sc. The commercial room in a roadhouse. MF

Road to Christmas, The. Anita B. Ferris. 19 or more b. or g. Sc. Anywhere. Everyland 8: 337–342, 349, Nov. 1917.

Roamy-e-owe and Julie-ate, burlesque on Romeo and Juliet. 9m., 2w. Sc. Garden before a balcony. WHP

Robbery, The. Clare Kummer. 3m., 2w. Sc. Sitting room. FSD

* **Robert Fulton.** Archie Marmer. 16b. Sc. Interior. MAR

* **Robert Morris and the Revolution.** Louise E. Tucker and Estelle L. Ryan. 3b., 2g. Sc. Street in Philadelphia. TRH

* **Robin Goodfellow.** Netta Syrett. 14c. and chorus. Sc. A farmhouse kitchen. SSE

* **Robin Hood becomes an outlaw.** Alice Cook Fuller. Robin Hood play. 16b. Sc. Sherwood forest. FU

Rocking chairs. Alfred Kreymborg. A concertino for Katydids. 3w. Chorus. Sc. Dining room in fairly prosperous home. STW

Rococo. Granville Barker. 3m., 3w. Sc. An ugly drawing room of an English vicarage. BT, CBI

Rohan the Silent. Evelyn G. Sutherland. Romantic drama of medieval England. 8m., 2w. Sc. Castle in the 12th century. SUP

† **Rolling stone gathers no moss, The.** Edith Brown-Evarts. 4b., 1g. Sc. Interior. BEY

Romance by porcelain, A. Rudolph Raphael. Comedy. 3m., 1w. Sc. Dental office. B

† **Romance by schedule.** Mabel H. Crane. Boarding School play. 8g. Sc. Sleeping room in a girls' boarding school. B

† **Romancers, The.** Edmond Rostand. Trans. from the French. 4m., 1w., chorus. Sc. Stage is cut in two by an old wall. WWS

Romantic Molly. Ada S. Macomber. 4m., 3w. Sc. Sitting room. BUP

Romantic rogue. Carrie W. Colburn. 2m., 3w. Sc. Room in a suburban home used as an office. B

Romany road. Rex Hanter. 2m., 5w., 1c. Sc. Clearing in a forest. HS

Romeo of the Rancho. James Francis Cooke. Comedy. 3m., 1w. Sc. Hotel bedroom. PPP

Room 83. Morton Weil elaborated by Marion Short. 2m., 2w. Sc. Hotel apartment. FSD

Room without a number. Robert H. Davis. 3m., 1w. Sc. Rich bachelor's apartment. Smart Set 51: 201–207, April 1917.

Rooms to let. M. N. Beebe. Play of college life. 3m., 4w. Sc. Room in a student's boarding house. FSD

Rope, The. Eugene O'Neill. 3m., 1w., 1c. Sc. Interior of old barn. OMC

Ropes. Wilbur Daniel Steele. 2m., 2w. Sc. Living room of keeper of a light house. Harper's Magazine 142: 193–208, Jan. 1921.

Rosalie. Max Maurey. Trans. by B. H. Clark. Comedy. Curtain raiser. 1m., 2w. Sc. Interior. FSD

Rosalind. Barrie, J. M. 1m., 2w. Sc. Parlor of a cottage by the sea. BH

Rosamond. Barrett Wendell. Historical, poetic. 2w. Sc. Bower at Woodstock, in mediaeval England. WR

Rosamund and Eleanor. Maurice Baring. Farce. 3w., 1s. Sc. Room in Rosamund's house. BA

Rose, The. Mary MacMillan. 1m., 1w., 1s. Historical background. Sc. An apartment—a tower room in castle in time of Elizabeth. MS

Rose garden, The. Frayne Williams. Play of Oriental philosophy and phantasy. 11m., 2w. Sc. Interior of a Chinese house in 13th century. WIT

Rose leaves and asparagus tips; or, Romance and reality. Fletcher Cowan. Symbolic poem treating of a present day problem. 1m., 2w. Sc. Dining room. Smart Set 8: 33-40, Dec. 1902.

Rose of the wind. Anna Hempsted Branch. Fairy play in verse. 2m., 2w. Sc. Cobbler's cottage. BRD, HOM

Rosedale sewing circle, The. Arlo Bates. Comedy. 10w. Sc. Parlor. G2

‡ **Rosie, the girl from Paris.** E. M. Peixotto. Farce. 9b. Sc. Parlor. PET

Rostof pearls. Mary Ross Nevitt. 7w. Sc. Boudoir. FSD

Rounding the triangle. David Quarella. 1m., 2w. Sc. Living room of bachelor's apartment. Smart Set 40: 131–140, May 1913.

Row at the Ruggles', A. C. N. Moller. (Harold Hale, pseud.) Farce. 2m., 5w. Sc. Room in a hotel. B

Royal reception, A. Anthony J. Schindler. A comedy of errors. 14m. Sc. Village street or country lane. SCP

* **Royal toy-mender, A.** Eleanor L. Skinner and Ada M. Skinner. 5b., 2g., chorus. Sc. A room in the king's palace. SSC

Ruben Rube; or, My invalid aunt. A. Z. Chipman. 2m., 1w. Sc. Parlor. APP

Ruby Red, an Oriental satire. Clarence Stratton. 2m., 2w. Sc. Room in Hotel Oriental, Biskra, on the edge of the desert. Drama 10: 192–195, Feb. 1920.

* **Ruler of the desert, The.** Virginia Olcott. 5b., chorus of b. Sc. Forest. OP

Rummage sale at Hickory Hollow, The. Elizabeth Whitehill. 2m., 10w. Sc. Living room. MAP

Rumpus on Olympus, A. Mabel H. Crane. Play of Classical mythology. 8w. Sc. Olympus home of the Gods. PPP

Rush light, The. Monica Barry O'Shea. 1m., 2w. Sc. Main room of a cottage in Ireland. Drama 7 : 602–615, Nov. 1917.

Rusty door, The. Howard Forman Smith. Sea fishing play. 7m. Sc. Cabin on board a trawler on the banks of Newfoundland. STV

* **Ruth's donation party.** Anita Ferris. 4b., 7g. Sc. Living room. MIS

Ryland. Thomas Wood Stevens and Kenneth Sawyer Goodman. Comedy. 5m., 2w. Sc. Cell in Wengate prison. MA, STG

S

S. O. S. Preston Gibson. Adapted from a short story by Leonard Merrick. 8m., 2w. Sc. On the deck of a yacht. FSD

Sabotage. Charles Hellem. W. Valcros and Poe d'Estoc. 3m., 2w. Sc. Living room and bedroom combined. Dramatist 5 : 425–437, Jan. 1914.

† **Sacred ground.** Giuseppe Giacosa. Trans. from the Italian. 2m., 2w. Sc. A dignified but simple room. MR

Sacrifice. Ruth L. Baugham. 2m., 2w. Sc. Living room. DAK

Sacrifice. Lawrence I. MacQueen. Story of Abraham and Isaac. 4m. Sc. Plain of deep sand. Drama 11 : 216–219, Mar. 1921.

Sacrifice. Rabindranath Tagore. 5m., 2w., 1b., chorus. Sc. A temple. TCS

Sad mistake, A. Tom Masson. 1m., 1w. Sc. Not given. Smart Set 16 : 159–160, July 1905.

Safety first, a vivisection. Randolph Bartlett. 1m., 2w. Sc. Living room. Smart Set 49 : 243–251, May 1916.

* **Sailor man, The.** Laura E. Richards. 3b. Sc. A doorway of a house beside the sea. RP

Saint Cecelia. Pauline Phelps and Marion Short. 1m., 7w. Sc. Sitting room. FSD

Saint-King. Thomas B. Rogers. Medieval England. 7m., 1w., chorus. Sc. Sheltered chamber in a natural fortress. RO

* **St. Nicholas.** Ruth Arkwright. 3b., 2g. Sc. Interior of a Dutch cottage. AB

St. Valentine's house. Frances Gillespy Wickes. 15c. Sc. Workroom in St. Välentine's house. WCB

Sallie-for-keeps. Frances M. Jackson. 4m., 1w. Sc. Fashionable drawing room. FSD

Salome. Oscar Wilde. Historical. 11m., 2w. Chorus of m. and w. Sc. A great terrace in the Palace of Herod. CBI Poet Lore 18 : 199–223, Summer 1907.

Salon Carre fantasy. Marguerite Merington. From the picture "The man with the glove" by Titian. 2m., 6w., chorus. Sc. In the Louvre gallery. MPZ

Salt of life. Alfred Sutro. Comedy. 1m., 1w., 1s. Sc. Boudoir. FSD, SFA

Saltimbank. Herman Heijermans. Trans. by Lilian Saunders and Caroline Heijermans-Houwink. 8m., 1w. Sc. Dressing room of traveling circus. Drama 13 : 363–367, Aug.–Sept. 1923.

* **Salvage.** Eleanore Hubbard. Conservation and thrift. 3b., 2g. Sc. Room. HUC

† **Sam Average.** Percy Mackaye. 3m., 1w. Sc. An intrenchment in Canada near Niagara Falls. LC, MA, MY

Sam Tucker. Paul Green. For the negro theatre. 2m., 2w. Sc. Negro cabin in N. C. Poet Lore 34: 220–246, Summer 1923.

Sam Weller and his father. Binney Gunnison. From Dickens' Pickwick Papers. Comedy. 3m. Sc. Tavern. GU

* **Sambo's party.** Marie Irish. 6b., 6g. Sc. Living room. IL

Same man The. Lida L. Coghlan. Comedy. 2w. Sc. Sitting room. B

Same old thing, The. Roi Cooper Megrue. 2m., 1w. Sc. Room furnished with good taste. Smart Set 29: 128–135, Nov. 1909.

Same to Ye!, The. R. J. FRY. Irish farce. 1m., 1w. Sc. Kitchen. APP

Samson's courtin'. O. E. Young. Rube farce. 1m., 1w. Sc. Old fashioned sitting room. BUP

* **Samuel Morse's telegraph.** Eleanore Hubbard. The invention of telegraphy. 3b. Sc. Morse's work room in New Jersey. HUD

Sancta Susanna, the song of a May night. August Stramm. Trans. by Edward J. O'Brien. 1m., 3w., others. Sc. Interior of a convent church. Poet Lore 25: 514–522, Winter 1914.

Sanctuary. Percy Mackaye. A bird masque. 6m., 1w., chorus. Sc. Sylvan glade of a bird sanctuary. MYS Century 87: 547–557, Feb. 1914.

Sandbar queen, The. George Cronyn. 6m., 1w. Sc. Low, box-like room. FS

Santa Claus. Doris F. Halman. 1m., 3w., 1b., 1c. Sc. Toy department of a large store. HAS

* **Santa Claus brigade, The.** Willis N. Bugbee. 4b., 4g. Sc. Interior. BUJ

* **Santa Claus' garden.** Ellen M. Willard. 5b., 3g. Sc. Garden. WY

* **Santa Claus gets his wish.** Blanche Proctor Fisher. Christmas play. 8c. Sc. Interior. B

* **Santa Claus in many lands.** Ellen M. Willard. 20c. Sc. Interior. WY

* **Santa Claus or papa.** Susan E. W. Jocelyn. 1b., 4g., chorus b. Sc. A room with a good sized closet. WEP

* **Santa's allies.** Anita B. Ferris. 16 to 56c. Sc. Anywhere. Everyland 8: 198–205, July 1917.

* **Santa's rescue.** Elizabeth F. Guptill. Christmas play. 4b., 5g., chorus groups. Sc. Before the curtain and North Pole. TMP

* **Saturday night in New England.** Louise E. Tucker and Estelle L. Ryan. 3b., 2g. Sc. Living room in old New England. TRH

Sauce for the Emperor. John Chapin Mosher. Roman history comedy. 5m., 4w. Sc. Room in Caesar's palace. MOS Smart Set 51: 199–208, Jan. 1917.

Saved! Percival L. Wilde. From the French of André de Lorde and Eugene Morel. 8m., 2w. Sc. Grounds of French consulate in China. Smart Set 46: 397–409, July 1915.

Savior, The. Aleister Crowley. 16m., 1w. Sc. Council room. International 12: 75–82, March 1918.

Savonarola and Lorenzo. Binney Gunnison. Adapted from "Savonarola" by Alfred Austin. Historical. 2m. Sc. Palace in Florence. GU

Sayonara; or, The testing of the poet. Ernest Hervilly. Englished and ed. by Kenneth Sylvan Guthrie. Verse. Japanese background. 2m., 2w. Sc. Suburbs of Yedda in ancient Japan. HES

Scales and the sword, The. Farnham Bishop. 5m., 2w., 1b., chorus. Sc. Cheap grocery in a suburban town. HD2

Scapegrace, The. Frances Aymar Mathews. 1m., 6w. Sc. Morning room. WEP

Scar, The. Wilfrid Wilson Gibson. Verse. 1m., 1w., Sc. Shepherd's cottage. GIA, GIP, GIS

Scaring off of Teddy Dawson, The. Harold Brighouse. Comedy. 2m., 2w. Sc. Interior of a small East End house. FSD

* **Scene at the ticket office.** Marie Irish. 6b., 6g. Sc. R. R. ticket office. IP

* **Scene from Robin Hood.** Lena Dalkeith. 9b., 2g., chorus. Sc. Open space in Sherwood forest. DLP

‡ **Scene from Uncle Tom's Cabin.** Lena Dalkeith. 3g. Sc. Bed room. DLP

Scene shifter's lament, The. Alfred Lester. Farce. 2m., 2w. Sc. Back of the scenes. FSD

Scheming lieutenant, The. Samuel A. Eliot, ed. From St. Patrick's Day by Richard Brinsley Sheridan. ELT1

Scholar bound for paradise, The. Hans Sachs. Trans. by Bayard Quincy Morgan. Shrove-tide comedy. 2m., 1w. Sc. Not given. Playbook 1: 16–27, Oct. 1913.

School board in our town, The. C. H. LeVitt. Tragic comedy. 4m. Sc. Interior. G1

School for mothers-in-law, The. Eugene Brieux. 2m., 4w. Sc. A parlor. International 3: 54–59, Mar. 1911. Smart Set 41: 1–16, Sept. 1913.

School of life, The. James Platt White. 1m., 4w. Sc. Library. Harvard Monthly 30: 198–209, July 1900.

* **School opera.** Mrs. C. F. Fernald and Olivia Lovell Wilson. 5b., 5g. Sc. Interior. BAB

* **Scold, the scoundrel and the scout, The.** C. I. Chambers. Scout play. 12b., 1g. Sc. Camp of Scout Troop. CB

Scoop; or, The Billionaire, The. Milton Francis Clark. Satire on oil magnate. 4m. Sc. Private apartments in an elegant home. CLA

Scoop, The. Harriet Holmes Haslett. Newspaper play. 2m., 1w. Sc Dining room. HAE

* **Scotch grace.** Madalene D. Barnum. Thanksgiving Day play. 1b., 6g. Sc. A kitchen. BS

Scotty, the cowboy. Frank Dumont. 3m. Sc. Room in a hotel. WHP

‡ **Scout's honor, A.** Clifton Lisle. Boy Scout play. 13b., chorus. Sc. A lakeside camp. LB, PPP

* **Scouts to the rescue.** C. I. Chambers. Scout play. 8b., 1g. Sc. Path through a meadow. CB

Scrambled eggs. Lawton Mackall and Francis R. Bellamy. A barnyard fantasy. 2m., 2w., chorus. Sc. A barnyard. STK

Scratch race, A. Walt Makee. (pseud. of W. H. Maguire.) 3m., 2w. Sc. Interior. B, PWP

Scruples. Octave Mirbeau, tr. from the French by Clyde Barrett. Thief play. 4m. Sc. Well furnished Louis XVI drawing room. LO

Sea, The. A. H. Hughes. Dramatic fantasy. 1m., 3w. Sc. Sea scene. FSD

Sealed silver; or, Volenti mon fit injuria. H. Field Etherington. 3m., 3w. Sc. Combined dining and living room. FSD

* **Search for Mother Goose, The.** Elizabeth F. Guptill. Christmas play. 8b., 9g. Sc. Interior. EP

Search me! Charles D. Morgan. 1m., 2w. Sc. Small bare room on dock of transatlantic liner. Smart Set 45: 379–388, Jan. 1915.

Seashell, The. Fullerton L. Waldo. Comedy. 5m., 3w. Sc. Lobby of a summer hotel. PPP

Seat in the park, a warning, A. Arthur Pinero. 2m., 2w. Sc. Lawn in Hyde Park, London. CH, FSD

Second childhood. W. C. Parker. Farce. 2m., 2w. Sc. Interior. DEP

Second-story man, The. Upton Sinclair. 2m., 1w. Sc. Luxuriously furnished room. SIP

Secret, The. Katharine Metcalf Roof. After Maeterlinck. 3m., 4w. Sc. Long corridor in Carnegie Hall. Smart Set 19: 108–111, Aug. 1906.

Secret of life, The. Leon Kobrin. Trans. from the Yiddish by Isaac Goldberg. 2m., 1w. Sc. A garden. PTT

Secret way, The. Preston Gibson. Comedy. 1m., 1w. Sc. Room in a hotel in Washington. FSD

Secretary, The. John G. Bartram. 4m., 3w. Sc. Interior. B

Seeing the animals. Clara J. Denton. Farce. 1m., 2w. Sc. Exterior. MAP

Seeing the pictures. Roy Melbourne Chalmers. 1w., 1b. Sc. Art gallery. Smart Set 8: 85, Nov. 1902.

Seeker of a secret, The. John Hanlon. Verse. 1m., 1w. Sc. Anywhere. Smart Set 63: 115–116, Nov. 1920.

* **Seeking information.** Clara J. Denton. 1b., 1g. Sc. Interior. MBP

See-saw. Louise Saunders. 2m., 2w. Sc. Garden in the moonlight. SAM

* **Selfish woman, The.** Augusta Stevenson. 2g. Sc. Kitchen. SC2
* **Senior, The.** Clara J. Denton. Graduation play. 16 or more c. Sc. A student's room. DAI

Sentence, The. Edith Wheeler. 2m., 1w. Sc. Library in a home. WIA

Sentimental journey, 1902, A. Francis M. Livingston. 4m., 1w. Sc. Cordlandt St. Station 6th Ave. Elevated. Smart Set 6: 105–110, Jan. 1902.

Separation of the Browns, The. Clara B. Batchelder. (Barbara Burbank, pseud.) 1m., 2w. Sc. Interior. B

Sequel, The. Percival Wilde. Comedy. 3m., 1w. Sc. Parlor. WE

Serpent's tooth, The. Essex Dane. Play of India. 5m., 1w. Sc. House in India at the present time. DAO

Settled out of court. Stanley C. West. 2m. Sc. Solicitor's office. FSD

Seven kings and the wind, The. Stark Young. Verse. 7m. Sc. Large chamber in a palace. YA

Seven leagued boots, The. Mildred Plew Merryman. 1m., 1w. Sc. Attic workroom of an astronomer. American Poetry Magazine 1: 19–24, Sept. 1919.

* **Seven little soldiers and seven little maids.** Willis N. Bugbee. 7b., 7g. Sc. An ordinary room. BUP

Seven princesses, The. Maurice Maeterlinck. Trans. from the French. 3m., 8w., chorus. Sc. A spacious hall of marble. MAH, MAI

* **Seven sleepers of Ephesos, The.** Marguerite Merington. Easter play.

10m., 14b., 1w. Sc. Beyond the city bounds, on a holiday. MFP

Seventh doctor, The. M. N. Beebe. Farce. 9m. Sc. Sitting room. FSD

Sevres tea-cups, The. Stuart Wishing. 2m., 2w. Sc. Drawing room. PLA

Sewing circle meets at Mrs. Martin's, The. F. M. Kelly. Comedy. 10w. Sc. Sitting room in a cottage in a suburban village. FP

Sewing machine, The. George Edward Barton. 3m., 3w. Sc. Room in a dingy tenement. BAR

Sewing society, The. Helen Sherman Griffith. 8w. Sc. Interior. DPP

Sganarelle; or, Imaginary horns. Philip Moeller. Freely trans. from Moliere. 6m., 5w. Sc. Before a house. ELT2

Shadow, The. Howard Mumford Jones. 3m., 3w. Sc. A forest. WIP2

* **Shadow, The.** Laura E. Richards. 2g., chorus b. and g. Sc. Out of doors. RP

Shadow in the White House, The. James Oppenheim. 2m. Sc. Room in the White House. Seven Arts 2 : 263–269, July 1917.

Shadow of the glen, The. John M. Synge. 3m., 1w. Sc. Cottage kitchen in Ireland. SYT, SYU

† **Shadowed star, The.** Mary Louise MacMillan. Play about late Christmas shopping. 1m., 6w. Sc. A very bare room in a tenement house. MAM, MS

Shadows. Mary Moncure Parker. Dream play of the south. 3m., 4w. Sc. Interior. DEP

Shadowy waters, The. William Butler Yeats. Verse. 4m., 1w. Sc. Deck of an ancient ship. YC2, YP2, YPP, YS

† **Shakespeare garden club, The.** Mabel M. Moran. Fantasy of Shakespeare's women characters. 16w. Sc. Room in Ann Hathaway's cottage at Stratford-on-Avon. MOA

‡ **Shakespeare up-to-date,** class day play for girls' schools. Ethelyn Sexton. 6g. Sc. Interior. MAP

Shakespeare's daughters. George Henry Trader. Fantasy of Shakespeare's women characters. 11w. Sc. A glade. FSD

† **Sham.** Frank G. Tompkins. A social satire. 3m., 1w. Sc. A darkened room. SL, STK

Shambles, a sketch of the present war. Henry T. Schnittkind. 3m., 1w., 1c. Sc. Interior of a shabby shanty in Europe. Poet Lore 25 : 559–571, Winter 1914.

Shamed life. Allan Monkhouse. Great War play. 1m., 3w. Sc. Sitting room of a small house. MW

Sharing, The. Agnes Lee. Poetic. 2m., 1w. Sc. Garden in front of a cottage. LEE Poetry 3 : 95–99, Dec. 1913.

She couldn't marry three. Joseph J. Slater. Farce. 3m., 2w. Sc. Interior. APP

She must marry a doctor. Solomon J. Rabinowitsch. 3m., 4w. Sc. Large parlor in disorder. PTS

She tells her daughter. Djuna Barnes. 2w. Sc. Handsome drawing room. Smart Set 72 : 77–80, Nov. 1923.

She who was fished. (Tsuri Onna) Ancient Japanese farce. Trans. by Michio Itow and Louis V. Ledoux. 2m., 2w. Outlook 133 : 218–219, Jan. 31, 1923.

* **Shepherd-boy who called wolf, The.** Augusta Stevenson. 6b. Sc. A hillside near a village. SC2

† **Shepherd in the distance, The.** Holland Hudson. A pantomine. 6m., 4w. Sc. A garden. SL

Sheriff of Tuckahoe, The. George M. Rosener. Western play. 3m., 1w. Sc. Interior of Sheriff's house. FP

Shewing-up of Blanco Posnet, The. Bernard Shaw. 5m., 7w., chorus groups. Sc. A big room. SHS

Ships on the sand, a play of the Suffolk Broads. Charles A. Myall. 2m., 2w. Sc. Kitchen of a wayside public house. Drama 12:153–156, Feb. 1922.

* **Shirkers, The.** Elizabeth F. Guptill. 10c. Sc. Any interior. FIL

Shirt, The. Wilfrid Wilson Gibson. Poetic. 2w. Sc. A room in tenements near the railway. GID, GIP

Shivaree. Mark O'Dea. 2m., 2w. Sc. Room in an Iowa farmhouse. OR Drama 11:11–15, Oct. 1920.

† **Shoes that danced, The.** Anna Hempstead Branch. Fanciful fantastic. 3m., 4w. Sc. Watteau's studio. BRA, WWS

Shojo. Ernest Fenollosa and Ezra Pound. Noh play of Japan. 2m., chorus. Sc. Japanese Exterior. FEN

Shop of perpetual youth, The. Katherine Morse. 2m., 3w., 1c. Sc. Beauty parlor. FSD

Shopping. Daisy McGeoch. Comedy. 5m., 1w. Sc. Simple. MAC

Short way with authors, A. Gilbert Cannan. Burlesque. 7m., 1w. Sc. Dressing room in a London theatre. CAP, REP

* **Shouting the battle cry of "Feed 'em."** Edna Randoph Worrell. Patriotic play. 1m., and many c. Ladies' Home Journal 34:40, Nov. 1917.

Show actress, The. J. C. McMullen. 3m., 4w. Sc. Dining room. B

Show of hands, The. W. R. Walker. Romantic comedy. 1m., 1w. Sc. Neatly furnished sitting room. PH

Shower, The: The Moon. Yone Noguchi. Noh play of Japan. 2m., 1w., chorus. Sc. None. Poet Lore 29:455–458, Autumn 1918. Poetry Review 8:189–193, Aug. 1917.

Shunamite, The. Yehoash, pseud. of Solomon Bloomgarden. Authorized trans. from the Yiddish by Henry T. Schnittkind. 3m., 1w. Sc. Inner chamber of King David's Palace. Stratford Journal 4:313–320, June 1919.

Sibyl, The. Isaac Rieman Baxley. Ancient Greece. 2m., 3w. Sc. An annex room to the Temple of Apollo at Delphi. BAX

Sic passim. Joseph Andrew Galahad. 1w., 2m. Sc. None given. Poetry 19:20–21, Oct. 1921.

Sicilian, The. Jean B. C. Moliere. Trans. from the French by Barrett H. Clark. 4m., 2w., chorus. Sc. A street with house in the background. FSD

Sicilian limes. Luigi Pirandello. Trans. from the Italian and edited by Isaac Goldberg. 2m., 2w., chorus. Sc. Hallway. VE
——Trans. by Elizabeth Abbott. Theatre Arts Magazine 6:329–344, Oct. 1922.

* **Sick deer, The.** Augusta Stevenson. 4b., Sc. A meadow. SC1

Side-show, The. John Kendrick Bangs. Farce. 6m., 4w. Sc. Stage of an improvised theatre. BAD

Sidhe of Ben-Mor, The. Ruth Sawyer (i. e. R. S. Durand) Irish folk play. 1m., 5w., 6 fairy women. Sc. Interior of cabin. Poet Lore 21 : 300–310, July–Aug. 1910.

Siege, The. Colin Campbell Clements. 3w. Sc. Room in an Oriental house. CLD, STW

* **Siefried:** a German folk play. Constance D'Arcy Mackay. 3b., 2g. Sc. A deep forest. MST

* **Siegfried and Brunhilde.** Alice Cook Fuller. 5b., 1g., chorus. Sc. Palace. FU

Silas Wegg's stall. Horace B. Browne. From Dickens' Our Mutual Friend. 2m. Sc. In front of a corner house. BD

Silent house, The. Agnes Lee. Poetic. 1m., 2w. Sc. Living room of a scholar. LEE Poetry 1 : 173–178, March 1913.

Silent waiter, The. Alfred Kreymborg. Satire 3m. Sc. One of the dimly lighted windows of a cafe seen from the street. KMA, STV

Silly ass, The, Adelaide C. Rowell. 2m., 2w. Sc. Living room. Drama 12 : 344–350, Sept. 1922.

Silver blade, The. Hermann Hagedorn, Jr. 3m., 2w., chorus. Sc. Room in a castle in ancient Scotland. HPS

† **Silver lining, The.** Constance D'Arcy Mackay. 1m., 1w., 1s. Sc. A pleasant room a trifle littered with books. MB, SS

Silver salt-cellars, The. Stuart Wishing. 2m., 2w. Sc. Sitting room in a flat. PLA

Simon the Cyrenian. Ridgely Torrence. Historical. 11m., 1w., chorus characters. Sc. Garden in Jerusalem. TPF

Simoon. Johann August Strindberg. Trans. from the German. 2m., 1w. Sc. Arabian burial chamber. MR; Trans. by Emil Schering. Poet Lore 17 : 21–28, Autumn 1906; Trans. by Edwin Björkman. Smart Set 40 : 135–141, July 1913.

Simp, The. George M. Rosener. Irish comedy. 4m., 3w. Sc. In front of an Irish cottage. WRP

Simpkins little breakfast party. Charles S. Bird. Farce. 4m., 3w. Sc. Combined sitting and breakfast room. FP

Sin of Ahab, The. Anna Jane Harnwell with an introduction by Clara Fitch. Biblical play. 5m., 1w. Sc. Private audience chamber in the palace of the king. HAT

Sing a song of seniors. Lindsey Barbee. Play of college life. 7w. Sc. Room in a girls' seminary. DEP

‡ **Sing a song of sleepy head.** James W. Foley. 19c. Sc. Drawing room. FO

Singer, The. Padraic H. Pearse. Irish play in verse. 5m., 2w. Sc. Wide clean kitchen of a country house. PRZ, PS

Singing pool, The. Helen L. Mobert. 4m., 2w. Sc. Outside of a cottage in India. Poet Lore 30 : 275–288, Summer 1919.

Singing soul, The. Mrs. Henry Backus. Chinese legend. 4m., 3w., chorus. Sc. Interior of Chinese home in Peking 500 years ago. FSD

Sinner, The. Sholom Ash. 15m., 1w., chorus. Sc. Jewish cemetery in a small town in Russian Poland. PTS

Sinstram of Skagerrak. Sada Cowan. (Mrs. Frederick James Pitt) Impressionistic episode. 1m., 1w. Sc. High bare cliff. MA

Sir Bob. George M. Rosener. 2m., 1w. Sc. Room handsomely furnished. Stagelore p. 157–, Feb. 1912.

† **Sir David wears a crown.** Stuart Walker. 13m., 4w., chorus. Sc. Gateway to the King's castle. SCO, STK, WA Ladies' Home Journal 38 : 6–7, 154, 157–159, June 1921.

Sister Masons. Frank Dumont. Burlesque. 11w. Sc. Large room. PPP

Sister to assist'er, A. John Le Breton. 2w. Sc. Shabby bed-sitting-room. FSD

Sisters, The. Harold Goddard. 5m., 5w., chorus. Sc. Interior. GJ

Sisters of Susannah. Philip Moeller. Biblical farce. 5m., 1w. Sc. Beautiful garden of Myrah. MF

Sisters' tragedy, The. Richard Hughes. 2m., 3w. Sc. Hall of a house used as a dining room. HUG

Six and eightpence. H. B. Tree. Comedy. 2m., 1w. Sc. Lawyer's office. FSD

Six men of Calais, The. Lascelles Abercrombie. 6m. Sc. Not given. Poetry Review 1: 529–533, Dec. 1912.

† **Six who pass while the lentils boil.** Stuart Walker. Fantasy. 5m., 2w., chorus. Sc. Kitchen. MA, MTC, SS, STK, WP, WS

68–70 Berkeley Place. Whitney Darrow. Comedy. 3m., 5w. Sc. Dining room of twin house. PPP

Skeptic's challenge, The. Henry Frank. 8 char. Sc. Vision of a revolving globe enwrapped in bright clouds. Open Court 36: 6–16, Jan. 1922, 36: 78–88, Feb. 1922.

* **Skirmish in Rensselaerswijck.** Louise E. Tucker and Estelle L. Ryan. New York in Colonial days. 5b., 3g. Sc. Living room in Dutch home in old New York. TRH

* **Skyboy.** Gertrude Knevels. 15c. Sc. Outdoor setting. CAM

Slacker, The. Jewell Bothwell Tull. Great War play. 2m., 7w. Sc. Living room. B

Slacker for the cause, A. B. A. Hedges. Great War play. 3m., 1w. Sc. Interior. FP

Slacks, The. David Carb. 12., 2w. Sc. Large white washed kitchen. Harvard Monthly 48: 20–27, March 1909.

* **Slave raiders, The.** Anita B. Ferris. 25 or more c. Sc. Unimportant. Everyland 8: 244–247, Aug. 1917.

Slave with two faces, The. Mary Caroline Davies. Allegory. 3m., 4w. Sc. Path in the woods. FLS, SL

* **Slight mistake, A.** Marie Irish. 2b., 4g. Sc. A sitting room. IP

Slippers. Anne Macfarlane. Fantasy. 1m., 1w., 1b. Sc. Living room. Poet Lore 32: 425–430, Autumn 1921.

Slump, The. Frederick L. Day. 2m., 1w. Sc. A dingy room in middle class American home. SL

Smile of Mona Lisa, The. Jacinto Benavente. Trans. from the Spanish by J. A. Herman. 4m., 1w. Sc. Studio of Leonardo da Vinci in Florence. BAG, BSM

Smith's unlucky day. Charles Nevers Holmes. Comedy. 1m., 1w. Sc. Interior. DEP

Snare and the fowler, The. Beulah Marie Dix. 3m. A narrow chamber in a chateau in Normandy. DA

Snaring the lion. E. C. Ehrlich. Based on an incident in Judges. 2m., 2w. Sc. Roof of a house in Palestine. Drama 9: 60–83, May 1919.

* **Snow image, The.** E. Antoinette Luques. Miracle play. 1b., 5g. Sc. Window overlooking garden. LS

Snow man, The. Laurence Housman. Verse. 2m., 1w., 1b., 1g. Sc. A poor peasant dwelling. CBI, FSD

AN INDEX TO ONE-ACT PLAYS 171

* **Snow-white and rose-red.** E. Harcourt Williams. Adapted from Grimm's story. 2b., 4g. Sc. Interior of cottage. WI
* **Snow witch, The.** Constance D'Arcy Mackay. A Russian folk play. 1b., 4g., chorus characters. Sc. A bare plain room. MST
Snowed-up with a Duchess. C. A. Castell. Comedy. 4w. Sc. Interior of a cottage. FSD
Snowstorm, The. Perez Hirschbein, tr. from the Yiddish. 7m., 4w., 2c. Sc. Room in a small farmhouse in Russia. BLK
Snubbing of Fanny, The. Winifred St. Clair. Early Victorian. 1m., 3w. Sc. Comfortable drawing room. SAI
* **Soap-box orator, The.** F. Ursula Payne. 5b., 3g., chorus. Sc. Corner near a small city park. PPC
Soap club, The. E. J. Freund. 9w. Sc. A large room. ANP
Sob sister. Lillian Saunders. 1m., 2w. Sc. Disorderly sitting room. Drama 11:354–357, July 1921.
Socialism and beauty. Bouvé Souther. 3m. Sc. A garden at night. Harvard Monthly 54:202–207, July 1912.
Society column, The. Stella T. Payson. 9m., 9w., 1g. Sc. Country editor's office. BEQ
Society notes. Duffy R. West. 6m., 3w. Sc. Handsome morning room. STK
* **Soft-soap day, The.** Eleanore Hubbard. Pilgrim play. 7b., 4g. chorus. Sc. Pilgrim village on the edge of a forest. HUD
Sojourners. Anna Harnwell and Isabelle Meeker. 5m., 2w. Sc. Yard of cottage in Leyden in 1620. Drama 10:357–364, July–Sept. 1920.
† **Solemn pride.** George Ross Leighton. U. S. Civil War play. 9w. Sc. Sitting room in New England village in 1865. WWS
Solomon's song. Harry Kemp. Historical. 3m., 2w. Sc. Throne-room of Solomon's royal palace about 100 B. C. SCO
Some mischief still. Joyce Kilmer. 4m., 1w. Sc. Living room of upper West side Apartment. Smart Set 43:131–142, Aug. 1914.
Somebody-nothing, a Japanese farce. Trans. by Michio Itow and Louise V. Ledoux. 3m. Sc. Room in a Japanese house. Asia 21:1011–1012, Dec. 1921.
Something to vote for. Charlotte Perkins Gilman. 2m., 7w., other club w. Sc. Room arranged for a meeting. Forerunner 2:143–153, June 1911.
Son of the greater Fatherland. Edward Morgan. Great War play. 4m., 1w., 1b., 1g., chorus. Sc. Interior of a room in a town not far from Liege. MOQ
Song at the castle, A. Evelyn G. Sutherland. Historical background. Romantic comedy. 6m., 2w. Sc. Drawing room in Dublin Castle. SUP
Song of Solomon, The. Mark O'Dea. 2m., 3w. Sc. Back room of a farm house. OR Drama 11:154–157, Feb. 1921.
Sons of Adam. Mariano Alarcon. 5m., 3w., peasants. Sc. Interior of humble home of a peasant. Stratford Journal 4:75–93, Feb. 1919.
Soothsayer, The. Verner von Heidenstam. Trans. from the Swedish. 5m., 6w., chorus. Sc. A laurel grove in ancient Greece. FOS, HVS
Sotoba Komachi. Ernest Fenollosa and Ezra Pound. Noh play of Japan. 2m., 1w. Sc. Along a bridge. FEN
Sotoba Komachi. Kwanami. Noh play of Japan. 2m., 1w., chorus. Sc. Stage. WAA

Sounding brass. Edward Hale Bierstadt. 3m., 1w. Sc. Living room of warden's quarters in prison. STK

Souvenir spoons. Irving Dale. Comedy. 2m., 2w. Sc. Small reception room in a fashionable hotel. B

Spark of life, The. Emma Beatrice Brunner. 2m., 2w. Sc. Luxurious living room. BRB

Sparks divine. Bessie Springer Breene. Comedy. 10w. Sc. Sitting room. FSD

Sparrow, The. Sabatino Lopez. Trans. from the Italian and edited by Isaac Goldberg. 2m., 4w., 1b. Sc. Room on the ground floor. VE

Special delivery. D. M. Henderson. Farce. 3m., 2w. Sc. Reception room. B

Special rehearsal. E. P. Churchill. 2m., 1w. Sc. Interior. CHU

Spectator No. 558. R. Clipston Sturgis, Jr. 3m. Sc. Corner in Will's coffee house. Harvard Monthly 36: 201-203, July 1903.

* **Spider and the fly, The.** Emma L. Johnston and Madalene D. Barnum. 3b. Sc. A dining room. JB

Spineless. Elsie Garretson Finch. 2m., 1w. Sc. Large living and drawing room in a country house. SCT

* **Spirit of Christmas, The.** Ellen M. Willard. 4b., 4g. Sc. Interior. WY

Spirit of Kiwanis, The. Edward Saxon. Patriotic play. 6m. Sc. Interior. SAX

* **Spirit of liberty, The.** Jessie M. Webb and Lucile Schamberger. 7c., 9 chorus groups. Sc. Children's nursery. FSD

* **Spirit of Memorial Day, The.** E. Antoinette Luques. 4b., 5g. Sc. Out-of-doors. LS

Spirit of Purim, The. Herman D. Levinson. Jewish holiday play. 1m., 1w. Sc. Room off the ball room. BLD

Spiritual boost at Sallytown, The. Alice Marie Donley. Comedy. 3w. Sc. Study. G3

Spoiling the broth. Bertha N. Graham. 2m., 2w. Sc. Kitchen in a Yorkshire house. JOA

† **Spreading the news.** Lady Gregory. 7m., 3w. Sc. Outskirts of a fair. Ci, CBI, GS, KP, LE, SS, Samhain pp. 15-28, 1905.

Spring in Bloomsbury. Harold Brighouse. 3m., 2w. Sc. Bed-sitting room in Bloomsbury. WIA

Spring recital, The. Theodore Dreiser. 15m., 3w., many chorus char. Sc. Prosperous church in the heart of a great city. DP, Little Review 2: 28-35, Dec. 1915.

* **Spring time fantasy.** Marjory Benton Cooke. Easter play. 9b., 8g. Sc. Unimportant. DPP

Spy, The. Malcolm W. Davis. 5m., 1w. Sc. Interior. DAA

Square deal, A. Edward Mumford. Comedy. 2m., 2w. Sc. Reception room. PPP

Square pegs. Clifford Bax. 2w. Sc. A garden. BAP, C2

Squashville fire brigade, The. Willis N. Bugbee. 3m., 2w. Sc. Sitting room. MAP

Squaw-man, The; an idyl of the ranch. Edwin Milton Royle. 7m., 1w. Sc. Ranch. Adobe house in the distance. Cosmopolitan 37: 411-418, Aug. 1904.

Squaw of Bear Clan. Evangeline M. Lent. Indian play. 3m., 1w. Sc. Interior of Indian-Agent's house. WEP

Stage struck boarding house. Frank Dumont. 6m., 2w. Sc. Interior. WHP

Staircase, The. Lascelles Abercrombie. Verse. 2m., 1w. Sc. Small room in an empty cottage without furniture. ABF

Standing moving. Mary MacMillan. 2m., 2w. Sc. Living room in a very old frame house. MTT

Standing room only. Dwight Spencer Anderson. 3m., 1w. Sc. Interior. FP

Star boarder, The. Charles Nevers Holmes. Boarding house comedy. 1m., 8w. Sc. Dining room. DEP

Star brave, The. Helen Fitzgerald Sanders. Verse. Based on Indian myth. 3m. Sc. Interior of a Blackfoot Indian lodge. SAD

Star dust path, The. Colin Campbell Clements. 1m., 1w., chorus. Sc. Pine woods on shore of a lake. Poet Lore 31: 181–186, Summer 1920.

Star in the trees, The. Stark Young. 2m., 15w. Sc. A secret wood. YA

Star of Bethlehem, The. Clay M. Greene. 5m. Sc. Cosy corner of a gentlemen's club. GD

* **Star of Bethlehem, The.** Mrs. Alice Corbin Henderson. Nativity play. 10b., 2g. Sc. Stable of the inn at Bethlehem. HAD

* **Star spangled banner, The.** Eleanore Hubbard. U. S. War of 1812 play. 5b. Sc. On board a British battleship. HUD

Star spangled banner, The. Katherine Stagg. Civil War episode. 2m., 1w. Sc. Interior. DPP

State forbids, The. Sada Cowan. Slum play. 1m., 2w., 1b. Sc. A desolate one room dwelling. COV

Station episode, A. Louise Rand Bascom. 1m., 1w. Sc. Waiting room of station. MBP

† **Stepmother, The.** Arnold Bennett. Farce. 2m., 2w. Sc. Study. BP, CBI

Step mother, The. A. A. Milne. 3m., 1w. Sc. Pleasant room. FSD, MSM

Stick-up, The. Pierre Loving. Wild west fantastic play. 3m. Sc. Inside the orbit of Uranos. STK, STV

* **Stockings' revolt.** Elizabeth Ferguson Seat. Christmas play. 15c. Sc. Living room. FIL

Stoic's daughter, The. Maurice Baring. Historical farce. 4m., 3w., 1s. Sc. Room in the house of Burrus. BA

Stolen horse, The. Louise Rand Bascom. Comedy. 3m., 2w. Sc. Sitting room. MBP

Stonefolds. Wilfrid Wilson Gibson. Verse. 2m., 2w. Sc. Living room of shepherd's hut. GIA, GIP, GIS

Store, The. Elizabeth Kellam. 3m., 3w. Sc. Back room of a grocery store. FSD

† **Storm, The.** John Drinkwater. Poetic. 2m., 3w. Sc. A mountain cottage. DPA, DR, Theatre Arts Magazine 4: 191–199, July 1920.

Storm, The. Mary MacMillan. Farce. 1m., 10w., 1s w. Sc. Drawing room. MTT

Storm in a tea shop. Stafford Hillard. 2m., 3w. Sc. Tea room. FSD

Stormy night, A. Katharine Kavanaugh. Comedy. 3m., 1w. Sc. Drawing room. FP

* **Stormy times.** Louise E. Tucker and Estelle L. Ryan. Rebellion in early New York. 5b., chorus char. Sc. On the road to a fort. TRH

Story of a famous wedding, The. Evelyn Greenleaf Sutherland. Early New England. 6m., 4w. Sc. Drawing room in mansion in early New England. SUO

Story of Corporal Bell, The. Cyril Wentworth Hogg. 3w. Sc. Living room. FSD

‡ **Story of Jacob, The.** Harris G. Hale and Newton M. Hall. 7b., 2g. Sc. Interior. HAL

* **Story of the poplar tree, The.** E. Antoinette Luques. 22c. Sc. Forest scene. LS

* **Strange boy, The.** Netta Syrett. 3b., 5g. Sc. Schoolroom. SSG

Strange host, The. Arthur Law. Fanciful. 3m., 2w. Sc. Old fashioned room in a cottage. WIA

Strange physician, The. May Bell. 3m., 1w. Sc. A hall furnished as a living room in Johannesburg. BRW

Stranger, The. Felix Gould. 3m., 2w. Sc. Before a house. GO

Stranger, The. Perez Hirschbein. Tr. fr. Yiddish. 3m., 2w. Sc. A small room with tiny windows. BLK

Stranger, The. David Pinski. Trans. from the Yiddish by Isaac Goldberg. 9m., 6w., many chorus characters. Market place of Birath Arba at the time of the destruction of the Temple at Jerusalem. PT, PTT

Strangers. Emma Beatrice Brunner. 2m., 1w. Sc. Luxurious living room. BRB

Strangers. Sada Cowan. 1m., 1w. Sc. Office. Smart Set 42: 115–116, Mar. 1914.

Sranger's visit, The. Horace B. Browne. 2m., 1w. Sc. Interior of cottage. BD

* **Strategy of Director Kieft, The.** Louise E. Tucker and Estelle L. Ryan. 6b., 1g., chorus char. Sc. A garden. TRH

Streaks of light. Hermann Sudermann. Trans. from the German. 2m., 1w. Sc. Small pavilion in a park. SU

Street singer, The. Jose Echegaray. Trans. by John Garrett Underhill. 2m., 2w., others. Sc. A public square. Drama 7: 62–76, Feb. 1917.

* **Strike in Santa Claus land, The.** Clara J. Denton. Christmas play. 5b., 6g. Sc. Room decorated for Christmas festivities. SI

* **Strike in Santa Claus land, A.** Effa E. Preston. 14c. Sc. Room in Santa's house. PAP

* **Strike Mother Goose settled, The.** Evelyn Hoxie. 5b., 7g. Sc. Interior. EP

Striker, The. Margaret Scott Oliver. 2m., 3w. Sc. A dining room in a workman's house. OS

Striped sweater, The. O. E. Young. 6m. Sc. Interior. B

Stroke of Marbot, The; or, The Emperor at Melk. Graham S. Rawson. Background of France in Napoleonic times. 13m., chorus. Sc. Great apartment overlooking the Danube. RA

Stronger, The. August Strindberg. 2w. Sc. Corner of a ladies' restaurant. LC, LO, STO, Trans. from the Swedish by Edith and Warner Oland. International 4: 58–59, Sept. 1911. Trans. by F. I. Ziegler. Poet Lore 17: 47–50, Spring 1906.

Stronger woman, The. August Strindberg. 2w. Sc. A nook in a ladies' cafe. STW

† **Studying for a test.** Edith F. A. U. Painton. 4g. Sc. School room. PAD

Stuff o' Dreams. Rex Hunter. 3m., 1w. Sc. Interior of a fisherman's cottage in Maine. HS
Stuffing. Dorothy Cleather. 7w., 1c. Sc. Cottage room. CH
Stuffing. George Paston. 1m., 2w., 1b. Sc. Living room. FSD
Subjection of Kezia, The. Mrs. Havelock Ellis. 2m., 1w. Sc. Interior of cottage kitchen in a Cornish fishing village. EL, ELA, SL
Substance of ambition. Marie Josephine Warren. 2m., 2w. Sc. Parlor of boarding house. B, PWP
Substitute, The. Effie Ellsler Weston. 3m., 1w. Sc. Interior of cobbler's shop. Smart Set 31 : 115–121, July 1910.
Substitute bride, The. Adelaide Stedman. 2m., 3w. Sc. Luxurious living room in New York. Smart Set 35 : 129–136, Oct. 1911.
* **Substitute for Santa Claus.** Carolyn Wells. 7b., 1g. Sc. Father Time's office. WJ
Success. Marjorie Benton Cooke. 1m., 1w. Sc. Garden. CO
Successful failure, A. George M. Rosener. Farce. 4m. Sc. Hotel parlor. FP
Such a charming young man. Zoe Akins. 6m., 3w. Sc. Balcony overlooking a fashionable restaurant. Smart Set 48 : 67–78, Apr. 1916.
Such extravagance. George Bloomquest. 2m., 1w. Sc. Interior. FSD
Suffragette, The. Helen G. Ludington. 7w. Sc. Sitting room. FSD
Suffragette baby, A. Alice C. Thompson. Comedy. 6w. Sc. Boarding house interior. PPP
Suffragette's redemption. Inglis Allen. 1m., 1w. Sc. Interior. FSD
Sugar house, The. Alice Brown. 4m., 3w. Sc. A sugar-house in a New England wood. BO
Suicides. Preston Gibson. 2m. Sc. Poorly furnished apartment. FSD
Suite B. Fannie Myers Langolis. 3m., 1w. Sc. Handsomely furnished hotel sitting room. DPP
Suited at last; or, Sauce bordelaise. Elizabeth Urquhart. Comedy. 1m., 7w. Sc. Living room. FP
Suitors three; or, Her test for true love. C. Gordon Kurtz. 3m., 2w. Sc. Interior. STB
Suma Genji. Ernest Fenollosa and Ezra Pound. Noh play of Japan. 3m. Sc. Japanese exterior. FEN
Sumida Gawa, adapted from the Japanese Noh drama by Motomasa by Colin C. Clements. 2m., 1w., 1c., chorus. Sc. Banks of the Sumida River. Stratford Journal 2 : 29–39, Jan. 1918.
Summer-dawn. Wilfrid Wilson Gibson. Verse. 1m., 1w. Sc. Cottage before dawn. GID, GIP
Sun, The. John Galsworthy. 2m., 1w. Great War play. Sc. Stile close to a river. GSS, LE, Scribner's Magazine 65 : 513–516, May 1919.
* **Sun goddess, The.** Constance D'Arcy Mackay. Masque of old Japan. 19c., 3 chorus groups. Sc. Not given. MBF
Sunbeam. Federico Mariani. 2m., 2w. Sc. Private parlor in apartment in fashionable N. Y. hotel. Smart Set 29 : 130–138, Oct. 1909.
Sunday on Sunday goes by. Henri Lavedan. 3m. Sc. Plateau in the country. Poet Lore 27 : 185–189, Spring 1916.
Sundial, The. Howard Mumford Jones. 2m., 4w. Sc. A garden. Texas Review 5 : 93–125, Jan. 1920.

† **Sunny morning, A.** Serafin Quintero and Joaquin A. Quintero. Trans. from the Spanish by Lucretia Xavier Floyd. 1m., 1w., 2s. Sc. Retired part of a park in Madrid. SL, WWS, Trans. by Isaac Goldberg. Stratford Journal 1 : 39–51. Autumn 1916.

Sunshine, an idyll. Charles Dickson. Southern play. 2m., 1w. Sc. Garden. WHP

Superior sex, The. Helen Bagg. Farce. 1m., 9w. Sc. Interior. PPP

Suppressed desires. George Cram Cook and Susan Glaspell. Satire. 1m., 2w. Sc. A studio. MA, P2

Surprises. C. Leona Dalrymple. Farce. 2m., 1w. Sc. Interior. FP

* **Surprising Santa.** Willis N. Bugbee. 3b., 2g., 2 chorus groups. Sc. Living room. BUJ

Survival. Horace Holley. 1m., 1w. Sc. Garden of a home in the suburbs. HOR

Susan's embellishments. Arthur Eckersley. 1m., 3w. Sc. Interior. FSD

Susan's finish. Alice C. Thompson. Comedy. 7w. Sc. Sitting room. B

* **Susie pays a visit.** Kittie Barne. (Mrs. Eric Streatfield) A play with a dance. 6b., 1g. Sc. Interior. BAS

Swan song, The. Anton Checkhov. Trans. from the Russian. 2m. Sc. Stage of a country theatre in Russia. CHE, SS

† **Swanwhite.** August Strindberg. Trans. from the Swedish. Fairy play. 10m., 7w. Sc. Large apartment in Mediaeval stone castle. SMS, STP

† **Sweeps of ninety-eight, The.** John Masefield. 7m., 1w. Sc. A parlor in an inn. MLS, MTA

Sweet-and-twenty. Floyd Dell. Comedy. 3m., 1w. Sc. Corner of a cherry orchard. DK, SCO, STK

Sweet elysium club, The. Alice E. Ives. Comedy. 14w. Sc. Club room. FSD

* **Sweet girl graduate,** a commencement play. Carolyn Wells. 9b., 14g. or all g. Sc. Gay garden. PPP, Ladies' Home Journal 38 : 19, 38, May 1921.

† **Sweetmeat game.** Ruth Comfort Mitchell. 2m., 1w., 1b. Sc. Living room in a Chinese house in the Chinese quarter. FSD

Swift's pastoral. Padraic Colum. Irish legend of St. Patrick's purgatory. 1m., 1w. Sc. Unimportant. CDL, Poetry 17 : 175–180, Jan. 1921.

Swimmin' pools. Belford Forrest. 5m. Sc. Dark stage—outside the city limits. B

* **Swineherd, The.** Evelyn Smith. From Hans Andersen. 6b., 4g. Sc. A room in a palace. SFR

Sympathetic souls. Sydney Grundy. From the French of Eugene Scribe. 2m., 2w. Sc. A sitting room. FSD

T

Tabarin's wife. Catulle Mendes. Trans. from the French by Frank R. Arnold. 5m., 3w. Sc. Square of the Dauphin in 1629. International 5 : 38–41, Feb. 1912.

* **Tables turned, The.** John Kendrick Bangs. Farce. 2b., 3g. Sc. A nursery. HB

Tabloid, A. Arthur Eckersley. Tragic farce. 3m. Sc. A bachelor's room. FSD, Smart Set 44 : 135–142, Oct. 1914.

* **Tadpole school, The.** Emilie Blackmore Stapp and Eleanor Cameron. A September play. 4b., 1g., 2 chorus groups b. and g. Sc. On the bank of a pond. SCH

Tag, der; or, The tragic man. J. M. Barrie. Great War play. 4m. Sc. A bare chamber. BET

* **Tailor's dummy, The.** Clara J. Denton. 2b., 1g. Sc. Interior. MBP

Taking father's place. W. C. Parker. Farce. 5m., 3w. Sc. Broker's office. DEP

* **Taking teacher's place.** Elizabeth F. Guptill. 4b., 4g. Sc. Not important. GUT

Taking the census. Elizabeth F. Guptill. Farce. 1m., 1w., 1b. Sc. At the door of a house in a poor neighborhood. TMP

Taking way, A. Innis G. Osborn. Farce. 4m., 2w. Sc. Interior. B

* **Tale of the tarts.** E. M. Fotheringham. 3b., 4g. Sc. Outside the palace of the King of Hearts. FSD

Talisman, The. Miss E. H. Keating. Proverb play "Truth may be blamed, but it cannot be shamed." 8m. Sc. Garden of a palace. KE

Tamura. Ernest Fenollosa and Ezra Pound. Noh play of Japan. 3m. Sc. Japanese setting. FEN

* **Tangled skein, The.** Laura E. Richards. 2g. Sc. Room. RP

Tangles. C. Leona Dalrymple. Farce. 4m., 2w. Sc. Interior. FP

Taniko. (The Valley-Hurling) Zenchiku. Pt. 1. Noh play of Japan. 2m., 1w., 1b., chorus. Sc. Stage. WAA

Tanks. Hugh Mytton. 2m., 2w. Sc. Bedroom of a Scotch Hydro. FSD

Tatters. Richard Burton. Juvenile Court character sketch. 3m., 1b. Sc. Lawyer's room. FSD, Drama 12 : 206–208, March 1922.

Tea and conversation. Colin C. Clements. A comedy of bad manners. 7w. Sc. Sitting room. FSD

Tea and politics. Irene Jean Crandall. Comedy. 2m., 7w. Sc. Interior. DEP

‡ **Teacher's pet, The.** E. M. Peixotto. Farce. 7b., chorus. Sc. School room. PET

Tears of dawn, a medieval phantasy. Faith Van Valkenburgh Vilas. 2m., 2w. Sc. Mountain pass. Poet Lore 33 : 105–113, Spring 1922.

Tears of the birds, The. Yone Noguchi. 2m., 1w., 1c., chorus. Sc. None given. Poet Lore 29 : 451–455, Autumn 1918.

Tecpancaltzin. Grace E. Taft. Verse. Ancient Aztec. 5m., 2w. Sc. Garden. TA

Teeth of the gift horse. Margaret Cameron. 2m., 4w. Sc. Interior. FSD

Teja. Hermann Sudermann. Early Mediaeval. 9m., 2w. Sc. King's tent. STZ

Telegram from Dad, A. J. M. Taylor. Farce. College play. 6m., 1w. Sc. A student's room. B

Telegrams, The. Horace Holley. 2m. Sc. Front of a shop in Paris. HOR

Telephone, The. Charles Ligory Fleming. Farce. 10m. Sc. A room with telephone boxes. FLE

Telling the truth. Louis Herman Hubbard. Farce. 1m., 9w. Sc. Sitting room. HUB

Temperament. Mary Aldis. 1m., 2w. Sc. 1. Library in a private house; sc. 2. A studio in Greenwich Village. AP

Temperament. Maverick Terrell. 2m., 2w. Sc. Star's dressing room in a theatre. Smart Set 50: 215–220, Sept. 1916.

Templeton tea pot The. Grace Cooke Strong. Farce. 4m., 4w. Sc. Library. B

Ten days later. Carl Glick. 4m., 2w., crowd. Sc. Street in small town in Palestine about 1 A. D. Drama 11: 159–165, Feb. 1921.

Ten fingers of Francois, The. Christmas play of old Provence. Delle Houghton Oglesbee. 2m., 2w., 3b., 2g., others. Sc. Kitchen of farm house. Drama 14: 65–69, Nov. 1923.

‡ **Ten minutes by the clock.** Mrs. Alice C. Riley. 7b., 2g. Sc. Breakfast room in a palace. RIT

Ten P. M., a problem play. Mary Aldis. 1m., 1w. Sc. A fireside, under shaded lamps. Drama 11: 187–188, March 1921.

Ten years after (with apologies to Dumas Pere). Baroness von Hutton. 1m., 1w. Sc. Not given. Smart Set 12: 75–77, Oct. 1903.

Tenor, A. Louis Gilmore. 2m., 2w. Sc. Boudoir in winter Palace, 1780 at time of Empress Catherine. Double-Dealer 3: 301–310, June 1922.

Tenor, The. Frank Wedekind. Trans. from the German by Andre Tridon. Comedy. 3m., 3w., 2s. Sc. A large hotel room. SL

Tents of the Arabs, The. Lord Dunsany. 5m., 1w. Sc. Outside gate of city of Thalanna. Smart Set 45: 229–239, Mar. 1915.

Teoteuctli. Grace E. Taft. Verse. Ancient Aztec. 7m., 3w. Sc. Interior of small Aztec temple. TA

Terrible Meek, The. Charles Rann Kennedy. 2m., 1w. Sc. A windswept hill. KT

Terror of a day, The. M. F. Hutchinson. 6w. Sc. A square sitting room. WIA

* **Tertulla's garden; or, The miracle of good St. Valentine.** Marguerite Merington. 3m., 3w., 1c., chorus. Sc. A room in the town house of Asterius. MFP

Test, The. Helen L. Willcox. Missionary play. 7m. Sc. A room in a hut in Morocco. MIS

Test kiss, The. John Keble Bell. (Keble Howard, pseud.) 1m., 1w. Sc. Room in a country house. FSD

* **Testing of Sir Gawayne, The.** Marguerite Merington. Hallowe'en. 8m., 4w., 1c., many chorus char. Sc. King Arthur's Court. MFP, MTC

† **Thankful for Jack.** Alice W. Chaplin. 6g. Sc. Sitting room. CHC

Thankful heart, The. Frances Gillespy Wickes. 8c. Sc. Cottage room which is both kitchen and living room. WCB

‡ **Thanksgiving conspiracy, A.** Marie Irish. 5b., 4g. Sc. Living room. PAP

* **Thanksgiving Day—1696.** Martha B. Bayles and Anna M. Lütkenhaus. American history play. 8g., chorus. Sc. New England kitchen. LU

* **Thanksgiving Day—"Anychild's vision of blessings."** F. Ursula Payne. 29c. Sc. A room in Anyhouse. PP

* **Thanksgiving dream, A.** Caroline A. Creevey and Margaret E. Sangster. 17c. Sc. Ethel's bedroom. HB

* **Thanksgiving dream.** Effa E. Preston. 15c. Sc. Interior. PAP

Thanksgiving festival. Arranged by normal students in the Dept. of

Hist. of the State Normal and Model Schools, Trenton, N. J. Any no. of children. Sc. Exterior of Jewish tabernacle. Ladies' Home Journal 30 : 39, 74–75, Nov. 1913.

‡ **Thanksgiving of Praisgod plenty, The.** Julia M. Martin. 3b., 2g. Sc. Interior of Puitan home. EP

That black cat. Bert C. Rawley. 6m., 2w. Sc. Interior. APP

That blessed lady. Edward Mumford. Farce. 1m., 1w. Sc. Seashore house. PPP

That blonde person. Helen Bagg. Farce. 6w. Sc. A pretty drawing room. PPP

† **That boy.** Alice W. Chaplin. 4g. Sc. Sitting room. CHC

That brute Simmons. Arthur Morrison and Herbert C. Sargent. Adapted from Arthur Morrison's story in "Tales of mean streets." 2m., 1w. Sc. Interior. FSD

That little rogue next door. Harold Sander. Farce. 2m., 3w. Sc. Drawing room. FP

Their anniversary. Alice C. D. Riley. 3m., 3w. Sc. Garden side of a house. Drama 12 : 157–162, Feb. 1922.

Their first dinner. Rufus H. Gillmore. Farce. 3m., 2w. Sc. Dining room. B

Their first quarrel. Charles Nevers Holmes. Comedy. 1m. 1w. Sc. Any room. DEP

Their Godfather from Paris. Lillian Pleasant. Comedy. 2m., 3w. Sc. Sitting room. PLN

† **Their point of view.** Wilfred T. Coleby. 2m., 1w. Sc. Chaplain's room in a government Industrial Home. FSD

Their wife. George Middleton. 1m., 1w., 1 chorus character. Sc. Room which apparently has been closed for many months. MIT

"**Them banns.**" Catherine Bellairs Gascoin. 1m., 2w. Sc. Back hall of the vicarage. GAL

Theodat. Rémy de Gourmont. Trans. by Richard Aldington. 7m., and clerks., 1w. Sc. Large hall in Bishop's palace at Clermont in 570. Drama 6 : 184–205, May 1916.

Theodore, Jr. Sally Shute. 1m., 7w. Sc. Library in a home. B

Theorist, The. R. M. Arkush. 1m., 3w. Sc. Small, plainly furnished room. Harvard Monthly 42 : 46–53, Mar. 1906.

There's a difference. Grover Theis. 2m., 1w. Sc. Professor Sharp's bedroom. TN

There's always a reason. Bernard Sobel. 10w. Sc. Living room. ST

These wild young people. J. M. O'Connor, Jr. 3m., 2w., 1s. Sc. A glassed porch. UW

They the crucified. Florence Taber Holt. Great War play. 7m., 2w. Sc. Living room of an old fashioned farm house, somewhere in northern France. HT

Thief, The. Clara J. Denton. 1m., 3w. Sc. Handsome interior. DAI

Thief in the house, A. R. M. Robinson. Comedy. 6m. Sc. Interior. B

Third chapter. Charles Dickson. 2m., 1w. Sc. Drawing room. WHP

Third man, The. Roderick Benedix. Trans. by Barrett H. Clark. 1m., 3w. Sc. Room in a small house in Germany. FSD

Thirst. Henry Gordon. Verse. Army play. 7m. Sc. In U. S. Army Recruit Depot on sea shore. GOR

Thirst. Eugene G. O'Neill. 2m., 1w. Sc. On a raft in a tropical sea. OT

13 Simon Street. Anthony P. Wharton. 3m., 1w. Sc. Tenement house. FSD

† **Thirteenth domino, The.** Harold S. Latham. 16b. Sc. College room in boy's preparatory school. FSD

This is so sudden. McPherson Janney. Farce. Bachelor girl play. 5w. Sc. Living room of small apartment. B

This is the law. Lillian P. Wilson. 5m. Sc. County jail. WIF

This room is engaged. Florence M. Millward. Farcical comedy. 3m., 5w. Sc. Room in a building let for concerts. MIF

This way out. Gladys Ruth Bridgham. 6m., 5w. Sc. Room in lodging house. EP

This youth.—Gentlemen! Margaret Scott Oliver. Fantasy. 1m., 1b. Sc. A narrow lane sharply ascending the hill-side. OS

Thompson's luck. Harry Greenwood Grover. Tragedy. 3m., 1w. Sc. Very plain farmhouse kitchen. SCO

Those dreadful Drews. Helen Morrison Howie. Comedy. 6w. Sc. Parlor. PPP

"**Those dreadful vity-mines!**" Rea Woodman. 1b., 3g. Sc. Sitting room. WO

Those husbands of ours. Jessie A. Kelley. Farce. 7w. Sc. Living room in disorder. FSD

Those landladies. Ina Leon Cassilis. Boarding house comedy. 2w. Sc. Sitting room of lodging house. PH

Those red envelopes. W. C. Parker. Farce. 4m., 4w. Sc. Interior. DEP

Thou shalt not steal. Edith Sessions Tupper. 3m., 1w. Sc. Comfortable living room. Smart Set 27:134–140, Feb. 1909.

* **Three bears, The.** Katharine Lord. 3b., 2g. Sc. Edge of a wood. LLS

* **Three bears, The.** Caroline W. Thomason. 3b., 1g. Sc. In the Bear's house. (Play for children to be given in English or French.) PPP, TH

Three bears, The. E. Harcourt Williams. 2b., 2g. Sc. Cottage with kitchen and bedroom. WI

Three blind mice. William Muskerry. A predicament. 1m., 2w. Sc. Sitting room. FSD

* **Three compromises of the Constitution.** Blanche Shoemaker Wagstaff. Colonial American history. 12b. Sc. Large dignified Colonial room. WCP

Three dear friends. Katharine Roof. Feminine episode. 4w. Sc. Corner in the drawing room. B

Three false women of Llanlar, The. Hermann Hagedorn. Verse. 3w. Sc. Unimportant. HP

Three from the earth. Djuna Barnes. 3m., 1w. Sc. Boudoir. Little Review 7:3–15, Nov. 1919.

Three graces, The. Edward Granville. Comedy. 4m., 2w. Sc. Hall used as a sitting room. B

Three is company. Alfred Brand. Comedy. 3m., 2w. Sc. Drawing room. BRI

Three lepers of Sul-El-Garab. Colin Campbell Clements. 3m. Sc. Corner in a narrow cobblestoned street. CLD

Three of a kind. Gladys Ruth Bridgham. Comedy. 1m., 6w. Sc. Interior. B

† **Three pills in a bottle.** Rachel Lyman Field. Fantasy. 5m., 3w. Sc. Room filled with sunlight. FS1

Three rogues and a rascal. Wilma Wigginton. Farce. 5m. Sc. Police night court. FSD, US

* **Three-score miles and ten.** Someple, pseud. 13c. Sc. Ticket office. SO

* **Three sleepy heads.** Clara J. Denton. New Year play. 1b., 2g. Sc. Study room in a Public Library. DAH

* **Three Sundays in a week.** Harriet Sabra Wright. From a story by Poe. 4b., 1g. Sc. Interior of a house. WN

Three travelers watch a sunrise. Wallace Stevens. 5m., 1w. Sc. Forest on a hilltop in Pennsylvania. SL, Poetry 8: 163–179, July 1916.

* **Three wishes, The.** Constance D'Arcy Mackay. A French folk play. 2b., 1g. Sc. A Breton kitchen. MST, STV

Three wishes. Thomas Wood Stevens. Comedy. 5m. Sc. An army billet somewhere in France. STG

Three women. Charlotte Perkins Gilman. 1m., 4w. Sc. Parlor. Forerunner 2: 115–123, 134, May 1911.

Threshold, The. Harold Chapin. Play of Welsh mining life. 1m., 1w., Sc. Simple room. FSD

Thrift. W. Lloyd Berridge. 4b., 2g. Sc. Sitting room. Ladies' Home Journal 35: 57, Nov. 1918.

Thrilling. Daisy McGeoch. Comedy. 3m., 2w. Sc. Dark stage. MAC

"Through Christmas bells." Clay M. Greene. 4m., 1w. Sc. The sacristy of a fashionable Church. GD

* **Through the looking-glass.** Anna M. Lütkenhaus. From the book by Lewis Carroll. 6b., 8g. Sc. Room with little furniture except a large arm chair. LU

Thumbscrew, The. Edith Lyttelton. 2m., 4w., 2b., 1g. Sc. Stage divided into two rooms. LYA

Thursday evening. Christopher Morley. Comedy. 1m., 3w. Sc. A small suburban kitchen in a modest home. SCO, STK

Thy kingdom come. Florence Converse. A drama for Easter Even. 3m., 8c., angels. Sc. Tomb of Christ. Atlantic Monthly 127: 352–362, Mar. 1921.

Tickets for the Sheffield choir. Edith Lowell. Dramatized from the story by Elizabeth Weir. Comedy. 6w. Sc. Sitting room. B

Tickets, please. Irving Dale. Comedy. 4w. Sc. Reception room in a hotel. B

Tickless time. Susan Glaspell and George Cram Cook. 2m., 4w. Sc. A garden. GP, SCO

"Tiddville and the radio." Harry Doty. Rural comedy. 3m., 5w. Sc. Sitting room. DOT

Tides. George Middleton. 2m., 1w. Sc. Simply furnished study. LE, MIM

Ties of blood. Lillian Sutton Pelee. 3m., 1w. Sc. Adobe house in San Gabriel, California. Poet Lore 32: 572–580, Winter 1921.

Tiger, a play of the Tenderloin. Witter Bynner. 2m., 3w. Sc. A room in a house in the Tenderloin district in N. Y. BB, BYT, Forum 49; 522-547, May 1913.

Tilda's new hat. George Paston. 1m., 3w. Sc. Living room in a tenement house. FSD

Till three P. M. Marvin Hadley. Farce. 2m., 1w. Sc. Well furnished apartment. FP

Time is money. Mrs. Hugh Bell and Arthur Cecil. 1m., 2w. Sc. Interior. FSD

Timothy Ryan's return. Harry L. Newton and A. S. Hoffman. Comedy. 2m. Sc. Interior. DPP

Tiny Tim's surprise-party. Arthur Guiterman. 5b., 5g. Sc. Kitchen. Woman's Home Companion 39 : 40, Feb. 1912.

Tired woman, The. Max Nichelson. 9w. Sc. Street of ugly red brick rooming houses. Poetry 11 : 255–259, Feb. 1918.

Tit-bits. Herbert Swears. Comedy. 2w. Sc. Room in furnished apartment. FSD

* **Tit for tat.** Marjorie Benton Cooke. 3b., 9g. Sc. Interior. DPP

To be perfectly frank. Josephine A. Meyer. 2m., 1w. Sc. Sitting room. Smart Set 65 : 69–79, June 1921.

To find our lives. Kenneth Hunter. 1m., 1w. Sc. Hill overlooking the city. Harvard Monthly 51 : 197–200, Feb. 1911.

* **To save his country.** Irma Kraft. Pesah. 7b., 3g. Sc. A room in a private home in a little village in southern France. KPP

Tobacco evil, The. A. P. Tchehoff. Trans. from the Russian by Henry James Forman. 1m. Sc. Platform of provincial clubhouse. Theatre Arts Magazine 7 : 77–82, Jan. 1923.

Told by the gate. Malcolm Morley. Love cycle. 2m., 2w. Sc. A picturesque country meadow. MOL

Told in a Chinese garden. Constance Wilcox. Fantastic. 6m., 3w., chorus characters. Sc. A Chinese garden. WCT, Drama 9 : 116–150, May 1919.

Tom, Tom, the piper's son. Irving Pichel. 3m. Sc. A kitchen. Harvard Monthly 57 : 80–88, Dec. 1913.

Tommy, short character play. Ethel Hale Freeman. 4m., 3w. Sc. Kitchen. FSD

* **Tommy's Thanksgiving party.** Willis N. Bugbee. 6b., 4g. Sc. Sitting room. EP

Tomorrow, a nightmare. Henry B. O'Hanlon. 4m. Sc. Interior of a morgue. Studies 6 : 48–57, Mar. 1917.

Tomorrow at ten. Lindsey Barbee. Movie play. 1m., 1w. Sc. Interior. DEP

"The Tongmen." Adolph Lehmann. 4m., 2w. Sc. Street corner in Chinese quarter. Little Theatre Monthly 1 : 50–52, July 1917.

Tongues of fire. Patrick Kearney. 2m., 2w. Sc. Room in poor apartment in N. Y. Drama 11 : 397–401, Aug.–Sept. 1921.

Too many wives. Sara Henderson. Domestic comedy. 4m., 2w. Sc. Living room. MAP

Too much Bobbie. Helen Morrison Hoxie. Farce. 6w. Sc. Living room. PPP

Too much Galatea. Arthur Lewis Tubbs. Dream play of Greece. 2m., 2w. Sc. Interior. PPP

Too much married. Charles Townsend. 3m., 2w. Sc. Interior. PPP

† **Too much monkey.** E. M. Fotheringham. 7b. Sc. Study of a rectory. FSD

Too much salt. George S. Bryan. Culinary comedy. 3m., 3w. Sc. Interior. B

Toolip, The. Catherine Bellairs Gascoin. 1m., 1w. Sc. Living room. GAL

* **Top of the world, The.** Emma Mauritz Larson. Christmas play. 6b., 2g. Sc. Interior of home of Father Christmas. Woman's Home Companion 46 : 43, 120, Dec. 1919.

* **Topsy turvy Christmas.** Elizabeth F. Guptill. 15c. Sc. Inner curtain and stage. PAP

* **Torch, The.** Josephine Thorp. Pageant. 57c. Sc. Time's garden. TKP

Torch of time, The. Laurence Housman. A study in revolution. 4m. Sc. Suburban interior. HAB

Torches. Kenneth Raisbeck. 2m., 2w., 2c. Sc. An upper terrace by the side of a castle. FS2

Touch of the child, The. Leon M. Lion. Adapted from Tom Gallon's story. 2m., 2w. Sc. Handsomely furnished room. FSD

Touch of truth, The. Henry M. Walbrook. Comedy. 2m. Sc. Dining room. FSD

Tourist agency, The. Herbert C. Sargent. Farce. 3m., 3w. Sc. Tourist office. SAR

Tower of silence, The. James Platt White. 3m., 2w. Sc. Circular room at top of tower. Harvard Monthly 33 : 188–208, Feb. 1902.

* **Toys' rebellion, The.** Edna Randolph Worrell. 5b., 7g., other c. Sc. Kris Kringle's workshop. Ladies' Home Journal 20 : 16, Dec. 1902.

* **Tracks to the den, The.** Augusta Stevenson. 3b., 4g. Sc. A forest. SC1

Tradition. George Middleton. 1m., 2w. Sc. Sitting room. LC, MIT

† **Tragedian in spite of himself, A.** Anton Chekov. 2m. Sc. A study. CHD, Poet Lore 33 : 268–273, Summer 1922.

Tragedy of true love, The. a warning to those contemplating matrimony. C. F. R. 1m., 1w. Sc. Drawing room. Smart Set 3 : 143–144, Apr. 1901.

* **Trained menagerie, A.** Marie Irish. Comedy. 7b. Sc. Menagerie with cages for animals. IPP

Train leaves in ten minutes, The. Louise Rand Bascom. Farce. 1m., 1w., 1g. Sc. Interior. MAP

Train to Morrow, The. Jeannette Joyce. 3m., 2w. Sc. Country railway station. MAP

† **Traitor.** Percival Wilde. Boer War play. 7m. Sc. Officer's tent in South Africa. B, WED

Tramp and a night's lodging, A. Mrs. Gudrun Thorne-Thomsen. 1m., 2w. Sc. Kitchen. TT

‡ **Tramp barbers, The.** E. M. Peixotto. 7b. Sc. Barber shop. PET

Transaction in stocks, A. Ralph W. Tag. Comedy. 4m., 1w. Sc. Office. FP

Traveller and peasant. Leo Tolstoy. Trans. by L. and A. Maude. 2m. Sc. Peasant's hut. English Review 5 : 617–624, July 1910.

* **Travellers and the hatchet, The.** Augusta Stevenson. 3b. Sc. A high road. SC3

‡ **Travelling man, The.** Lady Gregory. Miracle play. 1m., 1w., 1c. Sc. A cottage kitchen. GS, MTC

Travelling photographer, The. Kate Alice White. Farce. 3m., 2w. Sc. Back yard. MAP

Treason. S. A. Welldon. 6m., 1w., others. Sc. Front of a Southern colonial mansion. Harvard Monthly 37 : 14–29, Oct. 1903.

* **Treasure chest, The.** Josephine Thorp. Fairy play. Any number of children. Sc. Forest by the sea. THR

‡ **Treasure in the trunk, The.** William N. Blutt. Play of Jewish life. 3b., 3g. Sc. An attic room. BLD

Trecento. Hanns Heinz Ewers. 6m., 1w., servants. Sc. Hall in castle in 14th century. International 11 : 135–140, May 1917.

Trend, The. Manta S. Graham. 2m., 1w. Sc. Front of house in model factory village. GRL

‡ **Trial for the murder of the King's English.** Julia E. Park. Play for Good Speech Week. 28c. Sc. Court Room. EP

Trial of a heart, The. J. Raines Wilson. 4m. Sc. "Court of the soul." Smart Set 36 : 141–142, Feb. 1912.

* **Trial trip of the Clermont, The.** Eleanore Hubbard. 5b. Sc. The Clermont on the Hudson River. HUD

* **Trials of Christmas shopping.** Marie Irish. 1b., 3g. Sc. Sitting room. I

Triangle No. V333. Frank T. Kleber. Comedy. 1m., 2w. Sc. Well furnished boudoir. KLE

Triangled. Frank T. Kleber. Comedy. 1m., 2w. Sc. Well furnished boudoir. KL

Trick of the trade, A. Alice K. Bower. 1m., 1w. Sc. Living room. FSD

Trickery. Wilson Hicks. 3m. Sc. ·Inside of small pawnshop. Smart Set 66 : 79–85, Sept. 1921.

Trifles. Susan Glaspell. 3m., 2w. Sc. Kitchen in abandoned farm house. GP, SL

Trimming of the tree. E. Ethel Mould. 16c. Sc. Living room. Ladies' Home Journal 36 : 143–144, Dec. 1919.

Trimplet, The. Stuart Walker. 2m., 3w. Sc. A lonely place. WP

Triumph of earth. Eleanour Morton. Poetical phantasy. 5w. Sc. Wild and desolate shore of the sea. Poetry Review 10 : 89–95 Mar.–Apr. 1919.

Triumph of instinct, The. Rufus Learsi. 4m., 3w. Sc. Parlor. Drama 14 : 26–28, Oct. 1923.

Triumph of Pauline. John Jason Trent. 2m., 4w. Sc. Attractively furnished room. DPP

Triumph of peace. Anita B. Ferris. 35 char. Sc. Any platform of good size. Everyland 6 : 223–231, Sept. 1915.

Triumph of remorse. Gabriel Bellini. Great War play. 3m., 1w., voice., chorus. Sc. Commander's cabin on board a submarine. BEL

Troll King's breakfast, The. Zakarias Topelius. Trans. by Elizabeth J. Macintre. 5m., 1w., others. Sc. Mountain slope in Lapland. Poet Lore 28 : 589–595, Autumn 1917.

* **Troll magic**; a Norwegian folk play. Constance D'Arcy Mackay. 11c., chorus char. Sc. A field. MST

Troth, The. Rutherford Mayne. 3m., 1w. Sc. A farm kitchen in Ireland. MD, MDT

Trouble by mail. John M. Francis. 2m., 3w. Sc. Interior. FSD

* **Trouble in the toyroom.** Clara J. Denton. Christmas play. Any

number of b. and g. Sc. In front of the toy room of Santa Claus. SIA

Troubles of a house keeper. Comedy. 1m., 7w. Sc. Dining room. G2

* **Troublesome flock;** Mother Goose play for children. Elizabeth F. Guptill. 10b., 15g. Sc. Unimportant. B

Troublesome time. Harry L. Newton. 3m. Sc. Interior. DPP

* **True Christmas spirit, The.** Marie Irish. 1b., 4g. Sc. Interior. I

True hero. W. D. Howells. Melodrama. 3m., 1w. Sc. Pastor's study. Harper's Magazine 119: 866–875, Nov. 1909.

Trusted friend, The. William and Josephine Giles. 3m., 1w. Sc. A well furnished room. RE

Truth, The. Jacinto Benavente. Trans. from the Spanish. 1m., 1w., 1s. Sc. Bachelor's apartment. BJP3

Truth, The. Edna Wahlert McCourt. 2m., 4w. Sc. Living room. Seven Arts 1: 475–492, March 1917.

Truth about Jane, The. Alice C. Thompson. 7w. Sc. Interior. B

Truth about liars, The. Helene Mullins. 2m., 1w. Sc. A garden. Drama 34: 145–151, Spring 1923.

† **Truth for a day, The.** Helen T. Darby. Washington's birthday play. 5g. Sc. Room in girl's boarding school. EP

Truth, the mischief. A. Thompson. 4w. Sc. Interior. DPP

Trying a dramatist. William S. Gilbert. 12m., 2w., others. Sc. Criminal court. Century Magazine 83: 179–189, Dec. 1911.

Trying them out. Lillian Stoll. Comedy. 2m., 4w. Sc. A business office. STN

Trysting place, The. Booth Tarkington. 4m., 3w. Sc. Room just off the lounge in a fine hotel in the country. C2 STK Ladies' Home Journal 39: 3–5, 137, 138, 141, 142, 145, Sept. 1922.

Tsunemasa. Ernest Fenollosa and Ezra Pound. Noh play of Japan. 2m., chorus. Sc. Japanese temple. FEN

Tsunemasa. Seami. Noh play of ancient Japan. 2m., chorus. Sc. Stage. WAA

Tubby and Gawks. F. Kinsey Peile. 4w. Sc. Interior. FSD

Tuff's boarder. Robert Henry Diehl. 3m., 2w. Sc. Interior. APP

Tune of a tune, A. Dan W. Totheroh. 2m., 2w. Sc. Front parlor. Drama 10: 184–188, Feb. 1920.

† **Turtle dove, The.** Margaret Scott Oliver. 5m., 1w., chorus. Sc. None necessary. KP, OS

Turtle-doves. Mellis Twelve. 2m., 3w. Sc. Interior. FSD

Tweedledum. Otis Richardson. 2m., 1w. Sc. Plainly furnished room. UW

* **Tweedledum and Tweedledee.** Fannie Wyche Dunn. Alice in Wonderland play. 4b., 1g. Sc. A wood with a road running through it. DUN

Twelfth night at Fisher's crossing. John T. Frederick. 4m., 1w., 1g. Sc. Waiting room of a depot in a small town. Midland 2: 18–24, Jan. 1916.

Twelve good men and true. Bessie Springer Breene. Comedy. 12w. Sc. A jury room. FSD

† **Twelve pound look, The.** J. M. Barrie. 1m., 2w., 1s m. Sc. Room in a home. BH, LC

Twice one. Basil MacDonald Hastings. 2m., 2w. Sc. Hall of a bungalow in England. Smart Set 39: 129–142, Jan. 1913.

Twice-told tale, A. Anna Cantrell Laws. 1m., 3w. Sc. Living room of the shabby-genteel. Drama 8: 400–413, Aug. 1918.

Twilight of the Gods, The. Josephine Daskam Bacon. 20 or 30 char. of the Bible. Sc. Not given. Forum 53: 7–20, Jan. 1915.

Twilight saint, The. Stark Young. 2m., 2w. Sc. Rather poorly furnished room in Italian house of 13th century. C1, YA, YO

* **Twinkle-Twinkle.** Someple (pseud.) 13c. Sc. Stage. SO

Twins, The; a frothy fragment. Dorothy Cleather. 5w. Sc. Sitting room. CH

Twins and how they entertained the new mininster, The. Elizabeth F. Guptill. Farce. 1m., 1b., 1g. Sc. Reception room. TMP

Twins of Bergamo. Jean-Pierre Claris de Florian. Trans. from the French by Oliver Farnsworth. 2m., 2w. Sc. Terrace. Drama 8: 350–368, Aug. 1918.

Twisting of the rope. Douglas Hyde. Trans. by Lady Gregory. 2m., 3w., others. Sc. Large room in a farm house 100 years ago. C2, Samhain pp. 30–38, Oct. 1901. Poet Lore 16: 12–22, Spring 1905.

Two aunts and a photo. Maisie B. Whiting. 4w. Sc. College room in girl's school. DEP

Two bad fairies, The. Kathleen C. Greene. 4g. Sc. Audience room in the Palace. GDL

Two barrels, The. Ford Douglas. 8m. Sc. Club grill room. Smart Set 64: 65–71, April 1921.

Two blind beggars and one less blind. Philip Moeller. 3m., 1w. Sc. Rag picker's cellar. FLS

Two blind men and a donkey. Marthurin M. Dondo. 5m., a donkey. Sc. Public square of a walled town. Poet Lore 32: 391–402, Autumn 1921.

Two college tramps. Victor Allen. 2m., 3w. Sc. Interior. B

* **Two countrymen, The.** Augusta Stevenson. 5b. Sc. A quiet corner with a high wall in a large city. SC3

Two cowards, The. Eugene Labiche. Trans. from the French by Barrett H. Clark. Comedy. 3m., 2w. Sc. Parlor. FSD

† **Two crooks and a lady.** Eugene Pillot. 3m., 3w. Sc. Library in an old Fifth Ave. mansion. FS1, KP

Two domestics. Netta Syrett. 6w. Sc. Drawing room. FSD

Two girls and him. Harry L. Newton. 1m., 2w. Sc. Outside of depot in a small town. WHP

* **Two holes, The.** Augusta Stevenson. 2g. Sc. Living room. SC1

Two husbands. Henri Lavedan. Trans. from the French by R. T. House. 2m. Sc. A study. Poet Lore 19: 207–211, Summer 1908.

Two in a flat. Mary Elwes. 2m., 2w. Sc. Sitting room. ETE

Two in a fog. Madeline Bridges. 1m., 1w. Sc. Not given. Ladies' Home Journal 32: 8, Aug. 1915.

Two in a trap. Albert E. Drinkwater. 1m., 1w. Sc. Drawing room in a flat. FSD

Two in a tiff. Robert C. V. Meyers. 2m., 1w. Sc. Interior. PPP

Two jay detectives, a rural riot of comedy. Harry L. Newton. 3m. Sc. Interior. DEP

Two jolly girl bachelors. Edward Martin Seymour. Romantic farce. 2w. Sc. Parlor of a small flat. PH

Two merry wagers. Edna Randolph Worell. 2m., 2w. Sc. Breakfast room. MAP

Two of a kind. Dunne Douglas. 1m., 1w. Sc. Interior of a hansom cab. Smart Set 2: 79–80, Oct.–Nov. 1900.

Two of a kind. Granville Forbes Sturgis. Burglar play. 2m., 1w. Sc. Handsome bachelor suite. STR

Two prisoners. Judith Matlack. 3m., 2w. Sc. A stone courtyard. SCT

Two slatterns and a king. Edna St. Vincent Millay. Moral interlude. Verse. 2m., 2w. Sc. Before a stage curtain. SCO, STK

Two sociable friends. C. Lewis. 3m. Sc. Interior. AMP

Two sons, The. Nerth Boyce. 2m., 2w. Sc. A low room with fish nets and oilskins hanging on the walls. P3

Two talismans, The. George Calderon. Comedy. 6m., 1w., chorus. Sc. On a hilltop outside an Arabian city. CA

Two's company. Manta S. Graham. 2m., 4w. Sc. Dining room. GRL

Typewriter lady, The. Edward Mumford. 3m., 4w. Sc. Office. PPP

Tyrfing. Thomas Sturge Moore. Verse. Viking play. 6m., 2w. Sc. Sweep of the out of doors. MOT

U

Ukai. (The Cormorant-fisher) Enami No Sayemon. Noh play of Japan. 4m., chorus. Sc. Stage. WAA

Unborn, The. George Middleton. 1m., 2w. Sc. Simple cozy library. MIP

Uncertain Silas. H. P. Powell. Rural comedy. 1m., 3w. Sc. Either interior or exterior. PPP

Uncle Eben's s'prise party. W. T. Newton. 7m., 5w. Sc. Interior. BUP

* **Uncle Grouch.** Marie Irish. Christmas play. 2b., 2g. Sc. Interior. IPR

† **Uncle Jimmy.** Zona Gale. 3m., 5w. Sc. Porch and front yard of a village house. B, Ladies' Home Journal 38: 18–19, 98, 101–104, Oct. 1921.

‡ **Uncle Joe's will.** Elizabeth F. Guptill. 7b., 2g. Sc. Lawyer's office. GUT

Uncle Pat. Thomas King Moylan. Irish comedy. 4m., 3w. Sc. A country kitchen. MOY

Uncle Peter's proposal. W. T. Newton. 3m., 2w. Sc. Sitting room. BUP

* **Uncle Sam to the rescue; or, Saving Santa's job.** Margie A. Jerauld. Patriotic Christmas play. 16c., chorus. Sc. Large roomy stage. FIL

Uncle Sam's cooks. Lizzie May Elwyn. 7m. Sc. Interior. APP

* **Uncle Sam's council.** Eva Thomas Nettleton. 43c. Sc. Large stage or platform. FSD

* **Uncle Sam's flower garden;** allegorical temperance play. Mrs. W. H. Preston. 12c. Sc. A garden. EP

* **Uncle Sam's mistake.** Marie Irish. Christmas play. 2b., 1g. Sc. Interior. IPR

Under conviction. J. Milnor Dorey. 2m., 2w. Sc. Kitchen in a miller's house in a small town in Pennsylvania. Drama 9: 115–127, Feb. 1919.

Undercurrents. Harriet Holmes Haslett. A melodrama. 4m., 2w. Sc. Entrance hall of an underground café. HAE

* **Under distinguished patronage.** Constance E. Waugh. Christmas play. 9g. Sc. Dressmaker's workroom. WH

Under London. George M. Rosener. Dramatization of Oliver Twist. 5m., 2w. Sc. Garret in the slums of London. WRP

Under sailing orders. Helen P. Kane. 1m., 1w. Sc. Cabin of a yacht. FP

* **Under the greenwood tree,** a pastoral play. Major P. Trevor. 3b., 4g. Sc. Out of doors. FSD

Under the white flag. Caroline Newnes. 1m., 1w. Sc. Ball room of Del Monte hotel. Smart Set 7: 159–160, July 1902.

Under their skins. George Allen England. 5m. Sc. Handsome furnished bachelor apartment in N. Y. Smart Set 44: 107–113, Nov. 1914.

Underground opportunity, An. Clara J. Denton. 2m., 3w. Sc. Hotel parlor. DAI

* **Underground railroad, The.** Wallace Rice. 4b., 4g. Sc. A clearing in a wood. RIS

Understudy, The. Agnes M. Miall. 5w. Sc. Dressing room of leading lady. FSD

Undine. P. D. Notrebal. Based on De La Frouques story of the same title. Verse. 3m., 2w. Sc. Exterior of fisherman's cottage. American Poetry Magazine 1: 12–20, July 1919.

* **Undoing of Giant Hotstoff, The.** Samuel Milbank Cauldwell. A dream play. 3b., 1g. Sc. Nursery. CC

Unequal triangle, An. Van Tassel Sutphen. 2m., 1w. Sc. Upstairs living room of a house. Smart Set 36: 127–132, Feb. 1912.

* **Unexpected company.** Clara J. Denton. Christmas play. 4b., 5g. Sc. Interior. I

Unexpected guest, The. Edna I. MacKenzie. 6w. Sc. Sitting room. PAP

Unexpected meeting, The. Horace B. Browne. From Martin Chuzzlewit. 3m. Sc. Pawnbroker's shop. BD

Unhoodwinkable. Pierre Wolff. Trans. from the French by Barrett H. Clark. 1m., 2w. Sc. Living room in Paris. Smart Set 58: 85–93, March 1919.

Unimagined Heaven, The. Maxwell Bodenheim. 7m., 2w., 1c. Sc. Triangular green booth. Seven Arts 2: 193–198, June 1917.

* **Uninvited guest, The.** Bertha Irene Tobin. 5b., 7g. Sc. A garden. TO

* **Uninvited member, An.** Elizabeth F. Guptill. 11g. Sc. Boarding school room. DEP

Universal impulse, The. Mrs. Wilson Woodrow. 3m., 3w. Sc. Reception room. Smart Set 34: 71–72, June 1911.

Unknown hand, The. Clifford Bax. Satire. 2w. Sc. Room in a flat. BAP

Unlucky tip, An. A. Louis Elliston. 2m., 2w. Sc. Interior of a cottage. B

Unnecessary atom, The. John Jex. 2m., 1w., 1b. Sc. In a shanty in the Canadian northwest. JEP

† **Unprofitable poultry keeping.** Violet M. Methley. 2g. Sc. Sitting room. FSD

Unseen, The. Alice Gerstenberg. 1m., 1w., 1s. Sc. Dining room. GT

† **Unseen host, The.** Percival Wilde. Great War play. Sc. An improvised American hospital in Paris. B, WU, WWS

* **Unselfish host;** a bluebird play. Mrs. Arthur T. Seymour. 18g. Sc. Large room or stage. B

* **Unsuccessful hunt, An.** Clara J. Denton. Christmas play. Any number of b. and g. Sc. The woods. SIA

Untrue to type. Ina Duvall Singleton. 1m., 2w. Sc. Interior. FSD

Up against it. Innis Gardner Osborn. 5m., 3w. Sc. Interior. B

Upon the waters. Tacie May Hanna. 2m., 4w. Sc. Sitting room of a small house. Drama 14: 58-62, 69, Nov. 1923.

Upstroke, The. F. J. Newboult. 4m., 3w. Sc. Kitchen-living room. FSD

* **Up-to-date America; or, The sweet girl graduate's dream.** Effie Louise Koogle. 10b., 10g. Sc. Art museum. MAP

Up-to-date proposal, An. Jeannette Joyce. 2m., 2w. Sc. Modern living room. MAP

* **Useful coal, The.** Laura E. Richards. 3b., chorus of b. Sc. Interior of palace. RP

V

Vacuum, The. Preston Gibson. 2m., 1w. Sc. Laboratory. FSD

Vagabond, The. Robert E. Rogers. 3m., 1w. Sc. Enclosed garden in the heart of Paris. Harvard Monthly 42: 87-95, April 1906.

* **Vain jackdaw, The.** Augusta Stevenson. 4b., chorus char. g. Sc. A public park. SC2

† **Valentine problem, A.** Alice W. Chaplin. 3g. Sc. Sitting room. CHC

Valley of gloom, The. Marie Drennan. 4m., many others, 1b., 1g. Sc. The valley of gloom. Poet Lore 34: 449-457, Autumn 1923.

Valyrie! Percival Wilde. Great War play. 3m. Sc. A level plain. WU

Vampire cat, The. Gerard Van Etten. From the Japanese legend. 4m., 2w. Sc. Japanese room. DPP

Vampire cat of Nabeshima, The. Fuji-Ko. 4m., 2w., cat. Sc. Japanese house. Smart Set 30: 127-134, Jan. 1910.

Vanishing race, The. Constance D'Arcy Mackay. 7m., 1w., chorus characters. Sc. A cleared space in a forest. MPP

Veal breaded. John M. Francis. 3m., 3w. Sc. Interior. B

Veil of happiness, The. Georges Clemenceau. Trans. by T. M. Cleland. Chinese play. 5m., 4w. Sc. Chinese interior in Peking. CLE

Velasquez and the "Venus." Maurice Baring. Farce. 2m., 1w. Sc. Studio of Velasquez. BA

Vengeance of Catullus. Emil Bohnslav Frida. 5m., 1w. Sc. Rome. Poet Lore 25: 536-544, Winter 1914.

Very naked boy, The. Stuart Walker. 2m., 1w. Sc. Hallway with a heavily curtained doorway. WM

Veterans, The. James Henry Henle. 2m., 1w. Sc. Restaurant. International 5: 53–54, Mar. 1912.

Victorious surrender of Lady Sybil, The. Capt. Leslie T. Peacocke. 2m., 2w. Sc. Drawing room of country house in England. Smart Set 32: 127–133, Oct. 1910.

Victory of love, The. Rex T. Stout. 2m. Sc. House of the soul. Smart Set 35: 49–50, Oct. 1911.

* **Victory of the good citizen, The.** F. Ursula Payne. 8c. Sc. Street near a school. PPC

Village, The. Octave Feuillet. Trans. by Barrett H. Clark. Comedy. 2m., 2w. Sc. Parlor in a home in a suburban village. FSD

Villain and victim. W. R. Walker. Matrimonial comedy. 1m., 1w. Sc. Drawing room. PH

Villain in the piece, The. Percival Wilde. 2m., 1w. Sc. Just outside a ballroom. WC

Violet souls. John Jex. Satire. 2m., 2w. Sc. Elaborately furnished bedroom—violet in color. JEP

Violet under the snow, The. Dennis Cleugh. Christmas play. 4m., 1w. Sc. Interior of a hut built in a hollow. CLF, Drama 13: 52–58, Nov. 1922.

Violin maker of Cremona, The. François Coppée. Trans. from the French. Costume play. 3m., 1w., pages. Sc. Plain room. DPP

Virgin and the white slaver. Frank Wedekind. Adapted by André Tridon. 2m., 5w. Sc. Living room. International 7: 279–282, Oct. 1913.

* **Virgin children of long ago.** Louise E. Tucker and Estelle L. Ryan. 1b., 3g. Sc. Sunny room in a large country house on a southern plantation. TRH

‡ **Vision of Columbus, The.** F. Ursula Payne. Great War background. Pageant of democracy. 30 or more c. Sc. In front of a curtain. PPD

Vision of Paganini, The. Leo Sarkadi. 2m., 1w. Sc. Living room of Italian house. International 10: 54–57, Feb. 1916.

Vision of youth, A. Eleanor Colby. 40 char. Graduation play. Sc. Simple setting with throne in center. Ladies' Home Journal 30: 91, 102, Mar. 1913.

Vision splendid, The. Kathleen C. Greene. 5m. Sc. A tavern by the roadside. GDL

Visit, The. Richard Pryce. Adapted from Freddy's ship by Mary E. Mann. 2m., 3w. Sc. Drawing room in country rectory. FSD

* **Visit from the Brownies, A.** Marie Irish. 8b. Sc. Interior of a kitchen. IL

Visit in Brazil, A. William Cabell Brown. Missionary play of Brazil. 1m., 2w. Sc. A parlor in Brazil. DOF

Visit of the Tomiter, The; A Christmas play, Mabel R. Goodlander. Any no. of c. Sc. Village square. Woman's Home Companion 41: 66, Dec. 1914.

* **Visit to Santa Claus.** Marie Irish. 5b., 4g. Sc. Interior. I

Visiting Mamma. Myra Emmons. 3w. Sc. Living room. Harper's Bazar. 43: 860-864, Sept. 1909.

* **Visitors, The.** Florence Kiper Frank. 3b., 3g. Sc. Children's bedroom. DPP

Visitors from the Colonial period. Anita B. Ferris. 1w., 5g., 4b. Sc. Ordinary room. Everyland 7: 75–79, Feb. 1916.

Vital moments. Arthur Schnitzler. Trans. by Edward Goodman. 3m. Sc. Well kept garden. International 3: 7–9, 16, Dec. 1910.

Voice on the stair, A. Lillian P. Wilson. 1m., 2w., 1b. Sc. Tastefully furnished room. WIF

Voices. Hortense Flexner. Poetic drama. 2w. Sc. Main street of Domremy in front of a shattered church. MA, Seven Arts Magazine 1: 135–143, Dec. 1916.

Volcanic island, The. Clifford Bax. Satire. 2w. Sc. Sitting room. BAP

† **Vote by ballot.** Granville Barker. Comedy. 3m., 1w., 1s. Sc. Drawing room with open French window. BT

Vote the new moon. Alfred Kreymborg. Satire. 5m., 1w. Sc. A dark stage. KMA, STV

Voyage en Cythère, Le. Lady Margaret Sackville. Poetic. 1m., 1w. Sc. An old garden with high yew hedges. SAS

W

Wager, The. Clara J. Denton. Farce. 4m., 2w. Sc. Handsome interior. DAI

Wager, The. Giuseppe Giacosa. Trans. from the Italian by Barrett H. Clark. Poetic comedy. 4m., 1w. Sc. Palace in the valley of Aosta in the 14th century. FSD

* **Waif's Thanksgiving, The.** Elizabeth F. Guptill. 5b., 4g. Sc. Interior. MAP

Waiting. George Middleton. 1m., 1w., 1c. Sc. Living room. MIT

Waiting at the church. Franz Rickaby and Barbara Rickaby. Farce. 5m., 3w. Sc. A room in an Episcopal church. B

Waiting for the 'bus. Gertrude E. Jennings. 2m., 10w. Sc. Exterior. FSD

Waiting for the train. Charles Nevers Holmes. 2m., 1w. Sc. Interior small railroad station. DEP

* **Waiting for the train.** Marie Irish. 7b., 7g. Sc. Waiting room of depot. IPP

Wake up, John Bull political play. Winifred Dolan. 9m., 5w. Sc. A green. FSD

Wakuwapi, the hunting. Hartley Alexander. Play of the Dakotah Indians. 2m., 2w., 1c., others. Sc. Mouth of the canyon in the Bad Lands. Play Book 2: 7–32, Apr. 1915.

Wally and the widow. Ethel L. Newman. 1w., 1b. Sc. Living-room. FSD

* **Wampun belts.** Louise E. Tucker and Estelle L. Ryan. Story of Roger Williams. 5b., chorus characters. Sc. Interior of wigwam. TRH

Wanderer, The. Maxwell Bodenheim. 4m., 2w. Sc. Fronts of two village shops. Seven Arts Magazine 2: 603–607, Sept. 1917.

Wanderer, The. Auberon Kennard. A costume play of English life in 17th century. 2m., 2w. Sc. Parlor of a small country house. FSD

Wanderer, The. Katharine Metcalf Roof. 2m., 4w. Sc. Deck of steamer. Smart Set 23: 130–133, Nov. 1907.

Wandering scholar from Paradise, The. Hans Sachs. Trans. from the German. Medieval play. 2m., 1w. Sc. Outdoors with cottage in the background. ELT4

* **Wanted: a chimney.** Elizabeth F. Guptill. Christmas play. 3b., 2g. Sc. Living room. GUD

Wanted: a cook. Edith F. A. U. Painton. Comedy. 1m., 6w. Sc. Interior. DEP

Wanted, a housekeeper. Clement O'Neill. Comedy. 1m., 3w. Sc. Room in a flat. WIA

Wanted, a license to wed. Elizabeth F. Guptill. Irish farce. 2m., 1w.. Sc. Sergeant's office. MAP

Wanted—a pitcher. M. N. Beebe. Farce. 11m. Sc. Real estate office. B

Wanted—a valet. Benjamin L. C. Griffith. Ethiopian sketch. 4m. Sc. Office. GR

Wanted—a wife. E. J. Freund. Comedy. 2m., 2w. Sc. Living room for bachelors. ANP

War. Witter Bynner. 2m., 2w. Sc. Library in home of a Prussian officer. Stratford Journal 6: 44–48, Jan.–Mar. 1920.

"War." John E. Fillmore. 2m., 1w. Sc. Country district in Central Europe. Poet Lore 25: 523–533, Winter 1914.

War brides. Marion Craig Wentworth. Great War background. 3m., 4w., chorus. Sc. Room in a peasant's cottage. WEN, WW, Century 89: 527–544, Feb. 1915.

War committee, A.; and The little silver ring. (Each in one act) Edward Knoblauch. 1m., 10w. Sc. Committee room. FSD

War fly, The. Noel Leslie. 3m. Sc. Private dining room in London hotel. LET

War woman, The. Caroline C. Lovell. Play of the American Revolution. 8m., 2w. 10c. Sc. Inside a log cabin. Drama 13: 23–26, Oct. 1922.

‡ **Wardrobe of the king, The.** William J. McKiernan. Burlesque. 5b. Sc. Private grounds of the King of Borgoloo. FP

War's end. Henry A. Coit. 5m., 1w. Sc. Hunting lodge. COI

* **Washington's birthday.** "Washington's message to Anychild." F. Ursula Payne. 8c. Sc. A room in Anyhouse. PP

Washington's first defeat. Charles Frederick Nirdlinger. Comedy. 1m., 1w., 1s. Sc. Drawing room. FSD

Wasp, The. Essex Dane. 2m., 1w. Sc. Living room of a deserted inn. DAO

Waste. Noel Leslie. 2m., 3w. Sc. Sitting room in a cottage in England. LET

Watch, a wallet and a jack of spades, A. Lindsey Barbee. Detective comedy. 3m., 6w. Sc. Living room. DEP

Watchers, The. R. E. Rogers. A Christmas masque. 3m., 6w. Sc. Grove of ancient trees on a hill slope. Harvard Monthly 41: 166–174, Jan. 1906.

"Watchful waiting." Dorothy Potter. 3m., 1w. Sc. Headquarters of the General in a town in Northern Mexico. POT

Watching for Santa Claus. Horace Varney. 1m., 1w., 3g., 2b. Sc. Library. Ladies' Home Journal 21: 19, Dec. 1903.

Water that has passed, The. Edgar Morette. Dream playlet. 5m., 1w. Sc. Interior. DEP

Water upon fire. Ercole Luigi Morselli. Trans. from the Italian by Isaac Goldberg. 5m., 2w. Sc. Interior of a shepherd's hut. VE

† **Waterloo.** Sir Arthur Conan Doyle. Historical. 3m., 1w. Sc. A front room in a small house. FSD

Way of a woman, The. Irving Dale. Comedy of amateur dramatics. 2m., 1w. Sc. Interior. DEP

Way of Yu-Soo, The. William T. Demarest. A play in the Chinese style. 4m., 4w. Sc. None necessary. DEM

Way out, A. Robert Frost. 3m., and a crowd. Sc. Bachelor's kitchen bedroom in a farm house. Seven Arts 1 : 347–362, Feb. 1917.

Way the noise began, The. Don and Beatrice Knowlton. 1m., 1w. Sc. Living room. Drama 12 : 20–21, Oct.–Nov. 1921.

Wayside comedy, A. James Platt White. 1m., 2w. Sc. Reception room in apartment in hotel in Buffalo. Harvard Monthly 31 : 101–110, Dec. 1900.

† **Wayside piper, The.** Mary S. Edgar. Based on the story of the Pied Piper of Hamelin. 21g. Sc. A wayside place. EDG

We and our friends. Marie Irish. Kindness to animals play. 5b., 4g. Sc. Stage. IPP

We choose a name. Frank Roe Batchelder. 1m., 1w. Sc. Not given. Smart Set 10 : 73–75, June 1903.

We dine at seven. Angela Cudmore and Peter Davey. 2w. Sc. Interior. FSD

We live again. Thornton Gilman. 6m., 6w. Sc. Living room. WIP2

Weakest link, The. Beulah Marie Dix. 4m. Sc. Beneath walls of Pontivet in Brittany. DA

Wearin' o' the green, The. Mary S. Watts. Farce. 11m., 7w. Sc. Living room. WT

Weary Willie. Charles E. Taylor. Farce. 1m., 1w. Sc. Interior. APP

Weasel, The. George N. Roberts. Crook play. 4m., 2w. Sc. Living room. B

Web, The. Alice Brown. 2m., 2w., 1s. Sc. Shabbily furnished sitting room. BO

Web, The. Eugene G. O'Neill. 5m., 1w. Sc. Squalid bedroom in a rooming house in the lower East Side N. Y. OT

Wedded, a social comedy. Lawrence Langner. 1m., 2w. Sc. Best parlor in house in cheap district of Brooklyn. Little Review 1 : 8–18, Nov. 1914.

Wedding, The. Anton Chekhov. 7m., 3w., chorus. Sc. Dining room. BFR, CHD

Wedding guest, The. Rosalee Kerley. 6m., 2w., others. Sc. Large hall of Italian villa. Poet Lore 33 : 232–238, Summer 1922.

Wedding morning, The. Arthur Schnitzler. 2m. Sc. Bedroom in bachelor's apartment. SA

Wedding of Mah Foy, The. Grace Luce Irwin. 3m., 3w., chorus. Chinese farce. Sc. Empty stage. ID

Weight of wings, The. Lillian P. Wilson. 1m., 2w., 1g. Sc. Living room in farmhouse. WIF

* **Welcoming the New Year.** Alice Sumner Varney. 18c. Sc. A large room. VA

* **Well babies.** Anna M. Lütkenhaus. Little Mother's league play. 7g., chorus. Sc. Interior. LU

Well matched pair. Beryl Tanner. 2w. Sc. Interior. FSD

† **Well remembered voice, A.** J. M. Barrie. 4m., 2w. Sc. A dark room which becomes an artist's studio. BE

† **Welsh honeymoon.** Jeannette Marks. 3m., 2w. Sc. A Welsh kitchen. Ci, MT, Smart Set 38: 135–141, Nov. 1912.

West of Omaha. Rachel Barton Butler. Farce. 4m., 3w. Sc. Studio. B

Wet blanket. Margery Stanley Clark. 1m., 2w. Sc. Parlour of seaside lodging house. FSD

What about Katie? Mary Aldis. 2w. Sc. Neat bright kitchen. Journal of Home Economics 9: 515–519, Nov. 1917.

* **What can I do?** Carolyn Wilson. A fancy for school children. 49c. Sc. Office of Uncle Sam. St. Nicholas 45: 599–603, May 1918.

What charity covers. David Garrow. Comedy. 2m., 2w. Sc. Drawing room. FSD

‡ **What Christmas did for Jerusha Grumble.** 5g. Sc. Sitting room. TMP

* **What do you know about ghosts?** Elizabeth F. Guptill. Hallowe'en farce. 4b. Sc. Interior. GUC

* **What happened to Henry Penny.** Lady Bell. Comedy. 6c. Sc. Unimportant. BEJ

What King Christmas brought. Ruth Suckow. 8c. Sc. Room with fire place. GUB

What married men do. George M. Rosener. Comedy skit. 2m., 1w. Sc. Apartment. Stagelore p. 132–, Feb. 1912.

What of the night? May Bell. 3m., 1w. Sc. An isolated farmhouse. BRW

What Rosie told the tailor. Edith J. Broomhall. College farce. 7m., 3w. Sc. College boy's room. B

What society is coming to. Felicia Goddard. 2m., 2w., others. Sc. Dining room table set for 24. Smart Set 12: 55–57, Oct. 1903.

What's in a name? Fanny Cannon. 2m., 3w. Sc. Interior. DEP

What's in a name? Beulah King. 2m., 2w. Sc. Studio. MAP

What's the use? J. H. Kehoe. 1m., 4w. Sc. Interior. RE

What's wrong? Paul Eldridge. 3m., 1w. Sc. Backroom of a cafe. Stratford Journal 5: 83–96, Aug. 1919.

* **Wheat-field, The.** Laura E. Richards. 1b., 2g., chorus of b. and g. Sc. A wheat-field. RP

* **Wheatless meal, The.** H. M. Hartman. Great War background. 3g., chorus. Sc. Kitchen. CAM

When Anne was Queen; or, A gentleman of the road. Comedy, 18th century England. Marie Boileau and Jonathan Erle. 4m., 2w. Sc. A panelled parlor. FSD

* **When Betty saw the Pilgrims.** Margaret Howard. 1b., 2g., 7 chorus groups. Sc. Stage divided by curtains. EP

When Danny came marching home. Edgar Selwyn. Farce. 2m., 2w. Sc. Kitchen. US

* **When Do-it school entertained.** Mary Bonham. Christmas play. 18b., 6g. Sc. Stage with large Christmas tree. EP

When doctors disagree. O. E. Young. Farce. 8m. Sc. Interior of sailors' lodging house. PPP

When extremes meet. Frank Teipe Kleber. Tragicomedy. 1w., 2g. Sc. Central Park, N. Y. KL

When Greek meets Greek. Maverick Terrell. 1m., 1w. Sc. Table in Tortoni's restaurant. Smart Set 54: 125–128, Apr. 1918.

When Heine was twenty-one. Maude Morrison Frank. 6m., 1w., 1s. Sc. Living room in a house in Hamburg. FSP

‡ **When knights were bold;** an incident of King Arthur's court. Marjorie Benton Cooke. 6b., 1g. Sc. Early English setting. DPP

* **When liberty calls.** Josephine Thorp. Pageant. 32c. Sc. The palace of justice. TKP

When love is blind. Harriet Holmes Halett. Comedy. 1m., 1w. Sc. Living room. HAE

When love is young. Marjory Benton Cooke. 1m., 3w. Sc. Drawing room. CO

When Mother came to college. Louis Dudley Daird. College comedy. 2m., 1w. Sc. Typical college room. FL

* **When Polly was queen of the May.** Elizabeth F. Guptill. Any number of c. Sc. Out of doors. EP

When Shakespeare struck the town. Lillian F. Chandler. Comedy. 8w. Sc. Living room. EP

When the boys came home. Grace E. Richmond. 4m., 1b., 5w. Sc. Living room well furnished. Ladies' home Journal 35: 13–14, 72, 74, 76, 78, Sept. 1918.

‡ **When the cat is away.** E. M. Peixotto. 7b. Farce. Sc. Living room of a country home in England. PET

When the dew falleth. Perez Hirschbein. An idyl trans. from the Yiddish. 3m., 2w. Sc. An old orchard. BLK

† **When the fates decree.** Grant H. Code. Greece—Virgil—Aneid. 9b., 7g. Sc. No scenery necessary. COW

When the land was young. Lucie T. Burkham. Incident of the American Revolution. 3m., 8w. Sc. Grounds before a Colonial house. BUR

* **When the sun stayed in bed.** Doris Holsworth. 10c. Sc. Bedroom in a palace. B

* **When the toys awake.** Lindsey Barbee. 15b., 5g. Sc. A nursery. BLP

When the wheels run down. Maude M. Rogers. 3w. Sc. Interior. FSD

When the whirlwind blows. Essex Dane. 3w. Sc. Roughly furnished room. DAO

When the willow nods. Alfred Kreymborg. A dance-play. 2m., 1w. Sc. A dense wood. KMP, KMR, Poetry 11: 287–297, Mar. 1918.

When the young birds go. Pauline B. Barrington. 3m., 2w. Sc. Living room in a country house. BAQ

When two's not company. Mary MacMillan. 2m. Sc. Large comfortable room. MTT

* **When we are grown up.** Marie Irish. Sunday School play. 12b. Sc. Stage. IPP

* **When we are women.** Marie Irish. 9g. Sc. Stage. IPP

When witches ride, a play of Carolina folk superstitions. Elizabeth A. Lay. 3m., 1w. Sc. The storehouse of a cross roads store. CFP

When women rule. Agnes Electra Platt. Farce. 2m., 4w. Sc. Private office in Washington. FP

Where are those men? Alice Gerstenberg. 8w. Sc. Living room. DPP

† **Where but in America.** Oscar M. Wolff. 2w., 1m. Sc. Dining room. LC, MA, Smart Set 54: 79–87, Mar. 1918.

* **Where is happiness?** E. E. Bloxam. 18c. Sc. Out of doors. BL

Where is my coat? Frank Dumont. Comedy. 2m., 2w. Sc. Sitting room. PPP

* **Where love is, there God is also.** Rita Benton. From the story by Tolstoy. 8b., 8g. Sc. Interior of a peasant's shabby hut. BSC

Where shall we go? Henri Lavedan. Tr. from the French. 1m., 1w., 5g. Sc. Bedroom. MR, Poet Lore 28 : 397–402, Vacation 1917.

Where the cross is made. Eugene O'Neill. 6m., 1w. Sc. Room erected as a lookout post on the top of a house. OMC

Where the trail ends. George M. Rosener. Life in the Canadian woods. 2m., 1w. Sc. Cabin in the Canadian woods. RE

‡ **Where war comes.** Beulah Marie Dix. 2b., 5g. Sc. Simple comfortable room. AS

* **Which shall be king?** Anna Van Marter Jones. Christmas play. 17c., 3 chorus groups. Sc. Large stage. SAB

While the mushrooms bubble. Dan W. Totheroh. Fantasy. 1m., 2w. Sc. Room of Pierrette. Poet Lore 32 : 251–261, Summer 1921.

While you wait. Charles Newton Hood. 1m., 1w. Sc. Cozy breakfast room. Smart Set 1 : 101–106, June 1900.

* **Whiney-Piney.** E. M. Fotheringham. 2g. Sc. Bedroom. FG

Whiskers. Helen F. Bagg. Farce. 3m, 7w. Sc. Den. PPP

Whisperer, The. William Sharp. Imaginative, poetical, philosophic. 2m. Sc. Crowded thoroughfare of London. SHV

* **White chief, The.** Clara J. Denton. Thanksgiving play. 3b., 7g. Sc. Dining room of a farmhouse. EP

White Christmas, The. Walter Ben Hare. Morality play. 8m., 7w. Sc. Winter street in Bethlehem. HW

White dresses. Paul Greene. 2m., 2w. Sc. In a negro cabin. LC

White elephant. Margaret Cameron and Jessie Leach Pector. 3w. Sc. Small reception room. FSD

White elephants. Kenyon Nicholson. 3m., 1w. Sc. Living room of New York apartment on Riverside Drive. Smart Set 66 : 63–74, Oct. 1921.

White horse, The. Morley Roberts. 3m., 2w. Sc. Old oak-panelled hall in an ancient castle. RF

White lie, The. Marie Metz-Konig, tr. from the Dutch by May Tevis and Pierre Loving. 1m., 2w. Sc. An artist's studio. LO

* **White magic.** Netta Syrett. 2b., 3g., many chorus characters. Sc. A wood. SSF

White messenger, The. Edith M. Thomas. Poetic. Great War background. 7m., 1w., chorus. Sc. Village in Eastern Europe. THO

Who are you? Frank Hall Shepard. Comedy. 2m., 1w. Sc. Law office. B

* **Who is queer?** Ruth Horton. 4b. Sc. Not given. Everyland 5 : 87, Mar. 1914.

Who kissed Barbara? Lillian Rickaby and Franz Rickaby. Farce. 3m., 2w. Sc. Interior. B

* **Who trimmed the Christmas tree?** Marie Battelle Schilling. 3b., 2g. Sc. Plainly furnished room. BAC

* **Who was scared?** Elizabeth F. Guptill. Hallowe'en play. 6g. Sc. Room in a girl's boarding school. GUC

† **Who wins?** 1b., 3g. Comedy. Sc. Sitting room. BU

Who wins the bet? John M. Francis. 2m., 1w. Sc. Interior. FSD

Whole truth, The. Lindsey Barbee. Comedy. 5m., 4w. Sc. Interior. DEP

Whole truth, The. Louise Bronson West. Telling the whole truth for a single day. 2m., 9w. Sc. Interior. B

Whom the Gods destroy. Jaroslav Hilbert. Trans. from the Bohemian by Charles Recht. Drama of the war of 1866. 12m., 1w. Sc. A country church yard. Poet Lore 27 : 361–389, Vacation 1916.

Whom the sea calls. Hermann Ford Martin. 1m., 1w. Sc. Rocks at the sea shore. American Poetry Magazine 5 : 11–13, Dec. 1922.

Who's crazy now? Harvey Denton. 3m., 2w. Sc. Interior. DEP

Who's the boss? Ragnia Eskel. Comedy of a hen pecked husband. 3m., 6w. Sc. Interior. DEP

* **Whose dog?** Elizabeth F. Guptill. 3b. Sc. Street. MBP
* **Whose tree?** No author given. Christmas play. 6b., 2g. Sc. Plain stage. HOL

Whose widow? Helen C. Clifford. Comedy. 4m., 4w. Sc. Living room. FP

* **Why?** E. M. Fotheringham. 1b., 1g. Sc. Room. FG
* **Why Christmas was late.** Lizzie De Armond. 11 or more b. Sc. Any interior or platform. FIL
* **Why didn't you tell?** Anita B. Ferris. An Easter entertainment. 30c. Sc. Platform. Everyland 7 : 114–118, Mar. 1916.

Why Jessica! Annie Rogers Knowlton. Comedy. 1m., 9w. Sc. Interior. B

† **Why the chimes rang.** Elizabeth Apthorp McFadden. 1m., 1w., 2b., chorus. Sc. Interior of a woodchopper's hut. FSD

Why not Jim? Helen Bagg. Farce. 3m., 6w. Sc. Summer house. PPP

Widdy's mite, The. Dan Totheroh. 2m., 2w. Sc. Scantily furnished living room in home in Ireland. Drama 13 : 13–15, Oct. 1922.

† **Widow of Wasdale Head.** Arthur Pinero. Fantasy. 5m., 1w. Sc. Gloomy, ancient room. CBI, CH, Smart Set 43 : 63–82, May 1914.

Widow Sabrina, The. Granville Forbes Sturgis. Comedy. College play. 3m. Sc. Typical college room. STR

Widows. Herbert Swears. 3w. Sc. Shabby living room. FSD

Widow's might, The. Nathaniel Ladd Foster. Comedy. 2m., 2w. Sc. Sitting room. FSD

† **Widow's veil, The.** Alice Rostetter. 2w., 1 voice. Sc. Dumb-waiter shaft. FLS

Wife of Marobious, The. Max Ehrmann. 1m., 2w. Sc. Antechamber to bed room in house in ancient Rome. EW

Wife of Usher's Well, a tragedy of the fantastic based on an old English ballad. John Joseph Martin. 3m., 3w. Sc. A great hall. Poet Lore 30 : 94–111, Spring 1919.

Wife tamer, The. Katharine Kavanaugh. Comedy. 2m., 1w. Sc. Parlor. DEP

* **Wigwam; or, The little girl from town.** Lady Bell. Comedy. 3g. Sc. Unimportant. BEJ

Wild animal play, The. Ernest Seton-Thompson. 9b., 8g. Sc. Woods. Ladies' Home Journal 17 : 2–3, 28, July 1900.

Wild flower. Mildred Criss McGuckin. Fantasy. 3m., 4w., chorus. Sc. Garden surrounded with box hedges. BAG

Wild goose, The. Rex Hunter. 1m., 1w. Sc. Combined living and sleeping room. HS

Wiles of the widow, The. Kathleen Crighton Lion. Yorkshire comedy. 2m., 2w. Sc. Room in a cottage in a fishing village. FSD

Will, The. J. M. Barrie. 6m., 1w. Sc. A lawyer's office. BH

Will he come back? Felix Grendon. Comedy. 1m., 2w. Sc. Sitting room of a modern flat. GRF

Will Soakum's matrimonial bureau. Frank I. Hanson. 19m., 5w., 6b., 5g. Sc. Office. EP

† **Will-o'-the-wisp.** Doris F. Halman. Fantasy. 4w. Sc. Interior of a farmhouse. HAS, KP, MA

Will-o'-wisp, A. Anna Wolfrom. 5m., 2w. Sc. Kitchen of an old farm house. WOH

"William." W. C. Baker. Farce. 2m., 2w. Sc. Interior. B

* **William Penn's treaty with the Indians.** Louise E. Tucker and Estelle L. Ryan. 6b., 2g., chorus char. Sc. An open space. TRH

Willow tree. Yone Noguchi. 6m., 1w. Sc. Not given. Pacific Review 1 : 310–313, Dec. 1920.

Wind and lady moon, The. Emma Sheridan. 1m., 1w., many others. Drama 12 : 314–318, June–Aug. 1922.

Wind over the water, The. Philip Merivale. Poetic. Iceland in the 12th century. 3m., 2w. Sc. Interior of house. FOS

Window to the south, A. Mary Katharine Reely. 5m., 3w. Sc. Farm kitchen. REE

Winds of night, The. John S. Miller, Jr. 4 char. and chorus. Sc. A graveyard by the river. Harvard Monthly 47 : 160–166, Jan. 1909. (Can not be staged.)

Windy shot, The. Edward Harold Conway. A subterranean incident. 5m. Sc. A parting in a coal mine. Smart Set 45 : 367–377, Apr. 1915.

Wings, The. Josephine Preston Peabody. Poetic, historical. 2m., 1w., 1c. Sc. A low hut in Northumbria about 700 A. D. FSD, Harper's Magazine 110 : 947–956, May 1905. Poet Lore 25 : 352–369, Vacation 1914.

Wings in the mesh, a colloquy. Milnes Levick. 3w. Sc. Living room. Smart Set 59 : 95–103, July 1919.

Winning a husband. Granville Forbes Sturgis. Comedy. 2m., 2w. Sc. Library in a home. STR

Winning a prize. Willis N. Bugbee. Comedy. 3m., 2w. Sc. Photographer's studio. MBP

Winning of Fuji, The. Eunice T. Gray. A Japanese play. 3m., 3w. Sc. Interior of a Japanese house. DPP

Winning ways. Walter F. Rice. Farce. 4m., 2w. Sc. Reception room in hotel. B

Winter. Sholom Ash. 2m., 5w. Sc. A room in an old house in a provincial town. PTS

Winter bloom. Budget T. Hayes. 2m., 4w. Sc. Comfortable kitchen. Poet Lore 30 : 385–411, Autumn 1919.

Winter dawn. Wilfrid Wilson Gibson. Poetic. 1m., 2w. Sc. Shepherd's cottage. GIA, GIP, GIS

Wire entanglement. Robert Marshall. 2m., 2w. Sc. Newspaper office. FSD

Wireless. Alice Leal Pollock. 4m. Sc. Interior of wireless station. Smart Set 24: 96–103, Mar. 1908.

* **Wise crow, The.** Augusta Stevenson. 2g. Sc. A meadow. SC2

Wise men, The. Lee Simonson. Christmas play. 6m., 3w., others. Sc. New England barn. Harvard Monthly 45: 139–149, Jan. 1908.

* **Wish-bird, The.** Augusta Stevenson. 1b., 2g. Sc. Palace gardens. SC2

Witch, The. Margaret Macnamara. 5m. Sc. Veranda of a boarding house for women. DAN

Witch of coos, The. Robert Frost. 2m., 1w. Sc. Not given. Poetry 19: 175–181, Jan. 1922.

* **Witch of the woods, The.** Mrs. Isabel Anderson. 3b., 3g., chorus. Sc. Garden with trees. AE

* **Witchcraft story, A.** Blanche Shoemaker Wagstaff. Colonial play. 4g. Sc. A Puritan home. WCP

Witches' hour and candle light. Pauline Phelps and Marion Short. Hallowe'en play. 3m., 1w. Sc. Living room in colonial house. FSD

* **Witch's dream, The.** Laura Rountree Smith. 12c. Sc. Dimly lighted stage. SFH

With candle and crucifix. Paul Mariett. 4m., others. Sc. Large room of a log cabin. Harvard Monthly 49: 117–122, Dec. 1909.

With chains of gold. José Andres Vasquez, tr. by Willis Knapp Jones. 1m., 1w. Sc. Luxurious drawing room in Spain. Poet Lore 34: 417–425, Autumn 1923.

Witness, The. Emil Bohnslav Frida. Trans. by Charles Recht. 4m., 2w. Sc. Dining room of an apartment. Poet Lore 25: 546–558, Winter 1914.

Wives wanted in Squashville. O. E. Young. Farce. 3m. Sc. Interior. DEP

* **Wolf and the horse, The.** Augusta Stevenson. 4b., 1g., chorus char. Sc. A field of oats. SC2

* **Wolf and the lamb, The.** Augusta Stevenson. 1b., 1g. Sc. A pasture. SC2

Wolf-hunt, The. Verga Giovanni. Trans. from the Italian by Isaac Goldberg. 2m., 1w. Sc. A shepherd's hut. VE

Woman, The. Harold F. Norton. 1m., 2w. Sc. Richly furnished library in a country house. Yale Sheffield Monthly 20: 393–401, June 1914.

Woman intervenes, The. J. Hartley Manners. 3m., 1w. Sc. Interior. FSD, Smart Set 36: 113–123, Apr. 1912.

Woman juror, The. E. F. Parr. 2m., 2w. Sc. Prettily furnished room. FSD

Woman of it, The; or, Our friends, the anti-suffragists. Mary Shaw. Satirical comedy. 9w. Sc. Club room of Anti-Suffrage Club. DPP

Woman who was acquitted, The. Andre de Lorde. Trans. from the French. 5m., 1w. Sc. Judge's chambers of the criminal court. MR

Woman's a woman for a' that, A. Mary MacMillan. 2m., 3w. Sc. Sitting room in summer cottage. MS

Woman's choice, A. L. H. and C. T. Dazey. 1m., 3w. Sc. Showy apartment of dressmaker. Smart Set 30: 123–129, Apr. 1910.

Woman's forever, A. Frances Aymar Mathews. 1m., 1w. Sc. Private parlor in hotel. WEP

Woman's honor. Susan Glaspell. 3m., 6w. Sc. Room in a sheriff's house used for conferences. GP

Woman's way, A. Edith Wheeler. 3m., 2w. Sc. Comfortable room with fireplace. WIA

Woman's wiles. William Young. Comedy. 2m., 1w. Sc. Interior. FSD

Womenkind. Wilfrid Wilson Gibson. Verse. 2m., 3w. Sc. Living room in a lonely cottage. GIP, GW

Women's votes. Mrs. Arthur Hopkinson. 2w. Sc. A small sitting room. FSD

* **Won.** Kate Harvey. Fairy play. 23c. Sc. Bank of green. BHP

Won by a kodak. Harold Sander. Comedy. 2m., 3w. Sc. Nicely furnished sitting room. FP

Won by a wager. O. E. Young. 4m., 4w. Sc. Farmhouse. PPP

† **Wonder hat, The.** Ben Hecht and Kenneth Sawyer Goodman. Farce. 4m., 1w. Sc. Park in moonlight. MA, STG

* **Wonder-hill, The.** Virginia Olcott. Play of industry. 2b., 2g. Sc. A peasant's home. OPA

* **Wonderful rose, The.** Netta Syrett. 1b., 3g. Sc. A big kitchen in a farmhouse. SSF

Wonderful woman, A. Percival Wilde. Comedy. 3m., 1w. Sc. Living room in an apartment. WE

Wondership, The. Leon Cunningham. 3m., 2w. Sc. Lonely island. Poet Lore 30 : 362–376, Autumn 1919.

Wooden leg, The. Essex Dane. 1m., 1w. Sc. Public sitting room at hotel at Nice. DAO

* **Wooden shoe, The; or, St. Valentine's Day.** Rita Strauss. 3b., 4g. Sc. Village street. BHP

* **Woodland princess, The.** Louise Saunders. Fairy play. 12c. Sc. Cleared space in heart of the forest. FSD

Woods of Ida. Olive Tilford Dargan. Verse. 2m., 4w. Sc. Woods of Mount Ida. Century 74 : 590–604, Aug. 1907.

Wooing of Dionysus, The. Lady Margaret Sackville. Verse. Greek. 1m., 9w., chorus. Sc. Sea shore. SAS

Wooing of Lilinau, an Indian drama. John Kearns. Verse. 4m., 1w. Sc. Interior Indian wigwam. American Poetry Magazine 1 : 14–22, June 1919.

Wooing of Mary Magdela, The. Joan Alquist Alquist. Symbolic religions. 2m., 2w. Sc. A quaint humble house. ALQ

Workers at the looms, The. Essex Dane. 12m. and w., chorus. Sc. Designed to give atmosphere. DAO

† **Workhouse ward.** Lady Gregory. Farce. Irish background. 2m., 1w. Sc. Ward in an Irish workhouse. FSD, GS, SL

World beyond the mountain, The. Katharine Roof. 2m., 2w. Sc. Woods. International 7 : 322–324, Nov. 1913.

* **World-wide baby, A.** E. E. Blozam. 17c. Sc. A nursery. BL

* **Worm turns, The.** Elizabeth F. Guptill. Christmas play. 3b., 4g. Sc. A living room. GUD

Wound, The. Wilfrid Wilson Gibson. Verse. 1m., 2w. Sc. Room in tenements. GID, GIP

Wren, The. Oliver P. Parker. 6m., 9w. Sc. Living room. PAR

Wrens, The. Lady Gregory. 5m. Sc. Outside House of Commons, Dublin. GI

† **Writing a school play.** Edith F. A. U. Painton. 2b., 4g. Sc. Schoolroom. PAD
Wrong again. Catherine Bellais Gascoin. 2w. Sc. Yard. GAL
Wrong baby, The. Alice C. Thompson. Farce of day nursery. 8w. Sc. Day nursery. DEP
* **Wrong lessons, The.** Clara J. Denton. 2g. Sc. Sitting room. MBP
Wrong man, The. Alice Marie Donley. Comedy. 1m., 1w. Sc. Sitting room. G3
Wrong Miss Mather, The. Helen Sherman Griffith. 6w. Sc. Interior. B
Wrong numbers. Essex Dane. 3w. Sc. A quiet screened-off corner in one of the Department stores. B, DAO
Wrong package. Helen Sherman Griffith. Comedy. 4w. Sc. Interior. B
Wrong side of the road, The. Frank Howell Evans. 1m., 1w. Sc. Inn. FSD
† **Wurzel-Flummery.** A. A. Milne. 3m., 2w. Sc. Morning room of town house. C1, FSD, MSL

X

† **X = O: A night of the Trojan war.** John Drinkwater. Historical. 6m. Sc. Grecian tent on the plain before Troy. WWS
Xantippe and Socrates. Maurice Baring. Farce. 1m., 1w. Sc. Room in home of Socrates. BA, Yale Review 4: 590–607, April 1915.

Y

† **Yagowanea.** Helen Kane. Indian tragedy. 7m., 1w. Sc. Indian encampment. FSD
Yankee and the pagan, The. Earl Wright. 2m., 1w., other men. Sc. General store in small village. International 9: 350–51, Nov. 1915.
Yellow boots, The. Edwin Carty Ranck. 2m., 1w. Sc. Shoemaker's shop. Stratford Journal 4: 267–274, May 1919.
* **Yellow law, The.** Clara J. Denton. Play for Thanksgiving. 6b., 2g. Sc. Throne room of palace. DAG
Yellow yielding. Dorothy Potter. 1m., 1w. Sc. Cabin in the mountains. POT
Yesterday. Colin C. Clements. Comedy for Victorians. 1m., 1w. Sc. Secluded nook off the ball room of a London house. LO
Yoshiwara. A. J. Westermaye. Japanese comedy. 2m., 2w. Sc. Interior of a Japanese house. WES
† **Yot-che-ka.** Helen P. Kane. Indian play of 16th century. 4b., 1g. Sc. Woodland outside tent. FSD
You know? I know. Shake! Vance C. Criss. 2m., 2w. Sc. Interior. PPP
You never can tell about a woman. Maverick Terrell and H. O. Stechhan. 2m., 1w. Sc. Parlor of a suite in cheap hotel in N. Y. Smart Set 37: 133–141, Aug. 1912.
Young D'Arcy, a short play for the lawn. Jasmine Stone Van Dressen. 2m., 4w. Sc. Lawn of large home. Delineator 99: 24–25, 50–52, Aug. 1921.

* **Young gardener, The.** Fred L. Pauly. 2b. Sc. Interior. MBP

Young idea, The. Herbert Swears. Comedy. 2w. Sc. Den in country house. FSD

* **Young King Cole.** Clementia. 30b. Sc. Cave in a forest. SIS

* **Young Mr. Santa Claus, a Christmas fantasy.** Claudia Lucas Harris. 6b., 5g. Sc. Christmas eve on a city street. Drama 12:42–47, Oct.–Nov. 1921.

Young Napoleon. Wilfred T. Coleby. French Revolution. 3m., 2w. Sc. Interior. FSD

* **Young patriot's league, Washington's birthday play.** Willis N. Bugbee. 5b., 5g., chorus. Sc. Interior. EP

Young wonder, The. Eugene Pillot. Play of modern hero-worship. 1m., 1w., Sc. Living room. Drama 11:151–153, Feb. 1921.

Younger son, The. Della J. Evans. 7m., 2w. Sc. Office in a city in the Middle West. EV

You're it. H. P. Powell. Comedy. 2m., 2w. Sc. Interior. PPP

You're such a respectable person, Miss Morrison. Dorothy Kirchener Earle. 3m., 2w. Sc. Library of large city home in London. Smart Set 46:87–94, Aug. 1915.

* **Yussouf.** Rita Benton. From the poem of Lowell. 4b., chorus. Sc. Desert sands. BSC

Z

Zone police, The. Richard Harding Davis. 4m. Sc. Police station on the Isthmus of Panama. FSD

AUTHOR LIST

Abbott, Avery.
 Mr. Enright entertains
Abbott, Elizabeth.
 Sicilian limes, tr.
Abbott, H. R.
 Fortune tellers, The
Abbott, Keene.
 Hair trigger Smith
Abercrombie, Lascelles.
 Adder, The
 Deserter, The
 Ham and eggs
 Six men of Calais, The
 Staircase, The
Abrahamson, Rebecca P.
 Hooverizing Internationalle
Adams, Laura M.
 Aunt Deborah's first luncheon
Ade, George.
 Marse Covington
Akins, Zoe.
 Did it really happen?
 Magical city, The
 Portrait of Tiero, The
 Such a charming young man
Alarcón, Mariano.
 Sons of Adam
Alden, Audrey.
 Interlude, tr.
Alden, R. MacDonald.
 Burglar alarm, The
Aldington, Richard.
 Old King, tr.
 Theodat, tr.
Aldis, Mary.
 Drama class of Tankaha Nevada
 Extreme unction
 Letter, The
 Mrs. Pat and the law
 Temperament
 Ten P. M.
 What about Katie?
Alexander, Sigmund B.
 Bird in the hand
Allen, Harold B.
 At the movies
Allen, Inglis.
 Suffragette's redemption, The
Allen, Lewis.
 After-dinner speaker, The
Allen, Margaret F.
 Happy prince, The
Allen, Olive.
 Aunt Grundy
 Peter Grief
Allen, R. A.
 Gentlemen all
Allen, Victor.
 Two college tramps
Alquist, Joan Alquist.
 Wooing of Mary Magdela
Altrocchi, Rudolph.
 Dante in Santa Croce, tr.
Alvarez Qunitero, Joaquin.
 Bright morning, A
 By their words ye shall know them
 Sunny morning
Alvarez Qunitero, Serafin.
 Bright morning, A
 By their words ye shall know them
 Sunny morning
Amend, J. Gordon.
 Pandora's box
Amesbury, Howard.
 Finnigan's finish
Ammerman, Ada Tully.
 Reader, The
Ancey, George.
 Monsieur Lamblin
Anderson, Dwight Spencer.
 Caught at last
 Standing room only
Anderson, Mrs. Isabel.
 Everyboy
 Gee whiz, The
 Justice Whiskers' trial
 King Foxy of Muir Glacier
 Little doubt
 Merry Jerry
 Witch of the woods, The
Andrews, Kenneth L.
 America passes by

203

Crooked man and his crooked wife, A
Andreev, Leonid.
Incident, An
Love of one's neighbor
Andreyev, Leonid, see Andreev, Leonid.
Annunzio, Gabriel D'.
Dream of a spring morning, The
Dream of an autumn sunset, The
Archer William.
Interior, tr.
Arkell, Reginald.
Colombine
Arkush, R. M.
Electra
Theorist, The
Arkwright, Ruth.
Baby New Year
Bibi
St. Nicholas
Arlen, Michael.
Ci-devant, The
Armstrong, Louise Van Voorhis.
Dolls
Armstrong, Paul.
Mr. Lorelei
Arnold, F. R.
Tabarin's wife, tr.
Arnstein, Marc.
Eternal song, The
Ash, Sholom.
Night
Sinner, The
Winter
Askew, Claude.
Marquise and woman
Atkin, G. Murray.
Our lady of the moon
Augier, Emile.
Green coat
Post-script, The
Austin, Alfred.
Lesson in harmony, A
Austin, Helen H.
Almost everyman
Austin, Mary.
Man who didn't believe in Christmas, The

Backus, Mrs. Henry.
Singing soul, The
Bacon, Josephine Daskam.
Twilight of the Gods, The

Bagg, Helen.
Behind the lines
First aid
His model wife
If morning glory wins
Man outside, The
Superior sex, The
That blonde person
Whiskers
Why not Jim?
Bailey, Helen Cheyney.
Demigod, The
Bailey, Pearce.
Confession, The
Baily, F. E.
For the defendant—with costs
Baird, George M.P.
Mirage
Baker, Edwin.
Finish of Pete, The
Baker, Elizabeth.
Miss Tassey
Baker, George M.
Freedom of the press, The
Baker, Jessie.
Dream-toy shop, The
Baker, Rachel E.
Her picture
Baldwin, Charles Crittenton.
Mary! Mary!
Baldwin, Sidney.
Christmas eve
Christmas spirit, The
Enchanted gate, The
Marjorie's garden
Mother Nature's trumpeter
Balph, Effie Sammond.
Princess Rosy Cheeks
Bangs. John Kendrick.
Barrington's "At home," The
Minister's first "At home," The
Real thing, The
Return of Christmas, The
Side-show, The
Tables turned, The
Bantock, Leedham.
Man the life boat
Banville, Theodore de.
Charming Léandre
Gringoire
Barbee, Lindsey.
All for the cause
All on a summer's day
Bluebeard
Christmas tree joke, A
Ever-ever land, The

Forest of every day, The
Her first scoop
"If don't believe is changed into believe"
Little pink lady, The
Sing a song of seniors
Tomorrow at ten
Watch, a wallet and a jack of spades, A
When the toys awake
Whole truth, The

Barber, M. E.
Mechanical Jane

Barbour, Ralph Henry.
Conspirators, The

Barclay, Thomas.
Gambetta's love story

Bargate, John.
Prize, The

Baring, Maurice.
After Euripides' "Electra"
Ariadne in Naxos
Aulis difficulty, The
Blue harlequin, The
Caligula's picnic
Calpurnia's dinner-party
Catherine Parr
Death of Alexander, The
Don Juan's failure
Drawback, The
Fatal rubber, The
Greek vase, The
Jason and Medea
King Alfred and the Neat-Herd
Lucullus's dinner-party
Member for literature, The
Pious Aeneas
Rehearsal, The
Rosamund and Eleanor
Stoic's daughter, The
Velasquez and the "Venus"
Xantippe and Socrates

Barker, Granville.
Ask no questions and you'll hear no stories, ed.
Christmas present, A. ed.
Dying pangs, ed.
Episode, An. ed.
Farewell supper, A. ed.
Farewell to the theatre
Keepsakes, ed.
Rococo
Vote by ballot
Wedding morning, The. ed.

Barnard, Charles.
Katy in Gooseland

Barne, Kitty.
Susie pays a visit

Barnes, Djuna.
She tells her daughter
Three from the earth

Barnes, J.
Looking for trouble

Barnum, Madalene D.
Abraham Lincoln and the little bird
Bee hive, The
Brethren
Diego's dream
Echo
Fourth of July
Fox and the crow
French maid and the phonograph
George Washington and the cherry tree
Honest Abe
How sleep the brave
Lady bird
Little birds, The
Little sparrow
Lion and the mouse, The
Our aunt from California
Scotch grace
Spider and the fly

Barr, Robert.
Gentlemen, the King

Barrett, Clyde.
Scruples, tr.

Barrie, J. M.
Barbara's wedding
New word, The
Old lady shows her medals, The
Pantaloon
Rosalind
Tag, Der
Twelve-pound look, The
Well remembered voice, A
Will, The

Barrington, Pauline B.
When the young birds go

Barrios, Eduardo.
Papa and Mama

Bartlett, Randolph.
Respective virtues of Héloise and Maggie
Safety first

Barton, George Edward.
Pipe of desire, The
Sewing machine, The

Bartram, John G.
Secretary, The

Bascom, Louise Rand.
Bachelor club's baby, The
Boy who found Christmas, The
Claims, The

Etiquette of the occasion, The
Fresh air fiend, The
Look out for Hezikiah
Norah makes a cake
Plumber, The
Station episode, A
Stolen horse, The
Train leaves in ten minutes, The

Bassett, Willard.
Gold brick, The

Batchelder, Clara B.
Billy's chorus girl
Postman's knock, The
Separation of the Browns, The

Batchelder, Frank Roe.
We choose a name

Bates, Arlo.
Business meeting, A
Gentle jury, A
Good-bye
Her deaf ear
Interrupted proposal, An
Rosedale sewing circle, The

Bates, Esther W.
Engaging Janet
Garafelia's husband

Bates, Joshua.
Decree nisi, The

Bates, William O.
Asaph
Dryad and the Deacon, The
In the light of the manger

Baugham, Ruth L.
Sacrifice

Baukhage, Hilmar.
Boor, The. tr.
Marriage proposal, The. tr.

Bax, Clifford.
Galahad Green
Square pegs
Unknown hand, The
Volcanic island, The

Baxley, Isaac Rieman.
Aegean, The
Cleopatra
Fool, The
In the house of the poet
Lais
Parthenon, The
Sibyl, The

Bayles, Martha B.
Crowning of the Dryads, The
Thanksgiving Day—1696

Beach, Lewis.
Brothers
Clod, The
Guest for dinner, A

Love among the lions

Becque, Henri.
Quiet game, A

Beebe, M. N.
All American eleven, The
Half-back interference, A
Poet's club, The
Rooms to let
Seventh doctor, The
Wanted—a pitcher

Beede, Vincent Van Marter.
High jinks along the milky way

Beery, Adaline Hohf.
Christmas rainbow, A

Behrman, S. N.
Never stretch your legs in a taxi

Beith Ian Hay.
Crimson cocoanut, The
Late delivery, A
Missing card, The
Queen of hearts, The

Bell, Elliott Palmer.
Professor's truant gloves, The

Bell, Mrs. Hugh.
Time is money

Bell, John Joy.
Made in Heaven
Pie in the oven, The

Bell, Joh Keble.
Come Michaelmas
Compromising Martha
Dramatists at home, The
Embarrassed butler. The
Martha plays the fairy
Martha the soothsayer
Test kiss, The

Bell, Lady.
Best children in the world, The
Cat and dog
Cat and the fiddle, The
Foolish Jack
Little Petsy
Lucy Locket
Miss Dobson
Monster in the garden, The
Oranges and lemons
Polly put the kettle on
Quite by ourselves
Rather a prig
What happened to Henny Penny
Wigwam, The

Bell, May.
Bluebeard
Culprit, The
Marah
Strange physician, The
What of the night?

Bellamy, Francis R.
Scrambled eggs
Bellinger, Lancelot.
Last drop, The
Bellini, Gabriel.
Triumph of remorse, The
Belmont, Mrs. O. H. P.
Melinda and her sisters
Benavente, Jacinto.
His widow's husband
No smoking
Smile of Mona Lisa, The
Truth, The
Benedix, Roderich.
Law-suit, The
Third man, The
Bennet-Thompson, Lillian.
In the dark
Bennett, Arnold.
Good woman, A
Question of sex, A
Stepmother, The
Benson, Mrs. Mary A.
Fairies' Christmas, The
Bent, Newell.
Hypnotism
Little tiff, A
Bentley, L. D. G.
At Whitsuntide
Benton, Rita.
Call of Samuel, The
Christmas story, The
Daughter of Jephthah, The
Esther
Good Samaritan, The
Happy man, The
Judgment of Solomon, The
King Robert of Sicily
Life beyond, The
Manger service
Moses in the bulrushes
Where love is, there God is also
Yussouf
Benton, William Birdsley.
Jack and John
Beresford, J. D.
Perfect machine
Bergström, Hjalmar.
Birthday party, The
Beringer, Mrs. Oscar.
Bit of old Chelsea
Holly Tree Inn
Beringer, Vera.
Penny bunch
Bermann, Patty Pemberton.
Familiar quotations

Bernard, Tristan.
French as he is spoke
French without a master
I'm going
Berridge, W. Lloyd.
Thrift
Betts, Frank.
Ingiald Evilheart
Bierstadt, Edward Hale.
Fifth commandment, The
Sounding brass
Bigelow, Julie Helene.
Fascinating Mrs. Osborne, The
Binyon, Lawrence.
Bombastes in the shades
Bird, Charles S.
Advertising for a husband
At the Junction
Matrimonial venture, A
Pa's new housekeeper
Simpkins little breakfast party
Biro, Lajos.
Bridegroom, The
Grandmother, The
Bishop, Farnham.
Scales and the sword, The
Bitney, Mayme Riddle, pseud. *see*
  Irish, Marie, pseud.
Björkman, Edwin.
Creditors, tr.
Miss Julia, tr.
Pariah, tr.
Stronger, The, tr.
Simoon, tr.
Blackman, Carree Horton.
Eternal presence, tr.
Blair, Wilfrid.
Consarning Sairey 'Uggins
Blanchard, Arthur.
Night after, The
Bloch, Bertram.
Humpty Dumpty
Maiden over the wall
Morals and circumstance
Bloomgarden, Solomon.
Shunamite, The. tr.
Bloomquest, George.
Such extravagance
Bloxam, E. E.
Best wish, The
Brothers and sisters
Cuckoo!
Growing up
Manners make the man
Philosophy and fairies
Where is happiness

World-wide baby, A
Blunt, Arthur A.
 At retreat
Blutt, William N.
 Treasure in the trunk, The
Boak, E. M. B.
 Peacemaker, The
Boas, Harriet Betty.
 Madonna Dianora, tr.
Bodenheim, Maxwell.
 Cloud descends, The
 Gentle furniture-shop, The
 Poet's heart
 Unimagined Heaven, The
 Wanderer, The
Boileau, Marie.
 When Anne was Queen
Boleskine, Lord.
 Elder Eel
Bone, F. D.
 Daughter of Japan, A
 Pride of regiment
Bonham, Mary.
 Malinda and the Duke
 When Do-it school entertained
Bornstead, Beulah.
 Diabolical circle, The
Bottomley, Gordon.
 Crier by night, The
 Gruach
 King Lear's wife
 Loadice and Danae
 Midsummer eve
 Riding to Lithend
Bouchor, Maurice.
 Christmas tale, A
Boulton, E.
 Elegant Edward
Boulton, Matthew.
 Brass door-knob, The
 Burglar and the girl, The.
 His best day
Bower, Alice K.
 Trick of the trade, A
Bowker, Thayer Susan.
 His lucky day
Bowman, Louise Morey.
 And forbid them not
Boyce, Neith.
 Enemies
 Two sons, The
Boyce, W. Hanson.
 Hotel comfort
Boyesen, Algernon.
 Don Juan duped

Bradbury, L. A.
 Masqueraders, tr.
Branch, Anna Hempstead.
 Lazarus
 Rose of the wind
 Shoes that danced, The
Brand, Alfred.
 Did it really happen?
 Infernal masculine, The
 Three is company
Brandane, John.
 Change-house, The
 Glenforsa
Brandon, R. A.
 By mutual agreement
Bragdon, Claude.
 Gift of Asia, The
Branen, Jeff.
 Irish stew, An
Brantzell, Aura Woodin.
 Resemblance, The
Bray, Louise Whitefield.
 Harbor of lost ships, The
 Mis' Mercy
Breed, James E.
 Everycreditman
Breene, Bessie Springer.
 Gracie
 Sparks divine
 Twelve good men and true
Breiby, Orrin.
 Do men gossip?
Bretherton, Evangeline L.
 "Minister's messenger, The"
Breton, John Le.
 Sister to assist 'er, A
Brewster, Emma E.
 Aunt Mehetible's scientific experiment
Bridges, Madeline.
 Nowadays call, A
 Two in a fog
Bridgham, Gladys Ruth.
 Children's hour, The
 Her first assignment
 Not on the programme
 Queen of hearts, The
 Ring-around-a-Rosie
 This way out
 Three of a kind
Brieux, Eugene.
 School for mothers-in-law, The
Briggs, Caroline.
 One a day
Brighouse, Harold.

Converts
Doorway, The
Followers
Lonesome-like
Maid of France
Man about the place, The
Maypole morning
Oak settle, The
Paris doctor, The
Price of coal, The
Prince who was piper, The
Scaring off of Teddy Dawson, The
Spring in Bloomsbury

Brock, Howard F.
Bank account, The

Broido, Louis.
Enemies of Israel, The

Brooke, Rupert.
Lithuania

Brooker, Bertram R.
Efficiency

Brookfield, Charles H. E.
Excellent receipt, An

Brooks, C. F.
Fond delusion, tr.

Brooks, E. S.
Lord Malapert of Moonshine Castle.
New Red Riding-Hood, The

Brooks, F. M.
Fond delusion, tr.

Broomhall, Edith J.
Converting Bruce
What Rosie told the tailor

Brown, Alice.
Crimson lake, The
Doctor Auntie
Hero, The
Joint owners in Spain
Loving cup, The
March wind, A
Milly dear
Mistletoe
Sugar house, The
Web, The

Brown, Charles Ingersoll.
Dizzy's dilemmas

Brown, Curtis.
Mrs. Hazenby's health

Brown, Derby.
Peacemaker, The

Brown, Viola E.
Billy's mishap

Brown, William Cabell.
Visit in Brazil, A

Brown-Evarts, Edith.
Honesty's the best policy
Jones family, The
Last day of school, The
Military and medicine
Not so bad after all
Our mother's aid society
Pleasant surprise, A
Prize of learning, The
"Put to the test"
Rolling stone gathers no moss, The

Browne, Horace B.
At "Jenny Wren's"
Betsy Trotwood at home
Division between friends, A
Friendly waiter, The
Gentleman next door, The
Great Protestant association, The
Hatching a conspiracy
Miss Squeers' tea-party
Mr. George's shooting gallery
Mr. Guppy's proposal
Mr. Pecksniff's pleasant family party
Mr. Micawber's prospects
Mr. Venus's shop
Mrs. Snagby's guests
Mrs. Tibb's boarding house
Silas Wegg's stall
Stranger's visit, The
Unexpected meeting, An

Brown, Maurice.
King of the Jews, The

Browne, William Maynadier.
Red or white?

Brunner, Emma Beatrice.
Making a man
Over age
Spark of life, The
Strangers

Brunton, F. Carmichael.
Living dead, The

Bryan, George S.
Too much salt

Bryant, E. M. pseud.
see Boak, E. M. B.

Bryant, Louise.
Game, The

Buchanan, Fannie R.
Lighting of the torch, The

Buck, Gertrude.
Mother-love

Buckley, Reginald R.
Comala

Buckton, A. M.
Eager heart

Bugbee, Willis N.
After the bargain sale
Arrival of Reuben, The
Closing day at Beanville
Elder Jenkins' reception
Graduation at Gayville
Goose feather bed, The
Happyville school picnic, The
Hiram and the peddlers
Married to a suffragette
Molly's Christmas tree
Old class reunion, The
Physical torture club, The
Reception for Santa Claus, A
Santa Claus brigade, The
Seven little soldiers
Squashville fire brigade, The
Surprising Santa
Tommy's Thanksgiving party
Winning a prize
Young patriots' league
Bull, George.
By mutual agreement
Burbank, Barbara, pseud.
see Batchelder, Clara B.
Burbank, Maude.
Pan of fudge, A
Burgess, Minnie C.
Four little fir trees
Burghlie, James.
Lawyer's mistake, A
Burkham, Lucie T.
When the land was young
Burnet, Dana.
Impromptu
Rain
Burr, Amelia Josephine.
Masque of women poets
Burrill, Mary.
Aftermath
Burrows, Edith.
Behind the rain curtains
Christmas strike, A
Fairy frolic, A
Key, The
Burnstein, Abraham.
Casting of lots
Burt, E. W.
Paper match, A
Burton, Richard.
Brothers
Tatters
Bush, Bertha E.
Making a flag
Butler, Ellis Parker.
Revolt, The

Butler, Rachel Barton.
West of Omaha
Butts, Dorothy.
Avenues
Bynner, Witter.
Cycle
Iphigenia in Tauris
Little king, The
Night wind, A
Tiger
War
Byr, Robert.
Love conquers revenge
Byrne, Lee.
Quarry slaves

Cabell, James Branch.
Jewel merchants, The
Caesar, Lodovici.
L'eroica
Caesar, Arthur.
Napoleon's barber.
Caillavet, Gaston de.
Choosing a career
Caine, Hall.
Iron hand, The
Calderon, George.
Derelicts
Geminae
Lamp, The
Little stone house, The
Longing
Parkin Bros.
Peace
Two talismans, The
Calhoun, Dorothy Donnell.
Cupid's column
100 per cent American
Parlor patriots, The
Callaway, Emillie.
Miss Oliver's dollars
Calthrop, Dion Clayton.
Gate of dreams, The
Cameron, Margaret.
Burglar, The
Christmas chime, A.
Committee on matrimony, A.
Her neighbor's creed
Holly wreath, The
Kleptomaniac, The
Lost firewood, The
Little gray lady
Miss Doulton's orchids
Molly's New Year's party
Mr. February thaw
Pipe of peace, A

Piper's pay, The
Tadpole school
Teeth of the gift horse, The
White elephant, The
Campbell, Constance.
One of the old guard
Campbell, Evangeline.
Husking bee, The
Cann, Louise Gebhard.
Life is always the same
Cannan, Gilbert.
Everybody's husband
Gloves
James and John
Mary's wedding
Short way with authors, A
Cannon, Fanny.
Lady of the opera house, The
Meow!
What's in a name?
Capus, Alfred.
My tailor
Carb, David.
Neuters, The
New age, The
Other side, The
Slacks, The
Carey, Alice V.
New names for old
Carlyou, Kathrine F.
Crowning of Columbia, The
Carpenter, Grant.
Dragon's claws, The
Carpenter, Mrs. Myrtle B.
Her uncle's boots
Carr, Dr. Albert.
Cowboy and the baby, The
Carroll, Mrs. S. F.
Dress rehearsal, A
Carter, Elsie Hobart.
Babushka, The
Christmas brownie, The
Hundred, The
Minty-Malviny's Santa Claus
Carthew, Lily.
American idea, The
Carton, R. C. pseud.
see Critchett, R. C.
Cassilis, Ina Leon.
Those landladies
Castell, C. A.
Snowed-up with a Duchess
Castillo, Carlos C.
Bright morning, tr.
Cauldwell, Samuel Milbank.

Chocolate cake and black sand
Invention of the rat trap, The
Undoing of Giant Hotstoff, The
Cecil, Arthur.
Time is money
Cecil, Edward.
Fourth man
Chalmers, Roy Melbourne.
Quest of an ancestor, The
Seeing the pictures
Chamberlain, Basil Hall.
Death-stone, The
Life is a dream
Nakamitsu
Chamberlin, Grace Hilton.
Fortissimo music society, The
Chambers, C. I.
Pheasants' eggs
Redeeming their characters
Scold, the scoundrel and the scout, The
Scouts to the rescue
Chandler, Lillian F.
At the window
When Shakespeare struck the town
Chapin, Harold.
Augustus in search of a father
Autocrat of the coffee-stall, The
Dumb and the blind, The
Innocent and Annabel
It's the poor that 'elps the poor
Muddle-Annie
Philosopher of Butterbiggins, The
Threshold, The
Chapin, Harry Lorenzo.
Agression won
Love test, The
Chaplin, Alice W.
Because it rained
Behind the screen
Home and mother
Independent Flynn
Mad! Mad!
May
Merry Christmas
Pickles, bonbons and temper
Thankful for Jack
That boy
Valentine problem, A
Chapman, John Jay.
Christmas in Leipsic
Chatterji, Tapanmohan.
Light-bearer, The
Chekhov, Anton.
Anniversary, The

Boor, The
Jubilee, The
Marriage proposal, A
On the high road
On the highway
Proposal, The
Swan song, The
Tobacco evil, The
Tragedian in spite of himself
Wedding, The

Chenoweth, Lawrence.
After the circus

Cherryman, Myrtle C.
Old friends together

Chevalier, Haakon M.
King laughs, The

Childs, Irene M.
Bonnie's Christmas eve.

Chillingworth, Ethel.
Academy picture, An

Chipman, A. Z.
Ruben Rube

Christian, Frances E.
Kingdom of love, The

Chubb, Percival.
Old year and the new, The

Church, Virginia.
Pierrot by the light of the moon

Churchill, E. P.
Special rehearsal, The

Churchill, M.
On black ice

Clark, Barrett H.
Affected young ladies, tr.
After the honeymoon, tr.
Charming Leandre, tr.
Choosing a career, tr.
Christmas tale, tr.
Crispin, tr.
Fairy, tr.
Françoise' luck, tr.
French without a master, tr.
Gimlet, tr.
Good-bye, tr.
Grammar, tr.
I'm going! tr.
Indian summer, tr.
Jean-Marie, tr.
Little sheperdess, tr.
Marriage proposal, tr.
Law-suit, The, tr.
Legacy, The, tr.
Modesty, tr.
Monsieur Lamblin, tr.
My tailor, tr.
Panurge's sheep, tr.
Post-script, tr.

Rebound, The, tr.
Rosalie, tr.
Sicilian, tr.
Third man, tr.
Two cowards, The, tr.
Unhoodwinkable, tr.
Village, The, tr.
Wager, The. tr.

Clark, Bertha W.
Prince of Semberia

Clark, Homan.
Colonel and the lady

Clark, Margery Stanley.
Wet blanket

Clark, Milton Francis.
Scoop, The

Clarke, Ednah Proctor.
Revolt of Santa Claus, The

Clarke, Violet.
Power of flattery, The

Cleather, Dorothy.
Black trouble, A
Just like a story
Magic tabloid, The
Stuffing
Twins, The

Cleland, T. M.
Veil of happiness, The, tr.

Clemenceau, Georges.
Veil of happiness, The.

Clementia.
Frolic of the bees and the butterflies.
Young King Cole

Clements, Colin Campbell.
By the Sumida river
Cherry blossom river, The
Columbine
Desert, The
Father, The
Four who were blind
Growing old together
Harlequin
Ivory tower
Just women
Life is a dream
Living hours, tr.
Love in a French kitchen, tr.
Man and his wife, A
Modern Harlequinade
Moon tide
Pierrot in Paris
Pirates
Return of Harlequin, The
Siege, The
Star dust path, The
Sumida Gawa, tr.

Tea and conversation
Three lepers of Suk-El-Garab
Yesterday
Cleugh, Dennis.
Violet under the snow, The
Clifford, Helen C.
Alice's blighted profession
Whose widow
Cobb, Mrs. George.
Just advertise
Cobb, Thomas.
Quiet little dinner, A
Cockrell, Maud.
Golliwog in Fairyland
Code, Grant H.
When the fates decree
Coddington, Hester.
He is coming, tr.
Coghlan, Lida L.
Same man, The
Cohan, George M.
Farrell case, The
Coit, Henry A.
War's end
Colburn, Carrie W.
Romantic rogue, A
Colby, Eleanor.
Vision of youth, A
Coleby, Wilfred T.
Aunt Bessie
Bit o' stuff, A
Dusty path, The
Likes o' me, The
Their point of view
Young Napoleon, The
Collins, Louise.
Modern autocrat, The
Collins, Sewell,
Gaspers
Colman, Morris.
Philosophers
Colquhoun, Donald.
Jean
Colum, Padraic.
Betrayal, The
Miracle of the corn, The
Swift's pastoral
Condrin, J. R. *see* **Richards, James C.**
Conger, Margaret L.
Good housewife and her labors, The
Conrad, Joseph.
One day more

Converse, Florence.
Blessed birthday, The
Thy kingdom come
Conway, Edward H.
Windy shot, The
Conway, Lucie.
"D. H. S."
Cook, George C.
Suppressed desires
Tickless time
Cook, Leroy James.
Peace at home, tr.
Cook, Sherwin L.
Game of comedy, A
Cooke, Marjorie Benton.
Case of Sophronia, The
Child in the house, The
Christmas benefit, A
Confessional, The
Court comedy, A
Dinner,—with complications, A
Fairy ring, The
Finer shades of honor, The
First Thanksgiving, The
In the good greenwood
Lady Betty's burglar
Lion and the lady, The
Manners and modes
Page from the past, A
Reform
Romeo of the Rancho
Spring time fantasy, A
Success
Tit for tat
When knights were bold
When love is young
Coon, Hilton.
My wife's husband.
Coppee, Francois.
Fennel
Lord's prayer, The
Pater Noster
Violin maker of Cremona, The
Corbin, Alice *see* **Henderson, Mrs. Alice Corbin.**
Corbin, John.
Forbidden guests, The
Corneau, Perry B.
Masks
Napoleon and the sentry
Country man, May E.
Hiram Jones' bet
Miss Parkington
Courteline George, *see* **Moinaux, Georges Courteline.**
Cowan, Fletcher.

Rose leaves and asparagus tips
Cowan, Floyd P.
Hidden love
Putting up a prosperous front
Cowan, Sada.
In the morgue
Sinstram Skagerrak
State forbids, The
Strangers
Cox, Ethel L.
Combat and the dragon, The
Craig Anne A. T.
Course of true love, The
Greatest gift, The
Grasshoppers and the ants, The
Pool of answers, The
Crain, George A.
Kara
Craine, Edith J.
Pharaoh's knob
Crandall, Irene Jean.
For freedom
Last rehearsal, The
Tea and politics
Crane, Eleanor Maud.
Best man, The
Fads and fancies
Her victory
"His soul"
"Honor of the class, The"
Peggy's predicament
Crane, Mabel H.
At the milliner's
Girls, The
Romance by schedule
Rumpus on Olympus, A
Crary, Alice.
Holy scenes of Christmas, The
Craven, Arthur S.
Perfect machine, The
Craven, John V. Jr.
Monsieur Galespard and Mademoiselle Jeanne
Creevey, Caroline A.
Ninepin club, The
Thanksgiving dream, A
Cripps, A. K.
Hired man's courtship, The
Criss, Vance C.
His methodist foot
You know? I know. Shake!
Critchett, R. C.
Dinner for two
Critchton, Dorothy.
As ye sew

Crocker, Bosworth.
Baby carriage, The
Cost of a hat, The
Dog, The
First time, The
Last straw, The
Cronyn, George W.
Death in fever heat, A
Sandbar queen, The
Crothers, Rachel.
Criss cross
Katy did
Mrs. Molly
Rector, The
Crowley, Aleister.
Bonds of marriage, The
Saviour, The
Cruger, Mrs. Van Rensselaer, *see*
Gordon, Julien
Crummins, Agnes L.
Pride of the family, The
Cudmore, Angela.
We dine at seven
Culbertson, Ernest H.
Goat alley
Cunningham, Leon.
Dralda Bloom, The
Wondership, The
Cuppy, Elizabeth O.
Mollusk or suffragette?
Curry, Bara Jefferis.
Devil's gold, The
Cutting, Mary S.
Good dinner, A

Dabney, Julia P.
Children of the sunrise
Dale, Irving.
Friend husband
Souvenir spoons
Tickets, please
Way of a woman, The
Daly, Arnold.
Democracy's king
Dominant male, The
Dalkeith, Lena.
King Arthur and the cakes
Princess and the swineherd, The
Scene from Robin Hood
Scene from Uncle Tom's cabin
Dallas, Mary K.
Our aunt Robertina
Dalrymple, C. Leona.
Mrs. Forrester's crusade
Surprises

Tangles
Damianakes, Stephanie.
  Obstacle, The
Damon, S. Foster.
  Kiri no Meijiyama
Dana, H. Manley.
  Local and long distance
Dance, Charles.
  Morning call, A
Dane, Essex.
  Cul-de-sac
  Fleurette and company
  Happy returns
  Serpent's tooth, The
  Wasp, The
  When the whirlwind blows
  Wooden leg, The
  Workers at the looms, The
  Wrong numbers
Darby, Helen T.
  Truth for a day, The
Dargan, Olive T.
  Flutter of the goldleaf, The
  Journey, The
  Woods of Ida
Darrow, Whitney.
  Meredith's entertainment, The
  68–70 Berkeley Place
Davey, Peter.
  We dine at seven
David, Emily.
  Mirth-provoking, schoolroom, The
David, Louise Dudley.
  When mother came to college
Davies, Mary C.
  Slave with two faces, The
Davis, Allan.
  On vengeance height
Davis, Lillie.
  Bumps
Davis, M. E. M.
  Bunch of roses, A
  Christmas boxes
  His lordship
  Queen Anne cottages
Davis, Malcolm W.
  Locked door, The
  Spy, The
Davis, Marjorie H.
  Patriot's parade, The
Davis, Oswald H.
  Dream stone, The
Davis, Richard Harding.
  Efficiency
  Miss Civilization
  Orator of Zapata City, The
  Peace manoeuvers
  Zone police
Davis, Robert H.
  Room without a number, The
Day, Curtiss LaQ.
  Bootlegger, The
Day, Frederick L.
  Slump, The
Dazey, L. H.
  Woman's choice, A
Dean, Alexander.
  Just neighborly
De Armond, Lizzie.
  Why Christmas was late
DeBois, O. B.
  Biscuits and bills
Dell, Floyd.
  Angel intrudes, The
  Chaste adventures of Joseph, The
  Enigma
  Human nature
  Ibsen revisited
  King Arthur's socks
  Legend
  Long time ago, A
  Poor Harold
  Rim of the world, The
  Sweet-and-twenty
Demarest, William T.
  New day, The
  Way of Yu-Soo, The
DeMille, William C.
  "Deceivers"
  Food
  In 1999
  Martyrs, The
  "Noblesse Oblige"
  "Poor old Jim"
Denison, Emily H.
  Dolly Madison's afternoon tea
  Duped
  Little mother of the slums, The
  My friend's in town
  Mystery of Beacon Hill, The
Denison, T. S.
  Great doughnut corporation, The
  Is the editor in?
Dennis, O. M.
  His honor
Denton, Clara J.
  All his fault
  At the library
  Being a hero
  Blue pump, The
  Boastful weathervane, The

Bob's and Tom's Thanksgiving
Charlie's pop-corn
Christmas at Holly Farm
Day after the circus, The
Gentle janitor, The
Going shopping
Governor's proclamation, The
Great sale, The
Hanging up the stockings
In the east
"Isabel"
Juniper baby, The
"Look of things, The"
Mademoiselle's mistake
Making the best of things
Minister's daughter, The
New man in town, A
Next day, The
No crown
"No presents"
Old ship, The
On the dyke
Ph.D., The
Queen's offer, The
Quick news
Seeing the animals
Seeking information
Senior, The
Strike in Santa Claus land, The
Tailor's dummy, The
Thief, The
Three sleepy-heads
Trouble in the Toyroom
Underground opportunity, An
Unexpected company
Unsuccessful hunt, An
Wager, The
White chief, The
Who's crazy now?
Wrong lessons, The
Yellow law, The

De Pue, Elva.
Hattie

Dickinson, Thomas H.
In hospital

Dickinson, Charles.
Sunshine
Third chapter

Diehl, Robert H.
Tuff's boarder

Dix, Beulah Marie.
Allison's lad
Captain of the gate, The
Clemency
Dark of the dawn, The
Enemy, The
Glorious game, The
Hundredth trick, The
Legend of St. Nicholas

Snare and the fowler, The
Weakest link, The
Where war comes

Dixon, M. Q.
Blue pincushion, The

Djurichich, Luka.
Prince of Semberia, tr.

Dodge, Flora B.
Mrs. Mack's example

Dolan, Winifred.
Wake up, John Bull

Dondo, Mathurin M.
Two blind men and a donkey

Donley, Alice M.
Cranberry corners
Spiritual boost at Sallytown, The
Wrong man, The

Donnay, Maurice.
Gimlet, The

Doo, Ding U.
Empty city, The

Dopp, Katharine E.
Homer and David

Doran, Marie.
Eyes of faith
Girls over there, The
How Nellie made good
Liberty thrift girls, The

Dorey, J. Milnor.
Under conviction

Dorff, M. J.
Firefly night

Dorsen, Helen.
Power of loyalty

Doty, Harry M.
Jonesville board of assessors, The
Just plain Jones
Tiddville and the Radio

Doucet, Theodore A.
Jasper's troubles

Douglas, Charles N.
Hired girl's dream, The

Douglas, Ford.
Return trip, The
Two barrels, The

Down, Oliphant.
Maker of dreams, The
Quod wrangle, The

Downing, Mr. and Mrs. Henry Francis.
Placing Paul's play

Dowson, Ernest.
Pierrot of the minute, The.

Doyle, Sir Arthur Conan.
Waterloo

Drachmann, Holger.
　"Renaissance"
Dransfield, June.
　Blood o' Kings
Dreiser, Theodore.
　Blue sphere, The
　Dream, The
　Girl in the coffin, The
　In the dark
　Laughing gas
　Light in the window, The
　"Old Ragpicker"
　Spring recital, The
Drennan, Marie.
　Valley of gloom, The
Drey Sylvan.
　New Pygmalion and Galatea, The
Drinkwater, John.
　God of Quiet, The
　Honors easy
　Little Johnny
　Storm, The
　Two in a trap
　X = 0
Driscoll, Louise.
　Child of God, The
　Garden of the west, The
　Metal checks, The
　Poor House, The
Drovin, George A.
　His first case
Drury, Major William P.
　Calamity Jane, R.N.
　Privy council, A
Dubois, O. B.
　Night in Tappan, A
Dubry, Louis E.
　Masqueraders, The
Duer, Caroline.
　Ambassador's daughter, The
　Mr. Shakespeare at school
Duffy, Richard.
　Night of the wedding, The
Dumas, Andre.
　Eternal presence
Dumont, Frank.
　Depot lunch counter, The
　Doubtful victory, A
　How a woman keeps a secret
　Midnight marauders
　Not a bit jealous
　Quiet hotel, The
　Real doctor, The
　Rival speakers
　Roamy-e-owe and Julie-ate
　Scotty

　Sister Masons
　Stage struck boarding house
　Where is my coat?
Dunbar, Alice.
　Author's evening at home, The
Dunbar, Mrs. Paul Lawrence.
　see Dunbar, Alice
Dunbar, Olivia Howard.
　Blockade
D'Unger, Giselle.
　Jack's predicament
Dunham, Curtis.
　Blood money
　Mademoiselle Plato
Dunn, Fannie Wyche.
　Tweedledum and Tweedledee
Dunn, Gerald.
　Fancy dress
Dunne, Douglas.
　Two of a kind
Dunning, Ralph Cheever.
　Home-coming, The
Dunsany, Lord.
　Cheezo
　Compromise of the King of the
　　Golden Isles, The
　Fame and the poet
　Glittering gate, The
　Golden doom, The
　Good bargain, A
　If Shakespeare lived today
　Lost silk hat, The
　Night at an inn, A
　Queen's enemies, The
　Tents of the Arabs, The
Dunton, Edith K.
　Is your name Smith?
Duran, Leo.
　Daimyo, The, tr.
　Hands in the box, The, tr.
　Honor of Danzo, The, tr.
Durand, R. S.
　Sidhe of Ben-Mor, The
Duval, Mary V.
　Court of fame, The
Dyk, Victor.
　Ninth night, The
Earle, Dorothy K.
　You're such a respectable person
Earle, Georgia.
　Before the play begins
　Gettin' acquainted
　Lie that Jack built, The
Ebner-Eschenbach, Marie von.
　Man of the world, A

Echegaray, Jose.
   Street singer, The
Eckersley, Arthur.
   Boy's proposal, A
   Hartleys, The
   Susan's embellishments
   Tabloid, A
Edgar, Mary S.
   Wayside piper, The
Edridge, Joan.
   "First aid"
Edridge, Richard.
   "First aid"
Egbert, Frank H.
   Capitulation of Mr. Hyleigh
Egerton, Lady Alix.
   Masque of the two strangers, The
Ehrlich, E. C.
   Snaring the lion
Ehrmann, Max.
   Bank robbery, The
   Wife of Marobius, The
Elberon, George.
   Johnson's busy day
Eldridge, Paul.
   Carnival, The
   Jest, The
   Loser, The
   What's wrong
Eliot, Samuel A.
   Christmas miracle play, A, ed.
   Doctor Faustus, ed.
   Polyxena, ed.
Elkins, Fenton B.
   Belgian baby, The
   Figuratively speaking
   Quick and the dead, The
Ellet, Marion.
   Germelshausen
Ellis, Mrs. Havelock.
   Mothers, The
   Pixy, The
   Subjection of Kezia, The
Ellis, Kenneth M.
   Ketcham pardon, The
Ellis, William.
   Ketcham pardon, The
Elliston, A. Louis.
   By woman's wit
   Recoiling vengeance, A
   Unlucky tip, An
Elwes, Mary.
   In time of war
   Two in a flat
Elwyn, Lizzie May.
   Uncle Sam's cooks
Emerson, M. A.
   If I were Bob
Emerson, William D.
   Cabman and the baby, The
   Humble pie
Emig, Evelyn.
   China pig, The
   Old order, The
Emmons, Myra.
   Visiting Mamma
Emmy, Fred.
   Arrival of a rival, The
England, George Allan.
   "Under their skies"
Erle, Jonathan.
   When Anne was queen.
Ernest, Alice.
   Living hours, tr.
Erskine, John.
   Noblesse oblige
Ervine, St. John G.
   Critics, The
   Magnanimous lover, The
   Orangeman, The
   Progress
Eskil, Ragna B.
   Aunt Harriet's night out
   For the sake of Peggy
   In the trenches "over there"
   Lottie sees it through
   Me and Betty
   Who's the boss?
Esmond, H. V.
   Her vote
Estabrook, Anne L.
   Christening robe, The
Estoc, Poe d'.
   Sabotage
Etherington, H. Field.
   Sealed silver
Ettlinger, Karl.
   Altruism
Evans, Della J.
   "M. R. S."
   Younger son, The
Evans, Florence W.
   Marriage of Guineth, The
Evans, Frank H.
   Wrong side of the road, The
Evans, Gladys LaDue.
   Little mortal child, The
Evans, Margaret.
   Faith

Everett, Edith.
  Everystudent
Evreinov, Nicholas.
  Beautiful despot, The
  Merry death, A
Ewers, Hanns H.
  Dead eyes, The
  Trecento

Fahnstock, Edith.
  Magic theatre, tr.
Fairbanks, S. vK.
  Other voice, The
Farnsworth, Oliver.
  Twins of Bergano, The, tr.
Farrar, John.
  Magic sea shell, The
Farrell, J. R.
  Casey's daughter, Mary Ann
Farrington, James.
  Hulks, The
Fawcett, Marion Roger.
  Alarm, The
Faxon, Grace B.
  Bachelor's reverie, The
Fay, F. C.
  Peace at home, tr.
Fay, Frederick L.
  Lend a hand
Feist, Ella.
  Fly-away land
Felter, Will D.
  Jack for every Jill, A
Fendall, Percy.
  Arrival of a rival, A
Fenn, Frederick.
  Convict on the hearth, The
  Love child, The
  Not wanted—a wife
  Nelson touch, The
  Op-o'-Me-Thumb
Fenollosa, Ernest.
  Awoi no Uye
  Chorio
  Genjo
  Hagoromo
  Kagekiyo
  Kakitsubata
  Kayoi Komachi
  Kinuta
  Nishikigi
  Shojo
  Sotoba Komachi
  Suma Genji
  Tamura
  Tsunemasa

Fenollosa, Mary.
  Lady of the hair-pins, The
Ferguson, J. A.
  Campbell of Kilmhor
Fernald, Mrs. C. F.
  Cobbler's bargain, The
  Honeymoon, The
  Irish washerwoman, The
  Learning lessons
  Left
  School opera
Fernald, Chester B.
  Cat and the cherub, The
Farrar, Jules.
  In "The spirit of '76"
Ferrer, L. M.
  Bobby's dream
Ferrier, Paul.
  Codicil, The
Ferris, Anita B.
  Children of the Christmas spirit
  Road to Christmas, The
  Ruth's donation party
  Santa's allies
  Slave raiders, The
  Triumph of peace, The
  Visitors from the Colonial period
  Why didn't you tell?
Ferris, Helen J.
  Extra!
Fetherstonhaugh, V.
  Harrison
Feuillet, Octave.
  Fairy, The
  Village, The
Ffeil, Helena A.
  Bill Perkins' proposin' day
Field, Rachel Lyman.
  Everygirl
  Three pills in a bottle
  Rise up, Jennie Smith
Fillmore, John E.
  "War"
Finch, Elsie Garreston.
  Spineless
Finch, Lucine.
  At the sign of the silver spoon
Fisher, Blanche P.
  Finding the Mayflowers
  Santa Claus gets his wish
Fiske, Isabella Howe.
  Comedy of the exile, A
  Evening musicale, A
Fitzjohn, R.
  Plume of feathers

Fitzmaurice, George.
　Dandy dolls, The
　Magic glasses, The
　Pie-dish, The
Flanagan, Hallie F.
　Curtain, The
Flanner, Hildegarde.
　Mansions
Flanner, Mary H.
　Christmas burglar, The
　Bargain day
Fleming, Charles L.
　Telephone, The
Flexner, Hortense.
　Voices
Florance, Richard.
　It, the usual play with the usual ending
Flower, Elliott.
　His imitation sweetheart
Floyd, Lucretia Xavier.
　Sunny morning, A tr.
Foley, James W.
　Sing a song of sleepy head
Foley, Marie H.
　Gift, The
Folmsbee, Beulah.
　Princess and the crystal pipe, The
Footner, Hulbert.
　Mystery
Ford, Grace.
　Love pirate, The
Forrest, Belford.
　Failures
　Honors even
　Lost sheep
　Swimmin' pools
Forrest, Mark.
　At the turn of the year
Foster, Nathaniel L.
　Widow's might, The
Fotheringham, E. M.
　Bad temper bureau, The
　Brummy crock
　Cash concern, A.
　Good intentions
　Maggie Ann
　Middle of the night, The
　Mrs. Marconi
　Princess Parsimonia
　Tale of the tarts, The
　Too much monkey
　Whiney-Piney
　Why?
Foucher, Laure C.
　Effie's Christmas dream

Francis, John M.
　Aunty
　Bills
　Trouble by mail
　Veal breaded
　Who wins the bet?
Frank, Florence Kiper.
　Garden, The
　Jael
　Visitors
Frank, Henry.
　Skeptic's challenge, The
Frank, Maude Morrison.
　Christmas eve with Charles Dickens, A
　Fairies' plea, The
　Friend in need, A
　Miss Burney at court
　Mistake at the manor, A
　When Heine was twenty-one
Frederick, John T.
　Hunter, The
　Twelfth night at Fisher's crossing
Freed, Clarence I.
　Absent minded
Freeman, Ethel H.
　Tommy
Freund, E. J.
　Don't bother Anton
　Germ hunters, The
　Grapejuice
　Hatching the lucky egg
　Soap club, The
　Wanted—a wife
Freybe, C. E.
　In Garrison
Frida, Emil Bohnslav.
　At the chasm
　Vengeance of Catullus
　Witness, The
Frith, Walter.
　Miniature, The
Froome, John R.
　Listening
Frost, Robert.
　Way out, A
　Witch of coos, The
Fry, R. J.
　Same to Ye! The
Fuji-Ko.
　Vampire cat of Nabreshima, The
Fulda, Ludwig.
　By ourselves
Fuller, Alice Cook.
　Christmas idea, The
　Cinderella

Clytie
Gifted givers, The
Golden touch, The
Hans and Grethel
Juno's bird
Little John joins the band of Robin Hood
Little Red Riding Hood
Puss in boots
Rhoecus
Robin Hood becomes an outlaw
Siegfried and Brunehilde

Furniss, Grace L.
Dakota widow, A
Perhaps

Gage, Edward.
Luckiest man, The
Galahad, Joseph Andrew.
Sic passim
Galbraith, Esther E.
Brink of silence, The
Gale, Elizabeth.
Just a little mistake
Mrs. Coulson's daughter
Gale, Rachel B.
Clinging vine, The
Coats and petticoats
Gale, Zona.
Neighbors, The
Uncle Jimmy
Gallon, Thomas.
Man who stole the castle
Galsworthy, John.
Defeat
Hall-marked
Punch and go
Sun, The
Gamble, Mary R.
Aunt Columbia's dinner party
Gardener, Eden.
Behind the Purdah
Gardner, W. H.
Christmas for Santa Claus
Garland, Robert.
At night all cats are gray
Double miracle, The
Importance of being a roughneck, The
Love's young dream
Garnett, Louise Ayres.
Hilltop
Garrison, Theodosia.
Hour of earth, An
Literati, The
At the sign of the cleft heart

Garrow, David.
Patty packs a bag
What charity covers
Gascoin, Catherine Bellairs.
Fickle Juliet
Fortescues' dinner party, The
"John Arbery's dream"
Lumber room, The
P. G.'s, The
"Them banns"
Toolip, The
Wrong again
Gatty, Mrs.
Life beyond, The
Gauss, Louise Fallenstein.
Little helpers
Gavin, Mary.
Curtains
Geijerstam, Gustaf.
Criminals
Gemmell, John.
Authorship
Baby's ill!
Muffin man, The
Gentry, Helen.
Derby
Gerald, Florence.
For love and honor
Gerson, Emily Goldsmith.
Delayed birthday, A
Gerstenberg, Alice.
"Attuned"
Beyond
Buffer, The
Ever young
Fourteen
He said and she said
Hearts
Illuminatti in drama libre, The
Overtones
Pot boiler, The
Unseen, The
Where are those men?
Getchell, Margaret C.
Birthday candles, The
Colette of the Red Cross
Giacosa, Giuseppe.
Rights of the soul, The
Sacred ground
Wager, The
Gibbins, J. R.
Becoming an American
Gibson, A. H.
Pursuing a mother-in-law
Gibson, Preston.
Cupid's trick

Derelicts
S. O. S.
Suicides
Vacuum, The

Gibson, Wilfrid Wilson.
Agatha Steel
Betrothed, The
Bloodybush edge
Bridal, The
Call, The
Child, The
"Family's pride, The"
Ferry, The
Firstborn, The
Furnace, The
Garret, The
Holiday
Hoops
House of candles, The
Mates
Mother, The
Night-shift, The
On the road
On the threshold
Operation, The
Queen's crags, The
Scar, The
Secret way, The
Shirt, The
Stonefolds
Summer-dawn
Winter dawn
Womenkind
Wound, The

Gilbert, William S.
Trying a dramatist

Giles, Josephine.
Gabe's home run
Hoosier school, The
It was the Dutch
Jake and his Pa
Just like a woman
News from home
Trusted friend, The

Giles, William.
Gabe's home run
Hoosier school, The
It was the Dutch
Jake and his Pa
Just like a woman
News from home
Trusted friend, The

Gilman, Charlotte Perkins.
Something to vote for
Three women

Gilmore, Louis.
Long live the empress!
Prince Patiomkin

Tenor, A

Gillmore, Rufus H.
Their first dinner

Gilman, Thornton.
We live again

Girardeau, Claude M.
God of the wood, The

Givens, Helen M.
Bull-terrior and the baby, The
Improving a husband

Glaenzer, Richard B.
Louis Quinze salon, The

Glaspell, Susan.
Close the book
Outside, The
People, The
Suppressed desires
Tickless time
Trifles
Woman's honor

Glazer, Benjamin F.
Altruism, tr.
Autumn tides, tr.
Matter of husbands, A, tr.

Gleason, Orissa W.
How the ladies earned their dollar
How the story grew

Glenn, Byron P.
Pair of burglars, A

Glick, Carl.
Immortal, The
It isn't done
Outclassed
Police matron, The
Prologue
Ten days later

Goddard, Felecia.
On with the new
What society is coming to

Goddard, Harold.
Sisters, The

Goldberg, Isaac.
Abigail, tr.
Abishag, tr.
Bathsheba, tr.
Better son, The, tr.
Black sheep, The, tr.
Forgotten souls, tr.
Gastone the animal tamer, tr.
In the harem, tr.
In the dark, tr.
Life, tr.
Little heroes, tr.
Michael, tr.
Poetry and prose, tr.
On the threshold, tr.

Rights of the soul, tr.
Secret of life, The, tr.
She must marry a doctor, tr.
Sicilian limes, tr.
Sinner, The, tr.
Sparrow, The, tr.
Stranger, The, tr.
Water upon fire, tr.
Winter, tr.
Wolf-hunt, tr.

Goodlander, Mabel.
Elves and the shoe-maker, The
Honest woodcutter, The
Mistress Mary gives a garden party
Pine tree, The
Visit of the Tomiter, The

Goodman, Edward.
Colloquy in Hades, A
Eugenically speaking
Portrait on the wall, The
Vital moments, tr.

Goodman, Kenneth Sawyer.
At the edge of the wood
Back of the yards
Barbara
Behind the black cloth
Dancing dolls
Dust of the road
Ephraim and the winged bear
Game of chess, The
Green scarf, The
Hand of Siva, The
Hero of Santa Maria, The
Holbein in Blackfriars
Man can only do his best, A
Parting, The
Red flag, The
Wonder hat

Gordon, Charles, pseud.
see Baldwin, Charles Crittenton

Gordon, Henry.
Thirst

Gordon, Julien.
Modern child, A
Modern daughter, A
Modern Mother, A

Gordon-Lennox, Cosmo.
Impertinence of the creature, The

Gordon, Leon.
As a pal
Leave the woman out

Gornall, H. K.
George

Gough, Margaret.
One may spin a thread too finely, tr.

Gould, Ernest M.
On the sight-seeing car

Gould, Felix.
In the marshes
Marsh maiden, The
Stranger, The

Gourmont, Remy de.
Old king, The
Theodat

Gow, Ronald.
Breakfast at eight

Graf, Arturo.
Dante in Santa Croce of the Raven

Graham, Bertha W.
Spoiling the broth

Graham, Manta S.
Allied occupations
By-product, A
Goose, The
Trend, The
Two's company

Grahame, Arthur.
Iron Ann, The

Granville, Edward.
Three graces, The

Gray, Eunice T.
Case of spoons
Winning of Fuji, The

Greenbank, Percy.
Man the life boat

Greene, Clay M.
Awakening of Barbizon, The
Dispensation, The
Star of Bethlehem, The
"Through Christmas bells"

Greene, Kathleen C.
First Christmas eve, The
Little boy out of the wood, The
Night watch
Poppy seller, The
Princess on the road, The
Two bad fairies, The
Vision splendid, The

Greene, Paul.
Granny Boling
Last of the Lowries, The
Lord's will, The
Sam Tucker
White dresses
Our Uncle from the West

Gregory, Lady Isabelle.
Bogie men, The
Coats
Deliverer, The
Dervorgilla

Full moon, The
Gaol gate, The
Hanrahan's oath
Hyacinth Halvey
Jackdaw, The
Losing game, A
Lost saint, tr.
McDonough's wife
Poorhouse, tr.
Rising of the moon, The
Spreading of. the news
Travelling man, The
Twisting of the rope, tr.
Workhouse ward, The
Wrens, The

Grendon, Felix.
Will he come back?

Greve, Clifford.
Militant God

Gribble, Harry Wagstaff.
All gummed up

Griffin, Chester A.
Hicksville burglar, The

Griffith, Benjamin L. C.
Cloudy day, A
For her sake
Forget-me-nots
Mistake in identity, A
Not at home
Wanted—a valet

Griffith, Helen Sherman.
Alarm of fire, An
Borrowed luncheon, A
Case of duplicity
Dumb waiter, The
Fallen idol, A
Getting the range
Her service flag
Knitting club meets, The
Ladies strike, The
Large order, A
Maid to order,
Merry widow hat
Minister's wife, The
Reflected glory
Sewing society, The
Wrong Miss Mather, The
Wrong package

Griffith, William.
Before the fairies came to America
Before the Pixies came to America
City pastorals

Grinnell, John E.
John Bargrave, Gentleman

Grissom, Herbert.
Easy victim, An

Griswold, Grace.
Billie's first love
Haunted chamber, The
His Japanese wife

Grossman, Samuel S.
Purim players, The

Grossmith, Weedon.
Commission, A

Grosvenor, Johnston.
Plaie for Merrie May tyme, A

Grover, Harry Greenwood.
Thompson's luck

Grundy, Sidney.
Head of Romulus, The
In honor bound
Man proposes
Sympathetic souls

Guild, Thacher Howland.
Class of '56, The
Higher good, The
Portrait, The
Power of a God, The

Guiterman, Arthur.
Christmas stockings
Journey's end
Tiny Tim's surprise-party

Gunnison, Binney.
Becket saves Rosamund
Ben-Hur and Iras
Deacon Brodie
Disastrous announcement, A
Extracting a secret
Gentlemen, The King
Love conquers revenge
Matter of duty, A
Miss Judith Macan
Mrs. Hardcastle's journey
Mrs. Harwood's secret
Open or shut?
Pizarro and Rolla
Prairie princesses, The
Pride against pride
Princess and the countess, The
Queen Catherine
Raimond released
Sam Weller and his father
Savonarola and Lorenzo

Guptill, Elizabeth F.
Answering the phone
As it will be
Aunt Sabriny's Christmas
Baby show, The
Bo-Peep's Christmas party
Brave little Tom-boy, A
Brownies' vacation, The

Census man, The
Christmas at Punkin Holler
Christmas at Skeeter Corner
Christmas at the Cross Roads
Christmas dream, A
Christmas for all nations
Christmas joke, A
Christmas mystery
Color fairies, The
Discouraged worker, A
Dolls' symposium, The
Dose of his own medicine, A
Dot entertains
Fun at Five Point school
Going to school in Mother Goose land
Grandmother's cat
Imaginary Tommy
Joke, The
Jolliest Christmas ever, The
Little Jack's Christmas
Marie recites
Mother Goose's gosling
Playing Rabbit
Santa's rescue
Search for Mother Goose
Shirkers, The
Taking teacher's place
Taking the census
Topsy turvy Christmas
Troublesome flock
Twins and how they entertained the new minister, The
Uncle Joe's will
Uninvited member, An
Waif's Thanksgiving, The
Wanted: a chimney
Wanted, a license to wed
What do you know about ghosts?
When Polly was queen of the May
Who was scared?
Whose dog?
Worm turns, The

Guske, Carl W.
Fata Deorum

Guthrie, Kenneth Sylvan.
Sayonara, tr.

Gyalni, Wolfgang.
After the honeymoon

Gyp, *see* **Martel de Janville.**

Hadley, Marvin.
Till three P. M.

Hagedorn, Hermann.
Five in the morning
Horse thieves, The
Last faring, The
Three false women of Llanlar, The
Silver blade, The

Hageman, Maurice.
Love's diplomacy

Hale, Harold, pseud. *see* **C. N. Moller.**

Hale, Harris G.
Story of Jacob, The

Hale, Louise Closser.
Other woman, The
Paste cut paste

Halevy, Ludovic.
Indian summer
Panurge's sheep

Hall, Newton M.
Story of Jacob

Hall, W. Strange.
Mobswoman

Halman, Doris F.
Closet, The
Difficult boarder, The
Dog, The
Famine and the Ghost
It behooves us
Lady Anne
Playroom, The
Santa Claus
Will-o'-the-wisp

Halpern, J.
Mother and son

Halsey, Forrest.
Empty lamp, The

Hamilton, Cicely.
How the vote was won
Jack and Jill and a friend

Hamilton, Cosmo.
Aubrey closes the door
Jerry and a sunbeam

Hankin, St. John E. C.
Burglar who failed, The
Constant lover

Hanlon, John.
Pan passes northward
Seeker of a secret, The

Hanna, Tacie May.
Hyacinths
Upon the waters

Hannan, Charles.
Electric man, The

Hanshew, T. W.
Harvest, The

Hanson, Frank I.
Father Time's Christmas treat
Will Soakum's matrimonial bureau

Hapgood, Hutchins.
Enemies
Harbour, J. L.
Mrs. Elwell's paper
Hardy, Robert T.
Hidden love
Hare, Walter Ben.
Anita's secret
Christmas carol, A
Christmas with the Mulligan's
Her Christmas hat
Isosceles
White Christmas, The
Hargrave, Eustace.
Island sea-dreams, The
Harned, Mary.
Outcast, The. Tr.
Harnwell, Anna Jane.
Sin of Ahab, The
Sojourners
Harris, Ada L.
Cupid in the kitchen
Harris, Claudia L.
It's spring
Man who couldn't say "No," The
Young Mr. Santa Claus
Harris, Frank.
King of the Jews, The
Harris May.
Open door, The
Poet's wife, A
Harris Sheba.
Quiet game, tr.
Hartley, Alexander.
Wakuwapi
Hartman, H. M.
Wheatless meal, The
Harvey, Della S.
Easter miracle, An
Harvey, Kate.
Courage
Won
Hasbrouch, Louise S.
Elizabeth's young man
Haslett, Harriet Holmes.
Dolores of the Sierra
Inventor, The
Modern menage, A
Scoop, The
Undercurrents
When love is blind
Hastings, Basil M.
Fourth act, The
"Q"
Twice one

Hetteras, Owen.
Eugenical wedding, A
Hauptmann, Gerhart.
Assumption of Hannele, The
Dead are singing, The
Helios
Haviland, J. Butler.
Miss Jones, Journalist
Hawkridge, Winifred.
Florist shop, The
Price of orchids, The
Hay, Ian, *see* **Beith, John Hay.**
Hay, John.
Happy man
Hayes, Budget T.
Winter bloom
Hazard, Rowland Gibson.
How Robin Hood once was a wait
Head, Cloyd.
Curtains, The
Grotesques
Head, John, Jr.
Death of Titian, tr.
Healy, Joseph P.
Drama of the future, The
Heathcote, Arthur M.
His good genius
Hecht, Ben.
Hand of Siva, The, jt. auth.
Hero of Santa Maria
Wonder hat, The
Hedges, B. A.
Slacker for the cause, A
Heffner, Hubert.
"Dod gast ye both!"
Heidenstam, Verner Von.
Birth of God, The
Soothsayer, The
Heijermans, Herman.
Jubilee
Saltimbank
Heijermans-Houwink, Caroline.
Saltimbank, tr.
Helburn, Theresa.
Enter the hero
Hellem, Ch.
Sabotage
Helliar, Arthur.
Proposing by proxy
Hemmerde, Edward G.
Maid of honour, A.
Henderson, Mrs. Alice Corbin.
Adam's dream
Easter morning

Star of Bethlehem, The
Henderson, D. M.
 Special delivery
Henderson, Jessie E.
 Borrowers' day
Henderson, Sara.
 Cupid mixes things
 Too many wives
Henle, James H.
 Veterans, The
Henry, Re.
 Fast friends
Herbach, Joseph.
 Rehearsal, The.
Herford, Beatrice.
 Bride's Christmas tree, The
Herford, Oliver.
 Modern dialogue, A
Herman, J. A.
 Smile of Mona Lisa, tr.
Herrick, Gertrude.
 Full of the moon, The
Herring, E. C.
 Lady Flora's namesake
Herts, B. Russell.
 Builders, The
 Female of the species
Hertz, Henrik.
 King Rene's daughter
Hervieu, Paul.
 Modesty
 Sayonara
Hewlett, Maurice.
 Ariadne in Naxos
 Death of Hippolytus, The
 Minos King of Crete
Hicks, Wilson.
 Before the dawn
 Trickery
Higginbotham, Robert.
 Clearly and concisely
 Lucky Peter
Hight, Mary.
 Police matron
Hilbert, Jaroslav.
 Whom the Gods destroy
Hill, Edward G.
 House of Aegues, The
Hill, Frederick Trevor.
 "Dinner's served!"
 Heathen Chinee, The
 Knotty problem, A
Hill, Margaret F.
 Lost village, The

Hillard, Stafford.
 Storm in a tea shop
Hillyer, Robert.
 Dawn of the sunset, The
Hillyer, William S.
 Not in the regular army
Hinkley, Eleanor H.
 Flitch of bacon, A
Hinks, K. W.
 Cave of precious things
Hirschbein, Perez.
 In the dark
 On the threshold
 Snowstorm, The
 Stranger, The
 When the dew falleth
Hobart, George V.
 Cure for jealousy, A
Hobart, Margaret Jeffery.
 Inasmuch as ye have done it unto the least
Hoffman, A. S.
 Deacon's sweetheart
 Timothy Ryan's return
Hoffman, Phoebe.
 Martha's mourning
Hofmannsthal, Hugo von.
 Death and the fool
 Death of Titian, The
 Idyll
 Madonna Dianora
 Prologue for a marionette theatre
Hogg, C. W.
 Men who loved Mamie, The
 Mirror of time, The
 Story of Corporal Bell, The
Hogrefe, Pearl.
 Every Senior
Hollander, George C.
 Putting it across
Hollander, Lee M.
 Renaissance
Holles, Alfred.
 Duchess of Doherty Court, The
Holley, Horace.
 Ellen
 Genius, The
 Her happiness
 His luck
 Incompatibles, The
 Modern prodigal, A
 Pictures
 Rain
 Survival
 Telegram, The

Hollingshead, J.
　Bardwell vs. Pickwick
Holmes, Charles N.
　Paper wedding, A
　Please pass the cream
　Smith's unlucky day
　Star boarder, The
　Their first quarrel
　Waiting for the train
Holsworth, Doris.
　When the sun stayed in bed
Holt, Edwin.
　Bud's baby
Holt, Florence Taber.
　They the crucified
Home, Ina.
　Dream on Christmas eve, A
Hood, Charles Newton.
　While you wait
Hoornbeek, Helen P.
　Mary Ann
Hope, Winifred Ayres.
　Friends in bookland
Hopkins, Arthur.
　Moonshine
Hopkins, Hester A.
　Anybody family on Sunday morning, The
Hopkinson, Mrs. Arthur.
　Women's votes
Horton, Ruth.
　Who is queer?
Houghton, Stanley.
　Dear departed, The
　Fancy free
　Fifth commandment, The
　Master of the house, The
　Phipps
House, R. T.
　Little blue guinea-hen, The, tr.
　Man of the world, tr.
　Two husbands, tr.
Housman, Laurence.
　Apollo in Hades
　As good as gold
　Bird in hand
　Brother Sun
　Christmas tree, The
　Comforter, The
　Death of Alcestis, The
　Doom of Admetus, The
　Fool and his money, A
　His favorite flower
　House fairy, The
　Likely story, A
　Lord of the harvest, The
　Moonshine
　Nazareth
　Possession
　Queen, The
　Return of Alcestis, The
　Snow man, The
　Torch of time, The
Hovey, Richard.
　Blind, The, tr.
　Intruder, The. tr.
　Seven Princesses, The. tr.
Howard, Margaret.
　When Betty saw the Pilgrims
Howard, Homer Hildreth.
　Child in the house, The
Howard, Katharine.
　House of life, The
Howell-Carter, Josephine.
　Hilarion
Howells, W. D.
　True hero
Howie, Helen M.
　His father's son
　Those dreadful Drews
　Too much Bobbie
Hoxie, Evelyn.
　Strike Mother Goose settled, The
Hrbek, Cyril J.
　Ninth night, The. tr.
Hubbard, Eleanore.
　America pays her debt to France
　Banker's strategy, The
　Charter oak, The
　Colonial school, A
　Daniel Boone's snuff box
　Declaration of independence, The
　First American library, The
　"First in war, The"
　Forewarned is forearmed
　Gold in California
　Homesteaders' Christmas, The
　Independence Day
　Lucky Hallowe'en, A
　Mayflower compact, The
　Memorial Day
　No man is above the law
　One way to capture a fort
　"Only a girl!"
　"Price of liberty, The"
　Salvage
　Samuel Morse's telegraph
　Soft-soap day, The
　Star-spangled banner, The
　Trial trip of the Clermont, The
Hubbard, George.
　In the dark
　Narrow squeak

Hubbard Louis Herman.
   Telling the truth
Hubbard, Philip E.
   Love passage
Hudson, Holland.
   Action!
   Shepherd in the distance, The
Hueffer, Ford Madox.
   House, A
Hughes, A. H.
   Sea, The
Hughes, Glenn.
   Bottled in bond
Hughes, Glenn, jt. author.
   Madman on the roof, The
   Nari-Kin
   Razor, The
Hughes, Richard.
   Sisters' tragedy, The
Hughes, Rupert.
   For she's a jolly good fellow
Huizinga, A. V. C. P.
   Louise, tr.
Humason, Sarah.
   Masks and men
Humboldt, Archibald, pseud. see
   March, George Archibald.
Hung, Shen.
   Cow-herd, The
Hunter, Kenneth.
   To find our lives
Hunter, Rex.
   Hands and the man
   Romany Road
   Stuff o' Dreams
   Wild goose, The
Hunting, Emma M.
   Betty's ancestors
   Double dummy
Hurst, Brandon.
   Pressing matter, A
Hurst, Harry.
   Bridal trip, A
Hussey, Eunice G.
   Newsy wins
Hutchins, Will.
   Day that Lincoln died
   Jeanne D'Arc at Vaucouleurs
   Pater Noster, tr.
Hutchinson, M. F.
   Cresmans, The
   Terror of a day, A
Hutten, Baroness von.
   Ten years after

Huxley, Aldous.
   Among the nightingales
   Happy families
   Mortal coils
Hyde, Douglas.
   Lost saint, The
   Marriage, The
   Poorhouse, The
   Twisting of the rope, The
Hyde, V. D.
   Helping Charlie

Idzumo, Takeda.
   Bushido from "Terakoya" or "Matsu"
Ilsley, S. Marshall.
   Feast of the holy innocents, The
Inman, A. C.
   Group of poems—Fate
   " " " Dialogue
Ireland, D. L.
   Cottage on the moor
Irish, Marie.
   Adoption of Bob, The
   Baby show, The
   Boastful saint, The
   Brave foresters
   Broken picture, The
   Christmas cookies, The
   Christmas dinner, The
   Christmas eve at the Mulligans
   Christmas in the air
   Christmas influence
   Christmas journey, A
   Christmas speakin' at Skagg's Skule
   Christmas surprise for Mother Goose
   Christmas visitors from other lands
   Christmas wishes
   Christmas sympathy
   Days of long ago, The
   Doing away with Christmas
   Double Christmas gift, A
   Good little girl, A
   Grandfather's bright Christmas plan
   Hiawatha
   Herbert's discovery
   Joy of giving, The
   Little housekeepers
   Lost pocketbook, The
   Meeting of the ghosts, The
   Merry Christmas Jake
   Mother Goose and her flock
   No Christmas in the house
   North-pole expedition, A

Old Uncle Rat gives his consent
Pickett's Christmas party, The
Prindle's proposal
Pumpkin Pie Peter
Sambo's party
Scene at the ticket office
Slight mistake, A
Thanksgiving conspiracy, A
Trials of Christmas shopping
Trained menagerie, A
True Christmas spirit, The
Uncle Grouch
Uncle Sam's mistake
Visit from the Brownies, A
Visit to Santa Claus, A
Waiting for the train
We and our friends
When we are grown up
When we are women

Irwin, Grace Luce.
Art for art's sake
Close call, A
Domestic dilemma, A
Heroes
Innocent villain, An
Intimate acquaintance, An
Music hath charms
Wedding of Mah Foy, The

Irving, Laurence.
Phoenix, The

Irwin, Wallace.
Isle of chestnuts

Isenberger, Glenn H.
Betty Jane's Christmas dream

Isenberger, Susie E.
Betty Jane's Christmas dream

Itow, Michio.
Fox's grave
She who was fished
Somebody—nothing

Ivan, Rosalind.
Fantasie impromptu, The

Ives, Alice E.
Meow!
Sweet Elysium Club

Iwasaki, Yozan T.
Nari-Kin

Izumo, Takeda.
Pine-tree, The

J., R. B.
Glimpse into the theatres, A

Jackson, Frances M.
Sallie-for-keeps

Jackson, J. J.
Political pull, A

Jagendorf, Moritz.
Blue morning glory, A

Jakobi, Paula.
Chinese lily

Jacobs, W. W.
Admiral Peters
Boatswain's mate, The
Changeling, The
Ghost of Jerry Bundler, The
Gray parrot, The
In the library
Keeping up appearances
Love passage, A
Monkey's paw, The

James, Fred H.
Cowboy-Jim
David Garrick's masterpiece
Faro-Jane
Japanese romance, A
Mining agent, The
Pride and charity

Janville, Martel de, S. G. M. A. de R. de M. *see* **Martel de Janville**

Jaros, Ernest S.
Love potion, The

Jarrell, Myra W.
Case of Mrs. Kantsay Know

Jefferys, William H.
Evening rice
Paper money
Real price or stranger than fiction, The

Jenkins, E. Lawrence.
Lady cook, The

Jenkins, George B.
Beautiful thing, The

Jenkins, Hester D.
In a tenement
Judith and Ariel
Mother Goose up-to-date
Our friends the food

Jenks, Annabel.
Dinner at seven sharp

Jenks, Tudor.
Dinner at seven sharp
Drifting cloud, The

Jennings, Eulora M.
Dinner at the club
Prinzessin von Barnhof, Die

Jennings, Gertrude.
Acid drops
Allotments
At the ribbon counter
Bathroom door, The
Between the soup and the savoury

Bobbie settles down
Elegant Edward
Five birds in a cage
I'm sorry—it's out!
"Me and my diary"
Mother-of-Pearl
No servants
Pros and cons, The
Rest cure, The
Waiting for the 'bus

Jerauld, Margie A.
Uncle Sam to the rescue

Jerome, Jerome K.
Barbara
Fennel

Jess, Ellen.
Birth of a nation's flag

Jex, John.
Mr. Willoughby calls
Nest, The
Unnecessary atom, The
Violet souls

Jocelyn, Susan E. W.
Santa Claus or papa

John, Gwen.
"Edge o' dark"
Luck of war, The

Johnson, Martyn.
Mr. and Mrs. P. Roe

Johnson, Sherman F.
Boys will be girls

Johnston, Emma L.
Abraham Lincoln and the little bird
Echo, The
Fourth of July, The
Fox and the crow, The
George Washington and the cherry tree
Ladybird
Lion and the mouse, The
Little birds, The
Little sparrow, A
Spider and the fly, The

Johnston, Franklin.
His dinner for two
New reporter, The

Jome, Ellis O.
Mrs. Pipp's Waterloo

Jones, Ann van Marter.
Which shall be king

Jones, Henry Arthur.
Clerical error, A
Goal, The
Grace Mary
Her tongue

Jones, Horatio S.
Cracker, The

Jones, Howard Mumford.
Shadow, The
Sundial, The

Jones, Willis Knapp.
With chains of gold, tr.

Jordan, Elizabeth.
Confidence, A

Joyce, Jeannette.
Aunt Jane visits school
In a doctor's office
No peddlers admitted
Proposal in grandma's day, A
Train to Morrow, The
Up-to-date proposal, An

Judge, Jane.
Christmas mystery, A

Justema, William, Jr.
Chi-Fu

Kane, Helen P.
Capture of Ozah, The
Dianthe's desertion
Her nephew-in-law elect
Peregrinations of Polly, The
Under sailing orders
Yagowanea
Yot-che-ka

Kaplan, Louis.
Night of light, The

Kattenberg, Burns.
Martha Dixon's parlor

Kaufman, S. Jay.
Kisses

Kavanaugh, Katherine.
Bachelor's baby
Converted suffragist, A
Couple of heroes, A
Daughter of men, The
Easy terms
Four adventurers
Friendly tip, A
Girl and the outlaw, The
House across the way, The
In wrong
It ain't my fault
Man who came back, The
Minister pro tem, A
My Mexican rose
O Joy San
Professor of love, The
Queen of diamonds, The
Stormy night, A
Wife tamer, The

Kearney, Patrick.
Great noontide, The

Tongues of fire
Kearns, John.
Wooing of Lilinau, The
Keating, Miss E. H.
Incog
Plot of Potzentausend, The
Poor relations
Talisman, The
Keeler, Charles.
Pagoda slave, A
Kehoe, J. H.
What's the use?
Kellam, Elizabeth.
Store, The
Kelland, C. B.
His wife's place
Kelley, Jessie A.
Employment office, The
Her weekly allowance
Mrs. Jenkins' brilliant idea
Photographer's troubles, A
Those husbands of ours
Kelley, Laura F.
Mrs. Sullivan's social tea
Kelly, F. M.
Sewing circle meets at Mrs. Martin's, The
Kelly, George.
Finders-keepers
Kemble, Howard, pseud. *see* **Bell, John Kemble**
Kemp, Harry.
Boccaccio's untold tale
Prodigal son, The
Solomon's song
Kemper, Sallie.
Blood will tell
Moth balls
Kendall, John.
Fond of Peter
Laughter in court
Kennard, Auberon.
Wanderer, The
Kennard, Marietta C.
Flight of the herons, The
Kennedy, Charles Rann.
Necessary evil, The
Terrible meek, The
Kennedy, Frank.
Deacon's sweetheart, The
Kenyon, Bernice Lesbia.
Alchemist, The
Kerley, Rosialee.
Wedding guest, The
Kester, M. A., Jr.

Hard heart, The
Ketcham, Arthur.
Maid's prologue, The
Other one, The
Kikuchi, Kan.
Madman on the roof, The
Kilmer, Joyce.
Some mischief still
Kimball, Rosamond.
Call to the Youth of America, The
King, Beulah.
Henry, Where are you?
His sisters
Indifference of Jerry, The
Maid, The
Rev. Peter Brice, Bachelor, The
What's in a name?
King, Charles.
Leave the woman out
Kingsbury, Sara.
Christmas guest, The
Kingsley, Ellis.
Other woman, The
Kingston, Mary F.
My son Arthur
Kinkead, Cleves.
Four-flushers, The
Kinnick, Claude.
As advertised
Kirk, Sara E.
In Betsy Ross's time
Kirker, Katherine.
Lady compassionate, The
Klauber, Adolph.
Green-eyed monster, The
Klauber, Amy Josephine.
Exile, The
Kleber, Frank T.
Triangle No. V333
Triangled
When extremes meet
Knevels, Gertrude.
Fairies' child, The
Skyboy
Kniffin, H. A.
Mrs. Flynn's lodgers
Knight, Percival.
Detective Keen
Knoblauch, Edward.
Little silver ring, The
My lady's lace
War committee, A
Knowlton, Annie R.
Why Jessica!

Knowlton, Beatrice.
"Way the noise began, The"
Knowlton, Don.
"Way the noise began, The"
Knox, Florence Clay.
For distinguished service
Matrimonial fog, The
Knox, Margaret.
Our choice
America
Kobrin, Leon.
Black sheep, The
Secret of life, The
Koogle, Effie Louise.
Up-to-date America
Kraft, Irma.
Ambition in White chapel
Because he loved David so
Maccabean cure, A
Power of Purim, The
To save his country
Kreymborg, Alfred.
At the sign of the thumb and nose
Blue and green
Jack's house
Lima beans
Manikin and Minikin
Monday
People who die
Rocking chairs
Silent waiter, The
Vote the new moon
When the willow nods
Kummer, Clare.
Bridges
Chinese love
Choir rehearsal, The
Inspiration of the play
Robbery, The
Kummer, Frederick Arnold.
Love of women, The
Kurtz, C. Gordon.
Missing lines
Suitors three
Crooks

LaBeaume, Mrs. Edmond.
Elusive Alonzo, The
Price of popularity, The
Problem of the hour, The
Labiche, Eugene M.
Grammar
Two cowards, The
Laidlaw, Alexander H.
Captain Walrus
La Mare, Harry.
Prim Miss Perkins, The

Lang, Edith.
Christmas story, The
Langhanke, Helen.
Doll shop, The
Langlois, Fannie Myers.
Suite B
Langner, Lawrence.
Another way out
Family exit, The
Licensed
Matinata
Pie
Wedded
Larson, Emma.
Christmas of the little pines, The
Top of the world
La Shire, Louis A.
Book agent, The
Latham, Harold S.
Thirteenth domino, The
Lavedan, Henri.
Afternoon walk, The
Along the quays
For ever and ever
Fraternity
Not at home
Sunday on Sunday goes by
Two husbands
Where shall we go?
Law, Arthur.
Artful automaton
Bright idea
Castle Botherem
Strange host
Lawrence, C. E.
Hour of Prospero
Message of Lazarus, The
Laws, Anna C.
Twice-told tale, A
Lay, Elizabeth A.
When witches ride
Leacock, Stephen.
"Q"
Learsi, Rufus.
Triumph of instinct, The
Ledoux, Louis V.
Fox's grave, tr.
She who was fished, tr.
Somebody-nothing, tr.
Lee, Agnes.
Blunted age, The
Eastland waters
Red pearls
Sharing, The
Silent house, The
Lee, M. E.

Black death or Ta-ün, The
Honor cross, The
Lefuse, M.
At the Golden Goose
For lack of evidence
Mistress Runaway
Lehmann, Adolph.
"The tongmen"
Leighton, George R.
Solemn pride
Leinster, Murray.
Beautiful thing, The
Leland, Emily H.
Maw Moseley's courtin' lamp
Leland, Robert DeCamp.
Barbarians, The
Purple youth
Lent, Evangeline M.
Love-in-idleness
Rag doll, A
Squaw of Bear Claw
Leonard, William Ellery.
Glory of the morning
Dream of wings, The
Le Sage, Alain-René.
Crispin, Rival of his master
Leslie, Noel.
Cult of content, The
For king and country
War fly, The
Waste
Lester, Alfred.
Restaurant, A
Scene shifter's lament, The
Leverson, Darcy.
Bet, The
Le Vett, C. H.
School board in our town, The
Levi, Ruth E.
Chanukah sketch
King's choice, The
Levick, Milnes.
Wings in the mesh
Levin, Z.
Poetry and prose
Levinger, Elma Ehrlich.
Burden, The
Great hope, The
Jephthah's daughter
Levinson, Herman D.
"Riley"
Spirit of Purim, The
Levy, Edith M.
At the end of the rope
Lewis, C.

Two sociable friends
Lewisohn, Ludwig.
Garden, The
Lie, The
New England fable
Night in Alexandria
Lincoln, Florence.
Piece of ivory, A
Lincoln, J. Willard.
Father changes his mind
Rather rough on Robert
Lindau, Norman C.
Cooks and cardinals
Lindsay, C. M.
Looking for more
Lion, Leon M.
King who had nothing to learn, The
Man who stole the castle
Mobswoman, The
Playing the game
Putting it over on father
Touch of the child, The
Wiles of the widow, The
Lipscomb, Mrs. M. A.
Ladies of Athens
Lisle, Clifton.
Fair play
Scout's honor, A
Livingston, Ethel.
Difference in clocks, A
Livingston, Francis M.
Dark man at the feast, The
Double negative, The
Sentimental journey, A
Lloyd, Gladys, *see* **Someple.**
Logie, Elma M.
Old maid's venture, A
Loomis, Charles B.
Evening in truth, An
Piazza parleys
Lopez, Sabatino.
Sparrow, The
Lord, Katharine.
Buried treasure
Greatest gift, The
Honorable Miss, The
June magic
Katjen's garden
Lark, The
Masque of the Pied Piper, The
Minister's dream, The
Raven man, The
Three bears, The
Lorde, André de.
Saved!

Woman who was acquitted, The
Louys, Pierre.
 At the setting of the sun
 Crepuscule
Lovell, Caroline C.
 War woman, The
Loving, Pierre.
 Autumn
 Festival of Bacchus, tr.
 His helpmeet, ed.
 Hour of recognition, The. tr.
 Indian summer
 Literature, tr.
 Louise, tr.
 Prologue for a marionette theatre, ed.
 Stick-up, The
Lowell, Edith.
 Tickets for the Sheffield choir
Loy, Mina.
 Pamperers, The
Loyd, Gladys, *see* **Someple, pseud.**
Luck, H. R.
 Man who never worried, The
Ludington, Helen G.
 Lunch in the suburbs, A
 Suffragette, The
Luehrmann, Adele.
 "Butting in" in French
 Disciples of art
Luques, E. Antoinette.
 Snow image, The
 Spirit of Memorial Day, The
 Story of the poplar tree, The
Luther, Leslie.
 Law
Lütkenhaus, Anna M.
 Barnaby Lee
 Birds' story of the trees, The
 Every boy
 Fairy minstrel of Glenmalure, The
 Geographical squabble, A
 Grammar play, A
 Master Skylark
 Mrs. Pollywigs and her wonderful wax works
 Nature play in a city school, A
 Thanksgiving Day—1696
 Through the looking-glass
 Well babies
Lyall, Eric.
 Coming of Columbine, The
Lyons, A. Neil.
 Pennybunch, A
Lyttelton, Edith.
 Christmas morality play. A
 Nyanysa
 Thumbscrew, The

McArthur, C. H.
 New school-Ma'am, The
McCauley, Clarice V.
 Conflict, The
 Queen's hour, The
Macauley, Ward.
 His city girl
 Letter of introduction, A
 Mr. Editor
 Mrs. McGreevy's boarders
 Pat's matrimonial venture
McClellan, Walter.
 Delta wife, The
 Pollin picks a wife
McClure, John.
 Cruet of Marigolds, The
 Doom of Metrodorus, The
McConnell, Genevive K.
 Bone of contention, The
McCourt, Edna W.
 Truth, The
McCoy, Samuel D.
 Mrs. Potiphar pays a call
Macdonald, John D.
 Ola
 What Christmas did for Jerusha Grumble
Macdonald, Zellah.
 Markheim
McEvoy, Charles.
 Dew necklace, The
McFadden, Elizabeth A.
 Why the chimes rang
Macfarlane, Anne.
 Slippers
Macfarlane, W.
 Breakfast breeze, A
McGeoch, Daisy.
 Camping
 Mormonizing
 Packing
 Picturing
 Proposing
 Reading
 Shopping
 Thrilling
McGuckin, Mildred C.
 Wild flower
McGurrin, C. H.
 Light from another world, A
Machado de Assis, J. M.
 Life

McInroy, Harl.
   Honorable Togo
Macintire, Elizabeth J.
   Bride's crown, tr.
   Field of enchantment, tr.
   Ivory tower, The
Macintyre, John see **Brandane, John.**
Mackall, Lawton.
   Scrambled eggs
Mackay, Constance D'Arcy.
   Abraham Lincoln
   Ashes of roses
   Beau of Bath, The
   Benjamin Franklin
   Boston Tea Party, The
   Brewing of brains, A
   Christmas guest, The
   Council retained
   Dame Greel o' Portland town
   Daniel Boone
   Elf child, The
   Enchanted garden, The
   Festival of Pomona, The
   Foam maiden, The
   Forest spring, The
   Fountain of youth, The
   George Washington's fortune
   Gift of time, The
   Gooseherd and the Goblin, The
   Gretna Green
   House of the heart, The
   In witchcraft days
   Little Pilgrim's progress, A
   Masque of conservation, A
   Masque of Pomona, The
   May-day
   Memorial day pageant
   Merrymount
   Nimble-wit and Fingerkin
   On Christmas eve
   Pageant of Hours, The
   Passing of Hiawatha, The
   Pioneers, The
   Prince of Court painters, The
   Princess and the Pixies, The
   Princess Pocohontas
   Siegfried
   Silver lining, The
   Snow witch, The
   Sun goddess, The
   Three wishes, The
   Troll magic
   Vanishing race, The
Mackaye, H. S.
   Lucinda's whim
Mackaye, Percy.
   Antick, The
   Cat-boat, The
   Chuck
   Gettysburg
   Sam Average
   Sanctuary
MacKenzie, Edna I.
   Dearest thing in boots, The
   Unexpected guest, The
McKiernan, William J.
   Wardrobe of the king, The
McKinnell, Normal.
   Bishop's candlesticks
   Dick's sister
McKinney, Isabel.
   Mud
McLane, Fannie Moulton.
   Behind the khaki of the scouts
Maclaren, Ian, see **Watson, John.**
McLaurin, Kate.
   Discussion with interruptions, A
McMechan, F. Hoeffer.
   Last race, The
MacMillan, Dougald.
   Off Nags Head
MacMillan, Mary.
   Apocryphal episode, An
   At the church door
   Dress rehearsal of Hamlet, The
   Dryad, The
   Entr' acte
   Fan and two candlesticks, A
   Futurists, The
   Gate of wishes, The
   His second girl
   In heaven
   Modern masque, A
   Peter Donelly
   Ring, The
   Rose, The
   Shadowed star, The
   Standing moving
   Storm, The
   When two's not company
   Woman's a woman for a' that, A
McMullen, J. C.
   Boob, The
   Show actress, The
Macnamara, Margaret.
   Light gray or dark
   Love-fibs
   Witch, The
Macomber, Ada S.
   Romantic Molly
McPherson, Janney.
   This is so sudden
MacQueen, Laurence I.

Sacrifice
McVay, Sumner.
An amethyst remembrance
Maddox, D. S.
Mr. McArdle's guest
Madison, James.
Bubble's troubles
Maeterlinck, Maurice.
Blind, The
Home
Interior
Intruder, The
Land of unborn children, The
Seven Princesses, The
Maguire, W. H.
Scratch race, A
Makee, Walt, pseud. *see* **Maguire, W. H.**
Malleson, Miles.
Paddly pools
Manley, William F.
Crowsnest, The
Mann, Herbert A.
His chance
Manners, J. Hartley.
All clear
Day of dupes, The
God of my faith
God's outcast
Happiness
Just as well
Ministers of grace
Queen's messenger, A
Woman intervenes, The
Mapes, Victor.
Flower of Yeddo, A
Marble, Thomas L.
Giuseppina.
Mademoiselle Prudence
March, George A.
Feast in the wilderness, A
Laughter and song
Marcone, Theodora.
Rights of the soul, tr.
Mariani, Federico.
Sunbeam
Mariett, Paul.
With candle and crucifix
Marion, Paul.
As Molly told it
Courting the widow
Elopers, The
Marivaux, Pierre C. de C.
Legacy, The
Markham, Catharine.

How Christmas was saved
Marks, Jeannette.
Deacon's hat, The
Happy thought, The
Merry merry cuckoo, The
Welsh honeymoon
Marmer, Archie.
Robert Fulton
Marsh, Charles A.
Challenge of the cross, The
Marshall, Abigail.
Accomplice, The
Marshall, Robert
Wire entanglement, A
Marston, Westlund.
Donna Diana
Martel de Janville, S. G. M. A. de R. de M.
Little blue guinea-hen, The
Martin, Hermann Ford.
Whom the sea calls
Martin, John Joseph.
Charlie Barringer
Wife of Usher's well, The
Martin, Julia.
Barbara the great
Quest of Christmas, The
Thanksgiving of Praisgod Plenty, The
Martin, Percy O.
Proof of the pudding, The
Martin, T.
King Rene's daughter, tr.
Masefield, John.
Good Friday
Locked chest, The
Mrs. Harrison
Philip the King
Sweeps of ninety-eight, The
Fairy Good-will
Massingham, Dorothy.
Goat, The
Masson, Tom.
Husband's advice, A
Sad mistake, A
Masters, Edgar Lee.
Conversation, The
Masterson, Kate.
Man to order, A
Mather, Charles C.
Dispatches from Washington
Double-crossed
Mathews, Frances A.
At the Grand Central
Finished coquette, A

New professor, The
On the staircase
Paying the piper
Proposal, The
Scapegrace, The
Woman's forever, A
Matlack, Judith.
Two prisoners, The
Matthews, Elva De Pue, *see* **De Pue, Elva.**
Matthews, Walter R.
Price of fame, The
Maude, A.
Traveller and peasant, tr.
Maude, L.
Traveller and peasant, tr.
Maurey, Max.
Rosalie
Mawson, Harry P.
Placing a play
Maxwell, Elsie.
Melinda and her sisters
Maxwell, William B.
Last man in, The
May, Gordon V.
Little black devil, The
Mayer, Gaston.
French as he is spoke
Mayer, Otto S.
End of the game, The
Immortal Gulick, The
Mayne, Rutherford,
Red turf
Troth, The
Mazaud, Emile.
Holiday, The
Meblin, Rose C.
Dowry and romance
Meeker, Arthur, Jr.
Hardy perennials
Meeker, Isabelle.
Sojourners
Megrue, Roi Cooper.
Double cross
Interviewed
Same old thing, The
Meigs, Cornelia.
Primrose lane
Meilhac, Henri.
Indian summer
Panurge's sheep
Meloney, William B.
Knave's move, The
Mencken, H. L.
Artist, The
Mendel, Paula.
Journeys end in lovers' meeting
Mendes, Catulle.
Tabarin's wife
Merington, Marguerite.
Abe Lincoln and little A. D.
Artist—Mother and child
Christmas party, A
Dulce et Decorum club, The
Father Time and his children
First flag, The
Gainsborough lady, A
His mother's face
Last sitting, The
Millet group, A
Princess Moss-Rose
Priscilla, Myles and John
Queen and Emperor
Salon Carré fantasy, A
Seven sleepers of Ephesos, The
Tertulla's garden
Testing of Sir Gawayne, The
Merivale, H. C.
Husband in clover, A
Merivale, Philip.
Knut at Rosekilde
Wind over the water, The
Merriam, Lillie Fuller.
Aunt Abigail and the boys
Merriman, Effie W.
Bachelor's club, The
Emerson club, The
Merrill, Fenimore.
Avenue, The
Merryman, Mildred Plew.
Seven Leagued boots, The
Methley, Violet M.
Buster
Clever kid!
Freckles
Unprofitable poultry keeping
Metz-Konig, Marie.
White lie, The
Meyer, Anna Nathan.
P's and Q's
Meyer, Josephine A.
To be perfectly frank
Meyers, Robert C. V.
Cousin Tom
Dane's dress suit case
Dressing gown, The
Eether or eyther
Forced friendship, A
Two in a tiff
Miall, Agnes M.

AN INDEX TO ONE-ACT PLAYS 239

Love's young dream
Understudy, The
Michelson, Max.
Haunted hat-shop, The
Tired woman, The
Michelson, Miriam.
Bygones
Curiosity of Kitty Cochraine, The
Middleton, George.
Among the lions
Back of the ballot
Black tie, The
Cheat of pity, The
Circles
Criminals
Embers
Failures, The
Gargoyle, The
Good woman, A
Groove, The
House, The
In his house
Jim's beast
Madonna
Man masterful, The
Masks
Mothers
On bail
Possession
Reason, The
Their wife
Tides
Tradition
Unborn, The
Waiting
Middleton, Richard.
District visitor, The
Mildren, Nan L.
Brownie Night
Millay, Edna St. Vincent.
Aria da capo
Two slatterns and a king
Miller, Agnes.
Finding of the first arbutus, The
First Thanksgiving Day, The
Miller, John S. Jr.
Winds of the night, The
Miller, Max.
Imposition
Mills, Horace.
Admiral Peters
Millward, Florence M.
Alternative, The
Colonel and the lady, The
Henry wakes up
History repeats itself
Irene obliges

This room is engaged
Milne, A. A.
Boy comes home, The
Man in the bowler hat, The
Red feathers, The
Step mother, The
Wurzel-Flummery
Milne, J. R.
Dardanelles puff-box, The
Melodrama
Mirbeau, Octave.
Scruples
Mitchell, Anne M.
Mistletoe
Peg's little sister
Mitchell, Earle.
Bookmaker's shoes, The
Mitchell, Ruth Comfort.
Sweetmeat game, The
Miyanmasu.
Eboshi-ori
Mobert, Helen L.
Singing pool, The
Modell, David A.
On the highway, tr.
Moeller, Philip.
Helena's husband
Little supper, The
Pokey or the beautiful legend of
  the amorous Indian
Roadhouse in Arden, The
Sisters of Susannah
Two blind beggars
Moinaux, Georges Courteline.
Blank cartridge
Peace at home
Pitiless policeman, The
Moller, C. N.
Row at the Ruggles', A
Molnar, Ferenc.
Actress, The
Matter of husbands, A
Monkhouse, Allan.
Choice, The
Night watches
Shamed life
Monro, Harold.
One day awake
Monroe, Harriet.
After all
At the goal
It passes by
Modern minuet, A
Montague, Harold.
First aid to the wounded
Proposing by proxy

Montague, Leopold.
 Crystal gazer, The
Montgomery, Elizabeth.
 Light of the star of peace, The
Montgomery, James.
 Rather rough on Robert
Moore, Bertha.
 Bunkered
 Happy ending
Moore, E. Hamilton.
 Dance of death, A
 Dove uncaged, The
Moore, Low Wall.
 Happy prince, The
Moore, McElbert.
 Passé
Moore, Thomas Sturge.
 Medea
 Niobe
 Tyrfing
Moorman, Frederick W.
 All souls' night's dream, An
 Potter Thompson
Moran, Mabel M.
 Shakespeare Garden Club, The
More, Federico.
 Interlude
Morette, Edgar.
 Oh! Helpless man!
 Water that has passed, The
Morgan, Bayard Q.
 Scholar bound for Paradise, The; tr.
Morgan, Charles D.
 Search me!
Morgan, Edward.
 Son of the greater fatherland, A
Morgan, Edward J.
 Return, The
Morgan, Geoffrey F.
 First American flag, The
Morgan, J. L.
 Obsequies, The
Morgan, Jacque.
 At the club
Morin, Catherine A.
 Mushroom meadow, The
Morley, Christopher.
 Bedroom suite
 Rehearsal
 Thursday evening
Morley, Malcolm.
 Beauty versus the beast
 Cosher, The
 Masterpiece, The

 Motor mishap, A
 Recollections
 Told by the gate
Morris, B. M.
 Batch of proverbs, A
Morris, Edwin Batman.
 Man next door, The
 Millions in it
Morris, Neilson.
 River of light, The
Morrison, Arthur.
 Dumb-cake, The
 That brute Simmons
Morse, Katherine.
 Shop of perpetual youth, The
Morselli, Ercole Luigi.
 Gastone the animal tamer
 Water upon fire
Morstrom, Louis Cool.
 Doll shop
Morton, John Maddison.
 Betsy Baker
Moseley, Katharine P.
 Daggers and diamonds
Mosher, John C.
 Beanstalk, The
 Fee Fo Fum
 Quay of magic things, The
 Sauce for the Emperor
Moss, Harriet Calhoun.
 Drama class of Tankaha Nevada
Motokiyo.
 Kakitsuhata
 Kanawa
 Nishikigi
Motomasa.
 Sumida Gawa
Motoyazu, Komparu Zembo.
 Early snow
 Hatsuyuki
 Ikuta
Mould, F. Ethel.
 Trimming of the tree, The
Mowery, William B.
 Election of the Roulette, The
Moylan, Thomas King.
 "Movies"
 Oh lawsy me!
 Uncle Pat
Moyston, Guy.
 Last drop, The
Muggeridge, Marie.
 Rest cure, The
Mukerji, Dhan Gopal.
 Judgment of Indra, The

Mullins, Helene.
   Truth about liars, The
Mumford, Edward.
   Square deal, A
   That blessed baby
   Typewriter lady, The
Munger, Carabel L.
   Just like a woman
Murdock, Arthur W.
   In a park
Murphy, Elinor.
   I'll try
Murray, Josepha Marie.
   Dream lesson, A
Muskerry, William.
   He, she and it
   Imaginary aunt, An
   Make-believe
   Three blind mice
Musset, Alfred de.
   Caprice, A
   Door must be open or shut, A
   Green coat, The
   One cannot think of everything
Myall, Charles A.
   Ships on the sand
Mygatt, Tracy D.
   Bird's nest
   Grandmother Rocker
Mytton, Hugh.
   First locust, The
   Tanks

Nakamura, Kichizo.
   Razor, The
Narodny, Ivan.
   Fortune favors fools
Nathan, George J.
   Eternal mystery, The
Nathan, May R.
   Foothills of fame
Nathan, Robert G.
   Atoms
   Coward, The
Neall, W. H.
   Raising the wind
Neihardt, John G.
   Eight hundred rubles
Nelson, A. D.
   Fairy and the witch, The
Nethercot, Arthur H.
   Funeral march of a Marionette, The
   Grecian urn, The
Nettleton, Eva T.
   Uncle Sam's Council
Neumann, Sara.
   Old order, The
Nevitt, Mary R.
   Rostof pearls
Newboult, F. J.
   Devil's star, The
   Upstroke, The
Newman, Ethel L.
   Wally and the widow
Newnes, Caroline.
   Under the White Flag
Newton, Alma.
   Artist and the materialist, The
   Dawn, The
Newton, Harry L.
   Burglar's welcome, The
   Business is business
   College chums, The
   Darktown Social Betterment S'ciety, The
   Down in Paradise Alley
   Go-between, The
   Graft
   Her second time on earth
   Invitation to the ball, An
   Jack and his queen, A
   Keep your eye on the ball
   Little Miss Enemy
   Meet my wife
   Morning after the night before, The
   Outwitted
   Timothy Ryan's return
   Troublesome time, A
   Two girls and him
   Two jay detectives
Newton, W. T.
   Uncle Eben's s'prise party
   Uncle Peter's proposal
Nichols, Content S.
   Everychild
Nicholson, Kenyon.
   Anonymous letter, An
   Casino gardens, The
   Gentle assassin, The
   Marriage of little Eva, The
   White elephants
Nirdlinger, Charles F.
   Aren't they wonders?
   Big Kate
   Look after Louise
   Real people, The
   Washington's first defeat
Nisbet, Wallace.
   After the honeymoon

Noble, Kate W.
　Colonial tea, A
Noel, Louis.
　House of rest, The
Noguchi, Yone.
　By Miho's pine-clad shore, tr.
　Demon's shell, The, tr.
　Love's heavy burden
　Melon thief, The, tr.
　Mountain she-devil, The
　Perfect jewel maiden, tr.
　Shower, The
　Tears of the birds, The
　Willow tree, The
Nooshich, Branislav.
　Prince of Semberia, The
Nordenshield, Jeanette.
　Don't do that
Norris-Lewis, Alice.
　Exemption
Norton, Eleanor.
　Triumph of earth, The
Norton, Harold F.
　Woman, The
Norton, Ida G.
　Adopting an orphan
　Aunt Sally Saunders' health crusade
　How to reduce
Norton, Louise.
　Little wax candle
Notrebal, P. D.
　Undine
Noyes, Alfred.
　Belgian Christmas eve, A
　Rada
Noys, Georgi R.
　Protegee of the mistress, tr.
Nusbaum, Julia K.
　Golden gifts

O'Brien, Edward J.
　At the flowing of the tide
　Sancta Susanna, tr.
O'Brien, Seumas.
　Blind
　Duty
　Jurisprudence
　Magnanimity
　Matchmakers
　Retribution
Ochiai, T.
　Kanawa
O'Connor, J. M., Jr.
　These wild young people

O'Dea, Mark.
　Miss Myrtle says "Yes"
　Not in the lessons
　Shivaree
　Song of Solomon, The
Officer, Katherine.
　All souls' eve
Ogden, Janet.
　Going to school in China
Oglesbee, Delle Houghton.
　Ten fingers of François, The
O'Hanlon, Henry B.
　Tomorrow
O'Hanlon, Ruth.
　In my day
Oland, Edith.
　Stronger, The, tr.
Oland, Warner.
　Stronger, The, tr.
Olcott, Virginia.
　Dora
　Goody Grumble's cottage
　Little homemaker
　Little people of Autumn
　Onéida's dream
　Poor little boy
　Princess and a churn, A
　Puritan Christmas, A
　Ruler of the forest, The
　Wonder-hill, The
Oliver, Margaret S.
　Children of Granada
　Hand of the prophet, The
　Murdering Selina
　Striker, The
　This youth-gentlemen!
　Turtle dove, The
Oliver, Roland.
　Little face
O'Neil, George.
　Ladies at twelve
O'Neill, Clement.
　Wanted, a housekeeper
O'Neill, Eugene G.
　Before breakfast
　Bound east for Cardiff
　Dreamy kid, The
　Fog
　Ile
　In the zone
　Long voyage home, The
　Moon of the Caribbees, The
　Recklessness
　Rope, The
　Thirst
　Web, The

Where the cross is made
Oppenheim, James.
Night
Pioneers, The
Prelude to "Creation"
Shadow in the White House, The
Orange, B.
Acacia cottage
Orrick, Johns.
Hero in pink, The
Osborn, Innis G.
Easy mark, An
Taking way, A
Up against it
Osborne, Duffield.
Xanthippe on woman suffrage
Osborne, Harry W.
After the play
Little Co-ed
Peter
Osborne, Hubert.
"The good men do"
O'Shea, Monica B.
Rush Light, The
Ostrovsky, Alexander.
Protegee of the mistress, A
Overman, E. L.
Bright morning, tr.
Overstreet, H. A.
Hearts to mend
Overton, Gwendolen.
First love—and second
Owen, Harold.
Little fowl play, A
Owen, Marie B.
At old Mobile
Battle of Manbilla
De Soto and the Indians
How Bienville saved Mobile

Painton, Edith F. A. U.
Bairnies' Saturday night, The
Camp-fire girl, The
Class ship, The
Coming home to Grandma's
Country cousin, A
Doll show, The
Good-Bye All!
Graduate's choice, The
Just plain Dot
Lost colors, The
Mere man, A
Murdering the language
Organizing a society
Popular Dick, The
Provident society, The

Rehearsing the program
Studying for a test
Wanted: a cook
Writing a school play
Palmer, Anne.
Hat at the theatre
Palmer, Anne B.
Hanging out the wash
Palmer, Anne M.
At the depot
Buying a suit for Jimmy
Palmer, Belle E.
Christmas mix-up; or, Mrs. Santa Claus, Militant
Love flower, The
Men not wanted
Mrs. Santa Claus, Militant
Palmer, Mrs. George T.
His old sweethearts
Palmer, Helen M.
Man and a maid, A
Palmer, John.
Over the hills
Palmer, Josephine L.
Lighting of the Christmas tree, The
Palmer, Mrs. Martha R.
Best sellers, The
Pape, Lee.
Bravest thing in the world, The
Park, Julia E.
Trial for the murder of the King's English
Parker, Louis N.
Man in the street, The
Minuet, A
Monkey's paw
Parker, Mary M.
Art clubs are trumps
Bread, butter and romance
Killing time
Little Miss America and the happy children
Love behind the scenes
Mrs. Busby's pink tea
Mrs. Hoops-Hooper and the Hindu
Princess Innocence, The
Quiet evening at home, A
Rehearsal, The
Shadows
Parker, Oliver P.
Wren, The
Parker, W. C.
Art for breakfast
Breaking the engagement

Our first performance; or, Not accustomed to the stage
Second childhood
Taking father's place
Those red envelopes
"William"
Parkhurst, Winthrop.
Beggar and the king, The
Getting unmarried
Importance of being early
It never happens
Morraca
Parr, E. P.
Escape
Woman juror, The
Parry, Katharine.
Cease fire!
Parsons, James F.
Fun in a photograph gallery
Judge Offerheimer's first case
Parsons, Laura M.
Aunt Jerusha's quilting party
Parsons, Margaret G.
Christmas message, The
Fire-spirits
In a Valentine box
Jack-I-the-Green
'Neath the scepter of Susan
Potentate of Weatherdom, The
Pascal, Floy.
Facing reality
Paston, George.
Feed the brute
Parents' progress, The
Stuffing
Tilda's new hat
Patrick, A., Jr.
Jimmy
Patterson, Frederick C.
Jeanette
On the Veldt
Patterson, Marjorie.
Pan in ambush
Paull, H. M.
Hal, the highwayman
Last day of term, The
Other room, The
Paulton, Edward A.
Dormitory girls, The
Pauly, Fred L.
The young gardener
Payne, F. Ursula.
Arbor Day
Christmas
Columbus Day
Conversion of Mrs. Slacker, The
Decoration Day
Flag Day
Graduation Day
Humane citizens
Lincoln's birthday
New-Year's day
Old tight-wad and the victory dwarf
Parted sisters, The
Rich citizens
Soap-box orator, The
Thanksgiving day
Victory of the good citizen
Vision of Columbus, The
Washington's birthday
Payson, Stella T.
Society column, The
Peabody, Josephine P.
Fortune and men's eyes
Wings, The
Peacock, Leslie T.
Penultimate test, The
Victorious surrender of Lady Sybil, The
Pearce, Walter.
1588 (Fifteen hundred and eighty-eight)
Pearse, Padraic H.
Iosagan
Master, The
Singer, The
Pearson, Lilian.
How the Christmas song was found
Peile, F. Kinsey.
Tubby and Gawks
Peixotto, E. M.
Chips off the old block
Ding-a-ling
Evil that men do lives after them, The
Last rehearsal, The
Lost but found
Political promises
Rosie, the girl from Paris
Teacher's pet, The
Tramp barbers, The
When the cat is away
Pelée, Lillian S.
Ties of blood
Pemberton, H. L.
Backward child, A
Pemberton, May.
Christmas in Rhyme-land
Lost toys
Mistletoe and holly
Pender, Mrs. Frederick W.

His exceptional mother-in-law
Pendered, Mary L.
  Hymen á la mode
Penn, Gulielma.
  Plume of feathers, A
Perez, Isaac Loeb.
  Champagne
Pertwee, Roland.
  Loveliest thing, The
  Odd streak, The
  Postal orders
Peters, Rollo.
  Dream assassins, The
  Philosophers, The
Peterson, Frederick.
  Flutter of the goldleaf, The
Pfeiffer, Edward H.
  At the setting of the sun, tr.
  Lamp, The
Fhelps, Pauline.
  Box of powders, A, ed.
  Confederates, The, ed.
  Home from college
  Jack's brother's sister
  Saint Cecelia
  Witches' hour and candle light
Philips, Austin.
  Fourth man, The
  Playing the game
Phillips, Stephan.
  Nero's mother
Phillpotts, Eden.
  Pair of knickerbockers, A
Piaggio, Edward E.
  At the play
Picard, Louis B.
  Rebound, The
Pichel, Irving.
  Tom, Tom, the piper's son
Pierce, Carl W.
  Lady to call, A
  Laziest man in the world, The
  Mothers on strike; or, Local, number one
Pillot, Eugene.
  Gazing globe, The
  Hunger
  Just two men
  My lady dreams
  Two crooks and a lady
  Young wonder, The
Pinero, Arthur.
  Play goers
  Seat in the park, A
  Widow of Wasdale Head, The

Pinski, David.
  Abigail
  Bathesda
  Beautiful nun, The
  Cripples, The
  Diplomacy
  Dollar, A
  Forgotten souls
  God of the newly rich wool merchant, The
  In the harem
  Inventor and the king's daughter, The
  Little heroes
  Michael
  Phonograph, The
  Poland—1919
  Stranger, The
Pioneer, Gerald.
  Music hath charms
Piper, Edwin F.
  Land of the Aiouwas, The
Pirandello, Luigi.
  Sicilian limes
Pitt, Mrs. Frederick J. see **Cowan, Sada.**
Platt, Agnes E.
  Model growl
  When women rule
Pleasant, Lillian.
  Their godfather from Paris
Pohl, Frederick J.
  Laugh and grow wise
Pollock, Alice L.
  Resemblance, The
  Wireless
Poole, Evan.
  Blood Royal
  King's letters, The
  Post of honor, The
  Promise, The
Poole, Madeline.
  Christmas box, The
  Elf that stayed behind, The
  Goblins, The
  Lady to call, A
  Puritan prank, A
  Quaker way, The
Porter, B. C.
  Luck of Santa Claus, The
Porter, Eleanor H.
  Her old sweethearts
Porter, Helen T.
  Lady with the dagger, The, tr.
  Living hours, tr.
Porter, Laura S.

"Light of other days, The"
Porto-Riche, Georges de.
  Françoise' luck
Potter, Dorothy.
  "Bombast and platitudes"
  "Watchful waiting"
  Yellow yielding
Pound, Ezra.
  Anachronism at Chinoss, An
  Awoi no Uye
  Geiyo
  Hagoromo
  Kagekiyo
  Kakit Suhata
  Kayoi Komachi
  Kinuta
  Shojo
  Sotoba Komachi
  Suma Genji
  Tamura
  Tsunemasa
Powell-Anderson, Constance.
  Heart of a clown, The
Powell, H. P.
  Ain't women wonderful?
  Embalming Ebenezer
  Uncertain Silas
  You're it
Powers, Jay C.
  Bonnie's Christmas eve
  Day in court, A
  Elsie in Dreamland
Praigg, D. T.
  Marriage made easy
Prentiss, Janet.
  Inasmuch
Presbery, Eugene.
  Courtship of Miles Standish, The
Preston, E.
  A. D. 2000
  Gloom; or, Old grey barn, The
Preston, Effa E.
  Dolls on dress parade, The
  In a toy shop
  Party in Mother Goose land, A
  Strike in Santa Claus Land, A
  Thanksgiving dream, A
Preston, Harold P.
  Elopement, The
Preston, Mrs. W. H.
  Uncle Sam's flower garden
Price, Graham.
  Absolution of Bruce, The
  Coming of fair Annie, The
  Marriages are made in heaven— and elsewhere

Pritchard, George A.
  Prohibition Mother Goose
Prosser, William L.
  Free speech
Pryce, Richard.
  Dumb-cake
  Love child
  Op-o'-Me-Thumb
  Privy council
  Visit, The
Prydz, Alvilde.
  He is coming
Purcell, Lewis.
  Pagan, The
Putnam, Nina W.
  Orthodoxy

Quaife, Elise W.
  Emancipated ones, The
  Knitting girls count one, The
Quarella, David.
  Rounding the triangle
Quintero, Joaquin. see **Alvarez, Joaquin Quintero**
Quintero, Serafin. see **Alvarez, Serafin Quintero**
Quinton, Pauline B.
  Locust flower, The

Rabe, Margaret.
  Princess' choice, The
Rackstraw, E. C.
  "Make-believe"
Radcliffe, Claude.
  Holed out in one
Raeder, Henry.
  Dream of liberty, A
Raisbeck, Kenneth.
  Torches.
Raisin, Abraham.
  Bohemians
Ramsey, Alicia.
  Henkers Mahlzeit
Ranck, Edwin C.
  Yellow boots, The
Rand, Kenneth.
  Cliff of tears, The
Randall, William R.
  Gray overcoat, The
Randolph, Edith.
  Lammas eve
Raphael, Alice.
  Dormer windows
  Interlude in the life of St. Francis, An

Raphael, Rudolph.
  Professional visit, A
  Romance in porcelain, A
Rask, M. A.
  How the shrew was tamed
Rawley, Bert C.
  That black cat.
Rawson, Graham S.
  Dangers of peace, The
  Pastor of Jena, The
  Stroke of Marbot, The; or, Emperor at Melk, The
Recht, Charles.
  Bridegroom, The, tr.
  Grandmother, The, tr.
  Whom the Gods destroy, tr.
Rector, Jessie L.
  White elephant, The
Reed, Ethelyn.
  Intruder, The
Reed, John.
  Freedom
  Peace that passeth understanding, The
Reely, Mary Katherine.
  Daily bread
  Early Ohios and Rhode Island Reds
  Flittermouse
  Lean years, The
  Window to the south, A
Rees, Rosemary.
  Her dearest friend
Regnart, James.
  Mr. Brent's wife
Reim, Adolph E.
  Judge's secret, The
Reizenstein, Elmer L.
  Diadene of snow, A
  Home of the free, The
Relonde, Maurice.
  Farce of the worthy master, The
  In the dusk of the day
Renard, Jules.
  Carrots
  Good-bye!
Rethy, Joseph B.
  It might happen again
  Rialto and the drama, The
Reyher, Ferdinand.
  "Play's the things, The"
Rhoades, Nina.
  Girl who paid the bills
Rice, Cale Y.
  Ardiun
  Giorgione
  Immortal lure, The
  O-Ume's gods
Rice, Carolyn F.
  More time out
Rice, Katharine M.
  Mrs. Tubbs's telegram
Rice, Wallace.
  Children of France
  Children of the Civil War
  Children of the Great War
  Children of the Illini
  Pioneer boys and girls
  Underground railroad, The
Rice, Walter F.
  Winning ways
Richard, James C.
  Her busy day; or, Experience in housekeeping, An
Richards, Laura E.
  About angels
  Cake, The
  Child's play
  Cooky, The
  For you and me
  "Go and Come"
  Great feast, The
  Naughty comet, The
  "Oh Dear!"
  Sailor man, The
  Shadow, The
  Tangled skein, The
  Useful coal, The
  Wheat-field, The
Richardson, Frank.
  Bonnie Dundee
Richardson, Grace.
  Battle of the days, The
  Goblin guests
Richardson, Otis.
  Tweedledum
Richmond, Cecil J.
  Jimmy's ghosts
Richmond, Grace S.
  Honor—and The girl
  Perfect church, The
  When the boys came home
Richmond, Mrs. Herbert.
  Humpty dumpty
  Little Miss Muffet
Rickaby, Barbara.
  Waiting at the church
Rickaby, Franz.
  Fever ward, The
  His wife's place
  Waiting at the church

248　　　AN INDEX TO ONE-ACT PLAYS

Who kissed Barbara?
Rickaby, Lillian.
　Who kissed Barbara?
Ricketts, Alex.
　Assisted order, An
Riese, Edna.
　"Our career"
Riley, Mrs. Alice C.
　Poet's well, The
　Ten minutes by the clock
Riley, Alice C. D.
　Mandarin coat, The
　Their anniversary
Ring, Barbara T.
　$1,000,000 club paper, The
Rivoire, Andre.
　Little sheperdess. The
Robbins, Jack.
　Night, tr.
Roberts, Charles V. H.
　Octavia
Roberts, George N.
　Weasel, The
Roberts, Morley.
　Hour of greatness, The
　Lamp of God, The
　Lay figure, The
　White horse, The
Roberts, Octavia.
　Happy day, The
Robertson, Marion.
　"Afterwards"
Robins, Gertrude.
　Makeshifts
　Pot-luck
Robinson, Lennox.
　Clancy name, The
Robinson, Raymond M.
　Amateurs, The
　Fooling father
　Jerry's job
　Thief in the house, A
Robinson, Reed.
　His charity patient
Rock, Charles.
　Ghost of Jerry Bundler
　Gray parrot
Roeder, Ralph L.
　Holiday, The, tr.
　Nocturne
　Poole, The
Rogers, Fairfax S.
　Preferences
Rogers, Maude M.
　When the wheels run down
Rogers, Robert E.
　Behind a Watteau picture
　Boy will, The
　Cain
　Jester, The
　King, The
　Meeting, The
　Vagabond, The
　Watchers, The
Rogers, Thomas Badger.
　Eyes to the blind
　Forfeit, The
　Hall of laughter, The
　Heirloom, The
　Saint-King, The
Roof, Katharine M.
　Edge of the wood, The
　Secret, The
　Three dear friends
　Wanderer, The
　World beyond the mountain, The
Rosener, George M.
　Cure for husbands, A
　Great Winglebury duel, The
　Relations
　Sheriff of Tuckahoe, The
　Simp, The
　Sir Bob
　Successful failure, A
　Under London
　What married men do
　Where the trail ends
Rosenthal, Rosa.
　Realist, The
Ross, Clarendon.
　Avenger, The
　Derelict, The
　Murderer, The
　Prisoner, The
Ross, Jean.
　Magic chest, The
　Queen Loving Heart
Rossetti, Christina G.
　Months, The
Rostand, Edmond.
　Romancers, The
Rostetter, Alice.
　Widow's veil, The
Rowell, Adelaide C.
　Silly ass, The
Royle, Edwin M.
　Squaw-man, The
Ruck, Berta.
　G for George
Rupert, Everett H

AN INDEX TO ONE-ACT PLAYS

Matchmaker, The
Ruschke, Egmont W.
Death speaks
Echo, The
Intangible, The
Russell, Mary C.
Penelope's affinity
Russell, Mary M.
Outcome of a secret, The
Ryan, Estelle L.
Beginning of Negro slavery
Cherry pie
Christmas tree in New England
Departure, The
Easter rabbit
Encounter in the forest
First crop of apples
First winter
Gentlemen of Virginia
Indian gifts
Little pilgrims
Massasoit's illness
Narrow escape
Pilgrims in Holland
Pocahontas in London
Quakers in New England
Robert Morris
Saturday night in New England
Skirmish in Rensselaerswijck
Stormy times
Strategy of Director Kieft
Virginia children of long ago
Wampum belts
William Penn's treaty with the Indians

Sabao, Iao.
Gods, The
Sabin, Edwin L.
Dinner tale, The
Sackville, Margaret.
Coming of Hippolytus, The
Orpheus among the shades
Poet at the court of Pan, A
Voyage en Cythère, Le
Wooing of Dionysus, The
St. Clair, Winifred.
Snubbing of Fanny, The
St. Claire, Adelaide.
Iron Ann
St. John, Christopher.
Coronation, The
How the vote was won
Salten, Felix.
Count Festenberg.
Sander, Harold.

In other people's shoes
Larry
Lovebird's matrimonial agency
Married lovers, The
Matrimonial tiff
That little rogue next door
Won by a kodak
Sanders, Helen F.
Petalesharoo
Star brave, The
Sandiford, Betti P.
Crows
Sanford, Amelia.
Corner in strait-jackets
Sangster, Margaret E.
Nine pin club
Thanksgiving dream
Santayana, George.
Flight of Helen, The
Hermit of Carmel, A
Knight's return, The
Sargent, Fred L.
Object lesson, An
Omar and the Rabbi
Sargent, Herbert C.
Amateur rehearsal of Hamlet, An
American bar, The
Burlesque pantomime, A
Buying a house
Changeling, The
Emigration
"Hang it!"
In the library
Life insurance
Pavement artist, The
Prize picture, The
Registry office, The
That brute Simmons
Tourist agency, The
Sarkadi, Leo.
Line of life, The
Passing show, The
Vision of Paganini, A
Saunders, John M.
Love in a French kitchen
Saunders, Lillian.
Saltim bank, tr.
Night brings a counselor
Sob sister
Saunders, Louise.
Figureheads
King and Commoner
Knave of hearts, The
Our kind
See-saw
Woodland Princess, The
Saunders, Winnie.

Mother Goose's Christmas party
Sawyer, Ruth. *see* **Durand, Ruth S.**
Saxby, Charles.
  Reforming Bertie
Saxon, Edward.
  Spirit of Kiwanis, The
Sayemon, Enami No.
  Ukai
Schemberger, Lucille.
  Spirit of liberty
Scheneck, Frederick.
  Death and the dicers
Schering, Emil.
  Debit and credit, tr.
  Outcast, tr.
  Simoon, tr.
Schilling, Marie B.
  Who trimmed the Christmas tree?
Schindler, Anthony J.
  Home run, A
  Little mother, The
  Royal reception, A
Schlumberger, Jean.
  Césaire
Schnittkind, Henry T.
  Shambles
  Shunamite, The, tr.
Schnitzler, Arthur.
  Anatol's wedding morning
  Ask no questions and you'll hear no stories
  Big scene, The
  Christmas present, A
  Christmas shopping
  Countess Mizzie
  Dissolution
  Duke and the actress, The
  Dying pangs
  Episode, An
  Farewell supper
  Festival of Bacchus, The
  Gallant Cassian
  Green cockatoo, The
  His helpmate
  Hour of recognition, The
  Keepsakes
  Lady with the dagger, The
  Last masks
  Literature
  Living hours
  Mate, The
  Milestones
  Paracelsus
  Questioning fate
  Vital moments
  Wedding morning, The

Schreiner, Frances H.
  Betty's butler
  Cin 'n' buns
Schreiner, Lillian S.
  Jack's visitors; or, School boy's dream, The
  Miss Poinsettia
Schriever, Amelia.
  Sons of Adam, tr.
Schroll, Eleanor A.
  Christmas in Mother-Gooseville
  Highway robbers, The
Schuchert, Herman.
  Critics' catastrophe, The
Scott, Fitzgerald F.
  Débutanté, The
  Mr. Icky, the quintessence of quaintness
  Porcelain and pink
Scott, Margretta.
  Bag o' dreams, The
  Heart of Pierrot, The
Seaman, Abel.
  Looking for trouble
Seami.
  Atsumori
  Aya No Tsuzumi
  Hachi No Ki
  Hagoromo
  Haku Rakuten
  Ikeniye
  Kagekiyo
  Tsunemasa
Searle, Katharine.
  "Hatred"
  Her story
  March of truth, The
Searle, Margaret.
  Bad debts
Seat, Elizabeth F.
  Stockings' revolt, The
Seiffert, Marjory A.
  Old woman, The
Seitz, George B.
  Hildetna
Seldes, Gilbert V.
  Marionettes
  Outcasts
Selman, Harold.
  Mysterious will, The
  Doll's playhouse, The
Seltzer, Thomas.
  Love of one's neighbor, tr.
Selwyn, Edgar.
  When Danny came marching home

Seton-Thompson, Ernest.
  Wild animal play, The
Sexton, Ethelyn.
  Busy day in Bangville, A
  Miss Burnette puts one over
  Shakespeare up-to-date
Seymour, Mrs. Arthur T.
  Camp fire Cinderella, A
  Flossie's alphabet lesson
  Mystic seven; or, Law of the fire, The
  Protest of the trees, The
  Unselfish violet, The
Seymour, Edward M.
  Two jolly girl bachelors
Shapiro, Mathilde.
  Made in heaven
Sharp, L. A.
  King Christmas
Sharp, William.
  Birth of the soul, The
  Black Madonna, The
  Coming of the Prince, The
  Fallen God, The
  Finis
  Northern night, A
  Passing of Lilith, The
  Passion of Pére Hilarion, The
  Whisperer, The
Shaw, Frances.
  Person in the chair, The
Shaw, George B.
  Annajanska, the Bolshevik Empress
  Augustus does his bit
  Dark lady of the sonnets, The
  How he lied to her husband
  Inca of Perusalem, The
  O'Flaherty, V. C.
  Overruled
  Press cuttings
  Shewing-up of Blanco, The
Shaw, Mary.
  Parrot cage, The
  Woman of it, The; or, Our friends, the anti-suffragists
Sheehan, P. P.
  Efficiency
Sheldon, Edward B.
  Her final answer
Shepard, Frank H.
  Hunting for Hapgood
  Who are you?
Shephard, G. S.
  Before the rummage sale
Shepherd, Edmund E.
  Closed door, The
Shepherd, Esther.
  Jet
Sheridan, Emma.
  Wind and lady moon, The
Sherry, Laura.
  Mask, The
  On the pier
Shigeyoshi, Obata.
  Melon thief, The
Shipley, Joseph T.
  Echo
Shirley, Arthur.
  Gringoire, ed.
Shoemaker, Dora A.
  Patron of art, A
Short, Marion.
  Box of powder, A
  Confederates
  Jack's brother's sister
  Home from college
  Lights of happyland, The
  Pauline Pavlovna
  Room 83
  Saint Cecelia
  Witches' hour and candle light
Shute, Sally.
  Miss Todd's vampire
  Theodore, Jr.
Sierra, Gregorio Martinez.
  Love magic
  Lover, The
  Poor John
Simms, Evelyn.
  Divided attentions
  Hidden Harmonies
  Packet for Popsy
  Playing gooseberry
Simonson, Lee.
  Death and the young man
  Wise men, The
Simpson, Harold.
  Adam's apple
Sinclair, Upton.
  Second-story man, The
Singleton, Ina D.
  Untrue to type
Sites, Will C.
  Lady servant, A; or, Mistress for an hour
Skinner, Ada M.
  Mother Autumn and North Wind
  Nick Bluster's trick
  Professor Frog's lecture
  Royal toy-mender, A

Skinner, Eleanor L.
   Mother Autumn and North Wind
   Nick Bluster's trick
   Professor Frog's lecture
   Royal toy-mender, A
Slater, Joseph H.
   She couldn't marry three
Small, F. A.
   Love's diplomacy
Smedley, Katharine E.
   Hanging out the wash
Smith, Bessie B.
   Considerable courtship, A
   Parted by Patience
Smith, Beulah.
   Christmas shopping
Smith, Duckie.
   Pink scarf, The
Smith, E. E.
   Cottage on the moor, The
Smith, Edward H.
   Release
Smith, Evelyn.
   Cock and the fox, The
   Death of Balder, The
   Parlement of foules, The
   Perfect holiday, The
   Swineherd, The
Smith, Henry C.
   Bunk
   Junk; or, One of those Sunday mornings
   Punk; or, Amateur rehearsal, The
Smith, Howard Forman.
   Blackberryin'
   Rusty door, The
Smith, J. Kinchin.
   Mummers' play, The
Smith, Jay G.
   Forbidden fruit
Smith, Jennie S.
   Home guard, The
Smith, Jessica B.
   Lamp of heaven, The
Smith, Laura R.
   Hallowe'en carnival and wax-work show, A
   Hallowe'en Puppet play
   Historical Hallowe'en, An
   Jack Frost's surprise
   Witch's dream, The
Smith, Nora A.
   Crowning of peace, The
Smith, Rita C.
   Rescue, The
Smith, S. Decatur, Jr.
   Grandpa
   Jack and Jill
   Man's honor, A
   Mother Goose Christmas, A
   Restville auction sale, The
Smythies, W. Gordon.
   Love suit, A
Snook, Lee O.
   Mr. Richey changes his mind
Sobel, Bernard.
   Immortal
   Jennie knows
   Mrs. Bompton's dinner party
   Phoebe Louise
   There's always a reason
Sobel, Mae Stein.
   Call of God, The
   First temptation, The
   Golden calf, The
   Mother love finds a way
   Promised land, The
Solon, Israel.
   Biteless dog, The
Sombart, Petronelle.
   L'eroica, tr.
Someple, pseud.
   A. B. C. capers
   Bye, Baby Bunting
   Cock Robin
   Curly locks
   House that Jack built, The
   I have a little nut tree
   Nanny Etticoat
   Old Mother Goose
   Old woman and her pig, The
   Over the hills and far away
   Three-score miles and ten
   Twinkle-twinkle
Sommers, Hobart.
   All the world loves a lover
Soule, George.
   Last women, The
   Logical extreme, The
Souther, Bouve.
   Socialism and beauty
Sowerby, Githa.
   Before breakfast
Speare, Florence L.
   Bride and the burglar, The
   Jones versus Jones
Speenhoff, J. H.
   Louise
Spencer, Frances P.
   Dregs

Spenser, Willard.
　Carrying out a theory
Speyer, Lady.
　Love me, love my dog
Springer, Bessie W.
　Gassed
　Girl to order, A
Springer, Thomas G.
　Luckiest man, The
Stafford, John K.
　College days
Stagg, Katherine.
　Star Spangled Banner, The
Stange, Stanislaus.
　Man about town, A
Stanton, Frank J.
　Adam Goodwon
Stapp, Emilie B.
　Holly wreath, The
　Little gray lady, The
　Lost firewood, The
　Molly's New Year's party
　Mr. February Thaw
　Tadpole school, The
Stayton, Frank.
　Double cross, The
Stayton, Marianne.
　Mollie and the milliner
　Question of division, A
Stearns, Henry C.
　Mrs. Stubbins' book agent
Stechhan, H. O.
　Branded Mavericks
　Real "Q", The
Stedman, Adelaide.
　Substitute bride, The
Steele, Asa.
　Cure for hypnotism, A
　Greater than war
Steele, Wilbur Daniel.
　Ropes
Steell, Willis.
　Bride from home, A
　Brother Dave
　Faro Nell
　Fifth commandment, The
　Morning after the play, The
Stein, J. J.
　It's great to be crazy
Stephenson, B. C.
　Faithful James
Stephenson, Mary L.
　Dead are singing
Sterling, George.
　Dryad, The

　Rabbit-hutch, The
Sterling, Sara H.
　Hamlet's brides
Stevens, Caroline D.
　Elopements while you wait
Stevens, Henry B.
　All alone in the country
　Bolo and Babette
　Madhouse, The
　Meddler, The
Stevens, Thomas W.
　Gold circle, The
　Halbein in Blackfriars
　Nursery maid of heaven, The
　Ryland
　Three wishes
Stevens, Wallace.
　Carlos among the candles
　Three travelers watch a sunrise
Stevenson, Augusta.
　Beautiful song, The
　Bernard Palissy, Enameller to his
　　Majesty
　Blind men and the elephant, The
　Cat and the mouse, The
　Cat that waited, The
　Christmas pitcher, The
　Clever cock, The
　Clever kid, The
　Crow and the fox, The
　Each in his own place
　Endless tale, The
　Fairy and the cat, The
　Fishing on dry land
　Golden bucket, The
　Hare and the hedgehog, The
　Hare and the tortoise, The
　Honest critic, An
　Honest woodman, The
　House of brick, The
　How a prince was saved
　In bad company
　King Alfred and the cakes
　King's good friend, The
　Lafayette's toast
　Little fish, The
　Mill that ground hot porridge, The
　Miller, his son, and their donkey,
　　The
　Moon's silver cloak, The
　Old man and his grandson, The
　Pen and the inkstand, The
　Pot of gold, The
　Piece of cheese, A
　Proud finger-ring, The
　Puppet Princess, The; or, Heart
　　that squeaked, The
　Selfish woman, The

Shepherd-boy who called wolf, The
Sick deer, The
Tracks to the den
Travellers and the hatchet, The
Two countrymen, The
Two holes, The
Vain jackdaw, The
Wise crow, The
Wish-bird, The
Wolf and the horse, The
Wolf and the lamb, The

Stevenson, Edward I.
Revolt of the Holidays, The

Stewart, Anna B.
Belles of Canterbury, The

Stewart, Charles, pseud. see **Walsh, Charles Stewart**

Stewart, William C.
My milliner's bill

Stickney, Joseph T.
Prometheus Pyrphoros

Stigler, W. A.
Be sociable
Little owl

Stockbridge, Dorothy.
Jezebel

Stockton, Dora H.
Golden wedding, The

Stokes, Charles W.
Door, The

Stoll, Lillian.
Trying them out

Storer, Edward.
Helen

Stork, Charles W.
Idyll, tr.

Stout, Rex T.
Victory of love, The

Stramm, August.
Sancta Susanna

Stratton, Charles.
Coda, The
Ruby Red

Strauss, Rita.
"In bells and motley"; or, May Queen, The
Wooden shoe, The; or, St. Valentine's day

Streatfield, Mrs. Eric, see **Barne, Kitty**

Strindberg, August.
Creditor, The
Debit and credit
Link, The
Miss Julia
Motherly love
Outcast, The
Pariah
Simoon
Stronger, The
Stronger woman, The
Swanwhite

Strong, Austin.
Drums of Oude, The

Strong, Grace C.
Girl and the undergraduate, The
Marrying Belinda
Templeton tea pot, The

Stuart, Charles M.
Dent's office boy

Stuart, Muriel.
Andromeda unfettered

Sturgis, Granville Forbes.
Butcher's daughter, The
College joke, A
Fatal pill, The
Just before dawn
Little Colombine
Madame
Our Mary
Red roses
Two of a kind
Widow Sabrina, The
Winning a husband

Sturgis, R. Clipston, Jr.
Spectator No. 558

Sturgis, Rebecca Forbes.
One war babe

Suckow, Ruth.
What King Christmas brought

Sudermann, Hermann.
Far-away Princess, The
Eternal masculine, The
Fritzchen
Last visit, The
Margot
Morituri: Teias
Streaks of light
Teja

Susman, Harold.
In the Ballingers' box
Mrs. Potter Buys a Present

Sutherland, Evelyn G.
At the barricade
Bit of instruction, A
Comedie Royall, A
End of the way, The
Galatea of the Toy-shop
In Aunt Chloe's cabin
In far Bohemia
In office hours

Po' White trash
Quilting party in the thirties, A
Rohan the Silent
Song at the castle, A
Story of a famous wedding, The

Sutphen, Van Tassel.
Unequal triangle, An

Sutro, Alfred.
Boy and a girl, A
Bracelet, The
Carrots, tr.
Correct thing, The
Ella's apology
Game of chess
Gutter of time, The
Maker of men
Man in the stalls, The
Man on the kerb, The
Marriage has been arranged, A
Marriage will not take place, The
Mr. Steinman's corner
Open door, The
Salt of life, The

Sutton, Vida R.
Mantle of the Virgin, The
Pilgrims' holiday, The

Swain, Corrine R.
Christmas babes in the woods
Maeterlinckian moving day, A

Swan, Arthur.
Julie, tr.

Swanson, Roy W.
Criminals

Swears, Herbert.
Cupboard love
Dog days
Granny's Juliet
Hero and heroine
Tit-bits
Widows
Young idea, The

Symon, J. D.
Conscript Fathers, The

Symons, Arthur.
Barbara Roscorla's child
Cleopatra in Judaea
Dance of the seven deadly sins, The
Death of Agrippina, The

Synge, John M.
Riders to the sea
Shadow of the glen, The

Syrett, Netta.
Christening of Rosalys, The
Christmas in the forest
Dream-lady, The
Enchanted garden, The

Fairy doll, The
In Arcady
Little Bridget
Old toys, The
Princess Fragoletta
Queen Flora's court
Robin Goodfellow
Strange boy, The
Two domestics
White magic
Wonderful rose, The

Taft, Grace E.
Chimalman
Tecpancaltzin
Teo Teuctli

Taft, Linwood.
Christmas mystery

Tag, Ralph W.
Conquest of Helen, The
Handy Solomon
Transaction in stocks, A

Tagore, Rabindranath.
Chitra
Sacrifice

Taketomo, Torao.
Mulan

Tanner, Beryl.
Well matched pair, A

Tarkington, Booth.
Beauty and the Jacobin
Ghost story, The
Trysting place, The

Taylor, Charles E.
Weary Willie

Taylor, J. M.
Man from Brandon, The
Telegram from dad, A

Taylor, L. M.
Cockcrow

Tchekoff, Anton. *see* **Chekhov, Anton**

Teasdale, Sara.
On the tower

Teleki, Joseph.
Actress, The

Telford, Mary E.
Children's Christmas dream, The

Terrell, Maverick.
Branded Mavericks
Honi Soit
Other fellow, The
Real "Q," The
Temperament
When Greek meets Greek
You never can tell about a woman

Terry, J. E. Harold.
Master Wayfarer
Theis, Grover.
Between fires
Crack in the bell, The
Like a book
Numbers
There's a difference
Theuriet, André.
Jean-Marie
Thomas, Augustus.
Man upstairs, The
Thomas, Brandon.
Colour-sergeant, The
Thomas, Charles.
Breaking the ice; or, Piece of holly, A
Thomas, Edith M.
White messenger, The
Thomas, Kate.
Bit of nonsense, A
Evening at Helen's, An
Thomason, Caroline.
Bluebeard
Three bears, The
Thompson, Alice C.
Auction at Meadowville, An
Aunt Matilda's birthday party
Broken engagement, A
Coming of Annabel, The
Day of the Duchess, The
Fudge and a burglar
Good old days, The
Hannah gives notice
Her scarlet slippers
Honest Peggy
Irish invasion, An
Katie's new hat
Knot of white ribbon, A
Luckiest girl, The
Miss Deborah's pocket book
Miss Susan's fortune
Much too sudden
Oysters
Peck of trouble, A
Red parasol, The
Return of Letty, The
Susan's finish
Suffragette baby, A
Truth about Jane, The
Truth, the mischief
Wrong baby, The
Thompson, Blanche J.
Dream maker, The
Thompson, Harlan.
Geometrically speaking
Man hunt, The

One by one
Pants and the man
Thompson, Lillian B.
"Narrow squeak, A"
Thorne-Thomsen, Mrs. Gudrun.
Tramp and a night's lodging, A
Thornton, Clare.
Marriage of Dotty, The
Thorp, Annie L.
Lighting of the Christmas tree, The
Thorpe, Josephine.
Answer, The
Torch, The
Treasure chest, The
When Liberty calls
Thursby, Charles.
Coronation
Thurston, Althea.
Exchange, The
Tibbals, Seymour S.
Christmas beyond the trenches
In Dixie land
Letter from home, A
Pandora's box
Tilden, Freeman.
Enter Dora—exit Dad
Tildesley, A. L.
Cast rehearses, The
Marrying money
Tinsley, Lily.
Cinders
Tobey, James A.
Jewels of Cornelia, The
Tobin, Bertha I.
Land of vacation, The
Uninvited guest, The
Tomes, Margaret O.
Children and the Evangelists, The
Tompkins, Frank G.
In front of Potter's
Sham
Topelius, Zakarias.
Bride's crown, The
Field of enchantment, The
Troll King's breakfast, The
Torrence, Ridgely.
Granny Maumee
Rider of dreams, The
Simon the Cyrenian
Totheroh, Dan W.
In the darkness
Tune of a tune, A
While the mushrooms bubble
Widdy's mite, The

Tourgenieff, Ivan.
  One may spin a thread too finely
Towne, Charles H.
  Aliens, The
Townley, Morris M.
  Caught
Townsend, Charles.
  Other one, The
  Too much married
Trader, George H.
  Shakespeare's daughter
Tree, H. B.
  Six and eight pence
Trelawney, Dangerfield.
  Old stuff
Trent, John J.
  Owin' to Maggie
  Triumph of Pauline, The
Trevor, Major P.
  Under the greenwood tree
  Looking-glass, The
Tridon, Andre.
  Tenor, The, tr.
  Virgin and the white slaver, The
Tritch, Martha.
  Isotta's trummp
True, Mary E.
  In moonbeams
Tubbs, Arthur L.
  Double deception, A
  Not on the bills
  Too much Galatea
Tucker, Louise E.
  At anchor
  Beginning of Negro slavery, The
  Cherry pie
  Christmas tree in New England, A
  Departure, The
  Easter rabbit, The
  Encounter in the forest, An
  First crop of apples, The
  First winter, The
  Gentlemen of Virginia
  How the Indians planted powder
  Indian gifts
  Little Pilgrims
  Massasoit's illness
  Narrow escape, A
  Pilgrims in Holland, The
  Pocahontas in London
  Quakers in New England, The
  Robert Morris and the Revolution
  Saturday night in New England
  Skirmish at Rensselaerswijck, A
  Stormy times
  Strategy of Director Kieft, The
  Virginia children of long ago
  Wampum belts
  William Penn's treaty with the Indians
Tull, Jewell B.
  Slacker, The
Tupper, Edith S.
  Thou shalt not steal
Tupper, Wilbur S.
  Bargain, The
  Figs and thistles
  In Toscana tavern
  Mr. Fraser's friends
  Onesimus
Twelve, Mellis.
  Turtle-doves

Ukáinka, Lésya.
  Babylonian captivity, The
Ulrich, Charles.
  Editor-in-chief
  Political editor, The
  Road-agent, The
Underhill, John G.
  His widow's husband, tr.
  Love magic, tr.
  Lover, The, tr.
  No smoking, tr.
  Poor John, tr.
  Street singer, The, tr.
Upper, Joseph.
  At the movies
Urquhart, Elizabeth.
  Suited at last; or, Sauce bordelaise

Vail, Lawrence.
  Popopelka
Valcros, W.
  Sabotagi
Van Derveer, Lettie C.
  Christmas picture, The
  Lonely little evergreen, The
Van Dresser, Jasmine S.
  Eight-thirty sharp
  Young D'Arcy
Vane, Larry.
  Great medical dispensary, The
Van Etten, Gerard.
  Vampire cat
Van Vechten, Hostetter.
  Peace on earth
Van Volkenburg, Carlton.
  Found in a closet

Varney, Alice S.
 Christmas
 Circus, The
 Daisy, The
 Don't count your chickens until they are hatched
 In union there is strength
 Welcoming the New Year
Varney, Horace.
 Watching for Santa Claus
Vasquez, José Andrés.
 With chains of gold
Vercill, Cornelia C.
 On vengeance height
Verconsin, Eugene.
 Fond delusion
Verga, Giovanni.
 Wolf-hunt, The
Vermilye, Kate J.
 Pompadour's protégé, The
Vickers, George M.
 Public worrier
Viereck, George S.
 Butterfly, The
 From death's own eyes
 Game at love, A
 Mood of a moment, The
 Question of fidelity, A
Viets, Edward.
 Masque of morning, The
 Masque of evening, The
 Noon
Vilas, Faith Van V.
 Fiat Lux (Let there be light)
 Tears of dawn
Vizin, Denis von.
 Choice of a tutor, The
Vosburgh, Maude B.
 Health champions, The
 Miss Maria
Vrchlicky, Jaroslav, pseud. *see* **Frida, Emil**
Vreeland, F. J.
 Fleeing flyer, The

Waddell, Leila.
 Hippodrome horror, The
Wagstaff, Blanche S.
 Colonial Virginia
 Crepuscule
 First Thanksgiving, The
 Georgia debtors, The
 Greater voice, The
 Indian story, An
 Life in New York
 Pennsylvania incident, A

 Revolutionary days
 Three compromises of the Constitution
 Witchcraft story, A
Walbrook, Henry M.
 Touch of truth, The
Waldo, Dorothy.
 Idowanna
 Kid curlers
Waldo, Fullerton L.
 Seashell, The
Waley, Arthur.
 Early snow, ed.
Walker, Dugald S.
 Dream boats
Walker, Francis.
 Prince's pigeon, The
Walker, Stuart.
 Birthday of the Infanta, The
 Medicine show, The
 Nellijumbo
 Nevertheless
 Sir David wears a crown
 Six who pass while the lentils boil
 Trimplet, The
 Very naked boy, The
Walkes, W. R.
 Major explains, The
 Pair of lunatics, A
 Show of hands, A
 Villain and victim
Wallace, A. C.
 Chrysanthemums
Wallace, Emma G.
 Flag of courage, The
Wallis, Ellen L.
 Cissy's engagement
Walsh, Charles S.
 Chance at mid-night, A
Walsh, Thomas.
 Goya in the Cupola
Walter, Elizabeth.
 Death and the fool. tr.
Wangenheins, Alice.
 Cave of precious things, The
Warden, Florence.
 Dolly's week-end; or, Tale of the speaking-tube, The
Warnock, A. McClure.
 Ramlet o' Puce, A
Warren, Ernest.
 "Nettle, The"
Warren, Gladys E.
 Cherry-Blossom Princess, The
 Paradise of children, The

Warren, Marie J.
  Substance of ambition
  Mistletoe and Holly-berry
Warren, Prescott.
  Day that Lincoln died, The
Watkins, Dwight E.
  Freddy goes to college
Watson, Evelyn.
  Our minister's bride
Watson, John.
  Duchess entertains, The
  Estamine, The!
Watson, Malcolm.
  Conversion of Nat Sturge
  Pretty bequest, A
Watson, William.
  King without peer, The
Watts, Mary S.
  Civilization
  Wearin' o' the green, The
Waugh, Constance E.
  Aunt Penelope
  Under distinguished patronage
Webb, Jessie M.
  Spirit of liberty, The
Webber, James P.
  End of the rainbow, The
  Golden arrow
Wedekind, Frank.
  Court singer, The
  Heart of a tenor, The
  Tenor, The
  Virgin and the white slaver, The
Weil, Morton.
  Room 83
Weil, P. L. *see* **Wilde, Percival.**
Weinberger, Mildred.
  Elaine
Weir, F. Roney.
  Cuckoo's nest, The
Welldon, S. A.
  Treason
Wellman, Rita.
  Dawn
  For all time
  Funiculi Funicula
  Lady with the mirror, The
Wells, Carolyn.
  April's lady
  Christmas gifts of all nations
  Day before Christmas, The
  Dolly dialogue
  Fairest spirit, The
  Greatest day in the year, The
  Greatest gift, The
  Is Santa Claus a fraud?
  Meaning of Thanksgiving day
  Night-before, The
  Once upon a Christmastime
  Play lovers, The
  Queen Christmas
  Substitute for Santa Claus, A
  Sweet girl graduate, The
Welsh, Robert G.
  Jezebel
Wendell, Barrett.
  Rosamond
Wendt, Frederick W.
  Dies Irae
Wentworth-James, Gertie de S.
  Cure that failed, The
Wentworth, Marion C.
  War brides
West, Duffy R.
  Society notes
West, Louise Bronson.
  Whole truth, The
West, Stanley C.
  Settled out of court
Westermayr, A. J.
  Yoshiwara
Westlake, A. L.
  Boasts—and a Bruise
Weston, Effie E.
  Substitute, The
Wetzel, George J.
  Pride and charity
Weysz, Hans.
  Duke and the actress, tr.
Whaite, H. Hoyle.
  Fidelitas
Wharton, Anthony.
  Nocturne
  13 Simon Street
Wheeler, Edith.
  Sentence, The
  Woman's way, A
Wheelock, John Hall.
  Paris and Aenone
White, Clematis.
  Convert, A
White, Ernest G.
  Bad beginning, A
White, Florence D.
  Magic theatre, tr.
White, James P.
  Emancipated, The
  School of life, The
  Tower of silence, The

Wayside comedy, A
White, Kate A.
Traveling photographer, The
White, Lucy.
Bird child, The
Whitehill, Elizabeth.
Rummage sale at Hickory Hollow, The
Whitelock, William W.
All in the family
Whitford, Mary V.
Ingenuous grandmother
Whiting, Eleanor C.
Ashes
Common ground
Whiting, Evelyn G.
Gone abroad
No admittance
Whiting, Maisie B.
Mrs. Carver's fancy ball
Two aunts and a photo
Whitman, A. E.
Getting rid of father
Whitworth, Geoffrey.
Father Noah
Wick, J. Mae C.
Radio Christmas, A; or, Christmas in Room 326
Wickes, Frances G.
Baucis and Philemon
Captured year, The
First May baskets, The
Light, The
Thankful heart, The
St. Valentine's house
Wied, Gustav.
Autumn fires
Wigginton, Wilma.
Three rogues and a rascal
Wilbur, Harriette.
Haste makes waste
Keeping Christmas
Wilbur, Helen C.
Kidnapping, The
Wilcox, Constance.
Four of a kind
Mother Goose garden
Pan pipes
Princess in the fairy tale, The
Told in a Chinese garden
Wild, Caroline S. P.
Kettle sings, The; or, Domestic conscience, The
Wilde, Oscar.
Salome

Wilde, Percival.
According to Darwin
Beautiful story, The
Catesby
Confessional
Culprit, The
Dawn
Dyspeptic ogre, The
Embryo
Finger of God, The
His return
House of cards, A
In the net
In the ravine
Line of no resistance, The
Mothers of men
Noble lord, The
Pawns
Playing with fire
Previous engagement, The
Question of morality, A
Reckoning, The
Saved!
Sequel, The
Traitor, The
Unseen host, The
Valkyrie!
Villain in the piece, The
Wonderful woman, A
Wilder, Marion.
Another man's place
Wiley, Sara K.
Football game, The
Patriots
Wilkes, Wilhemen.
Outsider, An
Wilkie, John E.
Interrupted operation, An
Wilkins, Eva.
Brogues of Kilavain Glen, The
Wilkinson, Ella C.
Freddy's great aunt
Madame de Portment's school
Wilkinson, Geoffrey.
Cure for indifference, A
Willard, Ellen M.
All the year 'round
Boy's Christmas, A
Christmas bargain, A
First Christmas, The
King of the year, The
Mrs. Randy's Christmas
Santa Claus' garden
Santa Claus in many lands
Spirit of Christmas, The
Willard, George H.
Mustard plasters, The

Wilcox, Helen L.
  Test, The
Willett, Edith M.
  His lordship, the burglar
Williams, E. Harcourt.
  Little Tuk's dream
  Snow-white and Rose-red
  Three bears, The
Williams, Frayne.
  Blue vase, The
  Man with the bundle, The
  Rose garden, The
Williams, H. Isabelle.
  Pitiless policeman, The
Williams, Mrs. Harry A.
  On the stairway of life in seven ages
Williams, M. J.
  Helpless couple, A
Williams, Thomas J.
  Ici on parle francais
Williamson, Anne E.
  Christmas stars
Williamson, Harold.
  Peggy
Wilmarth, Phil. R.
  Goo-goo
Wills, Anthony E.
  Heirs-at-law
  Benjamin, Benny and Ben
Wilson, Bertha M.
  Mr. Spriggs' little trip to Europe
  Raggles' corner
Wilson, Carolyn.
  What can I do?
Wilson, J. Raines.
  Trial of the heart, The
Wilson, Leila W.
  Like father, like son
Wilson, Leisa G.
  Lady loses her hoop, The
Wilson, Lillian P.
  Being the fly
  Empty shrine, The
  Episode, An
  Fruit of toil, The
  Living
  Returning the calculus
  This is the law
  Voice on the stair, A
  Weight of wings, The
Wilson, Louise L.
  All on account of an actor
  Fortunes of war, The
  Little game with fate, A

  Parliament of servants, A
  Priscilla's room
Wilson, Olivia L.
  Cobbler's bargain
  Honeymoon, The
  Irish washerwoman
  Learning lessons
  Left
  School opera
Wishing, Stuart.
  Sevres tea-cups, The
  Silver salt-cellars, The
Wolff, Oscar M.
  Where but in America
Wolff, Pierre.
  Unhoodwinkable
Wolfrom, Anna.
  Danny
  Marriage certificate, The
  New race, The
  Old shoes
  Ripening wheat
  Will-o'-wisp, A
Woodbridge, Elizabeth.
  Christmas conspiracy, The
Woodhouse, Vernon.
  Affinities
  How they kept her
Woodman, Rea.
  Bad case of microbes, A
  Buying a day
  Fashionable calls
  In the market place
  January styles
  "Those dreadful vity-mines!"
Woodrow, Mrs. Wilson.
  Universal impulse, The
Woodruff, Robert W.
  Death
Woods, Marjory.
  Birthday ball, The
Woolf, Edgar A.
  Bit of the world, A
Woolf, Henry.
  Dream book, The
Wormser, Florine R
  Portrait, The
Wormwood, Edyth M.
  Haunted gate, The
  No girls admitted
Worrell, Edna R.
  Christmas harvest, The
  Corner in hearts, A
  Dream come true, A
  Flag makers, The

Messenger birds, The
Shouting the battle cry of "Feed 'em"
Toys' rebellion, The
Two merry wagers

Wright, Earl.
Yankee and the pagan, The

Wright, Harriet S.
Birthday of the Infanta, The
On the old plantation
Three Sundays in a week

Wupperman, Carlos S.
Helios, tr.

Wynne, Anna.
Broken bars, The
On the path of the child

Yasukiyo, Hiyoshi Sa-ami.
Benkei on the bridge

Yeats, William B.
At the hawk's well
Calvary
Cathleen in Hoolihan
Countess Cathleen, The
Deirdre
Dreaming of the Bones, The
Green helmet, The
Hour glass, The
King's threshold, The
Land of heart's desire, The
On Baile's strand
Only jealousy of Emer, The
Pot of broth, A
Shadowy waters, The

Yehoash, pseud. *see* **Bloomgarden, Solomon.**

Young, Laurence D.
Iceman, The

Young, O. E.
All stars; or, Manager's trials, A
Axin' her father

Back from the Philippines; or, Major Kelly's cork leg
Backtown spirits; or, Two under the table
Betsey's boarders
Little red mare, The
Pat the apothecary
Pickled polliwog
Popping by Proxy
Sampson's courtin'
Striped sweater, The
When doctors disagree
Wives wanted in Squashville
Won by a wager

Young, Rida J.
John Clayton, Actor
Last of the Cargills, The

Young, Roland K.
Missing guest, The

Young, Stark.
Addio
At the shrine
Dead poet, The
Madretta
Queen of Sheba, The
Seven kings and the wind, The
Star in the trees, The
Twilight saint, The

Young, William.
Woman's wiles

Yuill, A. W.
Glenforsa

Zamacois, Eduardo.
Passing of the magi, The

Zenchiku Ujinobu.
Aoi No Uye
Hoko Priests, The
Kumasaka
Taniko

Zeigler, Francis I.
Stronger, The, tr.

SUBJECT INDEX

ANCIENT HISTORY
Babylonian captivity, The
Cleopatra in Judea
Hermit of Carmel, A
King, The
Morraca
Page from the past, A
Salome

ARABIAN
Bluebeard
Hand of the Prophet, The
How a prince was saved
New day, The
Two talismans, The

ARBOR DAY
Arbor Day.—"Anychild helps the baby tree"
April's lady
Birds' story of the trees, The

ARTS
Aegean, The
Disciples of art
Parthenon, The
Prince of court painters, The
Seeing the pictures

AZTEC
Chimalman
Tecpancaltzin
Teoteuctli

BIBLE
Abigail
Call of God, The
Call of Samuel, The
Chaste adventures of Joseph, The
Comedy of the Exile, A
Daughter of Jephthah, The
Esther
Father Noah
First temptation, The
Gift, The
Golden calf, The
Good Friday
Good Samaritan, The

Jael
Jephthah's daughter
Judgment of Solomon, The
Lazarus
Message of Lazarus
Moses in the bulrushes
Mother love finds a way
Nazareth
Onesimus
Prodigal son, The
Promised land, The
Sacrifice
Shunamite, The
Sin of Ahab, The
Sisters of Susannah
Snaring the lion
Solomon's song
Story of Jacob
Wooing of Mary of Magdela, The

BOARDING SCHOOL
All the world loves a lover
Bit of nonsense, A
Case of Sophronia, The
Fudge and a burglar
Honor of the class, The
In other people's shoes
Mad! Mad!
Madame de Portment's school
Maid to order
Miss Burnett puts one over
'Neath the scepter of Susan
Outsider, An
Pan of fudge, A
Romance by schedule
Sing a song of seniors
Uninvited member, An

BUSINESS
Boob The
Dent's office boy
Everycreditman
Great doughnut corporation, The
Maker of men
Taking father's place

CAMP FIRE
Camp Fire Cinderella, A
Camp-fire girl, The

Mystic seven, The
Oneida's dream
Taming of Horrors, The

CANADA

Door, The
Crows
Pathfinder
Unnecessary atom, The
Where the trail ends

CHINESE

Blue vase, The
Cat and the cherub, The
Chi-Fu
Chinese love
Cow-herd and the weaving maid, The
Dragon's claws, The
Empty city, The
Invention of the rat trap, The
Journey, The
Lamp of heaven, The
Mulan
Singing soul, The
Sweetmeat game, The
"Tongmen, The"
Turtle dove, The
Veil of happiness, The
Wedding of Mah Foy, The

CHRISTMAS

All his fault
All the Year 'Round
Anita's secret
Aunt Sabriny's Christmas
Bachelor Club's baby, The
Betty Jane's Christmas dream
Boastful giant, The
Boastful weathervane, The
Bonnie's Christmas Eve
Bo-Peep's Christmas party
Boy who found Christmas, The
Boy's Christmas, A
Bride's Christmas tree, The
Broken picture, The
Brownie's vacation, The
Bye, Baby Bunting
Children of the Christmas spirit
Children's Christmas dream, The
Christmas
Christmas at Holly Farm
Christmas at Punkin Holler
Christmas at Skeeter Corner
Christmas at the Cross Roads
Christmas babes in the woods, The
Christmas bargain, A
Christmas benefit, A

Christmas box, The
Christmas boxes
Christmas Brownie, The
Christmas Carol, A
Christmas chime, A
Christmas conspiracy, The
Christmas cookies, The
Christmas dinner, The
Christmas dream, A
Christmas eve
Christmas Eve at the Mulligans
Christmas for all nations
Christmas for Santa Claus, A
Christmas gifts of all nations
Christmas guest, The
Christmas harvest, The
Christmas idea, The
Christmas in Mother-Gooseville
Christmas in Rhyme-land
Christmas in the air
Christmas in the forest
Christmas influence
Christmas joke, A
Christmas journey, A
Christmas message, The
Christmas mix-up, A
Christmas morality play, A
Christmas mystery, A
Christmas of the Little Pines, The
Christmas party, A
Christmas picture, The
Christmas pitcher, The
Christmas rainbow, A
Christmas shopping
Christmas speakin' at Skagg's Skule
Christmas spirit, The
Christmas stars
Christmas stockings
Christmas story, The
Christmas strike, A
Christmas surprise for Mother Goose, A
Christmas sympathy
Christmas tree, The
Christmas tree joke, A
Christmas visitors from other lands
Christmas wishes
Christmas with the Mulligan's
Conspirators, The
Corner in hearts, A
Day before Christmas, The
Discouraged worker, A
Doing away with Christmas Dolls
Double Christmas gift, A
Dream on Christmas Eve
Dream-toy shop, The
Eager heart

AN INDEX TO ONE-ACT PLAYS

Fairies' Christmas, The
Fairy Good-will
Father Time's Christmas trial
Feast in the wilderness, A
Fiat Lux. (Let there be light)
First Christmas, The
First Christmas Eve, The
Four little fir trees
Gift of time, The
Gifted givers, The
Grandfather's bright Christmas plan
Great sale, The
Greatest gift, The
Hanging up the stockings
Herbert's discovery
Holly wreath, The
Holy scenes of Christmas, The
How Christmas was saved
How the Christmas song was found
In a toy shop
In the East
Inasmuch
Is Santa Claus a fraud
Jolliest Christmas ever, The
Joy of giving, The
Keeping Christmas
King Christmas
Kingdom of love, The
"Light of other days, The"
Lighting of the Christmas tree, The
Little helpers
Little Jack's Christmas
Luck of Santa Claus, The
Man who didn't believe in Christmas, The
Manger service
Merry Christmas
Merry Christmas Jake
Messenger birds, The
Minister's daughter, The
Minty-Malviny's Santa Claus
Miss Poinsettia
Mistletoe
Mistletoe and holly
Mistletoe and Holly-berry
Molly's Christmas tree
Mother Goose Christmas, A
Mother Goose's Christmas party
Mr. Richey changes his mind
Mrs. Randy's Christmas
Mrs. Santa Claus, Militant
Next day, The
Night-before, The
No Christmas in the house
"No presents"
Ola
Old friends together

On Christmas Eve
Once upon a Christmastime
Our Uncle from the West
Pickett's Christmas party, The
Pink scarf, The
Plaie for Merrie May Tyme, A
Puppet princess, The
Queen Christmas
Quest of Christmas, The
Radio Christmas, A
Reception for Santa Claus, A
Revolt of Santa Claus, The
Revolt of the Holidays, The
Road to Christmas, The
Santa Claus brigade, The
Santa Claus gets his wish
Santa Claus in many lands
Santa Claus or papa
Santa Claus' garden
Santa's allies
Santa's rescue
Search for Mother Goose, The
Spirit of Christmas, The
Star of Bethlehem, The
Stockings' revolt, The
Strike in Santa Claus land, The
Substitute for Santa Claus, A
Surprising Santa
Ten fingers of François, The
"Through Christmas bells"
Top of the world, The
Topsy turvy Christmas, A
Toys' Rebellion, The
Trials of Christmas shopping
Trimming of the tree, The
Trouble in the Toy room
True Christmas spirit, The
Uncle Grouch
Uncle Sam to the rescue
Uncle Sam's mistake
Under distinguished patronage
Unexpected company
Unsuccessful hunt, An
Violet under the snow, The
Visit of the Tomiter, The
Visit of Santa Claus, A
Wanted: a chimney
Watchers, The
Watching for Santa Claus
What Christmas did for Jerusha Grumble
What King Christmas brought
When Do-it school entertained
Which shall be king?
White Christmas, The
Who trimmed the Christmas tree?
Why Christmas was late
Wise men, The
Worm turns, The
Young Mr. Santa Claus

COLLEGE

Arrival of Reuben, The
Aunt Abigail and the boys
College joke, A
Football game, The
Fortunes of war, The
Fraternity
Girl and the undergraduate, The
Girl to order, A
Music hath charms
Priscilla's room
Returning the calculus
Rooms to let
Telegram from dad, A
When mother came to college
Widow Sabrina, The

COLUMBINE

Colombine
Coming of Columbine, The
Little Columbine
Vision of youth, A

COLUMBUS DAY

Columbus Day.—"Columbus helps Anychild"
Diego's dream

COMMENCEMENT DAY

Class ship, The
Fairest spirit, The
Good-Bye All!
Graduate's choice, The
Graduation Day
Just plain Dot
Land of vacation, The
Last day of school, The
Our choice
Senior, The
Sweet girl graduate, The
Up-to-date America

CONSERVATION

Brave foresters
Salvage

DETECTIVE

Gray overcoat, The
Queen of diamonds, The
Watch, a wallet and a jack of spades, A

DRAMATIZATIONS

Alcott, Louise M.
Effie's Christmas dream
Jack and Jill
Perfect holiday, The

Aldrich, Thomas Bailey.
Pauline Pavlovna
Austin, Alfred.
Savonarola and Lorenzo
Barr, Robert.
Gentlemen, the King
Beaumont and Fletcher.
Ricardo and Viola
Bennett, John.
Barnaby Lee
Master Skylark
Brown, Alice.
Mistletoe
Browning, Robert
Omar and the Rabbi
Byr, Robert.
Love conquers revenge
Carroll, Lewis.
Through the looking-glass
Chaucer.
Cock and the fox, The
Death and the dicers
Parlement of foules
Colman, George.
Military and medicine
Coppee, Francois.
Fennel
Crawford, F. Marion.
Extracting a secret
Curry, Sara Jefferis.
Devil's gold, The
Deland, Margaret.
Miss Maria
Dickens, Charles.
At "Jenny Wren's"
Bardwell vs. Pickwick
Betsey Trotwood at home
Christmas carol
Christmas eve
Disastrous announcement, A
Division between friends, A
Friendly waiter, The
Gentleman next door, The
Great Protestant association, The
Great Winglebury duel, The
Hatching a conspiracy
Holly Tree Inn
Miggs' revenge
Miss Squeers' tea-party
Mr. George's shooting-gallery
Mr. Guppy's proposal
Mr. Micawber's prospects
Mr. Pecksniff's pleasant family party
Mr. Venus's shop
Mrs. Snagsby's guests

AN INDEX TO ONE-ACT PLAYS 267

Mrs. Tibbs boarding-house
Sam Weller and his father
Silas Wegg's stall
Under London
Unexpected meeting, An
Ellis, William.
Ketcham pardon, The
Euripides.
Iphigenia in Tauris
Polyxena
Ford, John.
Duchess of Pavy, The
Fouque, Friedrich de la Motte.
Undine
Gallon, Tom.
Touch of the child, The
Gatty, Mrs. Margaret.
Life beyond, The
Goldsmith, Oliver.
Innocence rewarded
Mrs. Hardcastle's journey
Hale, Edward E.
Homer and David
Hawthorne, Nathaniel.
Derelict, The
Old year and the new, The
Hay, John.
Happy man, The
Hemans, Mrs. Felicia D. B.
Raimond released
Hope, Anthony.
Matter of duty, A
Hugo, Victor.
Bishop's candlesticks
Kelland, C. B.
His wife's place
Knowles, Sheridan.
Helen and Modus
Lagerlof, Selma.
Lighting of the Xmas tree, The
Lever, Charles.
Miss Judith Macan
Longfellow, Henry W.
Class ship
Hiawatha
King Robert of Sicily
Lowell, James R.
Yussouf
Mann, Mary E.
Visit, The
Marlow, Christopher.
Doctor Faustus
Marston, Westland.
Pride against pride

Mendenhall, Susan.
Slave raiders, The
Merrick, Leonard.
S. O. S.
Moliere, Jean-Baptiste P.
Affected young ladies, The
Sicilian, The
Sganarelle
Morrison, Arthur.
Tales of mean streets
Oliphant, Mrs. Margaret.
Mrs. Harwood's secret
Omar Khayyam.
Omar and the Rabbi
Peele, George.
Old wife's tale, The
Poe, Edgar A.
Three Sundays in a week
Poole, Madeline.
Lady to call, A
Sachs, Hans.
Wandering scholar, The
Sheridan, R. B.
Pizarro and Rolla
Scheming lieutenant
Stevenson, Robert L.
Deacon Brodie
Markheim
Princess and the Countess, The
Tennyson, Alfred Lord.
Becket saves Rosamund
Falcon, The
Tolstoy, Leo.
Where love is, there God is also
Wallace, Lew.
Ben-Hur and Iras
Wilde, Oscar.
Birthday of the Infanta
Happy Prince, The

DREAM PLAY

Assumption of Hannele, The
Chocolate cake and black sand
Elsie in Dreamland
Good old days, The
Hired girl's dream, The
"John Arbery's dream"
Mr. Spriggs' little trip to Europe
Shadows
Undoing of Giant Hotstoff, The
Water that has passed, The

EASTER

Easter miracle, An
Easter morning

Seven sleepers of Ephesos, The
Spring time fantasy, A
Thy Kingdom Come
Why didn't you tell?

ENGLAND—HISTORY AND SOCIAL LIFE

At the Golden Goose
Bonnie Dundee
Captain of the gate, The
Catherine Parr
Comedie Royal, A
Comforter, The
Cottage on the moor, The
Court comedy, A
Cupboard love
Fan and two candlesticks, A
1588 (Fifteen hundred and eighty-eight)
Flitch of Bacon, A
For lack of evidence
Fortune and men's eyes
"Good men do, The"
His favorite flower
Holbeim in Blackfriars
Honors easy
Hundredth trick, The
King Alfred and the cakes
King Alfred and the meat-herd
King without Peer, The
Maid of honor, A
Masks and men
Master Wayfarer
Maypole morning
Mistress Runaway
Nance Oldfield
Nelson touch, The
Queen Catherine
Queen: God Bless Her! The
Rohan the Silent
Rosamond
Rose, The
Saint-King, The
Spectator No. 558
Sweeps of ninety-eight, The
Traitor
Wanderer, The
When Anne was Queen
Wings, The

FAIRY

Before the Pixies came to America
Bone of contention, The
Brogues of Kilavain Glen, The
Dream lesson, A
Dryad and the Deacon, The
Dyspeptic ogre, The
Enchanted gate, The
Fairies' plea, The
Fairy frolic, A

Firefly night
Golliwog in Fairyland
Fairy ring, The
Marjorie's garden
Paddly pools
Pan Pipes
Rose of the wind
Swanwhite
Treasure chest, The
Won
Woodland Princess, The

FAMOUS MEN AND WOMEN

Absolution of Bruce, The (Robert Bruce)
As good as gold (St. Francis of Assisi)
Benjamin Franklin: Journeyman
Big Kate (Catherine the Great of Russia)
Bombastes in the Shades (Historical characters)
Boy Will, The (William Shakespeare)
Brother Sun (St. Francis of Assisi)
Christmas Eve with Charles Dickens, A
Court of fame, The (Play of great women)
Dante in Santa Croce of the Raven
Dark lady of the sonnets, The (Shakespeare)
David Garrick's masterpiece
Dolly Madison's afternoon tea
Exile, The (Dante)
Friend in need, A (Goldsmith, Oliver)
Fortune and men's eyes (Shakespeare)
Gambetta's love story
Giorgione
Goya in the Cupola
Hour of Prospero (Shakespeare)
Holbein in Blackfriars
Interlude in the life of St. Francis, An
Jeanne d'Arc at Vaycouleurs
Lady compassionate, The (Dante)
Long live the empress! (Empress Catherine of Russia)
Mary! Mary! (Shakespeare)
Miss Burney at Court
Napoleon and the sentry
Napoleon's barber
Paracelsus
Prince Patiomkin (Empress Catherine of Russia)

AN INDEX TO ONE-ACT PLAYS

Privy council, A (Pepys)
Shoes that danced, The (Watteau)
Smile of Mona Lisa, The (Leonardo da Vinci)
Tenor, A (Empress Catherine of Russia)
Velasquez and the "Venus"
When Heine was twenty-one

FLAG DAY

Birth of a nation's flag, The
Flag Day
First American flag, The
First flag, The
Flag makers, The
Fourth of July

FRANCE—HISTORY AND SOCIAL LIFE

At the barricade
Beauty and the Jacobin
Blood Royal
Crispin, rival of his master
Dangers of peace, The
Farce of the worthy master Pierre Patelin, The
Fatal rubber, The
Hulks, The
Incog
King's letters, The
Legacy, The
Little king, The
Little supper, The
Lord's prayer, The
Love in a French kitchen
Marquise and woman
Marriage of Guineth, The
Minuet, A
Pastor of Jena, The
Pater Noster
Pompadour's protege, The
Post of honour, The
Promise, The
Stroke of Marbot, The
Tarbarin's wife
Three wishes, The
Waterloo
Young Napoleon, The

GOOD ENGLISH

Grammar play, A
I'll try
Mrs. Forester's crusade
Murdering the language
Popular Dick, The
Trial for the murder of the King's English

GREAT WAR—BACKGROUND

All clear
All for the cause
America pays her debt to France
Barbara's wedding
Barbarians, The
Behind the lines
Belgian Christmas eve, A
By-product, A
Children in the Great War
Christmas beyond the trenches
Conversion of Mrs. Slacker, The
Defeat
Democracy's king
Duchess entertains, The
Estaminet, The
Exemption
First aid
Four who were blind
Getting the range
God of my faith
God's outcast
Hand of Siva, The
"Hatred"
Her service Flag
Her story
Hooverizing Internationalle
In heaven
In the ravine
In "The spirit of '76"
In the trenches "over there"
Iron hand, The
It behooves us
Knitting club meets, The
Knitting girls count one, The
Liberty thrift girls, The
Lottie sees it through
Maid of France
March of truth, The
Mothers of men
New word, The
Night watches
Old lady shows her medals, The
One a day
100 per cent American
One war babe
Parlor patriots, The
Pawns
Power of loyalty
Rada
Rise up, Jennie Smith
Shamed life
Slacker, The
Slacker for the cause, A
Son of the greater fatherland, A
Sun, The
Tag, Der
They the crucified
Three wishes

Triumph of remorse, The
Unseen host, The
Valkyrie!
Vision of Columbus, The
War brides
Well remembered voice
Wheatless meal, The
White messenger, The

GREECE, ANCIENT—HISTORY AND MYTHOLOGY

After Euripides' "Electra"
Apollo in Hades
Ariadne in Naxos
Aulis difficulty, The
Cliff of tears, The
Coming of Hippolytus, The
Death of Alcestis, The
Death of Alexander, The
Death of Hippolytus, The
Doom of Admetus, The
House of Aegues, The
Jason and Medea
Ladies of Athens
Lais
Loadice and Danaë
Medea
Minos, King of Crete
Niobe
Pandora's box
Paris and Aenone
Return of Alcestis, The
Rumpus on Olympus, A
Sibyl, The
Soothsayer, The
Too much Galatea
When the fates decree
Woods of Ida
Wooing of Dionysus, The
X = O: A night of the Trojan War
Xantippe and Socrates

HALLOWE'EN

"Brownie Night"
Fairy and the witch, The
Fire spirits
Hallowe'en carnival and wax-work show, A
Hallowe'en Puppet play
Haunted gate, The
Historical Hallowe'en, An
Jack Frost's surprise
Jimmy's ghosts
Magic chest, The
Testing of Sir Gawayne, The
What do you know about ghosts?
Who was scared?
Witches' hour and candle light

HARLEQUINADE

Aria da Capo
Course of true love, The
Harlequin
Heart of a clown, The
Merry death, A
Return of Harlequin, The
Wonder hat, The

HEALTH

Health champions, The
Jewels of Cornelia, The
Judith and Ariel
Mother Goose up-to-date
"Those dreadful vity-mines!"

HOLLAND—HISTORY, LEGEND AND SOCIAL LIFE

Katjen's garden
My lady's lace
On the dyke
St. Nicholas
Sojourners

HUMANITARIAN

Brothers
Humane citizens
We and our friends

INDIA—BACKGROUND AND PHILOSOPHY

Behind the Purdah
Chitra
Drums of Oude, The
Immortal lure, The
Judgment of Indra, The
Sacrifice
Serpent's tooth, The
Singing pool, The

INDIANS OF AMERICA

Capture of Ozah, The
Glory of the morning
Lark, The
Little owl
Mirage
Passing of Hiawatha, The
Petalesharoo
Squaw of Bear Claw
Star brave, The
Wakuwapi
Wooing of Lilinau, The
Yagowanea
Yot-che-ka

INVENTION

Samuel Morse's telegraph
Trial trip of the Clermont

IRELAND—HISTORY, BACKGROUND AND SOCIAL LIFE

At the flowing of the tide
Betrayal, The
Blind
Bogie men, The
Cathleen ni Hoolihan
Clancy name, The
Coats
Countess Cathleen, The
Deirdre
Dreaming of the Bones, The
Foam maiden, The
Full of the Moon, The
Gaol gate, The
"Good housewife and her labors, The"
Green helmet, The
Hyacinth Halvey
In the shadow of the glen
Iosagan
Jurisprudence
King, The
Kings threshold, The
Land of heart's desire, The
McDonough's wife
Magnanimous lover, The
Master, The
Miracle of the corn, The
O'Flaherty V. C.
"Oh Lawsy Me!"
On Baile's strand
Orangeman, The
Pagan, The
Pot of broth, A
Ramlet o' Puce, A
Red turf
Riders to the sea
Rising of the moon, The
Rush light, The
Shadow of the Glen, The
Sidhe of Ben-Mor, The
Singer, The
Spreading the news
Swift's pastoral
Traveling man, The
Troth, The
Twisting of the Rope, The
Widdy's mite, The
Workhouse ward, The
Wrens, The

ITALY—HISTORY, BACKGROUND AND SOCIAL LIFE

Alchemist, The
Dove uncaged, The
Dream of a spring morning, The
Dream of liberty, A
Forest spring, The
Hour of greatness, The
Jewel merchants, The
Portrait of Hiero, The
Quarry slaves
Smile of Mona Lisa
Twilight saint, The

JAPAN—HISTORY, DRAMA AND SOCIAL LIFE

Aoi No Uye
Atsumori
Awoi No Uye
Aya No Tsuzumi
Benkei on the bridge
Bibi
Bushido from "Terakoya"
By Miho's pine-clad shore
Case of spoons
Chorio
Chrysanthemums
Daimyo, The
Daughter of Japan, A
Death-stone, The
Demon's shell, The
Early snow
Eboshi-ori
Flower of Yeddo, A
Fox's grave
Genjo
Hachi No Ki
Hagoromo
Haku Rakuten
Hands in the box, The
Hatsuyuki
Hōka priests, The
Honor of Danzo, The
Honorable Miss, The
Ikeniye
Ikuta
Kagekiyo
Kakitsuhata
Kanawa
Kayoi Komachi
Kinuta
Kiri no Meijiyama
Kumasaka
Kyōgen
Life is a dream
Love's heavy burden
Madman on the roof, The
Man and his wife, A
Melon thief, The
Mountain she-devil, The
Nakamitsu
Nari-Kin
Nishikigi
O Joy San
O-Ume's gods
Perfect Jewel maiden, The

Pine-tree, The
Prince's pigeon, The
Razor, The
Sayonara
She who was fished
Shojo
Shower, The
Somebody—nothing
Sotoba Komachi
Suma Genji
Sumida Gawa
Sun goddess, The
Tamura
Taniko
Tears of the birds, The
Tsunemasa
Ukai
Vampire cat, The
Willow tree, The
Winning of Fuji, The
Yoshiwara

JEWISH HOLIDAYS
Ambition in White chapel
Because he loved David so
Casting of lots
Chanukah sketch
Delayed birthday
Dream book
Enemies of Israel
Golden gifts
King's choice, The
Maccabean cure, A
Night of light, The
Power of Purim, The
Purim players, The
Spirit of Purim, The
To save his country

LABOR
Eternal song, The
Miss Tassey
Price of coal
Sabatage

LABOR DAY
Bee hive, The
Play lovers, The

LINCOLN'S BIRTHDAY
Abe Lincoln and Little A. D.
Abraham Lincoln
Abraham Lincoln and the little bird
Day that Lincoln died, The
Honest Abe
Lincoln's birthday

LITERARY CHARACTERS
End of the way, The (Robin Hood)
How Robin Hood once was a wait
In the good green wood (Robin Hood)
Little John joins the band of Robin Hood
Potter Thompson (King Arthur)
Robin Hood becomes an outlaw
Ryland (Literary Characters—Eng. 18th. cent.)
Silver blade, The (King Arthur)
Shakespeare Garden Club, The
Shakespeare's daughter
When knights were bold (King Arthur)

MAY DAY
Crowning of the Dryads, The
First May baskets, The
Greatest gift, The
"In bells and motley"
Jack-I-the-Green
Making the best of things
May-day
Potentate of Weatherdom, The
Primrose lane
Queen Loving Heart
When Polly was queen of the May

MEDIEVAL
Fool, The
Gringoire
Knight's return, The
Swanwhite
Tears of dawn

MEMORIAL DAY
Decoration Day
How sleep the brave
Memorial day
Memorial day pageant
Spirit of Memorial Day, The

MIRACLE
Abraham and Isaac
Adam's dream
Blessed birthday, The
Christmas guest, The
"Isle of chestnuts"
Mantle of the Virgin, The
Nursery maid of heaven, The
Snow image, The

MISSIONARY

As ye sew
Going to school in China
Inasmuch as ye have done it unto the least
Paper money
Real price, The
Ruth's donation party
Test, The
Visit in Brazil, A

MORALITY

Broken bars, The
Butterfly, The
Cult of content, The
Every boy
Every senior
Everychild
"Everygirl"
Everystudent
Figs and thistles
Game, The
Garden, The
House, A
House of the heart, The
Human nature
Lord of the Harvest, The
Old woman, The
On the path of the child
One by one
One day awake
Queen's hour, The

NATURE

Mother Nature's trumpeter
Protest of the trees, The
Queen Flora's court
Sanctuary
Under the greenwood tree
Unselfish violet, The
When the sun stayed in bed
Wild animal play, The

NEGRO

Aftermath
Black tie
Darktown Social Betterment S'ciety, The
Dreamy kid
Elder Jenkins' reception
Faith
Gabe's home run
Goat alley
Granny Boling
Granny Maumee
Hanging out the wash
In Aunt Chloe's cabin
Not in the regular army
Rider of dreams, The
Sam Tucker
Wanted—a valet
White dresses

NEW YEAR'S DAY

Baby New Year
Father Time and his children
Molly's New Year's party
New Year's Day
Old year and the new, The
Three sleepy-heads
Welcoming the New Year

NEWSPAPER

Editor-in-chief
Extra! The newspaper minstrels are out!
Freedom of the Press, The
Her first assignment
Her first scoop
Hicksville Bungler, The
Is the editor in?
Miss Jones, journalist
Mr. Editor
New reporter, The
People, The
Political editor, The
Scoop, The
Society column, The
Wire entanglement, A

ORIENTAL

Beggar and the King, The
Black death, The
Gold circle, The
Man with the bundle, The
Pagoda slave, A
Rose garden, The
Ruby Red
Siege, The

PATRIOTIC

Aunt Columbia's dinner party
Becoming an American
Crowning of Columbia, The
Crowning of peace, The
Dora
Eyes of faith
Girls over here, The
Little Miss America and the happy children
Parted sisters, The
Patriot's parade, The
Spirit of Kiwanis, The
Star-spangled banner, The

PEACE

Brethren
Clemency

Enemy, The
Glorious game, The
Peace that passeth understanding, The
Triumph of peace, The
Where war comes

PHILANTHROPY
Locked door, The
Tramp and a night's lodging, A

PIERROT
Dream maker, The
End of the rainbow, The
Heart of Pierrot, The
Hearts to mend
Love and magic
Maker of dreams, The
Matinata
Moonshine
Pierrot by the light of the moon
Pierrot in Paris
Pierrot of the minute, The
While the mushrooms bubble

PLAYS WITHIN A PLAY
Aria da Capo
In the trenches "over there"
Way of a woman, The

POLITICAL
Daughter of men, The
Graft
His honor
Member for literature, The
Tea and politics

POVERTY
According to Darwin
Back of the yards
Cost of a hat, The
Daily bread
Dog, The
Down in Paradise Alley
First time, The
Little mother of the slums, The
Mother-of-Pearl
Man on the kerb, The
State forbids, The

PRISON
Fifth commandment, The
Freedom
Release
Sounding brass

PUBLIC LIBRARY
Best seller, The
First American Library, The
Friends in bookland
I'm sorry—it's out!
Newsy wins
Quest of an ancestor, The
In the library

ROME, ANCIENT
Caligula's picnic
Calpurnia's dinner-party
Death of Agrippina, The
Cleopatra
Fata Deorum
Fidelitas
In the house of the poet
Lucullus's dinner-party
Nero's mother
Octavia
Pious AEneas
Sauce for the Emperor
Stoic's daughter, The
Wife of Marobius, The

RUSSIAN LIFE, COSTUMES AND MANNERS
Anniversary, The
Babushka, The
Boor, The
Diadem of snow, A
Free speech
Jubilee, The
Little stone house, The
Love of women, The
Marriage proposal, A
On the highway
Protégée of the mistress, A
Snow witch, The
Tobacco evil, The
Tragedian in spite of himself, The
Wedding, The
Where love is, there God is also

ST. VALENTINE'S DAY
At the library
Cupid mixes things
Cupid's trick
Goblin guests
In a Valentine box
St. Valentine's house
Tertulla's garden
Valentine problem, A
Wooden shoe, The

SCANDINAVIAN HISTORY AND LEGEND
Combat with the dragon, The
Death of Balder, The

AN INDEX TO ONE-ACT PLAYS

Hildetua
Ingiald Evilheart
Knut at Roeskilde
Troll magic
Tyrfing
Wind over the water, The

SCOTLAND—HISTORY AND SOCIAL LIFE

Absolution of Bruce, The
Bairnies' Saturday night, The
Campbell of Kilmhor
Coming of Fair Annie, The
Glenforsa
Gruach
Jean

SCOUT

Behind the khaki of the scouts
Clever kid!
Fair play
If I were Bob
Jerry's job
Knotty problem, A
Lend a hand
Pheasants' eggs
Redeeming their characters
Scold, the scoundrel and the scout, The
Scout's honor, A
Scouts to the rescue

SEA AND SAILORS

Admiral Peters
Boatswain's mate, The
Bound east for Cardiff
Changeling, The
Consarning Sairey 'Uggins
Crowsnest, The
Fog
Gee Whiz, The
Ghost of Jerry Bundler, The
Gray parrot, The
Love passage, A
Ile
In the Zone
Keeping up appearances
Moon of the Caribees, The
North-pole expedition, A
Rusty door, The
Sea, The
Thirst
Under sailing orders
Wanderer, The

SOUTH AFRICAN BACKGROUND

Culprit, The
On the Veldt
Strange physician, The

SPAIN—HISTORY AND SOCIAL LIFE

Bright morning, A
By their words ye shall know them
Children of Granada
His widow's husband
Passing of the magi, The
Philip the king

TEMPERANCE AND PROHIBITION

Child in the house, The
Flag of courage, The
Prohibition Mother Goose
Uncle Sam's flower garden

THANKSGIVING

Bob's and Tom's Thanksgiving
Charlie's pop-corn
Coming home to Grandma's
First Thanksgiving Day, The
First Thanksgiving dinner, The
Governor's proclamation, The
Letter from home, A
Meaning of Thanksgiving Day, The
Priscilla, Myles and John
Pumpkin Pie Peter
Puritan prank, A
Scotch grace
Thanksgiving conspiracy, A
Thanksgiving Day
Thanksgiving dream, A
Thanksgiving festival, A
Thanksgiving of Praisgod plenty, The
Tommy's Thanksgiving party
Waif's Thanksgiving, The
White chief, The
Yellow law, The

THRIFT

Provident society, The
Thrift

UNITED STATES—HISTORY AND SOCIAL LIFE

Colonial
    Another man's place
    At anchor
    Cherry pie
    Colonial school, A
    Colinial Virginia
    Departure, The
    Diabolical circle, The
    Dowry and romance
    Easter rabbit, The
    Encounter in the forest, An
    Finding the May flowers

First crop of apples, The
First winter, The
Gentlemen of Virginia
Georgia debtors, The
How the Indians planted powder
In Betsy Ross's time
In witchcraft days
Indian gifts
Indian story, An
John Bargrave, gentleman
Lady Betty's burglar
Life in New York
Little Pilgrims
Lost village, The
Massasoit's illness
Minister's dream, The
Narrow escape, A
One way to capture a fort
Pennsylvania incident, A
Pilgrim's holiday, The
Pilgrims in Holland, The
Quakers in New England, The
Skirmish at Rensselaerswijck, A
Soft-soap day, The
Stormy times
Story of a famous wedding, The
Strategy of Director Kieft, The
Three compromises of the constitution
Virginia children of long ago
Visitors from the Colonial Period
Wampum belts
William Penn's Treaty with the Indians
Witchcraft story, A

U. S.—Revolutionary War
Birthday ball, The
Boston Tea Party, The
Colonial tea
Declaration of Independence, The
Dianthe's desertion
Dispatches from Washington
"First in war, The"
For love and honor
Independence Day
Just before dawn
Making a flag
Patriots
Quaker way, The
Revolutionary days
Robert Morris and the Revolution
War woman, The
When the land was young

U. S.—Civil War
At retreat
Children of the Civil War
Clod, The
"Cracker, The"
Gate of dreams, The
Solemn pride

Star spangled banner, The
Underground railroad, The

UNITED STATES—PIONEER

Children of the Illini
Daniel Boone: patriot
Daniel Boone's snuff box
Gold in California
Homesteaders' Christmas, The
Lucky Hallowe'en, A
"Only a girl!"
Pioneer boys and girls
Pioneers, The

UNITED STATES, SOUTH—HISTORY AND SOCIAL LIFE

At old Mobile
Battle of Maubilla, The
De Soto and the Indians
How Bienville saved Mobile
Last of the Cargills, The
Lights of happyland, The
Shadows
Sunshine, an idyll

UNITED STATES, WEST—BACKGROUND

Branded Mavericks
Death in Fever Flat
Girl and the outlaw
Orator of Zapata City
Road-agent, The
Sheriff of Tuckahoe, The
Squaw-man, an idyl of the ranch, The

WASHINGTON'S BIRTHDAY

George Washington and the cherry tree
George Washington's fortune
Truth for a day, The
Washington's birthday
Young patriots' league

WOMAN SUFFRAGE

Andromeda unfettered
Back of the ballot
Converted suffragist, A
Coronation, The
Dominant male, The
How the vote was won
Melinda and her sisters
Suffragette, The
Woman of it, The
Women's votes
Xanthippe on woman suffrage

COLLECTIONS

Abercrombie, Lascelles. Four short plays. Lond. Martin Secker, 1922.
  The Adder
  The staircase
  The deserter
  (Also "The end of the world," two acts)

Alabama Centennial Commission. Series of Children's plays in commemoration of the close of a century of statehood. Montgomery, Ala. Paragon Press. 1919.
  At old Mobile
  The battle of Maubilla
  De Soto and the Indians
  How Bienville saved Mobile
  (Also "Alabama," a longer play)

Aldis, Mary. Plays for small stages. N. Y. Duffield, 1915.
  Mrs. Pat and the law
  The drama class of Taukaha, Nevada
  Extreme unction
  The letter
  Temperment

Anderson, Mrs. Isabel. Everyboy and other plays for children. N. Y. Shakespeare Press, 1914.
  Everyboy
  King Foxy of Muir Glacier
  Little Doubt
  Merry Jerry
  The Gee Whiz
  Justice Whisker's trial
  The witch of the woods
  (Also a longer play)

Arkwright, Ruth. Brownikins and other fancies. Music by J. W. Wilson. Lond. Wells, Gardner, Darton, n. d.
  Bibi; or, The Japanese foundling
  St. Nicholas
  Baby New Year
  (Also three longer plays)

Baker, George M. and others. Ten plays for boys. Bost. Walter H. Baker, 1918.
  Not wanted—a wife — Fenn, Edward B.
  The freedom of the Press — Baker, George M.
  Dizzy's dilemmas — Brown, Charles I.
  Hypnotism — Bent, Newell
  (Also five plays copyrighted before 1900, and a longer play)

Baker, Walter H. Co., Publishers. Plays in Pinafores. Bost. Walter H. Baker. 1916.
  An Easter miracle — Harvey, Della Shaw
  The Doll's playhouse — Selman, Ruth
  School opera — Fernald, Mrs. C. F. and Wilson, Olivia L.
  The honeymoon — Fernald, Mrs. C. F. and Wilson, Olivia L.

277

    Left   Fernald, Mrs. C. F. and Wilson, Olivia L.
    Migg's revenge   Dickens, Charles
    The Irish washerwoman   Fernald, Mrs. C. F. and Wilson, Olivia L.
    The cobbler's bargain   Fernald, Mrs. C. F. and Wilson, Olivia L.
    Learning lessons   Fernald, Mrs. C. F. and Wilson, Olivia L.
(Also six other plays of different types)

Baldwin, Sidney. Five plays and five pantomimes. Phila. Penn, 1923.
    The Christmas spirit
    Christmas eve
    Marjorie's garden
    Mother nature's trumpeter
    The enchanted gate
    (Also five pantomimes)

Bangs, John K. The real thing and three other farces. N. Y. Harper, 1909.
    The real thing
    The Barringtons' "At home"
    The return of Christmas
    The side-show

Barbee, Lindsey. Let's pretend. Chic. T. S. Denison, 1917.
    The little pink lady
    The Ever-Ever Land
    When the toys awake
    The forest of Every Day
    A Christmas tree joke
    "If Don't-Believe is changed into Believe"

Baring, Maurice. Diminutive dramas. Lond. Secker, n. d.
    Catherine Parr
    The drawback
    Pious AEneas
    The death of Alexander
    The Greek vase
    The fatal rubber
    The rehearsal
    The blue Harlequin
    The member for literature
    Caligula's picnic
    The Aulis difficulty
    Don Juan's failure
    Calpurnia's dinner-party
    Lucullus's dinner-party
    The Stoic's daughter
    After Euripides' "Electra"
    Jason and Medea
    King Alfred and the Neat-Herd
    Rosamund and Eleanor
    Ariadne in Naxos
    Velasquez and the "Venus"
    Xantippe and Socrates

Barker, Granville. Three short plays. Bost. Little, Brown, 1917.
    Rococo
    Vote by ballot
    Farewell to the Theatre

Barnum, Madalene D. School plays for all occasions. Newark, N. J. Barse & Hopkins, 1922.

The bee hive
Diego's dream
Scotch grace
Honest Abe
Brethren
How sleep the brave
Past, present and future
(Also four longer plays)

Barrie, James M. Echoes of the war. N. Y. Scribner, 1918,
The old lady shows her medals
The new ward
Barbara's wedding
A well-remembered voice

Barrie, James M. Half hours. N. Y. Scribner, 1917
Pantaloon
The twelve pound look
Rosalind
The will

Barton, George E. The pipe of desire and other plays. Bost. Old Corner Book Store, 1905.
The pipe of desire
The sewing machine
(Also "The Image of God," a dramatic story, and "The thing to be done," two acts)

Bax, Clifford. Polite satires. Lond. Medici Society, 1922.
The unknown hand
The volcanic island
Square pegs

Baxley, Isaac R. Poems and plays, Vol. 1. San Francisco. A. M. Robertson, 1921.
Cleopatra
In the home of the poet
Lais
The Aegean
The Parthenon
The fool
The Sibyl
(Also "The Fire-Woman," two acts)

Beach, Lewis. Four one-act plays. N. Y. Brentano's, 1921
The clod
A guest for dinner
Love among the lions
Brothers

Bechhofer, C. E. Five Russian plays with one from the Ukrainian. N. Y. Dutton, 1916.
A merry death, a Harlequinade — Evréinov, Nicholas
The beautiful despot — Evréinov, Nicholas
The choice of a tutor — Vizin, Denis von
The wedding — Chékhov, Anton
The jubilee — Chékhov, Anton
The Babylonian captivity — Ukráinka, Lésya

Beith, John H. (Ian Hay, pseud.) The crimson cocoanut and other plays. Bost. Walter H. Baker, 1913.
The crimson cocoanut
A late delivery
The missing card

Bell, Lady, and Richmond, Mrs. Herbert. The cat and the fiddle book. N. Y. Longmans, Green, 1922.
   The cat and the fiddle
   Lucy Locket
   Polly put the kettle on
   Oranges and lemons
   Little Miss Muffet
   Humpty Dumpty
   (Also two longer plays)

Bell, Lady. Nursery comedies. N. Y. Longmans, Green, 1918.
   What happened to Henny Penny
   Little Petsy
   Rather a prig
   The monster in the garden
   Cat and dog
   Miss Dobson
   The wigwam; or, The little girl from town
   Foolish Jack
   Quite by ourselves
   The best children in the world
   (Also two longer plays)

Bell, May. What of the night? and other sketches. Lond. Arthur H. Stockwell, (1918)?
   The culprit
   What of the night
   Bluebeard
   The strange physician
   Marah
   (Also "Britannia goes to war," a pageant)

Bennett, E. Arnold. Polite farces. N. Y. Doran, n. d.
   The stepmother
   A good woman
   A question of sex

Benton, Rita. Shorter Bible plays. N. Y. Abingdon Press, 1922.
   Moses in the bulrushes
   The call of Samuel
   The judgment of Solomon
   The Good Samaritan
   Manger service
   (Also six longer plays)

Benton, Rita. The star-child and other plays. N. Y. Writers Pub. Co., 1921.
   Where love is, there God is also
   The happy man
   King Robert of Sicily
   Yussouf
   The life beyond
   (Also three longer plays)

Block, Etta, tr. One-act plays from the Yiddish. Cincinnati. Stewart Kidd, 1923.
   Champagne — Perez, Isaac L.
   Mother and son — Halpern, J.
   The stranger — Hirschbein, Perez
   The snowstorm — Hirschbein, Perez
   When the dew falleth — Hirschbein, Perez
   The eternal song — Arnstein, Marc

Bloxam, E. E. Little pageant plays for children. Lond. Wells, Gardner, Darton, n. d.
   A world-wide baby

Where is happiness?
Brothers and sisters
The best wish
Manners makyth the man
Cuckoo!
Growing up
Philosophy and fairies

Bottomley, Gordon. King Lear's wife; The crier by night; The riding to Lithend; Midsummer eve; Laodice and Danaë. Bost. Small, Maynard, n. d.
King Lear's wife
The crier by night
The riding to Lithend
Midsummer eve
Laodice and Danaë

Brand, Alfred. The infernal masculine and other comedies. Bost. Cornhill Co., 1918.
The infernal masculine
Three is company
Did it really happen?

Brighouse, Harold. Plays for the meadow and plays for the lawn. N. Y. French, 1921.
May pole morning
The Paris doctor
The Prince who was a piper
The man about the place

Brown, Alice. One act plays. N. Y. Macmillan, 1921.
The hero
Doctor Auntie
The crimson lake
Milly dear
The web
The loving cup
Joint owners in Spain
The sugar house
A March wind

Browne-Evarts, Edith. Young folks' dialogues and dramas. Chic., M. A. Donohue, 1902.
Not so bad after all
Our mother's aid society
The last day of school
A pleasant surprise
Put to the test
The prize of learning
The Jones family
A rolling stone gathers no moss
Honesty's the best policy
Military and medicine
(Also two longer plays and six dialogues)

Browne, Horace B. Short plays from Dickens. Lond. Chapman & Hall, 1908.
Mrs. Tibbs boarding-house
Miss Squeers' tea-party
The gentleman next door
Hatching a conspiracy
The stranger's visit
Mr. Pecksniff's pleasant family party
An unexpected meeting

A division between friends
The friendly waiter
Betsey Trotwood at home
Mr. Micauber's prospects
Mr. Guppy's proposal
Mrs. Snagsby's guests
Mr. George's shooting gallery
Silas Wegg's stall
Mr. Venus' shop
At "Jenny Wren's"
(Also two longer plays)

Brunner, Emma B. Bits of background in one act plays. N. Y. Knopf, 1919.
Over age
The spark of life
Strangers
Making a man

Bugbee, Willis N. Jolly Christmas book. Syracuse, N. Y. Willis N. Bugbee, 1919.
Molly's Christmas tree
The Santa Claus brigade
Surprising Santa
A reception for Santa Claus
(Also two plays in two scenes, and many recitations, monologues, etc.)

Bullivant, Cecil H. Home plays, a collection of new, simple, and effective plays for boys and girls. N. Y. Dodge Pub. Co., n. d.
The mushroom meadow
The paradise of children
Won
Courage
The Cherry-Blossom Princess
Peter Grief
Aunt Grundy
"In bells and motley"
The wooden shoe
(Also seventeen longer plays and one play in the French language)

Burbank, Barbara and others. Comedies for young folks. Bost. Walter H. Baker, 1902.
Beresford Benevolent Society
Love's Stratagem
Who wins?
The Postman's knock
(Also six longer plays)

Burrows, Edith; Bridgham, Gladys R. and others. Short plays for small players. Bost. Walter H. Baker, 1915.
The key
The children's hour
Bouquet of rose spirits
Pat's excuse
(Also four longer plays)

Bynner, Witter. A book of plays. N. Y. Knopf, 1922.
The little king
A night wind
Tiger
Cycle
Iphigenia in Tauris

Calderon, George. Eight one-act plays. Lond. Grant Richards, 1922.
Peace

The little stone house
Derelicts
Geminae
Parkin Bros.
The two talismans
The lamp
Longing

California University, Little Theatre workshop. Plays of the University of California. Little Theatre Workshop. Univ. of Calif. Little Theatre Press, 1922.
Derby   Gentry, Helen
The man who never worried   Luck, H. R.
The King laughs   Chevalier, Haakon M.
The obstacle   Danuariakes, Stephanie

Cameron, Margaret. Comedies in miniature. N. Y. McClure, Philips, 1903.
Miss Doulton's orchids
The burglar
The kleptomaniac
A pipe of peace
A Christmas chime
The committee on matrimony
Her neighbor's creed
(Also four monologues)

Cannan, Gilbert. Four plays. Lond. Sedgwick & Jackson, 1913.
James and John
Mary's wedding
A short way with authors
(Also Miles Dixon, two acts)

Carolina folk-plays. N. Y. Holt, 1922.
When witches ride   Lay, Elizabeth A.
Peggy   Williamson, Harold
"Dod gast ye both!"   Heffner, Hubert
Off Nags head; or, The Bell Buoy MacMillan, Dougald
The last of the Lowries   Greene, Paul

Carter, Hobart. Christmas candles; plays for boys and girls. N. Y. Holt, 1915.
The Christmas Brownie
The Babushka
Minty-Malviny's Santa Claus
The hundred
(Also eight longer plays)

Cauldwell, Samuel M. Chocolate cake and black sand, and two other plays. N. Y. Putnam, 1917.
Chocolate cake and black sand
The undoing of Giant Hotstoff
The invention of the rat trap

Chambers, C. I. The Boy Scouts' book of plays. Lond. Wells, Gardner, Darton, 1914.
Pheasants' eggs
The scold, the scoundrel
Scouts to the rescue
Redeeming their character

Chapin, Harold. Three one-act plays. N. Y. Samuel French, 1921.
It's the poor that 'elps the poor
The autocrat of the coffee-stall
Innocent and Annabel

Chaplin, Alice W. A play a month for female characters. Bost. Walter H. Baker, 1917.
Pickles, bonbons and temper
A Valentine problem
Mad! Mad!
Because it rained
May
That boy
Independent Flynn
Home and mother
Behind the screen
Thankful for Jack
Merry Christmas
(Also one longer play)

Chékhov, Anton. (Tchekoff, pseud.) Plays. Second series. N. Y. Scribner, n. d.
On the high road
The proposal
The wedding
The bear
A tragedian in spite of himself
The anniversary
(Also "The three sisters," four acts, and "The cherry orchard," four acts)

Clark, Barrett H., ed. Representative one-act plays by British and Irish authors. Bost. Little, Brown, 1921.

The widow of Wasdale Head	Pinero, Arthur
The goal	Jones, Henry A.
Salome	Wilde, Oscar
The man in the stalls	Sutro, Alfred
Op-'o-Me-Thumb	Fenn, Frederick and Pryce, Richard
The impertinence of the creature	Gordon-Lennox, Cosmo
The stepmother	Bennett, E. Arnold
Rococo	Barker, Granville
James and John	Cannan, Gilbert
The snow man	Housman, Laurence
Fancy free	Houghton, Stanley
Lonesome-like	Brighouse, Harold
Miss Tassey	Baker, Elizabeth
Makeshifts	Robins, Gertrude
The maker of dreams	Down, Oliphant
The land of Heart's Desire	Yeats, William B.
Riders to the sea	Synge, J. M.
Spreading the news	Gregory, Lady
Magnanimous lover	Ervine, St. John G.
The golden doom	Dunsany, Lord

Cleather, Dorothy. A handy book of plays for girls. Chic. Saalfield Pub. Co., n. d.
A black trouble
Just like a story
The twins
Stuffing
The magic tabloid
(Also "A burning question," two acts)

Clements, Colin C. Plays for a folding theatre. Cincinnati. Stewart Kidd, 1923.
Pierrot in Paris
Columbine
The return of Harlequin
Three lepers of Suk-El-Garab

The desert
The siege
Moon tide

Cohen, Helen L., ed. One-act plays by modern authors. N. Y. Harcourt, Brace, 1921.

The boy will	Rogers, Robert E.
Beauty and the Jacobin	Tarkington, Booth
The Pierrot of the minute	Dowson, Ernest
The maker of dreams	Down, Oliphant
Gettysburg	MacKaye, Percy
Wurzel-Flummery	Milne, Alan A.
Maid of France	Brighouse, Harold
Spreading the news	Gregory, Lady
Welsh honeymoon	Marks, Jeannette
Riders to the sea	Synge, John M.
A night at an inn	Dunsany, Lord
The twilight saint	Young, Stark
The masque of the two strangers	Egerton, Lady Alix
The intruder	Maeterlinck, Maurice
Fortune and men's eyes	Peabody, Josephine P.
The little man	Galsworthy, John

Cohen, Helen L. The junior play book. N. Y. Harcourt Brace, 1923.

Jephthah's daughter	Levinger, Elma E.
The forfeit	Rogers, T. B.
The trysting place	Tarkington, Booth
Square pegs	Bax, Clifford
The twisting of the rope	Hyde, Douglas
Paddy pools	Malleson
Followers	Brighouse, Harold
Brother Sun	Housman, Laurence

(Also three longer plays)

Cooke, Marjorie B. Dramatic episodes. Chic. Dramatic Pub. Co., 1904.
  A court comedy
  Manners and modes
  The confessional
  The child in the house
  The lion and the lady
  Success
  Lady Betty's burglar
  A dinner—with complications
  Reform
  When love is young

Craig, Anne A. T. The dramatic festival. N. Y. Putnam, 1912.
  The grasshoppers and the ants
  The greatest gift
  The course of true love
  The pool of answers
  (Also "Minka's wedding," a longer play)

Crocker, Bosworth. Humble folk. Cincinnati. Stewart Kidd, 1923.
  The last straw
  The baby carriage
  The dog
  The first time
  The cost of a hat

Dakota Playmaker plays. First series. Four one-act plays on Colonial themes. Bost. Walter H. Baker, 1923.

The diabolical circle	Bornstead, Beulah
John Bargrave, Gentleman	Grinnell, John E.

Another man's place   Wilder, Marion
Dowry and romance   Meblin, Rose C.

Dalkeith, Lena. Little plays. Lond. T. C. & E. C. Jack, n. d.
The Princess and the swineherd
King Alfred and the cakes
Scene from Robin Hood
Scene from Uncle Tom's Cabin
(Also a longer play)

Daly, Arnold. The dominant male, essays and plays. N. Y. Moffat, Yard & Co., 1921.
The dominant male
Democracy's king

Dane, Essex. One act plays. Bost. Walter H. Baker, 1923.
When the whirlwind blows
The wasp
Wrong numbers
A serpent's tooth
Happy returns
The workers at the looms
Cul-de-sac
Fleurette & Company
The wooden leg

Dargan, Olive T. and Peterson, Frederick. The flutter of the goldleaf, and other plays. N. Y. Scribner, 1922.
The flutter of the goldleaf   Dargan, Olive T. & Peterson, Frederick
The journey   Dargan, Olive T.
(Also "Everychild" in five scenes, and "Two doctors at Akragas")

Davis, M. E. M. A bunch of roses and other parlor plays. Bost. Small, Maynard, 1903.
A bunch of roses
Queen Anne cottages
His lordship
Christmas boxes
(Also two longer plays)

Dell, Floyd. King Arthur's socks, and other village plays. N. Y. Knopf. 1922.
Human nature
The chaste adventures of Joseph
The angel intrudes
Legend
Sweet-and-Twenty
A long time ago
Enigma
Ibsen revisited
King Arthur's socks
The rim of the world
Poor Harold

Denison, Emily H. The little mother of the slums, and other plays. Bost. Gorham Press, 1915.
The little mother of the slums
Duped
My friend's in town
The mystery of Beacon Hill
Dolly Madison's afternoon tea
(Also "The Yeggman," two scenes, and "The dawn of music," a wordless drama)

Denton, Clara J. All the holidays. Chic. A. Flanagan Co., 1905.
 Three sleepy-heads   Denton, Clara J.
 At the library   Denton, Clara J.
 Making the best of things   Denton, Clara J.
 Bob's and Tom's Thanksgiving   Denton, Clara J.
 Charlie's popcorn   Denton, Clara J.
 The Governor's proclamation   Denton, Clara J.
 Hanging up the stockings   Denton, Clara J.
 Old friends together   Cherryman, Myrtle C.
 (Also recitations, dialogues, and exercises)

Denton, Clara J. When the curtain rises. Program book, Volume 2. N. Y., J. Fischer & Bros., 1909.
 The senior
 No crown
 The Queen's offer
 The wager
 An underground opportunity
 The gentle janitor
 A new man in town
 "Isabel"
 The thief
 (Also recitations, drills, duologues, and longer plays)

Dix, Beulah M. Allinson's lad, and other martial interludes. N. Y. Holt, 1910.
 Allison's lad
 The hundredth trick
 The weakest link
 The snare and the fowler
 The captain of the gate
 The dark of the dawn

Domestic and Foreign Missionary Society. Voices from everywhere N. Y. The Domestic and Foreign Missionary Society, 1914.
 Inasmuch as ye have done it unto the least   Hobart, Margaret J.
 The real price; or, Stranger than fiction   Jeffreys, William H.
 Paper money   Jeffreys, William H.
 Evening rice   Jeffreys, William H.
 A visit in Brazil   Brown, William C.
 At the door of the Igloo   An Alaskan Missionary
 (Also six dialogues)

Dreiser, Theodore. Plays of the natural and the supernatural. N. Y. Lane, 1916.
 The girl in the coffin
 The blue sphere
 Laughing gas
 In the dark
 The spring recital
 The light in the window
 "Old Rag picker"

Drinkwater, John. Pawns: three poetic plays. Lond. Sidgwick & Jackson, 1917.
 The storm
 The God of Quiet
 X = O: A night of the Trojan War

Dunsany, Lord. Five plays. Bost., Little, Brown, 1914.
 The golden doom
 The glittering gate
 The last silk hat
 (Also two longer plays)

Dunsany, Lord. Plays of gods and men. Bost. Luce & Co., 1917.
   The queen's enemies
   A night at an inn
   (Also "The tents of the Arabs," two acts, and "The laughter of the Gods," three acts)

Dunsany, Lord. Plays of near and far. N. Y. Putnam, 1922.
   The compromise of the King of the Golden Isle
   Cheezo
   A good bargain
   If Shakespeare lived to-day
   Fame and the poet
   (Also "The flight of the Queen," a longer play)

Duran, Leo, tr. Plays of old Japan. N. Y. Thomas Seltzer, 1921.
   The Daimyo
   The honor of Danzo
   The hands in the box
   (Also two longer plays)

Eliot, Samuel A., Jr., ed. Little theatre classics, Vol. 1. Bost. Little, Brown, 1917.
   Polyxena, from the "Hecuba" of Euripides
   A Christmas miracle-play: the pageant of the Shearmen and Tailors in the Coventry Cycle of Miracles
   Doctor Faustus, by Christopher Marlow
   Ricardo and Viola, from "The Coxcomb" of Beaumont and Fletcher
   The scheming lieutenant, from "St. Patrick's Day," by Richard Brinsley Sheridan

Eliot, Samuel A., Jr., ed. Little theatre classics, Vol. 11. Bost. Little, Brown, 1920.
   Pateliu
   Abraham and Isaac
   Sganarelle
   (Also two longer plays)
   Alécis, Giullaume
   Brome & Chester, Cycle of Miracles
   Moliere

Eliot, Samuel A., Jr., ed. Little theatre classics, Vol. III. Bost. Little, Brown, 1921.
   Bushido
   Old wife's tale
   The Duchess of Pavy
   (Also one longer play)
   Idzumo, Takeda
   Peele, George
   Ford, John

Eliot, Samuel A., Jr., ed. Little theatre classics, Vol. IV. Bost. Little, Brown, 1922.
   The wandering scholar from Paradise
   All for love
   The martyrdom of Ali
   (Also a longer play)
   Sachs, Hans
   Dryden, John
   Miracle play of Hasan and Husain

Elkins, Fenton B. Three tremendous trifles. N. Y. Duffield, 1919.
   The Belgian baby
   The quick and the dead
   "Figuratively speaking"

Ellis, Mrs. Havelock. Love in danger. Bost. Houghton, Mifflin, 1915.
   The subjection of Kezia
   The pixy
   The mothers

Elwes, Mary. Temporary engagements and other plays. Lond. Francis Griffiths, 1920.
   Two in a flat
   In time of war
   (Also "Temporary engagements," two acts)

Ervine, St. John G. Four Irish plays. Dublin. Maunsel, 1914.
  The magnanimous lover
  The critics
  The Orangeman
  (Also "Mixed marriage," four acts)
Evans, Della J. Two plays and a preface. Bost. Richard G. Badger, 1921.
  "M—R—S"
  The younger son
Fay, Frederick L. and Emerson, M. A. Three plays for boys. N.Y. Association Press, 1919. (The International Commission of the Young Men's Christian Ass'n)
  Lend a hand
  If I were Bob
  (Also "A regular fellow," three acts)
Fenollosa, Ernest and Pound, Ezra. 'Noh;' or, Accomplishment, a study of the classical stage of Japan. N. Y. Knopf, 1917.
  Sotoba Komachi
  Kayoi Komachi
  Suma Genji
  Shojo
  Tamura
  Tsunemasa
  Kinuta
  Hagoromo
  Kagekiyo
  Awoi no Uye
  Kakitsubata
  Chorio
  Genjo
  (Also "Kumaska," two acts, and "Nishikigi," two acts)
Fitzmaurice, George. Five plays. Bost. Little, Brown. 1914.
  The pie-dish
  The magic glasses
  The dandy dolls
  (Also "The country dressmaker," three acts, and "The moonlighter," four acts)
Flying Stag plays. N. Y. Egmont Arens, 1918.
  The Sandbar queen   Cronyn, George
  Night   Oppenheim, James
  The angel intrudes   Dell, Floyd
  Enter the hero   Helburn, Theresa
  Two blind beggars and one less blind Moeller, Philip
  The slave with two faces   Davies, Mary C.
  Blind   O'Brien, Seumas
47 Workshop. Plays. First series. N. Y. Brentano's, 1918.
  Three pills in a bottle   Field, Rachel L.
  "The good men do"   Osborne, Hubert
  Two crooks and a lady   Pillot, Eugene
  Free speech   Prosser, William L.
47 Workshop. Plays. Second series. N. Y. Brentano's, 1920.
  Torches   Raisbeck, Kenneth
  Cooks and cardinals   Lindan, Norman C.
  A Flitch of Bacon   Hinkley, Eleanor H.
  The playroom   Halman, Doris F.
47 Workshop. Plays. Third series. N. Y. Brentano's, 1922.
  The crowsnest   Manley, William F.
  The hard heart   Kister, M. A., Jr.

Mis' Mercy   Bray, Louise W.
The other one   Ketchum, Arthur

Fotheringham, E. M. and Gemmell, John. Tiny plays for tiny people. N. Y. French, 1921.
Good intentions
The Muffin man
The middle of the night
Why?
Whiney-Piney
Baby's ill
Mrs. Marconi
Authorship
Maggie Ann

Frank, Maude M. Short plays about famous authors. N. Y. Holt, 1915.
A mistake at the manor
When Heine was twenty-one
Miss Burney at Court
A Christmas Eve with Charles Dickens
The fairies' plea

Fuller, Alice C. Dramatized stories, myths, and legends. Franklin, Ohio. Eldridge Entertainment house, 1913.
Puss in boots
Hans and Grethel
Little John joins the band of Robin Hood
Robin Hood becomes an outlaw
Cinderella
Rhoecus
Little Red Riding Hood
The golden touch
Juno's bird
Clytie
Siegfried and Brunehilde
(Also two longer plays and a dialogue)

Galsworthy, John. Six short plays. N. Y. Scribner, 1915–21.
Hall-marked
Defeat
The sun
Punch and Go
(Also "The first and the last," three scenes, and "The little man," three scenes)

Gascoin, Catherine B. The lumber room, and other plays. N. Y. Vaughan & Gomme, 1914.
The lumber room
Fickle Juliet
The Fortescues' dinner party
John Arbery's dream
The P. G.'s. (two scenes)
Them banns
The Toolip
Wrong again

Gerstenberg, Alice. Ten one-act plays. N. Y. Brentano's, 1921.
He said and she said—
Overtones
The unseen
The buffer
Attuned
The pot boiler
Hearts

Beyond
Fourteen
The illuminatti in drama libre

Gibson, Wilfrid W. Battle and other poems. N. Y. Macmillan, 1917.
Stonefolds
The bridal
The scar
Winter dawn
The ferry
On the threshold
(Also many poems)

Gibson, Wilfrid W. Borderlands and Thoroughfares. N. Y. Macmillan, 1914.
The queen's crags
Bloodybush edge
Hoops

Gibson, Wilfrid W. Daily Bread. N. Y. Macmillan, 1916.
The house of candles
On the road
The betrothed
The first born
"The family pride"
The garret
The shirt
The mother
The furnace
The child
The night-shift
Agatha Steel
Mates
The operation
The call
The wound
Summer-dawn
Holiday

Gibson, Wilfrid W. Poems (1904–1917). N. Y. Macmillan, 1912–1917.
Stonefolds
The bridal
The scar
Winter dawn
The ferry
On the threshold
The house of candles
On the road
The betrothed
The first-born
"The family's pride"
The garret
The shirt
The mother
The furnace
The child
The night-shift
Agatha Steel
Mates
The operation
The call
The wound
Summer-dawn

Holiday
Womenkind
The Queen's Crags
Bloodybush Edge
Hoops
(Also includes many poems)

Gibson, Wilfrid W. Stonefolds. Lond. Elkin Mathews, 1916.
Stonefolds
The bridal
The scar
Winter dawn
The ferry
On the threshold

Glaspell, Susan. The people and Close the book. N. Y. Shay, 1918.
The people
Close the book

Glaspell, Susan. Plays. Bost. Small, Maynard, 1920.
Trifles
The people
Close the book
Woman's honor
Tickless time (In collaboration with George C. Cook)
The outside
(Also "Bernice," three acts, and "Suppressed desires," two scenes)

Goodlander, Mabel R. Fairy plays for children. Chic. Rand McNally, 1915.
The honest woodcutter
Mistress Mary gives a garden party
The pine tree
The elves and the shoe-maker
(Also five longer plays)

Goodman, Kenneth S. More quick curtains. Chic. The Stage Guild, 1923.
The green scarf
The red flag
The parting
Behind the black cloth
At the edge of the wood
Dancing dolls

Goodman, Kenneth S. Quick curtains. Chic. the Stage Guild, 1915.
Dust of the road
The game of chess
Barbara
Ephraim and the winged bear
Back of the yards
Dancing dolls
A man can only do his best

Gould, Felix. The marsh maiden and other plays. Bost. Four Seas, 1918.
The marsh maiden
The stranger
In the marshes

Graham, Manta S. Light weights. Bost. Cornhill Pub. Co., 1921.
The goose
The trend
Two's company
A By-product
Allied occupations

Grange plays—Number one. One-act plays compiled by J. A. Darrow. N. Y. Chatham, 1914.
His lordship
The golden wedding
The school board in our town
The drifting clouds
The burglar alarm
(Also two longer plays and recitations, tableaux, and entertainments)

Grange plays—Number two. One-act plays, compiled by J. W. Darrow. N. Y. Chatham, 1915.
Troubles of a housekeeper
The Rosedale sewing society
Maw Moseley's courtin' lamp
Mrs. Elwell's paper
(Also two longer plays and dialogues, pantomimes, etc.)

Grange plays—Number three. One-act plays. Pub. by J. W. Darrow. N. Y. Chatham, 1915.
The spiritual boost at Sallytown
The wrong man
Cranberry corners
(Also one longer play)

Greene, Clay M. The dispensation and other plays. N. Y. Doran, 1914.
The dispensation
The star of Bethlehem
"Through Christmas Bells"
The awakening of Barbizon

Greene, Kathleen C. The little boy out of the wood and other dream plays. Lond. John Lane, 1917.
The little boy out of the wood
Night watches
The poppy seller
The first Christmas Eve
The vision splendid
The Princess on the road
The two bad fairies

Gregory, Lady Isabelle A. The image and other plays. N. Y. Putnam, 1922.
Hanrakan's oath
The wrens
(Also "The image," three acts, and "Shanwalla," two acts)

Gregory, Lady Isabelle A. New comedies. N. Y. Putnam, 1913.
The Bogie men
The full moon
Coats
McDonough's wife
(Also "Danner's gold," two acts)

Gregory, Lady Isabelle A. Seven short plays. N. Y. Putnam, 1903.
Spreading the news
Hyacinth Halvey
The rising of the moon
The Jack daw
The workhouse ward
The travelling man
The Gaol Gate

Griffith, Benjamin L. C. Plays and monologues. Phila. Penn Pub. Co., 1901.
Forget-me-not

A cloudy day
Wanted—a valet
For her sake
A mistake in identity
Not at home

Guild, Thacher H. The power of a God and other one-act plays. Urbana, Ill. University of Illinois Press, 1919.
The class of '56
The higher good
The power of a God
The portrait

Gunnison, Binney. New dialogues and plays for young people. N. Y. Hinds, Hayden, Eldredge, 1905.

Mrs. Hardcastle's journey.	Goldsmith, Oliver
A matter of duty	Hope, Anthony
Pride against pride	Marston, Westland
A disastrous announcement	Dickens, Charles
Miss Judith Macan	Lever, Charles
Helen and Modus	Knowles, Sheridan
Sam Weller and his father	Dickens, Charles
Extracting a secret	Crawford, F. M.
Open or shut?	Musset, Alfred de
The Prairie Princesses	Gunnison, Binney
"Gentlemen, the King!"	Barr, Robert
Ben-Hur and Iras	Wallace, Lew
Savonarola and Lorenzo	Austin, Alfred
Love conquers revenge	Byr, Robert
Becket saves Rosamund	Tennyson, Alfred Lord
The Princess and the Countess	Stevenson, Robert L.
Queen Catherine	Shakespeare, William
Deacon Brodie	Henley and Stevenson
Pizarro and Rolla	Sheridan, Richard B.
Raimond released	Hemans, Mrs. Felicia
Mrs. Harwood's secret	Oliphant, Mrs. M. O. W.
Innocence rewarded	Goldsmith, Oliver

(Also five longer plays)

Guptill, Elizabeth F. and Hunting, Ema S. and others. Bright ideas for Christmas. Lebanon, Ohio. March Bros., 1920.
The messenger birds
The boy who found Christmas
The jolliest Christmas ever
What King Christmas brought
(Also a longer play and many recitations, drills, exercises)

Guptill, Elizabeth F. The complete Hallowe'en book. Lebanon, Ohio. March Bros., 1915.
Who was scared?
What do you know about ghosts?
(Also a longer play and many recitations, dialogues, drills, etc.)

Guptill, Elizabeth F. Guptill's new Christmas book. Lebanon, Ohio. March Bros., 1915.
A discouraged worker
The worm turns
Wanted—a chimney
(Also recitations, dialogues, and drills)

Guptill, Elizabeth F. Twelve plays for children. Chic. Beckley-Cardy Co., 1916.
The Census man
The baby show

The color fairies
Taking teacher's place
Grandmother's cat
Imaginary Tommy
Marie recites
Playing Rabbit
Uncle Joe's will
A dose of his own medicine
(Also two longer plays)

Halman, Doris F. Set the stage for eight. Bost. Little, Brown, 1923.
Lady Anne
Santa Claus
The playroom
Fannie and the ghost
The difficult border
The closet
The dog
Will-o'-the-wisp

Hare, Walter B. The white Christmas and other merry Christmas plays. Chic., T. S. Denison, 1917.
The white Christmas
Anita's secret; or, Christmas in the steerage
Christmas with the Mulligan's
A Christmas Carol; or, The Miser's Yuletide dream
Her Christmas hat
(Also "The wishing man," three acts)

Harper's book of little plays. Selected by Madalene D. Barnum. N. Y. Harper, 1910.

The revolt of the Holidays	Stevenson, Edward I.
The Ninepin Club	Creevey, Caroline A. & Sangster, Margaret E.
Familiar quotations	Bermann, Patty P.
The tables turned	Bangs, John K.
A Thanksgiving dream	Creevey, Caroline A. & Sangster, Margaret E.

(Also "The frog party," three acts)

Harvard Dramatic Club. Plays. N. Y Brentano's, 1918.

The florist shop	Hawkridge, Winifred
The bank account	Brock, Howard
The rescue	Smith, Rita C.
America passes by	Andrews, Kenneth

Harvard Dramatic Club. Plays. Second series. N. Y. Brentano's, 1919.

The harbor of lost ships	Bray, Louise W.
Garafelia's husband	Bates, Esther W.
The scales and the sword	Bishop, Farnham
The four-flushers	Kinkead, Cleves

Haslett, Harriet H. Dolores of the Sierra, and other one-act plays. San Francisco, Calif., Paul Elder, 1917.
Dolores of the Sierra
The scoop
Undercurrents
A modern menage
The inventor
When love is blind

Henderson, Mrs. Alice C. (Alice Corbin). Adam's dream and two other miracle plays for children. N. Y. Scribner, 1909.
Adam's dream
The star of Bethlehem
Easter morning

Hewlett, Maurice. Agonists: a trilogy of God and man. N. Y. Scribner, 1911.
Minos, King of Crete
Ariadne in Naxos
The death of Hippolytus
Hill, Frederick T. High school farces. N. Y. Stokes, 1920.
"Dinner's served!"
The heathen Chinee
A knotty problem
Holley, Horace. Read-aloud plays. N. Y. Kennerley, 1916.
Her happiness
A modern prodigal
The incompatibles
The genius
Survival
The telegram
Rain
Pictures
His luck
Holt, Florence T. They the crucified and Comrades. Bost. Houghton, 1918.
They the crucified
(Also "Comrades," two scenes)
Houghton, Stanley. Five one-act plays. N. Y. French, 1913.
The dear departed
Fancy free
The master of the house
Phipps
The fifth commandment
Housman, Laurence. Angels and ministers. Lond. Cape, 1921.
The Queen, God Bless Her!
His favorite flower
The comforter
Housman, Laurence. Angels and ministers; four plays of Victorian shade and character. N. Y. Harcourt, Brace, 1922.
The Queen, God Bless Her!
His favorite flower
The comforter
Possession
Housman, Laurence. False premises: five one-act plays. Oxford. Basil Blackwell, 1922.
The Christmas tree
The torch of time
Moonshine
A fool and his money
The house fairy
Houseman, Laurence. The wheel: three poetic plays on Greek subjects. N. Y. French, 1920.
Apollo in Hades
The death of Alcestis
The doom of Admetus
Hubbard, Eleanore. Citizenship plays: a dramatic reader for upper grades. Chic. Benjamin H. Sanborn, 1922.
The Mayflower compact
The Charter Oak
The Declaration of Independence
A Colonial school
The first American library

"The price of Liberty"
The banker's strategy
The homesteader's Christmas
Salvage
Forewarned is forearmed
No man is above the law
(Also twenty longer plays)

Hubbard, Eleanore. Little American history plays for little Americans. Chic. Benjamin H. Sanborn, 1919.
The soft-soap day
"The first in war"
Independence day
The Star-Spangled Banner
One way to capture a fort
"Only a girl!"
A lucky Hallowe'en
Daniel Boone's snuff box
Gold in California
The trial trip of the Clermont
Samuel Morse's telegraph
Memorial day
America pays her debt to France
(Also fourteen longer plays)

Hunter, Rex. Stuff o' Dreams and other plays. Chic., T. S. Denison, 1919.
The wild goose
Stuff o' Dreams
Hands and the man
The Romany Road

Irish, Marie. Choice Christmas dialogues and plays. Dayton, Ohio. Paine Pub. Co., 1922.
The boastful giant
The broken picture
Herbert's discovery
Doing away with Christmas
Merry Christmas, Jake
The joy of giving
The Pickett's Christmas party
The Christmas dinner
A double Christmas gift
Grandfather's bright Christmas plan
(Also many dialogues, two longer plays, and plays of another type)

Irish, Marie. Little people's plays. Chic., T. S. Denison, 1913.
A good little girl
Prindle's proposal
Sambo's party
A visit from the Brownies
(Also nine longer plays)

Irish, Marie. Plays and comedies for little folks. Chic., A. Flanagan, 1912.
Hiawatha
Mother Goose and her flock
The baby show
Brave foresters
The days of long ago
Little house keepers
The lost pocket book
A North-pole expedition
Old Uncle Rat gives his consent
A trained menagerie

Waiting for the train
We and our friends
When we are grown up
When we are women
(Also longer plays and entertainments)

Irish, Marie. The primary Christmas book. Dayton, Ohio. Paine Pub. Co., 1922.
Uncle Sam's mistake
Uncle Grouch
The Christmas cookies
(Also recitations, drill, dialogues)

Irish, Marie, Denton, Clara J., Smith, Laura R., and others. Thirty new Christmas dialogues and plays. Chic. Flanagan, 1909.

A Christmas surprise for Mother Goose	Irish, Marie
A Christmas journey	Irish, Marie
Christmas wishes	Irish, Marie
The boastful weather vane	Denton, Clara J.
A visit to Santa Claus	Irish, Marie
The next day	Denton, Clara J.
Christmas visitors from other lands	Irish, Marie
"No presents"	Denton, Clara J.
All his fault	Denton, Clara J.
Christmas influence	Irish, Marie
Christmas sympathy	Irish, Marie
"The book of things"	Denton, Clara J.
The true Christmas spirit	Irish, Marie
Unexpected company	Denton, Clara J.
Christmas at Holly Farm	Denton, Clara J.
No Christmas in the house	Irish, Marie
Trials of Christmas shopping	Irish, Marie
Christmas in the air	Irish, Marie
The great sale	Denton, Clara J.

(Also eleven other dialogues and sketches)

Irwin, Grace L. Drawing room plays. San Francisco, Calif., Paul Elder, 1903.
A domestic dilemma
Heroes
An innocent villain
Art for art's sake
An intimate acquaintance
The wedding of Muh Foy
Music hath charms

Iwasaki, Yozan T. and Hughes, Glenn. Three modern Japanese plays. Cincinnati. Stewart Kidd, 1923.

The razor	Nakamura, Kichizo
The madman on the roof	Kikuchi, Kan
Nari-Kin	Iwasaki, Yozan

Jenkins, Hester D. Five playlets, written for the Department of Social Betterment. Brooklyn, N. Y., Bureau of Charities, 1915.
Mother Goose up-to-date
Judith and Ariel
Our friends, the foods
In a tenement
(Also "Killing giants," three scenes)

Jennings, Gertrude. Four one act plays. N. Y. French, 1914.
The rest cure
Between the soup and the savoury

The pros and cons
Acid drops
Jex, John. Passion playlets. Bost. Cornhill Co., 1918.
Violet souls
The nest
Mr. Willoughby calls
The unnecessary atom
Johnson, Gertrude E. Dialects for oral interpretation. N. Y. Century, 1922.
A Ramlet o' Puce
Spoiling the broth
The rider of dreams
"The Philosopher of Butterbiggins"
Warnock, A. McClure
Graham, Bertha N.
Torrence, Ridgeley
Chapin, Harold
(Also Discussion of dialect, poems, and recitations)
Johnston, Emma L. and Barnum, Madalene D. A book of plays for little actors. Chic. American Book Co., 1907.
The lion and the mouse
The echo
A little sparrow
The spider and the fly
The little birds
Abraham Lincoln and the little bird
Ladybird
George Washington and the cherry tree
The fox and the crow
The Fourth of July
(Also eight longer plays)
Jones, Henry A. The theatre of ideas: a burlesque, allegory, and three one-act plays. N. Y. Doran, 1915.
The goal
Her tongue
Grace Mary
Keating, Miss E. H. Dramas for boys. N. Y. French, n. d.
Plot of Potzentausend
Incog
The poor relation
The talisman
Kleber, Frank T. Three plays. N. Y. Kleber, 1922.
Triangled
When extremes meet
(Also "Men of Fame," in eight scenes)
Knickerbocker, Edwin Van B., ed. Plays for classroom interpretation. N. Y. Holt, 1921.
The golden doom
Two crooks and a lady
Will o' the wisp
Spreading the news
The turtle dove
Allison's lad
Dunsany, Lord
Pillot, Eugene
Halman, Doris F.
Gregory, Lady
Oliver, Margaret S.
Dix, Beulah M.
(Also scene II, act III of "Ulysses," by Stephen Phillips)
Kraft, Irma. The power of Purim and other plays. Designed for Jewish religious schools. Phila. Jewish Publication Society of America, 1915.
The power of Purim
A Maccabean cure
To save his country
Ambition in White chapel
Because he loved David so
(Purim)
(Hanukkah)
(Pasach)
(Shabuot)
(Closing of school)

Kreymborg, Alfred. Plays for Merry Andrews. N. Y. The Sunwise Turn, 1920.
  Vote the new moon
  At the sign of the thumb and nose
  The silent waiter
  Monday
  (Also "Uneasy street," two scenes)

Kreymborg, Alfred. Plays for poem-mimes. N. Y. The Other Press, 1918.
  When the willow nods
  Jack's house
  Lima beans
  Manikin and Minikin
  People who die
  (Also "Blue and Green," three scenes)

Kreymborg, Alfred. Puppet plays. N. Y. Harcourt, Brace, n.d.
  When the willow nods
  Blue and green
  Manikin and Minikin
  Jack's house
  Lima beans
  People who die
  Pianissimo

Langner, Lawrence. Five one-act comedies. Cincinnati. Stewart Kidd, 1922.
  Matinata
  Another way out
  The family exit
  Pie
  Licensed

Lee, Agnes. The sharing. Bost. Sherman, French, 1914.
  The sharing
  The silent house
  (Also many poems)

Leslie, Noel. Three plays. Bost. Four Seas, 1920.
  Waste
  The war-fly
  For king and country

Lewis, B. Roland. Contemporary one-act plays. N. Y. Scribner, 1922.
  The twelve-pound look   Barrie, James M.
  Tradition   Middleton, George
  The exchange   Thurston, Althea
  Sam Average   Mackaye, Percy
  Hyacinth Halvey   Gregory, Augusta
  The gazing globe   Pillot, Eugene
  The boor   Tchekov, Anton
  The last straw   Crocker, Bosworth
  Manikin and Minikin   Kreymborg, Alfred
  White dresses   Greene, Paul
  Moonshine   Hopkins, Arthur
  Modesty   Hervieu, Paul
  The Deacon's hat   Marks, Jeannette
  Where but in America   Wolff, Oscar M.
  A dollar   Pinski, David
  The diabolical circle   Bornstead, Beulah
  The far-away princess   Sudermann, Hermann
  The stronger   Strindberg, August

Lisle, Clifton. Boy scout entertainments. Phila. Penn Pub. Co., 1918.
  A scout's honor

Fair play
Jerry's job
(Also "On the Greenboro Nine"; "The Daniel Boone pageant"; "A Semaphore Flag Drill," longer plays)

Lord, Katharine. The little playbook. N. Y. Duffield, 1920.
Katjen's garden
June magic
The minister's dream
(Also three longer plays)

Lord, Katharine. Plays for school and camp. Bost. Little, Brown, 1922.
The Raven man
Buried treasure
The three bears
The Pied Piper
The Honorable Miss
(Also "Kris Kringle makes a flight")

Loving, Pierre, ed. Ten minute plays. N. Y. Brentano's, 1923.

Prologue for a Marionette Theatre	Hoffmannstahl, Hugo von
Echo	Shipley, Joseph T.
Living hours	Schnitzler, Arthur
In the darkness	Totheroh, Dan
Pandora's box	Amend, J. Gordon
Scruples	Mirbeau, Octave
Firefly night	Dorff, M. J.
A matter of husbands	Molnar, Ferenc
Philanthropy	Tompkins, Frank G.
At the setting of the sun	Louys, Pierre
Yesterday	Clements, Colin C.
The stronger	Strindberg, August
Indian summer	Loving, Pierre
The white lie	Metz-Konig, Marie

Luques, E. Antoinette. The snow image. Bost. Walter H. Baker, 1914.
The snow image
The spirit of Memorial Day
The story of the poplar tree
(Also "A dramatization of Hiawatha's childhood," three acts)

Lütkenhaus, Anna M. Plays for school children. N. Y. Century, 1915.

Master Skylark	Bennett, John
Barnaby Lee	Bennett, John
Through the looking glass	Carroll, Lewis
The fairy minstrel of Glenmalure	Leamy, Edmund
A nature play in a City School	Burroughs Nature Club. Public School 188 and 15, Manhattan
Our choice	Knox, Margaret
Every boy	Lütkenhaus, Anna M.
Thanksgiving Day—1696	Bayles, Martha B. & Lütkenhaus, Anna M.
The crowning of the Dryads	Bayles, Martha B.
The birds' story of the trees	Lütkenhaus, Anna M.
Well babies	Lütkenhaus, Anna M.
A geography squabble	Lütkenhaus, Anna M.
A grammar play	Lütkenhaus, Anna M.
Mrs. Pollywigs and her wonderful wax works	Lütkenhaus, Anna M.

(Also six plays of another type)

McGeoch, Daisy. Concert Cameos. N. Y. French, 1922.
Shopping
Mormonizing

Proposing
Packing
Picturing
Thrilling
Camping
Reading
(Also two longer plays)

Mackay, Constance D. The Beau of Bath and other one-act plays of eighteenth century life. N. Y. Holt, 1915.
The Beau of Bath
The silver lining
Ashes of roses
Gretna Green
Counsel retained
The prince of court painters

Mackay, Constance D. The Forest Princess and other masques. N. Y. Holt, 1916.
The gift of time
The masque of conservation
The masque of Pomona
The sun goddess
(Also two longer masques)

Mackay, Constance D. The house of the heart and other plays for children. N. Y. Holt, 1909.
The house of the heart
The gooseherd and the goblin
The enchanted garden
Nimble-wit and Fingerkin
A little Pilgrim's progress
A pageant of hours
On Christmas eve
The elf child
The Princess and the Pixies
The Christmas guest

Mackay, Constance D. Patriotic plays and pageants for young people N. Y. Holt, 1912.
Abraham Lincoln : rail-splitter
Benjamin Franklin : journeyman
The Boston tea party
Daniel Boone : patriot
George Washington's fortune
In witchcraft days
Merrymount
Princess Pocahontas

Mackay, Constance D. Plays of the pioneers. N. Y. Harper, 1915.
A book of historical pageant-plays
The pioneers
The fountain of youth
May-day
The vanishing race
The passing of Hiawatha
Dame Greel o' Portland Town

Mackay, Constance D. The silver thread and other folk plays for young people. N. Y. Holt, 1910.
The forest spring
The foam maiden
Troll magic
The three wishes

A brewing of brains
Siegfried
The snow witch

Mackaye, Percy. Yankee fantasies. N. Y. Duffield, 1912.
Chuck: an orchard fantasy
Gettysburg: a woodshed commentary
The antick: a wayside sketch
The cat-boat: a fantasy for music
Sam Average: a silhouette

MacMillan, Mary. More short plays. Cincinnati. Stewart Kidd, 1917.
His second girl
At the church door
The dress rehearsal of Hamlet
The dryad
(Also three longer plays)

Macmillan, Mary. Short plays. Cincinnati. Stewart Kidd, 1913.
The shadowed star
The ring
The rose
Entr' Acte
A woman's a woman for a' that
A fan and two candlesticks
A modern masque
The futurists
The gate of wishes
(Also "Luck," four acts)

MacMillan, Mary. Third book of short plays. Cincinnati. Stewart Kidd, 1922.
The storm
In heaven
When two's not company
Peter Donelly
An Apocryphal episode
Standing moving
(Also "The week-end," three acts)

Maeterlinck, Maurice. The intruder. tr. by Richard Hovey. N. Y. Dodd, Mead, 1911.
The intruder
The blind
The seven Princesses
(Also one longer play)

Maeterlinck, Maurice. Plays of Maurice Maeterlinck, Vol. I. tr. by Richard Hovey. Chic. Herbert S. Stone, 1894.
The intruder
The blind
The seven Princesses
(Also one longer play)

Manners, J. Hartley. Happiness and other plays. N. Y. Dodd, Mead, 1914.
Happiness
Just as well
The day of dupes

Manners, J. Hartley. Thre plays. N. Y. Doran, 1920.
All clear
God of my faith
God's outcast

March Brothers, Publishers. Petite plays. Lebanon, Ohio. March Bros., 1912.

After the bargain sale	Bugbee, Willis N.
The etiquette of the occasion	Bascom, Louise R.
The joke	Guptill, Elizabeth F.
As it will be	Guptill, Elizabeth F.
Whose dog?	Guptill, Elizabeth F.
Winning a prize	Bugbee, Willis N.
The young gardener	Panly, Fred C.
The plumber	Bascom, Louise R.
The fresh air fiend	Bascom, Louise R.
The stolen horse	Bascom, Louise R.
Norah makes a cake	Bascom, Louise R.
The claims	Bascom, Louise R.
A station episode	Bascom, Louise R.
Quick news	Denton, Clara J.
The tailor's dummy	Denton, Clara J.
Seeking information	Denton, Clara J.
Being a hero	Denton, Clara J.
The wrong lessons	Denton, Clara J.
Going shopping	Denton, Clara J.
The blue pump	Denton, Clara J.
The Junipes baby	Denton, Clara J.
The day after the circus	Denton, Clara J.
The Ph.D.	Denton, Clara J.

Marks, Jeannette. Three Welsh plays. Bost. Little, Brown, 1912.
The merry, merry cuckoo
The deacon's hat
Welsh honeymoon

Masefield, John. The locked chest and The sweeps of Ninety-eight. N. Y. Macmillan, 1916.
The locked chest
The sweeps of Ninety-eight

Masefield, John. Poems and plays. Vol. II. N. Y. Macmillan, 1918.
Mrs. Harrison
The locked chest
The sweeps of Ninety-eight
Philip the king
Good Friday
(Also four longer plays)

Mayorga, Margaret G., ed. Representative one-act plays by American authors. Bost. Little, Brown, 1919.

Sam Average	Mackaye, Percy
Six who pass while the lentils boil	Walker, Stuart
"Voices"	Flexner, Hortense
The merry merry cuckoo	Marks, Jeannette
Sinstram of Skagerrak	Cowan, Sada
Will-o'-the-wisp	Halman, Doris F.
"Beyond"	Gerstenberg, Alice
A good woman	Middleton, George
Funiculi Funicula	Wellman, Rita
Hunger	Pillot, Eugene
In the zone	O'Neill, Eugene G.
The brink of silence	Galbraith, Esther E.
Allison's lad	Dix, Beulah Marie
Mrs. Pat and the law	Aldis, Mary
Lima beans	Kreymborg, Alfred
The wonder hat	Hecht, Ben and Goodman, Kenneth S.
Suppressed desires	Cook, George C. and Glaspell, Susan
Where but in America	Wolff, Oscar M.

A question of morality   Wilde, Percival
Martha's mourning   Hoffman, Phoebe
Ryland   Stevens, Thomas W. and Goodman, Kenneth S.
The last straw   Crocker, Bosworth
Hattie   De Pue, Elva
Dregs   Spencer, Frances P.

Merington, Marguerite. Festival plays. N. Y. Duffield, 1913.
Father Time and his children
Tertulla's garden; or, The miracle of good St. Valentine
The seven sleepers of Ephesos
Princess Moss Rose
The testing of Sir Gawayne
A Christmas party

Merington, Marguerite. Holiday plays. N. Y. Duffield, 1910.
Priscilla, Myles and John
The first flag
Abe Lincoln and Little A. D.
The Dulce et Decorum Club
(Also "Washington Birthday pageant.")

Merington, Marguerite. Picture plays. N. Y. Duffield, 1911.
The last sitting
A Salon Curre fantasy
His mother's face
A Gainsborough lady
Artist-mother and child
Queen and Emperor
Millet group

Middleton, George. Embers and other one-act plays. N. Y. Holt, 1911.
Embers
The failures
The gargoyle
In his house
Madonna
The man masterful

Middleton, George. Masks. N. Y. Holt, 1920.
Masks
Jim's beast
Tides
Among the lions
The reason
The house

Middleton, George. Possession. N. Y. Holt, 1915.
Possession
The groove
A good woman
The black tie
Circles
The unborn

Middleton, George. Tradition. N. Y. Holt, 1913.
Tradition
On bail
Their wife
Waiting
The cheat of pity
Mothers

Millward, Florence M. Four short plays. Lond. Joseph Williams, 1922.
Irene obliges
The alternative
Henry wakes up
This room is engaged

Milne, A. A. First plays. Lond. Chatto & Windus, 1919.
Wurzel-Flummery
The boy comes home
The red feathers
(Also two longer plays)

Moeller, Philip. Five somewhat historical plays. N. Y. Knopf, 1916.
Helena's husband
The little supper
Sister Susamiah
The roadhouse in Arden
Pokey; or, The beautiful legend of the Indian amorous

Monroe, Harriet. The passing show: five modern plays in verse. Bost. Houghton, Mifflin, 1903.
At the goal
After all
A modern minuet
It passes by
(Also "The thunderstorm," two acts)

Moore, Thomas S. Tragic mothers. Lond. Grant Richards, 1922.
Medea
Niobe
Tyrfing

Morley, Malcolm. Told by the gate and other one-act plays. Bost. Gorham Press, 1916.
Told by the gate
The masterpiece
Recollections
The Cosher
Beauty versus the Beast
A motor mishap

Morningside plays. N. Y. Frank Shay, 1917.
Hattie — De Pue, Elva
One a day — Briggs, Caroline
Markheim — Macdonald, Zellah
The home of the free — Reizenstein, Elmer L.

Moses, Montrose J., ed. Representative one-act plays by continental authors. Bost. Little, Brown, 1922.
Countess Mizzie — Schnitzler, Arthur
Death and the fool — Hofmannsthal, Hugo von
The blind — Maeterlinck, Maurice
The birthday party — Bergström, Hjalmar
The woman who was acquitted — Lorde, Andre de
Among the quays — Lavedan, Henri
For ever and ever — Lavedan, Henri
Where shall we go? — Lavedan, Henri
The afternoon walk — Lavedan, Henri
Not at home — Lavedan, Henri
Françoisé Luck — Porto-Riche, Georges de
Morituri: Teias — Sudermann, Hermann
The Court singer — Wedekind, Frank
Sacred ground — Giacosa, Giuseppe
An incident — Andreyev, Leonid

AN INDEX TO ONE-ACT PLAYS 307

A merry death — Evréinov, Nikolai
By their words ye shall know them — Quintero, Serafin & Quintero, Joaquim A.
The lover — Sierra, Gregorio M.
Simoon — Strindberg, Johann A.

Moses, Montrose J., ed. A treasury of plays for children. Bost. Little, Brown, 1921.
The testing of Sir Gawayne — Merington, Marguerite
Punch and Judy — Anon
Six who pass while the Lentils boil — Walker, Stuart
Master Skylark — Lütkenhaus, Anna M.
The months: a pageant — Rossetti, Christina G.
The traveling man — Gregory, Lady
(Also eight longer plays)

Moylan, Thomas K. "Oh Lawsy Me!" and "Movies." Dublin. James Duffy, 1917.
"Oh Lawsy Me!"
"Movies"

Musset, Alfred de. Barberine and other comedies. Chic. (Sergal) Dramatic Pub. Co., 1911.
A door must be open or shut
A caprice
One cannot think of everything
(Also three longer plays)

Nirdlinger, Charles F. Four short plays. N. Y. Kennerly, 1916.
Look after Louise
Big Kate
The real people
Aren't they wonders?

Norton, Ida G. Club stunts. La Junta, Colo., Ida G. Norton, 1922.
Aunt Sally Saunders' health crusade
How to reduce
Adopting an orphan
(Also a monologue and an entertainment)

O'Brien, Seumas. Duty and other Irish comedies. Bost. Little, Brown, 1916.
Duty
Jurisprudence
Magnanimity
Matchmakers
Retribution

O'Dea, Mark. Red Bud women: four dramatic episodes. Cincinnati. Stewart Kidd, 1922.
The song of Solomon
Shivaree
Miss Myrtle says "Yes"
Not in the lesson

Olcott, Virginia. Patriotic plays for young people. N. Y. Dodd, Mead, 1918.
Goody Grumble's cottage
Dora: her flag
Little homemaker
The wonder-hill
Oneida's dreams
Poor little boy
A Princess and a churn
(Also two longer plays)

Olcott, Virginia. Plays for home, school and settlement. N. Y. Moffat, Yard, 1916.
The ruler of the forest
A Puritan Christmas
Little people of Autumn
(Also three longer plays)

Oliver, Margaret S. Six one-act plays. Bost. Richard T. Badger, 1916.
The hand of the Prophet
Children of Granada
The turtle dove
This youth—gentlemen!
The striker
Murdering Selina

O'Neill, Eugene G. The moon of the Caribbees and six other plays of the sea. N. Y. Boni and Liveright, 1919.
The moon of the Caribbees
Bound east for Cardiff
The long voyage home
In the zone
Ile
Where the cross is made
The rope

O'Neill, Eugene G. Thirst and other one act plays. Bost. Gorham Press, 1914.
Thirst
The web
Fog
Recklessness
(Also "Warnings," two scenes)

Painton, Edith F. A. U. Dialogues and plays for entertainment days. Chic. Beckley-Cardy, 1917.
Studying for a test
Writing a school play
Organizing a society
The Popular Dick
The Bairves' Saturday night
Rehearsing the program
Murdering the language
The lost colors
The Camp-fire girl
A country cousin
(Also one longer play and several dialogues)

Painton, Edith F. A. U. Specialty entertainments for little folks. Chic. Beckley-Cardy, 1917.
The doll show
Good-bye all!
Coming home to Grandma's
The Provident society
(Also many entertainments)

Parker, Mary M. Monologues, stories, jingles and plays. Chic. Frederick J. Drake, 1917.
Killing time
Love behind the scenes
The Princess Innocence
A quiet evening at home
The rehearsal
(Also dialogues, jingles and "Powder and patches," a play in two acts)

Payne, Fanny U. Plays and pageants of citizenship. N. Y. Harper, 1920.
The soap-box orator
The victory of the good citizen
Old tight-wad and the victory dwarf
Rich citizens
Humane citizens
(Also three longer pageants)

Parsons, Margaret G. Red letter day plays. N. Y. Womans Press, 1921.
Fire-spirits
The Christmas message
In a Valentine box
Jack-I-The-Green
The potentate of Weatherdom
'Neath the scepter of Susan
(Also ten longer plays)

Payne, F. Ursula. Plays for Anychild. N. Y. Harper, 1918.
New Year's Day
Lincoln's birthday
Washington's birthday
Arbor Day
Decoration Day
Flag Day
Graduation Day
Columbus Day
Thanksgiving Day
Christmas Day

Payne, F. Ursula. Two war plays for schools. Brooklyn, N. Y. Training School for teachers. Bulletin II., 1918.
The vision of Columbus
The conversion of Mrs. Slacker

Pearse, Padraic H. Collected works. Dublin. Maunsel, 1917.
The singer
The king
The master
Iosagan
(Also many stories and poems)

Pearse, Padraic. The singer and other plays. Dublin, Maunsel, 1918.
The singer
The king
A morning call
Those landladies
Breaking the ice
A pair of lunatics

Pinski, David. King David and his wives. tr. fr. Yiddish by Isaac Goldberg. N. Y. Huebsch, 1923.
Michal
Abigail
Bathsheba
In the harem
Abishag

Pinski, David and others. Six plays of the Yiddish Theatre. tr. and ed. by Isaac Goldberg. Bost. John W. Luce, 1916.
Abigal   Pinski, David
Forgotten souls   Pinski, David
She must marry a doctor   Rabinowitsch, Solomon J.
Winter   Ash, Sholom
The sinner   Ash, Sholom
In the dark   Hirschbein, Perez

Pinski, David and others. Six plays of the Yiddish Theatre. Second series tr. & ed. by Isaac Goldberg. Bost. John W. Luce, 1918.
  Little heroes — Pinski, David
  The stranger — Pinski, David
  On the threshold — Hirschbein, Perez
  Poetry and prose — Levin, Z.
  The black sheep — Kobrin, Leon
  The secret of life — Kobrin, Leon

Pinski, David. Ten plays tr. from the Yiddish. N. Y. Huebsch, 1920.
  The phonograph
  The God of the newly rich wool merchant
  A dollar
  The cripples
  The inventor and the king's daughter
  Diplomacy
  Little heroes
  The beautiful nun
  Poland—1919.
  The stranger

Playbits: fragments for concert folk. N. Y. French, 1922.
  A breakfast breeze
  "Hand it!"
  Gloom
  A. D. 2000
  (Also dialogues, a monologue and one scene series)

Plays for amateur actors. (New ed.) Lond. Pearson, 1921.
  G for George — Ruck, Berta
  The silver salt-cellars — Wishing, Stuart
  The Sevres tea-cups — Wishing, Stuart
  Cupid in the kitchen — Harris, Ada L.
  The proof of the pudding — Martin, O. Percy
  The marriage of Dotty — Thornton, Clare
  A quiet little dinner — Cobb, Thomas
  For the defendant—with costs — Baily, F. E.
  The cure that failed — Wentworth-Jones, Gertie de S.
  (Also "The black and white Pierrot," two acts)

Plays with a punch. Bost. Walter H. Baker, 1916.
  A crooked man and his crooked wife — Andrews, Kenneth L.
  His chance — Mann, Herbert A.
  The alarm — Fawcett, Marion R.
  A bride from home — Steell, Willis
  Brother Dave — Steell, Willis
  Faro Nell — Steell, Willis
  A game of comedy — Cook, Sherwin L.
  A scratch race — Makee, Walt
  The substance of ambition — Warren, Marie F.
  Her picture — Baker, Rachel E.
  Red or white? — Browne, William M.

Poole, Evan. An age of steel. Lond. Heath, Cranton & Ouseley, 1913.
  The post of honour
  Blood Royal
  The promise
  The King's letters

Poole, Madeline. The elf that stayed behind and other plays for children. Bost. Walter H. Baker, 1918.
  The elf that stayed behind
  The master
  (Also "Iosagan," a longer play)

Peixotto, Eustace M. Ten boys' farces. Bost. Walter H. Baker, 1916.
  Ding-a-ling
  The last rehearsal
  Rosie, the girl from Paris
  The teacher's pet
  Lost but found
  Political promises
  When the cat is away
  Chips off the old block
  The tramp barbers
  (Also one longer play)
Pemberton, May. Christmas plays. N. Y. Crowell, 1915.
  Lost toys
  Mistletoe and holly
  Christmas in Rhyme-Land
Phelps, Pauline and Short, Marion, ed. Sixteen two-character plays. N. Y. Edgar S. Werner, 1906.
  A box of powders
  A husband in clover
  Villain and victim
  Fast friends
  A happy ending
  Two jolly girl bachelors
  A show of hands
  A backward child
  The crystal-gazer
  The confederates
  "The nettle"
  He, she and it
  The goblins
  The Quaker way
  The Christmas box
  A Puritan prank
Potter, Dorothy. Under the eagle: three plays with a prologue and epilogue. Bost. Gorham Press, 1916.
  "Watchful waiting"
  Yellow yielding
  "Bombast and Platitudes"
  (Also a Prologue and Epilogue)
Practical Publishing Co. Christmas plays for children. Series I. Westfield, N. J. Practical Pub. Co., 1916.
  Little helpers
  Christmas stars
  King Christmas
  Four little fir trees
  (Also two long plays and three plays of a different type)
Provincetown plays. First series. N. Y. Shay, 1916.
  Bound east for Cardiff — O'Neill, Eugene G.
  The game — Bryant, Louise
  King Arthur's socks — Dell, Floyd
Provincetown plays. Second series. N. Y. Shay, 1916.
  Freedom — Reed, John
  Enemies — Boyce, Neith & Hapgood, Hutchins
  Suppressed desires — Cook, G. C. & Glaspell, Susan
Provincetown plays. Third series. N. Y. Shay, 1916.
  The two sons — Boyce, Neith
  Lima beans — Kreymborg, Alfred
  Before breakfast — O'Neill, Eugene G.

Rawson, Graham S. The stroke of Marbot and two other plays of Napoleonic times. Lond. T. Fisher Unwin, 1917.
  The stroke of Marbot
  The dangers of peace
  The Pastor of Jena

Reely, Mary K. Daily Bread; A window to the south; The lean years; one-act plays. N. Y. Wilson, 1919.
  Daily bread
  A window to the south
  The lean years

Rice, Cale Y. The immortal lure. Garden City, N. Y. Doubleday, Page, 1911.
  Giorgione
  Arduin
  O-Umè's gods
  The immortal lure

Rice, Wallace. Suggestions for giving six little plays for Illinois children. Illinois Centennial Commission. State of Illinois, 1918.
  Children of the Illini
  Children of France
  Pioneer boys and girls
  The underground railroad
  Children of the Civil War
  Children in the Great War

Richards, Laura E. The pig brother play-book. Bost. Little, Brown, 1915.
  The shadow
  For you and me
  The useful coal
  The sailor man
  The cooky
  "Oh, dear!"
  "Go" and "Come"
  Child's play
  The naughty comet
  The tangled skein
  The cake
  About angels
  The great feast
  The wheat-field
  (Also "The pig brother" and "Hokey Pokey," longer plays)

Richardson, Grace. Summer snow and other fairy plays. Chic. Saalfield Pub. Co., 1916.
  The battle of the days
  Goblin guests
  (Also two longer plays)

Roberts, Morley. Four plays. Lond. Nash, 1911.
  The hour of greatness
  The lamp of God
  The white horse
  The lay figure

Rogers, Thomas B. Five plays. Lond. Philip Allan, 1920.
  The forfeit
  The hall of laughter
  Eyes to the blind
  The Saint-King
  The heirloom

Ruschke, Egmont W. "The echo" and "A bit o' verse." Bost. Stratford Co., 1918.
  The echo
  Death speaks
  The intangible
  (Also many poems)

St. Nicholas book of plays and operettas. Second series. N. Y. Century, 1916.

The dream-toy shop	Baker, Jessie M.
Christmas babes in the woods	Swain, Corinne R.
Which shall be king?	Jones, Anna Van Marter
The Christmas conspiracy	Woodbridge, Elizabeth
How Christmas was saved	Markham, Catharine
The first Thanksgiving	Miller, Agnes
Everychild	Nichols, Content S.
"Everygirl"	Field, Rachel Lyman
Lord Malapert of Moonshine Castle	Brooks, E. S.
A friend in need	Frank, Maude M.
The new Red Riding-Hood	Brooks, E. S.

  (Also two operettas and a Shadow play)

Sanders, Helen F. Petalesharoo, and The Star Brave. Butte, Montana. McKee Printing Co., 1910.
  Petalesharoo
  Star Brave

Sargent, Herbert C. Pierrot playlets. N. Y. French, 1920.
  A burlesque pantomime
  The registry office
  The pavement artist
  The tourist agency
  An amateur rehearsal of Hamlet
  Buying a house
  Emigration
  Life insurance
  The American bar
  The prize picture

Saunders, Louise. Magic lanterns, a book of plays. N. Y. Scribner, 1923.
  Figureheads
  Our kind
  See-saw
  King and Commoner
  (Also "Poor Maddalena," a longer play

Schafer, Barbara L., ed. A book of one-act plays. Indianapolis. Bobbs-Merrill, 1922.

Nevertheless	Walker, Stuart
The heart of Pierrot	Scott, Margretta
The bank robbery	Ehrmann, Max
The Dryad and the Deacon	Bates, William O.
In the light of the manger	Bates, William O.
Phoebe Louise	Sobel, Bernard
Ever young	Gerstenberg, Alice
The man who couldn't say "No"	Harris, Claudia L.
The Deacon's hat	Marks, Jeannette
The exchange	Thurston, Althea

Schnitzler, Arthur. Anatol. (Paraphrased by Granville Barker) Bost. Little, Brown, 1917.
  Ask no questions and you'll hear no stories
  A Christmas present
  An episode

Keepsakes
A farewell supper
Dying pangs
The wedding morning

Schnitzler, Arthur. Anatol; Living hours; The Green Cockatoo. tr by Grace Isabel Colbron. (The Modern library of the World's Best Books) N. Y. Boni & Liveright, 1917.
Anatol—Questioning fate
Anatol—Christmas shopping
Anatol—Episode
Anatol—Milestones
Anatol—The farewell supper
Anatol—Dissolution
Anatol—Anatol's wedding morning
Living hours
The lady with the dagger
Last masks
Literature
The green Cockatoo

Schnitzler, Arthur. Comedies of words and other plays. Cincinnati. Stewart Kidd, 1917.
The hour of recognition
The big scene
The festival of Bacchus
Literature
His helpmate

Schnitzler, Arthur. The green Cockatoo and other plays. Lond. Gay & Hancock, n. d.
The green Cockatoo
The mate
Paracelsus

Searle, Katharine. Three war sketches. Cambridge, Mass. Powell Pub. Co., 1916.
Her story
The march of truth
"Hatred"

Seymour, Mrs. Arthur T. The protest of the trees and Flossie's first alphabet lesson: two blue bird plays. Bost. Walter H. Baker, 1918.
The protest of the trees
Flossie's alphabet lesson

Sharp, William. Vistas, the gypsy Christ and other imaginings. N. Y. Duffield, 1912.
Finis
The passion of Pére Hilarion
The birth of a soul
A northern night
The black Madonna
The fallen God
The coming of the Prince
The passing of Lilith
The whisperer

Shaw, George B. Heartbreak House; Great Catherine, and playlets of the war. N. Y. Brentano's, 1919.
O'Flaherty, V. C.
The Inca of Perusalem
Augustus does his bit
Annajanska, the Bolshevik Empress
(Also "Heartbreak House," three acts; and "Great Catherine," four scenes)

Shay, Frank, ed. Contemporary one-act plays of 1921. (American) Cincinnati. Stewart Kidd, 1922.

Mirage	Baird, George M. P.
Napoleon's barber	Caesar, Arthur
Goat alley	Culbertson, Ernest H.
Sweet and twenty	Dell, Floyd
Tickless time	Glaspell, Susan & Cook, George C.
The hero of Santa Maria	Goodman, Kenneth S. & Hecht, Ben
All gummed up	Gribble, Harry Wagstaff
Thompson's luck	Grover, Harry G.
Fata Deorum	Guske, Carl W.
Finders-keepers	Kelly, George
Solomon's song	Kemp, Harry
Matinata	Langner, Lawrence
The conflict	McCauley, Clarice V.
Two slatterns and a king	Millary, Edna St. V.
Thursday evening	Morley, Christopher
The dreamy kid	O'Neill, Eugene
Forbidden fruit	Smith, George J.
Jezebel	Stockbridge, Dorothy
Sir David wears a crown	Walker, Stuart

(Also "Pearl of Dawn" by Holland Hudson, ten scenes)

Shay, Frank. A treasury of plays for men. Bost. Little, Brown, 1923.

Four who were blind	Clements, Colin
The Devil's gold	Curry, Sarah J.
Blood o' Kings	Dransfield, Jane
It isn't done	Glick, Carl
Outclassed	Glick, Carl
The hand of Siva	Goodman, K. S. & Hecht, Bess
Action!	Hudson, Holland
The Alchemist	Kenyon, Bernice L.
The silent waiter	Kreymborg, Alfred
Vote the new moon	Kreymborg, Alfred
The stick-up	Loving, Pierre
The accomplice	Marshall, Abigail
The judgment of Indra	Mukerji, Dhan G.
The beggar and the King	Parkhurst, Winthrop
Just two men	Pilot, Eugene
Freedom	Reed, John
Release	Smith, Edward H.
The rusty door	Smith, Howard F.
The gold circle	Stevens, Thomas W.
Three wishes	Stevens, Thomas W.
In front of Potter's	Tompkins, Frank G.

Shay, Frank, ed. A treasury of plays for women. Bost. Little, Brown, 1922.

The siege	Clements, Colin C.
Columbine	Clements, Colin C.
The china pig	Emig, Evelyn
Ever young	Gerstenberg, Alice
For distinguished service	Knox, Florence Clay
Rocking chairs	Kreymborg, Alfred
Manikin and Minikin	Kreymborg, Alfred
The conflict	McCauley, Clarice V.
Rehearsal	Morley, Christopher
Before breakfast	O'Neill, Eugene
My lady dreams	Pillot, Eugene
Blackberryin'	Smith, Howard Forman
The stronger woman	Strindberg, August
Motherly love	Strindberg, August

(Also a monologue and two longer plays)

Shay, Frank & Loving, Pierre, ed. Fifty contemporary one-act plays. Cincinnati. Stewart Kidd, 1920.

Madonna Dianora	Hofmannsthal, Hugo von
Literature	Schnitzler, Arthur
The intruder	Maeterlinck, Maurice
Interlude	More, Federico
Monsieur Lamblin	Ancey, George
Francoise Luck	Porto-Riche, Georges de
Altruism	Ettlinger, Karl
The tenor	Wedekind, Frank
A goodwoman	Bennett, E. Arnold
The little stone house	Calderon, George
Mary's wedding	Cannan, Gilbert
The baby carriage	Crocker, Bosworth
The Pierrot of the minute	Dawson, Ernest
The subjection of Kezia	Ellis, Mrs. Havelock
The constant lover	Hankin, St. John
The judgment of Indra	Mukerji, Dhan G.
The workhouse ward	Gregory, Lady
Louise	Speenhoff, J. H.
The grandmother	Biro, Lajos
The rights of the soul	Giacosa, Giuseppe
Love of one's neighbor	Andreyeo, Leonid
The boor	Tchekoff, Anton
His widow's husband	Benevente, Jacinto
A sunny morning	Alvarez, Serafin Q. & Alvarez, Joaquin Q.
The creditor	Strindberg, August
Autumn fires	Wied, Gustav
Brothers	Beach, Lewis
In the morgue	Cowan, Sada
A death in fever flat	Cronyn, George W.
The slave with two faces	Davies, Mary C.
The slump	Day, Frederic L.
Mansions	Flanner, Hildegarde
Trifles	Glaspell, Susan
The pot boiler	Gerstenberg, Alice
Enter the hero	Helburn, Theresa
The shepherd in the distance	Hudson, Holland
Boccaccio's untold tale	Kemp, Harry
Another way out	Langner, Lawrence
Aria da capo	Millay, Edna St. V.
Helena's husband	Moeller, Philip
The shadowed star	MacMillan, Mary
Ile	O'Neill, Eugene G.
The nursery maid of heaven	Stevens, Thomas W.
Three travellers watch a sunrise	Stevens, Wallace
Sham	Tompkins, Frank G.
The medicine show	Walker, Stuart
For all time	Wellman, Rita
The finger of God	Wilde, Percival
Night	Asch, Sholom
Forgotten souls	Pinski, David

Sindelar, Joseph C. Bright entertainments for Christmas. Chic. Beckley-Cardy, 1922.

In the east	Denton, Clara J.
The minister's daughter	Denton, Clara J.

The strike in Santa Claus Land   Denton, Clara J.
(Also recitations, drills, dialogues, and duologues)

Sindelar, Joseph C. The new Christmas book. Chic. A. Flanagan, 1910.
An unsuccessful hunt   Denton, Clara J.
Trouble in the toy room   Denton, Clara J.

Skinner, Eleanor L. & Skinner, Ada M. Children's plays. N. Y. Appleton, 1918.
Nick Bluster's trick
Professor Frog's lecture
Mother Autumn and North Wind
A royal toy-mender
(Also seven longer plays)

Smith, Alice M., ed. Short plays by representative authors. N. Y. Macmillan, 1920.
The Merry Merry Cuckoo   Marks, Jeannette
The locked chest   Masefield, John
Six who pass while the lentils boil   Walker, Stuart
The silver lining   Mackay, Constance D.
By ourselves   Fulda, Ludwig
The rider of dreams   Torrence, Ridgely
Spreading the news   Gregory, Lady
The Swan song   Chékhov, Anton
The man on the Kerb   Sutro, Alfred
The shadowed star   MacMillan, Mary
(Also "The Hraun farm," by Sigurjonsson, three acts, and "The post office," by Tagore, two acts)

Smith College. Theatre workshop plays—an anthology, 1918–1921. The Theatre workshop. Smith College, Northampton, Mass. 1921.
Isotta's triumph   Tritch, Martha
Made in heaven   Shapiro, Mathilde
Spineless   Finch, Elsie G.
Ingenuous grandmother   Whitford, Mary V.
At the end of the rope   Levy, Edith
The two prisoners   Matlack, Judith
The realist   Rosenthal, Rosa
In my day   O'Hanlon, Ruth
Avenues   Butts, Dorothy
Germekhausen   Ellet, Marion

Smith, Evelyn. Form-room plays. Junior book. N. Y. Dutton, 1920.
The swineherd   (fr. Hans Andersen)
The Parlement of Foules   (fr. Chaucer)
The death of Balder   (Norse legend)
The cock and the fox   (fr. Chaucer)
The perfect holiday   (fr. Alcott—Little women)
(Also eight longer plays)

Smith, Laura R. Helps and hints for Hallowe'en. Lebanon, Ohio. March Bros., 1920.
Jack Frost's surprise
A historical Hallowe'en
The witch's dream
A Hallowe'en carnival and wax-work show
Hallowe'en puppet play
(Also exercises, drills, and dialogues)

Sobel, Bernard. Three plays. Bost. Gorham Press, 1913.
Jennie knows
Mrs. Bompton's dinner party
There's always a reason

Soble, Mae Stein. (Mrs. John J. Soble) Bible plays for children. N. Y. Jas. T. White, 1919.
The first temptation
Mother love finds a way
The call of God
The golden calf
The promised land
(Also a longer play and four story interpretations)

Someple, pseud. Mother Goose dramatized. Lebanon, Ohio. March Bros., 1923.
Old Mother Goose
Three-score miles and ten
Cock Robin
The old woman and her pig
Curly locks
Over the hills and far away
Bye, Baby Bunting
I have a little nut tree
Twinkle-Twinkle
Nanny Etticoat
(Also two longer plays)

Stapp, Emilie Blackmore & Cameron, Eleanor. Happyland's fairy grotto plays. Bost. Houghton, Mifflin, 1922.
The tadpole school
The lost firewood
The little gray lady
The holly wreath
Molly's New Year's party
Mr. February than

Stevens, Henry B. A cry out of the dark. Bost. Four Seas, 1919.
The meddler
Bolo and Babette
The madhouse

Stevenson, Augusta. Children's classics in dramatic form. Book I. Bost. Houghton, Mifflin, 1911.
The two holes
The little fish
The hare and the tortoise
How a prince was saved
A piece of cheese
In bad company
The sick deer
The golden bucket
The house of brick
The cat that waited
The honest woodman
The tracks to the den
The moon's silver cloak
The clever cock
The King's good friend
The fairy and the cat
The beautiful song
The mill that ground hot porridge
The Christmas pitcher
(Also five longer plays)

Stevenson, Augusta. Children's classics in dramatic form. Book II. Bost. Houghton, Mifflin, 1909.
The clever kid

The wolf and the horse
The wise crow
The wolf and the lamb
The selfish woman
The blind men and the elephant
The shepherd-boy who called wolf
The wish-bird
The proud ring-finger
The vain jack daw
The endless tale
The pot of gold
The hare and the hedgehog
Fishing on dry land
King Alfred and the cakes
(Also eight longer plays)

Stevenson, Augusta. Children's classics in dramatic form. Book III. Boston. Houghton, Mifflin, 1908.
The travellers and the hatchet
The old man and his grandson
The crow and the fox
The miller, his son, and their donkey
Each in his own place
The cat and the mouse
The two countrymen
(Also nine longer plays)

Stevenson, Augusta. Children's classics in dramatic form. Book IV. Bost. Houghton, Mifflin, 1910.
The pen and the inkstand
An honest critic
Bernard Palissy, Enameller to his majesty
Lafayette's toast
(Also eleven longer plays)

Stigler, W. A. Three plays. Memphis, Tenn. National Drama Co., 1923.
Be sociable
Little owl
(Also "Where east meets west," three acts)

Strindberg, August. Plays. Second series. tr. by Edwin Bjorkman. N. Y. Scribner, 1913.
Miss Julia
The stronger
Creditors
Pariah

Sturgis, Granville F. Little plays for all occasions. Bost. Cornhill Pub. Co., 1923.
Madame
The fatal pill
Red roses
Two of a kind
Just before dawn
Winning a husband
Little Colombine
Our Mary
A college joke
The butcher's daughter
The widow Sabrina
One war babe
Sturgis, Rebecca F.

Sudermann, Hermann. Morituri: three one-act plays. N. Y. Scribner, 1910.
  Teja
  Fritzchen
  The eternal masculine

Sudermann, Hermann. Roses: four one-act plays. N. Y. Scribner, 1916.
  Streaks of light
  The last visit
  Margot
  The far-away princess

Sutherland, Evelyn G. In office hours and other sketches. Bost. Walter H. Baker, 1900.
  In office hours
  A quilting party in the thirties
  In Aunt Chloe's cabin
  The story of a famous wedding

Sutherland, Evelyn G. Po' White trash and other one-act dramas. Chic. Herbert S. Stone, 1900.
  Po' White trash
  In far Bohemia
  The end of the way
  A comedié Royall
  A bit of instruction
  A song at the castle
  Rohan the Silent
  At the barricade
  Galatea of the toy-shop

Sutro, Alfred. Five little plays. N. Y. Brentano's, 1914.
  The man in the stalls
  A marriage has been arranged
  The open door
  The man on the kerb
  The bracelet

Sutro, Alfred. Women in love: eight studies in sentiment. Lond. George Allen, 1902.
  The correct thing
  The gutter of time
  Ella's apology
  A game of chess
  The salt of life
  Mr. Steinmann's corner
  A maker of men
  (Also "Maggie," a monologue)

Symons, Arthur. Tragedies. N. Y. John Lane, 1916.
  The death of Agrippina
  Cleopatra in Judaea
  (Also "The harvesters," three acts)

Synge, J. M. The shadow of the glen, and Riders to the sea. Lond. Elkin Mathews, 1911.
  The shadow of the glen
  Riders to the sea

Synge, J. M. The Tinker's wedding; Riders to the sea; and The shadow of the glen. Dublin, Maunsel, 1911.
  The riders to the sea
  The shadow of the glen
  (Also "The Tinker's wedding," two acts)

Syrett, Netta. The fairy doll and other plays for children. N. Y. Dodd, Mead, 1922.
The fairy doll
Christmas in the forest
The Christening of Rosalys
The enchanted garden
The strange boy

Syrett, Netta. Robin Goodfellow and other fairy plays for children. Lond. Lane, 1918.
Robin Goodfellow
Princess Fragoletta
The old toys
Queen Flora's court
(Also "Venus and Cupid," and "The Dryad's awakening," both sketches for a ballet)

Syrett, Netta. Six fairy plays for children. N. Y. John Lane, 1903.
The dream lady
Little Bridget
White magic
The wonderful rose
In Arcady

Taft, Grace E. Chimalman and other poems. N. Y. The Cameo Press, 1916.
Chimalman
Tecpancaltzin
Teoteuctli
(Also seven poems)

Theis, Grover. Numbers and other one-act plays. N. Y. Nicholas L. Brown, 1919.
Numbers
Between fires
The crack in the bell
There's a difference
Like a book

Thorp, Josephine and Kimball, Rosamond. Patriotic pageants of today. N. Y. Holt, 1918.

The answer	Thorpe, Josephine
When Liberty calls	Thorpe, Josephine
The torch	Thorpe, Josephine
The call to the Youth of America	Kimball, Rosamond

Torrence, Ridgley. Plays for a Negro Theatre. N. Y. Macmillan, 1917.
Granny Maumee
The rider of dreams
Simon the Cyrenian

Tucker, Louise E. and Ryan, Estelle L. Historical plays of Colonial days for fifth year pupils. N. Y. Longmans, 1912.
The departure
William Penn's Treaty with the Indians
Cherry pie
The Quakers in New England
Gentlemen of Virginia
Massasoit's illness
Little Pilgrims
The beginning of Negro slavery
The strategy of Director Kieft
An encounter in the forest
Wampum belts
The Pilgrims in Holland
Pocahontas in London

The Easter rabbit
The first crop of apples
A skirmish at Rensselaerswijck
How the Indians planted powder
Indian gifts
A Christmas tree in New England
Robert Morris and the Revolution
At anchor
A narrow escape
Stormy times
The first winter
Virginia children of long ago
Saturday night in New England

Tupper, Wilbur S. Six short plays. Bost. Four Seas, 1922.
Mr. Fraser's friends
In Toscana tavern
Onesimus
The bargain
Figs and thistles
(Also "The wise man of Nineveh," two acts)

University of Washington Plays. First series. Seattle, Wash. University of Washington Press, 1921.

Jet	Shepherd, Esther
Imposition	Miller, Max
These wild young people	O'Connor, J. M., Jr.
Tweedledum	Richardson, Otis

Vagabond plays. First series. Baltimore. Norman, Remington Co., 1921.

The double miracle	Garland, Robert
On Vengeance Height	Davis, Allan and Vencill, Cornelia C.
Pan in ambush	Patterson, Marjory
Release	Smith, Edward H.
The importance of being a roughneck	Garland, Robert
The conflict	McCauley, Clarice Vallette

Varney, Alice S. Story plays old and new. Book III. N. Y. American Book Co., 1915.
The daisy
In union there is strength
Don't count your chickens until they are hatched
The circus
Christmas
Welcoming the New Year
(Also twelve longer plays)

Verga, Giovanni and others. Plays of the Italian Theatre. tr. by Isaac Goldberg. Bost. John W. Luce, 1921.

The wolf-hunt	Verga, Giovanni
Water upon fire	Morselli, Ercole L.
Gastone, the animal tamer	Morselli, Ercole L.
The sparrow	Lopez, Sabatino
Sicilian times	Pirandello, Luigo

Viereck, George S. A game at love and other plays. N. Y. Brentano's, 1906.
A game at love
The mood of a moment
From death's own eyes
A question of fidelity
The butterfly: a morality

Viets, Edward. The masque of morning and other poems. Bost. Four Seas, 1921.

The masque of morning
Noon, an interlude
The masque of evening
(Also poems)

Wagstaff, Blanche S. Colonial plays for the school-room. Bost. Educational Pub. Co., 1912.
Colonial Virginia
The first Thanksgiving
A witchcraft story
A Pennsylvania incident
Life in New York
The Georgia debtors
An Indian story
Revolutionary days
Three compromises of the Constitution
(Also "The Columbus story," a longer play)

Waley, Arthur. The Nō plays of Japan. N. Y. Knopf, 1922.

Atsumori — Seami
Ikuta — Zembō Motoyasu
Tsunemasa — Seami
Kumasaka — Zenchi Ku Ujinobu
Eboshi-ori — Miyamasu
Benkei on the bridge — Hiyoshi Sa-ami Yasukiyo
Kagekiyo — Seami
Hachi No Ki — Seami
Sotoba Komachi — Kwanami
Ukai — Enami No Sayemon
Aya No Tsuzumi — Seami
Aoi No Uye — Zenchiku Ujinobu
Kantan — Anon
The Hōka Priests — Zenchika Ujinobu
Hagoromo — Seami
Taniko — Zenchiku
Ikeniye — Seami
Hatsuyuki — Koparu Zembo-Motoyasu
Haku Rakuten — Seami
Kyogen — Esashi Juo

Walker, Stuart. Portmanteau adaptations. Cincinnati. Stewart Kidd, 1921.
The birthday of the Infanta
Sir David wears a crown
Nellijumbo
(Also "Gammer Gurton's needle," five acts)

Walker, Stuart. Portmanteau plays. Cincinnati. Stewart Kidd, 1917.
The trimplet
Nevertheless
The medicine show
The six who pass while the lentils boil

Washington Square plays. Garden City, N. Y. Doubleday, Page, 1916.
The clod — Beach, Lewis
Eugenically speaking — Goodman, Edward
Overtones — Gerstenberg, Alice
Helena's husband — Moeller, Philip

Watt, Mary S. Three short plays. N. Y. Macmillan, 1917.
Civilization
The wearin' o' the green
(Also "An ancient dance," two acts)

Waugh, Constance E. Holiday plays for girls. Lond. Wells, Gardner, Darton, n. d.
    Under distinguished patronage
    Aunt Penelope
    (Also "Wanted a governess," two acts)

Webber, James P. and Webster, Hanson H., ed. One-act plays for secondary schools. Bost. Houghton, Mifflin, 1923.

The boy comes home	Milne, A. A.
Followers	Brighouse, Harold
A sunny morning	Alvarez, Serafin Q. & Alvarez, Joaquin Q.
The falcon	Tennyson, Alfred Lord
The coming of Fair Annie	Price, Graham
The Romancers	Rostand, Edmond
My Lady's lace	Knoblach, Edward
The Lord's prayer	Coppée, François
The cottage on the moor	Smith, E. E. and Ireland, D. L.
Solemn pride	Leighton, George R.
X = O: A night of the Trojan War	Drinkwater, John
The rising of the moon	Gregory, Lady
Nevertheless	Walker, Stuart
Manikin and Minikin	Kreymborg, Alfred
The Beau of Bath	Mackay, Constance D.
The unseen host	Wilde, Percival
The shoes that danced	Branch, Anna H.
Colombine	Arkell, Reginald

Wells, Carolyn. Jolly plays for holidays. Bost. Walter H. Baker, 1903.
    The greatest gift
    Christmas gifts of all nations
    The greatest day in the year
    Is Santa Claus a fraud?
    A substitute for Santa Claus
    The day before Christmas

Wickes, Frances G. A child's book of holiday plays. N. Y. Macmillan, 1916.
    The captured year
    The light
    St. Valentine's house
    The first May baskets
    The thankful heart
    Baucis and Philemon
    (Also three longer plays)

Wilcox, Constance. Told in a Chinese garden and four other fantastic plays for out-doors or in-doors. N. Y. Holt, 1920.
    Told in a Chinese garden
    Pan pipes
    Four of a kind
    The Princess in the fairy tale
    Mother Goose garden

Wilde, Percival. Confessional and other American plays. N. Y. Holt, 1915.
    Confessional
    The villain in the piece
    A question of morality
    The beautiful story
    (Also "According to Darwin," two scenes, same setting)

Wilde, Percival. Dawn with The Noble Lord; The traitor: A house of cards; Playing with fire; The finger of God. N. Y. Holt, 1915.
    Dawn
The Noble Lord

The traitor
A house of cards
Playing with fire
The finger of God

Wilde, Percival. Eight comedies for little theatres. Bost. Little, Brown, 1922.
The sequel
The previous engagement
The dyspeptic ogre
In the net
A wonderful woman
Catesby
His return
Embryo

Wilde, Percival. The unseen host and other war plays. Bost. Little, Brown, 1917.
The unseen host
Mothers of men
Pawns
In the ravine
Valkyrie!

Willard, Ellen M. Yuletide entertainments. Chic. T. S. Denison, 1910.
All the year 'round
A boy's Christmas
A Christmas bargain
The first Christmas
The King of the year
Mrs. Randy's Christmas
Santa Claus' garden
Santa Claus in many lands
The spirit of Christmas
(Also recitations, monologues, drills etc.)

Williams, E. Harcourt. Four fairy plays. N. Y. French, 1920.
Snow-white and Rose-red
Little Tuk's dream
The three bears
(Also "Puss in Boots," a longer play)

Williams, Frayne. Three Oriental plays. Los Angeles, Calif., J. A. Alles, 1921.
The rose garden
The blue vase
The man with the bundle

Wilson, Lillian P. The fruit of toil and other one-act plays. Indianapolis, Bobbs-Merrill, 1916.
The fruit of toil
An episode
Being the fly
A voice on the stair
The empty shrine
The weight of wings
This is law
Living

Wisconsin plays. ed. by Thomas H. Dickinson. N. Y. Huebsch, 1914.
The neighbors   Gale, Zona
In hospital   Dickinson, Thomas H.
Glory of the morning   Leonard, William E.

Wisconsin plays. Second series. N. Y. Huebsch, 1918.
The Feast of the Holy Innocents   Ilsley, Marshall S.

On the Pier   Sherry, Laura
The shadow   Jones, Howard M.
We live again   Gilman, Thornton

Wolfrom, Anna. Human wisps: six one-act plays. Bost. Sherman, French, 1917.
The marriage certificate
Old shoes
A will-o'-wisp
Ripening wheat
The new race
Danny

Woodman, Rhea. The Bobby Bennett plays for children. Chic. Dramatic Pub. Co., 1922.
Fashionable calls
A bad case of microbes
In the market place
Buying a day
January styles
Those dreadful Vity-Mines

Wright, Harriet S. New plays from old tales. N. Y. Macmillan, 1921.
The birthday of the Infanta
Three Sundays in a week
On the old plantation
(Also five longer plays)

Yeats, William Butler. Collected works. Vol. II. Lond. Chapman & Hall, 1908.
The King's threshold
On Baile's strand
Deirdre
The shadowy waters

Yeats, William Butler. Four plays for dancers. N. Y. Macmillan, 1921.
At the Hawk's well
The only jealousy of Emer
The dreaming of the Bones
Calvary

Yeats, William Butler. The King's threshold and On Baile's Strand. (Vol. III of Plays for an Irish theatre) Lond. A. H. Bullen, 1904.
The King's threshold
On Baile's strand

Yeats, W. B. Plays in prose and verse written for an Irish theatre. N. Y. Macmillan, 1922.
Cathleen in Hoolihan
The pot of broth
The hour-glass (in prose)
The King's threshold
On Baile's strand
The shadowy waters. (stage version)
Deirdre
The green helmet
The hour-glass (in verse)

Yeats, W. B. The hour-glass and other plays. N. Y. Macmillan, 1904.
The hour glass
Cathleen Ni Hoolihan
A pot of broth

Yeats, William B. Poetical works. Vol. II. Dramatic poems. N. Y. Macmillan, 1907.
The Countess Cathleen

The land of Heart's Desire
The shadowy waters (stage version)
On Baile's strand
The King's threshold
Deirdre

Yeats, William B. and Gregory, Lady Isabelle A. The Unicorn from the stars. N. Y. Macmillan, 1908.
The Unicorn from the stars   Yeats, William B. & Gregory, Lady
Cathleen Ni Hoolihan   Yeats, William B.
The hour-glass   Yeats, William B.

Young, Stark. Addio; Madretta and other plays. Chic. Dramatic Pub. Co., 1912.
Addio
Madretta
The star in the trees
The twilight saint
The dead poet
The seven kings and the wind
The Queen of Sheba

Young, Stark. Three one-act plays. Cincinnati. Stewart Kidd, 1921.
Madretta
At the shrine
Addio